I0138188

VIOLENCE AS A GENERATIVE FORCE

VIOLENCE AS A GENERATIVE FORCE

IDENTITY, NATIONALISM, AND MEMORY IN A BALKAN COMMUNITY

MAX BERGHOLZ

CORNELL UNIVERSITY PRESS
Ithaca and London

Publication of this book was made possible, in part, by a grant from the First Book Subvention Program of the Association for Slavic, East European and Eurasian Studies

First published 2016 by Cornell University Press

Printed in the United States of America

Library of Congress Cataloging-in-Publication Data

Names: Bergholz, Max, author.
Title: Violence as a generative force : identity, nationalism, and memory in a Balkan community / Max Bergholz.
Description: Ithaca : Cornell University Press, 2016. | Includes bibliographical references and index.
Identifiers: LCCN 2016025961 | ISBN 9781501704925 (cloth : alk. paper)
Subjects: LCSH: Massacres—Bosnia and Herzegovina—Kulen Vakuf—History. | Ethnic conflict—Bosnia and Herzegovina—Kulen Vakuf—History. | Violence—Bosnia and Herzegovina—Kulen Vakuf—History. | Nationalism and collective memory—Bosnia and Herzegovina—Kulen Vakuf—History. | Communalism—Bosnia and Herzegovina—Kulen Vakuf—History. | Kulen Vakuf (Bosnia and Herzegovina)—Ethnic relations. | World War, 1939–1945—Bosnia and Herzegovina.
Classification: LCC DR1785.K85 B47 2016 | DDC 940.53/49742—dc23
LC record available at https://lccn.loc.gov/2016025961

Cornell University Press strives to use environmentally responsible suppliers and materials to the fullest extent possible in the publishing of its books. Such materials include vegetable-based, low-VOC inks and acid-free papers that are recycled, totally chlorine-free, or partly composed of nonwood fibers. For further information, visit our website at www.cornellpress.cornell.edu.

Cloth printing 10 9 8 7 6 5 4 3 2 1

For everyone who helped,
i svima koji su vjerovali,
from Pittsburgh to Toronto,
od Beograda do Kulen Vakufa,
and all the places,
i velika i mala,
along the way.

Contents

Illustrations

Figures

Maps

Acknowledgments

This book began after a chance encounter with a stack of remarkable documents bound in frayed string, which I discovered after I was unexpectedly given access—for fifteen minutes—to an archive's basement storage depot. Noticing them in a flashlight's beam, and later reading them carefully, gave me the feeling of cresting a sand dune and gazing out on the wide ocean. I could almost feel a warm breeze picking up speed behind me. And I wanted to raise the sails of my imaginary ship as fast as possible, and pursue the story whose tantalizing outline I could already sense protruding in that stack of dusty papers. This book would not exist without the people and institutions that made such moments possible. They helped prepare me to be ready to seize opportunities to discover something new before the fleeting windows closed. They supported me on the long and winding road of uncovering and writing this history. And they challenged me to keep going and see this project through to the end.

For financial support, I thank the Harry Frank Guggenheim Foundation, the International Research and Exchanges Board, the American Council of Learned Societies, the American Historical Association, the Fulbright Program and the United States Department of State, American Councils for International Education, the Government of Ontario, Le Fonds québécois de la recherche sur la société et la culture, the University of Toronto, and Concordia University. Special thanks are due to Mr. James M. Stanford, whose generous support of my professorship in genocide and human rights studies helped make this book possible. None of these institutions and individuals is responsible for my interpretations.

Writing this book could not have happened without guidance from many great scholars. In Pittsburgh, Orysia Karapinka, Neal Galpern, Bill Chase, Alexander Orbach, Dennison Rusinow, and Alejandro de la Fuente provided the foundation. Michael F. Jiménez did that too, and much more. In Toronto, Lynne Viola offered a superior model of professionalism and always exuded inspiration. Derek Penslar, Jeff Kopstein, and Doris Bergen pushed me to see the broader horizons. Since taking up my position at Concordia University in Montreal,

I have been fortunate to meet some amazing scholars currently working on cutting-edge research about violence and nationalism. Scott Straus generously read my work, shared his deep knowledge, and continues to inspire. Edin Hajdarpašić offered voluminous, incredibly helpful feedback on the entire manuscript, which reflects his profound knowledge of Balkan, Yugoslav, and Bosnian histories. Evgeny Finkel has been a wonderful political science critic who read every word and, while appreciating me as a historian, always pushed to deepen my social scientific analyses. So too did Anastasia Shesterinina, whose perceptive feedback on the whole manuscript sharpened its analytical edges. Nikica Barić poured over everything I sent, offered expert comments based on his unparalleled knowledge of the archives, and never tired of sending me books, articles, and amazing materials for the book's maps. For advice and support over the years, I am grateful to Maria Todorova, Charles King, Theodora Dragostinova, Alex Toshkov, and Dave Gerlach.

This project benefitted greatly from opportunities to present parts of it at conferences and workshops, where the audiences' questions pushed me to sharpen my ideas and arguments. I am especially grateful to those who invited me to speak at the Program on Order, Conflict, and Violence at Yale University; the Center for Russia, East Europe, and Central Asia at the University of Wisconsin-Madison; and the conference, "Beyond Mosque, Church, and State: Negotiating Religious and Ethno-National Identities in the Balkans," held at Ohio State University.

At Cornell University Press, Roger Haydon's belief in this project, his professionalism, and support have made the publication phase of finishing this book exciting and energizing. I am grateful to the two thoughtful anonymous readers whom he selected, whose close engagement with the manuscript helped me improve it in a number of critical ways. Many thanks to Karen Laun and Susan Barnett who worked proficiently to prepare the book for publication. Bill Nelson expertly transformed my scans, scribbles, and drawings into the maps I had long envisioned. I thank Oxford University Press for permission to republish here parts of my article "Sudden Nationhood: The Microdynamics of Intercommunal Relations in Bosnia-Herzegovina after World War II," which appeared in *American Historical Review* 118, no. 3 (June 2013): 679–707.

This book would not exist without a group of extraordinary archivists and librarians. I am grateful to everyone who assisted me in the institutions where I conducted research. In Zagreb, Branislava "Zoja" Vojnović taught me as much as any scholar, and maybe more; her knowledge of history and sources dazzled and inspired me. Angelika Milić made the day-to-day workable and got things done when others could not. In Banja Luka, I had great luck to meet Verica Stošić—a kindred spirit—whose expertise and profound devotion to understanding the past propelled me forward. Her protégé, Vladan Vukliš, gave me hope for the future. In Bihać, Fikret Midžić did his best to prevent this story from being told. Asija Filan decided to intervene and help, and I was able to move forward because of her goodwill and generosity. Nijazija Maslak provided a room in the local museum with a wood-burning stove where I could quietly continue my work. Dženita Halilagić found sources, worked the phones, and transformed many of my dead ends into open doors, while making me laugh and feel at home. In Sarajevo, Mina Kujović and Fahrudin Kulenović helped me take the first steps through their enormous knowledge of sources. Šaban Zahirović graciously released materials that opened up new, breathtaking vistas. Sandra Biletić made everything possible in the archive, while providing hope and lots of laughter. In Belgrade, Marina, Dragana, Mića, Suzana, Nada, Boro, Goran, Marijana, and Ljiljana made the archives not just exciting places to explore the past, but also homes.

A sizable amount of this research unfolded in places far outside of official institutions. In Kulen Vakuf and its surrounding villages, I met many remarkable people who enthusiastically supported my work. Among them, Nataša "Đina" Kadić—moja stara i zločesta prijateljica!—was an inspiration and taught me to see people in all their complexity. Mehmed Anadolac's local knowledge—and warm generosity—opened windows to the past that I never would have discovered on my own. Derviš Dervišević shared his story and insisted on teaching me how to eat canned meat with a large knife. Muhamed "Crni" Handžić, whom I met on my first visit to Kulen Vakuf while walking across the bridge over the Una River, pointed me in the right direction. These people—and all the others I encountered during my fieldwork—changed my life, and helped make this book possible.

I am deeply grateful to Zoran Bibanović who shared with me his late father's unpublished manuscripts and research materials on the history of Kulen Vakuf, and whose trust and enthusiasm inspired me. Sadeta Ibrahimpašić and Josip Pavičić kindly provided eye-opening photographs, and gave me permission to publish them. Abas Mušeta spoke with me on multiple occasions about living through the history told in these pages, and shared his research materials. Amela Mujagić always offered support and friendship during my stays in Bihać, and gave sound advice (such as to avoid the discos in Cazin). Jasna Karaula intuitively understood my path, and offered expertise and warmth as I walked forward. Writing this book could not have happened without three great friends in Belgrade. Saša Ilić showed me that beliefs matter, and that while history demands explanation, it must also be told as stories. Jovan Pešalj's introduction to Belgrade's intellectual terrain was unforgettable, as was his raw excitement for the past. Saša Glamočak—moj profesor zauvek!—taught me language(s) and about humanity, and showed me that it's possible to write late into the night in dimly lit hallways, if need be.

Sue Van Doeren and Andy Sheehan provided light at critical moments. Eleanor Mallet was the first and last reader of everything. Her editorial magic ensured that my best could always be made better. My parents never expected to learn so much about a small corner of the Balkans, but they absorbed my relentless interest with ceaseless support and an inspiring curiosity about the world. They reminded me to stay the course when the path forward became hazy.

Ayla unexpectedly appeared on a summer night in the midst of this project, and has insisted on joy and laughter ever since. I hope that she never stops teaching me what matters most.

Abbreviations

ABiH	Arhiv Bosne i Hercegovine (Archive of Bosnia-Herzegovina)
AJ	Arhiv Jugoslavije (Archive of Yugoslavia)
AMUSK	Arhiv Muzeja Unsko-sanskog kantona (Archive of the Museum of the Una-Sana Canton)
ARS PJF	Arhiv Republike Srpske, Područna jedinica Foča (Archive of the Serb Republic, Territorial Unit of Foča)
ARSBL	Arhiv Republike Srpske Banja Luka (Archive of the Serb Republic, Banja Luka)
AS	Arhiv Srbije (Archive of Serbia)
ASPC	Arhiv Srpske pravoslavne crkve (Archive of the Serbian Orthodox Church)
AUSK	Arhiv Unsko-sanskog kantona (Archive of the Una-Sana Canton)
AHRP	Arhiv za historiju radničkog pokreta (Archive for the History of the Workers' Movement)
CK SK BiH	Centralni komitet Saveza komunista Bosne i Hercegovine (Central Committee of the League of Communists of Bosnia-Herzegovina)
DAKA	Državni arhiv Karlovac (State Archive of Karlovac)
DKUZ	Državna komisija za utvrđivanje zločina okupatora i njihovih pomagača (State Commission for Determining the Crimes of the Occupiers and their Collaborators)

HDA	Hrvatski državni arhiv (Croatian State Archive)
KBUVB	Kraljevska banska uprava Vrbaske Banovine (Royal Banovina Administration for the Vrbas Banovina)
KI	Komesarijat za izbeglice (Commissariat for Refugees)
LAEB	Lični arhiv Esada Bibanovića (Personal Archive of Esad Bibanović)
MINORS NDH	Ministarstvo oružanih snaga Nezavisne Države Hrvatske (Ministry of Armed Forces of the Independent State of Croatia)
MUP Kraljevine Jugoslavije	Ministarstvo unutrašnjih poslova Kraljevine Jugoslavije (Ministry of Internal Affairs of the Kingdom of Yugoslavia)
MUP NDH	Ministarstvo unutarnjih poslova Nezavisne Države Hrvatske (Ministry of Internal Affairs of the Independent State of Croatia)
NDH	Nezavisna Država Hrvatska (Independent State of Croatia)
NOV	Narodnooslobodilačka vojska (People's Liberation Army)
OIVB Bihać	Okružni inspektorat Vrbaske Banovine Bihać (District Inspectorate of the Vrbas Banovina, Bihać)
OK SK BiH Foča	Opštinski komitet Saveza komunista Bosne i Hercegovine Foča (Municipal Committee of the League of Communists of Bosnia-Herzegovina, Foča)
OK SK BiH Kulen Vakuf	Opštinski komitet Saveza komunista Bosne i Hercegovine Kulen Vakuf (Municipal Committee of the League of Communists of Bosnia-Herzegovina, Kulen Vakuf)
OKUZ za Liku	Okružna komisija za utvrđivanje zločina okupatora i nijhovih pomagača za Liku (District Commission for Determining the Crimes of the Occupiers and their Collaborations for Lika)
RAVSIGUR NDH	Ravnateljstvo za javni red i sigurnost Nezavisne Države Hrvatske (Directorate

	for Public Order and Security of the Independent State of Croatia)
RMZDL	Radni materijal za Zbornik Donji Lapac (Working Material for the Collection Donji Lapac)
SUP BiH	Sekretarijat unutrašnjih poslova Bosne i Hercegovine (Secretariat of Internal Affairs of Bosnia-Herzegovina)
SUP SRH	Sekretarijat unutarnjih poslova Socijalističke Republike Hrvatske (Secretariat of Internal Affairs of the Socialist Republic of Croatia)
SUBNOR BiH	Savez udruženja boraca Narodnooslobodilačkog rata Bosne i Hercegovine (Union of the Associations of Fighters of the People's Liberation War of Bosnia-Herzegovina)
SK SK BiH	Sreski komitet Saveza komunista Bosne i Herzegovine (Regional Committee of the League of Communists of Bosnia-Herzegovina)
USPBVBBL	Ustaški stožer i povjereništvo za bivšu Vrbasku banovinu Banja Luka (Ustaša Leader and Commission for the Former Vrbas Banovina, Banja Luka)
VA	Vojni arhiv (Military Archive)
ZKUZ BiH	Zemaljska komisija za utvrđivanje zločina okupatora i nijhovih pomagača Bosne i Hercegovine (Territorial Commission for Determining the Crimes of the Occupiers and their Collaborators of Bosnia-Herzegovina)

VIOLENCE AS A GENERATIVE FORCE

PART I

History

Introduction

On a September afternoon in 2006, while I was sifting through uncatalogued documents in the Archive of Bosnia-Herzegovina in Sarajevo, a handful of arresting words on a bundle of tattered blue folders stopped me in my tracks: "Examination of sites of mass executions in the Socialist Republic of Bosnia-Herzegovina" (*Pregled stratišta u SR BiH*). The documents inside revealed that in 1983 the then communist authorities ordered a confidential, republic-wide investigation. Its objective was to gather information about all sites where the mass executions of civilians had occurred during the People's Liberation War (Narodnooslobodilački rat), which referred to the years 1941–1945. Several questions framed the investigation: How many civilians were killed in each local community, and where? What were their "nationalities" or "ethnicities"? And had these sites been marked with monuments? Local war veterans affiliated with the communist authorities surveyed each community during the next few years, and then sent the findings to their central organization in Sarajevo for analysis.[1]

Completed in 1985–1986 (but not released publicly), the investigation's final reports repeatedly mentioned the wartime experience of a largely unknown community: Kulen Vakuf, a small town in a rural region of northwest Bosnia that straddles the Una River, just a few kilometers from the present-day border with Croatia. There, in September 1941, the report said that as many as 2,000 people—men, women, and children "of the Muslim population"—were killed. Who exactly was guilty for their deaths was discussed in a few complicated, unclear sentences. The "Partisans," who fought under communist leadership during the war, were declared not to have been responsible. Neither was any foreign army, such as the German and Italian forces, which invaded the Kingdom of Yugoslavia in April 1941 and dismembered the country. Nor was any role mentioned of "Serb" or "Croat" nationalist forces (i.e., "Chetniks" or "Ustašas"), which historians generally identify as among the main perpetrators of violence against civilians in this part of Europe during 1941–1945. Instead, the report named an amorphous group that has not figured prominently—or even at all—in most wartime histories as perpetrators: the "insurgents" or *ustanici*, who appeared to have been neighbors of those whom they killed. Yet strangely, in the decades after 1945 the communist authorities did not designate the approximately 2,000 victims in Kulen Vakuf as "Victims of Fascist Terror" (*žrtve fašističkog terora*), the category created for official civilian war victims. Thus, they were not counted among the region's wartime dead, and no monument had been built for them. The report said that lack of clarity about what happened in Kulen Vakuf remained an ongoing "political problem." Solving it—and finally breaking the public silence about the existence of these victims—would require clear and precise answers about the violence of 1941.[2]

The next morning at the archive, an experienced librarian placed two texts on a table for me: a memoir and a few pages marked in a monograph.[3] These were the only materials he knew of that might shed light on the 1941 mystery in Kulen Vakuf. Instead, they added more layers of complexity. According to these writings, it appeared that during the summer of 1941 much of the region's multi-ethnic population had, in fact, become both perpetrators and victims in a series of locally executed massacres that swept thousands to their deaths. Local residents called "Orthodox Serbs" had first become the victims of militias called "Ustašas," who were composed of their Muslim and Catholic neighbors. They had been empowered by the leaders of the newly established Independent State of Croatia (Nezavisna Država Hrvatska [NDH]), which had been created in the aftermath of the Axis invasion of the Kingdom of Yugoslavia in April 1941. They wished to create a state only for those, such as these local Catholics and Muslims, whom they considered to be "Croats." But those initially persecuted soon took up arms; they transformed themselves from victims into "insurgents"; and they took revenge on their former neighbors. Some of these new victims had been among the initial Ustaša perpetrators, while many others were killed because of a perceived ethnic association with them.

The documents from the blue folders, along with these few writings, offered only a glimpse into a perplexing story of a multi-ethnic community's sudden descent into intercommunal violence, and the dramatic transformation of its residents' lives as a result. But this snapshot also suggested a potentially compelling micro lens through which to embark on a search for answers to several broader questions: What causes intercommunal violence among neighbors in multi-ethnic communities? And how does such violence then affect their identities and relations? This book represents the culmination of that search, the first steps of which began during those two days in the archive, with the rest lasting nearly the next decade. This journey led to the examination of thousands of largely never-before-seen documents from archives and libraries in Bosnia-Herzegovina, Croatia, and Serbia. Many were discovered in cities, such as Sarajevo, Banja Luka, Zagreb, and Belgrade, while others were found in smaller towns, such as Bihać and Karlovac. Highly skilled archivists and librarians located many of these materials, while power-hungry provincial figures jealously guarded others, which were pried free only after considerable time and struggle. This search required extended conversations with residents in the Kulen Vakuf region. They were reached by local bus, borrowed bicycle, and sometimes on foot through river valleys, forests, and along mountain pathways. And this pursuit entailed seeking out unpublished histories, memoirs, and documents mentioned during these conversations, which were not held in any official institution, but had been kept for years in shoeboxes buried in people's closets.

Each of the sources slowly revealed more about what took place in September 1941 in Kulen Vakuf. But telling that story required the opening of doors to a distant past, to a history of a local community living through the rise and fall of empires, the creation and destruction of states, and the shifts in local solidarities and conflicts that such upheavals brought. Telling this story also entailed following the community into the decades after the cataclysmic events of 1941 and the rest of the war, to when communism was built, during which identities and social relations continued to be deeply influenced by the experience and memory of local violence. Slowly, the seed of the brief story discovered in those tattered blue folders sprouted and grew into a detailed history of a local community's forms of social identification, its bases of cohesion and conflict, the factors that made local killing possible, and the ways that neighbors found to live together again after intercommunal violence.

The challenge of reconstructing this world meant grappling with multiple vocabularies of community, often erased or ignored in histories of the wider region, among which categories of "ethnicity" or "nationality" were only one option that competed with others. This local history that emerged did not reveal a clear, linear path to the intercommunal violence of 1941, which some might believe a majority of local residents consciously paved through widespread, deeply rooted ethnic conflicts. The community's largely unknown past counter-intuitively suggested that the profound saliency of ethnicity as an axis that would soon determine life and death in 1941 did not, in fact, result from decades of local nationalism and antagonistic ethnic cleavages. Rather, a unique confluence of events rapidly empowered small groups, whose members correctly perceived the unprecedented opportunity to profit and settle local conflicts once and for all by employing violence on an ethnic axis. In the Kulen Vakuf region, the violence that they soon unleashed to realize these objectives would quickly cascade into more killings, ultimately culminating with the massacres of September 1941 briefly mentioned in those blue folders.

The story revealed that these acts of violence triggered a host of difficult-to-perceive, yet far-reaching transformations, which the lens of the local community brought into sharp focus. For some, the violence led to sudden surges in the salience of ethnicity; for others, its equally rapid irrelevance. Some sought to escalate killing on an ethnic axis at all costs. Others sought just as fiercely to restrain it. The upheavals that the local killing wrought thus created new perceptions of ethnicity—of oneself, of supposed "brothers," and those perceived as "others." As a consequence, this violence forged new communities, new forms and configurations of power, and new practices of nationalism. The history of this small community was thus one marked by an unexpected burst of locally executed violence by the few, which functioned as an immensely generative force in transforming the identities, relations, and lives of the many.

As such, telling the story of Kulen Vakuf in 1941 blossomed into a way to do more than just better explain what took place in a small town during that fateful year. It became, in fact, a means through which to rethink fundamental assumptions about the inter-relationships among ethnicity, nationalism, and violence. By carefully excavating the history of this largely unknown corner of Europe, we discover a compelling way through which to confront a major puzzle at the epicenter of these subjects, both among scholars and among the wider public: Does ethnicity and nationalism lead to violence, as many would assume? Or can violence on an ethnic axis actually produce profoundly antagonistic waves of ethnic identification and nationalism? The double take that the blue folders caused me to take on that September day in the archive led to the largely forgotten story of Kulen Vakuf in 1941. And the long journey to tell that intricate story of intimate killing in a small Bosnian town ultimately leads to the very heart of a globally significant challenge: How to explain the causes of intercommunal violence and its effects in multi-ethnic communities?

Approaching the subjects of ethnicity, nationalism, and violence by posing these kinds of broad questions has generally not been how historians and others have written histories of World War II in this part of the Balkans. Until recently, little sustained scholarly attention has been devoted to explaining the causes, dynamics, and effects of intercommunal violence in the NDH, especially in its rural areas (such as the Kulen Vakuf region), where the killings were most widespread.[4] Among the large number of works written during the past decades in the South Slavic languages, perhaps the most striking characteristic is how the description of atrocities overwhelmingly substitutes for explanation. Although basic information often abounds about instances of violence (e.g., dates, locations, estimates of victims), most authors have employed what could be called the "bloodlands" approach.[5] Like the title and one of the main thrusts of historian Timothy Snyder's recent book, this refers to graphic descriptions of violence, the presentation of large, yet precise body counts, and disturbing survivor testimonies.[6] Although this style can make for page-turning reading, its explanatory capacity often leaves much to be desired, as several prominent historians have noted in critical reviews of Snyder's book.[7] The "bloodlands" approach leaves us shocked by the horror of violence. But that shock can also lead us to forget to ask questions about the causes, dynamics, and effects of violence, particularly at the local level where perpetrators and victims—who are often neighbors—meet face-to-face.

Another general characteristic of much of this literature is its striking level of ethnicized selectivity. Frequently, these histories and document collections focus on the killing of people understood as members of a particular "ethnic group" or "nation." Writings on the killings of "Serbs" in the NDH often start with the persecution of those considered to be of this category; yet they often abruptly end without mentioning the subsequent Serb-led insurgency that resulted in retaliatory killings of those considered as "Croats" and "Muslims."[8] In the same way, writings about the killings of these "Croats" and "Muslims" generally begin with the "Serb" attacks on these groups, but usually without much (or even any) attention to the prior NDH violence against those singled out as "Serbs."[9] As such, these histories often propose divergent and mutually incompatible visions of the past, even when dealing with the same locations and time periods. And the version of this fragmented history that we receive depends almost entirely on which "ethnic group" an author wishes to demonize or portray as martyrs.

Toward that end, authors often decontextualize killings by stringing together acts of violence against a particular group from different locations and times—as if a list of massacres is a sufficient explanation—yet without accounting for their specific causes and often bewildering temporal and geographical variation. This approach has made it easier for some to suggest the existence of an overarching, exclusionary nationalist ideology by "ethnic group x" for "ethnic group y," and to identify this as the primary cause of inter-group violence.[10] The motivation in doing so often has roots in a desire to argue that a particular group's killings constitute genocide. Thus, there is the imperative to show premeditated intent in the form of a supposedly deeply rooted, exclusionary ideology. As Zdravko Dizdar and Mihael Sobolevski claim in their study and document collection of Chetnik ideology and violence in the NDH: "All of these documents show that these Chetnik crimes of genocide against Croats and Muslims were planned out in advance."[11]

Two key elements thus emerge from much of the South Slavic literature on violence in the NDH: on the one hand, there is a sense that whole "ethnic groups" should be seen as our main historical actors, both as perpetrators and victims; on the other, the violence among these "groups" emanates from their supposed deeply rooted nationalist ideologies.[12] Rarely do we get even a rough sense of the specific causes of the violence in a given instance, or why it occurs when and where it does (and not at other times and in other places), or what the relationship might be among violence, ethnicity, and nationalism. Instead, all of these factors appear aggregated into one unchanging portrait in which "ethnic groups" kill other "ethnic groups," or are killed by them. In this framework, violence is seemingly foreordained by distant historical factors, and so the task of the historian is merely to depict the horror of killing. Donald Horowitz's observation of much of the literature on riots in South Asia resonates here: "Violence is either beyond explanation or not in need of explanation."[13]

Given this state of much of the South Slavic literature on violence in the NDH, one can perhaps understand why some North American historians, such as Tara Zahra, have suggested more generally that it may be time to "rescue Eastern Europe from the tropes of violence [and] nationalism." Yet such voices have not called for more sophisticated approaches to researching and explaining the perplexing episodes of intercommunal killing that have occurred. Rather, their 'rescuing' would seem to entail abandoning this supposed "relentless focus on violence" by historians and others, and instead to take up the study of other subjects. New fields of inquiry, such as transnational history, can certainly be enlightening. Yet if one sees the historiography of Eastern Europe (or the Balkans), as Zahra has suggested, as mired in "old stories of pathological . . . ethnic conflict" and "violence," a productive way forward would be to produce more analytically sophisticated studies of such phenomena. Carrying out such studies would not further "pathologize" the region's history, as some might fear; rather, they would actually "de-pathologize" it by shedding light on the still poorly understood causes and dynamics of violence, and its relationship with nationalism and "ethnic conflict."[14]

Fortunately, during the past decade, interest has grown in the history of the NDH among scholars, particularly those based outside the South Slavic lands, which has resulted in several new studies. We now know much more about life in Sarajevo during World War II; the overarching political objectives of the Ustašas and Chetniks, as well as their violent policies and practices; the conflict between the Chetniks and communist-led Partisans; and the cultural politics of the NDH regime.[15] It is indisputable that today English-language readers can learn more than ever before about the history of the NDH, and some aspects of the violence that occurred during its existence. Nonetheless, when we are challenged with questions about the causes, dynamics, and effects of local intercommunal violence, this literature offers surprisingly few answers.

Common in these studies is the presence in one way or another of what the political scientist Stathis Kalyvas has called "the urban bias," which until relatively recently has been a feature of many studies on mass violence and civil war in various contexts. By this he meant not just literally the absence of the countryside in such works, as well as a preference among researchers for conducting research in large cities; it also entails a "more general tendency to interpret phenomena acontextually and in an exclusively top-down manner."[16] In both subject choice and research methodology, some of this newer work on the NDH displays a clear interest in probing the specific dynamics of wartime life in that state's handful of urban areas. Among the works that do purport to study events in rural communities, their authors generally use brief examples from the localities to illustrate more macro-level ideologies, policies, and trends, but without making the local rural community a central, sustained focus. Moreover, nearly all these studies rely on sources housed almost exclusively in urban centers, and eschew fieldwork in provincial archives and ethnographic research in villages.

While this newer work has indeed brought real gains, it is striking how little we still know about the local rural community in the NDH, despite a consensus among scholars that the vast majority of intercommunal violence took place there. The ongoing existence of this historiographical lacuna is further perplexing given the shift in research on mass violence during the past decade in other contexts, such as Asia and Africa, in which the local level, especially in the countryside, has become a central subject for analysis.[17] This has also been true in research on other parts of Europe during World War II, such as Poland and Eastern Galicia. One need only note that Jan Gross's groundbreaking study on locally executed mass killing, *Neighbors: The Destruction of the Jewish Community in Jedwabne, Poland*, was published almost fifteen years ago.[18] And yet, no historian has taken up the challenge of writing a similar micro-level study on a small town or village in a rural region of the NDH, even though the phenomena of neighbors killing neighbors on an ethnic axis was arguably more widespread than in German-occupied Poland.[19]

Among the newer works on the NDH that do deal with the countryside in some way, one does not see a dismissal of the widespread phenomena of rural violence. But there is a tendency to adopt a largely top-down explanatory framework to account for it, usually by stressing the importance of nationalist ideologies and elite decision-making. Life and death at the local level thus appears as essentially the last (and usually passive) chain in a causal process that generally begins far away in capital cities among key political leaders.[20] State-sanctioned violence by the NDH authorities was undoubtedly of great importance in 1941 (and during the years that followed). No scholar can afford to discount this when trying to explain the violence in that state. But questions about the participation by local residents in killing their neighbors on an ethnic axis; the high levels of temporal and geographical variation in the occurrence of this violence; and its relationship with, and effects on ethnicity and nationalism—these questions cannot be adequately addressed without close, sustained attention to local social relations, both before and during 1941.[21]

The continued dominance of a largely top-down explanatory framework remains puzzling given the voluminous evidence suggesting how weak the NDH government actually was in many of its rural localities, specifically with regard to directing the violence of its own local militias—the Ustašas. Consider the words of an NDH official in the Bosnian town of Jajce writing in September 1941 to his superiors about the violence of Ustašas: "[In Jajce] there is no authority, nor government, nor central leader, nor gendarmerie, nor army—there are only these Ustašas."[22] Or the NDH military commander, who in May 1941 wrote about the attitude of local Ustašas in the Kulen Vakuf region: "they answered that for them there doesn't exist any kind of [higher] authority, and that they can do whatever they want."[23] Such evidence suggests the limitations of relying solely on top-down explanations in accounting for dynamics of local violence in the NDH. The continued prevalence of such an approach reflects a lack of sustained attention to the site where an enormous amount of the killing actually took place: the local rural community. This discrepancy between wanting to explain the causes and dynamics of mass violence, yet not devoting sufficient attention to researching the communities where it occurred on the ground, is not new in the scholarship on mass violence. It characterized the study of the Holocaust for decades, particularly with regard to Eastern Europe as Omer Bartov has argued, and began to be overcome only in the last fifteen years or so.[24]

But a similar shift has yet to take place in the study of violence in the NDH. This ongoing limitation is closely connected to the kinds of research questions that have retained importance. Historians of the NDH have tended to focus on a set of widely debated subjects that have long dominated their field: how many people were killed in the NDH; whether certain killings constituted "genocide"; the wartime experience of "ethnic groups"; the struggle between communist-led Partisans and Serb nationalist Chetniks; whether the years should be understood as three-sided or four-sided civil war; and whether Bosnia's "Muslims" were somehow a "natural" ally of the Nazis or instead "antifascists."[25] It can be argued that all of these questions have their place and deserve attention. But their continued prominence has also helped to maintain a certain inward focus in discussions about this history. A consequence of this has been a lack of engagement with broader scholarly debates currently taking place about the causes, dynamics, and effects of political violence in various contexts throughout the world.[26] And that is unfortunate because historians of the NDH potentially have much to contribute given the prevalence of locally executed intercommunal violence in that state.

Important theoretical and empirical work during the past decade, largely by political scientists and anthropologists, has illuminated the frequent sizable disjuncture between the macro cleavages of a conflict and the nature of local, or micro-level violence, especially in rural regions.[27] This insight has helped to spur more sustained engagement in accounting for what is often the puzzling temporal and geographical variation in instances of local violence, particularly through micro-comparative research.[28] Increased attention to variation has led to the challenge of explaining the presence and absence of violence within the same subnational units, and thus to the question of accounting for both the escalation and restraint of violence in such areas.[29] Studying the ebb and flow of violence and its results has generated work on how wartime dynamics then shape the prospects for further violence. This has helped focus attention on the extent to which prewar political cleavages and local wartime dynamics matter in accounting for whether intercommunal violence happens, where it happens (or does not), and in what ways.[30] This work on the endogenous dynamics of violent conflict has suggested that violence may, in fact, dramatically transform identities and forms of social categorization in ways that differ strikingly from what existed prior to violent conflict.[31] All of these findings, which have so animated the field of political violence in recent years, provide compelling ways of approaching and rethinking how to better explain local violence in the NDH. Yet virtually none have been applied to this case.

A fruitful path forward would consist of two closely connected approaches, which can help us to better account for the perplexing explosion of killing in places like Kulen Vakuf in 1941, and its subsequent effects on local life. On the one hand, we urgently need to make the rural community—where so much of the violence in the NDH actually took place—the central lens of analysis. Increased analytical focus on the micro-level in the countryside, where civil war and mass killing often occurs, has yielded important advances in the scholarship on other cases of violence, such as those in Africa. Yet even among researchers who work on that part of the world, one still hears calls for increased local-level research, if only to provide a basic reconstruction of the often poorly understood flow of events in villages where neighbors killed neighbors.[32] Given the much greater paucity of such research on rural localities in the NDH, the need to shift analytical attention in this direction is even more acute.

On the other hand, an analytical bridge needs to be built between the specific history of the local rural community in the NDH and the broader scholarly debates about the causes, dynamics, and effects of violence throughout the world. A way to take up this challenge is not only to excavate the local history of the Kulen Vakuf region, but also to chart a course by using the kinds of questions, and a more global set of comparative cases, that emerge by engaging in this broader conversation about violence. In that way, we can attempt to navigate the uncharted waters of the NDH's rural communities with new research questions and data for comparison, which can help us focus attention on discerning causes, dynamics, and effects. And posing them to this particular corner of the world holds the promise of better illuminating what still remains largely mysterious: How and why did neighbors in multi-ethnic communities, who had generally lived in peace for long periods, descend suddenly in 1941 into shocking levels of intercommunal violence? And how did this experience affect their identities and relations?

This book represents a sustained attempt to meet these challenges. It draws on questions and findings from the fields of political violence, ethnicity, and nationalism to tell the story of Kulen Vakuf before, during, and after 1941; yet along the way, the rich empirics of this story will become a means to critically engage key debates in these fields. As such, this book sheds analytical light on the local dynamics of intercommunal violence and its effects in a rural Balkan community, a subject strikingly absent in the literature on political violence. Yet while this study draws on key questions and findings in this scholarship, it does not apply them to the Balkans to merely illustrate well-known theories. Rather, the story of this Balkan community provides us with a way to expand this research on political violence—much of which has been concerned with non-ethnic civil wars. The objective here is to enhance this work by extending it to a type of violence less frequently analyzed in this literature: what many people might perceive as "ethnic violence."

The rest of Part I ("History") is a reconstruction of the history of the Kulen Vakuf region prior to 1941, with focus on the subjects of ethnicity and conflict. We begin at the end of the seventeenth century, when a small town was established in the Una River valley near several military fortifications built as a result of the ongoing wars that the Ottoman Empire was fighting in its western borderlands. The town eventually became known as Kulen Vakuf. Two questions frame our inquiry into the history of this town and its surrounding region: What meaning did "ethnicity" (or "nationality") have prior to 1941 at the local level? To what extent was ethnicity and nationalism a relevant category and ideology through which conflict was channeled? Here it is necessary to investigate their local prewar saliency, or lack thereof. Rich, under-utilized archival sources, particularly those created by the Austro-Hungarian authorities (1878–1918) and the interwar Yugoslav governments (1918–1941) exist to help in this search: court documents related to land disputes; crime statistics; police reports on political cleavages and inter-personal conflicts; programs and activities of political parties; election results; and reports about the existence of extremist groups and their activities (or their absence). If a sense of antagonistic ethnicity did become an available vocabulary in local politics and social relations, was it dominant? If so, when and why?

After excavating the prewar, local dynamics of identification, conflict, and cohesion, Part II ("1941") turns to an analysis of 1941, with specific focus on the period of April–September during which the Kulen Vakuf region witnessed unprecedented levels of locally executed violence. The German-led invasion of the Kingdom of Yugoslavia in early April 1941 resulted in the dismemberment of that state, and the establishment of the NDH. Voluminous archival sources left behind by its civil and military authorities on the building of their new state at the macro (central), meso (regional), and micro (local) levels, along with the contemporary press, make it possible to piece together how this sudden transformation unfolded. They also allow us to discern what its effects were on local forms of identity and social relations. How did that government's creation of a new political field, in which "ethnicity" had a dramatically enhanced salience, affect local inter- and intra-ethnic relations? What were the new categories of inclusion and exclusion? The key actors at the local level who drove these transformations were the men who joined the government's Ustaša militias. Documents from a wide array of archives, along with unpublished manuscripts and memoirs written by local residents, make it possible to use the case of the Kulen Vakuf region to provide a detailed social portrait of this group and illuminate its dynamics of mobilization at the local level.

One of the first effects of the government's policies in this region was the sanctioning of mass plunder of the property of "non-Croats" by the Ustaša militias and others whom the authorities defined as "Croats." How did opportunities for inter-ethnic plunder affect both inter- and intra-ethnic relations? Initially, those defined as "ethnic others" (i.e., "Serbs") were the only victims. But soon the Ustašas targeted their own supposed "ethnic brothers" (i.e., "Croats") once they had stolen everything from the "others." What does this tell us about the salience of ethnicity in such moments of upheaval? Documents from the NDH's civil and military authorities provide us with the materials to compose a vivid local picture of these difficult-to-discern and under-researched dynamics. Here, it is important to distinguish between how the newly politicized salience of ethnicity affected opportunities for violence versus simply viewing violence and plunder as outgrowths of supposedly pre-existing antagonistic "ethnic" cleavages. In so doing, we can question whether deeply rooted nationalist sentiment or ethnic cleavages are necessary to drive violent behavior on an ethnic axis at the local level.

By early July 1941, massacres of those considered to be "non-Croats" (i.e., "Serbs") began in many local communities, generally in response to mutually reinforcing fears. The NDH authorities instituted policies of ethnicized persecution, which caused many of the persecuted to flee to the forests, where local leaders feared they were preparing a rebellion. This triggered pre-emptive government-sanctioned attacks on their villages, which resulted in mass killings. Archival documents written before, during, and shortly after these events by the NDH's civil and military authorities make it possible to carry out a detailed reconstruction of these massacres, as do testimonies and memoirs of those who survived. These sources make it possible to explain why this local violence occurred when and where it did. They also enable us to explore how the killings affected intercommunal relations, and perceptions of group identities. Did perpetrators and survivors change their views of neighbors, and of themselves, in moments during and immediately following this violence? While these killings took place, instances of inter-ethnic rescue and intervention to save potential victims emerged in some locations, but not in others. The challenge is to explain this puzzling geographical variation. What made it possible for some to save their neighbors? Pre-1941 factors (such as long-standing inter-ethnic friendships) certainly mattered. But our search for an explanation suggests the importance of endogenous factors of the violence, since evidence of positive prewar inter-ethnic relations was widespread, but instances of rescue were highly varied.

Less than a month after these Ustaša killings began, a sizable part of the Orthodox population began an insurgency. During August and early September, they struck Catholic and Muslim villages where they committed large-scale retaliatory killings. Many of those who took up arms later wrote memoirs about their experiences. These sources are of varying quality, and often tend to be hagiographic when it comes to the role of the Communist Party, which months later managed to assume leadership over many of these local fighters. Yet many of these firsthand recollections convey a complex picture of local events, often discussing in rich detail the insurgency's weaknesses, acts of inter-ethnic rescue, and instances of intercommunal violence. Archival documents of the insurgents' public manifestos and private correspondence written during the rebellion also exist, which can help us evaluate to what extent these memoirs exaggerate, minimize, or omit information.

When compared with one another, these sources provide a window into the motivations, actions, and objectives of local insurgents. They allow us to pose several questions: How did violence on an ethnic axis affect both how local people saw themselves, and those whose violence had inscribed ethnicized categories of inclusion and exclusion upon them? How fixed were the new forms of identification that emerged during such acts? The earlier mass killings of the Orthodox population not only triggered a rapid collective categorization of the "ethnic other" as enemy. They also led to a process of collective categorization within the newly hardened group boundaries. Survivors of massacres often demanded ethnicization, or a closing of ranks on an ethnic axis, among their supposed "brothers" in response to their collective persecution.

A key objective in examining the insurgency is to try to push beyond analyzing only how violence on an ethnic axis can produce a rapid sorting of people into categories of ethnic "others" or "brothers." We also need to consider how intercommunal violence might actually fuel simultaneous processes of ethnicization, which unfold rapidly in multiple directions. Perpetrators may inscribe ethnicity on victims through acts of violence; victims, in turn, can both internalize this externally imposed ethnic categorization and, through acts of revenge, can inscribe ethnicity on the initial perpetrators and those associated with them. Yet ethnicization may also spread rapidly within perpetrator/victim groups through acts of violence and threats—against both ethnic "others" and "brothers." A working-hypothesis in analyzing this violence is thus our need to better appreciate the power of violence not simply as a destructive force, but also as a highly generative one in radically shaping the limits and possibilities for individual and group identification.

Yet a danger here is how selection bias—the initial choice to analyze the Kulen Vakuf region, where a number of communities were ravaged by high levels of mass violence—might lead us to believe that "ethnic" violence only produces cascading "ethnic" polarization. We can guard against this bias by employing a micro-comparative approach. Doing so allows us to identify "negative cases," that is, instances in this same region where violence did not occur, or where inter-ethnic rescues and interventions restrained and prevented killing. Memoirs and archival documents produced by insurgents are the key sources in identifying and reconstructing these understudied instances in which violence seemed likely, yet did not take place; so too are memoirs written by local residents who were spared being subjected to violence in such cases. The puzzle is that the areas where violence did not occur had similar prewar structural features as those that experienced mass killings, and both were subjected to similar NDH policies of persecution during the summer of 1941. How can we explain this puzzling subnational variation in violence? How did inter-ethnic acts of rescue and efforts to restrain violence affect ethnic identification and intercommunal relations? Here, we may be dealing with an understudied, counter-intuitive dynamic. While waves of killing can rapidly create antagonistic collective categorization on an ethnic axis, they may also produce their opposite: waves of inter-ethnic rescue and a sense that behavior—not ethnicity—is paramount in distinguishing enemies from friends.

The last chapter of Part II ("Forty-Eight Hours") is a detailed reconstruction and analysis of the snapshot discovered in the blue folders in the Archive of Bosnia and Herzegovina: the mass killings by insurgents of mostly civilians in Kulen Vakuf during a few days in early September 1941. A wide array of sources are necessary for the telling of this history: archival documents from the civil and military authorities of the NDH; memoirs and documents produced by insurgents; the contemporary NDH press; survivor testimony (both written and oral); and unpublished manuscripts (e.g., histories and memoirs written by local residents). Having carried out a micro-comparative study of insurgent violence, we can analyze this violence with different categories and questions than what might seem obvious. Rather than ask: Why did insurgents (whom many would simply define as "Serbs") kill large numbers of civilians Kulen Vakuf (i.e., "Muslims"), we can pose a different, more analytically useful question: How did the "advocates of escalation" among the insurgents manage to overcome the resistance of "the advocates of restraint" within their ranks, and then commit a series of massacres in Kulen Vakuf on an ethnic axis?

By approaching our analysis in this way, we can avoid reducing this history to a simplistic clash of whole "ethnic groups" in which one, with a supposedly powerful desire for revenge against the other, commits large-scale retaliatory violence. Instead, this history challenges us to explain how those who sought to escalate violence first faced the task of defeating their opponents, who were nominally on the same side and of the same ethnicity, yet opposed to killing. In doing so, we can illuminate the precise mechanisms whereby a desire for violence on an ethnic axis transforms into acts of killing in a particular time and place, but without relying on factors such as supposed long-term "ethnic antagonisms" or even a powerful situational desire for revenge, as primary causal factors. These may be necessary causes in some cases, but they are not sufficient as an explanation. As our previous micro-comparative analysis of negative cases will suggest, even when "ethnic antagonisms" and a desire for revenge on an ethnic axis appear to be high in a given region, violence may still not take place. Reconstructing several days of extreme violence in early September 1941 in Kulen Vakuf thus provides us with a unique challenge: How can we explain what exactly transforms a situation conducive to intercommunal violence into actual large-scale killing?

In Part III ("After Intercommunal Violence"), we turn to exploring how experiences and memories of violence affected local forms of identity, relations, and nationalism during several decades after the war. How did the killings of 1941 shape people's perceptions of themselves and each other? In what ways did people speak—or not speak—the language of nationalism after such high levels of intercommunal violence, yet now under the authority of a communist government intent on eradicating all forms of antagonistic nationalism? Newly available archival sources on local intercommunal relations during the 1950s and 1960s, which were compiled by municipal committees of the League of Communists, make such a micro-level examination possible. When supplemented with the views of some local residents, they open a rare window into the micro-dynamics of local nationhood in the shadow of intercommunal killing, during which perpetrators and survivors—whose identities could be held by the same people—often lived once again as neighbors. Did the killings of 1941 affect how people would react to attempts by their neighbors to spread a sense of antagonistic nationalism, especially in response to incidents of local conflict? What accounts for some people remaining indifferent to such efforts and others who sought to restrain them? A primary objective here is to provide new micro-level answers to a major question in the field of nationalism studies: How do ordinary people come to speak, remain indifferent, or resist the language of nationalism?

In the epilogue, we return to the present day by considering three striking local portraits: the unveiling of the first ever war monument in the town of Kulen Vakuf in 1981; the selection at a bridge spanning the Una River in June 1992 by Bosnian and Croatian Serb forces of 210 local Muslim men and boys for arrest and interrogation; and a reflection about the current landscape of war memory in the region. The purpose of bringing our story forward to the present through these portraits is not only to create a context in which to better illuminate its main scholarly contributions; it is also to suggest how this history—and the way(s) it has been told, silenced, and forgotten—continues to have far-reaching consequences for people in this part of the world. This has included fueling the potential for subsequent violence (i.e., during 1992–1995), and the casting of a shadow over present-day sensibilities about what kind of future is possible—or not.

Ultimately, our journey from the blue folders discovered in the archive into the distant past, through the violence of 1941, and then forward to the present-day, will suggest locally specific and empirically rich answers to several questions with global significance: What is the relationship between violence, on the one hand, and identity, nationalism, and memory, on the other? What creates a perception of one's local community as composed of mutually exclusive, antagonistic "ethnic groups?" How do certain people in such communities come to view their history as driven by seemingly endless cycles of "ethnic violence?" And what is our responsibility in telling the history of the violent past in such places?

Before we embark on this journey, a few words are in order about methodological and conceptual issues. This study makes extensive use of primary sources in reconstructing nearly *all* parts of this story. These archival documents, memoirs, and oral testimonies open new windows to life at the local level in the countryside. The substantial effort to obtain such sources was not taken simply to provide more local color. Rather, this approach enables us to stay close to the ground throughout the telling of this history. Doing so makes it possible to attempt to reconstruct this past without frequently resorting to an uncritical use of ethnicized, groupist language by casually dividing the region's people into "groups" called the "Serbs," the "Croats," the "Muslims," and so on, an approach that is common in most histories of this part of the world. Instead of projecting a sense of clearly defined "ethnicities" or "nationalities" onto our historical actors, the large quantity and high quality of primary sources enable us instead to listen closely to what they actually have to say about such categories of identification. Thus, in this book the word "nominally" will often precede ethnic categories, or they will sometimes be written in quotations, whenever primary sources do not exist to illuminate how historical actors themselves deployed ethnic names. This is a purposeful decoupling of our categories of historical analysis from the daily practice of historical actors. What they have said should guide how we use—and do not use—ethnic categories in the telling of this history. We should resist the urge to project our own perceptions of such categories onto those whose history we seek to tell. Remaining vigilant about this issue is essential in order to take up the challenge of discerning how ethnic categories come to matter—and not matter—to people, and how and why these categories change in meaning and relevance over time.

To better grasp and explain this fluidity, we need to resist a notion that "ethnicity" and "nation" are living things in the world, or abstract collective actors to which people somehow naturally belong and act through. Instead, we need a sense that they are "a perspective on the world," as the sociologist Rogers Brubaker has argued. They are mental frames, or ways of seeing and interpreting one's world, which are not simply deep and enduring, but can also suddenly "happen" among people in certain moments.[33] The challenge for the historian is to uncover the specific factors that imbue an "ethnicized" perspective with meaning and political salience at a particular time—or not. In searching for these factors, it will be useful to focus particular attention on the contingent events, particularly at the local level, which can rapidly transform peoples' perspectives about identities and social relations in dramatic, and often unexpected ways.[34] Employing this kind of "eventful analysis" holds the promise of better illuminating how and why categories of "ethnicity" or "nation" come to matter (or not) among ordinary people in small communities.

Here, a main focus is on instances of violence. As our story vividly suggests, such instances can be a crucial means through which a powerful sense of ethnicity can rapidly crystalize, amplify, or transform. Violence, in short, is a generative force in shaping forms of ethnic identification and social relations. This is, perhaps, a counter-intuitive proposition for many, who may strongly believe that deeply rooted and long-standing forms of ethnic identification, along with mutually exclusive nationalist ideologies, are necessary to cause "ethnic violence." Resisting the adoption of such a belief may be difficult when confronted with the existence of instances of violence on an ethnic axis. But here, we have to strive to avoid conflating results with causes. And so it is essential to proceed differently by not assuming that a strong and widespread sense of antagonistic ethnicity must automatically be a necessary precondition for conflict and violence on an ethnic axis. Instead, we seek to identify and explain the events that precede and trigger more widespread ethnicized perspectives on the world. Paying close attention to the sequencing of these events is essential if we wish to more clearly illuminate, and account for the causal relationship between ethnic polarization and violence, which too often is assumed rather than demonstrated with convincing evidence. What is the real relationship here? Does the former precede the latter, as many would assume? Or can violence be an underappreciated, yet crucial force in producing and amplifying not just ethnic polarization, but a sense of ethnicity more generally?

Our search for answers to these broad questions promises to be more successful if we root our analysis in a specific place where we know that both violence and ethnicity have mattered decisively in particular moments. And our investigation is likely to yield new answers to questions about the relationship between the two if we make the effort to closely examine life there—before, during, and after violence—through the sustained use of micro-level data. The blue folders discovered by chance one afternoon in the Archive of Bosnia and Herzegovina provide us with that place: the Kulen Vakuf region. And years of hunting down sources on its history—from central archives to unpublished manuscripts; from capital cities to mountain villages—provide the critical means to take us deeply into that multi-ethnic world, to discover what made it possible for neighbors to live together, to kill one another, and then live together once again.

Chapter 1

Vocabularies of Community

The Una River flows out of the mountains that straddle northwestern Bosnia on one side, and the Lika region of Croatia on the other. When sunlight beams down, its frigid and crystal-clear waters appear "agleam with gold and emerald," as the British archeologist Sir Arthur Evans wrote during his travels in the region in the 1870s.[1] Occasionally cascading over waterfalls, but mostly flowing along quietly, the Una is eventually joined by a much smaller river called the Ostrovica. It emerges from the base of mountain and flows on its own for a few hundred meters. At the confluence between the two, one looks up from the valley and sees an old fortress dominating the heights of a nearby ridge. Its ancient walls, although crumbling and decaying, still appear today impossible to breach.

It was here at the end of the seventeenth and beginning of the eighteenth century that the region's recent Slavic converts to Islam began arriving from Lika. Having fled from their homes in towns such as Udbina in the aftermath of the Ottoman defeat at Vienna in 1689, they began to build a town on a small island between the two rivers. Its Turkish name, pronounced in the local Slavic language as Džisri-kebir (Great or Long Bridge), referred to the wooden bridge that they built over the Una River to connect the town with the rest of Bosnia. But to local residents, the town was also known as "The Province of Pasha Mahmut Kulenović" (Palanka Mahmut-paše Kulenovića), named after a man who during the first half of the eighteenth century had been an Ottoman commander of the fortress. He ordered that a mosque be built in the center of the town in honor of Ottoman Sultan Ahmed II. It had a towering white minaret that reached for the sky, and a small walking street ran through an arch built underneath that was filled with small shops selling spices, produce, and gold work. Pasha Mahmut Kulenović declared that after his death most of his property was to be left to the mosque. According to Islamic tradition, such a religious endowment is known as a *wakf* (as transliterated from Arabic). Local residents pronounced the word in their language as "vakuf." And so, from around the second half of the eighteenth century on, the town became known as "Kulen Vakuf," as a sign of respect for the man whose wealth had built its largest and most famous mosque.[2]

Both the founding and subsequent growth of Kulen Vakuf in the first half of the eighteenth century was due to a series of wars and postwar crises that transformed the western borderlands of the Ottoman Empire. As a result of the Austro-Ottoman War of 1683–1699, as well as subsequent wars

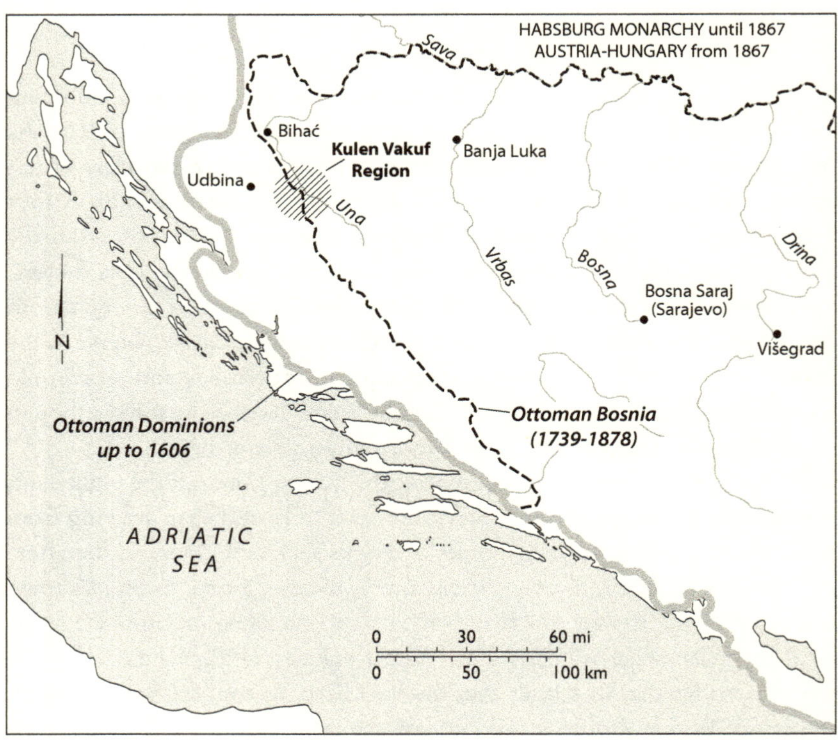

MAP 1. The Kulen Vakuf region in relation to the western borders of the Ottoman Empire, ca. early seventeenth century until 1878.

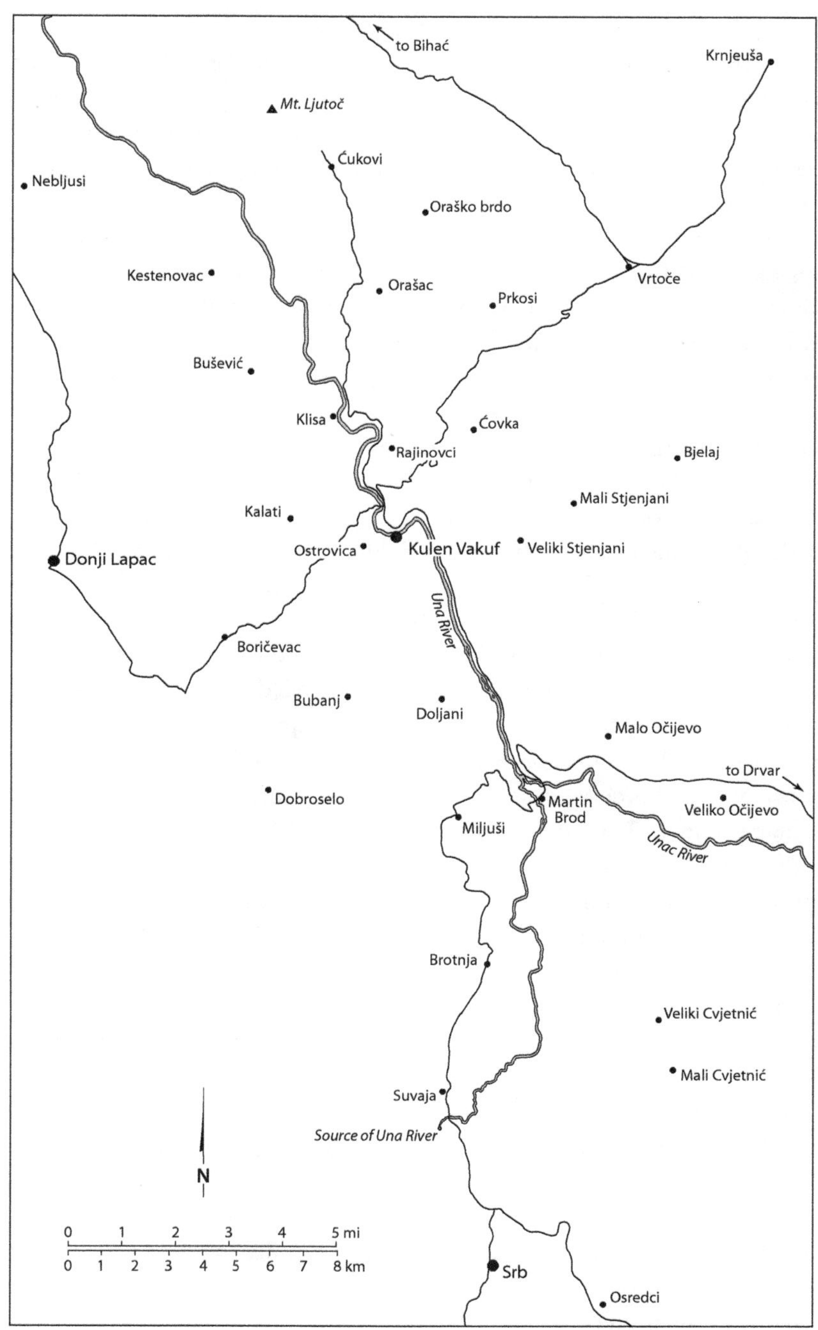

to Bihać
Krnjeuša
Mt. Ljutoč
Ćukovi
Nebljusi
Oraško brdo
Kestenovac
Orašac
Prkosi
Vrtoče
Bušević
Klisa
Ćovka
Rajinovci
Bjelaj
Mali Stjenjani
Kalati
Ostrovica
Kulen Vakuf
Veliki Stjenjani
Donji Lapac
Una River
Boričevac
Bubanj
Doljani
Malo Očijevo
to Drvar
Dobroselo
Martin Brod
Veliko Očijevo
Miljuši
Unac River
Brotnja
Veliki Cvjetnić
Mali Cvjetnić
Suvaja
Source of Una River
N
0 1 2 3 4 5 mi
0 1 2 3 4 5 6 7 8 km
Srb
Osredci

Map 2. The Kulen Vakuf Region

during the 1710s and 1730s, the Ottomans lost a sizable amount of territory, particularly along their northwestern border. To forestall further losses, they reorganized their military units, and created a series of new defensive subdivisions known as *kapetanije*. Each covered a town, its main roads, and the nearby countryside. A commander known as a *kapetan* was in charge of these precincts.[3]

The growth of the town of Kulen Vakuf came about because a kapetanija was established in the fortress, known as Old Ostrovica (Stara Ostrovica), which was located on the ridge above the confluence of the Una and Ostrovica rivers. The location provided complete visibility in all directions of the densely forested mountains of oak, beech, maple, and ash trees, whose leaves on summer days reflected ever-changing hues of brilliant green as the sun moved across the sky. The first commander of the precinct was Salih-aga Kulenović. Like many among the region's Islamic population, he likely came from Udbina not long before 1699, when the Ottoman Empire lost control to the Austrians of that town, along with its foothold in Lika. From this time on, members of the Kulenović family ran the kapetanija and established themselves as the most powerful clan in the region. While officially appointed by the Sultan, the Kulenović kapetans policed public order, gained significant authority in military matters, controlled trade, and oversaw the collection of many taxes. They served life-long appointments and, over time, transformed the position of kapetan into a hereditary office.[4] The ongoing wars along the borderlands resulted in the steady increase of taxes to finance military actions. This empowered the small local Muslim landowning elite, with the Kulenović kapetans at the helm, to exploit the region's largely peasant population. Among the Christian part of the peasantry, a majority were Orthodox and a minority Catholic, and most lived in villages located in the hills and mountains surrounding Kulen Vakuf.[5]

Hours away by foot—often up steep pathways and along narrow, dusty roads—life in their stone homes and rocky fields was a world apart from that in Kulen Vakuf. Freezing mountain winds swept across the highland meadows in winter, while the sun beat down mercilessly during summer months. Theirs was a world of never-ending work: grazing sheep, goats, and cattle, which they kept inside their homes during harsh weather; and cultivating plots of potatoes, beans, and wheat in the generally poorer rocky soil of the hills and mountains. Feeding their families was a constant worry not only because of the unfavorable conditions for intensive agriculture, but also due to the need by the local Muslim elite to finance the ongoing border conflicts in the region. Because of this, corrupt economic practices ensued, such as tax farming, whereby the local elite paid the Sultan a set fee in order to collect taxes from the peasantry. In lean years, these power holders paid the Sultan's fee out of their own pockets. But in better times they were able to extract a sizable profit from local peasants. This impoverished most, and transformed many during the second half of the eighteenth and first half of the nineteenth centuries into essentially landless sharecroppers.[6]

Despite holding a superior economic position in the localities, during the eighteenth and nineteenth centuries a more general hostility developed among Muslim elite toward Orthodox and Catholic Christians in Bosnia. This was due in large part to the international context. Ongoing Ottoman military losses to the Austrians and Russians led to the suspicion that the local Catholic and Orthodox populations were sympathizing with the external "Christian" enemy. Repressive practices ensued, such as prohibiting the construction of churches from the 1740s on.[7] The Habsburg war of the 1780s and the Serbian Uprising of 1804–1813 only increased fears among the Muslim elite about the "Christian" encroachment around this part of the Ottoman Empire. This led to more anxiety about the sympathies of local Christians, which in turn fueled Muslim hostility toward them, particularly among the elite. The establishment of regional consuls in Bosnia during the 1840s for Austria, France, Russia, Italy, England, and Prussia introduced new political actors into the region who often asserted themselves as the protectors of Christians in Bosnia. This development added to the suspicions that the Muslim elite already had toward the local Christians.

By the first part of the nineteenth century, arbitrary abuse, both physical and verbal, of Bosnian Christians by embittered Muslim notables had become more frequent. Echoes of such behavior can be seen in travel accounts written decades later, such as that by Sir Arthur Evans who visited the Kulen Vakuf region in the 1870s. He wrote that a Muslim merchant told him that landowner Tahir-beg Kulenović was known to visit the nearby Orthodox monastery in Rmanj, which was located on property he owned. "He rode on horseback into the church . . . after that he was in the habit of dismounting, and, seizing the priest's vestments, he made them into a kind of saddle, set them on the priest's back, and then mounting on it himself, made the wretched pope crawl around on all fours and serve the purpose of a beast till the poor man sank with exhaustion."[8]

Such types of behavior, while perhaps exaggerated in Evans's example due to its occurrence during the peasant uprising in Bosnia in the mid-1870s, reflected more broadly the Muslim elite's anxieties about the changing place of Christians in Bosnia. The ongoing wars on the borderlands; the resulting militarization of the region; the manipulative tax practices by the kapetans and other landowners; and the increased interest by foreign "Christian" powers in the fate of Ottoman Bosnia—all these factors coalesced to bring about a strong conflation of class and religious identities, making for increasingly antagonistic relations along such an axis. These transformations led to growing tension between the small Muslim landowning elite and the Christian part of the peasant population. During the end of the eighteenth and beginning of the nineteenth century, this growing fault-line transformed the connotation of the word *raya* or *reaya*—literally "the flock," but better understood as "subjects." While it had once referred to the entire peasantry and other small-scale wealth-producing segments of the population (e.g., urban peddlers, small-time traders), it now came to be conflated in negative ways only with those who were "Christians."[9] Located near the volatile northwestern border of the Ottoman Empire, social relations in the Kulen Vakuf region reflected these internal transformations brought on throughout Bosnia in response to the changing international context.

The rise in power of the kapetans and other Muslim provincial notables, and their tendency to abuse or disobey the laws of the Ottoman authorities, was a result of these broader historical changes. In the first half of the nineteenth century, the Ottoman authorities instituted a series of reforms in Bosnia in an attempt to break the entrenched power of the local Bosnian Muslim elite, such as the Kulenovićes in the Kulen Vakuf region. In 1835, they decided to abolish the kapetanije. At the same time, they adopted a more conciliatory attitude to Bosnian Christians in order to show other European powers that this population was indeed protected under the law.[10] Members of the local Bosnian Muslim elite, however, felt strongly that they should both be exempt from the regulations of the central Ottoman authorities, and continue to maintain a dominant position over the raya. As a local Muslim notable remarked in 1840, when discussing new taxes that the Ottoman Pasha sought to levy on the local Muslim elite: "And why are we taxed, as if we were Vlachs (a derogatory word for Orthodox Christians), and not Turks like him!?"[11] Breaking the power of the Muslim provincial elite would eventually prove so difficult that the Ottoman authorities decided to undertake a series of military offensives against them in the middle of the nineteenth century.[12]

During these transformations, social relations in the Kulen Vakuf region took several forms, not all of which were antagonistic. Despite the tensions that had grown along religious lines, there were points of close intercommunal contact, which had specific local and regional roots. The town of Kulen Vakuf was populated predominately by Muslims, some of whom were landowners and soldiers. Others were traders and merchants, who arose in response to the economic opportunities available given the town's close location near the border with the Habsburg Monarchy.[13] During the sixteenth and seventeenth centuries, when Ottoman control had stretched across that border, many of the ancestors of these individuals had once lived on the other side in Lika. Because of trading relations, more than a few had maintained close ties with the Catholic and Orthodox populations, particularly in towns such as Udbina and Donji Lapac, which had come under Austrian control at the end of the eighteenth century.[14] These Christians had converted to Islam when the Ottomans conquered the region in the fifteenth and sixteenth centuries. When control was lost at the end of the seventeenth century, some departed with the retreating Ottoman forces for Bosnia, while others stayed and converted back to Christianity. However, family connections—now divided by an international border and different religions—were often maintained. Some even continued to share the same last names, such as Osmanić and Abdulić, despite their changes in religion.[15] The region's local history thus produced the basis for a long-term tradition of close, quasi-familial intercommunal contact among a part of the population.

On the Ottoman side of the border, Muslims lived in the upper Una River valley, both in the town of Kulen Vakuf and in the nearby village of Klisa, located two kilometers down the river, just beyond a gorge known as the *buk*. Others settled in a narrow strip of land about twelve kilometers farther along the valley to the north, but built their houses and mosques slightly east of the riverbank. These lands, which were suitable for agriculture, stretched for nearly twenty kilometers to the north toward Mount Ljutoč, a pointed peak that juts forth from the valley. Along this part of the valley floor, two other Muslim villages—Orašac and Ćukovi—were established during the eighteenth and nineteenth centuries.[16] Their inhabitants felled the dense forests as far as possible up each side of the steep valley, and planted fields of corn and other crops. Mosques, such as those in Klisa and Orašac, were built on small hills and ridges so that their minarets appeared to reach even higher for the sky. A small number of the inhabitants of these villages, like their neighbors in Kulen Vakuf, were landowners. Their existence depended on collecting dues from their mostly Orthodox Christian tenants who lived in nearby villages high above the valley's fertile fields, in Prkosi, Ćovka, Stjenjani, Kalati, Bušević, and others. Yet a majority of those living in the valley were Muslim villagers. Like their Orthodox and Catholic neighbors in the nearby hills and mountains, they were poor peasants and engaged in small-scale agriculture. As Muslim subjects under the Ottoman authorities, however, they had more rights than these Christians, such as paying less taxes and having the right to own small plots of land. But many were essentially

FIGURE 1. The Una River Valley as seen from the Ostrovica Fortress above Kulen Vakuf. The peak in the distance is Mt. Ljutoč, and below the Una snakes its way past the village of Klisa, whose mosque can be seen in the center. The village of Orašac is in the upper right. Image taken by the author.

sharecroppers and lived in difficult material conditions similar to their non-Muslim neighbors.

The paucity of archival sources makes it difficult to tease out the dynamics of local intercommunal relations on the Ottoman side of the border prior to the twentieth century. But what evidence does exist suggests that we should be careful of assuming that deep-seated polarization along a religious or "ethnic" axis was widespread in this region during the second half of the nineteenth century. Sir Arthur Evans, who visited the Kulen Vakuf region during 1877, noted that some of the local Muslim elite held contempt for Orthodox Christians, with one referring to them simply as "the *raya* dogs."[17] However, other sources suggest that some landlords treated their tenants well and, in turn, were well liked.[18] Evans himself acknowledged the existence of a multiplicity of views among other Muslims in the region, such as a merchant whom he met in Kulen Vakuf; the man despised the insults that some Muslim landowners heaped on the Christian population.[19]

Among the Orthodox population, Evans noted that their perceptions of their Muslim landlords were formed not only by the economic exploitation that they often experienced, but also by stories passed down about the Ottoman conquest. A group of Orthodox peasants told him: "In this village was an ancient graveyard, and an old cross over-thrown and half buried in the earth. The people said that when the Turks first conquered Bosnia a marriage was going on here; that the Turks rushed in, killed the wedding guests and bridegroom, and carried off the bride, and this cross was set up in memory of the tragedy."[20] Whether such a story was true is less important than the fact that it was told and retold among local peasants, thus making it "psychologically true," as scholars of oral history have long observed about such testimonies.[21] The existence of such tales, which contained the gendered trope of violence not only against the Christian community, but also against its "women," played a role in forming the historical consciousness of Orthodox Christians in the region. Such stories contributed to a more general negative perception of the "Turks" (*Turci*), which was a formulation that local peasants often used to refer to their present-day, Slavic-language speaking Muslim landlords and neighbors.

But more than centuries-old stories told and retold of suffering during the Ottoman conquest, the difficult economic conditions that the Christian peasantry faced on a day-to-day basis were what fueled resentment among many toward their Muslim landlords. By the mid-1870s, this tension helped to produce the region's first major instance of intercommunal violence.[22] During the summer of 1875, the Ottoman authorities decided that the traditional tax of a tenth of a peasant's produce would now need to be paid in cash, which was nearly impossible for most peasants. This triggered an armed rebellion of Christians, which began in Herzegovina.[23] By late summer, Christians in the Kulen Vakuf region (most of whom were Orthodox) had joined, as well as many others throughout the frontier zone that separated the Ottoman Empire from the Habsburg Monarchy, known to local people as the Bosnian Krajina (Bosanska Krajina)—literally, "the Bosnian frontier." Orthodox insurgents, supported and often led by volunteers living on the Austrian side of the border, attacked Ottoman fortifications and set them on fire. They also sought out Muslim landlords and tax collectors, killing some and destroying much of their property.[24] According to Evans, who traveled with several insurgent commanders during 1877 (as well as other contemporary sources), the insurgent violence in the Kulen Vakuf region toward the "Turks" was brutal. Decapitation of prisoners captured and mutilation of those killed in battles was common, as was setting fire to Muslim villages. This violence brought a sizable influx of Muslim refugees from the nearby villages of Klisa, Orašac, and Ćukovi to the town of Kulen Vakuf to seek safety.[25]

These were not the only refugees on the move. As the violence escalated during the summer and autumn of 1875, thousands of Orthodox peasants fled from their villages to nearby mountains and caves, as well as to more secure locations across the border.[26] In the Kulen Vakuf region, what drove many to leave was the violent response of the Ottoman authorities to the rebellion, and especially that of the local Muslim elite. With a small number of Ottoman gendarmerie on hand to respond to the insurgents, the local Muslim elite organized their own units of irregular troops made up of local Muslims who were known as the *başibozuk* (bashi-bazouk). Witnesses living near the Orthodox monastery in Rmanj, located about twelve kilometers south of Kulen Vakuf, told Evans that these armed groups had damaged the church in September 1875, and then killed numerous men, women, and children. They staged similar attacks on nearby villages during the rest of 1875 and into 1876, such as Veliki and Mali Cvjetnić, Veliko and Malo Očijevo, Bjelaj, and others nearby Kulen Vakuf. This resulted in massacres of villagers unable to flee and the burning of their homes. Those who escaped in time sought refuge in the forests and the mountains.[27]

The local notables who organized and commanded these units, such as landowner Tahir-beg Kulenović from Kulen Vakuf, quickly transformed themselves into warlords. They were responsible to no one but themselves, as the region's Ottoman authorities (at least initially) proved too few and weak to deal effectively with the insurgents.[28] As the monopoly over the means of violence devolved to local leaders, aggression toward the Orthodox population increased. This included not just killings, but also widespread plunder of property, such as the seizure of clothing, crops in storage (i.e., corn), and livestock. Putting down the rebellion thus became an unexpected opportunity for those mobilized into the armed units to enrich themselves at their neighbors' expense.

Like the insurgent violence, the killings that these armed groups committed, which were under the command of the local Muslim elite, often included decapitation and treatment of corpses that was both symbolically humiliating and communicated a sense of domination. As Evans noted after speaking with a wife of a village elder: "A Bashi-bazouk seized him on either side, while a third dispatched him with pistol shots. The Turks then made off with their booty to Kulen Vakuf, carrying with them in triumph the head of the village elder. A Christian in Kulen Vakuf saw the Turks kicking the head in the streets of the town."[29]

Yet not all of the region's Muslim elite gave their approval to these violent acts. Evans noted that during this same attack "the women and girls [of the village of Očijevo] were stripped of the girdles and other ornaments that they possessed, and the irregulars were proceeding to outrages of a more shameful kind when stopped by the timely arrival of Ali-Beg Kulenović (a landowner), who succeeded on this occasion in restraining his retainers."[30] There were other local Muslims who opposed some or all of the violence against their non-Muslim neighbors. The merchant Mehmed Omić deplored the ongoing atrocities, but did not assign guilt to his Orthodox Christian neighbors for the violence. "We are ruined; trade is stopped; public security in abeyance; and who is to blame? First and foremost, the Begs [Muslim landowners]. It is their savagery and their oppression of the rayah that has brought all this evil upon us."[31] Others tried to persuade landowners to order their başibozuks to take a more moderate approach in their attacks on the Orthodox villages.[32]

This local intercommunal violence was a reflection of the broader structural dynamics of the agrarian question, in which the conflation of class and religion had pitted Muslim landlords against the Kulen Vakuf region's largely Orthodox Christian peasantry. At stake were not only the questions over how much tax should be paid, but also the more fundamental issue of who should own the land. Nonetheless, during the rebellion that lasted from 1875 to 1878, a series of alliances crystalized that crossed, or at least attempted to cross, ethnic lines. It appears that some local Muslim notables held discussions with several insurgent commanders about ending the violence and coming to a more equitable solution over the agrarian question. In the end, however, their meetings did not yield results. This was due to threats that more extreme elements—on each side—issued to their own moderates.[33] Such threats were not simply posturing; insurgents often set fire to the houses of Orthodox villagers who refused to participate in the rebellion.[34] This period of intercommunal violence thus also brought with it a significant element of intracommunal violence.

Still, several alliances continued despite the violence against ethnic "others," as well as supposed "brothers" who were identified as being too moderate. There was a small number of Christians who continued living in the town Kulen Vakuf during the rebellion. And a handful of Muslim merchants managed to maintain trade relations with their Christian counterparts in the wider region.[35] Throughout Ottoman Bosnia, intercommunal alliances of a different sort emerged. Most importantly for the fate of the rebellion were the Orthodox merchants who chose to support the Ottoman authorities and local Muslim elite against the largely Orthodox peasant rebellion. This Orthodox elite obtained a sizable part of its wealth by engaging in tax farming, and thus was complicit with Muslim landowners in exploiting the largely Christian peasantry. They did not wish for any change in the existing structure of agrarian relations.[36] In the end, the rebellion lost direction and disintegrated, mostly because of the inability of its Orthodox leadership, composed mostly of merchants, to unite behind common objectives. Those who engaged in tax farming did not wish to expropriate lands from the Muslim landowners. Their stance alienated the Christian peasantry. As a result, the position of the Muslim landowning elite remained structurally unchanged after the rebellion.

In its aftermath, Austria-Hungary was granted the right in 1878 to occupy Bosnia and Herzegovina. This was a reward for agreeing to stay neutral in the Russo-Ottoman War, which had begun in 1877 in part in response to the diplomatic crises that the rebellion triggered. The new Austro-Hungarian administration did not try to solve the agrarian question, but rather sought to maintain the existing land tenure system as established under the Ottoman Empire. As landownership laws remained the same, the dominance of the Muslim elite was preserved, particularly in the countryside and small towns. This

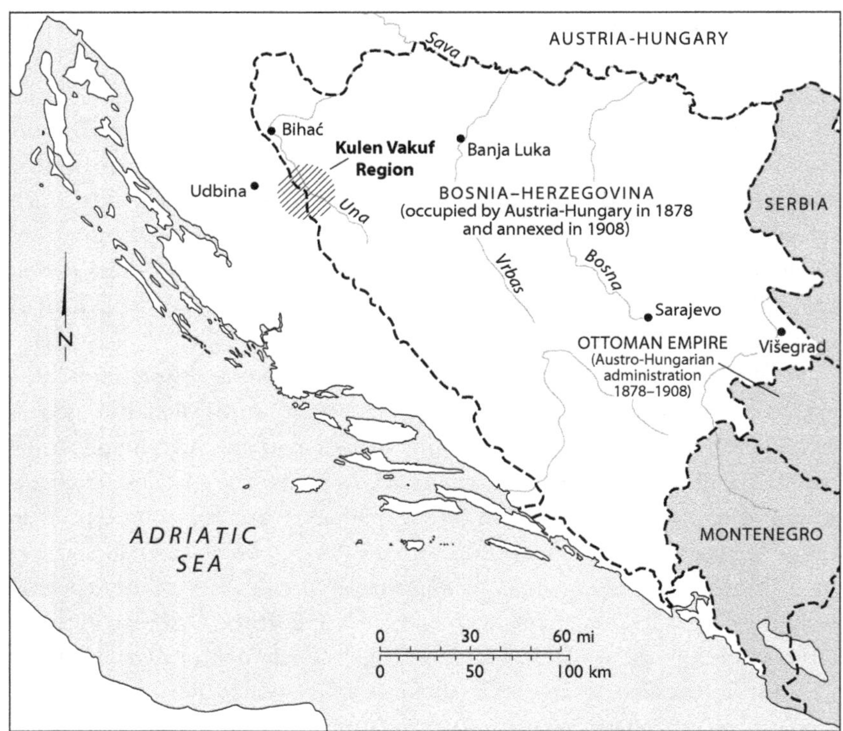

MAP 3. The Kulen Vakuf region after the Austro-Hungarian occupation of Bosnia-Herzegovina in 1878.

merely maintained tensions between Muslim landlords and their largely Christian tenants, as well as the basis for future conflicts along this ethnic/class axis.

Although religion had long been the key identifier of a sense of "us" and "them" in this part of the Balkans, it was increasingly the language of ethnicity, or "nation" (*narod*), that began to take precedence during the second half of the nineteenth century. As was the case in many other parts of Europe, this shift was largely confined to the intellectual classes. Nationalist activists of various stripes, often from regions outside of Bosnia-Herzegovina proper, began to imagine and redefine the region's Orthodox and Catholic Christians as individual parts of supposedly nationally conscious collectivities called "Serbs" and "Croats." They projected these groupist conceptions back into the distant past while simultaneously imbuing these "nations" with future destinies, usually in the form of creating nation-states. For some, "Muslims" now appeared less as a merely religious category, and more akin to a quasi-national group, on par with its Christian "Serb" and "Croat" counterparts.

Yet even here the complexities abounded, and defy any attempt at easy categorization and explanation. The slow and uneven penetration of the ideology of nationalism resulted in some so-called Muslims, especially among intellectuals, sometimes seeing themselves at various points more as "Serbs" or "Croats," despite their Islamic heritage. And perhaps even more common, as historian Edin Hajdarpašić has argued, it was the region's non-Muslim nationalist activists who looked toward the Islamic population of Bosnia simultaneously as "(br)others," who could be alternatively thought of as potential co-ethnics and/or culturally distinct enemies.[37] The arrival of the ideology of nationalism, which had already begun decades before the occupation of 1878, added new categories of potential identification to the social and political landscape, without automatically removing older forms of classification and self-identification. The categories of "Muslim," "Catholic," and "Orthodox" continued to exist after the Austro-Hungarian occupation in 1878, often in confusing and contradictory ways, alongside newer more "national," or "ethnic" understandings of "Muslim," and especially "Catholic Croat," and "Orthodox Serb." As Hajdarpašić has convincingly argued, the development of nationalism here was neither evolutionary nor linear. Instead, it is better characterized as an ongoing and conflict-ridden process, moving in multiple directions without a clear endpoint of forming so-called nations.

Although most of the Muslim elite in the Kulen Vakuf region appear to have opposed the occupation, almost no violent resistance occurred in 1878 in response to the arrival of Austro-Hungarian troops.[38] According to a local history of the region, residents recalled that the new foreign administrators simply imposed an increased level of order and stability, in particular when it came to economic relations between Muslim landowners and the predominately Christian peasantry. Each now faced much greater pressure from the new authorities to fulfill their obligations toward the other.[39] Of course, this did not change the structural basis for conflict between the two groups. But the Austro-Hungarian occupation does appear to have curbed the more extreme and widespread abuses that were common in the region under Ottoman rule, such as tax farming and violent methods of tax collection, which had triggered the rebellion in 1875. Archival documents of court cases over land disputes and the payment of rents in the Kulen Vakuf region during the first decade and a half of the twentieth century reflect this increased level of order. The evidence does not suggest that the Austro-Hungarian authorities were heavily biased for or against any particular party. One finds cases brought by Muslim landlords against Orthodox tenants for supposedly illegally dividing up lands and giving them to relatives. One can also read cases brought by tenants against their Muslim landlords for attempting to take more than the agreed upon share of crops. And there were cases of intra-ethnic disputes, especially among family members, over land ownership.[40]

Two other local developments further suggested that the new authorities of Bosnia-Herzegovina were not particularly interested in promoting the interests of one community at the expense of another. Kulen Vakuf's first primary school—built for all the region's children, regardless of religion and ethnicity—opened its doors in 1880. Above its entrance was written: "Blind is the one who does not know how to read." And in 1892, the steeple of a Serbian Orthodox church appeared on a hillside not far from the center of town, which joined the minaret of the Sultan Ahmed II mosque in stretching toward the sky. The call to prayer in Arabic throughout the day now co-mingled from time to time with the ringing of church bells.

During the late nineteenth and early twentieth centuries, with the increased political stability brought by Austro-Hungarian rule, it was no longer the dispute over land rights and obligations that appeared to threaten local peace. In the town of Kulen Vakuf, it was the natural world that often posed a greater danger. The rushing waters of the Una River could quickly become a menacing and destructive force, particularly in the fall and spring, when heavy rains caused flooding. Houses were often built on stilts in order to withstand the rapidly rising waters. But their wooden construction offered no defense against fire. The year 1775 was the first time that fire almost completely destroyed the town. On June 16, 1903, flames once again consumed nearly every structure. During the years in between, smaller-scale fires regularly caused significant damage. The dominance of nature over the town gave rise to a fatalistic saying among local residents: "Fire will either burn or the Una will flood Vakuf" (*Vakuf će ili vatra zagorjeti ili Una poplaviti*).[41] In their powerlessness over the calamities brought on by the natural world, some local people even sought an explanation for contemporary political events. The Ostrovica River was said to sometimes suddenly cease flowing from its source at the base of the mountain. Local people came to believe that the dry riverbed was a sign of impending political upheaval. Many claimed that the river had dried up just before the Austro-Hungarian occupation of 1878. It supposedly did so again shortly before 1914.[42]

The assassination in Sarajevo on June 28 of that year of Arch Duke Franz Ferdinand by Gavrilo Princip triggered World War I. This act compelled the Austro-Hungarian authorities to institute a series of repressive measures against much of the Orthodox population in Bosnia, which they defined collectively as "Serbs." This was due to a perception that the Kingdom of Serbia was involved in the assassination, and had pretensions to lead Bosnia's Orthodox population, which Serb nationalists in Serbia and Bosnia considered as Serbian brethren. The repression of the Orthodox population was

FIGURE 2. A postcard drawing of Kulen Vakuf as it appeared several years after the 1903 fire that nearly destroyed the entire town. Image courtesy of Buybook, Sarajevo.

perhaps most severe in Sarajevo, but was also present in the eastern regions of Bosnia that were close to the border with Serbia and Montenegro. The Austro-Hungarian military authorities believed that the civilians whom they identified as Serbs, as well as guerrilla forces from Serbia and Bosnia, were preparing for war against the Empire. In response, Austrian army units took hostages whom they believed were involved in such activities and carried out a series of executions.[43]

Some authors have suggested that some Muslims, as well as those who saw themselves as Catholic Croats, were recruited to join an auxiliary militia called the Schutzkorps to assist the Austro-Hungarian authorities in this repression. Their activities are said to have included hostage taking, stealing, demolition of property, and murders. Yet these units may not have been composed exclusively of those considered as "Muslims" and "Croats"; contemporary observers have noted that some who saw themselves as "Serbs" also joined this militia. They apparently took part in the persecution of their perceived co-ethnics rather than be sent to the frontlines to fight for the Austro-Hungarian Empire. In any event, the context of war; long-term resentments against the "Turks" for exploitation suffered during the years of Ottoman rule; and the violence of the Schutzkorps—these factors eventually triggered "Serb attacks" on Muslims. Several massacres took place, especially in eastern Bosnia.[44] Due the lack of archival sources, however, it remains unclear if these inter- and intra-ethnic dynamics of violence were similar in the Kulen Vakuf region during the early years of the war.

As World War I came to a close, local residents remembered that 1918 was another instance in which the Ostrovica River suddenly ceased to gush forth from the mountain. As had been the case in 1878 and 1914, there were townspeople in Kulen Vakuf who believed that some kind of upheaval was imminent. Whether the river's water actually vanished or not, they were correct in anticipating a major change. The year 1918 marked the creation of the Kingdom of Serbs, Croats, and Slovenes, commonly known as "The First Yugoslavia." Prior to the official proclamation of the new state on December 1, the government declared that agrarian reform would soon be instituted.[45] The essence of the reform was that the land would be redistributed to those who till it, and that former landowners would receive a "just indemnity."[46] In Bosnia-Herzegovina, the vast majority of the population—close to 90 percent—was peasant. Given that landownership laws were created during the centuries of Ottoman rule, and had been preserved by the Austro-Hungarian Empire (1878–1918), the question of agrarian reform was one of the most sensitive issues for both the people and the political leadership in Bosnia. And because of the long-term entwinement of the agrarian question

MAP 4. The Kulen Vakuf region in the Kingdom of Serbs, Croats, and Slovenes.

with class and "ethnic" disputes, any attempt to alter the existing situation was bound to incite tension and conflict.

In the wake of the government's decrees on agrarian reform in late 1918 and early 1919, many former peasant tenants did not wait for the authorities to redistribute land. They often took matters into their own hands. The words and deeds of two such tenants from the Kulen Vakuf region—the brothers Mile and Lazo Tintor—who sent letters to the central authorities in Belgrade, provide us with an evocative window into the frustration among former tenants. Anxious to assume ownership over the land they tilled, as the government had promised, they were impatient with the slow pace of the reforms, and furious that their landlord thus far had refused to step aside:

> After 530 years of sad slavery and the immeasurable pain and suffering that we have had to endure, the sun of freedom and the dawn of better days has risen . . . the words of your highness the king: the land belongs to those who till it. We sincerely hope that this concerns us, who for sixty years have soaked this land with our blood and sweat. And so we

> never dreamed that our landlord [*spahija*] would demand that we pay him in the year 1919.[47]
>
> In the hour when everyone is joyous, we are grieving; while everyone sings, we must pay; while everyone has been liberated, we remain enslaved. And we are not enslaved by foreigners, such as the Italians, somewhere on the periphery of our state. Rather, we are enslaved right here in the heart of our state by our landlord Alajbeg Kulenović of Kulen Vakuf.
>
> We gave this landlord what was his right up until we heard [King] Aleksandar's words: that neither serfdom nor landlords will exist anymore in his state.[48]

Mile and Lazo Tintor did not simply use words to express their frustration. Several days earlier they had harvested the wheat, corn, barley, hay, and beans from the lands they tilled. They carried away whatever they could store, and then destroyed the rest. Several prominent local Muslim landowners observed them, including their former landlord, Alajbeg Kulenović. Mile Tintor noticed him standing there, and with a few words alerted him to the sea change in landlord/tenant relations that he and his brother had just wrought: "Get lost, and get out of here!"[49]

Throughout Bosnia-Herzegovina, such confrontations between former landlords and their tenants were sometimes much more violent. Armed groups of so-called Green Cadres (zeleni kaderi), often made up of Orthodox peasants, began to seize land from their landlords. They stole property, burned down houses, and killed Muslims, both their former landlords and others. In some cases, they destroyed entire Muslim villages.[50] Some researchers in Bosnia have argued that these groups killed as many as several thousand Muslims in Bosnia-Herzegovina between 1918 and 1921, which they justified by claiming that they were taking revenge on the "Turks." It has been suggested that no one was brought to justice for these killings.[51] The historian Ivo Banac has argued that this anti-Muslim violence was only partly the result of long-standing class antagonisms. Orthodox peasants carried out violent acts not only against the small number of Muslim landlords who possessed large estates, but against Muslims more generally, the majority of whom were smallholders.[52] This resulted in free Muslim peasants, who were often just as poor as former Orthodox tenants, choosing to align themselves with former Muslim landlords out of fear.[53] The killings of Muslims in the first years after 1918 thus appeared to contemporary observers—as they have to many historians since—less as a class-driven revenge of impoverished tenants against landlords, and more as a form of "ethnic violence": that is as "Serb revenge" against the "Turks" for centuries of exploitation under the Ottomans. The killings have also been interpreted as a response to the repressive measures against the Orthodox population that some Muslims and Catholics had taken part in following the Sarajevo assassination of 1914.[54]

Yet such interpretations appear less clear-cut when one changes the analytical lens from the macro to the micro level. According Esad Bibanović, one of the few local historians of the Kulen Vakuf region, it appears that a part of the Orthodox population that lived in the hills and mountains surrounding Kulen Vakuf did indeed attempt to carry this wave of violence to the town's Muslims. Not long after the creation of the Kingdom, a large group marched to the town with the intention of attacking its Muslim residents. However, they were stopped before anyone could be killed. Perhaps surprising to those who would characterize this period as one based on clear, ethnically based enmity, those who brought about the successful intervention were not fellow Muslims, but rather the local Serbian Orthodox priest, Father Vukosav Milanović and Jovan Knežević, a well-known Orthodox peasant from the nearby village of Palučak.[55] Father Milanović happened to be in the town that day and met the armed group as they approached. "If you have come as liberators," he declared, "then enter and you will be received warmly and well cared for. But if you have come to commit any kind of evil against our Muslim brothers, then I will call on my entire parish to rise up against you."[56] In another instance, the former Orthodox tenants of Muslim landowner Muhamed Kulenović-Bajbutović, known to locals simply as "Pašabeg," guarded him and his property day and night throughout this unstable period. They were aware that other local Orthodox peasants wished to murder former Muslim landlords. Because Pašabeg had always treated them fairly, they protected him and his property from attacks that their supposed co-ethnics were perpetrating.[57]

The sparse archival record makes it difficult to determine definitively what motivated these interventions. A tradition of intercommunal friendship and good neighborly relations among some in the region may be part of the explanation. Perhaps even more important, however, was a perception that some of those perpetrating the violence were not merely doing so to take revenge on their former landlords, or to overturn a centuries-old pattern of land tenure, or to take revenge in the name of "Serbs" against the "Turks." Instead, under the guise of such explanations, they were taking advantage of the chaotic situation to rapidly enrich themselves, not unlike the local Muslim başibozuks during the rebellion of 1875–1878, many of whom were motivated by the opportunity to plunder. As a report sent to the Ministry of Internal Affairs in Belgrade suggests, among those "Serbs" involved in this violence "were a number of criminal and failed types who, under the guise of 'Serbianism' and the mask of various political parties, are mercilessly and unlawfully destroying muslims, secretly killing them, and stealing their property. They are doing this for their personal gain and to cover up their old sins."[58]

Reports from the region in 1921 suggest that armed groups, whose members appear to have been Orthodox Serbs (such as the leader of one such gang, Stevan Obradović "Langa," from the village of Doljani in Lika), were indeed roaming around and terrorizing the population. But their primary activity was noted as "robbery" (*razbojstvo*). And it remains far from clear whether they were doing so solely along an ethnic axis.[59] One of the victims of their robberies in 1921 was a Muslim merchant in the Kulen Vakuf region named Mustajbeg Kulenović, whom they killed.[60] But another target for plunder, which took place around the same time and in the same region, was the Serbian village of Ćovka, whose residents were attacked and robbed.[61] Various individuals, with histories of engaging in unlawful acts, seized upon a moment of upheaval to perpetrate violence and especially plunder, sometimes on an ethnic axis, and sometimes not, but largely for their own enrichment. It was not difficult for prominent local residents to identify such individuals and their motivations for engaging in violence at this moment. This may have been the reason why those such as Father Vukosav Milanović and Jovan Knežević intervened decisively to stop the violence and plunder in order to prevent the further destabilization their communities. They likely also sought to protect themselves, given that the perpetrators of violence were not choosing their targets solely along an ethnic axis.

While the local violence was stopped before it engulfed the Muslim population of Kulen Vakuf, some isolated acts did eventually take place in the wider region in which former tenants murdered their Muslim landlords.[62] The general atmosphere of disorder began to slowly dissipate during the first half of the mid-1920s, although local court records suggest that some individuals continued to seek out ways to enrich themselves during this period of instability. Suspected illegal trafficking of livestock, for example, and the supposed acceptance of bribes by some local officials to look the other way, elicited conflicts and alliances. Two such officials—Cvijetin Đurić (nominally "Serb") and Abdulah Kulenović (nominally "Muslim")—were sentenced in 1922 for working together in mistreating and exploiting local Orthodox villagers who wished to sell hogs.[63] Such conflicts thus had both inter- and intra-ethnic dimensions. By 1925, local officials reported that "peace and order" had been largely established.[64] Yet implementation of the agrarian reforms continued to drag on for several years, leading to ongoing tension between not only former landlords and their former tenants, but also between some tenants who fought with each other over who would receive redistributed parcels of land.[65] Evidence suggests that these intra-ethnic struggles among those former tenants quickly became the central flashpoints for local conflict.[66]

Part of the problem with quickly and effectively carrying out the agrarian reforms was that the government did not establish a sufficient number of local offices and staff with appropriate qualifications to deal with the complex litigations related to land redistribution. These deficiencies were why in the county (*srez*) of Bosanski Petrovac, where the municipality of Kulen Vakuf was located, and where such disputes existed in sizable numbers, not a single one was addressed during 1923.[67] Complaints written during the late 1920s suggest that local officials often did not implement decisions of higher authorities regarding the payment of indemnities. This meant that compensation was frequently not paid to former landlords whose lands were redistributed, which caused them hardship.[68] And so the agrarian reforms unfolded in slow motion during the 1920s and 1930s. The laws were altered several times, and in fact the entire internal territorial distribution of the state was dramatically reorganized after the establishment of royal dictatorship in 1929 (with the country then renamed the Kingdom of Yugoslavia [Kraljevina Jugoslavije]). This resulted in the creation of "banovinas," which were akin to internal states or provinces. Their leaderships (the ban and the banska uprava) now became responsible for handling the implementation of agrarian reform and any accompanying disputes. Such sweeping changes in internal administration and jurisdiction did not bode well for quick solutions to long-standing land disputes, for which a sizable cadre of experts was needed, especially those with local knowledge.[69]

Some local historians have suggested that the agrarian reform impoverished many of the former Muslim landowners who lived in and nearby Kulen Vakuf. The government apparently paid them an inadequate amount of compensation, and none of the poorer Muslims received any new parcels of land.[70] Archival documents show that former landlords and their family members continued to request proper compensation from the regional authorities as late as the 1930s.[71] However, it is not clear from the existing evidence whether such individuals were reduced to poverty, as some historians have suggested more generally for all of Bosnia-Herzegovina.[72] The agrarian reforms are said to have affected about 4,000 Muslim families (i.e., landlords and their families). This constituted a transfer of land away from them largely toward the rural Orthodox population, which comprised the bulk of landless tenants.[73] Although it is indisputable that former Muslim landlords lost much of their land holdings, in the Kulen Vakuf region it appears that some members of these families managed to switch to careers as successful merchants. In fact, such transitions were already underway prior to the establishment of the Kingdom of Serbs, Croats, and Slovenes. This substantially mitigated their economic losses due to the agrarian

Map 5. The Kulen Vakuf region in the Kingdom of Yugoslavia after the establishment of the banovinas.

reforms. They also managed to remain as influential members in their local communities.

Despite the hardships that ensued for some due to the agrarian reforms, the town of Kulen Vakuf began to slowly expand after 1918 as a regional center for trade and business activity. A group of influential local merchants crystallized during the 1920s. By 1930, they were sufficiently established to found a local association for advancing trade and transportation links to broader markets.[74] Yet the real impetus for the town's economic growth was the state-initiated construction in 1936 of railroad lines through the upper Una River valley, with a section of track crossing through Kulen Vakuf. Once finished, the railroad made possible a much larger amount of sustained trade between the town's merchants and their counterparts in the wider region.[75] The traditional weekly market in Kulen Vakuf now attracted merchants from as far away as the Dalmatian coast. They were drawn because of the diversity and quality of the livestock sold there, which was produced in the nearby Orthodox villages, as well as for other produce and crafts.[76]

The increased amount of trade helped to transform Kulen Vakuf's weekly market into a place of mixing between the largely Orthodox peasant population and the town's predominately Muslim merchants. The market day was not only for buying and selling, but was a means to hear news, and cultivate and maintain friendships. Local peasants would sell their livestock, eggs, cheese, and *kajmak*, and then spend hours talking with Muslim acquaintances and friends about all subjects, including local and national politics.[77] Later in the day on their way home, bouncing along the bumpy dirt roads in their horse-drawn carts, they would sometimes argue and complain about the prices in the market for this or that. But according to memoirs, rarely did any speak in negative collective terms about the merchants in Kulen Vakuf.[78]

Alongside the market, the construction of railroad lines along this part of the Una River provided further opportunities for the growth of intercommunal connections. Friendships were formed as men of all backgrounds cleared trees, pounded in spikes, and dug for hours each day in dark tunnels. Working together under difficult conditions created opportunities for interethnic friendships and acts of mutual assistance.[79] The building of the railroad did much to stimulate the growth of trading and crafts, as well as taverns in Kulen Vakuf, due to the town's designation as one of the headquarters for workers charged with constructing about thirty kilometers of track. People whose land was needed for the railroad lines were well compensated, and many others found work as laborers. Money, contemporaries recalled, appeared to be pouring out everywhere in the town.[80]

Yet these favorable economic changes in the town of Kulen Vakuf do not appear to have had much effect in the nearby countryside, which had long existed in difficult conditions. On the eve of the Great Depression, local officials described the region's villages as mired in "primitivism and poverty." Most did not have schools. The villagers' main source of subsistence was raising livestock, such as sheep, goats, cattle, and hogs. Their lands, which were largely in the hills and mountains, were too weak to support intensive agriculture. Most villagers usually kept their animals inside their homes (in stables directly below their own rooms) when not grazing them. This was done to both protect them during the winter from the elements, and more generally from anyone who might steal them.[81] Although many sold their livestock in Kulen Vakuf's weekly market, there was little improvement in their economic situation during the late 1920s and first half of the 1930s.[82] They survived by cultivating their small fields of wheat, rye, barley, and corn, along with gardens of beans, cabbage, and potatoes. Harvests were better some years than others depending on temperatures and rainfall. Sometimes their plum, apple, pear, and cherry orchards yielded fruit, and sometimes not.

In general during the 1930s, the region's villagers struggled to extract a sufficient amount of food from the land.[83]

As a result, increasing numbers of men sought work at the few factories in the town of Drvar, about forty-five kilometers southeast of Kulen Vakuf. They worked in wood and bauxite processing, but employment was often unstable due to market fluctuations during the late 1920s and early 1930s. Thus, these peasants-workers sometimes worked only a handful of days per month. Local officials noted with alarm that such men were often unable to feed their families.[84]

Despite the unstable economic conditions in the region during the 1920s and 1930s, the factories in Drvar and the construction of the railroad nonetheless fueled the growth in numbers of permanent and seasonal workers. Some men who had worked in industry in Belgrade and abroad attempted to spread ideas about class solidarity and the international workers' movement.[85] During the first half of the 1920s, the local authorities took note of meetings of hundreds of disgruntled workers, which were held near the large factories in Drvar. "Patriotism ends," one speaker declared during a gathering in November 1923, "if the stomach is empty." Such a statement foreshadowed a different kind of local politics in which loyalty to the new state, and especially the "nation" or "ethnicity," would not trump the need to resolve pressing socio-economic problems.[86] The spread of working-class politics outside of Drvar was contingent on the growth of industrial wage laborers. Given that industry remained confined to the town, the expansion of the embryonic workers' movement throughout the region was quite modest during the 1920s.[87]

This changed, however, in the second half of the 1930s with the construction of the railroad. By far the region's largest ever construction project, the railroad required the mobilization of thousands of workers, many of whom were local peasants. From villages such as Suvaja, Nebljusi, Begluk, and Doljani came scores of men who eagerly took on the difficult work of building the railroad as a way to solve their economic difficulties. Working long days under difficult conditions for generally low wages was acceptable for most during 1936. But 1937 brought sharp increases in prices for most household items, which triggered strikes. They quickly assumed large-scale proportions, with between 3,000 and 4,000 workers walking off the job, as well as other smaller actions in which groups of striking workers forcibly attempted to prevent others from working.[88] The local authorities noted that their demands were of an entirely "economic basis," specifically fewer working hours, higher pay, and more jobs reserved for local men rather than workers from outside the region.[89]

The strikes reflected popular dissatisfaction. Yet they also had a crucial organizational component, which was driven by a handful of local men with prior experience in the workers' movement in larger cities, some of whom were imbued with socialist and communist ideas. Josip Hodak, who was born in the village of Kliško Poljice just a few kilometers from Kulen Vakuf, was the principle organizer in 1937–1938 of most of the region's strikes. He was secretary of the local organization of construction workers, and a dedicated activist on their behalf. As such, he was popular with most workers, regardless of which village they came from.[90] His focus was on resolving the conflict between his men and their employer—and not on "ethnic conflict." In this regard, he led by example, forming alliances to advance the workers' cause, which were often inter-ethnic. While organizing a strike in the Orthodox village of Martin Brod in 1938, Hodak (nominally Catholic) arranged for the baker Hamdija Kulenović of Kulen Vakuf (nominally Muslim) to supply the workers with bread. The loaves would be received and distributed to the strikers by a local merchant in Martin Brod, Marko Vladetić (nominally Orthodox).[91]

While "ethnicity" may have been of importance among strike organizers in some way, it did not appear to have much significance in determining how they forged local political solidarities, other than being a potential cleavage to be bridged. For Hodak's role in organizing the railroad workers in the Kulen Vakuf region, the authorities issued orders to have him removed from the area, and banned him from returning.[92] More than a few former railroad workers would later suggest in memoirs and local histories, that participating in these strikes during their late teens and early twenties was formative. This was their first experience with collective political action. And it was one in which economic—not ethnic—factors were paramount in distinguishing friends from opponents.[93]

Even though the 1920s and 1930s witnessed the birth of regional and local working-class politics, local historians have claimed that formal political affiliation remained on an almost exclusively ethnic basis. About 95 percent of the Muslims in Kulen Vakuf, and throughout the Muslim villages of the immediate region, were said to be supporters of the Yugoslav Muslim Organization (Jugoslavenska muslimanska organizacija [JMO]), the main political party formed in Bosnia-Herzegovina after 1918 that purported to protect "Muslim" interests. The small Catholic Croat population in villages such as Vrtoče, Kalati, Brotnja, Boričevac, and Krnjeuša was said to support the Croat Peasant Party (Hrvatska seljačka stranka), whose leaders sought to create a Croat federal unit in the Kingdom of Yugoslavia. And the vast majority of the Orthodox population was said to support the

National Radical Party (Narodna radikalna stranka), which had a "Serb" nationalist orientation.[94]

However, these local histories only occasionally make use of archival documents. More often, they are based on the personal recollections of their authors, and do not reflect the election data. The election results found in archives lack complete data for most years. Nonetheless, what does exist suggests a more complicated picture in which categories of ethnicity (e.g., nationality or religion) do not always suggest clear "ethnic" voting patterns. For example, the main candidates at the national level in the 1938 elections were Milan Stojadinović and Vladimir "Vladko" Maček. The local list of candidates for each in the county of Bosanski Petrovac included those who were nominally Orthodox Serbs and Muslims. Interestingly, those voters classified as "Muslim" divided their votes between the Muslim candidates on each list, Adem Kulenović and Hasan Saračić. But they also voted in high numbers for Serb candidates, Dušan Novaković and Đuro Smiljanić. Those voters classified as "Orthodox" (i.e., Serb) barely gave any support to either of the Muslim candidates, but divided their votes among various local Serb political leaders. Voters classified as "Catholic" (i.e., Croat) voted almost entirely for those local candidates on Maček's list, but all of the candidates whom they supported appear to have been nominally Serb; they gave no support to the local Muslim leader on the list, Hasan Saračević.[95]

In short, we do not see what local historians have suggested: that the population voted along clearly defined ethnic lines and for single, ethnically oriented parties. Instead, voters classified according to their nominal religion/ethnicity voted in more complex ways: Muslims supported two different Muslim candidates, but also voted in large numbers for one who was Serb; Orthodox voters did not vote for Muslim candidates, but divided their votes among Serb candidates; Catholic voters did not support Muslims (nor Catholics, as there were none on the list), but divided their votes among various Serb candidates. Such local election data does not suggest an overly clear link between perceptions of one's "ethnic group" and voting behavior.

We should also not assume that more than a small minority of people devoted much time, thought, or energy to party politics. For example, in reports about the region's political situation that the local authorities complied during March of 1924, they noted that Hasan Saračević, the president of Kulen Vakuf's local council of the Yugoslav Muslim Organization, was elated with the recent fall of the cabinet in Belgrade. His hope was that Stjepan Radić, the longtime leader of the Croat Peasant Party would come to power, and along with him Mehmed Spaho, the leader of the JMO. However, the same reports also noted: "A majority of people [in the region] are not partaking in politics, let alone are they concerned in any way about the composition of the cabinet. They are much more worried about plowing their fields and obtaining food."[96] Examples abound of such wide discrepancies between the daily concerns of local politicians and the region's rural population.[97]

Awareness and support of other more "extremist" political groups, which the government sometimes banned for various periods of time, was even more limited. A small group of local supporters of the Communist Party of Yugoslavia, which the government banned in 1920, formed a small branch of the party in Kulen Vakuf in 1940. These few communists were only peripherally involved with their equally small number of counterparts in nearby towns and villages.[98] The authorities in the wider region, such as those in Donji Lapac, submitted reports during the mid-1930s in which they regularly indicated that communist-oriented individuals and organizations did not exist in that town or in its nearby villages. These officials noted that communist pamphlets or other printed materials were not in circulation.[99] It was toward the end of the decade when a host of groups united in a larger political opposition bloc (Udruženje opozicije [UO]) began to form, that the local police mentioned the existence of a handful of youthful "communist oriented" activists. These included the prominent organizer of railroad workers, Josip Hodak of the village of Kliško Poljice near Kulen Vakuf, along with Milojko Majstorović of Doljani (who in 1939 became the president of the municipality of Donji Lapac), among a few others.[100]

Evidence from the 1930s suggests that Croat nationalists affiliated with the Ustaša movement, who wished to destroy the Kingdom of Yugoslavia and create an exclusively Croatian nation-state, were few in number and without influence in Kulen Vakuf and its region. A 1933 report suggests that several meetings took place in the Catholic village of Boričevac among those who could be considered as actual and potential supports of the Ustašas. In autumn of that year, Juko Pavičić visited the village (where it seems he was born). It was said that he maintained direct connections with well-known Ustašas who were in exile, such as Mile Budak.[101] During his visit, he spoke with several local Muslims from Kulen Vakuf, such as a merchant named Husein Zelić. According to police reports, they discussed "separatism," "anti-state activities," "the slavery of the Croat people and its need for freedom," and sang songs about "Ustaša actions." The local authorities kept this handful of individuals under close surveillance during the 1930s, and it does not appear that they engaged in overt political activity during the second half of the decade.[102] Most of the movement's supporters were based in the wider region in the cities of Banja Luka and Bihać, and in larger towns, such as Bosanski

Petrovac and Cazin. Lists complied by the Ministry of Internal Affairs during the late 1930s of Ustaša supporters living in exile in Italy did not include any names from the Kulen Vakuf region. The movement also appears to have had few visible supporters at the village level, aside from what appears to have been a few in Boričevac. In fact, their activity does not appear to have become noticeable, at least to the local authorities, until 1940. Real and potential members were under heavy surveillance by the local gendarmerie.[103]

The Ministry of Internal Affairs in the Vrbaska Banovina was increasingly concerned with the "tribal animosity and hatred" that Chetnik societies were said to be stirring up, especially during the second half of the 1930s. These were nationalist associations, largely composed of those who considered themselves Serbs.[104] But the evidence does not suggest that such organizations were either large or influential in the Kulen Vakuf region. As of 1938, the regional authorities did not list a single Chetnik society in existence in the county of Bosanski Petrovac.[105] The evidence thus suggests that political groups with more extremist ideologies—whether of a nationalist (e.g., Serb or Croat) or communist character—were small to non-existent in the region.

During the 1930s, intra-political party conflicts were what the local authorities mostly took note of. Party leaderships often tended to be composed of those who saw themselves as co-ethnics, which suggests that intra-ethnic conflict was more common, or at least publicly visible, than inter-ethnic. For example, police reports sent to Belgrade between 1936 and 1938 indicated that conditions were "very good," and that most people's disposition toward each other, and the government, was generally positive. No overt ethnic clashes were reported.[106] But significant tensions, due frequently to "personal quarrels," between members of two factions within the Yugoslav Radical Union (Jugoslovenska radikalna zajednica [JRZ]), whose members were considered to be mostly Serb, caught the authorities' attention on several occasions. Conflicts also occurred among Muslim political figures. One of the leaders of the municipality of Kulen Vakuf, Adem Kulenović, refused to attend the welcoming ceremony for Džafer Kulenović, a minister without portfolio who was originally from the region (from the village of Rajinovci), when he visited Kulen Vakuf in July 1938. He declined to attend the minister's speech and chose not to hang a flag in front of his tavern as a public indication of his disrespect during Kulenović's visit.[107]

These conflicts were often personal and intra-ethnic. A regional inspector noted in 1932 that several ongoing conflicts in Kulen Vakuf were the result of "old hatreds" between Ivan Topalović, the local administrative authority (*starešina ispostave*), and Milan Stakić, the former head of the municipal council, both nominally "Serb."[108] On September 7 of the same year, in a tavern in the nearby town of Drvar, several people testified that Jovan Đurđević, a well-known critic of local and national political affairs, especially when intoxicated, yelled out: "Bogoljub Kujundžić [a member of the parliament], Milan Srškić [minister of Internal Affairs], and Vaso Jovanović [a retired minister]—they can all kiss my ass!" He went on to curse the mother of local merchant Todor Tadić and finally criticized the work of the local leader [*načelnik*] of the municipality of Drvar, Jovo Kreco.[109] Đurđević's targets occupied diverse positions, from the national to the local level. Yet uniting them all with Đurđević was a nominal sense of Serbian nationality; his was definitely not an "inter-ethnic" rant.

The data on crime in the region suggests similar dynamics, in which a main axis for conflict was intra-ethnic and often personal, rather than inter-ethnic. While statistics on local crime for all the interwar years are lacking, the numbers that do exist for the years 1935–1936 suggest several trends. The county in which the municipality Kulen Vakuf region was located generally had a low murder rate compared to others in northwest Bosnia. It was usually less than one killing per month. Conflict that did exist, whether inter- or intra-ethnic, did not tend to end in death. But the region had a generally high rate of physical assaults, arson, and theft, often times among the highest in the region. It is likely that much of this fighting, intentional burning, and stealing was of an inter-personal and intra-ethnic nature given that most communities in this county were villages, often where people of only one nominal ethnicity lived, and where most people knew each other face-to-face.[110]

The qualitative evidence suggests that this crime, as well as more violent incidents such as rapes and murders, tended to be of an intra-, rather than inter-ethnic nature. For example, one of the few instances of rape concerned two male relatives who raped a thirteen-year-old girl. The perpetrators and victim were all nominally "Serb."[111] In a report about a murder, one man shot another with a pistol. The perpetrator appeared to have been having an affair with the victim's wife. All were from the same locality (in the region of Lika, just to the west of the Kulen Vakuf region); all were nominally "Orthodox" or "Serb."[112] In March of 1939, Ilija Majstorović from the village of Doljani stabbed Stevan Polovina of Dobroselo in the back. Both men were from neighboring Orthodox villages within walking distance of each other.[113] In the village of Suvaja, two members of the Keča clan fought each other, with one killing the other with an axe; and not far from the town of Donji Lapac, two from the Obradović clan fought, with one killed after being struck with a rock. In both instances, all the men involved were nominally of the same ethnicity.[114]

None of these examples would surprise criminologists, who have long shown that much violent crime occurs among people in small communities or social circles. Frequently, perpetrators and victims are well acquainted with one another.[115] As was the case after a violent robbery in the Orthodox village of Doljani in May 1930, local residents complained about having been attacked yet again by two well-known local convicts, Todor Medić and his accomplice Avram Jovanić (known as "Buzdum") both of whom were nominally "Serb," just like their victims.[116] And in the town of Donji Lapac, where most people were considered to be nominally "Serb," local inspectors noted during the same year that several stables were burned down because of a desire for "revenge" (*osveta*) by some neighbors against others.[117] What is noteworthy in these examples is the degree to which local incidents of violence do not suggest that nationality, ethnicity, or religion were the main axes around which violent crime took place. Personal, local intra-ethnic tensions and disputes among villagers and townspeople are more often what one finds in the archival sources written during the 1930s, rather than voluminous evidence suggesting that overt "ethnic" conflicts were predominant or steadily crystalizing.

In fact, evidence suggests that intercommunal cooperation among local leaders was a feature of local political life, at least to some extent. For example, records of the meeting minutes of Kulen Vakuf's municipal council (*opštinsko vijeće*) from 1930 show a group of local leaders, often composed of relatively equal numbers of those who were nominally Serbs and Muslims, engaged in the daily business of striving to improve their region's economy and social welfare. Their main concerns were securing new doctors and veterinarians, and debating how much assistance to provide to poverty-stricken families whose dilapidated homes were on the edge of ruin. Pressing the regional authorities for permission to amalgamate the Kulen Vakuf municipality with that of Donji Lapac for the purpose of increasing economic development was a concern, as was developing their region's hydro-electric capacity, railroads, and roads. The mixed nature of the leadership of the council, and their primary focus on social welfare, infrastructure, and economic issues does not suggest that deep polarization among them along ethnic lines was the order of the day.[118]

The birthday celebration of Yugoslavia's king, Petar II, on September 6, 1938, further exemplifies the region's atmosphere of general peace and lack of overt, sustained ethnic conflict. Local gendarmes noted that in Kulen Vakuf the day came and went "with complete order and peace, without any kind of incident." The municipality's two leaders, Adem Kulenović and Vlado

Milanović, both gave short speeches about the importance of the King and his dynasty, which were followed by applause from the crowd of town residents, peasants from nearby villages, and the many workers who were in the region building the railroad through the Una River valley. Kulenović was known for his thorny relations with fellow Muslim political leaders. Milanović was the son of Father Vukosav Milanović, the local Orthodox priest who had intervened decisively in 1918 to stop local Orthodox peasants from attacking Kulen Vakuf's Muslim population during the period of agrarian reform. Their personal histories and the way they practiced politics suggest that they fostered cooperation during the late 1930s, not "ethnic conflict."[119]

Internal government reports on the emergence of the "Serbs, Rally together!" movement (*Srbi na okup!*), which emerged during the fall of 1939 and spring of 1940 in many locations in response to the creation of the Banovina of Croatia (a new administrative unit created within the Kingdom of Yugoslavia), further support a sense that inter-ethnic conflict was low in the Kulen Vakuf region. The movement's supporters held meetings in cities and towns such as Mostar, Glina, Vukovar, Otočac, Gradačac, Brčko, Derventa, and Osijek. Prominent merchants and especially the local Orthodox clergy were the key actors in staging these meetings, organizing local villagers to attend, and drafting resolutions about the imperative for their respective counties to secede from the newly created Croatian banovina and join a future Serbian one.[120] Yet no such meeting in support of this proposal was held in any town or village in the Kulen Vakuf region. The local authorities noted that some individuals here and there were sympathetic to the movement, but their sentiments do not appear to have manifested into overt action. Only a handful, such as Stevo Rađenović from the town of Srb, made the effort to attend meetings in towns outside the immediate vicinity where they lived.[121] While nationalistic rhetoric was strong at these events, and inter-ethnic incidents of conflict sometimes took place before and after them, they had little to no overt impact on political leaders in the Kulen Vakuf region.[122]

Among those not active in politics, evidence suggests that everyday interactions among neighbors tended to be generally peaceful, with little noticeable conflict on an ethnic axis during the 1930s. Local historians have noted that in the town of Kulen Vakuf, individuals who were nominally "Muslims" and "Orthodox Serb" would sometimes argue passionately in the weekly market or in taverns about the latest political developments and scandals taking place in Belgrade. Yet a few days later many of the same people could be seen walking together to the local soccer field. There they drank and joked together while watching teams such as Mladost (Youth) and Una face off against each other. Each included players who were nominally Serb and

Figure 3. The multi-ethnic members of the soccer team Mladost in Kulen Vakuf posing together for a photograph in 1937. Standing from right to left: Bogdan Došenović, Muharem Džigumović, Mahmut Ćehić, Esad Ibrahimpašić, Esad Bibanović, Rasim Čeliković, and Hamdija Bibanović. Seated from right to left: Ibrahim Demirović–Seno, Stevo Vladetić, Muhamed Kulenović–Brk, Đuro Cvjetnićanin, Ale Alajbegović and Huse Demirović. Sitting on the ground: Boro Kecman. Image courtesy of Zoran Bibanović.

Muslim. In photographs from the period of these teams, one can discern a difference among the young men only by the handful who chose to wear the *fez*, a traditional hat generally worn by Muslims in the region.[123] In some cases, these friendships between those of nominally different ethnicities, which sometimes had roots in experiences such as playing sports together as children, were so deep that they were eventually formalized. When such men married, they sometimes became *kumovi* (akin to godfather) to each other.

According to oral testimonies, such intimate, quasi-familial connections between those who saw themselves as Orthodox Serbs and Muslims were not uncommon, especially in the town of Kulen Vakuf and its immediate region.[124] Some religious leaders of different faiths in the wider region also appear to have been close friends. Local historians who interviewed Catholics in the village of Krnjeuša discovered that their priest, Father Krešimir Barišić, who took up his position in 1937, was close to his Orthodox counterpart, Father Drago Savić. They were frequently seen walking and joking together, and would regularly visit each other's homes. Savić was notorious for asking his Catholic, and therefore celibate friend: "When are you going to get married, so that I can come to your wedding?"[125]

Despite this evidence of intra-ethnic conflict being just as common—if not more—than inter-ethnic, as well as the existence of intercommunal friendships, there is reason to believe that different mental templates also existed, at least for some. In such ways of seeing and interpreting, the language of ethnicity mattered significantly, or could suddenly surface in certain situations in antagonistic ways. Conversations that regional inspectors had with local residents reveal that some harbored negative views of their neighbors according to ethnic categories, which structured their behavior toward whole groups of people as perceived along an ethnic axis. For example, Mahmud Kulenović-Haračlija, who was a member of Kulen Vakuf's municipal council, was said to have been negatively disposed toward "Serbs." This was because of the murder of his father immediately after the establishment of the Kingdom of Serbs, Croats, and Slovenes in 1918. According to police reports, his father had poorly treated his Orthodox tenants during World War I, and one killed him as a consequence. Kulenović-Haračlija expressed his negative sentiments toward "Serbs" more generally by dismissing all Serb employees from the municipal council when he joined in 1928. He also made sure to reverse the council's decision to give a parcel of land to the Serbian Orthodox Church in Kulen Vakuf.[126]

In other situations, it appears that local residents used ethnic categories in negative ways to account for their problems, even when such conflicts did not involve individuals of different nominal ethnicities. In the late 1920s, David Opačić illegally built a house on state property near the source of the Ostrovica River in Kulen Vakuf. At the time of construction, the local administrative authority knew about this, but had looked the other way. By 1930, Opačić was now poised to build an outhouse and stables for cows. The excrement from both would flow directly into the river, the water many people in Kulen Vakuf used for drinking. The new local administrative authority, Ivan Topalović, confronted him about these offenses. The regional inspectorate (*okružni inspektorat*) reported the incident in this way: "If I were a Turk" (a derogatory word for "Muslim"), Opačić erupted, "then I would be able to get away with anything that I want."[127]

Here, even in a conflict that concerned two individuals who were nominally "Serb," which had to do with one's clearly illegal actions, there was a sudden attack on "Muslims," or in this case, the "Turks." They apparently held a monopoly on political power, and thus could carry on in ways irrespective of existing laws. Reports written by inspectors based in the nearby city of Bihać regarding the reorganization of the territorial make-up of the municipality of Kulen Vakuf suggest there may have been some truth, or at least a perception of truth, underlying this accusation. "It is a public secret," wrote the inspectors, "that the municipality [of Kulen Vakuf] has been structured in this way so that the Muslim population can assure itself a majority, and that in this way will guarantee itself a majority in the municipal council, and thus in the municipality's administration."[128]

Such evidence suggests that mental templates existed in which one's actions or interpretations of conflicts could take on a strong—and especially antagonistic—ethnic coloring. To what extent this way of thinking was widespread is difficult to definitively assess given the limited number of archival sources. But the evidence here is revealing for what it suggests about the prevalence of ethnic categories as a prism for interpreting conflictive situations, especially in negative ways. And this appears to have been present both among those in leadership positions, such as Mahmud Kulenović-Haračlija, and those not, such as David Opačić—regardless of their perceived "ethnicity."

The basis for such antagonistic views could be rooted in experiences and memories of violence in the past, or in perceptions of a group's dominance in the present. How far one would be able go in putting such ways of seeing the world into actual practice would depend on the receptivity of others, and especially whether the authorities would condone or condemn these ethnically divisive acts and interpretations. Archival evidence suggests that at least some of the local authorities in the Kulen Vakuf region were not tolerant of such views during the 1930s. Around the time that the local administrative authority, Ivan Topalović, confronted David Opačić about his illegal construction that would have polluted the drinking water, an anonymous letter arrived to the regional inspectorate in the city of Bihać. Its author, who was most likely David Opačić, complained of "terror and difficult conditions" due to Topalović's apparently harsh law enforcement methods. There was even a suggestion that Topalović was practicing ethnic discrimination. But after investigating, the regional inspectors noted that in response to Opačić's anti-Muslim statement, "if I were a Turk, then I would be able to get away with anything that I want," Topalović had simply responded sarcastically, "Sure, whatever you say, if you were a Turk."[129]

The connotation here was that it was of no consequence what Opačić's ethnicity was. He was breaking the law. He was upset that Topalović would not look the other way (as the previous local administrative authority had done). And so he resorted to the language of antagonistic ethnicity as another method to successfully maneuver through the confrontation. But his approach fell on deaf ears and elicited a sarcastic dismissal. Why this seemingly minor incident deserves our attention is because it sheds light on a much broader subject: the capacity of some people in the region to invoke an antagonistic language of ethnicity in certain moments of conflict. Yet it also shows us that the question of whether such interpretations would gain traction would be contingent on the receptivity of others in the community, and especially the reaction of the authorities.

The dominance of an ethnicized interpretation of a local conflict, and a practice of politics along such lines, was not a foregone conclusion. It required people to take forceful action to frame situations along this axis, and for them to overcome any resistance that might come their way. The evidence does not suggest that the final years of the interwar period was a time during which anything close to a majority of the local authorities and population would have had much incentive to support an antagonistic form of ethnicized politics. But a government with a radically different ideology and politics could change the political field so as to empower individuals such as David Opačić and Mahmud Kulenović-Haračlija. It was neither a historical necessity nor inconceivable that a political context in which their highly ethnicized ways of seeing the local community could be rapidly created, and quickly become much more influential.

In 1877, while traveling on foot through the Kulen Vakuf region during the rebellion with Orthodox insurgents, Sir Arthur Evans observed: "To-day, in this unhappy land, look where we will, we see nothing but divisions—barriers political, social, and religious. But whenever we go back a step . . . whenever we turn our gaze, our search reveals the still existing bonds of union."[130] In many ways, his observation still applied during the early months of 1941, when, unbeknownst to the region's residents, their country—the Kingdom of Yugoslavia—would exist for only a few more months. An examination of the history of this corner of the Balkans, from the establishment of the town of Kulen Vakuf at the confluence between the Una and Ostrovica rivers at the end of the seventeenth century until the spring of 1941, presents us with a major historiographical challenge, which is visible in Evans's observation. Can we tell this history in a way that does justice to the divisions and lines of conflict, but also takes account of the "bonds of union," yet without erasing the historical contingency of both as potentially dominant practices of politics and everyday life? None of the people whose lives we wish to explain knew what would happen in the future; and our responsibility is to tell their stories in such a way that recognizes this. To write this history means to suppress any desire we may have to use our knowledge of future events as an explanatory tool, and to resist suggesting any kind of inevitability of subsequent events that we—rather than contemporaries—know about.

Choosing to tell this history from the perspective of the local community, and reconstructing it with sources that take us close to the ground, can help provide us with the tools to meet these challenges. With local evidence in hand, we are less likely to make sweeping assumptions and generalizations that erase the complexities and nuances of the community's history. Specifically, we will be much less likely to resign ourselves to simplified master narratives in which the local community's history might appear a reflection of a seemingly inexorable development of clearly defined and mutually antagonistic "ethnic groups" or "nations," and their inevitable violent clash conflict along a predictable "ethnic" axis.

Instead, what is perhaps most striking in this investigation of the history of the Kulen Vakuf region is that the two periods of the most intense social conflict prior to 1941—the rebellion of 1875–1878 and the years from 1918 through the early 1920s—defy any easy characterization of the nature of the region's conflicts. Killings and plunder occurred on an ethnic axis, yet intra-ethnic violence was also central during each of these periods. Various individuals and groups made significant attempts to prevent or stop intercommunal violence, and to create a basis to resolve social conflicts in their myriad forms. A longer-term sense of "us" and "them" in the region, rooted in religious identities and the social, economic, and political structures of Ottoman society, should not blind us to the fact that conflicts often unfolded along lines other than religion and "ethnicity." The slow and even penetration of the ideology of nationalism at the local level during the nineteenth and first half of the twentieth century did not change this general dynamic. Ethnic categories became an available vocabulary for conflict in specific moments, but this language did not cancel out other axes of conflict.

The history of this region suggests that the period of turmoil after the establishment of the Kingdom of Serbs, Croats, and Slovenes, which historians often depict as solely fueling inter-ethnic conflict, also produced various forms of intercommunal solidarity.[131] As social and economic structures in the region changed from landlord-tenant to those between town (i.e., merchant) and village (i.e., peasant producers), new relationships of mutual interdependence arose. Large-scale construction projects, such as the railroads in the Una River valley, along with the development, albeit in fits and starts, of industry in Drvar, contributed to the increasing growth of a small group of construction and industrial workers, which was composed of people of all backgrounds. All of these changes created new points of contact, which included economic relations, friendships, and political solidarities. These

FIGURE 4. The Una River between Martin Brod and Kulen Vakuf. Image taken by the author.

transformations also brought conflict, some of which had an inter-ethnic component. But the divisions were just as much—if not more—intra-ethnic, intra-party, and inter-personal.

The potential for multiple forms of conflict therefore surely existed, but so too did the potential for peace and manageable tension. The historian's challenge, particularly when aware of what would soon occur in the community during 1941, is to remember that neither direction was foreordained. What would be crucial in the future would be which kinds of social categories would become primary in any future creation of policies of inclusion and exclusion. This would determine along which axis, and to what extent, groups and individuals would be able to act out their ongoing tensions and conflicts, or rapidly create new lines of division. In the spring of 1941—if we endeavor to tell this history forward to that year, rather than by projecting backwards our knowledge of subsequent future events—no dramatic shift appeared likely in the Kulen Vakuf region. As winter gave way to longer and warmer days, local life seem destined to continue as it had during the previous years, ambling along slowly, much the same as the emerald green waters of the Una River.

Part II

1941

Chapter 2

A World Upended

It is not known whether the crystal clear waters of the Ostrovica River suddenly ran dry in late March 1941. If they did continue flowing from the base of the mountain in Kulen Vakuf, then according to local legend neither the townspeople nor the region's 16,000 or so residents would have had warning that a new, much larger upheaval was now looming on the horizon.[1] In response to a military officer–led coup in Belgrade on March 27, Hitler ordered his army to invade and destroy the Kingdom of Yugoslavia. German bombers attacked the city on April 6. The rest of the country fell to the German, Italian, and Hungarian blitzkrieg during the ensuing weeks.[2]

German tanks and troops arrived to northwest Bosnia, but did not remain as a formal occupying force.[3] Instead, this region, along with most of what constitutes present-day Croatia, Bosnia-Herzegovina, as well as parts of Serbia, was incorporated into a newly established state called the Independent State of Croatia (Nezavisna Država Hrvatska [NDH]). Established on April 10, its fascist leadership—known as the Ustašas (*ustaše*)—was committed to creating a nation-state exclusively for "Croats." Formed as political movement in the late 1920s and early 1930s, this group crystalized into a small terrorist organization whose members violently opposed the existence of the Kingdom of Yugoslavia. In alliance with other anti-Yugoslav elements, they had succeeded in assassinating the Serb King of the country, Aleksandar, in 1934 while he was visiting France. They had also attempted to stir up a rebellion in the Lika region in September 1932, but without success.[4] For much of the 1930s, the bulk of its membership, which appears to have numbered only in the hundreds, lived in exile abroad, mostly in Italy, but also Hungary and Germany. By the late 1930s, the largest number of supporters who were still in the Kingdom of Yugoslavia—perhaps at least half—resided in Zagreb. Much smaller numbers were in towns such as Karlovac, Gospić, and in the western regions of Herzegovina. In Bosnia, there were a handful of supporters in the city of Banja Luka and in towns like Bihać and Travnik, among a few others.[5]

Initially, Hitler approached leading non-Ustaša political leaders in the former Banovina of Croatia, such as Vladko Maček of the Croat Peasant Party, and invited them to become the leaders of the NDH. When they declined, he settled for the Ustašas. At their helm was Ante Pavelić, a lawyer who had lived in exile in Italy for most of the 1930s. He and his like-minded colleagues accepted Hitler's offer to lead the new state, whose creation was another method, along with brute military force, that the Axis powers used to destroy the Kingdom of Yugoslavia. Pavelić and his associates unexpectedly found themselves in control of a large territory whose population they believed should be exclusively "Croat." At its center was the former frontier region between the former Austro-Hungarian and Ottoman Empires—the Krajina. Here lived people of different religions, some of whom also saw themselves as members of national/ethnic collectivities, of which the category "Croat" was only one among several. Here was also the Kulen Vakuf region, which straddled both sides of the former international border, with its inter-connected communities in both the Krajina and Lika. Its residents, like that of other local communities in the NDH, were not asked whether they wished to become part of this new nation-state, and be subjected to its leadership's nationalist vision of the future. However, such sudden and radical shifts in government and policy were nothing new to the region's people. Especially from 1878 on, they had become accustomed to a world in which, as Ivo Andrić put it in his novel *The Bridge on the Drina* (1945), "everything happened far away and unbelievably quickly. Somewhere far away in the world the dice had been thrown, the battles fought, and it was there that the fate of each one of the townsfolk was decided."[6]

Disagreements between the NDH authorities and some of their foreign allies over the borders of the new state dragged on for some time, but had little to no impact on daily life in communities in the Kulen Vakuf region, which were located far from such sites of dispute. What would be crucial here at the local level, however, would be the state's new internal policies,

Map 6. The Kulen Vakuf region in the Independent State of Croatia in 1941 after the establishment of the velike župe.

most especially those that would define who—and who was not—to be a part of the Croat national community. Like other fascists in Europe at the time, the Ustaša ideologues made use of racial concepts in this task. Yet they also did so within specific limitations. As adherents of Nazi-style racial ideology with regard to "Jews," the NDH authorities issued a series of decrees in which they defined this group as a racial category. Other categories that the new authorities defined as "races" included "Gypsies, Blacks, Tatars, Armenians, Persians, and Arabs," among others, the majority of which were not even considered to be present in the NDH. "Orthodox Serb," "Catholic Croat," and "Muslim"—which were contemporary categories used at the time both by the NDH elites and many ordinary people to refer to the vast majority of the population of the new state—were *not* officially defined as "races," although some comments by certain officials did on occasion have a racial tinge.[7]

The supreme leader (*poglavnik*) of the NDH, Ante Pavelić, considered "Muslims" to actually be "Croats of the Islamic faith." "The muslims are the blood of our blood," he stated, "they are the flower of our Croatian nationality."[8] Other high-level NDH officials, such as Mile Budak (appointed Minister of Religion and Education in 1941), defined the Croat nation (*hrvatski narod*) as multi-confessional: "We [Croats] are a people of the Catholic and muslim faiths."[9] Intellectual fellow travelers joined this chorus by writing texts in which they invoked a combination of historical, linguistic, anthropological, and quasi-racial arguments about how the Bosnian-Herzegovinian muslims and Catholic Croats were one coherent unit, united by Croatianness. The key elements of this sense of groupness included: past Serbian persecution of Muslims and Croats, particularly during the interwar period; the supposed darker physical features of Serbs versus the lighter characteristics of Croats and Muslims; a notion that Muslims and Croats engaged in agriculture, while Serbs raised livestock; and supposed differences in spoken and written language.[10]

It was an open question what the wider population that considered itself Muslim thought of these arguments. Intellectuals such as Mehmed Alajbegović declared early on after the establishment of the NDH that, "the Croatianness of the Bosnian-Herzegovinian muslims can be considered as an indisputable fact."[11] Yet other contemporary thinkers, such as Muhamed Hadžijahić, remarked that, "'Croatian-ness' has yet to decisively emerge among the muslim masses."[12] Whatever the case, the claim by the NDH elite and their supporters that Bosnia-Herzegovina's Islamic community was in fact "Croat" provided some Muslim leaders with the sudden opportunity to publicly voice grievances about those whom they perceived as their past persecutors: the Orthodox Serb community. NDH newspapers published articles during the first few months of the state's existence about the past Serbian persecution of Muslims, such as during World War I, and especially after the establishment in 1918 of the Kingdom of Serbs, Croats, and Slovenes.[13] The subject of the agrarian reforms, and specifically how by instituting them "[the interwar] Belgrade government wanted to materially destroy all muslims," was one that received attention in the press and internal NDH government documents.[14] The newspapers also provided accounts of Catholic Croats who had suffered at the hands of Serbs, particularly during the years 1918–1941.[15]

Playing up real and supposed past sufferings was one way of attempting to mobilize those now perceived as "Croats" both to support the NDH, and to turn against the "Serb" population. Here, the new NDH authorities were explicit about redefining as solely "ethnic" the axis around which conflict was to now unfold. As one regime newspaper put it in an announcement in late April 1941, which was directed to "Muslims" in northwest Bosnia: "Brother soldiers! Turn your weapons on our enemies, the Serbs. Do not back down or give up your weapons. Take power, because from now on you are the rulers of your house in your country."[16]

Aside from those defined in racial terms, such as Jews (as well as "Gypsies" [Roma]), the perceived Serb Orthodox community was the main population group the NDH elite viewed as standing in the way of creating an ethnically pure Croatian nation-state. This was a major problem because, according to NDH statistics, this group comprised a large part of the state's population.[17] Using the last census carried out in the Kingdom of Yugoslavia (1931), the authorities first calculated what they believed was the religious composition of their territory (i.e., according to faith [*po vjeroizpoviesti*]). For Bosnia-Herzegovina, they believed that there were 550,000 Catholics, 718,000 Muslims, 1,030,000 Orthodox, and 29,000 "others." Drawing on these numbers, they claimed that the ethnic composition was 1,238,000 "Croats" (which included those considered as "Catholic Croats" and "Muslims") and 1,024,000 "Serbs."[18] Here was a crucial part of the logic in claiming that the Islamic community of Bosnia-Herzegovina was "Croat": it allowed the NDH elite to assert that there were, in fact, more "Croats" than "Serbs."

Speeches by the NDH elite, such as Minister of Justice Mirko Puk, during the first several months of the new state's existence, illustrated elite conceptualizations of "Serbs," and what needed to happen to them:

> Besides the Jews and communists in our homeland, there is another enemy, and that is the Serbs, who for twenty years have beat us into a creation [i.e., the interwar Yugoslav kingdom] that has been called with justification the prison of the Croatian nation. The Serbs came to our lands with the Turkish detachments as thieves, as dregs, and as garbage from the Balkans. We cannot allow two peoples to lead our national state. There is one God, and there is one people who lead, and that is the Croat people. Let those who came to our homeland 200–300 years ago return to where they came from. Either leave our homeland willingly, or we will drive you out by force.[19]

Because of its historic place as the border between the Habsburg (and later Austro-Hungarian Empire) and Ottoman Empire, northwest Bosnia and Lika—which composed much of the Krajina region—were areas to which the NDH leadership attached special importance. With a large Orthodox population, due to the former empires' policies of offering land to Orthodox settlers in exchange for military service in guarding the border, the Ustaša elite viewed the region as a place in urgent need of being "cleansed" of non-Croat influence. The key strongman whom they selected to carry out their policies in the region was a former judge and reserve captain of the Yugoslav Army from Banja Luka. His name was Viktor Gutić. Politically engaged with the Ustaša movement since the mid-1930s, he maintained regular contact with its supporters who lived abroad prior to the Axis invasion of the Kingdom of Yugoslavia.[20] Gutić's Croatian nationalism was particularly virulent. His statement to a group of Serbian Orthodox priests in northwest Bosnia during the first half of May exemplified the hardline Ustaša stance on what such individuals represented, and what would need to be done with them: "There are no more Serbs. I don't recognize Serbs anymore. Get out of here. This is the heart of Croatia, and a heart must be cleansed of poison. You are that poison."[21]

It appears that Pavelić and his associates in Zagreb gave Gutić the task of personally organizing the NDH authorities in northwest Bosnia. They saw him as ideologically committed to the Ustaša cause, and he was believed to be politically reliable. He carried out this task almost immediately after the establishment of the NDH in the region's towns of Bihać, Bosanka Krupa and Bosanski Novi, and sent close associates to do the same in Cazin and Velika Kladuša. By May, Gutić had installed at least ten key Ustaša leaders. These men then appointed those below them. All owed their unexpected positions as the new undisputed holders of local power to Gutić, who attempted to maintain detailed knowledge of their activities.[22]

A key method that Gutić used to attract men into this regional network of Ustaša leaders was to promise them the right to appropriate the property and wealth of those people whom the government now defined as "non-Croats," such as Jews and Serbs. There was, therefore, a sizable economic incentive to join the new regime. As such, becoming an Ustaša was especially attractive to previously politically and economically disenfranchised individuals. Gutić led by example. Among his first acts was to order some of the wealthiest Serb merchants and industrialists of Banja Luka to bring him large sums of money within a twenty-four-hour deadline, or else face dire consequences.[23] In late April, he created the position of the commissar of Jewish property and apartments. All rent due to Jewish landlords would now be paid to this commissar—in effect, directly to Gutić's government in Banja Luka.[24] He forbid the purchasing of property from those defined as "Serbs" and "Jews," or to agree to care for their property, except for the NDH authorities under Gutić's command.[25] The creation of the NDH government thus provided the new regional and local leaders with enormous and unprecedented power to expropriate the wealth and property of their former neighbors on an ethnically defined axis.

A significant part of what would soon cause difficulty for the NDH elite in Zagreb in controlling their supposed allies in the localities was the way in which they delineated spheres of authority. The creation of the NDH state apparatus proceeded on several levels. There was the creation of civil authorities, whose staff was not necessarily composed of those deeply sympathetic to the Ustašas' nationalist cause. Often, they were simply the regional and local officials who were deemed to be "Croat," and who were available for such work because they had already been employed in the administration of the former Kingdom of Yugoslavia. This was less true for many in the NDH's military (called the Croatian Homeguard [Hrvatsko domobranstvo]), as well as its gendarmerie forces (oružništvo). In particular, the military was envisioned as a heavily Croatianized force that would be composed of former officers from the Army of the Kingdom of Yugoslavia who were thought to be sympathetic to the Croatian national cause, as well as some retired officers who had served in the military during the period of Austro-Hungarian rule.[26]

The Ustaša organization, however, constituted a largely separate, vertically integrated authority structure. This was where generally the most extreme nationalists gravitated, though certainly not all who would become Ustašas should be thought of in this way. The Ustašas had organizations at the village level (*roj*), at the level of rural municipalities, which included many villages (*tabor*), for groups of municipalities (*logor*), and at the county level (*stožer*)—all of which were theoretically commanded by the Main Ustaša Headquarters (*Glavni ustaški stan*). Most levels had armed units, akin to local militias.[27] Significantly, there were few formal horizontal links between the civilian authorities, military and police, on one side, and the Ustaša organizations, on the other. Of equal importance, the armed Ustaša units were not under the command of the military nor the gendarmerie; instead, they had their own command structures, and were not accountable to any other armed group in the NDH. In general, it was only the most prominent Ustaša elite who were capable of exerting power over all of these de-facto separate branches of the new state. In this way, the Ustaša organizations constituted an essentially parallel authority structure, with almost no non-Ustaša institutionalized check on their power. In northwest Bosnia, Gutić and those immediately below him were the undisputed leaders of this group.[28] This division of authority had two key implications. First, it meant that regional and local strongmen could empower their Ustašas to carry out policies as they saw fit. Second, the NDH's military, gendarmerie, and civil authorities did not have the formal authority to intervene in Ustaša activities.

The supreme leader of the NDH, Ante Pavelić, called Gutić to a meeting in Zagreb during the third week of April. He gave Gutić a new title and sphere of authority. Beginning on April 20, 1941, he was to be known as the "Ustaški stožernik," or the Ustaša leader for the entire territory of the former Vrbaska banovina, the former administrative unit in the Kingdom of Yugoslavia that had encompassed all of northwest Bosnia and parts of Lika.[29] Later, Gutić officially began to refer to himself in more grandiose terms, as the Ustaša Leader for Bosnian Croatia (*Ustaški stožernik za bosansku Hrvatsku*). This reformulation of his position appears to have been an attempt to carve out a sphere of authority even larger than northwest Bosnia.[30]

While in Zagreb, Gutić met with key members of the NDH elite, including the minister of Internal Affairs, Andrija Artuković, and the supreme commander (*vojskovođa*) of the NDH military, Slavko Kvaternik.[31] From May 20 to May 24 he attended more meetings in Zagreb during which explicit discussions took place about future measures to restructure the ethnic composition of the population of northwest Bosnia. After his return to Banja Luka, Gutić publicly announced the task that lay ahead: "Now I will be approaching the grandiose task of cleansing the Croatian Bosnian Krajina [northwest Bosnia] of unwanted elements."[32] Who these "unwanted elements" were was already clear. The primary means through which they would be cleansed from the region was still being formulated, and would soon take shape, driven by the elite in Zagreb and regional leaders' own policies.

Already in April, Gutić had taken the initiative in delineating new lines of inclusion and exclusion along an ethnic axis, even without receiving direct orders from Zagreb. Through his newspaper *Hrvatska Krajina* (The Croatian frontier), he began issuing public orders and declarations to accomplish this objective. His first task was to de-Serbianize and aggressively Croatianize the physical landscape. In Banja Luka, all writing in Cyrillic on stores and other public establishments, which was considered to be evidence of "Serbdom, Byzantinism, and Balkanism," was now banned.[33] All emblems, flags, and photographs that had any connection to the former Kingdom of Yugoslavia were to be immediately removed from public spaces, and especially those connected with the Serbian Karađorđević dynasty and Serb politicians.[34] Streets previously named after Serb historical figures were now renamed after Ustaša leaders, as well as other personalities viewed as "Croat," including Catholics and Muslims.[35]

Yet it was the ethnic composition of the human landscape that was Gutić's central concern. Just weeks after the establishment of the NDH, he made a first attempt to de-Serbianize the population. On April 24, he issued an order for "all persons" who were born, or had roots in "the former Serbia and Montenegro," to leave the NDH within five days.[36] He had received no directive from Zagreb to issue this order. In the days that followed this sweeping pronouncement, which took no account of the fact that many people originally from these areas did not see themselves as Orthodox Serbs, he had to issue qualifications granting Muslims and Catholics from these regions the right to stay in the NDH.[37]

Un-mixing the local population of northwest Bosnia along a clear ethnic axis was a crucial concern. Gutić established evening curfews for those considered to be Serbs and Jews, and barred Jews from entering all public places.[38] Ethnic lines of inclusion and exclusion were applied to employment. Large numbers of those considered Serbs, as well as others considered "enemies of the state," were fired from their government jobs, and their names were printed in the newspaper.[39] Utilizing public transportation also now turned on an ethnic axis. Those considered "Croats" were to be given preference in riding buses (yet how individual drivers were to make these distinctions was left unclear).[40]

Of importance in these orders and new regulations was the forceful act of publicly sorting individuals into positive and negative categories according to ethnic criteria. This was also simultaneously an act of inclusion and exclusion of individuals from the new national community. Gutić's newspaper, *Hrvatska Krajina*, printed articles that focused on the "anti-Croat" behavior of individual Serbs and others considered as non-Croats "whose presence is unwanted in our lands."[41] Following statewide laws from late April, he also required Jews to wear an identifying yellow patch on the left side of their chests with a Star of David and large "Ž" to designate them as Jews (*židovi*), and barred them from public places.[42] Yet this sorting and classification on an ethnic axis appeared less as a final objective, and more as a step toward erasing certain "groups" from existence, at least in their current incarnation. On May 17, Gutić issued an order that all those who were members of the Serbian Orthodox Church (as well as those who were members of the Russian Orthodox Church) were now to be categorized as "Greek-Easterners" (*grko-istočnjaci*). This order effectively annulled use of the category "Serb." It seems to have been instituted nearly two months before the central authorities in Zagreb did the same.[43]

What was striking about many of these orders, declarations, and new laws was that they frequently were not the result of directives from the central NDH authorities. Rather, regional leaders, such as Gutić, sometimes took the initiative in instituting their own policies of persecution. Some even had counter-productive results for Zagreb, such as the order for all those from Serbia and Montenegro to leave the NDH, which included sizable numbers of people who were not considered "Serbs."[44] The plunder of wealth by these regional leaders for their own use from those targeted for persecution was equally counter-productive for the central authorities. This suggests that while a top-down process of discrimination was certainly occurring in the NDH in April and May, it appears to have had multiple engines driving it forward. Regional leaders were able to create policies on their own volition, which began to cause problems of control for the NDH elite in Zagreb. The process of persecution through new laws and declarations, which was initiated by the central authorities, thus included a fair amount of poor coordination with, and supervision over, the regions and localities. And so it was in the smaller towns and villages that discriminatory policies began to crystalize in a myriad of forms—driven forward both from above and below, often in conflicting ways.

Such attempts by the regional elite, such as Gutić, to chart an independent course in carrying out persecution have been under-analyzed in the literature on the NDH. But knowledge of the inner-workings of the Ustašas in even smaller subnational units, such as towns and villages, is virtually non-existent during this crucial period. Even basic information, such as who the Ustašas actually were in these places, remains murky in the literature, including the newest studies, whose authors tend to rely on the uni-dimensional rubric: "the Ustašas." Memoirs of participants in wartime events provide us with glimpses into these communities, as do largely untapped archival material produced by NDH officials and others in the localities. Yet scholars have generally yet to make critical use of these sources in order to excavate and reconstruct the micro dimensions of the rapid and sweeping historical changes that took place in the largely rural local communities of the NDH during 1941.[45] What did the establishment of the NDH mean in the countryside, which composed the vast majority of the new state? The Kulen Vakuf region was such an area. An analysis of its history during April–June 1941 thus provides us with a new lens through which to better understand how local communities in the NDH responded to, and participated in, the major political and social changes that unfolded after the destruction of the Kingdom of Yugoslavia.

Following the establishment of the NDH on April 10, the mayor of the town of Kulen Vakuf was Adem-beg Kulenović. He was known for being a political moderate and for his thorny relations with fellow Muslim politicians. He was also a friend of the former mayor of the town, Vlado Milanović, the son of Father Vukosav Milanović, the Orthodox priest who had defended the town's Muslim population from an angry mob of Orthodox peasants in 1918. There had been no official members of the Ustaša movement in the region prior the 1941, though some local residents appear to have had links to proponents of what the Yugoslav authorities during the 1930s called "separatism," a euphemism for Croatian nationalism and, in certain cases, the interwar Ustaša movement. As a result, regional NDH leaders, such as Gutić and his associates, often sought out new men in the smaller towns and villages whom they felt would be reliable leaders. Kulenović was an unlikely choice given his prewar politics. It is unclear who exactly arrived to mobilize the first local Ustašas, but the main actors here were likely NDH officials from the nearby city of Bihać or perhaps the equally close town of Bosanski Petrovac. Another choice may have been Juko Pavičić, originally from the Catholic village of Boričevac, located about ten kilometers to the west of Kulen Vakuf. He had lived outside the region prior to 1941, but was now active in the region's Ustaša organization. On several occasions during the 1930s he met with local Catholics and Muslims to discuss "[Croat] separatism."[46] But whoever it was, the man approached to become the leading Ustaša in the Kulen Vakuf region was called Miroslav "Miro" Matijević.[47]

Born in 1908 in the village of Vrtoče, located on the high plateau above the hills and mountains northeast of Kulen Vakuf, Matijević came to the town several years prior to 1941 with his wife and children. A burly man with a square face and dark hair, he was thirty-three years old in the spring of 1941. He had opened a tavern around a kilometer outside of the center of Kulen Vakuf during the late 1930s, which was located near a spot on the bank of Una River called the *buk*, where the river bottlenecks around a long curve, causing the water to rush through a small gorge. His tavern was within shouting distance of Kulen Vakuf's gendarmerie station, which was on the road leading toward the village of Klisa.[48] In the late 1950s, members of the post–World War II Yugoslav state security claimed that Matijević had been a prewar member of the Ustaša movement; so too have some local residents in their memoirs. Yet none have provided specific evidence to support this claim, and no other archival evidence exists as corroboration. In fact, Matijević's name does not appear in any prewar documents that would suggest the nature of his pre-1941 political involvement (if any), or participation in incidents that could be interpreted as "ethnic conflict."

If he held a strong nationalist orientation, it certainly did not prevent him from close socialization with "non-Croats" during this time. In a memoir about the region, he appears in a photograph from a local wedding in Kliško Poljice taken during the autumn of 1938. On that day, the future Ustaša leader can be seen posing with his neighbors, some of whom were Orthodox. A well-liked Orthodox neighbor, Mića Rudić, sat on the ground with a platter on which a small pig's head can be seen, a clear symbol of the wedding's festive atmosphere. Not far from him was another Orthodox neighbor, Đurenda Kuga. Intermingled with local Catholics, among whom stood future Ustaša Miroslav Matijević, these Orthodox men who attended the wedding are described as "good neighbors" (*dobri susjedi*), with one even called a "blood-brother" (*pobratim*).[49]

Figure 5. A wedding in Kliško Poljice in 1938. Miroslav Matijević, a tavern owner in Kulen Vakuf and future Ustaša leader, can be see standing in the second row, second from left, wearing a leather overcoat with a sash across his chest. On this day he celebrated not only with fellow Catholics, but also with his Orthodox neighbors, such as Mića Rudić, who can be see sitting in the front row, second from left, holding a plate with a pig's head. Image courtesy of Josip Pavićić.

Figure 6. A postcard drawing from 1906 of the buk in Kulen Vakuf, where the Una River rushes though a small gorge. Ustaša leader Miroslav Matijević's house and tavern was located not far from the houses on the right. Image courtesy of Buybook, Sarajevo.

There was an incident that took place immediately after the fall of the Kingdom of Yugoslavia that may be significant in accounting for Matijević's eventual participation in the Ustašas. When German tanks and soldiers rolled past his home village of Vrtoče during the first week of April, Matijević's father, Josip, greeted them by waving a Croatian flag. Some witnesses claim that he even saluted them Nazi style. A Serb gendarme standing nearby was disgusted by his acts and shot him in the leg, which later had to be amputated. Local residents have suggested in their memoirs that Josip's son, Miroslav, was enraged; he wanted revenge on the "Serbs."[50] If true, this incident suggests that Matijević's father was sympathetic to Croatian nationalism, which may have exerted some influence on his son's level of receptivity. It also suggests that the gendarme's attack on his father was an event that tipped Matijević in the direction of becoming an Ustaša.

Local historian Esad Bibanović, who lived in Kulen Vakuf during this period, has suggested that Matijević took up his new position as Ustaša commander (*Ustaški tabor*) of the region's municipalities on or about April 15, 1941. The actual date may have been somewhat later. While some regional NDH leaders such as Gutić immediately went about issuing new discriminatory laws and orders, in Kulen Vakuf nothing of great consequence seems to have changed during the second half of April after Matijević assumed his new position. There were no new regulations nor policies of persecution issued that were aimed at the population perceived to be "non-Croat." The establishment of the NDH and the appointment of Matijević did not bring with it a spontaneous eruption of "ethnic violence" among local residents. Instead, the region's population continued to meet peacefully at Kulen Vakuf's weekly market. Local residents attended dances and played soccer together, with teams composed of men of different nominal ethnicities, just as they had before April 1941.[51] This should not come as a surprise. The pre-1941 history of the region does not suggest that widespread conflict was a central dynamic of local social relations, let alone widespread conflict along an ethnic axis.

If "ethnic conflict" was to become the new order of the day, then conscious work would be necessary to decisively transform the region's political field. A first task would be to assemble a group of local men to join the Ustašas. Matijević devoted time during the second half of April and much of May to visiting the region's Muslim and Catholic villages in search of volunteers. He may have also conducted some of these conversations in his tavern, as well as in others in Kulen Vakuf, which sizable numbers of local men visited, particularly on the weekly market day. According to Bibanović, he found six volunteers in Kulen Vakuf, one of whom was Catholic and the rest Muslim. In the nearby village of Kalati, he found six Catholics. In Orašac, he found five, and another five in Ćukovi—all Muslims.[52] Bibanović's research is pioneering and invaluable, but part of his purpose was to disprove a post–World War II perception that the Kulen Vakuf region was a so-called Ustaša place (*ustaško mjesto*). This appears to have led him to minimize the number of local volunteers. He also did not consult archival material, and most likely did not have access to archives during the 1970s and 1980s when he conducted his research.

Documents from archives in Bosnia-Herzegovina, Croatia, and Serbia suggest that the number of men who joined was, in fact, much higher. Instead of the thirty-two individuals cited by Bibanović, at least 111 names appear in various documents, of which 72 have names suggesting they would have been perceived as "Muslims," while thirty-nine would have been perceived as "Catholic Croats." We cannot be completely sure that each of these men was an active Ustaša, given that some files only briefly mention their names. Others, however, include substantial and compelling testimony about their deeds from multiple witnesses.[53] While nearly four times the size of Bibanović's figure, this group of suspected Ustašas nonetheless constituted less than 1 percent of the total population of nominal Muslims and Croats in the Kulen Vakuf region. This should give us pause when assessing the popularity or mass nature of the region's Ustaša movement during the late spring and early summer of 1941. It was a small group of men who became Ustašas.[54]

Mobilizing these local men to join the Ustašas could be a difficult, and sometimes fruitless endeavor. For example, in the nearby town of Donji Lapac a significant section of the perceived "Croat" population viewed the establishment of the NDH government with suspicion. Several of the local NDH leaders, such as Vinko Marinković, as well as those who were sent to the town from other areas, encountered sizable difficulties in convincing young local men to join the Ustašas, despite a combination of promises, pressure, and even threats. These leaders registered complaints with the regional authorities in Bihać and the town of Gospić. And, in frustration, they soon requested that manpower be sent in from other areas, which eventually arrived during mid-June in the form of twenty to thirty men. The inability of the local NDH authorities in Donji Lapac to mobilize local men into the Ustašas for nearly two months, and their eventual reliance on outsiders, suggests that strong indigenous support for the NDH was indeed often lacking in parts of the Kulen Vakuf region.[55]

But there were local men who did join the Ustašas. Who were they? And what led them to do so? One of the greatest weaknesses in the archival

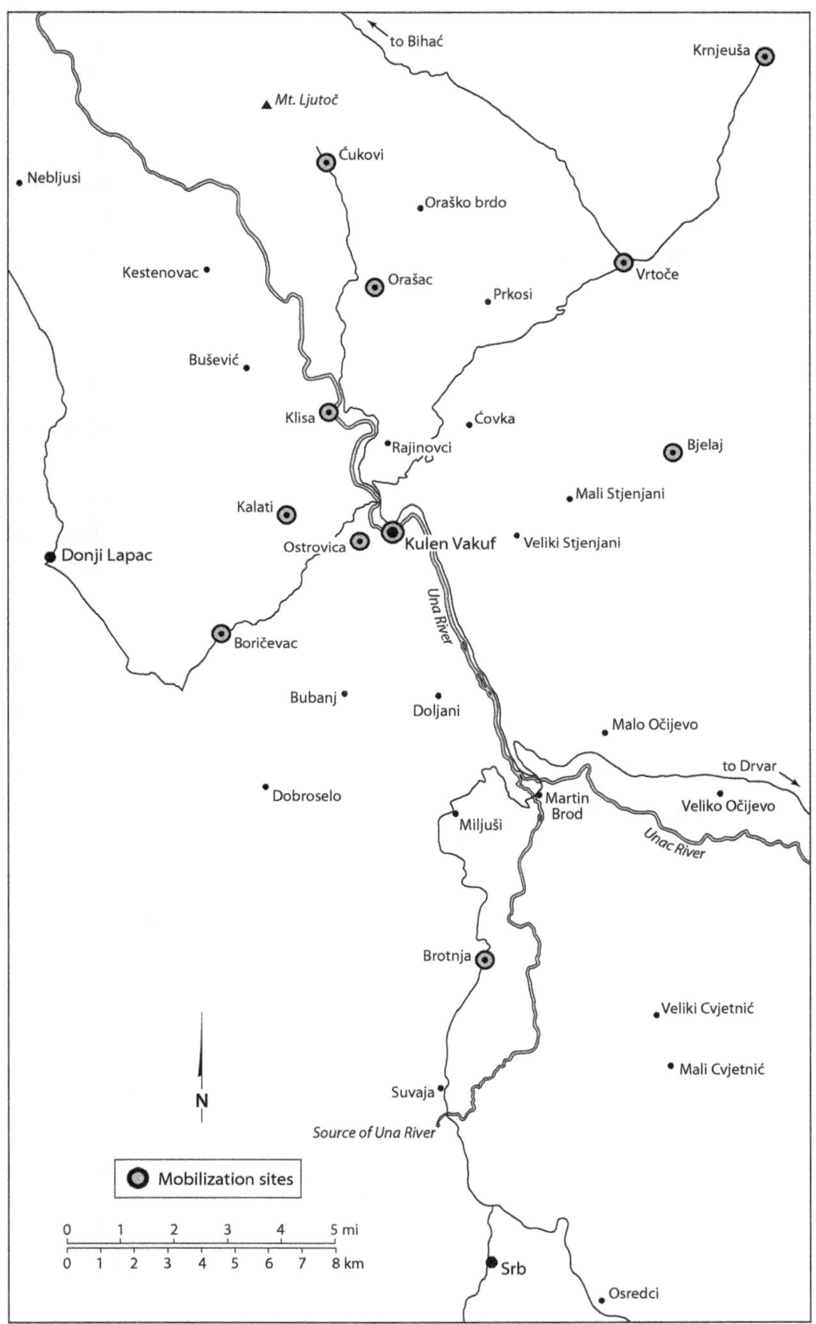

Map 7. Main sites of Ustaša mobilization in the Kulen Vakuf region, April–July 1941.

holdings for the NDH, most especially for the critical months following the establishment of the state in April 1941, is the paucity of fine-grained data on the local Ustašas throughout the new state. An abundant amount of detailed biographical information that would allow us to reconstruct an expansive "thick description" of their pre-1941 lives, motivations for joining the Ustašas, and subsequent actions, is generally lacking, although exceptions exist here and there. A sizable amount of research in multiple archives, both central and provincial, is usually necessary to determine even basic information, such as names and dates of birth. And quite frequently, no information exists. These significant source limitations should be kept in mind when the inevitable blanks spots appear in the historical record.

Among the local men who joined forces with Matijević was Mustajbeg Kulenović from Kulen Vakuf. He appears to have been a relative of the man with the same name killed by the gang led by Stevan Obradović "Langa." They had robbed and killed Muslims and Orthodox Serbs during the period of instability after the establishment of the Kingdom of Serbs, Croats, and Slovenes. Another appears to have been the local politician Hasan Saračević. He had been a leading member of the local council of the Yugoslav Muslim Organization, was active in local elections through the late 1930s, and tended to support Croat political leaders. While not well liked by all who perceived themselves as Muslims, he certainly had received the electoral support of some according to interwar election results. Another with political motivations rooted in the prewar period was Husein "Huća" Zelić. During the 1930s, the local authorities noted that he had been in contact with several Croat nationalists while they visited the nearby village of Boričevac, such as Juko Pavičić. Among their subjects of discussion was "the slavery of the Croat people" and the need for "[Croat] separatism."[56] Such individuals had obvious tendencies toward supporting a movement like the Ustašas, whose leaders aimed to redefine the local political field along antagonistic ethnic lines, in particular, in ways that would now exclude those considered to be "Serbs."

There were several merchants who appear to have joined, among them both Catholics and Muslims. Evidence suggests that one was Mehmed "Meho" Mušeta, who had been a member of the association of merchants in Kulen Vakuf prior to 1941, as well as a member of the municipal council.[57] A former officer in the Austro-Hungarian Army, he was said to have once fired several bullets into a photograph of King Aleksandar on the wall of a local tavern during the late 1930s.[58] Here too was his neighbor Husein "Huća" Zelić who, aside from his prewar interest in Croat separatism, was said to have been a chronic speculator and generally among the least successful in Kulen Vakuf's business community.[59] Another was Grga "Grco" Pavičić from the village of Boričevac. Numerous contemporaries have said that his wife Marija was also a strong supporter of the Ustašas.[60]

The sudden political shifts taking place presented these individuals with an unexpected opportunity to radically change the rules of local business that had been in place for years. For example, following the establishment of the NDH, a merchant from Kulen Vakuf named Mehmed, who was said to have joined the Ustašas, now told Orthodox peasant Petar Karanović, from whom he frequently purchased lamb skins: "Listen, you better take whatever amount I offer you for these [skins], because later you'll give them to me for nothing." The opportunity to join the Ustašas was also an easy way for local merchants to relieve themselves of a host of debts that they owed to local residents now classified as Serbs, from whom they had previously purchased goods. A Muslim merchant from Kulen Vakuf owed Spira Karanović a sizable amount of money for livestock that he bought before April 1941. When Karanović sent his son to collect the money shortly after the establishment of the NDH, the eighteen-year-old was beaten severely and sent home. For the local merchants who joined the Ustašas, this was their sudden opportunity to erase the local business conventions in the community, restructure them in entirely in their favor, and rapidly enrich themselves.[61] This dynamic has echoes in many other contexts during which sudden (often violent) change can open up lucrative opportunities among merchants and others for personal gain. As M.J. Akbar has written in regard to riots in India: "The history of riots shows clear efforts by landlords or traders to use the conflagration as a camouflage to do what they couldn't have achieved legally."[62]

There were others who seem to have viewed the opportunity to join the local Ustaša units as a moment to quickly and decisively settle ongoing local disputes, particularly over the use of land and other natural resources. It seems that several members of the extended Pehlivanović clan in the village of Ostrovica had been locked in regular disputes with some of their Orthodox neighbors in the village of Bubanj over the use of pastures located on the borders of their villages. There were also ongoing, local disputes, which stretched back decades (and perhaps even longer), over who had the right to cut down trees in the forests that surrounded such villages. Difficult winters and general poverty compelled people to cut trees for heating, without making any payment for them. And those they selected to fell were frequently not located on their property. Often, they carried out such illegal acts in forests near the borders between villages. This created a basis for disputes, which could quickly take on a strong inter-ethnic dimension if the sides involved happened to come from villages where they were considered to be of different nominal ethnicities. Local forestry officials often exacerbated such conflicts. They were usually from the region, and frequently looked the other way when residents of their villages (who were often members of their extended families) illegally cut trees. This preferential treatment usually had a clear inter-ethnic aspect to it.[63] It is likely that the sudden opportunity to decisively resolve such long-term conflicts in their favor was what led some local men, such as Ibrahim and Suljo Pehlivanović of the village of Ostrovica, to join the Ustašas. There is also evidence to suggest individuals were driven toward the Ustašas for the opportunity to now "get even" for other kinds of past wrongs. Some local residents who joined the Ustašas were embittered for having been denied employment in the past by other local residents who happened to be considered "Serb."[64] Now that the NDH authorities were defining inclusion and exclusion along an ethnic axis, any dispute that had previously involved individuals who were nominally of different ethnicities could now be politicized. This was a rare opportunity for those now classified as "Croats" to take the initiative to settle accounts with neighbors whom they had previously had conflicts, who were now classified as "Serbs." Archival evidence suggests that this was a widespread dynamic among many local men who joined the Ustašas throughout the NDH.[65]

Another factor that seems to have been significant when considering local mobilization patterns among the Ustašas in the Kulen Vakuf region was family relation. It was not by chance that groups of men from the same extended families, who lived together in the same small villages, made up a sizable number of the Ustašas. There were three other Matijevićes, two of whom came from the Catholic village of Krnjeuša, located close to Ustaša leader Miroslav Matijević's place of birth in Vrtoče. There were four men from the Kozlica clan in the village of Orašac. There were perhaps as many as ten men from the Markovinović clan from the village of Boričevac, and nearly the same number of Kulenovićes from Kulen Vakuf. The archival records suggest that there were at least thirteen other groups of men (usually between two to five individuals) from families in the region's Catholic and Muslim villages. This included some of the Maričićes of Vrtoče, the Pavičićes of Boričevac, Vojićes of Orašac, the Pehlivanovićes of Ostrovica, and Selimovićes of Ćukovi. The widespread pattern of groups of men from the same extended families joining the Ustašas suggests that mobilization often took place through these familial networks. This is not to say that whole extended families should be seen as Ustaša, as the evidence does not point to all men from certain clans joining. Rather, it was groups of between two to ten men from much larger families. They were usually in their twenties and thirties, though the youngest was sixteen and the oldest forty-nine. Most were married and fathers of several children.

There was likely a degree of social pressure from those who felt strongest about the necessity of joining. Their act of becoming Ustašas, and what was most likely their subsequent application of social pressure, may have compelled their relatives to follow suit, especially if there was a local conflict involving their family that could be quickly resolved by doing so. The Pehlivanovićes, we should recall, had been in a long-standing conflict with their Orthodox neighbors in Bubanj over the use of local natural resources such as forests and pastures. What deserves attention is the role of social structure—in this case the extended family—and its influence in small villages as a mechanism for mobilization. Other researchers, such as Omar Shahabudin McDoom, who have been able to acquire more fine-grained data on those who joined militias in communities in Rwanda, have noted similar dynamics at work. Again, local social structure and pressure through local networks are often primary channels through which relatives and neighbors can be transformed into potential perpetrators.[66]

In the Kulen Vakuf region, there were some individuals who appear to have come from families that had been among the Muslim landowning elite prior to 1918. But their numbers were quite small. While there were perhaps as many as ten Kulenovićes, there were only two Bibanovićes, one Islambegović, one Kadić, and one Kurtagić, to cite a handful of examples of individuals from the region's most prominent former landowning elite. Why this matters is because it suggests that losing land in 1918 *was not* an automatic historical trigger for Muslim participation in the Ustaša movement, or at least support for it, contrary to what some NDH officials argued at the time.[67] For every individual from a former landowning family who appears to have joined and supported the Ustašas, many more did not.

The evidence suggests that a majority of the local men who joined the Ustašas were from relatively poor families or had been unsuccessful in attaining steady employment. Local historian Milan Obradović has described many of these men as unemployed "stragglers," more than a few of whom were alcoholics, who tended to live economically and socially on the margins of their communities. They thus had little standing with any their neighbors—regardless of whatever nominal ethnic categories supposedly bound or separated them.[68] This was a similarity shared by many local Ustašas in other parts of the NDH, such as Herzegovina, which NDH officials noted in their reports during 1941.[69] This general characteristic suggests that the local volunteers were attracted to the Ustašas out a sense that participation could bring with it a rapid and easy enhancement in their marginal economic and social status.

This social profile contrasts with evidence about the composition of the Ustašas who existed in northwest Bosnia prior to the establishment of the NDH. According to post–World War II investigations by the communist government's state security, prewar supporters of the Ustaša movement tended to be educated, and included lawyers, bank employees, teachers, and engineers. They were also state employees, skilled workers, and business owners, along with gendarmes, clerks, blacksmiths, tavern owners, merchants, and butchers. It appears that there was awareness among them of the Ustaša movement's nationalist ideology and, to at least some extent, a commitment to it.[70]

However, evidence suggests that only a miniscule number of these kinds of supporters of the Ustašas existed in the Kulen Vakuf region prior to the establishment of the NDH. And so once local mobilization began during the second half of the April 1941, the composition of the men who became Ustašas "overnight" was quite different, with just a handful fitting the general pre-1941 profile.[71] The local Ustaša leader, Miroslav Matijević, was a tavern owner in Kulen Vakuf. His counterpart in the nearby town of Donji Lapac, Vinko Marinković, was a judge. Mehmed Mušeta, Husein Zelić, and Grga Pavičić were merchants. Memoir and archival evidence suggests that some or all of these individuals may have had some degree of pre-1941 sympathy for the Ustaša movement.[72] Together these men constituted the head of the Ustašas in the Kulen Vakuf region, and were few in number; the body, however, was much larger and was composed primarily of poor Catholic and Muslim peasants and the unemployed—more Muslim than Catholic—who were now considered to be "Croat." As far as the limited sources allow us to reconstruct, their primary motivations in joining the Ustašas were to take advantage of the unexpected and unique opportunity to "settle scores" and rapidly enhance their economic and social positions at the expense of neighbors whom the new government now defined as "non-Croats."

The primary axis for future conflict at the local level was thus to be ethnic. This was not because a significant number of individuals demanded that conflict be structured along such lines; or because there was a critical mass that had a history of political activism on behalf of the Ustaša movement and a clear understanding of the ideological objectives of the NDH elite. Rather, the stage was now being set for "ethnic conflict" because the new authorities were offering certain local residents—especially those previously at the margins of economic, social, and political life—an unexpected opportunity and sizable incentives to act out pre-existing, or initiate new local conflicts on an ethnic axis. Although many local residents expressed shock that their neighbors became Ustašas, this sudden shift was not mysterious.

There was a certain logic and rationality at work among the men who joined. Unexpected opportunities for personal gain and settling conflicts crystalized clearly in response to the radical transformation of local political life. They saw these opportunities in concrete terms, and quickly moved to take advantage of them.

While this process of mobilization and political realignment along ethnic lines occurred in local communities such as the Kulen Vakuf region between April and June, the NDH elite in Zagreb debated how to solve the "Serb question." The policies that emerged from these conversations would affect how the new local elite and newly mobilized Ustašas would behave in the coming weeks toward their non-Croat neighbors. But this was not merely a matter of the center formulating policies and then sending out directives for the obedient local holders of power to enact. On the contrary, the ways that the central leadership may have imagined such policies unfolding would soon prove to be closely dependent on the desires and will of their local collaborators, and the specific local circumstances in which they operated—little of which was ideal for effectively carrying out the center's wishes. Moreover, the central authorities' complex methods of conceptualizing who was—and who was not—to be a part of the nation state offered local leaders even more space for autonomous policy implementation. None of this boded well for a swift, top-down resolution of the so-called Serb question.

Initially, the central authorities considered two main policies to deal with what they saw as the large "Serb minority." The first was to rapidly convert a sizable part of this population from Orthodoxy to Catholicism, and in some cases to Islam, in order to make "Serbs" into "Croats."[73] Archival documents suggest that the NDH elite were not opposed to Orthodox Christianity in principle. Indeed, special orders were issued to ensure that individuals practicing Orthodoxy in the NDH, such as those considered to be "Montenegrins," "Romanians," or "Macedonians," would be protected from conversion policies. Rather, the NDH elite viewed Serbian Orthodoxy as the foundation of Serbian identity. And because of its apparent function in creating this ethnic community, whose members had in history proven to be dangerous to Croats, it was seen as negative. Thus, it was the adherents of the Serbian Orthodox Church, including any Christians who "felt themselves to be Serbs," who were seen as the potential converts.[74] As the central pillars of the Serb Orthodox community, Serb priests and their families fell outside of this pool of converts because of their central role as the main propagators of "Serbdom" (*srpstvo*).

Viktor Gutić clarified the matter of conversions of "Greek Easterners" to Catholicism for the public in late June 1941 in a newspaper article, titled "Objašnjenje" (Explanation):

> Serb nationalist propaganda, which was skillfully and tirelessly led from Belgrade, especially by Orthodox priests and teachers in religious schools, and through all of its state authorities and institutions of [the Kingdom of] Yugoslavia, succeeded in Serbianizing nearly all Greek Easterners to a fanatical degree.
>
> If these individuals have realized that they have been alienated and driven mad, and now wish to assimilate themselves into the Croat people, and as a first step in that direction wish to leave that [Orthodox] Church, in which one can only be a Serb and nothing else, when they renounce Serbdom and those who propagate it there is no reason that these kinds of people should not be recognized as full-fledged members of the Croat nation with all the accompanying rights and responsibilities, if they wish and desire this.[75]

So even among the most committed Croat nationalists, such as Gutić, there was a belief that followers of Serbian Orthodoxy, that is "Serbs," could—at least theoretically—become part of the "Croat nation." The ethnic identity of such individuals was rooted in religion, education, and state propaganda. Nationality or ethnicity was thus the result of a specific set of external influences on a person; it was not an immutable, intrinsic essence of a person. Religious conversion, therefore, could be a way to reduce the significant number of those whom the NDH authorities perceived to be "Greek Easterners," that is "Serbs."[76]

An important finding in the NDH documents concerns which people among those seen as "Greek-Easterners" had the right to convert. In a circular sent from the Ministry of Justice and Religious Affairs on July 30, 1941, the authorities indicated that, "[Serb] peasants can receive [conversion] certificates without difficulties, except in exceptional cases." At the same time, "attention should be paid not to give certificates to teachers, priests, merchants, well-off craftsmen and peasants, and members of the intelligentsia, except in certain cases when those in question show honesty, because it is the official stance of the government not to give certificates to these groups of people."[77] Anyone seen as an active transmitter of Serb culture, and thus nationality, was singled out as more likely to be unredeemable.[78] Again, such stipulations suggest that the NDH government did not employ a racial, or even primordialist view of ethnicity, when conceptualizing the

"Serb" population—all those considered to be "Serbs" were not viewed as permanently fixed members of this community.[79]

Instead, one's occupation, education, and level of perceived participation in fostering a sense of "Serbdom," or "Serb" national/ethnic feeling, were the central factors in distinguishing the dangerous members of the "Greek-Easterners"—such as the intelligentsia and clergy—from those who could be safely converted to Catholicism and thus become "Croats," such as ordinary peasants. The NDH category "Greek-Easterner"—"Serb"—thus referred to types of behavior and level of perceived participation in building and maintaining a "Serb" community. This way of conceptualizing what constituted a "Serb" was radically different from how the NDH government defined the categories "Jews" and "Gypsies," in which clear Nazi-style biological language was employed. This difference made it much more likely that a set of policies would be instituted with the aim of the total physical removal of those considered to be members of these groups.[80]

Perhaps because of the complex distinctions of categorizations, a striking degree of variation occurred at the regional and local level. With regard to religious conversion, the Ministry of Justice and Religious Affairs gave the regional authorities significant discretion in terms of formulating a policy.[81] For example, a local Ustaša leader in Donji Lapac, located not far from the town of Kulen Vakuf, employed his own understanding on the matter of religious conversion. He offered the following reply to a request by a young Orthodox man to convert to Catholicism: "A black sheep always remains black," he replied, after which he struck a match and lit the man's written request on fire.[82]

Conceptualized as a key aspect of the central government's approach to remaking the human landscape of the NDH, the conversion policy was ultimately subject to local interpretation, and therefore could mean little to nothing in practice, especially at the town and village level. In northwest Bosnia, this was not simply due to the complicated definitions, and the lack of personnel in the countryside, which made it difficult for the NDH's central authorities to enforce a uniform approach to implementing the religious conversion policy. Of greater importance was that the central authorities explicitly exempted the leaders of the region, which was called the Velika župa Krbava i Psat, along with those in a neighboring region (the Velika župa Gora, located to the north and stretching past Zagreb), from even having to follow the instructions. Instead, they were to approach the issue of religious conversion by coming to an agreement with local Ustašas "according to local conditions."[83] As historian Fikreta Jelić-Butić has argued, the exemptions for these regions, where the perceived Serb population was considered to be among the largest in the NDH, strongly suggests that religious conversion was not intended as the primary solution to the "Serb question" in these territories.[84] So while some "former Serbs" in the NDH began attending Catholic mass each Sunday, which made them into "Croats," others, such as many in northwest Bosnia, were seen as unchangeable "black sheep." Their fate now rested in the hands of local NDH officials and Ustaša militias, who were to employ their own understanding of the feasibility of religious conversion.

For some of the NDH elite, like their counterparts in Romania, Nazi Germany, and other parts of Europe at the time who saw "unwanted populations" within their states, a more preferable way of solving the Serb question was "resettlement" (*iseljavanje*), or the forced migration of the perceived Serb population outside of the NDH's borders.[85] This was the second main policy that the NDH elite formulated to deal with the Serb question.[86] Documents from the State Office for Renewal (Državno ravnateljstvo za ponovu), which was established on June 24, 1941 to plan and direct the arrests and resettlement of the Serb population, reveal a bewildering array of rules, and what specifically determined whether an individual was to be expelled from the NDH or could remain.[87] In a set of internal instructions that the Office issued on July 24 regarding which families of mixed religious marriages should be resettled, several rules illuminate how the NDH elite understood what constituted a "dangerous" individual:

> In response to the numerous and diverse questions about the resettlement of those in mixed marriages, we are providing the following answers:
>
> 1. If the husband is Orthodox and the wife Catholic, and the children are Orthodox, then the entire family can stay only so long as the husband has not personally engaged in anti-Croat political activities and is not too economically successful, which would make him dangerous.
> 8. If the family is Orthodox, and one member from the family is actively serving in the Croatian Army, then the entire family may remain, so long as it meets the criteria as outline in point 1.
> 10. A bachelor or family of the Orthodox faith, which has for the entire period from 1918 until today behaved loyally to the Croat people, and has tried to help the nation morally, politically, and materially in its struggle, that family or bachelor may remain.[88]

Like the declarations about religious conversion, these stipulations regulating which mixed-marriage families could stay in the NDH strongly suggest that one's behavior—and not a sense of immutable biological or primordial "ethnic" characteristics—was decisive in determining whether one was to be resettled or not. Here, political and economic activities, service in the army of the NDH, and behavior vis-à-vis the "Croat people" during the interwar period are what matter most in determining one's level of danger to the NDH, and thus whether one would have to be resettled. "Orthodox," that is "Serb," thus was a category into which one did, or did not fit, according to one's past actions.

Present-day sentiments mattered too, as can be seen in a directive called, "Who is considered to be a Serb," which the NDH supreme military command issued later in 1941. While stating that, "in principle, a Serb is considered a person who is of the Orthodox/Greek-Eastern faith," exceptions were to be made for those serving in the NDH armed forces. After all, "faith is not the sole criterion that makes a person a Serb nationalist in his heart."[89] Again, what deserves attention is the extent that documents produced by the NDH elite reveal an exceptionally subjective understanding of what it meant to be categorized as a "Serb." At least at the higher levels of government, what one felt "in his heart" appears to have mattered as much, if not more, that any supposedly objective criteria such as religion, language, or "ethnicity" in determining who was a Serb. This elastic understanding of ethnic identity left significant space for multiple interpretations, exceptions, and reinterpretations, which resulted in an increased case-by-case treatment of those believed to be "Serbs." Taken together, the murky, subjective definition of "Serb" handed the local authorities significant latitude to decide whom they believed was—and was not—part of this category.

Evidence from NDH military documents suggests that large-scale plans were drawn up for the resettlement of all or most of the perceived "Serb" population of northwest Bosnia.[90] The State Office for Renewal was given responsibility for organizing these resettlements. The central authorities in Zagreb sent the Office precise instructions about how to carry out this task, which was described as being of "a strictly secret and urgent nature." This included the procedures for arresting those to be resettled, what they could bring with them, and especially how the state authorities—and not ordinary citizens—were to appropriate their wealth once they had left.[91]

The resettlement plans were not only designed to help solve "the Serb question" in the NDH; they were also geared toward enabling the government to engage in large-scale plunder. A mid-July circular, which was sent to all regional governors, made this explicit: "In order to more easily obtain the bank deposits, cash, and valuables of those arrested, it is to be suggested to them—and is permitted—to bring everything from their homes that they can carry."[92] In practice, however, it appears that much of the deported Serbs' wealth, like that of Jews, fell into the hands of local leaders and common citizens who rushed to plunder their former neighbors as soon as they departed.[93] The clique gathered around Viktor Gutić appears to have been one of the most active in this regard. During the first half of July, once the resettlements had begun, they took advantage of the chaos, and the inability of the State Office for Renewal to effectively expropriate the property of the deportees, to plunder large amounts money and property. Gutić was said to have given properties and businesses to his inner circle, and to have sold them to others.[94] That the State Office for Renewal was aware of this, can be seen in a directive issued at the end of July, in which it loudly reminded the local authorities—in capital and underlined letters—that "all property of the resettled Serbs, like that of those who have yet to be resettled, is the property of the Independent State of Croatia, with the State Office for Renewal having sole power over its administration and management."[95]

In response to this locally executed plunder, the NDH authorities in Zagreb attempted to force those targeted for resettlement to first register their property with the central authorities. This was an attempt to steer expropriation in the localities away from individuals such as Gutić and toward the central authorities.[96] Yet internal NDH investigations would later show that the expropriations by regional leaders continued largely unfettered. Such documents indicated that this plunder was "not in the interests of the state, but rather for the use of individuals, their families, their friends."[97] Empowering regional and local leaders to carry out ethnically defined policies of "resettlement" thus set the stage for mass local plunder along such an axis, which also stymied the central authorities' attempt to appropriate this wealth.

Like the NDH's plans for religious conversion, attempts at resettling the large perceived Serb population unfolded with significant regional variation, which suggests the existence of a sizable gap between central planning and local practice. In northwest Bosnia, large-scale deportations were organized in some areas, such as in the city of Bihać during the second half of June and early July, while a much slower and more selective approach to deportation was taken in Banja Luka.[98] In the Kulen Vakuf region, there is no archival evidence that a branch of the State Office for Renewal was even established. As we shall see, instead of resettlement and religious conversion of the perceived Serb population, stealing and a much more violent approach would soon take shape there. This suggests that the wide latitude of interpretation built into these policies—from categorization to implementation—meant that local leaders could enact policies toward "non-Croats" in radically different ways according to their own needs.[99]

Successfully pursuing a large-scale resettlement policy in northwest Bosnia was daunting for the NDH's central leadership whose authority did not always extend very far into the rural regions where the population was often overwhelmingly Orthodox. In some municipalities, sometimes there were less than a hundred Ustašas for thousands—even tens of thousands—of "Serbs."[100] Quickly deporting a sizable part of this population was therefore a daunting task in this region where their numbers were thought to be in the hundreds of thousands. What emboldened NDH supreme leader Ante Pavelić and his closest associates was their agreement with the German Army, which they made during the first week of June. It stipulated that thousands of Catholic "Slovenes" would be transferred into the NDH, and then an equal number of Orthodox "Serbs" would be deported to Serbia, which was under German occupation. The State Office for Renewal sent out instructions to the regions and localities about the importance of closely following the terms of this agreement, or else the possibility of resettling a sizable part the NDH's Serb population to German-occupied Serbia would be brought into question.[101]

But the archival record suggests that adhering to international agreements was not merely the prerogative of the central authorities; the success or failure of the ambitious resettlement plans also lay very much in the hands of regional and local holders of power. A brief examination of events in northwest Bosnia is instructive. On June 16, Ljubomir Kvaternik was appointed as Veliki župan, or supreme leader, of the newly created administrative unit (akin to a large county) that encompassed much of northwest Bosnia and part of Lika, which was called "Velika župa Krbava i Psat." On June 20, he ordered that all those considered to be "Serb" and "Jewish" were to be expelled from the town of Bihać.[102] Here, there was no careful sorting among individuals according to past and present behavior in order to determine who had to leave; the order was sweeping. At 5:00 a.m. on June 24, those who assembled were loaded on buses. The Ustašas in Bihać forced them to hand over most of their valuables and money, as well as the keys to their homes and apartments. One part of the group was taken fifty kilometers to Kulen Vakuf, while the others were taken east and left in various Serbian villages in the Bosanski Petrovac region. The deportees were allowed to bring a small amount of money and valuables, which the NDH authorities later took from them.[103]

The level of disorganization and improvisation during the expulsions was evident, which suggests that Kvaternik's main objectives, like that of other local NDH authorities, were clearing "unwanted elements" from their stronghold in Bihać and plundering their property. The meticulous plans for resettlement of the central authorities in Zagreb, along with a careful consideration of the definitions of who should be resettled, were nowhere to be seen. The ordeal had just begun for those robbed and expelled from Bihać, and then sent on buses to Kulen Vakuf. There they disembarked, waited for hours without any food or water, and then were made to walk fifteen kilometers to the village of Martin Brod, where they spent the night in fields. The next day, the few NDH authorities in the village told them they were to now return the same way they came to Kulen Vakuf. After another day or so spent there, they were ordered to walk thirty to forty kilometers to the Bosanski Petrovac region.[104]

The expellees thus spent days wandering the region under armed guard, sometimes returning multiple times to the same locations, before being told to move again. No plan for deportation outside the borders of the NDH seemed to exist. Some of the expellees, particularly the elderly and small children, died during these marches. However, the evidence does not suggest that mass killing was the ultimate objective of these resettlements. Instead, we see a central state administration attempting to rid its territory of unwanted groups, but plagued in the regions and at the local level by a lack of coordination, poor planning, and especially the pursuit of local agendas. Indeed, what seemed primary to regional leaders like Kvaternik and other local officials was not pushing "non-Croats" outside the borders of the NDH, but simply robbing them, and then pushing them somewhere else within the NDH, so long as this was outside of the immediate vicinity of their towns and villages. The NDH authorities in Bosanski Petrovac responded to the expulsion of Serbs from Bihać in a similarly self-interested way by placing a ban on the refugees coming from within five kilometers of their town.[105]

This level of local autonomy in directing the "resettlements" not only called into question whether implementing a policy of forced migration was even feasible, which the Italian vice consul in Banja Luka doubted would continue given the kinds of problems that arose during the operation in Bihać in June.[106] More importantly, it would soon trigger serious internal security problems in northwest Bosnia. The NDH's military was the institution most concerned about the effects that these poorly planned and executed resettlements would have on the level of "order" in the region.[107] As one military analyst remarked in an internal report about the June 24 deportations from Bihać:

> The situation is difficult in the Bosanski Petrovac region [in northwest Bosnia], where about 2,700 of the Orthodox population were

> removed from Bišće [Bihać] and Plitvica. They were dumped in the vicinity of the towns of Kulen Vakuf and Drvar and then moved to poor villages without any preparations and plans, and without means for food. This sudden movement of entire villages with women and children in desperate condition has disturbed the entire region, which is predominately Orthodox [Serb]. Although peace still remains, it is not inconceivable that a revolt of the people could break out, as they have been forced to leave their homes and then to wander through villages without food and real accommodations. Due to this, intervention should be taken with the civilian administration to organize food, housing and employment for this population as soon as possible. These people are being exposed to hunger and theft in this poor (passive) region, and this can only be a germ for the growth of disorder and dissatisfaction.[108]

Others in the military did not believe that better caring for the expellees would, at this point, contain what they saw as an impending Serb rebellion in response to the resettlements. A few weeks later, in mid-July, some commanders in northwest Bosnia and Lika were already requesting troop reinforcements to ensure that "an insurgency would not break out . . . due to the insufficiently organized resettlement of Serbs and Jews, which has worsened the atmosphere and made it much more difficult to calm the political conditions."[109] This fear was based less on what the largely urbanized deportees from Bihać might do in the countryside, and more on how the military expected the rural Orthodox population to react to the impending threat of resettlement. Being forced to move would deprive these peasants of their fields, livestock, and homes. Fear of this fate, as NDH military analysts noted, was sweeping through much of the countryside, and "stirring up" the Orthodox villages. By early July, increasing numbers of men from these villages were now spending their nights in nearby forests, afraid to stay at home. More than a few were armed because of their recent military service in April when the former Yugoslav Army had mobilized to resist the German invasion. In some localities, incidents of unknown persons firing shots at NDH officials from the forests nearby villages were starting to take place.[110]

By late June, the central NDH authorities were slowly losing control over the implementation of policies of persecution in northwest Bosnia that they had recently helped to unleash. The "resettlements" had not removed the perceived Serb population; on the contrary, they had rapidly laid the foundation for a serious security threat. At the local level, the sudden empowerment of men to join the Ustaša units was supposed to provide the necessary muscle to realize the objective of remolding the ethnic composition of the NDH's population. Yet the subsequent behavior of these local men does not suggest they had much understanding and commitment to this primary ideological task of the central authorities. In the Kulen Vakuf region, among the first activities that local Ustašas engaged in was neither facilitating religious conversion nor resettlement of the perceived Serb population; rather, it was stealing from their neighbors. This did not rid the region of the non-Croat population; rather, like the poorly executed resettlements, it created rising levels of fear and insecurity. The local plunder also led to a growing atmosphere of anarchy, which blurred the supposed hard ethnic lines of division that the central authorities envisioned conflict unfolding along, and soon began to endanger "Croats."

As Gutić had already begun in April, the Ustaša leader in the Kulen Vakuf region, Matijević, began to make use of his new position in May, and increasingly during June, to steal money and property from those whom he considered as the region's most prominent Orthodox. He sent orders to such individuals in the local villages to appear in the town of Kulen Vakuf with a specific sum of money. He usually arrested those who arrived, took their money, and then held them prisoner for a period of time.[111] Matijević was not simply acting on his own volition. He was following in the footsteps of the regional leaders Gutić and Kvaternik. The latter was explicit about the need for Serbian property to "fall into the [Croat] people's hands." This was a primary means through which to mobilize local Catholics and Muslims to assist in the elite-led project of reshaping of the NDH's ethnic composition. The opportunity to plunder freed leaders such as Gutić and Kvaternik from the worry of whether their Ustaša foot soldiers were deeply committed nationalists.[112] And the local Ustašas, many of whom had previously lived on the margins of their communities prior to the establishment of the NDH, were only too ready to respond to this unprecedented opportunity for rapid personal gain. One NDH military officer minced no words, calling these men "a bunch of good-for-nothing troublemakers [*nekolicini nevaljalaca*], who for years have walked the streets . . . without work, and now are making use of today's circumstances for their personal gain."[113] Scholars have noted similar social profiles among many of those mobilized into militias during conflicts in other parts of the world, such as Africa. There, the socially marginal have been attracted to participate in "ethnic" persecution by suddenly receiving the unexpected opportunity to plunder along such lines. Deeply rooted and widespread antagonistic ethnic sentiments do not have to be present among such individuals to trigger their participation; rather, situational opportunity to profit is often sufficient.[114]

This was a central dynamic in many parts of the NDH, such as Herzegovina. In a frank assessment made in early July 1941 of the situation there, a regional NDH official noted:

> Often the first men gathered up [to join the Ustašas] were those found on the streets [i.e., without jobs], whom by their past behavior were not even qualified to be the most ordinary clerks, let alone Ustašas. These same people were then armed and given full power to decide the life and death of all residents.
>
> These armed men were only interested in their personal gain . . . as I have seen with my own eyes that not even the smallest item has been left in the [Serbian] houses. They have carried away everything. Officers of the Croatian Army have told me that . . . they have witnessed people with rifles who were carrying stolen goods on their backs. When one was asked why he was carrying these things, he responded: "Because I'm an Ustaša." Here . . . there are twelve men who have sworn an oath to become Ustašas and who have been armed. Out the twelve, six are unsuitable because of their political and social background, as among them are men who have been previously convicted for stealing.[115]

Of significance here is the notion that one had the right to steal "because I'm an Ustaša." This suggests that the new position that the NDH government gave to these men, which carried with it an expectation that they would have a wide latitude of authority in their local communities, played a key role in restructuring their future behavior. Social psychologists have noted that giving a subject a new identity label can have profound effects on his/her subsequent actions, regardless of personal dispositions prior to the attachment of this label.[116] At work in the localities of the NDH was a dynamic in which local men, who often existed on the margins of society prior the establishment of the NDH, suddenly became "Ustašas," which empowered them in unprecedented ways to mistreat others in their communities. This label then became the justification they invoked for their deeds, even for those that transgressed the new state's official laws.

The unprecedented opportunity to plunder one's neighbors by becoming an Ustaša was at work among the local Ustašas in the Kulen Vakuf region. NDH documents demonstrate that units at the village level used their newfound authority to demand, on multiple occasions, increasing amounts of money and goods from prominent individuals whom they categorized as Serbs. One was Marko Vladetić from the village of Martin Brod, who was widely known in the region as a wealthy merchant. Ustašas robbed him on multiple occasions.[117] According to memoir accounts, the village of Boričevac quickly became one of the centers where stolen property was taken, which increasingly included the materials taken after the complete stripping of houses. "Even bricks, boards, beams . . . were taken to Boričevac," as one local resident recalled. "And the furniture vanished from the houses of those [Serbs] who fled, along with livestock and farm tools—everything that could be removed from the walls and rooftops was taken."[118]

What deserves attention when examining this stealing is how it was a mobilizational tool that the macro and meso levels of the NDH government used to attract local men, many of whom had little to no connection to the Ustašas prior to 1941, into the new Ustaša units. Yet these micro-level actors quickly began to behave in ways that soon thwarted the large-scale ideological plans of those who empowered them. This was because their stealing quickly transcended the solely ethnic axis on which the central and regional NDH authorities wished to steer it along, and began to negatively affect "Croats" in various ways. This was a more general trend throughout the NDH at the local level.

According to the authorities in eastern Bosnia, for example, during the first part of the summer of 1941 Muslim Ustašas committed "unlawful" acts of plunder, which they followed by issuing death threats against those "Muslims" and "Croats" who indicated that they would report them to the authorities. For some local NDH officials, the stealing had to be stopped to prevent "damage to the appearance of the Ustaša movement," as well as that "of all good and respectable people of the muslim faith." Reports from June and July show that local Muslim men made use of their new status as Ustašas to maraud through the region's Serbian villages, stealing wine, wheat, and clothing, demanding money, and removing wedding rings from women after failing to find a sufficient amount of valuables in their homes. As was the case with some of the local Ustašas in the Kulen Vakuf region, many of those who participated were familiar faces in their localities, described by the NDH gendarmerie as men with long-time reputations as "well-known thieves." Some were not even formally enlisted in the Ustaša units, choosing instead to present themselves to their victims as Ustašas and then "taking whatever came into their hands." They informed anyone who might threaten them, as one local official put it, "that there are no limits on their power in the NDH, that they are Gods, that they can search anyone's home, and could even arrest [NDH] gendarmes."[119]

The threats that local Ustašas now began to issue to supposedly fellow "Croats" and "Muslims" who questioned their behavior were not mere words. NDH military reports from late May show that Ustašas—whether official or not, remains unknown—arrested an NDH army officer, and broke into the room of another to steal shoes and fuel.[120] During July in northwest Bosnia, the military noted with dismay that local Ustašas were searching officers' houses for items to steal, and carrying off uniforms from soldiers. In Bihać around the same time, Ustašas arrested two NDH lieutenants, whom they refused to release, and then fired their rifles at the captain who came to free them.[121] Reports from NDH civil authorities in other regions suggest that the Ustašas also stole from, and abused Muslim villagers and townspeople. They forced some to roast their own sheep for them, and shot at others while drinking alcohol. All this caused spiraling fear among the Muslim villages.[122]

This evidence suggests that what began as inter-ethnic plunder also quickly took on intra-ethnic dimensions. One should thus be cautious about making any quick conclusions about the explanatory power of "ethnic conflict" in helping us understand the dynamics of this stealing that snowballed not long after the establishment of the NDH. A cursory glance at events from the early summer of 1941 might suggest to some that "Muslims" and "Croats" were those pre-disposed to engage in theft of their "Serb" neighbors' property. But the local evidence suggests that intra-ethnic theft also quickly became a problem, as the example of the Ustašas robbing NDH military officers demonstrates. The central and regional NDH authorities did not expect this when they mobilized local "Croats" into the Ustaša units.

This general dynamic—of theft outside the axis of "Croats" versus "non-Croats"—was present in the Kulen Vakuf region, yet manifested in ways that are even more surprising. On June 13, 1941, three men dressed as Ustašas approached the wealthy Serb merchant, Marko Vladetić, in his store in the village of Martin Brod. They demanded money. However, he recognized one of them, Ilija Ćubrilo, as "a Serb" from the region. Ćubrilo, along with his two accomplices, had decided to capitalize on the new situation in the region by impersonating Ustašas in order to rob well-off Serbs.[123] Here we see intra-ethnic theft among those (i.e., "Serbs") whom the NDH authorities had singled out for persecution along an ethnic axis.

Such evidence further suggests that the mass theft now taking place throughout the NDH could be just as much, if not more, rooted in making use of the newly politicized salience of ethnic categories, as in any actually existing antagonistic cleavages along such lines. More "Croats" and "Muslims" stole from "Serbs" because they could, given the politics and policies of the central NDH authorities at the time. Yet some enterprising individuals categorized as "Serbs" soon found ways to rob their supposed co-ethnics by capitalizing on the NDH government's policies of persecution of the Serb community. And being an "Ustaša" certainly did not mean that one was inclined to rob only "Serbs," as the designation quickly became an unofficial license to plunder, regardless of a victim's supposed ethnic category. The opportunities of the new political context often ruled over supposed "ethnic" affinities and antagonisms.

The flood of local theft thus suggests that nationalist ideology and "ethnic hatred" was much less important that one initially might assume. The new political field that the central and regional authorities created was conducive to local theft along an ethnic axis. And some who participated did have prior grievances on an ethnic basis that could now be acted upon. But the rapid emergence of intra-ethnic theft at nearly the same time also suggests a different dynamic at work: the new circumstances empowered certain people to steal, which they did along an ethnic axis when it suited them, and also along an intra-ethnic axis when that proved feasible. Other scholars have noted similar dynamics in conflicts in Africa, such as in Rwanda and Darfur, in which it has sometimes been assumed that perpetrators in various militias "naturally" represent the violent incarnation of a supposed long-term cultural cleavage. In fact, just like the Ustaša recruits, these men, while certainly mobilized due to a perception of their supposed common cultural traits, capitalized in particular situations on the unexpected opportunity that came with suddenly being handed a monopoly over the means of violence.[124]

The process of mobilizing local men into the Ustašas thus carried with it a certain level of destabilization for the local NDH authorities, and the daily lives of the local Catholic and Muslim population. This was the case because more than a few of the new Ustašas did not appear to share the deeply ethnicized worldview of the NDH elite, in which the only enemies that existed were "Serbs" and other non-Croats, such as "Jews" and "Roma," as well as political opponents, such as communists. Or, if they did, they applied it in a situational way, according to their prospects for material gain. These were men who stole from their neighbors along an ethnic axis when it could be accomplished easily, yet a moment later, when the situation appeared favorable, could pay little attention to the ethnic criteria of their victims.

In an important sense, then, the initial mobilization of local men into the Ustašas was a situational convergence of divergent agendas that suited both national and regional leaders—and local residents—but in general, for different reasons. For the former, men were needed, and incentives were needed to mobilize them, to carry out the removal of non-Croats from the NDH, and to deal with supposed security threats. For the latter, to be suddenly armed and to be able to behave however they wished toward their neighbors was an unprecedented and, for most, irresistible opportunity to rapidly enrich themselves. There was rationality to each side's behavior; and there was an obvious conflict between the two, which would grow in the coming months.

We now have the pieces in place to explain the main dynamics of the sweeping changes that took place in the Kulen Vakuf region during the first two months after the establishment of the NDH. The interactions among the macro, meso, and micro levels upended the world of the local community that existed prior to early April 1941, which then recrystallized in response to a radically different political field. The elite of the NDH redefined the population as composed of ethnic categories of inclusion and exclusion. These tended to be based more on subjective factors such as past and present behavior, rather than a perception of unchangeable essence, such as race. This meant that while the central axis for future conflict would be ethnic, in practice ethnicity was to be understood in local, subjective ways. The state's elite did not simply unleash deeply rooted, widespread, and pre-existing hatreds along such lines, although for a minority of people prewar political and inter-personal conflicts mattered in explaining their participation in the Ustaša units; rather, they created a set of exclusive, antagonistic categories, and then offered local actors concrete incentives to use them in order to undertake ethnic persecution, which the central authorities hoped would assist in their creation of a new nation-state.

Mobilization of local actors did indeed occur in a top-down fashion, yet bottom-up forces were significant in the transformations taking place. Only for a small number did their prewar political disposition matter in any serious way. For the rest, the unexpected opportunity for personal enrichment was paramount. Some merchants looked to change the rules of local business, erase their debts, and enrich themselves. Peasants in disputes with neighbors over the use of natural resources saw the chance to resolve conflicts in their favor or get even for past wrongs. Family members often teamed up and joined the Ustašas in pursuit of these objectives.

Several factors made the new local Ustaša units very much a new power unto themselves: the specific authority structure of the NDH state, in which there were few horizontal links between the civil authorities, gendarmerie, and military on one side, and the Ustašas on the other; the near monopoly of the Ustašas on local power, especially the capacity to use violence in the local community; and the overall lack of a sizable non-Ustaša NDH authority presence in the countryside—all these factors accentuated the local power of the Ustaša units, in spite of their small size and general lack of widespread support from the communities in which they operated.

This meant that patterns of persecution in the NDH quickly took on a regional and local quality, as the independent behavior of Viktor Gutić, Ljubomir Kvaternik, and Miroslav Matijević demonstrates. These local strongmen took the lead in putting the new policies of exclusion into practice in ways that suited them. The latitude available to such men in implementing policies of persecution, such as resettlement, helped to facilitate in northwest Bosnia and Lika an enormous amount of plunder, but also produced chaos and rapidly triggered a worsening security situation. In the Kulen Vakuf region, the mobilization of men into the Ustašas did not even bring about attempts at forced migration or religious conversion; rather, the main result was mass local theft and social destabilization.

Herein lay the paradox of the relationship between the central NDH authorities and their allies in the regions and localities. To carry out their ideological objectives, the elite in Zagreb needed local manpower, and they mobilized it by allowing individuals to plunder. Yet their plunder quickly transcended the "ethnic" axis because the new political field also facilitated intra-ethnic plunder in a myriad of ways by a host of local actors. The central authorities thus quickly faced the challenge of steering the behavior of the local Ustašas toward realizing their broader ideological objectives, when the basis on which they mobilized them often thwarted the realization of such goals. And so in northwest Bosnia, Lika, and in the Kulen Vakuf region, the result after two months or so of NDH power was not successful resettlement or religious conversion of the perceived Serb population; rather, it was mass theft, growing fear among most local people, and the government's perception of spiraling insecurity. This was setting the stage for a radicalization in policies to solve the "Serb question," a resolution of which the Ustaša elite had long desired. By mid-June 1941, it was for them rapidly becoming an immediate necessity.

What made escalation more likely was the increasing marginalization of more moderate NDH officials in the regions and localities of northwest Bosnia and Lika, a process that had already begun germinating toward the end of May and into June. Viktor Gutić set the stage for this internal cleansing. "Every Croat who intercedes on behalf of our enemies," he said, "is not merely no kind of good Croat, but stands against and hinders our plan for cleansing our Croatia of unwanted elements."[125] The arrival of Ljubomir Kvaternik as the Veliki župan of the newly established administrative unit for much of northwest Bosnia and Lika, the Velika župa Krbava i Psat, exemplified a major shift in the region toward radicalization.[126] Little mass persecution of non-Croats had occurred there prior to early June. It appears that Gutić, as well as Pavelić in Zagreb, were displeased with the NDH leaders in Bihać for being too moderate, particularly in a region where the Serb population was considered to be so large.[127] In response, Pavelić appointed Ljubomir Kvaternik, who was the brother of Slavko Kvaternik, the supreme commander of the NDH's military.[128] It appears that he arrived to Bihać on June 16.[129] With him came other Ustašas—Enver Kapetanović, Pero Šimić, and Jakov Džal, among others—some of whom had been in exile prior to the war. They were intent on immediately instituting policies of persecution against those they considered as non-Croats.[130] Within a week, Kvaternik and his clique began issuing proclamations designed to separate and remove "unwanted elements"—those considered Serbs and Jews—who were seen as guilty of damaging the "honor of the Croatian homeland and Croat nation." They then moved quickly to expel these populations from Bihać.[131]

After plundering the expellees' property, Kvaternik ordered that the Serbian Orthodox Church in Bihać be destroyed on June 28, known as Vidovdan—the Serbian religious holiday of St. Vitus and the day when the Serbian Orthodox Church commemorates its martyrs who are believed to have fallen during the Battle of Kosovo in 1389. This act exemplified the ideological commitment by the Ustaša elite to purifying the NDH of all things Serbian, and demonstrated their capacity to undertake policies that were bound to provoke confrontation. Yet the moderate mayor of Bihać, Abdulah Ibrahimpašić, opposed Kvaternik's order. He argued that such measures would surely lead to a rebellion that no one would be able to stop. In protest, he indicated that he would remain in his position only if the town's Catholic churches and mosques were also razed along with the Serbian Orthodox Church. He was immediately removed and replaced, and the destruction of the Orthodox Church eventually began. Under the direction of Kvaternik, the local authorities intensified their internal cleansing by carrying out as many as fifty arrests of Ibrahimpašić's supporters, several of whom had previously held positions in the NDH government.[132] Younger Ustaša supporters, such as university student Pero Šimić, who had been a supporter of the movement since 1939, and Jakov Džal, a lawyer, now assumed their positions. The internal cleansing of the NDH authorities in Bihać continued unabated. Vicko Dračevac, the head of the municipality, was quickly removed from his position after it became known that he had recently intervened on behalf of several well-known local Serbs.[133]

These intra-Croat struggles between those in favor of radicalization and those with a more moderate stance continued even after the mass expulsions of the non-Croat population from Bihać. Internal NDH directives sent out as late as a month after the mass exodus warned all lower level officials that there would be severe consequences for anyone who did not stop all "Vlahs" (a derogatory words for Serbs) from coming to the city, and especially for those who were continuing to interact with such individuals.[134] The situation was similar in other regions of the NDH, such as the town of Knin, where Ustaša-oriented officials described local Croat merchants as having an "enemy disposition" because "they had always been in the best and closest relationships with Serbs."[135]

As the cleansing of internal enemies intensified, some of the region's NDH officials, such as Rifat Kulenović in Bosanski Petrovac, resigned rather than be implicated in acts of persecution of non-Croats.[136] Yet much more common was the identification and subsequent removal of NDH officials and others considered too moderate. NDH military officer Tomislav Gržeta, who was stationed in Drvar, was described as a "Yugophile" because of his marriage to a Serb woman, and his attempts to disarm the local Ustašas. His lieutenant, whose last name was Čengić, was said to be socializing with local Serbs, with whom he frequently had lunch. Both were removed from their positions. Outsiders sometimes replaced such individuals when no suitable local replacements were available. Đuro Kuharski came to Drvar from Herzegovina in order to take over the local government, which the regional authorities considered insufficiently radical in persecuting non-Croats. Along with immediately dismissing all "Serbs" from their jobs, Kuharski targeted Drvar's Catholic priest, Father Martin Vujević, supposedly a fellow "Croat." He received death threats for advocating on behalf of his town's Orthodox population, and eventually fled Drvar.[137]

Archival documents contain similar examples of NDH civil, military, and religious figures in other parts of northwest Bosnia and Lika who were noted for their opposition to "Ustaša policies."[138] Those who wished to intensify the persecution of "non-Croats" needed first to orchestrate the removal of these individuals and their replacement with those amenable to implementing more radical policies.[139] The push toward persecuting the external ethnic "other" thus went hand-in-hand with an internal identification, persecution and disciplining of those co-ethnics viewed as too moderate. Scholars have noted similar dynamics in other contexts, such as Rwanda in 1994, during which pursuing any escalation of "ethnic" persecution first (or simultaneously) required removing moderate elements from one's own perceived community.[140]

In the localities, the top-down imperative to remove moderates from power provided more radical or opportunistic elements with the opening to now push their local rivals from power. In Kulen Vakuf, during the period from late May until the middle of June, a series of conflicts began over who would run the government in the town and its municipality, and who would control the incipient Ustaša units. Since the establishment of the NDH state, the town's mayor was Adem-beg Kulenović, a political moderate. The tavern owner Miroslav Matijević was in charge of the Ustašas. It appears that Matijević had concerns about certain local powerholders, such as Kulenović, being too "lenient" toward the non-Croat population. This concern could have been rooted in Matijević's supposed Croatian nationalism. But it also could have easily been a convenient way to orchestrate Kulenović's removal from a leadership position, which would have allowed Matijević and his associates an even greater degree of latitude to steal. On at least one occasion, he traveled to Zagreb to meet with Jure Pavičić, who had roots in the region. He was also a high-level member (*doglavnik*) of Pavelić's inner circle gathered in the Main Ustaša Headquarters. It appears that Matijević discussed with him the need to replace the moderates in Kulen Vakuf. By mid-June, it appears that Husein "Huća" Zelić had become the new mayor of Kulen Vakuf, while Matijević had even more firmly established his control over the mobilization and direction of the region's Ustaša units.[141] Zelić was known in Kulen Vakuf as an unsuccessful merchant, "notorious speculator," and having had contacts with Croat nationalists prior to 1941.[142] Other evidence suggests that he may have been favorably disposed to the Nazis.[143] Like the other local Ustašas whom he had mobilized, Matijević had already benefitted greatly by this time from his position due to the opportunity to freely plunder his "non-Croat" neighbors.

When the year 1941 began, it is unlikely that these men entertained the notion that they would ever be anything more than a tavern owner and marginal merchant. Now they were leading the local community. The establishment of the NDH and the formation of its authority truly upended the world of the localities, catapulting such previously marginal individuals into positions of unprecedented power. Any policy change ordered from above would now be channeled out into the lives of the region's residents through their interpretation of it. As the days of the second half of June passed, it was increasingly likely that the central and regional authorities were leaning toward a more radical approach to solve the "Serb question." Its implementation would depend on these local men and those now associated with them.

Chapter 3

Killing and Rescue

As July approached, the Kulen Vakuf region remained relatively quiet. Arrests, widespread plunder, and some incidents of physical violence had occurred, including several instances of killing.[1] But the atmosphere there was radically different from other parts of the NDH. Severe outbreaks of mass violence against the perceived Serb population had already taken place in numerous communities. In the village of Gudovac, near the town of Bjelovar, Ustašas killed 184 peasants during April 27–28. In Blagaj, they called on all men from the village of Veljun to gather, and then killed about 250 during the night of May 4–5. On the night of May 11–12, Ustašas went from house to house in the town of Glina, rounded up men and boys and killed more than 300 of them. On June 2, near the town of Ljubinje in Herzegovina, Ustašas killed about 140 peasants. Three days later, they killed about 180 from the village of Korita near the town of Gacko. On June 23, again near Ljubinje, they killed about 160 people, and then another 80 in three villages near Gacko. And nearly 260 were killed during two days in the Herzegovinian municipality of Stolac. Historians of the NDH are aware of these killings. But explanation of their causes, and the reasons for the temporal and geographical variation of this violence, remain bewildering in the literature. Most are usually content to list the massacres, often describing the violence in graphic detail, but generally without providing much, if any causal explanation, aside from Ustaša nationalist ideology. It has been as if recording the number of killings and victims (however imprecise), and the methods of their deaths by murderous nationalists, are somehow sufficient for us to understand how and why such violence could happen.[2]

It is difficult to determine the precise chain of causation of these usually locally executed massacres because the paper trail left behind by organizers and perpetrators is at best thin and fragmentary, or in some cases even absent. Yet reconstructing the micro-dynamics of these local killings, and explaining their causes, remains a central historiographical challenge for scholars. Ideologies of utopian cleansing, or in this case the "genocidal" nature of the NDH regime's ideology and state practice, may—and often do—matter significantly in creating a context conducive to mass violence. But such ideational frameworks do not explain why and when mass violence becomes the policy of choice in certain locations and moments, but not others.[3] What is needed is not only a "thick description" of both the chain of events that leads to local violence, and how it unfolds; we also need a careful analysis that seeks to explain the interactions among the macro, meso, and especially micro mechanisms that make such dramatic shifts possible.

In the Kulen Vakuf region, a three-day period of July 1–3 marked the turning point when local Ustašas shifted from sporadic arrests, plunder, and selective violence into full-blown mass killing. As such, it provides us with a local lens through which to search for an answer to a major—and still highly debated—question in the literature on mass violence: Why in certain locations and at certain times does mass killing become the order of the day? Scholars have long been interested in determining why state leaders choose to engage in such violence rather than employ less draconian measures of repression and persecution. This once "unsolved puzzle," as Barbara Herff put it in a thought provoking critique several decades ago, has received serious attention from scholars, mostly in macro-level studies of violence.[4] In recent years scholars have devoted increased attention to uncovering the causes of violence through more micro-level studies, particularly in contexts such as Africa, Asia, and some parts of Eastern Europe.[5] But in the NDH, empirically detailed and theoretically engaged research on the rural communities where the violence was most severe is still largely absent. And so a detailed analysis of what took place in the Kulen Vakuf region during July 1–3 holds the potential to tell us something new—both in this context and more generally—about why local communities, which do not have long-term histories of violence, can suddenly explode into episodes of local killing.

What stands out when closely examining this region's history is how mutually reinforcing fears at the local level can drive some local actors to compel higher-level authorities into ordering acts of pre-emptive, "self-defensive" mass violence. These can then trigger further waves of locally driven violence. Yet the motivations of those who order such violence and those who carry it out on the ground can differ sharply. Their violence can deeply polarize a multi-ethnic community, and lead to a rapid hardening of inter-ethnic boundaries. But it can also simultaneously produce new, or amplify pre-existing forms of inter-ethnic solidarity through acts of inter-ethnic rescue.

The search for the specific causes of the shift to mass violence in the Kulen Vakuf region takes us back to a policy that the NDH authorities attempted to implement to better control the non-Croat population. Documents from the NDH's military from late April indicate that disarming the perceived Serb population was called "the most important part of our work." To realize this objective, the use of force and taking of prisoners was sanctioned.[6] Slavko Kvaternik, the army's supreme commander, issued public announcements that anyone who failed to turn over military equipment and arms would be arrested and placed on trial for treason.[7] This imperative to disarm the Orthodox population—especially former soldiers of the Army of the Kingdom of Yugoslavia—was an essential step before any major confrontational policy to reshape the ethnic composition of the NDH, such as resettlement, could be implemented.

Attempts to disarm this population began in April in the Bihać region, which soon spread to all of northwest Bosnia, and to neighboring communities in Lika. However, by mid-May, little to no progress had been made. This greatly worried the authorities given their perception of the region as overwhelmingly "Serb."[8] According to NDH statistics, it was believed that the ethnic composition of most municipalities was between 60 and 80 percent Serb.[9] Memoirs suggest that it was only in the most ethnically mixed areas, which constituted only a small part of the region, that former Orthodox soldiers were more likely to respond positively to the call to turn in their weapons. The men from these areas had previously served together in the army with their Catholic and Muslim neighbors during the short war in early April against the Axis powers. Often, they had returned together to their communities, and the Catholic and Muslim soldiers knew that their Orthodox neighbors were still armed. They were thus afraid that some of their neighbors would report them to the authorities for failing to hand over their military equipment. In areas where the majority of population was Orthodox, by contrast, such fears did not exist. So these men were more likely to hold on to their rifles and ammunition, which they often hid in the forests nearby their homes. Such acts would be important in determining a village's capacity for armed resistance in the event of any violent escalation in NDH policies.[10]

The attempt in May and June by local Ustašas in the Kulen Vakuf region to disarm former Orthodox soldiers yielded only about 100 rifles, which left them fearful.[11] They believed that local villagers had hidden sizable quantities of weapons and ammunition (especially by burying them) in the mountainous forests along the border between Lika and Bosnia, which the Kulen Vakuf region straddled.[12] This fear was not entirely unfounded. After returning home following the dissolution of the former Yugoslav army, a sizable number of local men brought with them rifles, pistols, a small number of light machine guns, and ammunition, which most kept in hiding.[13] Of the seventy-one men from the village of Osredci who participated in the defense of the Kingdom of Yugoslavia in April 1941, more than half were said to have returned home with their rifles and some ammunition. It does not appear that any of these men turned in their weapons.[14] From the perspective of the authorities, there was some justification for concern about what these former soldiers might do with their arms.

In May, NDH military reports began noting sporadic incidents of individuals shooting at Ustašas in locations in Lika and parts of northwest Bosnia, including near Kulen Vakuf. This heightened the tension, fear, and suspicion of the male Serb population, which the authorities increasingly believed were preparing an attack.[15] Whether such incidents took place frequently, as well as what their actual causes were, remain unclear. Some sources suggest that NDH authorities sometimes opened fire on villagers who fled from them. Neighbors in nearby villages, after hearing these shots, and thinking that this was a signal for a rebellion to begin, would then fire their weapons into the air.[16] Memoirs suggest that the sporadic shooting was sometimes in defense when Ustašas entered a village, due to their propensity to steal. Moreover, the reports by NDH officials of shootings by Serbs may have been made up, at least in part, because often it was actually Ustašas who fired off rounds when entering a village in order to frighten residents into fleeing to the forest. This made it easier to enter their homes and steal their belongings. Ustašas were also known to shoot during the night, which heightened tensions, and then would explain such events the next day by referring to acts of "Chetniks" (Serb rebels) in the woods.[17]

All of this served to create and amplify a "psychosis" of fear among NDH officials, military personnel, and local Ustašas of what the "Serbs" were doing in the forests. It was increasingly believed that these men, referred to as "Chetniks," were planning some kind of rebellion.[18] This belief, and the mounting atmosphere of fear, then made it easier to mobilize more Catholic and Muslim villagers to join the Ustašas in their patrols. And the increasing numbers of men in these patrols helped to create a growing chasm at the village level between neighbors who nominally happened to be of different religions, or thought of as belonging to different ethnicities.[19]

Here, the role of local "non-Serbs" was significant in fueling the fears of the regional NDH authorities, who often had no capacity to verify events in the hard-to-reach localities. Communication with the villages in Lika and northwest Bosnia was generally spotty. So it fell to a small, select group of individuals in each locality, such as Mile Knežević in the village of Boričevac or Tomo Delač in the village of Doljani (both located near the town Kulen Vakuf), who were responsible for keeping their superiors in regional centers such as Bihać and Gospić apprised of the local situation. Because regional leaders had little capacity, or perhaps desire, to verify these reports, these local gatherers of information held a sizable capacity to influence regional policy, specifically through their assessments of the threat that the local Orthodox population posed. When they submitted reports that large numbers of "Chetniks" had fled to the forests and were preparing to attack, their superiors received confirmation of their worst fears. This would set in motion plans for pre-emptive military operations.[20] What deserves our attention here is how a context for violent escalation, which many scholars have argued is created by a state's elite, can also be driven in surprising ways by local actors, who can compel higher authorities into action, particularly in weaker states.[21]

The wider context was important in how the regional and local NDH authorities conceptualized the supposed activities of the local Orthodox population. At the end of May, the NDH military indicated that rumors were spreading of a possible rebellion in Bosnia.[22] By early June, these predictions became reality when Orthodox insurgents began fighting Ustašas and the NDH military in Herzegovina, where mass killings of the Orthodox population, which began earlier in the month, had sparked a regional armed uprising.[23] By late June, the military noted that "Chetnik actions" in Herzegovina, and the desire for revenge by the rebels against the non-Serb population because of the "Ustaša cleansings," had assumed "wide and serious dimensions." In Lika and northwest Bosnia, where an insurgency had not broken out, NDH military documents suggest that fear was rapidly growing that the unrest in Herzegovina would soon spread to this region. There, the Orthodox men who had fled to the forests in response to Ustaša persecution appear in NDH documents as large groups of so-called Chetniks—believed to exist in the thousands. Rather than hiding from the authorities, who were attempting to "resettle" many of them, and who had empowered local

Ustašas to steal from them, these men appear in NDH documents as "rebels" who had fled to the hills to prepare for an attack on the state.[24]

Ustaša leaders in the Lika region, such as Vinko Marinković in the town of Donji Lapac, reported that ultimatums were being sent during the last week of June to "the Chetniks" hiding in the hills east of the town of Srb, near the village of Suvaja. They were to return home within forty-eight hours, or else they would be attacked with all available force, and their families would be subjected to "reprisals." In response, many women and children returned from the forests, but without any men. Local leaders grew increasingly fearful. As one NDH military report speculated in late June: "The men who have fled are supposedly preparing themselves to attack the Ustašas." Some were even said to have machine guns. During the last days of June, Ustaša leaders in Bihać and Gospić, in conjunction with the regional military command, began making plans to undertake an operation to reassert control over the region that they believed was rapidly slipping out of their hands.[25]

They received crucial support from the central authorities, specifically from the supreme leader of the NDH, Ante Pavelić. Rumors were spreading of an impending Serb rebellion that was supposed to begin in various parts of the NDH on June 28, known as Vidovdan—the Serbian religious holiday of St. Vitus. As the atmosphere of fear grew, Pavelić issued "extraordinary orders" on June 26 that set the stage for the escalation of violence in the localities where "Chetniks" were supposedly preparing their rebellion:

> All officials of Ustaša organizations and all commanders of Ustaša armed units are personally responsible for every disturbance . . . and it is their responsibility to use all means necessary to stop any kind of disturbance.
>
> Wherever on the territory of the Independent State of Croatia would appear any individuals in a group of so-called Chetniks, or as remnants of the Serbian [i.e., Yugoslav] Army, or any other such [armed] persons, who are not authorized to wear an Ustaša or any other military uniform, it is the duty of all the authorities to use arms against them. This includes the police, Ustaša units, and if necessary, support is to be sought from the military.[26]

Pavelić's orders included a caveat warning Ustašas that any unlawful act by them would be harshly sanctioned. But it was clear that his overwhelming concern was to give local NDH authorities a green light to use violence to deal with any "disturbance" coming from the perceived Serb population.

What emerges is the critical importance of mutually reinforcing fears and suspicions—both real and imagined—at work in driving the escalation of tensions. Invoking a notion of mutuality is useful because it helps us to better understand the local dynamics of escalation; it should not, however, be taken to imply an equal balance of power between the two sides. Empowered by the state elite, which was deeply committed to radically reshaping the NDH's ethnic composition, the region's Ustašas had pursued various policies of persecution, such as disarming and resettling the Serb population, and much stealing of Serb property had already occurred by late June. Fearful of suffering further negative consequences, the persecuted fled to the forests. This left the local Ustašas, as well as the NDH military and regional authorities, fearful that these men, who they believed were armed, were now preparing an attack. Eventually, even the central authorities grew concerned about a rebellion. And so it appears that all levels of the NDH government began preparing some kind of preventive attack to counteract the violence that they believed was imminent. This was a context of mutually reinforcing fears—of the Orthodox population facing greater persecution by Ustašas, and Ustašas facing what they believed was an impending attack by those whom they were persecuting—that was making a major escalation increasingly likely. Analysis of the behavior of both sides—the persecutors and persecuted—and especially their interactions over time and at multiple levels of authority are essential to illuminate the mechanisms that can tip scales in favor of resorting to increased violence.

Two local sparks then provided the pretext for these fears to be rapidly transformed into large-scale acts of violence. During the final days of June, local officials reported that they were shot at while driving between the town of Srb and the village of Suvaja. The "bandits" responsible were reported to have been "Chetniks." Second, an unknown Ustaša was supposedly attacked while in Suvaja, returning home beaten with his clothes torn.[27] These incidents provided the regional Ustaša leadership with a pretext to order a "cleansing" action—in essence, preemptive mass violence—against the entire village, which was now seen as supporting the "Chetniks" in the forests.

Previous incidents of such shootings had already resulted in threats that 100 "former Serbs" (*bivši Srbi*)—the euphemism now used for the community—were to be shot for every Ustaša killed.[28] Such incidents of resistance to the Ustašas resulted in increasingly vitriolic calls for "revenge." After several Ustašas were killed in Herzegovina around this same time, Viktor Gutić—the NDH strongman in northwest Bosnia—suggested the following recommendations for responding to the "Serbs" in that region: "Here is the answer for those who have been weak and intervened on behalf of certain Serbs, and have attempted to protect them. . . . The Serbs do not deserve any kind of consideration because they belong to that evil breed that is trying in every possible way to strike the greatest blow possible against the Croat people, even against those who have been honorable and tolerant toward them. . . . Not weakness, but the taking of revenge is what we owe our [Ustaša] heroes who have fallen in the hills of Herzegovina."[29]

Gutić's counterpart in Bihać—Ljubomir Kvaternik—appears to have had the same sentiment in mind when unknown persons fired those shots at the NDH officials as they drove between the town of Srb and the village of Suvaja. What made the report of the shooting even more incendiary were rumors that quickly emerged not only about shots fired, but that some local NDH men had been killed. Moreover, their heads had supposedly been sliced off and then placed on top of sticks, while their tongues had apparently been cut out and strung together on a wire, and then hung for all to see.[30] Whether such acts were true is impossible to verify. What matters, however, is that such rumors almost certainly contributed to motivating local Ustašas to participate in a pre-emptive strike against those Orthodox villages where the trouble appeared to be rooted.

These local dynamics of escalation compare to other contexts throughout the world. As Donald Horowitz has suggested in his wide ranging analysis of riots and other acts of violence, in which he devotes particular attention to the South Asian context: "Rumors have a certain predictive utility . . . the magnitude of events depicted in rumors of aggression is often a reliable predictor of the magnitude of the aggression to follow."[31] Others have echoed this emphasis on the role of rumors, such as Jonathan Spencer in his work on violence in Sri Lanka during the early 1980s. For him, appreciating the role of "collective panic" and "savage paranoia," particularly in out-of-the way rural regions, is crucial in helping us make sense of how a context for violence, beyond the world of the extremist elite, can crystalize on the ground.[32] Similar forces were at work in the Kulen Vakuf region, which helped bring about a surge in tension, and then the decision to order mass violence.

The afternoon of July 1 was the turning point. As many as 300 armed men swept into the village of Suvaja, a majority of whom were Ustašas from the region, but among them were also about 100 NDH soldiers. According to NDH documents, they were sent under the combined orders of the Gendarmerie of the Velika Župa Lika i Gacka (located west of the Kulen Vakuf region) and Ljubomir Kvaternik, the Veliki župan of the Velika Župa Krbava i Psat. Their violence was a sea change from anything that had occurred thus far in the region. In about two hours they killed perhaps as many as 300 men, women, and children, and set about twenty-five houses on fire.[33] Their methods of violence were not just aimed at erasing the physical presence of the village and its residents; they were also designed to terrorize the men who had previously fled to the forests by inflicting humiliating torture on the women whom they had left behind. The Ustašas found Ljubica Lavrnje, the pregnant wife of the local Orthodox priest whom they had recently arrested and killed. They stabbed her to death, and then cut out the fetus of her unborn child, which they sliced into pieces along with her body—all of which they left to be found later by the village's men. Another woman met the same fate.[34] This gendered dimension of the violence, in which inflicting maximum psychological pain on the victim's surviving community members, has echoes in other instances of violence, such as some lynchings of females in the United States. The comparison with acts of gendered mass violence in Rwanda in 1994 is even stronger.[35]

The Ustašas and NDH military forces continued on their rampage. They stabbed women and children in their chests. Others they gathered together and locked inside a house, which they set on fire. They caught one woman who escaped the flames and threw her back inside, while the rest burned to death. They gathered together other groups and killed them in similar ways, while the rest—about 170 victims—they threw into three nearby deep vertical caves.[36] The extent to which notions about "Chetniks" had permeated the perpetrators' thoughts comes clear in survivor accounts. Rade Dubajić Čkaljac was ten years old when five Ustašas attacked his house in Suvaja. He managed to escape after they killed his mother and younger brother. While hiding nearby in tall grass, he listened as they attacked his neighbor's house. "Beat down the Chetniks!" one yelled out. "Fuck their mothers!"[37] Notable here was both the attachment of the label "Chetniks" to the entire village, and the sense that killing defenseless women and children constituted a way to deal with the perceived threat of rebellion. Once the killings ended, the Ustašas plundered the homes not yet on fire, and then led away a considerable amount of livestock, which was the main form of the villagers' subsistence.[38]

NDH military reports written just after the attack are striking because they reveal the extent to which erroneous information was used to justify and explain the attack. In Bihać, the Veliki župan Kvaternik claimed that 500 "Chetniks," with the support of about 2,500 local residents—all of whom were apparently armed with "modern weapons"—had started a rebellion. His reports, along with those of the army commanders who collaborated with him in conducting the operation, indicated that after a three-hour battle about "fifty Chetniks had been killed and fifteen captured."[39] Military officials in the town of Gospić claimed that the villagers of Suvaja were, in fact, responsible for violence. Among the victims "were a small number of women and children" who were killed due to their own "lack of attention and fear," especially because shots had supposedly been fired from certain houses in their village. As for the scores of burned houses, it was "the Chetniks [who] set about ten on fire when fleeing from our forces."[40]

However, other members of the army who visited the village during the following week offered a different interpretation. "It appears that the information of the Veliki župan [Ljubomir Kvaternik] and the local Ustaša authorities about the organized Chetnik activities and disorder was exaggerated." They concluded that resistance in Suvaja to the Ustašas was barely present; that which eventually materialized actually emerged in response to the attack: "The disorder in Suvaja was caused when the Ustašas killed part of the population, expelled others, and burned the village."[41] The regional authorities' report about large numbers of well-armed "Chetniks" was, in the eyes of army investigators, even more improbable given that "insignificant forces were needed to put down the resistance, and only two Ustašas were wounded. The resistance and the number of Chetniks were small, and these Chetniks—local residents who were killed in the village—may have been unarmed."[42] Further suggesting the exaggerated nature of the initial claims about the existence of thousands of "Chetniks" is the fact that the extra 200 soldiers sent to the region to deal with the "disorder" were returned to their base in Gospić on July 6—less than a week after the attack—because "there ceased to be a need for them."[43]

What is significant in these post-attack reports is the degree to which fear of an impending "Chetnik" attack led to exaggerations of the threat, and then subsequent acts of mass violence. The mechanism at work in transforming an ideological context conducive to violence into actual killing was a spiraling sense of fear, which reached a tipping point with minor incidents of local isolated shootings, and subsequent rumors of atrocities. This provided a justification for attacking villages where the existence of actual armed resistance was unconfirmed, and where the targets were almost entirely unarmed civilians.

As NDH army officers noted after similar Ustaša cleansing operations in other regions, in such cases it was actually "the non-fighters who were cleansed," while the fighters who were believed to exist (i.e., the men who had fled) "remained in the forest."[44] In many cases, such as that in Suvaja, the so-called fighters did not even exist in sizable numbers before the mass killings. This tendency by the local and regional NDH authorities to drastically exaggerate the number of rebels would continue, and fears of impending threats provided a pretext for preemptive mass killing.[45] Yet it was the violence of the Ustašas—which was often said to be a response to "Serb" resistance, both real and especially imagined—that was, in fact, creating a context for the rapid growth for armed resistance by the Orthodox population. As the

NDH military concluded after investigating the July 1 attack on Suvaja: "The Orthodox population is terrified and dejected. The unlawful and unjust acts of the self-styled Ustašas are spreading unrest and fear to the people, while the killings, burning and plunder are the reasons that the population—especially the men—have left their homes and fled to the forests."[46] The NDH's policies of persecution, which caused these men to flee to the forests, and the fears of armed Serb resistance against local Ustašas, were combining to create a context in which preemptive mass killing was rapidly becoming the order of the day. State-sanctioned persecution thus created fear of victim resistance, and this fear, when triggered by incidents—either real or imagined—led to a radical escalation in violence against victims.

Word of the attack on Suvaja quickly spread. In the nearby village of Osredci, terrified people fled to the forests, leaving the village practically empty. But a small number chose to remain in their homes, hoping that the violence would not engulf them. The day after the burning of Suvaja, on July 2, about 130–150 Ustašas attacked their village. They captured about thirteen people, twelve of whom they killed, while one escaped.[47] Like the day before, the Ustašas plundered the houses of those who fled, making sure to take their livestock.[48] They returned the next day and captured a group of mostly elderly people, most of whom they killed. This brought the village's death toll to more than thirty. None of the villagers who had fled dared return, as the Ustašas appeared to be waiting in the immediate vicinity ready to catch them.[49] An NDH report written by an official who visited the village shortly after the attack painted a stark portrait: "Today I was in the village of Osredci, which has been burned. The bodies of the men, women, and children who were killed on July 2 and 3 are lying everywhere. There is a terrible odor. Dogs and pigs are chewing on the bodies, and the Ustašas from Srb have forbid their burial. There is fear of infection. Whoever is still alive has fled to the forest. There they are dying of hunger."[50]

The killings in Suvaja and Osredci sowed intense fear among the Orthodox population in neighboring villages. Retold countless times by local villagers was the story from Suvaja of the unborn baby cut from its mother's womb, and then hacked into pieces. This left people silently shaking their heads, unable to absorb what had happened. Many feared, and one young survivor later remembered, "that the evil would soon come to us." People began sleeping in the forests near their houses with extra food and clothes packed, ready to flee further into the mountains at any moment.[51]

It would be difficult to exaggerate the shock and trauma that this violence caused among survivors. As suggested by the report from Osredci, which was similar to other instances of mass killing in the NDH, the Ustašas often left the mutilated corpses of their victims in plain view, or buried the dead (or those badly injured, yet still alive) in shallow graves. In some areas, such as in eastern Bosnia, dogs dragged the corpses out of the ground and began eating them. NDH officials noted that villagers who managed to flee in time would sometimes return to these killing sites. The experience of seeing the remains of their relatives and neighbors in this condition "brought about the greatest revolt and fear among the Serbs." These traumatic moments were what compelled survivors to take to the forests in large numbers.[52] Convincing them to return to their villages would be nearly impossible. Many of their relatives and neighbors had been brutally killed. Most, if not all of their livestock, had been stolen. And nearly all of their houses had been burned. As one NDH army officer asked in a report: "How would they return, when they had nothing and no one to return to?"[53]

The killings in Suvaja and Osredci quickly generated their own local, endogenous dynamics that led to the further escalation of violence in the region, even though it does not appear to have been directly ordered by regional leaders. The sudden violence had a deeply polarizing effect on intercommunal relations, leading to a rapid transformation of neighbors into collective categories of enemies, and calls for retaliation along such lines. The nature of the violence—in which people were killed because they were perceived as part of an ethnic category—altered how many survivors saw themselves and those whom they viewed as now being in conflict with. The experience of violence triggered a rapidly crystallizing sense of the local community as now divided into ethnically defined, antagonistic collectivities.

These hard-to-discern micro-dynamics can be seen vividly through an incident that occurred on July 3, the day after the first attack on Osredci. In a field in the nearby village of Bubanj, three men, apparently armed with rifles, approached Stana Pavičić, a local woman. Obviously aware of recent mass killings in Suvaja and Osredci, they called out to her: "You Croats are now filling bottomless pits with us, but when our time comes we will do the same with you." They then supposedly threatened to cut her throat.[54] Such threats—characterized by collective categorization of whole "ethnic groups" as enemies, and followed with promises of revenge—were increasingly common in areas where local Ustašas committed similar acts of violence. In the Sanski Most region at the end of June, NDH military analysts noted that Serbs were heard saying, "You Turks and Catholics won't forget what you have done . . . everything of yours will be burned." Others added: "You Turks want to take our land . . . fuck Pavelić's mother, you won't be here long, you'll be slaughtered."[55]

Such evidence allows us to capture the process whereby in moments during, and especially immediately following, acts of local intercommunal violence, people can rapidly reconfigure their views of neighbors by suddenly categorizing and subsuming them as parts of a much larger enemy collectivity. Stana Pavičić was no longer an individual neighbor; rather, she had become an individual manifestation of "You Croats." Others had been subsumed into "You Turks!" or "You Catholics!" Similar to the dynamics of mass violence in Rwanda in 1994, the initial acts of killing in the Kulen Vakuf region produced a rapid "collective categorization of the other," in which the soft boundaries of ethnicity among former neighbors, who historically had generally interacted peacefully, quickly transformed into hard, lethal lines of division.[56] Many of the survivors of the massacres in Suvaja and Osredci that the Ustašas committed suddenly viewed all "Muslims" and "Croats" as guilty.[57] The violence in the region thus rapidly created new perceptions of extremely polarized group identities by inscribing hard boundaries through the act of killing. This counter-intuitive dynamic—in which acts of violence create antagonistic perceptions of identities rather than antagonistic identities leading to violence—is one that scholars have recently begun calling attention to in other contexts, such as in the civil war in Greece and in riots at various points in South Asia.[58] While theoretically useful, this emerging literature often lacks the on-the-ground data to help capture the moments when such a process actually happens.[59] The archival records and testimonies about the incident in Bubanj, by contrast, provide us with a concrete instance through which to make this theoretical proposition both vivid and understandable.

Stana Pavičić managed to escape from the three men who seemed poised to take revenge because they now saw her as an embodiment of the Croat community. She immediately informed the young Ustašas in Bubanj about the incident. Three claimed that unknown individuals hiding in a nearby forest had recently shot at them.[60] With the threats apparently multiplying, they contacted Vinko Marinković, the Ustaša commander in the nearby town of Donji Lapac. He quickly organized as many of the region's Ustašas as possible, about sixty men, including a significant number of men from the village of Boričevac, to launch an attack on the Orthodox villagers in Bubanj.[61] According to NDH military reports, "the Ustašas then went to Bubanj and slaughtered everyone they encountered, killing them with rifles and machine guns, regardless of whether they were at home or in their fields, and they killed without regard to age or sex. They also burned a number of houses in the village."[62] Witness accounts suggest that the villagers were taken completely by surprise when the attack began, with instances of Ustašas bursting into homes and killing entire extended families as they ate together.[63]

The attack on Bubanj illustrates how the top-down ordered violence in Suvaja and Osredci, which included the participation of regional army units, then set off another, much more locally driven wave of mass violence, which had its origins in the local effects of the previous two days of killing. In Bubanj, the threats that the handful of armed Serbs supposedly made to Stana Pavičić were in response to the previous days of violence. The reaction to these threats, and to the isolated shootings that apparently occurred around the same time, was yet another massive attack. But this time it was carried out exclusively by local Ustašas, and under the orders of local leaders.[64] It seems that the regional NDH authorities in Bihać and the NDH military may have not even known that the operation in Bubanj had been ordered. Military reports produced later noted the key role of the local Ustašas in producing a third straight day of violence: "Order was established everywhere [after the attacks on Suvaja and Osredci], but the Ustašas continued to search for weapons and Chetniks. And so on July 3 they burned down the village of Bubanj."[65] Nevertheless, reports written later by the NDH's Ministry of the Interior still attributed the root cause of killings in Bubanj to "provocations" from the Serb side.[66]

Here, one must examine the interaction among the macro, meso, and micro levels in order to explain the continuation and trajectory of the violence. Top-down orchestrated violence in Suvaja and Osredci produced mass destruction at the local level, which then led to threats of revenge by survivors. This then compelled the local and regional Ustašas to order more violence in Bubanj to deal with the increased local instability, which central-level leaders did not seem aware of, or perhaps necessarily even wanted. Yet the capacity for violence to be instigated and escalated at multiple levels of authority was, in fact, very much a logical reflection of the specific way that the main holders of power in northwest Bosnia and Lika, such as the Veliki župan Ljubomir Kvaternik, chose to conduct their affairs.

The rare written record of a remarkable series of exchanges between local NDH officials and Kvaternik provides us with an eye-opening source about the organization and management of violence in the region. Their exchanges were in response to the commander of Italian forces in Bosanski Petrovac, Lieutenant Colonel Lohengrin Giraud, who took note with concern of the dramatic shift to mass violence in the wider region. He requested an urgent meeting on June 21, 1941 with the town's main representative of the NDH authorities, Branko Crnić. Speaking loudly and gesticulating intensely, Giraud said to him:

> I have determined that in recent days things are happening that I do not like in the least, things that in Italy we would call murder. Several days ago

> the commander of the Ustaša unit arrested a number of Serbs, and that commander gave his word—the honorable word of an officer—to the Italian major Tarzi that these men would not be shot, but rather would be taken to Banja Luka to be placed on trial. However, I discovered that all of these individuals were murdered, and this is horrendous and barbaric. It was the Ustašas who did this, not the regular [NDH] authorities. In Croatia, I only recognize the regular authorities and the gendarmerie. I don't even want to hear about the Ustašas. In the future, whatever happens, I will hold the regional military captain responsible, who is to inform me about everything that takes place. If the Ustašas are not able to act peacefully, I will use force against them. I have 2,000 rifles and machine guns, so there is no need for me to speak anymore about this.[67]

The record of the reaction to this threat from lieutenant colonel Giraud is short, but reveals crucial, hard-to-discern dynamics about the organization of violence by the NDH authorities: "The regional [NDH] representative informed the vice governor in Bihać by telephone about this incident, who told us [the NDH representatives in Bosanski Petrovac] to come immediately [to Bihać] the same day—June 21—to give a verbal report to the Veliki župan [Ljubomir Kvaternik] about what we have done. He told us not to carry out the order given to us by the Italian commander, but rather to continue doing what we have done up until now, that is, the commander of the Ustaša forces should act according to regulations [*propisi*]."[68]

Several dynamics here deserve our attention. First, it is telling that telephone and face-to-face conversations were the primary modes of communication used on the NDH side to handle this kind of incident. The written archival record of such exchanges among the regional elite and officials about their dealings with local Ustašas, particularly with regard to violence, is extremely rare. Yet this document is suggestive as to why it has proven difficult for researchers to reconstruct the decision-making process, particularly in the localities, about the organization of violence in the NDH. Conversations about sensitive matters frequently took place on the telephone; instructions "to act according to regulations" were given face-to-face.[69] Second, it is clear from this incident that the Veliki župan Kvaternik was the key authority in the region, and thus policies of mass violence had a crucial top-down organizational component, both in conception and management. Evidence collected after the war from NDH archives by the Yugoslav communist war crimes commission suggests that, unlike many of the civil authorities in the NDH, the figure of the Veliki župan was often intimately involved with managing his region's civil administration, military, and Ustaša organization—the latter often personally.[70] Third, although it would seem that local Ustašas were operating under orders from local and regional officials to arrest members of the Serb community, they had a certain degree of latitude to engage in acts of violence as they saw fit, killing their prisoners according to their own will, and doing so in their own ways, viewed here as "horrendous and barbaric." It is likely that this autonomy was not merely given out by the higher authorities, but was also something that local Ustašas felt entitled to. As one NDH military commander in a nearby region noted in mid-May, when anyone attempted to curtail their violent actions they insisted on their right "that authority remain in their hands."[71] Another, who wrote about the behavior of Ustašas operating near the villages of Martin Brod and Doljani (located south and west of Kulen Vakuf), described their attitudes in response to his criticisms of their behavior in an early July report: "they answered that for them there doesn't exist any kind of [higher] authority, and that they can do whatever they want."[72] This finding may help to explain why, among other factors, the violence against the Orthodox population unfolded with such significant regional variation during 1941. Empowered by the central and regional authorities, but often able to operate in the localities with little-to-no supervision, these groups could deploy violence when and where they wished. This dynamic has echoes in other contexts, such as the Java region of Indonesia during the mass violence in that country during 1965. "While encouraged and in some instances even armed by the state," as Robert Hefner has noted, "lowland activists in the first stages of the killing acted with considerable independence of the government or military."[73]

This rare record of the angry protests of an Italian military officer, the worried telephone call from local NDH officials to their superiors in Bihać, and their subsequent face-to-face meeting with Kvaternik, thus illuminates a key micro-mechanism of the initial phase of local violence in the region. The regional NDH authorities gave orders for the physical persecution of a section of the perceived Serb community, but left space for the local interpretation of their implementation, which local actors appear to have felt entitled to have authority over. And everything was done with almost no paper trail.

In the village of Bubanj, this sense of entitlement to carry out violence according to local conditions resulted in a yet another day of mass killing. In the end, NDH military reports suggested that the Ustašas killed 152 of the village's residents and burned approximately twenty of their houses. But commanders later acknowledged that some bodies had been completely burned and in some households not a single member was left alive, thus making it difficult to precisely count the dead.[74] Survivor testimonies suggest about 270 victims.[75]

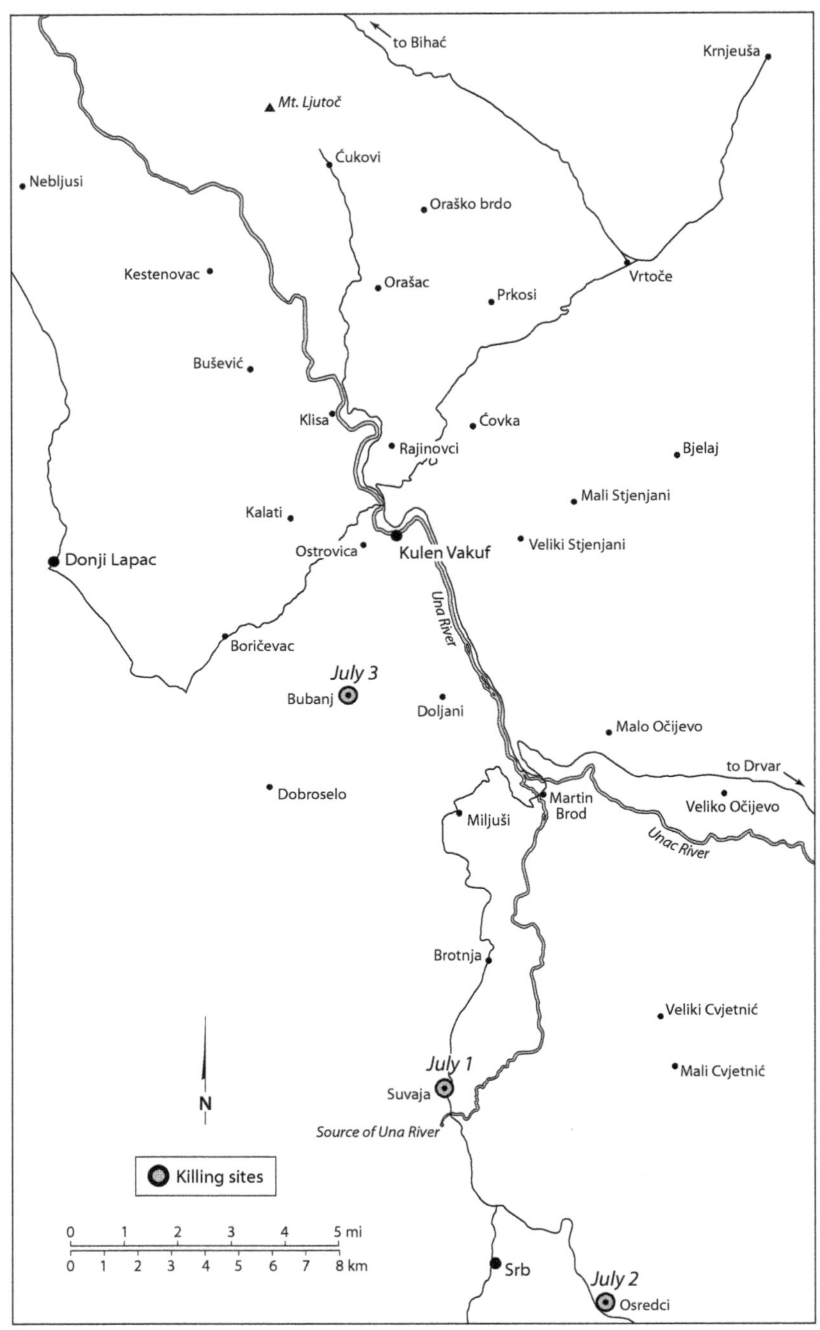

Map 8. First wave of Ustaša violence, July 1–3, 1941

What made the quick mobilization of Ustašas possible was the perceived security threat from the local Orthodox population, as suggested by the shooting at local Ustašas from unknown persons and the threats made to Stana Pavičić. But local Catholics and Muslims also participated who had not been directly threatened, particularly some from Kulen Vakuf and the nearby villages of Ostrovica and Boričevac.[76] The sources suggest that their motives for joining in the attack were closely connected with the opportunity to plunder their neighbors. Survivors returned to Bubanj a few days later to salvage whatever was left in their homes. They discovered only bare walls and bloodstains; local Catholics and Muslims had carried away everything else.[77] NDH military commanders later noted that "Muslims from Kulen Vakuf also came and engaged especially in stealing livestock from stables and pastures, as well as taking items from homes." Among them were Suljo and Ibrahim Pehlivanović, both from Ostrovica. Some were well-known neighbors of the villagers in Bubanj, having bought their sheepskins in the past. NDH documents suggest that what drove their participation in the plunder were previous local tensions and conflicts: "Because of the forests that make the border between Bubanj and Ostrovica, there had been fights and mutual revenge taking" over the use of these resources during the years that preceded the war.[78] Similar tensions existed between some Orthodox villagers in Bubanj and their Catholic counterparts in the nearby village of Boričevac, whose fields bordered each other's. According to local historians, conflicts and even fights had taken place among them over the borders of their property.[79] It appears that in some cases local Ustašas fanned the flames of these ongoing interpersonal conflicts in order to mobilize local men for their attacks.[80] This may explain the participation of at least seven men of the Markovinović clan from Boričevac.[81]

Evidence from other parts of the NDH supports a notion that local Ustaša leaders were able to drum up local manpower by providing villagers with the unexpected opportunity to "get even" for past wrongs. In early June in Herzegovina, for example, Ustašas killed almost 170 Orthodox villagers and then distributed more than 5,000 of their livestock to local Muslims to care for until the Ustašas decided how to make use of them. In a report about these killings, regional NDH military officials, who were supportive of the violence, noted that taking this livestock "does not even come close to representing the value of the livestock that Serbs in the Gacko region took from Muslims in 1918."[82] Righting perceived past wrongs was part of the rationale for the violence in the local community, and the same was true in the Kulen Vakuf region. "I was certain," recounted one survivor, "that the Ustašas from Boričevac would blame me and my father for every little thing that had happened in the past."[83] Survivors of the attack on Bubanj noted that many of their neighbors-turned-Ustašas from Boričevac took revenge for perceived past wrongs not only by killing; they also made off with at least 750 of the village's livestock.[84]

These conflicts over the use of natural resources and ownership of livestock were often personal and intense, and could easily serve as a catalyst for rapid antagonistic collective categorization, as scholars have noted in other contexts, such as South Asia.[85] For example, in June 1941 in the Sanski Most region of northwest Bosnia, Trivun Stojković got into a fight with his Muslim neighbors over what he felt was their unjust use of land that he considered as his pasture. "You Turks," he yelled out to them, "I'll fuck your mothers. You know this [pasture] is Serbian. Fuck your state, fuck your government, and fuck those who made it, and who allow you to do such things."[86] Evidence from witnesses and accused persons compiled during postwar communist war crimes trials suggests that some relationships among neighbors in the vicinity of Bubanj and Kulen Vakuf were filled with similar tensions over long-standing disputes. And under the right circumstances, they could erupt. In some cases, fights over the use of land prior to the war led to some people building fences to keep neighbors from using pastures, which fueled simmering personal resentments.[87] It should not be surprising that some men could be quickly mobilized to attack their neighbors when the opportunity presented itself.

Here, we need to resist assuming that those who live in close proximity, and know one another—that is, "neighbors"—should somehow enjoy more positive relations with each other than those who do not. Criminological and sociological evidence has shown for decades that violence is more likely to occur among people who know each other well.[88] Yet this finding continues to puzzle some scholars of political violence and genocide who appear to view mass violence among "neighbors" as somehow more shocking and perplexing, as if physical proximity and everyday familiarity somehow should provide people with increased immunity from conflict and physical violence.[89] The evidence from the Kulen Vakuf region suggests that the opposite can be true: being "neighbors" can, in fact, lay the foundation for conflict-ridden social relations. Their existence, however, *need not produce violence under stable conditions*—which deserves emphasis—but nonetheless can explode into violent behavior if a situation provides one party with the opportunity to decisively settle a local conflict through force.

This history of personal tensions among some neighbors was combined with a local, intimate knowledge of what each possessed. "Especially the local [Ustaša] men," recalled a survivor from the attack on Bubanj, "the Kovačevićes,

Markovinovićes, Pehlivanovićes, and others—they knew every inch of land in Bubanj and didn't need a guide."[90] This intimate knowledge of their neighbors' property placed these men in an ideal position to effectively engage in plunder, the act of which could then trigger conflicts among them. As one survivor recalled from the attack: "The Ustašas from the rocky hills around Bubanj, or who lived nearby them, such as Stević Kovačević, Ilija and Dujo Pavičić, Milan Miškulin, Josina Markovinović, and others, were those who decided whose houses to burn, and whose to leave alone, whose property to wreck and destroy, where to take the livestock, whom to give it to, and whom to give other stolen items, such as the grain, and other things. The greatest conflicts took place when money, watches, and similar things were found. The Ustašas stole it all. They even fought amongst themselves over it."[91]

The desire to plunder diffused rapidly out to parts of the non-Ustaša Catholic and Muslim population, which then created tension between them and the NDH military. As a report by a military officer who visited Bubanj on July 4 demonstrates: "Upon arriving to Bubanj our unit caught two peasants who were stealing from abandoned houses. I should mention that these peasants tried to persuade the soldiers that they had just seen two Chetniks in the forests. It was clear that they wanted the soldiers to leave so that they could continue stealing."[92] The opportunity to suddenly enrich oneself easily produced such attempted deceptions of those considered to be at least nominally on the same side. While the killing and stealing in Bubanj had certainly unfolded along an ethnic axis, the post-massacre stealing reveals how such a distinction was highly situational. A mere twenty-four hours after the killing had stopped, the NDH military now was in conflict with local non-Serb peasants over what to do with the remaining Serb property.[93] Scholars have noted similar intra-group fights over how to distribute the spoils of plunder after intercommunal violence in other contexts, such as Rwanda and German-occupied Poland.[94] "Ethnicity" here deserves our attention only as one axis around which conflict was unfolding; it co-existed with others, and its relevance ebbed and flowed according to the rapidly changing situational dynamics on the ground. One's perceived ethnic category did not somehow automatically determine one's range of behavior.[95]

Driving local participation in the attack on Bubanj were other short-term resentments, some of which were not based on economic grievances, or a desire to steal, but rather on earlier conflicts from the spring of 1941. After the defeat of the Yugoslav army in April, a group of Orthodox soldiers from Suvaja supposedly beat a group of Catholics who were speaking favorably about the establishment of the NDH. According to one contemporary, "[local] people believed that this [incident] caused the Ustašas to want revenge."[96] Such incidents do not explain why the attacks on the Orthodox villages occurred when and where they did, but they do provide us with another piece of the micro-level context that helps explain why some people, when given the opportunity, could be suddenly mobilized to launch an attack on their neighbors.

Finally, the brutality of the attacks—the hacking to death of the victims, the multiple gunshots, the burning alive of unarmed women and children, the cutting out of fetuses from pregnant women, and the intentional leaving of their corpses in the open to be eaten later by animals—these exceptionally cruel methods of killing and corpse disposal suggest that some kind of locally rooted desire for vengeance may have been at play. Psychologists and criminologists have noted that murders among people who previously knew each other and who held deep resentments, such as those involving family members, are often characterized by much higher levels of violence—far beyond what is necessary to cause death. When guns are used in such cases, the numbers of shots fired is significantly higher; when knives are the weapon of choice, perpetrators tend to stab their victims many times.[97] Similar dynamics are likely at work in violence among close neighbors, especially those who are involved in frustrating, everyday disputes that flare on a regular basis. When an unexpected opportunity for vengeance arises in such cases, the methods of violence may appear severe and overwhelming; but they may also have an internal logic given the intimacy of many social conflicts in local communities.

So while a perceived security threat provided the spark that set off the decision to attack Bubanj, a wider mobilization of local men was possible by appealing to the previous resentments of some of the region's Muslim and Catholic population. This finding has echoes in other contexts throughout the world. Scholars of violence in South Asia, such as the anthropologist Veena Das, have noted similar dynamics in small communities, arguing that "violence offered the possibility of acting on long-standing problems and resolving them at one stroke."[98] In his work on the local dynamics of the genocide in Rwanda, Timothy Longman found that the roadblocks, where so many victims met their fate, often "became instruments for carrying out personal vendettas."[99] In Guatemala during the early 1980s, a village schoolteacher noted that "it has become conveniently easy to get rid of a person for reasons of revenge or other personal differences," especially through denunciation to the army.[100] In guerilla conflicts in Missouri during the American Civil War, Michael Fellman has shown that "militia troops joined the armed forces or used their military status to get even for wrongs done to them and their families."[101] And in their analysis of the mass violence in Indonesia in

1965, Leslie Dwyer and Degung Santikarma suggest that "much of the violence was in fact . . . motivated by social conflicts that were local, diverse, and shifting," with local residents telling stories "of people being killed over land, over inheritance and over more personal problems such as long-remembered insults or sexual jealousy."[102]

All of these insights fall under the evocative rubric of "the privatization of politics"—the "getting even" that people sometimes engage in during unexpected opportunities in moments of upheaval—which the historian Jan Gross coined in his seminal study of the Sovietization of parts of Eastern Europe.[103] The attack on Bubanj not only provided local Catholics and Muslims with the unprecedented opportunity to steal enormous quantities of livestock and other goods, which otherwise they could not easily and quickly attain; it also allowed them to use violence to quickly get even for past wrongs.[104]

So two important micro-dynamics emerge from examining the three consecutive days of killing in Suvaja, Osredci, and Bubanj, when between 400 and 500 people were killed, with a majority being women, children, and the elderly.[105] The first is that mutually reinforcing fears were a crucial factor. Those classified as "Serbs" fled to the forests out of fear of suffering more Ustaša persecution. Regional and local NDH leaders then feared that these men were preparing to attack them, and the ongoing Serb rebellion in Herzegovina gave them reason to believe that an armed insurgency could soon break out in their region. In this sense, the subsequent explosion of mass killing by Ustašas of Serbs appears like it was driven by a self-generated sense of defensive mass violence. This is a general dynamic that scholars have noted in other contexts, such as during campaigns against Indians in the American southwest, the genocide in Rwanda, and in instances of violence in Sri Lanka. Each case demonstrates how perpetrators can dramatically intensify their violence due to fear of *potential* victim retaliation.[106]

The second micro-dynamic was the existence of a sizable disjuncture between those who ordered this operation, most of whom were concerned with cleansing the area of non-Croats and crushing the perceived Serb threat, and a majority of the foot soldiers who carried out the killing and stealing. Among the perpetrators on the ground, long-standing personal grievances and a situational desire for rapid material enrichment were the main factors that made it possible to mobilize their participation. There is no evidence to suggest that the local perpetrators received any kind of systematic training in submitting themselves to the state authorities and in following their orders to inflict violence on their neighbors. In other cases, such as among police torturers in Greece during the late 1960s and early 1970s, social psychologists have shown that elaborate training programs were created—and, moreover, were necessary—to teach "normal" men to obey their authority figures and carry out intimate acts of violence over extended periods. The implication here is that without such systematic training in performing violence, the previous dispositions of such individuals, whom are often referred to as "anyone's sons" or "ordinary men," would most likely not have led them to become torturers. In the Kulen Vakuf region, by contrast, this elaborate training that some consider necessary in order to produce "violence workers" was strikingly absent.[107] Instead, there was a substratum among a minority of individuals of locally rooted inter-personal conflict, desire for revenge, and a tendency toward plunder, which predisposed certain individuals to violence. Under stable conditions, such tendencies found little to no expression. But when given the unexpected opportunity in the early summer of 1941, this substratum burst forth. And virtually no training or habituation appears to have been necessary for these individuals to unleash a wave of killing, plunder, and destruction.

The attack on Bubanj only furthered the process of intercommunal polarization and collective categorization. Nearly all those who escaped fled to the forests where they hid from their non-Serb neighbors. A handful of survivors, such as Rade Radaković, managed to play dead among the bodies of their families inside burning houses, before taking the chance to run to the woods. Arriving sometimes with wounds still bleeding, they told their surviving relatives and neighbors what had happened, relating horrific scenes of children stabbed by bayonets, mothers shot with dough still in their hands as they prepared meals, and bodies of loved ones burned inside their homes.[108] Others who had managed to flee later returned to Bubanj where they witnessed with their own eyes the carnage that the Ustašas had wrought. Shock and fear were the dominant initial reactions, as was the instinctual desire to save oneself and family. "The crimes that the Ustašas committed," one contemporary later noted, "represented an enormous earthquake in the consciousness of the people: all previous understandings about the world, society, and justice were shaken."[109] Another, who was a child at the time, remembered the sudden shift: "The news [of the first killings] were received with great difficulty. This could be seen on the faces of our people and in their comprehension . . . something huge, enormous, and strange had changed."[110] It was only another day or two before many others in the region's Orthodox villages heard about the violence. As the stories were told, the shockwaves reverberated from house to house.[111]

What emerged among some was a desire to fight back. One local historian, who interviewed survivors during the late 1960s, noted that many local men quickly began "imagining what the first battle would look like with the enemy who had spared neither the old nor the young in Bubanj."[112] Memoirs suggest that it was after the attack on Bubanj that such men began to gather together weapons, and to organize guards and patrols to resist the Ustašas if they ventured into the forests.[113] One need only examine the numbers and composition of the dead to appreciate their sense of devastation and desire not only for self-defense, but also for retaliation. In Suvaja, at least twenty-six extended families in the village lost multiple members, with some nearly completely wiped out.[114] The men who had fled earlier to the forests returned to this village to discover the mutilated and burned bodies of their mothers, wives, sisters, and small children.[115] The Ustašas murdered at least forty-five members of the village's large Keča clan, along with about 115 of their neighbors.[116] In Bubanj, each of the forty-three households lost at least one family member. Of the forty-eight villagers killed, more than half were children under the age of fifteen, ten of whom were five or younger. In the aftermath of the attacks, the words of one survivor—"I will take revenge"—quickly became the mantra of many others.[117]

The level of intercommunal fear and polarization ballooned after the attacks of July 1–3. Most the survivors whom the NDH military commanders later spoke with in order to reconstruct what happened in Bubanj were reluctant to give testimonies out of fear of provoking more violence from local Ustašas. Some, who months later gave depositions to the Commissariat for Refugees (Komesarijat za izbeglice) after arriving to German-occupied Serbia, recalled how, from their hiding places in the forests, they witnessed local Ustašas eating and drinking with their families while calmly watching Bubanj being destroyed and plundered. The experience profoundly altered their perceptions of their former neighbors. "These were our neighbors whom we had done favors for . . . [and now] they no longer had any feelings for us. Their only wish was for the Serbs to disappear, to seize their property, to put Serbian corn in their barns."[118] What shocked many was how the violence broke down—literally overnight—local connections among people that had existed for decades, or longer. One local historian, who lived through the war years, recalled that the killings suddenly altered the custom among much of the local youth of herding livestock together in mountain pastures. Prior to the summer of 1941, they had socialized together in the same places where "their fathers, grandfathers, and great grandfathers had together cared for such animals." This tradition abruptly halted as news of the violence spread.[119]

The sudden shock of mass violence did not just sever such long-term patterns of local interaction; its aftershocks fueled a growing fixation on vengeance, which suggested that further waves of killings might soon come. A Catholic from Bubanj told the NDH military authorities that his Orthodox neighbor, Vojin Šarac, approached him while the attack was still unfolding. "You Croats are now throwing us alive into bottomless pits," he said. "But we will be the ones who will finish this."[120] This third straight day of unprecedented mass violence was making some kind of retaliation increasingly likely. The preemptive cleansing operations, which were undertaken ostensibly to enhance security, were now causing reactions that, as the political scientist Barry Posen has noted in other contexts, were actually making the perpetrators of mass violence less secure.[121] The nature of their killings, in which they targeted people without regard to their actual behaviors, erased the principle of transgression. Their violence vividly demonstrated that previous understandings about the relationship between crime and punishment no longer existed. Now, simply being thought of as a member of a group in a particular location under attack was sufficient to bring about lethal sanction.[122] For those targeted, the nature of the Ustaša violence left them two stark options: be killed or somehow fight back. Through their own policies of persecution, the NDH authorities were thus rapidly creating the conditions for the emergence of violent resistance, and potentially triggering their own destabilization.

Strikingly, the explosion of the July 1–3 violence did not engulf the rest of the region. To the immediate west, east and north of Kulen Vakuf, the sizable number of Orthodox villages did not suffer mass destruction during this same period, nor during the several weeks that followed.[123] Instead, local Ustašas in Kulen Vakuf and its vicinity continued to employ a much more selective approach of using violence to extract economic resources from their Orthodox neighbors. The question is why?

This pattern had been in place since mid-May, when local Ustašas began visiting these villages to steal household items and livestock, as well as to demand sums of money.[124] Evidence suggests that while threats and beatings certainly occurred during these robberies, there were few killings, and no large-scale massacres. By June, the Ustašas began sending men to inform some of the most prominent individuals in these villages that they would need to bring certain sums of money to Kulen Vakuf.[125] Most appear to have complied, either alone or accompanied by Ustašas, as most felt that they had done nothing wrong and thus had little to fear. "This is a government like every government," some said. "They are [only] looking for those who mistreated Croats in the old [Kingdom of] Yugoslavia," said others.[126] Sometimes these individuals were allowed to return home after producing sums of money, and spending some time in the town's improvised jail, while

Ustašas executed others. One who met this fate was the former mayor of Kulen Vakuf, Vlado Milanović, whose father, Vukosav, was the Orthodox priest who had defended the town's Muslim residents from revenge-seeking Orthodox peasants in 1918.[127] Many of the individuals killed were the former holders of political and economic power in the region, thus suggesting the selective nature of the violence, with its objective being the rapid transfer of this power to the local Ustašas.

What is striking, however, is that this selective approach to violence remained more or less in place even after the mass killings that occurred on July 1–3 in Suvaja, Osredci, and Bubanj. This variation suggests that the decision to resort to mass violence was not to be applied more widely, even in a region where persecution—including selective killing—of those perceived as Serbs was already taking place. Without outside pressure from the higher authorities, and a real or perceived security threat, the local Ustašas in Kulen Vakuf and its vicinity seemed content to continue to use threats and targeted terror in order to successfully plunder their Orthodox neighbors.

In the case of Suvaja and Osredci, by contrast, the regional authorities in Bihać were alarmed because of incidents in which "Chetniks" had supposedly attacked local NDH authorities, and were apparently preparing themselves for a large-scale rebellion. When the local Ustašas there called for assistance in the immediate aftermath of a series of supposed shootings and threats, the regional authorities—who were already anxious to implement a solution to the "Serb question"—quickly deployed overwhelming force. Yet even there, the local participants showed a strong appetite for plunder and the use of violence for settling longer-term local disputes. Their fear of the supposed security threat of the Orthodox population as a motivating factor in committing violence is more difficult to ascertain due to the paucity of archival evidence. But it is telling that they did not rush to launch similar assaults on the rest of the region's Orthodox villages during the coming days and weeks. Instead of mimicking the violence that took place in Suvaja, Osredci, and Bubanj, the local Ustašas reverted to a more restrained approach of plundering, arresting and selectively killing—but also sometimes releasing—their prisoners. In general, they endeavored to rob their neighbors of their property and money, rather than to physically exterminate them.

The killings of July 1–3 happened when and where they did—and not in other locations in the same region at the same time—because of the need by regional and local Ustaša leaders to protect themselves against perceived security threats, specifically the supposed rebellion that they believed Serb men were organizing. The evidence does not suggest that the regional authorities in Bihać, such as the Veliki župan Ljubomir Kvaternik, issued explicit orders for large-scale violence to then be spread widely throughout the region. In fact, some evidence suggests that the central authorities in Zagreb may have even reprimanded the leaders in Bihać because of their exaggerated claims about the nature of the Serb threat, and the destabilizing violence that they unleashed in response. For example, the Ustaša leader in Donji Lapac, Vinko Marinković, was removed (at least temporarily) from his position soon after the killings in Bubanj. The Veliki župan Kvaternik was the one who made this decision.[128] Both Marinković and Kvaternik had been closely involved in organizing the attacks on Suvaja and Osredci. It is highly unlikely that Kvaternik suddenly had a change of heart with regard to using mass violence against the Orthodox population. Rather, the abrupt change of direction and the removal of Marinković suggest that higher levels of authority were displeased by the cascading local violence, whose propulsion was slipping out of the higher authorities' control already by July 3, and leading to destabilization. Kvaternik mostly likely received instructions from higher authorities.

Further implementing this de-escalation of violence in the region was Juko Pavičić, a state secretary (državni tajnik) in the NDH government who had close prewar ties to some of the men who were now Ustašas in Boričevac. After the killings of July 1–3, he issued an order that "this could not be allowed to happen again."[129] According to local historians who interviewed contemporaries, Pavičić then requested a meeting with an acquaintance from Bubanj, Nikica Medić. "The killings were the independent work of individual Ustašas," he assured him, and that no one in the higher echelons of the NDH government knew about their intentions. Medić recalled Pavičić saying, "that all the livestock that the Ustašas had taken from Bubanj would be returned to their rightful owners . . . and if anyone touched me I was to come to him personally." The extreme violence of the previous days obviously made such claims and promises difficult to take seriously. "I understood what he said," Medić remarked, "as a deception."[130]

So the dramatic change in the behavior of Ustašas immediately after the killings of July 1–3 was surprising and difficult for local residents to comprehend and believe. Nonetheless, their violence came to an abrupt halt. It even appears that it became possible for some survivors to search in Croatian villages for their stolen livestock.[131] NDH military documents from two weeks after the killings in Bubanj confirm these observations, adding that the local authorities even began issuing certificates to survivors for their stolen property so that they could reclaim it at some point. The military mobilized Catholic peasants to help bury the bodies of the dead, and instructed them to gather the stolen livestock and care for it until the survivors returned to their homes.[132]

Nevertheless, there was a sizable gap between regional orders and local implementation, as had been the case since the establishment of the NDH. In the Kulen Vakuf region, local Ustašas continued to operate according to their own needs, robbing the Orthodox population and committing targeted executions of influential men. But they did not resort to mass violence after the killings of July 1–3. Their behavior does not suggest that exterminatory killing was their preferred strategy—or even ultimate objective—despite the recent officially sanctioned use of mass killing in Suvaja, Osredci and Bubanj. Part of what may account for this variation is that the NDH military does not appear to have noted incidents of shootings by "Chetniks," or incidents of attacks by Serb villagers against Ustašas, in the forests and villages to the immediate west, north, and east of Kulen Vakuf. Without a clear sense that the men from these villages were armed and using their weapons against representatives of the NDH, the local Ustašas appear to have been content to employ selective violence in order to plunder and "settle scores" on a more individual, rather than group basis.

More broadly, this variation suggests that deploying mass violence is a risky policy choice, especially in contexts in which the central authorities have weak control over their subordinates. Fractions within perpetrator groups can decide to back away from killing when the costs begin to multiply, and the violence can no longer be easily controlled. In the case of the NDH, the higher authorities appear to have sensed that they were rapidly losing control over the violence that they had empowered their regional and local subordinates to commit. In the Kulen Vakuf region, the violence of July 1–3 immediately created a widespread sense of cascading disorder. This caused the regional and perhaps even central authorities to recoil and order de-escalation. For at least some of the local Ustašas, this shift was perhaps welcome. Employing more selective violence was, at least for the moment, an effective way to plunder and resolve their local conflicts case-by-case.

Yet little during the summer of 1941 would remain stable. Witness and survivor accounts suggest that during the second half of July the local Ustašas, under the orders of local strongmen such as Miroslav Matijević of Kulen Vakuf, as well as Vinko Marinković of Donji Lapac and Grga Pavičić of Boričevac, increasingly abandoned the strategic use of terror to plunder their Orthodox neighbors. Instead, they embarked on an intensifying series of arrests and massacres, which steadily began to resemble sustained, group selective killing. Beginning on or around July 15, they began to kill more of those whom they ordered to appear in Kulen Vakuf, or whom they arrested in villages and then brought to town. The primary locations for the killings and the disposal of the corpses were a ditch near the town's Orthodox Church and another near the school. They also began to commit killings in nearby villages, such as Bušević and Dobroselo. Their victims were now not only prominent men, but also increasingly women, children and the elderly.[133] In other instances, local Ustašas, such as a group from Orašac, brought their prisoners back to their village, where they tortured and killed them.[134] A common feature of these killing operations was the participation of local residents from the region's Muslim and Catholic villages. During the second half of July, they increased their use of deep vertical caves into which they threw their victims, especially one located near Boričevac.[135] Dara Škorić Popović, a young woman from the village of Nebljusi, survived one of these massacres. Nearly a week after being thrown into the Boričevac pit with her neighbors, she managed to climb out. Later, she recalled how she recognized some perpetrators, among whom she said included Miroslav Matijević, Mehmed Altić, Huća Zelić, and Mehmed Mušeta—all local men from Kulen Vakuf.[136]

The rare testimony from another survivor of one of these killings sheds further light on the changing dynamics of the violence. Vladimir Tankosić was born in 1916 in Veliko Očijevo, located in the mountains southeast of Kulen Vakuf. On July 23, 1941, five men came to his village, two of whom—Hilmija Altić and Mahmut Kadić—were Ustašas from Kulen Vakuf. They arrested about thirty men.[137] They said that the men were being taken for questioning, as well as work projects, and that they would return home shortly.[138] Instead, they brought them to Kulen Vakuf and then held them prisoner in the town's school. Throughout the night the Ustašas beat them with clubs. The next day they marched them toward Boričevac. That they were being led to mass executions appears to have been an incomprehensible mental leap for most. This may explain why there was no resistance during this march, as was the case during most others for which survivor testimonies exist.[139]

Just before reaching the village they turned off the road onto a path. At its end was a hole in the ground that was the opening of a deep vertical cave. The local residents aware of its existence attributed mystical qualities to it. It was believed that the pit had no bottom, or that it was filled fearsome animals, or that its bottom was a vast lake.[140] Miroslav Matijević and several other local Ustašas stood waiting. Yet again showing how their use of violence was intimately connected to material gain, they ordered the prisoners to hand over whatever money they still had. Matijević and the other Ustašas took each prisoner to the edge of the pit.[141] Tankosić's testimony tells us what then happened:

> One Ustaša grabbed me, pulled my head up, and [Miroslav] Matijević shot a bullet into my head. The bullet stayed inside. Blood came out

> of my nose, mouth and ears, and I fell into the pit. It was around thirty meters deep. Then they threw a large stone in after me. Then they threw in Nikola Rodić, and then another stone after him. The whole time I was only half-conscious. They killed six more after that.
>
> The pit was full of dead, rotting bodies. The stench was unbelievable. Worms and maggots crawled all over me, going into my mouth and ears. I was among corpses. During the day there was enough light that I could see that there were around ten cradles in which there were dead children. Many of the dead bodies had their eyes poked out. There were pieces of human flesh. There were men and women of all ages. I could barely move. Every night around eight to ten more people were killed and dumped into the pit.
>
> On the third night Mile Pilipović from the village of Rajinovci jumped into the pit. Matijević killed his son, two brothers, and three uncles. When he saw that, he jumped. I climbed over to where he was. He was terrified when he saw me! It was easier after that because I had someone to talk to. The whole time we didn't eat or drink. We survived by licking water off the rocks.[142]

The victims were now the entire Orthodox community—men, women, and children. Their killing without regard to behavior, and the disposal of their bodies in deep pits, speaks to a shift toward physical extermination. Throughout the last week of July 1941, this scenario of killing repeated itself nearly each day, as Tankosić recalled. The Ustašas gathered victims from the villages in the Kulen Vakuf region, such as Rajinovci, Malo and Veliko Očijevo, and Veliki Stjenjani. They marched them back to Kulen Vakuf. And after a night or two of beatings in the school, they murdered these prisoners in the same way as they had tried to kill Vladimir Tankosić and Mile Pilipović. During the final days of July, they both still lay at the bottom of the pit near Boričevac. They were exhausted, covered in worms and maggots, yet still remained half-alive in a steadily growing pile of mutilated, decomposing corpses.[143]

For night-time killings in Kulen Vakuf, in addition to the ditches near the Orthodox Church and school, the Ustašas dug a large hole near the town's train station. Witnesses reported that Matijević and other local Ustašas would come nightly to the improvised jail in the school and select around ten individuals. With battery-operated lamps, they led them up the hill toward the train station. There they cut their throats and dumped their bodies into the hole. When the Ustašas returned from these killings, witnesses remembered that their arms were often covered in blood up to their elbows.[144]

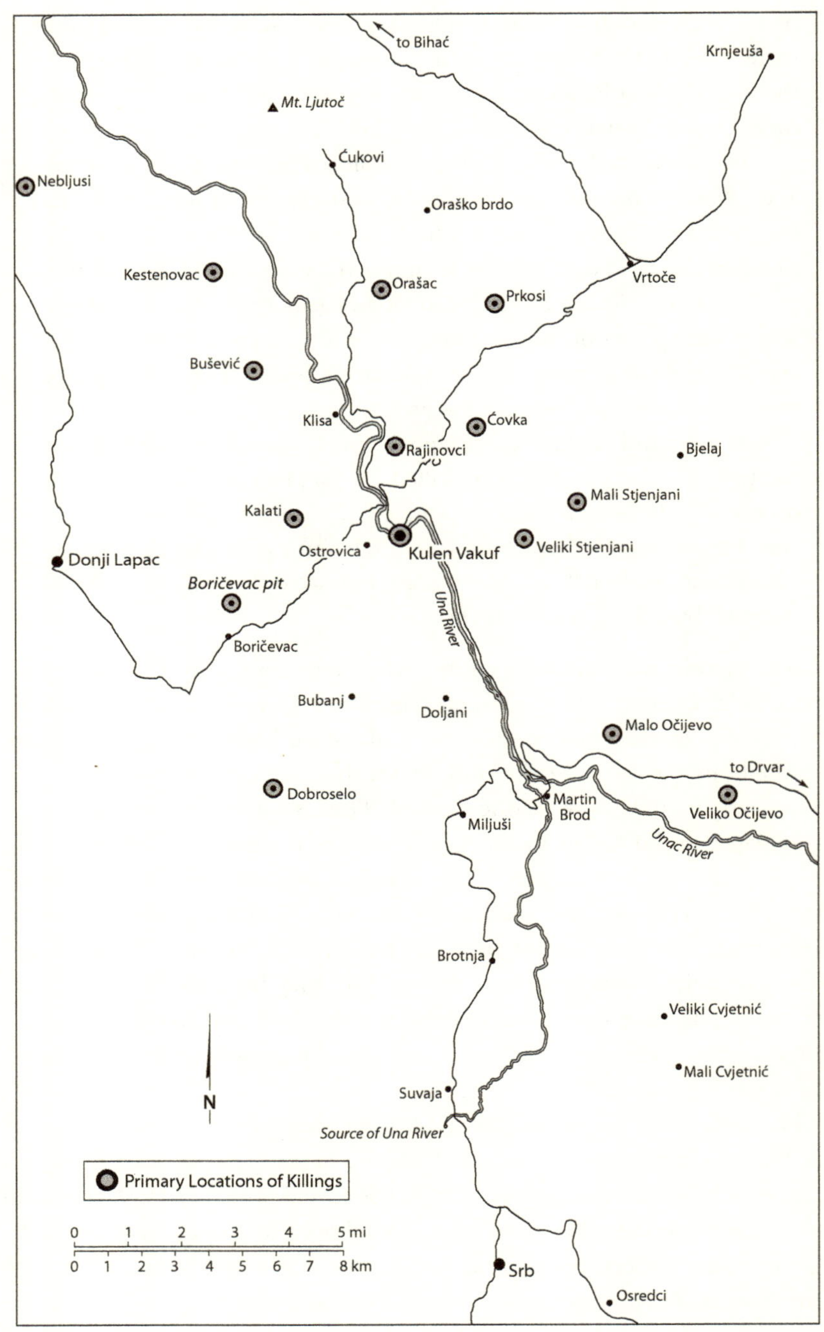

Map 9. Second wave of Ustaša violence, late July–August 1941

FIGURE 7. Postcard drawing of Kulen Vakuf from 1935. This postcard was sent on May 15, 1941, about a month after local Ustašas took power, and about six weeks before they would unleash a massive wave of violence. In Kulen Vakuf, their killing sites included the Orthodox Church, visible here just above the mosque's minaret, and the school—the larger building in the center, slightly above the town center up the hill. Postcard in the author's possession.

What explains why the local Ustašas in the Kulen Vakuf region shifted during the second half of July into the mass killing of nearly all their prisoners? It is difficult to provide a precise answer this question. No archival records exist to shed light on the decision making by men like local Ustaša strongman Miroslav Matijević. There is no evidence suggesting that regional leaders, such as Ljubomir Kvaternik or Viktor Gutić, issued specific written orders to begin the mass killing, although it is possible that such leaders were involved in some way. After all, we know that they could give the green light for violence over the telephone, or in face-to-face meetings. Most of what we know about this phase of the violence comes not from NDH documents, but rather from survivor testimonies, as well as from the few memoirs of non-Serbs who lived in Kulen Vakuf during July 1941. From such sources we can piece together what happened, but it is much more difficult to tease out why, given that such individuals were victims and observers rather than decision makers. So our search for an explanation must remain speculative for why the period of relative calm after the mass killings of July 1–3 transformed by the second half of July into mass killing.

Part of what may explain the shift was how the news of the first wave of violence of July 1–3 affected the region's Orthodox villages. Word of the massacres, burning, and plunder in Suvaja, Osredci and Bubanj had spread to most of the Orthodox villages by mid-July. As a result, most men, aside from the elderly, fled to the forests. As one local man recalled in his memoirs, by mid-July "they [the Ustašas] couldn't find a young man anywhere."[145] The local Ustašas became aware of these changes because they regularly visited these villages in order to steal. As was the case at the end of June, this appears to have a created a sense of fear that the men hiding in the forests were preparing an attack. As a result, the Ustašas began to ratchet up their violence against those who remained in the villages as a way of crushing the perceived threat. In this sense, their behavior began to mimic what happened weeks earlier in Suvaja, Osredci, and Bubanj. Even though it was their violence that caused the Orthodox men to flee their villages, they nevertheless responded to the perceived threat by intensifying their violence against the region's Orthodox population. At work may have been a sense of an imperative to destroy the threat before those in the forests rose up and took revenge.

This transformation may have affected one of the central factors that led many local men to join the Ustašas: stealing. Once the Orthodox villages began to empty, the living could no longer be so easily robbed. Their homes could, of course, be plundered and livestock taken. But other kinds of wealth, such as gold and money, could be taken into the forests and mountains. Arrest and killing were more radical ways of extracting these more portable economic resources. Jan Gross has shown in the case of German-occupied Poland how, for local residents, killing and corpse disposal of Jews was not merely about removing an unwanted population; these activities also constituted lucrative opportunities for enrichment, specifically by taking gold teeth and any other wealth still located on (or in) the bodies of the victims.[146] In the Kulen Vakuf region, local Ustašas such as Matijević were careful to steal the money that their prisoners had in their pockets just before throwing them into vertical caves or ditches. Evidence from the wider region suggests that some Ustašas would check the teeth of their victims and pull out any gold before disposing of the corpses.[147] With a stream of new victims nearly each day, killing now provided the local Ustašas a steady supply of plundered wealth once robbing the living in their homes had become unfeasible. With each intensification of violence, the opportunities for easy plunder narrowed, which may have contributed to further violent escalation.

Missing from our analysis of this ebb and flow of local violence is consideration of the behavior of another significant part of the population. How did the "non-Serb" but non-Ustaša population react to the unprecedented violence against their neighbors? To better understand why killing on an ethnic axis could become the order of the day in a given place and time, it is essential to examine the behavior of those in a community not targeted for plunder or elimination. The evidence suggests that many of those whom the authorities considered to be "Croats" were, in fact, appalled by the violence. In NDH surveillance reports, military commanders noted that in many Catholic villages one could hear protests, often made publicly, particularly from the most prominent residents. "Until now we had God," said one, "but now the devil has come," speaking here about killings of his Orthodox neighbors by local Ustašas. Another asked: "Why are the Orthodox being slaughtered when they are Christians just like us?" The mass executions of entire families baffled others: "What could children, women, and the elderly be guilty of that it is necessary to kill them?"[148] In NDH reports on the "mood of the people" (*raspoloženje naroda*), it was noted by mid-July that hostility among many non-Serbs toward the Ustašas was growing, due largely to their violence. Calls for them to be disarmed were becoming more frequent.[149] Accounts from refugees expelled from Bihać, who made their way to German-occupied Serbia, corroborate this evidence from NDH archives. As one put it: "The relationship of the local Croat and muslim population [toward Serbs] was good, one could even say friendly. The measures that the Ustaša authorities took against the Serbs did not find approval among local Croats and muslims."[150] Such sentiments were echoed in other regions of the NDH, such as Kordun. There, local Catholics called the Ustaša violence "a shame for the Croatian nationality, culture and Catholic faith." They were deeply disturbed that their Orthodox neighbors, with whom they had been in good relations prior to 1941, were now being killed.[151]

Such feelings of disapproval and verbal protests were insufficient for some; instead, they undertook interventions to save their neighbors' lives. When Nikica Medić ventured into Kulen Vakuf to buy oil and other household items, his Muslim friend, a carpenter whose last name was Muratović, immediately hid him in his shop, and then bought the things that Medić needed. He warned him that the Ustašas were killing Serbs, but also said that, "the respectable people cannot stand this." He then led Medić safely out of town. A blacksmith named Murat warned his friends Joce and Rade Medić that the local Ustašas who were killing Serbs "were drunks and unemployed riffraff," and that they "should hide in the forests . . . and tell the people not to come to town anymore."[152] Members of the Catholic Hodak family who lived near the village of Klisa, several of whom had connections to organizing prewar strike actions in the region, took measures to protect their Orthodox neighbors. Obrad Banjac, who lived in the village of Bubanj, received warnings of impending Ustaša attacks both from Božo Markovinović and Mile Krpan Jalšin, who were Catholics from Boričevac, and from a blacksmith named

Adžekovac, as well as a merchant named Alija—both Muslims from Kulen Vakuf. Some of these men used their personal connections to prevent arrests or to free those already arrested. They warned their neighbors not to go to Kulen Vakuf, where it was likely that the Ustašas would kill them. When aware that the Ustašas were en route to attack an Orthodox village, such as Buševič, they traveled ahead of them in order to warn their neighbors to flee. They also saved some villagers in Rajinovci, located opposite their village on the other side of the Una River, by taking them across the water by boat and then hiding them in their homes.[153]

A former landowner (*beg*) from Kulen Vakuf also warned villagers in Rajinovci about impending Ustaša attacks. His intervention significantly reduced the number of victims.[154] Ahmet Pehlivanović, who lived in Ostrovica above the town of Kulen Vakuf, traveled on several occasions to the nearby village of Kalati to warn its villagers about impending Ustaša attacks. Ivan Đukulović, a Catholic from the same village, regularly warned his neighbors about the dangers they faced, and once even ran ahead of a group of Ustašas who were on their way to attack the village to tell its residents to flee. Those who listened to him survived, while the rest were killed. Sveto Zorić recalled how a Muslim from the village of Orašac came to his village and warned him that the Ustašas were planning to kill all of the men. Thanks to him, 150 lives were saved.[155]

Even some local "non-Serbs" who collaborated with the Ustašas nevertheless took actions to save their Orthodox neighbors. Muharem Dervišević from the village of Klisa was one such individual. Even though he received a rifle from the Ustaša mayor of Kulen Vakuf, Husein "Huća" Zelić, he traveled to the nearby village of Buševič the night before a planned Ustaša attack to tell his neighbor Obrad Ljiljak and his fellow villagers to flee to the forests.[156] If they were unable to issue advance warnings, then some even tried to intervene while the Ustaša attacks were underway. It was said that Ibrahim Vojić approached a group of Ustašas who were in the midst of killing, and asked desperately: "Why are you killing these perfectly fine people [*zdravi ljudi*]!?" Their reply: "If it's not clear to you, we'll kill you too!" They then executed Vojić.[157]

However, such instances of physical violence against non-Serbs for attempted interventions appear to have been rare. In general, the evidence does not suggest that local Catholic and Muslim Ustašas regularly used force against those whom they perceived as community members, even when such individuals openly challenged them.[158] As such, fear of reprisal for non-participation in violence, which some scholars have suggested is crucial for fueling participation in local killings in other contexts, such as during the genocide in Rwanda, does not appear to have been of sizable importance in northwest Bosnia and Lika in 1941.[159]

In some cases, it appears that prewar inter-ethnic friendships, as well as relationships that some non-Ustaša Catholics and Muslims had with local Ustašas, were important factors in making such interventions possible. Milan Alivojvodić, for example, saved several of his Orthodox friends, including one who was a prominent communist, by using his connections with the Ustašas who regularly ate and drank in his tavern in the Donji Lapac region.[160] Such connections also occurred in the town of Donji Lapac, where a group of fifteen to twenty local Catholics demanded that one of the Ustaša leaders, whose last name was Kokotović, release their Orthodox neighbors who had been imprisoned, and to cease their violence against, and plunder of these "innocent people." As one recalled: "We emphasized that we local people know best because we have all lived together, and not one of them [among the prisoners] has done anything wrong to anyone."[161] It appears that the local Ustašas eventually gave in to their demands after realizing they had little to no support from the community for their policies of persecution.

In areas where "non-Serbs" who opposed the persecution of their Orthodox neighbors outnumbered or matched the numbers of Ustašas, regular incidents of conflict occurred between them. In Donji Lapac on the day of the town's weekly market sometime in July, the local Ustašas marched a group of prisoners down a main street. Their hands were bound and nearly all showed signs of having been recently beaten. A group of residents assembled and began protesting, yelling out: "Shame on you all for what you have done!" On other occasions, local residents brazenly confronted Ustašas, calling them in public "butchers" and "thieves." Such incidents would sometimes result in the Ustašas drawing their guns, but it does not appear that anyone was shot for such verbal attacks.[162] This was most likely due to the fact that the small Catholic population of Donji Lapac seems to have been largely ill disposed to the Ustašas. This meant they enjoyed little authority or respect among their supposed co-ethnics, which made it difficult for them to assert themselves however they wished.

Yet even in Boričevac, one of the main centers of Ustaša power and activity in the region, confrontations of this sort took place. Milan Vranić, an older, respected Catholic resident of the village, approached a group of younger Ustašas who were trying to take local Orthodox residents Nikola and Marko Vučković out of the village. "You scum," he shouted angrily, "where are you taking these respectable men? They haven't done anything to anyone, especially you."[163] At work here, it seems, were prewar systems of hierarchy. Authority figures knew the types of usually young men who joined the Ustašas, and often had little respect for them. Once they began persecuting the Orthodox community, this lack of respect turned quickly into open disdain and disgust. Again, evidence does not suggest that such altercations and protests by Catholics generally resulted in Ustaša retaliation against them. Vranić, for example, was warned that his interventions would bring severe consequences, but such threats were mere posturing by local Ustašas; he does not appear to have been harmed.[164]

There were also cases in which local residents sheltered neighbors who managed to escape Ustaša attacks. Nine-year old Rajko Srdić managed to survive a mass shooting during which his mother, grandmother, and uncle were killed. Unfamiliar with the area, he wandered alone through the forest until he saw a mosque's minaret. He had unwittingly returned to Kulen Vakuf where he, his family, and many others had previously been held prisoner. A local Muslim man, Mujo Kulenović, found him and took him home. He and his family then hid Srdić for more than two months. As Srdić later recalled: "In the beginning, Mujo's neighbors looked at me suspiciously, but his authority among the people of [Kulen] Vakuf was so great that I didn't need to be too afraid. Still, this didn't mean there was no risk in what he did. The decency and humanity of these people cannot be exaggerated."[165]

In another instance, Manda Krpan, a young Catholic woman from Pištalska Draga, came to the house of Petar Pilipović on the morning of June 27. She had long been a friend of the family, and sometimes did housework for them. She found nothing expect pools of semi-dried blood at their door. The previous evening, local Ustašas from Boričevac had come and executed nearly the entire family. They planned to give the house and land to one of their local strongmen. Manda found four-year old Milica Pilipović, the only survivor of the attack, who had managed to escape from the house with her brother (who was later shot). During the attack, Milica lost her parents, grandparents, a second brother, and her sister. Manda immediately took the child into her care, where she remained safely for several more months. After the war, Milica described Manda as "my other mother."[166]

While it is difficult to arrive at a precise overall figure, the evidence that local historians have collected, especially through oral histories conducted with survivors during the 1960s and 1970s, suggests that local Muslims and Catholics managed to save a significant number of their Orthodox neighbors.[167] For example, according to Esad Bibanović, who interviewed scores of the region's residents, Muslims saved fifty-nine of the 106 Orthodox residents who lived in the town of Kulen Vakuf.[168]

Such evidence of rescue not only strongly suggests that local non-Serbs were far from united behind the violence of the Ustašas. It also points to a prewar tradition in the region of intercommunal friendship, which appears to have actually grown deeper among some as the persecution of the Orthodox community intensified and some neighbors chose to take risks to save their neighbors. This finding is significant for scholars of violence and ethnicity, some of whom have suggested that violence in multi-ethnic societies tends to harden antagonistic ethnic identities.[169] This finding is important, but the history of the Kulen Vakuf region suggests that an opposite process—also driven by violence—can be at work at the same time: the rapid growth of inter-ethnic solidarity based on acts of intervention and rescue in the midst of inter-ethnic persecution and killing. What emerges is perhaps a counter-intuitive notion that contexts of extreme inter-ethnic violence, which often produce the antagonistic collective categorization that may further intensify violence, can also simultaneously strengthen inter-ethnic social ties, or create new ones.

What accounts for the occurrence of these acts of intervention and rescue, however, is a more difficult question. It is tempting to argue that long-standing prewar friendship was an important, if not the most important factor. Although not common, there were instances in which even local Ustašas protected their longtime Orthodox friends. For example, Ilija Rašeta discovered one of the vertical caves where some of his neighbors had been killed. One of his childhood friends, now among the Ustašas, saw him wandering there one day. He returned home and instructed his mother to speak immediately with Rašeta's mother in order to warn him to never again go to the site, which would endanger his life. Rašeta believed that this long-term friendship was critical in making such an intervention possible.[170]

Yet research in other contexts suggests pre-violence friendships are generally poor indicators of whether rescue or other forms of intervention will take place. Studies on the genocide in Rwanda, for example, show that intercommunal friendship (and even intermarriage) was widespread prior to 1994; yet intercommunal killing nevertheless took place on a mass scale, including among those who shared these pre-genocide connections, while intervention much less common.[171] How can we explain the significant number of interventions in the Kulen Vakuf region by local non-Serbs to save their neighbors? There are two main reasons. First, high levels of latent fear and resentment were not widespread. Local Catholics often viewed the Orthodox population as "fellow Christians," while some Muslims (and Catholics) considered them as "perfectly fine people." Among both, many saw their Orthodox neighbors as not guilty of any crime. This made it difficult to see any reason for their persecution, which may have played a role in decisions to intervene. Still, psychological research, such as Stanley Milgram's well-known experiments on obedience to authority, suggests that we should not assume that widespread feelings of fear and resentment are necessary factors for people to commit violence. One of Milgram's important contributions was showing that a majority of people, who previously did not harbor hatred toward certain individuals, can nonetheless subject them to high levels of pain under orders from a perceived legitimate authority.[172]

This perception of a "legitimate authority"—and especially the lack thereof—was the second crucial element at work in the acts of rescue and intervention. The local Ustašas were well-known local men and boys, and most were not well thought of. After visiting the village of Doljani, located not far from Kulen Vakuf, one NDH military official reported in early July: "The members of the Ustaša unit are mostly boys between sixteen to twenty years old, not sufficiently serious, have almost no knowledge about laws and, based on their appearance, have little respect for their elders."[173] And evidence suggests that "their elders" had little respect for them. Ilija-Icalj Ivaniš, the father of one of the local Ustaša leaders in Kulen Vakuf, Tomo Ivaniš, openly opposed his son's activities. He made a habit of traveling to Serbian villages such as Kalati, Kestenovac, and Bušević, to tell their residents to hide in the forests after hearing his son speak about impending attacks.[174] Mara and Ivica Ivezić—the mother and father-in-law of the local Ustaša leader Miroslav Matijević—condemned the violence of the Ustašas. So too did Matijević's own wife, Anica. Evidence from multiple memoirs suggests that they took measures to warn their neighbors in Kalati that "not one of them should come to Kulen Vakuf," lest they fall into the hands of the Ustašas.[175] Such examples demonstrate that family ties—even between wife and husband—did not prevent such interventions. Some family members of Ustašas thus did not regard the authority of their Ustaša spouses and other relatives as legitimate and unquestionable.

Among people not related to Ustašas, evidence suggests that many held them in low regard. Like their counterparts in other parts of the NDH, the local Ustašas were often known prior to April 1941 as "drunks and unemployed riffraff," "good-for-nothings," "notorious alcoholics," and "unworthy, corrupt people who steal and drink"—all of whom overnight had unexpectedly become the new holders of power.[176] As such, they had a certain level of authority by virtue of having an official monopoly on political life and especially the means of violence. Yet they did not enjoy the respect of many of their fellow non-Serb citizens, who saw them at best as entirely ordinary men, and more likely, as some would later describe them, as the "garbage of the Croat people" who overnight had become authority figures.[177] As Milgram's various experiments have suggested, people tend not only to ignore orders to comply with policies they do not agree with, but also frequently protest and resist them—even by taking physical action—if they perceive the authority figure as "a common man" and therefore illegitimate.[178] This is the perception that many individuals in the Kulen Vakuf region had of the local Ustašas.

This sense of an illegitimate authority, combined with a feeling among many that their neighbors were not enemies but rather friends, mostly likely explains why many non-Serbs not only engaged in acts of rescue, but even felt ready to resist calls by the new authorities to participate in acts of violence. As Kulen Vakuf resident Bećo Mašinović yelled out in response to Ustaša Miroslav Matijević, who had called a town meeting in late July and demanded that all local residents join him in killing and burning everything Serbian: "Miro, who are we supposed to attack? Our neighbors? You really are crazy."[179]

Comparative evidence from other regions of the NDH further strengthens this notion that people are more likely to resist those whom they know and whose authority they do not consider legitimate. In September 1941, 117 Ustašas from Herzegovina arrived at the Bosnian town of Jajce. They were completely unknown to the local residents. They marauded around for several days terrorizing local residents before deciding to herd 158 "Serbs" into the town's Orthodox church. They killed some inside it, and took the rest to a location not far from a nearby Catholic village where they butchered their victims.[180] According NDH reports, local Catholic and Muslim residents "strongly condemned this anarchy" and "expressed their disgust with the bloody deeds, which not only deprived their fellow citizens of life, with whom they had lived for decades in good relations, but also deprived them of their most beautiful memories."[181] Yet aside from harshly criticizing the Ustašas when speaking privately amongst themselves, it appears that few non-Serbs in Jajce took actions to rescue their Orthodox neighbors, aside from some members of the NDH military who protected the handful still employed in the town's government.[182]

Again, people's perception of what constituted a legitimate authority was central in determining the possibilities and limits for intervention. In Jajce, none of the Ustašas in question were local men. And they acted in extremely violent ways, which terrified the local non-Serb population. Even the most prominent members of the town's NDH government were afraid of them. Several insisted that armed guards accompany them wherever they went. Another was changing apartments every night out of fear that these Ustašas would kill him. This "passivity" on behalf of the local Catholic and Muslim population in confronting the Ustašas is something that was noted in NDH military reports from other regions. The main reason was "that people feared for their lives, that is, that they would become victims of the so-called 'cleansings' carried out by irresponsible individuals from the [Ustaša] organization."[183] In the words of an NDH report from Herzegovina: "During the time of the "Ustaša regime, not one [NDH] official, not one officer, not one citizen, not one woman, and not even one child could be sure of staying alive—day or night. The Ustašas marauded around everywhere they attacked."[184]

These dynamics resulted in the only local authority becoming these unknown and violent men who displaced all others by their unchallenged capacity to kill whomever they wished. As a report from Jajce eloquently put it: "There is no authority, nor government, nor Veliki župan, nor gendarmerie, nor army—there are only these Ustašas."[185] Here, intervention and rescue were rare because those with control over the means of violence were unknown and deeply feared. Moreover, their threats and acts of violence also endangered non-Serbs, including local NDH officials. As such, they constituted de facto a "legitimate authority," due almost entirely to fear. This left space for quiet criticism; but actual intervention to save one's neighbors was frightening and, most of all, life threatening, and thus much less frequent.

This dynamic compares to some extent with the relationship between the German authorities and Polish peasants in the countryside of German-occupied Poland. There, local residents often took part in the "hunt for the Jews," which historian Jan Grabowski has described. For some, a main reason was fear of reprisals from the German police and military, as well as local denunciation to them by their neighbors. The extent of German power, and the willingness to use violence to bring about conformity to its policies, was such that acts of rescue were often infrequent, while active collaboration in persecution was much more common.[186] The parallels are perhaps even stronger to the Rwandan case. Scott Straus has shown that participation in the genocide was neither immediate nor the natural outgrowth of pre-genocide antagonisms between "Hutus" and "Tutsis." Initially, local leaders often attempted to prevent the wave of killing from engulfing their communities, and some even succeeded for a brief time in doing so. However, as those committed to violence gained the upper hand and the pursuit of non-violent policies became life threatening, space for rescue quickly evaporated, despite strong desires of more than a few to protect their neighbors.[187] These examples suggest that when open defiance to the advocates of violence becomes extremely dangerous, acts of rescue will decline. A similar process took place in Jajce in 1941, despite the town's history of positive inter-ethnic relations, and the disgust that many non-Serb residents felt about the persecution of their neighbors.

The opposite was true in the Kulen Vakuf region, where levels of respect for, and especially fear of the Ustašas as a legitimate authority, were lower than in other locations, such as Jajce, because they were well-known local men and often not well thought of. This difference helps to account for why intervention and rescue were much more common there than during the massacres in Jajce, despite what appears to have been similar pre-1941 levels of intercommunal friendship in both areas. This finding suggests caution in explaining the micro mechanisms of rescue during instances of extreme violence as being rooted predominately in an individual's morality, as some scholars have argued.[188] In both Jajce and Kulen Vakuf, many people valued their neighbors and did not wish for them to be persecuted. However, the variation in levels of rescue between the two towns had little to do with their residents' morality. Instead, the central factor was strikingly different perceptions of the legitimacy of the Ustašas' authority, which was based largely on the extent to which these armed men posed a lethal threat to would-be rescuers. In short, it was whether the circumstances made rescue possible or not—rather than a potential rescuer's prior disposition—that best explains the variation in levels of intervention.

There were also non-Serb villagers in the Kulen Vakuf region who opposed the Ustašas because they intuitively understood that their violence was likely to trigger retaliation from the Orthodox population. Local communist Gojko Polovina recounts in his memoirs a conversation that took place in early July in Boričevac. Ustašas had just returned from their attack on Bubanj. Wanting to celebrate, they ordered all local residents to gather. An elderly peasant, whose last name, like many of the Ustašas, was Markovinović, approached and asked the group: "Children, if you believe in God and his holy son Jesus Christ, then tell me what are you doing?" One answered: "Our time has come, grandfather. We're slaughtering the Serbian dogs in Bubanj." The old man replied: "A year may go by, or two, or even three, but you won't have to wait long . . . people will come one day and say: 'the village of Boričevac used to be here, but now no longer exists. People seeking revenge came and burned it to the ground.'" One Ustaša supposedly struck the elderly man in response. Yet from that night on, many local peasants began sleeping in the forest, fearful that their Orthodox neighbors would soon come and take vengeance by destroying their village.[189]

Fear of retaliation supposedly infected the Ustaša leaders in Boričevac, with most electing not to sleep in their village after the killings in Bubanj. Those who did chose to sleep in the school among other armed Ustašas.[190] It seems that nearly the entire Catholic population—Ustaša or not—was coming to believe, as one local resident put it, that "the forests are full of irate, persecuted people." NDH military reports produced during the second half of July echoed these sentiments, noting that, "the people are afraid of what might happen because of the [Ustašas'] treatment of the Orthodox population." Others indicated that the "political situation is not normal" because of the "feelings of fear and insecurity."[191] Now it seemed to some that it was only a matter of time before a wave of revenge came, which some intuitively sensed would target the whole Croat population—not just the Ustašas who had started the violence and enriched themselves along the way. "The rich men in Boričevac [i.e., the Ustaša leaders] have wrecked the Croat people in this region," said one local man. "If an [armed] uprising begins they will hide, but the rest of us will be left to perish."[192] These fears of being swept up in the process of collective categorization were not unfounded. "The majority of [Serb] peasants," one local resident recalled when describing this period, "aimed their intense hatred at all muslims and Croats for the atrocities that the Ustašas committed against the Serb population."[193]

These dynamics were similar in other regions, such as Herzegovina, where local Catholics and Muslims grasped that the Ustaša violence had implicated them as well. Muslims in the village of Berkovići sought protection from the NDH military after realizing that the violence some from their community had committed against their Orthodox neighbors, whose houses and property they had seized after expelling them, was now sure to bring about "blood vengeance" (*krvna osveta*).[194] In other villages, residents began to realize that they could not escape the process of collective categorization, despite their opposition to the Ustašas. "Why are they killing and plundering in the name of us Croats," asked one prominent peasant, "when we are not in favor of this?"[195] In the Herzegovinian village of Popovo Polje, NDH military reports from late July indicated that agricultural work had ceased after Ustašas killed nearly 150 Orthodox peasants in late June, which caused the rest of the population to flee to the hills. Local Muslims and Catholics were now terrified to continue working in their fields. At any moment, they expected their neighbors to return and kill them as retribution.[196]

With daily life and work grinding to a halt in many villages because of the fear of revenge, much of the non-Serb population appeared increasingly unsupportive of the Ustaša violence. Many believed that there was no justification for the attacks on their neighbors. And when the circumstances permitted, some risked intervening to protect them. The acts of rescue and intervention not only saved lives; they also appeared to change how the local Ustašas practiced violence. In mixed regions, such as in the immediate vicinity near the town of Kulen Vakuf, the Ustašas were increasingly inclined to lead their victims away from the non-Serb population, in order to kill them and then drop their bodies into pits, so they were not in view. Killing and disposing of the corpses in this way appears to have been employed to avoid further destabilizing the non-Serb population and provoking increased resistance and intervention. However, in the regions where the Orthodox were considered to be the majority, the Ustašas seem to have been willing to leave the mutilated and decomposing corpses in the open, especially once the days of easy plunder ended. This had the effect of terrifying those who remained.

Regardless of the method of corpse disposal, as NDH officials wrote with regard to killings elsewhere, "this [violence] has created fear among the people, as well as indignation, all of which now makes any kind of reconciliation [between the Serb and non-Serb population] unthinkable."[197] The sudden disappearance of relatives and neighbors; the stories told by the often single, blood-soaked survivor who managed to crawl out of a vertical cave; the explosive attacks on villages; the experience of finding the hacked-up bodies of parents and siblings, with their limbs gnawed off by livestock and dogs—all this was, as one local man put it when recalling his experiences in July 1941, "the greatest tragedy that could happen to a person."[198] NDH military analysts noted the dramatic results of the "Ustaša cleansing actions:" "It is difficult to conceive of collective life of the Croat-Muslim part of the population with the Serb part. The chasm that now exists is too big."[199] The cause of the tremendous and sudden instability in the region, which was mirrored in many others throughout the NDH, was clear to the military: "the Ustašas are guilty in large part for today's unrest."[200] As a mid-July report concluded: "The Orthodox element is fearful and battered. Unlawful acts by the 'self-styled' Ustašas have brought unrest and fear to the people, and the stealing, burning of houses, and killings are why the population—especially the men—have left their homes and fled to the forests."[201]

By the last week of July, the evidence suggests that the local Ustašas in the Kulen Vakuf region had killed approximately 700 people whom they defined as "Serbs." The first wave of violence was largely selective, with the Ustašas targeting mostly men, and especially merchants, heads of households, priests, and others of influence. Later waves widened the group-selective nature of the violence, with entire villages destroyed simply for what their residents were perceived to be—"Serbs." Yet by empowering these local Ustašas to arrest, plunder, and kill, the central and regional NDH authorities simultaneously triggered the beginnings of their own destabilization. Serious weaknesses existed in their capacity to effectively govern the localities, and especially in exerting control over the means of violence. Poorly organized attempts to "resettle" parts of the Serb population outside of the borders of the NDH had not solved the "Serb question," nor had mass conversions of Orthodox Serb peasants to Catholicism. In fact, neither of these policies had even been much practiced in the Kulen Vakuf region. Plunder and then mass killings were more the order of the day, and they had ravaged local eco-systems of long-standing inter-ethnic co-existence. They were rapidly replaced with cascading levels of intercommunal polarization. The emergence of intercommunal rescue in response to the killing provided a glimmer of hope that the violence might somehow be contained, or perhaps even stopped. But the space for non-violence was rapidly disintegrating by the end of July as Ustašas, such as Miroslav Matijević, led victims each day to the Boričevac pit, where their corpses fell into the pile in which survivor Vladimir Tankosić was still alive, licking the rocks to quench his thirst. If those now targeted for physical elimination decided to fight back, how could the NDH authorities respond effectively, when the brute force of their Ustašas was already causing more failure than success?

Chapter 4

Rebellion and Revenge

The mass killings of the Orthodox population presented survivors with a stark choice: be killed or fight back. At the end of July, groups hiding in the forests banded together and chose to resist. An insurgency broke out in northwest Bosnia and Lika at different times and in different locations during the last week of July.[1] A detailed reconstruction of this uprising at the local level reveals that these fighters, contrary to those who might wish to depict them at this time as coherent groups of communist "Partisans" or nationalist "Chetniks," were actually quite heterogeneous in outlook and behavior. Lacking strong political organizations, they ranged from men who sought blood vengeance against all whom they viewed as "Catholics" and "Muslims," to others who hoped for a more restrained approach to violence—and those who oscillated between these two tendencies. Among restraint advocates, the strongest tended to be the few local communist oriented fighters, some of whom had been away from the region for many years. However, they were also the weakest in terms of influence and authority. And so they struggled greatly to control the powerful urge among many others to take revenge on an ethnic axis. Yet micro-level analysis illuminates how inter-ethnic retaliation could be practiced simultaneously alongside intra-ethnic plunder and threats against supposed ethnic "brothers" who did not automatically choose revenge as a response to the Ustaša violence. Telling the story of this rebellion thus shows us how intercommunal violence can propel multiple processes of ethnicization at the same time, with perceptions of ethnic categories hardening and softening on both inter- and intra-ethnic axes.

The NDH persecution was, of course, the immediate trigger causing local men to take up arms. Yet a longer-term tradition of armed resistance, such as during the peasant rebellion of 1875–1878, and more recent military activity in the first half of the twentieth century, such as during World War I, provided these fighters with a mental outlook and the concrete skills to quickly organize themselves. "Our grandfathers waged war with the Turks [the Ottoman authorities]," as one local man recalled. "Our fathers were veterans [*Solunaši*] from World War I, and stories from these experiences were constantly discussed. I was listening to terrible war stories from the time that I knew I existed, and they were mentioned more frequently as another war seemed possible [in 1941]."[2] To these stories were added the experience that many local men shared of the recent mobilization to resist the German-led Axis invasion in April. Most still had their uniforms and weapons from the former military forces of the Kingdom of Yugoslavia. A long-term oral tradition that depicted the community as one that regularly took up arms to defend itself, and the more immediate experience of having just been mobilized, provided local men with a mind-set in which armed resistance against the Ustašas was logical and possible.

The small number of communists in the region, such as Gojko Polovina, Đoko Jovanić, Stojan Matić, and Stevan Pilipović Maćuka, among a handful of others, had already been discussing the need for armed resistance. During the second half of June, some began forming embryonic underground "revolutionary councils." They began making more concrete plans during the second half of July, especially those in the towns of Srb and Drvar.[3] Yet the role of any formal political organization, such as the Communist Party of Yugoslavia, in organizing the insurgency was minimal to non-existent. As one local communist activist said: "There was no party leadership nor a sufficient number of party members."[4] The situation was not much different in the wider Lika region, as exemplified in the memoirs of the communist commander Kosta Nađ: "Except in rare instances, our [communist] party organizations did not play a role in the organization of the insurgency."[5] So the few local communists collaborated with the much more numerous non-communist groups of villagers interested in waging armed resistance. Together, they devoted themselves to creating "peasant councils" in Orthodox villages of three to five men, whom they attempted to mobilize to protect their villages from Ustaša attacks, to gather weapons, and to prepare themselves and their neighbors to fight.[6]

This method of organizing ensured that the nuclei of insurgent units were fellow villagers. Not unlike the Ustaša units, potential insurgent groups were often composed of relatives and neighbors. And they looked to the prominent, well-known men from their villages as their authority figures. One was twenty-six year-old Nikola Karanović, a short man with dark hair and a mustache, who was a former army officer from the village of Ćovka located in the hills about six kilometers east of Kulen Vakuf. He had worked the fields until he was fifteen when he left to study in an officers' school. Karanović returned to his village shortly after the collapse of the Yugoslav Army in the spring of 1941. As a local military figure, he had enjoyed the respect of his Orthodox neighbors for years. Now with them in the forests hiding from the Ustašas, he declared: "We will fight against this evil that has happened to us."[7]

According to insurgent testimonies, no more than one-quarter of the peasant fighters had firearms, which included military and hunting rifles. The rest carried axes and other farm tools.[8] Like those who rose up against their Muslim landlords and the Ottoman authorities in 1875, most referred to themselves as "insurgents" (*ustanici*). Beginning on July 24 in the village of Nebljusi, they emerged from the forests and began launching attacks. The fighters immediately overran at least four villages and towns, killing several Ustašas, burning their commands to the ground, and capturing their weapons and ammunition.[9] Many of these commands were quite small, as NDH military reports later indicated, and were isolated bases in areas where the Orthodox population vastly outnumbered anyone else. For example, NDH reports from the Drvar district (*kotar*) expressed worry that the Ustaša command had only eleven men for an area considered to be 25,000 Serb and only about 100 Croat. Similar concerns were voiced about the low numbers of Ustašas vis-à-vis the Serb population in other parts of northwest Bosnia.[10] These command posts thus were extremely vulnerable to attack, while the insurgents enjoyed the advantage of support from the Orthodox population and had local knowledge of the terrain. They attacked more villages during the last few days of July, with varying degrees of success, destroying not only NDH commands, but also cutting many telegraph and telephone lines, and blocking roads and disrupting railroad lines.[11]

The success of the attacks caused local NDH military officials to send a flurry of telegrams to their superiors, which described their regions' conditions as "desperate" and "urgent." Some noted that "panic" was already widespread among the non-Serb population. This sudden atmosphere of emergency, combined with unexpectedly being put on the defensive in multiple locations at the same time, led many local commanders to estimate the numbers of fighters they faced in the thousands.[12] What is striking is the degree to which the NDH military forces in northwest Bosnia and Lika were rapidly placed on the defensive by various groups of relatively unorganized fighters, the vast majority of whom did not have access to much military equipment and were operating in the forests. Less than a week after the insurgents fired their first shots, regional and local NDH commanders faced cut telegraph lines, attacks on their command posts, an Orthodox population that had largely fled to the forests, Catholics and Muslims fleeing with their children and livestock to the safety of nearby towns, and fields of un-harvested wheat. One military commander concluded: "the present conditions, which are now unbearable, will become hopeless if urgent measures are not undertaken."[13] Such reports suggest the overall weakness of the NDH state in the localities where the insurgency began.

The insurgents who had caused this panic were a mixed group. Some wore their old uniforms of Army of the Kingdom of Yugoslavia. Others dressed in their civilian clothes, which were all that many had when they fled their villages during Ustaša attacks. Some waved hand-made tricolor Serbian flags, while a handful of others preferred red, possibly to symbolize communism and solidarity with the Soviet Union. Yet even among these men could be heard calls for the "resurrection" of Serbia and the "disappearance" of Croatia.[14] Many more had no visible political affiliation. Their primary common motivation was to save their lives and those of their families, as NDH military commanders noted in a report written several days after the fighting began: "It is a relatively small number of Chetniks [Serb rebels] who are taking part in these actions. Most are peasants from the vicinity of Srb [located south of Kulen Vakuf] who are participating, along with their families, wives and children. This is simply a reaction by them to the cleansing that our Ustaša formations have carried out. Cleansing should be understood as destruction—the killing and slaughtering of Serbs, regardless of their age and sex, as well as the destruction of their property."[15]

The nature of the Ustaša "cleansings," in which perpetrators were often well acquainted with those whom they were stealing from and killing, produced in many victims—now insurgents—more than just a desire to save themselves. "Those whom had been robbed were prone to rob, even their closest neighbors. Those whose relatives and neighbors the Ustašas had killed were prone to seek revenge. It was especially difficult for those whose entire families had been killed, and whose houses and everything they owned had been burned and destroyed," as one local fighter said.[16] Among many insurgents who had just suffered enormous losses at the hands of the Ustašas, there was thus a powerful desire to "get even."

In the Kulen Vakuf region, a handful of communists who considered themselves "Serb" hoped to eventually transform the insurgents into a disciplined guerrilla army. But they encountered serious difficulties in exerting control over the peasant fighters. As was the case in other parts of the NDH, such as Herzegovina, the number of local communists was small. They often lacked the necessary authority that other prominent local men had, such as former gendarmes and military officers like Nikola Karanović from the village of Ćovka. For example, twenty-three year-old communist activist Đoko Jovanić was born in the village of Suvaja, but had left for Vojvodina (northern Serbia) when he was five. He spent most of his life outside of the Kulen Vakuf region, and returned only in May 1941. While he certainly could claim local roots, he was personally unknown to most local villagers, many of whom were also unfamiliar with the communist movement that he supported.[17] Significantly, none of the incipient insurgent units in the region had Communist Party organizations during the summer of 1941.[18] Even in the main towns, Donji Lapac had only eight Communist Party members before April 1941, and Kulen Vakuf had three. They had some sympathizers among their fellow residents, and a few allies here and there in the villages. Communist influence and organizational capacity thus was limited when the insurgency broke out in late July.[19]

These limitations affected how the uprising crystallized during its initial period. As the communist Đoko Jovanić recalled, the first days of the insurgency had a certain level of "randomness" (*stihijnost*): "It wasn't led . . . from one center. [Our communist] leaders had some influence, but that influence was minimal. Already by the second or third day, and especially in the days that followed, plans were created on the fly, on the basis of unconfirmed news, and ideas that emerged in the moment."[20] A report produced months later by communists in Lika about these days echoed this assessment: "The condition of the [communist] party organizations is unsatisfactory in its entirety. It is understood that the party is not in the position to be the real leader of the insurgency, as in a majority cases it following rather than leading events [*jašilo na recu događaja*]."[21] Others from the region, who eventually became communists, characterized these early days of fighting as chaotic, with a noticeable lack of communist leadership: "The question was how to initiate and organize the struggle. With regard to that, disorientation and a confusion of ideas were what dominated. Some people connected to the struggle with communists, but truthfully they did not exist in those days."[22] Gojko Polovina, from the village of Dobroselo and another of the region's few communists with local roots, described the time in similar terms, critiquing in the process former fighters who later exaggerated the coherence and influence of the communists: "The historical claims of some participants are wrong when it is said that individuals, at least those who were communists, imposed everywhere a shape on that amorphous peasant mass, designated commanders . . . and that they commanded the masses of people with their conceptions and initiatives. As far as I know, in the sector of southern Lika [the western edge of the Kulen Vakuf region], that kind of imposition of organization and command was impossible."[23] This great gap between the would-be communist commanders and the peasant insurgents is important given the extent to which communists—and not only in the Kulen Vakuf region—would soon encounter serious difficulties in controlling these fighters' retaliatory violence.[24]

The insurgency had a chaotic and spontaneous quality. Some fighters took up arms not only to defend themselves and their families, or to take revenge; like their Ustaša enemies, they also sought to capitalize on the opportunity to plunder, which the instability created. In some instances, this included stealing the property of other fellow "Serbs." Not long after the start of the insurgency, local fighter Đuro Štikovac of Dobroselo, who had worked prior to 1941 as the treasurer of his village's administration, broke into the store of merchant Marko Vladetić in the village of Martin Brod. Only a handful of days earlier local Ustašas had arrested Vladetić, along with his two sons, and then taken them to Kulen Vakuf. Flush with plundered goods, Štikovac pronounced himself commander of the local insurgents. He sought to cement his position by giving out brandy (*rakija*), which he just had stolen from Vladetić. Other insurgents, whose sympathies lay more with the communists, disagreed over how to deal with men such as Štikovac. Some insisted that they be executed immediately. But others argued that such measures could cause a revolt among those fighters who considered such individuals as "local men," and held them in high regard.[25]

Similar behaviors appeared among another group of fighters, who were from villages near the town of Donji Lapac, which the insurgents took control of in early August. Plunder—especially the stealing of livestock—seems to have been at least as important to them, if not more, than taking revenge along ethnic lines. When no more Catholics remained to steal from, they immediately turned on local Orthodox families, including those of their fellow insurgents, and plundered their property.[26] This stealing of "Serb" property by insurgents was not a local phenomenon; it was also noted in other regions, such as Herzegovina, during the early weeks of the insurgency there, and it continued for months.[27]

Such behaviors—plunder, poor discipline, and an overall lack of organization—have been noted by other observers and analysts of guerilla fighters during their early actions in various contexts, perhaps most famously by Mao Tse-tung in *On Guerrilla Warfare* (1937).[28] The insurgency in northwest Bosnia and Lika contained serious internal tensions and conflicts among the fighters who wished to fight against the Ustašas and NDH authorities. Saving their own lives and those of their families, taking revenge, and plundering their neighbors—often regardless of perceived ethnicity—were primary motivations. These sentiments appear to have often co-existed and fluctuated.

The intra-ethnic plunder that manifested during the early days of the insurgency suggests that we should be cautious when analyzing—as well as characterizing—contexts in which significant "inter-ethnic" violence is occurring. A strong "inter-ethnic" dynamic of conflict does not mean that concurrent and subsequent violence will automatically unfold along the same axis. The plunder of Marko Vladetić's store in Martin Brod suggests that people in such contexts can easily choose their targets based on non-ethnic criteria—such as personal conflicts and desire for enrichment, or simply ease of attack. Vladetić was one of the wealthiest merchants in Martin Brod. He had already been a target of thieves earlier in the year, when the NDH authorities noted him being robbed by some of his Orthodox neighbors who were impersonating Ustašas.[29] He may have been in conflict with such individuals prior to 1941, who most likely knew of, and coveted his wealth. Moreover, the Ustašas had recently arrested him, along with his two sons, and they were being held in jail in Kulen Vakuf when the insurgency began. His absence thus made his store an easy target for plunder. Even in a moment when violence appeared to be unfolding along ethnic lines, local actors channeled their activities toward attacking their neighbors whom one might assume they would be allied with. Micro-level analysis helps us avoid assuming "ethnicity" is primary in discerning what drives violence, even when this factor appears at first glance to be dominant, such as during 1941 in the NDH.

And yet, the nature of the Ustaša violence during the past weeks—in which victims were overwhelmingly selected based on what ethnic category they were perceived to belong to—did over determine a retaliatory wave along an ethnic axis. For many insurgents, the Ustaša killings caused a sudden shift in perception of their Muslim and Catholic neighbors. "Among one part of the [Orthodox] population, who had lost their closest family members [*najrođenije*] to the Ustašas," as Đoko Jovanić described, "there was a desire for revenge against the entire Croat population because they did not differentiate the Ustašas from the Croat people."[30] Local encounters attest to these sentiments. NDH soldiers whom the insurgents captured reported that they heard constant discussions of the fighters' plans to take revenge against all Croats.[31] Another prisoner noted that, "the [Serb] population is full of hatred," while others said that Orthodox villagers would call out to them as they passed through their villages: "When are the pits going to be filled [with you]?"[32]

The Ustaša violence made it difficult for many of the peasant fighters to differentiate those responsible for these killings from the rest of the non-Serb population.[33] "For them," one contemporary recalled, "every Croat was an Ustaša."[34] Another described the atmosphere immediately after the fighters entered the town of Donji Lapac: "Certain Serbs were already saying out loud that all Croats needed to be killed, and they needed to be killed because they were Croats."[35] One's previous behavior no longer mattered. As one insurgent remembered, there were people "who were not in the mood to differentiate between those who were bandits and those who were innocent among the Croats."[36]

Some fighters extended this way of thinking to non-Serb women and children, whom they now also conceived of as enemies in need of extermination, even going so far as to compare them to animals whose reproductive ability needed to be stopped. As one insurgent yelled out after killing a woman and her child during the first week of the insurgency: "Stop these dog-bitches from breeding more puppies" (*neka se paščad ne ligu*).[37] Others sought to apply this mental template, in which the perception of belonging to an ethnic category now determined how one should be dealt with. Insurgent Brato Šašić was from an Orthodox village near Donji Lapac. He had worked off and on in Belgrade before the war as a stevedore, and was known as a communist sympathizer. Nonetheless, he immediately arrested Jakov Blažević, the secretary of the regional committee (okružni komitet) of the Communist Party, when he came to his village with other communist activists. Why? "Because he's a Croat," Šašić later admitted to an insurgent commander.[38]

A similar situation occurred in the village of Veliki Cvjetnić. In early August, it seems, the communist Marko Orešković Krntija and his counterpart Đoko Jovanić came to the village to explain that the insurgents were intent on fighting the Ustašas, but not all Croats and Muslims. While villagers prepared eggs for them, the son of the local Orthodox priest approached Jovanić. While pointing at Orešković Krntija, he asked: "It that one a Croat?" Jovanić replied: "He is, and so what?" The priest's son fired back: "Let's kill him . . . Croats and Muslims cannot be trusted."[39] For some people, even for those who were not known as nationalists before the war, all those perceived as non-Serbs—including those who were fighting with the insurgents—had suddenly become parts of abstract, enemy categories. "Croats" were among these categories, and they now needed to be destroyed.

The same was true for some fighters in how they now conceptualized their neighbors whom they saw as "Muslims." "The dominant slogan," as one insurgent commander recalled, "was that all Croats and Muslims are Ustašas."[40] Some even felt they were now specifically fighting a war against what they called the "Turks" or the "balijas" (*balije*), which were derogatory words for local Muslims.[41] This reflected a perception that it was not outsiders who had killed their relatives and fellow villagers, but rather their Muslim neighbors, whom they referred to as "Turks." For some, the logical response to their persecution was "to kill everyone who is Turkish," as one insurgent commander from Herzegovina put it, in the aftermath of Ustaša killings in that region in June and July 1941.[42] The comments by others reflected the limits that many now felt about the possibility of intercommunal resistance, specifically with their Muslim neighbors, against the Ustašas: "The Turks are against us, they are killing us, slaughtering us, throwing us into pits. With them there is not—and cannot be—any collective struggle together."[43] Many insurgents in northwest Bosnia felt the same.[44]

This type of antagonistic collective categorization that the Ustaša mass killings triggered led to regular requests by Orthodox villagers for insurgent commanders to hand over any captured enemy soldiers so that "they could slaughter them."[45] For some insurgents, this seemed to be the primary goal of their attacks. As one fighter reportedly called out to his comrades as they surrounded an NDH military command in the village of Doljani: "Capture them alive and I'll fuck their mothers!"[46] Those who protested against the executions of NDH soldiers were sometimes referred to in derogatory ways as "Croat protectors." Insurgents threatened to kill them and burn down their houses.[47]

For those who did not automatically come to these conclusions, there were insurgents who set out to persuade them. Lazo Tešanović was a teacher before the war, and a lieutenant in the former army of the Kingdom of Yugoslavia. He attempted to convince the survivors of killings, and the relatives and neighbors of those massacred, that the Ustašas were not a select group of Muslims and Catholics, but rather that all Muslims and Catholics were in fact Ustašas.[48] Toward this end, Tešanović, and others like him, explicitly sought out only "Serbs" to join them in their fight.[49] There appeared to be more than a few men who conceived of themselves in this ethnically categorical way. As one put it in a letter he had delivered to his Catholic neighbors, whose surrender he demanded in the aftermath of an Ustaša attack: "This letter is from a Serb, Iso Stanić, who is a son of a Serb, and who is the king of the forest."[50]

One important method that such individuals used to spread a sense of antagonistic collective categorization was the telling of stories of Ustaša massacres, especially by fighters who survived or witnessed killings, to their counterparts whose villages had not yet been attacked. Moving stories circulated about the destruction during July 1–3 in the villages of Suvaja, Osredci, and Bubanj. As one who listened recalled: "Their stories of the atrocities that the Ustašas under the command of Miroslav Matijević committed in the villages near Kulen Vakuf were shocking. Some fighters told of twenty girls and women who were tied together around a haystack, and then the hay was set on fire . . . with more women thrown alive into the fire. Other fighters told about Ustašas who grabbed whomever they found in a village—the elderly, women, children—and then forced them into a hut, which they set on fire."[51] This experience of listening to atrocity stories bonded the fighters, both by creating feelings of fear and a sense of common suffering due to their perceived ethnicity, which most likely helped to cement a desire among many for revenge along ethnic lines.

Yet there were those who did not so easily adopt a sense that all of their Muslim and Catholic neighbors were now enemies. And so some insurgents used the threat of violence to discipline these supposed co-ethnics. The case of Ilija Rašeta is striking. He was born in the Donji Lapac region and grew up with his best friend, Pejo Šikić, a Catholic. Rašeta's childhood friend did want to join the Ustašas, and was in regular conflict with his brother because he refused to cooperate with them and condemned their atrocities. "He even told us whose names were written on the Ustaša lists and who was going to be sentenced to death, and immediately came to tell us what the Ustašas from Gospić were doing in [Donji] Lapac," said Rašeta. Yet none of these actions saved his life when insurgents entered Donji Lapac in early August 1941. "I saw him as he ran from them through a field, like a rabbit in front of hunters, and I began crying," Rašeta recalled. "My godfather [*kum*], Stevo Lavrnje, then said to me: 'Stop it or you'll be killed like him.' I had to stop or I would have lost my life."[52]

Collective categorization of others as enemies was not merely a disposition that traumatized and angry individuals adopted in response to Ustaša killings. Nor was it something they were easily convinced of by explanations and moving atrocity stories told by friends, neighbors, and relatives. Despite the fact that much of the violence was indeed unfolding along an ethnic axis, one's perceived ethnicity did not automatically correspond to, nor determine one's behavior. However, there were those, such as Ilija Rašeta's godfather, who saw individuals only as parts of ethnic categories that now had negative collective identities. For them, it made sense to resort to the threat of intra-ethnic violence—even against their own relatives—in order to enforce a sense of collective categorization among the region's Orthodox population about the "enemy" character of their Catholic and Muslim neighbors. This was the logic that the mass killing of whole categories of people along an ethnic axis was rapidly producing. As one insurgent reportedly yelled out to his neighbors, after calling on them to gather weapons, ammunition, horses, and join the fight against the Ustašas: "Kill those [Serbs] who are not with us!"[53]

Perhaps paradoxically, inter-ethnic mass killings were what caused these intra-ethnic threats of violence, as some fighters sought ways to enforce antagonistic collective categorization as a mobilizational tool in response to the Ustaša violence. This seems to be a feature of insurgencies more generally, in which disciplining one's own perceived "people" is a necessary component of successfully waging war against the "enemy." As much work on political violence has shown, such as in the case of Latin America, the use of violence by insurgents to police those on whose behalf they claim to be fighting is an often underappreciated, yet crucial dynamic of many rebellions, insurgencies, and civil wars.[54] But when this process occurs in a multi-ethnic conflict, it also sheds light on a central mechanism through which actors may attempt to bring about a sense of antagonistic ethnicization. In such a context, the adoption of a hard sense of who is an "ethnic other," and who is an "ethnic brother," often does not emerge automatically, even in a context of extreme intercommunal violence. Rather, such a sentiment often has to be made through sustained, conscious human effort, and specifically through threats or acts of violence.

This focus by many fighters on enforcing conformity through hostility to non-Serb participation in the insurgency, and by discouraging other inter-ethnic connections, gave the insurgency a pronounced ethnic slant during its early days. As local communist Gojko Polovina noted: "The insurgency in Lika began as an uprising whose immediate objective was the defense and protection of the lives of the Serb population."[55] An NDH military report on the outbreak of attacks indicated that while "the rebellion has a communist character," due mostly to the visible participation of a small number of local activists, "it is in fact is a Serb insurgency."[56] German military reports about the political situation in the NDH echoed this assessment by down playing the role of communism: "the Serb peasant is not any more inclined toward communism than the Croat peasant . . . without the crimes of the Ustašas no amount of propaganda would have been able to convince the Serb peasant to wage a life and death struggle for communist goals."[57]

Still, this portrait of a "Serb insurgency" in which fighters nominally of the same ethnicity sought revenge along ethnic lines, while certainly reflecting an important aspect of events at the time, must be balanced with another reality. For some insurgents, antagonistic collective categorization along ethnic lines was not their guiding principle. Stevo Atlagić, who was from the village of Vrtoče, remarked while hiding in the forest with his neighbors: "They killed my father, but I don't want revenge on them all, and we will not give weapons to those who want this. We will kill those who have killed ours."[58] Of a similar mind-set was the insurgent commander Stojan Matić, a twenty-six year-old former Yugoslav army officer from the village of Nebljusi, who had studied at the Military Academy in Belgrade and the Faculty of Law in Zagreb. Local Ustašas murdered about seventy of his neighbors and relatives and then threw their bodies into the Boričevac pit. Among them was his mother. Yet he did not advocate collective punishment of all Catholics and Muslims.[59] Others, such as Stevan Pilipović Maćuka, the insurgent commander of fighters from the villages of Veliki and Mali Cvjetnić, explicitly ordered his fighters prior to attacking the Ustašas that they were not to burn any non-Serb house or harm any non-Serb residents.[60] This need to differentiate among Catholics and Muslims could be expressed even while characterizing the insurgency as an essentially Serb movement. As a group of insurgents from western Bosnia and Lika put it in late August: "We Serbs are fighting for the national liberation of our people from the occupiers and their mercenaries. But the goal of our struggle is not just the liberation of the Serb people, but rather all of the enslaved peoples of our fatherland. We offer a brotherly hand to the Croat people . . . and to our brothers who are Muslims to unite with us and to wage a merciless battle against the occupiers and domestic traitors."[61]

Gojko Polovina, a local communist and would-be insurgent commander, was perhaps the most explicit about the imperative to appeal to "Serbs" and "non-Serbs" in the fight against the Ustašas. During the first week of August, in the aftermath of the outbreak of the insurgency, he wrote a remarkable manifesto directed explicitly to the "Serb" and "Croat" populations of Lika, especially those in the western part of the Kulen Vakuf region. Born in the village of Dobroselo, and educated at the Faculty of Law in Belgrade, Polovina was a pre-1941 communist activist. He was active in the Kulen Vakuf region during the late 1930s as part of the political opposition to the government. Along with others, he regularly gave speeches in villages—such as Osredci, Dobroselo, Nebljusi, and Doljani—often in people's homes. In this way, he established himself at the local level as a well-known advocate for the rights and welfare of both peasants and workers.[62] He had become the leader of the Main Command of Guerilla Units for Lika (Glavni štab gerilskih odreda za Liku), which he helped form on August 3 or 4. Yet during late July and early August, he had yet to have any direct contact with other communists in the region, let alone the leadership of the Communist Party of Yugoslavia.

His manifesto thus reflected his own thinking about what he was witnessing in the Kulen Vakuf region. It is worth quoting at length. First, it demonstrates that the local insurgency at this point was made up overwhelmingly of persecuted Orthodox peasants who were fighting for their lives, rather than any other ideological objective. Second, it vividly shows how some commanders, such as Polovina, insisted on differentiating between the Ustašas and the rest of the Catholic and Muslim population—a distinction that many fighters were refusing to make. Third, it presents an embryonic appeal to the "Croat" population—understood here as distinct from the Ustašas—to see the violence against their "Serb" neighbors also as a form of violence against themselves; the only way to liberation was, therefore, a collective struggle of both communities. Finally, the document shows us that revenge killings along ethnic lines were starting to occur. For activists such as Polovina, this vengeance had to cease immediately.

Serbs in Lika!

The crimes of Pavelić's Ustašas have exceeded all limits. We Orthodox Serbs are sentenced to death and complete destruction regardless of our age and sex. All the caves and pits in our canyons are already full of the bodies of our innocent brothers and sisters. We have kept quiet and suffered for a long time, but we cannot any longer. We have prepared weapons and we are fighting a life and death struggle. Our only rallying cry is this: to victory or we all perish.

Serbs, in our suffering and in the beginning of our struggle, we have the friendship of the whole world. We have to show everyone that we deserve the freedom that we are fighting for and the help that we expect. That is why, brother Serbs, we cannot allow ourselves in any way to be like the Ustašas.

The whole world condemns the Ustaša way of killing and burning. We cannot allow people to appear among us who, because of a need for revenge, seek to kill innocent people and destroy the property of innocent Croats and Muslims. If we act like the Ustašas we will not have a single friend in the world. If our comrades whose families the

Ustašas have killed are not able to find a way to master their pain and find an expression for it in destroying those who are really guilty—the Ustašas—then we will lose the friendship and every prospect for help from the whole of the respectable world, whose help we are counting on.

Croats in Lika!

You are the best witnesses of the crimes that the Ustaša bandits have committed in Lika. What is most unfortunate is that these bandits say that what they're doing is in your name. We know that the Croat people are not criminal and do not wish to spill blood. They have been chained and have not been able to find their words. But the links on those chains of slavery in which the Ustašas and their masters have held the Serb and Croat people have now been broken. The time has come for the Croat people to erase the bloody stain from their history and past [*istorija-povijest*]. The time has come for the Croat people to cleanse their own ranks and to join with other peoples in the struggle for a new and more just life.

Croats, the Ustašas have caused damage to your body. And the Ustašas have caused terrible wounds to the body of the Serb people.

Croats, cleanse your body of the rotten Ustaša movement and in that way you will contribute the most to your own liberation and to the liberation of people throughout the world.

Serbs, accept the brotherly hand that the authentic and honorable sons of the Croat people are offering to you. Don't equate the whole Croat people with the Ustašas. We will show ourselves to be honorable fighters, worthy of our ancestors. The only way we can replace the blood of our brothers and sisters who have been killed is to catch those who are the real criminals and those who are really guilty, and not by spilling the blood of those who are innocent. We will fall again into slavery if we behave as the Ustašas have. That is why we are joining forces and we will offer a brotherly hand to those honorable Croats and Muslims who are ready to fight with us until the destruction of the enemy.[63]

Such sentiments were also visible among fighters who do not appear to have had connections with the communist movement. In these cases, it appears that local traditions of neighborliness were what motivated calls to non-Serbs to join the insurgency. Yet deserving our attention among such insurgents is how threats of retaliatory violence co-mingled with calls to join the fight. This suggests the extent to which intercommunal ties were fraying in the shadow of the ongoing Ustaša violence. As one insurgent wrote to his neighbors in a village in Lika:

> Croat brothers and neighbors,
>
> For years and years our neighborly harmony and love have been the standard in all of our villages. That standard should have continued in this Croatian state [the NDH]. Unfortunately, it has not. Among you have emerged monsters. They have lit the sparks of hatred, which have broken out into flames. Today we are counting 100 new graves, but we are still not thirsting for your blood, and we are not looking to take revenge on your hardworking and peaceful population. We are passing across that and will not touch anything of yours. Instead, we only come with kind words.
>
> Every honorable Croat who has not stolen from Serbs or done any kind of evil to them is still our friend. Let them freely come and join us, and work together.
>
> Do not forget that so long as you continue to shoot at our peaceful population—and at our women and children—we will answer your fire with that of our own.[64]

Or the mixed messages present in a letter sent from the "People's Liberation Army of Grmeč," based just north of the Kulen Vakuf region:

> Brother Muslims,
>
> It's already been a month and a half since you have been forced to leave your homes, forced to be hungry, to be unclothed, to be barefoot, and to hide with your women and children in the homes of others or in the cold forest. Why has this happened? You know yourselves that we Serbs are not guilty for this because you are the ones who have burned the majority of our homes and property, surely under the influence of thieves and Ustašas. Even though at any moment we could burn your homes and property, we won't do this because we know that they have been acquired with the blood and sweat of the hard-working and honorable peasant. And we won't do it because we believe that you, dear brothers, will one day see that we are honorable people, and that we won't hurt or kill any peaceful person.
>
> We give you our word that there is no power that can destroy us, and if you continue in the way that you have you will succeed in provoking us so much that we will come from [the mountains of] Grmeč with all of our forces and we won't leave a single one of you alive or any of your houses unburned. We tell you once more that we are honorable Serbs, and not bandits. We are protectors and liberators of our homes

and those of all people, regardless of whether they are Serbs, Croats, or Muslims.

We invite you as brothers—and this is what is in your best interest—to return to your homes. Do not leave your weapons behind with the enemy. Instead, bring them to us and join with us as brothers to fight against our collective enemy.[65]

Such attempts to forge intercommunal resistance, however much they were also suffused with threats of retaliation, were nonetheless few and far between during the early weeks of the insurgency. The vast majority who took up arms had recently lost close relatives and neighbors to the Ustašas, which left many unable to see their Catholic and Muslim neighbors as anything other than enemies. This set the stage for a wave of retaliation against them. Milan Alivojvodić, the tavern owner from the Donji Lapac region who had intervened with local Ustašas earlier in the summer to save his Orthodox friends, felt no need to flee with the rest of his Catholic neighbors as the insurgents approached. He was sure that his previous behavior would provide a guarantee of security. Yet in these moments when collective categorization had suddenly become the order of the day for many, his perceived ethnicity and the negative traits now associated with this category—rather than his acts of rescue—had become paramount. Several insurgents killed him during the last days of July.[66]

Sometimes the experiences that took place during insurgent attacks could rapidly erode whatever shaky support may have existed for a more selective or restrained approach to dealing with the perceived enemy. This is what occurred during insurgent attacks on Croatian villages in late July and early August 1941, which included Brotnja, Krnjeuša, Vrtoče, and Boričevac. In some cases, commanders who sought a more restrained approach, such as Stevo Atlagić, were killed during the attacks.[67] Their absence then played a role in enabling those who wished to take vengeance to assume a leading role in instigating the violence that followed. The evidence suggests that those who shared these sentiments constituted a significant number of the fighters. "Hatred toward the Ustašas," one insurgent remembered, "dominated during the attack, as did the desire to take revenge on them for the relatives and friends [of the insurgents] they had killed."[68] The critical question, however, was who constituted the "Ustašas?" For many fighters, that category had merged with those of "Catholics" and "Muslims" more generally. And so, when the few advocates of restraint suddenly disappeared, or were not even present, the stage was set for retaliation against all those seen as parts of these categories—regardless of their previous behavior.

During these killings the insurgents treated their victims and their corpses in ways that deserve closer examination in order to better understand what fueled the intensity of the local violence, and shaped its subsequent dynamics. In some cases they immediately sought to physically obliterate the entire perceived Croat community. Only days after the outbreak of the insurgency, a group of fighters stormed into the village of Brotnja and rounded up nearly its entire Catholic population, where most were of the Ivezić clan. They brought them to the edge of a nearby vertical cave, and threw them one at a time—while still alive—to their deaths. As many as thirty-seven people were killed.[69]

The evidence suggests the importance of the revenge motive in fueling this massacre. Already by mid-July, local Ustašas in the region, especially those stationed in the town of Donji Lapac and village of Doljani, had come to Brotnja to arrest Orthodox men, most of whom they later killed.[70] But the main connection between the previous Ustaša violence and this insurgent retaliation was the July 1 attack on the village of Suvaja. According to Gojko Polovina, at least two Ustašas from Brotnja had participated in the slaughter of villagers in Suvaja. Several insurgents, such as Joco Keča, who then participated in the killing of Catholics in Brotnja, were from that village.[71] Others, such as the commander Đoko Jovanić, also suggested that among those who participated in the killings in Brotnja were several from Suvaja, whose families the Ustašas had completely destroyed a month earlier.[72]

The insurgent retaliation in Brotnja mirrored the Ustaša violence in Suvaja: the fighters sought to kill whole families; at least half the victims were women, elderly, and children.[73] This dynamic was similar in other regions, such as eastern Herzegovina. There, insurgent commanders noted that the fighters who were often prominent in committing mass killings of non-Serbs were those who had survived Ustaša massacres by climbing out of pits, or who had fled earlier only to later discover that local Catholics and Muslims had butchered their families. These individuals were often among the most active participants in retaliatory killings.[74]

The visible participation of such embittered men suggests that these revenge killings were about more than just "getting even." Drawing on Nico Frijda's work on vengeance, their behavior could also be understood as a way of restoring one's sense of being the cause of one's acts, especially vis à vis those perceived to have violently taken this agency away, in this case, those perceived as "Ustašas." Conceptualized this way, taking vengeance was a concrete way to alleviate a profound sense of helplessness brought about by the previous wave of Ustaša killings. Moreover, it was a brutally effective means through which to replace feelings of utter powerlessness in the world with those of total power.[75]

At the edge of the vertical cave not far from Brotnja, where the victims were thrown to their deaths, two young Catholic men managed to escape into the forest just before they were to be killed with their neighbors. Not long after fleeing, other insurgents captured them. The two men presented themselves as Orthodox Serbs. Suspicious of their claim, one of the insurgents demanded that they pray to God as Orthodox Christians would. They did so perfectly. Vividly exemplifying how the perception of belonging to a certain ethnic category could mean life or death, the insurgent, after hearing their prayers, patted them on their shoulders and said, "these are Serb children," and sent them on their way.[76] Such successful escapes, however, were rare during this first wave of insurgent killings. This was because the perpetrators frequently knew the victims, which made this kind of deception impossible. And so the revenge-driven violence was often intimate and personal, as the case of men from Suvaja killing their neighbors in Brotnja shows us.[77]

Like the Ustaša killings, the insurgent violence had a profoundly destructive effect on intercommunal relations. It appears that the two male survivors from Brotnja, along with a young woman who also managed to escape on her own, were eventually captured and brought to one of the main insurgent commands located in the nearby town of Srb. The communist-oriented commander Đoko Jovanić tried to explain to them that he and others like him were against the taking of collective revenge on innocent Catholics and Muslims. He condemned the mass killings of their relatives from the Ivezić clan in Brotnja. "They just stared blankly at me," Jovanić recalled, "and then tried to hide their faces. It was unpleasant and difficult to see how they didn't believe a word I said, and how much they feared me." Such encounters demonstrated the great difficulty that some insurgent commanders faced in attempting to portray the insurgency as inclusive of non-Serbs—and against collective punishment on an ethnic axis—while fighters supposedly under their command sought to kill those whom they viewed as "Catholics" and "Muslims." When Jovanić returned the next day to check on the terrified Ivezićes, he discovered they were missing. In the meantime, they had been taken away and shot.[78]

During the insurgent killings, fighters often first sought out specific targets and their methods of violence tended to have strong symbolic meaning. After attacking the village of Krnjeuša on August 9, several searched for the local Catholic priest, thirty-four-year-old Krešimir Barišić. Having arrived to the village in 1937, he was known to many local villagers for his close friendship with his Orthodox counterpart, Father Drago Savić, who regularly joked with his Catholic friend about when he was finally going to marry.[79] For the insurgents who attacked Krnjeuša, Father Barišić was simply a key representative of the entire Croat community, which they now viewed as enemies. There is some evidence to suggest that some fighters believed he was a key organizer of the village's Ustašas.[80] Once they captured him, several began cutting him all over his body. They sliced off his nose and ears, and poked out his eyes—but left him alive in agony, for the moment.[81] They tortured Krnjeuša's municipal chief (*općinski načelnik*), Ivan Matijević, in similar ways, cutting his face open and hacking off his fingers, and then also setting him on fire. After rounding up many other local residents, they locked them inside the village's Catholic church, along with Father Barišić, now blinded and slowly dying. They set the building on fire, with everyone inside burning to death.[82] Specifically desecrating such religious sites—the key physical symbols of the Catholic Croat community—seems to have been an intentional part of the insurgent violence. In other villages, such as Boričevac, insurgents used the shells of burnt-out Catholic churches to hold their livestock. This was a further humiliation to the Catholic community, and could be seen as a symbolic form of revenge.[83]

Villagers whom the insurgents did not kill inside Krnjeuša's burning church were taken to the nearby village of Zelinovac. There, the insurgents locked them inside several buildings. They set them on fire and began slaughtering livestock. In this case, the violence shifted to wholesale destruction, with the killing of perhaps as many as four hundred Catholics—all those who did not escape in time—and the burning of nearly every single structure.[84] Only a handful survived. One was a child, who, while fleeing, encountered "Chetniks" (how many local people at the time referred to the insurgents). "[They] took mercy on me," the boy recalled, "and told me to run."[85] But the evidence suggests that such moments of intercommunal assistance were rare during this attack, which was characterized by violent retaliation against the entire Catholic community.

Some insurgents explicitly sought out relatives of Ustašas during their attacks, which further suggests the prevalence of the revenge motive in driving their behavior. They made a point of mutilating their bodies in ways that would communicate that they had taken blood vengeance. Memoirs suggest that insurgents killed fathers, brothers, and other kin of Ustašas, despite the fact that many such individuals had committed no violence. "They paid for the sins of their relatives and their namesake with the Ustašas," as one fighter put it.[86] During the attack on the village of Vrtoče on August 2, insurgents searched for the father of Miroslav Matijević, the local Ustaša leader in Kulen Vakuf. His name was Josip Matijević. After capturing him, they cut off his head. They then placed it on top of a stick and carried it around the village while killing others, including his wife, whom they also decapitated and whose head they also placed on a stick. Among their subsequent victims were at least eight other members of the Matijević family, including several children.[87] When the NDH military re-entered Vrtoče in mid-August, they found only a handful of women and children who somehow managed to survive the attack. Josip Matijević's store and tavern had been plundered, wrecked, and burned, along with nearly every other structure.[88] Here was the insurgents' response for his son Miroslav—along with the other local Ustašas whom he helped recruit—for what they had done to the Orthodox population during the previous weeks.

We can better understand the meaning of placing the heads of Matijević's father and mother on sticks by situating the act in local historical context. The Ottoman authorities, as well as the *kapetani* (local Muslim military commanders of the fortifications along the region's Ottoman-Habsburg military border), used such techniques for those whom they considered to be enemies, including both Christians and Muslims. This was not merely a method of execution. It also transmitted feelings of fear to the local population, clearly showing who was in control, and publicly demonstrating that the enemy had been killed in a shameful and humiliating way. Such methods of violence were a mix of revenge and spectacle.

FIGURE 8. The remains of Josip Matijević's store and tavern in Vrtoče as photographed by NDH military forces in 1941. Insurgents not only decapitated Matijević and burned his tavern; it also appears they made an effort to erase his first name from the sign. Image courtesy of the Military Archive in Belgrade.

The beheadings here share similar characteristics with scalpings, mutilations, decapitations, and hangings in other contexts, such as during the French Revolution, incidents of violence in the American southwest during the nineteenth century, and in Indonesia during the mass killings of 1965.[89] These forms of mutilation and dismemberment of the body are not employed simply to cause death. They also have a powerful communicative function with the perceived enemy. Far better than any words, they graphically inform a target population about what is to be expected in response to behaviors that the damage-inflictors deem inappropriate.[90] In some cases, using such methods of terror against the opposing side's bodies can be a way to change future behaviors of those still alive, that is, to bring about their compliance.[91] In others, however, mutilation and public display of body parts can be less about changing future actions, as it is geared toward "getting even," often in vastly disproportionate ways. Both dimensions appear to have been at work during insurgent attacks in the Kulen Vakuf region in early August 1941.

The particular method of decapitation that the insurgents employed in Vrtoče had deep historical roots, having been the standard practice of the region's Ottoman authorities and their local collaborators since at least the first third of the nineteenth century, if not earlier. The head was placed on a stick and then positioned on or near the site of an Ottoman military fortification to look like a gravestone, which would be visible to all local villagers. Being executed in this way was considered to be a disgrace.[92] Based on the nearly identical execution style of Miroslav Matijević's father and mother, and the subsequent placing of their heads on sticks, we can hypothesize that the insurgents preserved the memory of these Ottoman-era practices through their local oral tradition. They drew on these stories of violent practices in this moment of profound crisis in order to find an effective method through which to take revenge on their neighbors and humiliate them.[93]

The insurgent killings of Catholics several days earlier in Brotnja has some aspects in common with what took place in Vrtoče. While the peasant fighters there threw most villagers into a deep vertical cave, memoirs suggest that they intentionally left the corpse of Mile Markovinović, an Ustaša who had participated in the massacre of Orthodox villagers a month earlier in Bubanj, in the open for animals to eat. Within days, only Markovinović's skull remained. According to a contemporary, the insurgents had no intention of burying it. Rather, they left it in a visible location to send a message that they had taken vengeance.[94] In short, certain aspects of the insurgents' violence and their methods of corpse disposal reflected the history of violent practices during the region's period of Ottoman rule, especially those related to taking revenge.

As for the rest of the Catholics in Vrtoče, the insurgents made a point of executing most by cutting their throats, as they would slaughter their livestock, which perhaps is not surprising given that most fighters were peasants who practiced animal husbandry. Survivors specifically recalled this method of killing in their testimonies. In an NDH newspaper article about a similar attack, journalists noted that "when children talk about how the Chetniks killed their mothers and fathers they do not use the word 'killed' [*ubili*], but rather all say 'slaughtered' [*poklali*] or 'butchered' [*zaklali*]"—both of which are words in the local Slavic languages used to describe the slaughter of livestock or the killing of a person by the cutting of his or her throat.[95] Some scholars have suggested that such methods of killing could be interpreted as simply rooted in the insurgents' lack of ammunition; in some instances, this may have been true.[96] Yet there is evidence to suggest that these techniques of violence had symbolic dimensions. In some cases, the methods of torture and killing appear to have been deployed to reduce victims to the level of animals, which could be seen as another means through which to take revenge.[97]

Dehumanizing techniques of violence, such as cutting off genitalia or removing a victim's heart, and then placing these body parts on a corpse's face or stomach for others to later see, were noticed by NDH officials in other regions.[98] In some instances, evidence suggests that insurgents took the time not just to kill a victim, but also to methodically cut the still living body apart into many pieces. This could begin by removing fingers, hands, and feet, or gouging out eyes, and progress to tearing out ribs and cutting the rest of the body into small parts—until death. These torturous methods of killing were done to inflict immense pain on a victim in a highly dehumanizing way. Survivor testimonies suggest how such methods literally made victims feel like animals. The cutting off of body parts, as one survivor recalled, was done "to make you howl and die like a dog" (*prostiš kao pašće*). These methods of killing, which would have reminded anyone in the countryside of the slaughtering and butchering of animals, served to terrify and humiliate those who would later find the mutilated and dismembered corpses.[99] Similar methods of killing have been noted in other conflicts, such as in Algeria during the 1950s and 1960s and Guatemala during the early 1980s. In at least some instances in these cases, the torturous methods of violence were employed to achieve similar symbolic effects as what we see in the Kulen Vakuf region in 1941.[100]

Insurgents carried out other forms of torture for the same purpose. In one such instance in Herzegovina in late August, they captured a Muslim man during a retaliatory attack and, in addition to cutting off one of his ears and beating him, forced him to kiss their pigs and then get down on the ground and eat with them. They then brought him to a Serbian village where they took him from house to house, calling out to local women, "We've caught a Turk!" likening him to a captured animal.[101] In another instance that the NDH press reported on, "Chetniks" captured an imam (a Muslim religious official) from the former Yugoslav army. In addition to beating him, they apparently forced him to eat the excrement of one their fighters, then pork, and finally to drink alcohol.[102]

Such dehumanizing forms of torture, along with their religiously symbolic overtones, recall the violence in Anatolia against Armenian Christians. There, examples of men nailed to crosses and then delivered to their families suggests a more generic tendency among perpetrators to seize upon sacred elements of victims' cultural practices as ways not only to kill and torture, but also to dehumanize and humiliate them, their families, and communities.[103] The persecution of Jews in Germany, and later in other locations in Nazi-occupied Europe, is replete with similar examples of violence employed specifically to debase victims' sacred practices, such as burning synagogues (along with people inside them) and the Hebrew Bible. Such acts also constituted forms of communication—both with victims and also with perpetrators' own perceived people.[104] The insurgents' violent practices should be viewed in this way, as forms of intimate communication with perceived enemies, and those perceived to be fellow victims, here of Ustaša violence. They graphically transmitted a message that vengeance had been taken, and that their targets had been deeply humiliated and dehumanized. As such, this type of violence helped to further propagate the notion of the local community as now divided into antagonistic groups.

Their acts of violence may have also been of critical importance to them from a psychological perspective, which crystalized in the specific historical circumstances that fueled insurgent revenge killings. Such behavior communicated unambiguous evidence of their total power over those whom they tortured and killed. A total lack of power is exactly what many experienced during the previous months at the hands of the Ustašas and their followers. This experience was not only painful; it was also profoundly humiliating and disempowering. The extreme cruelty they now meted out could be interpreted as a way to graphically demonstrate that the tables had been decisively turned; they were now anything but victims. Similar dynamics of torture and mutilation can be seen in other instances of guerilla warfare, such as during the American Civil War. For example, in his analysis of violent practices in Missouri, Michael Fellman has noted that, "some groups of fighters wished to push on to some final place of total destruction, some land where 'we' in all of our force are all and 'they' are made of nothing at all."[105] In the Kulen

Vakuf region, the insurgents who took vengeance in such brutal ways may have found a highly effective way to restore their sense of power after it had been so violently taken away. This could be construed as the "rationality" that underpinned their extreme cruelty, which appears to most as baffling, senseless, and irrational.[106]

Here we have to be careful to pay close attention to the historical context that frames such violent episodes, and resist the urge to interpret these extreme acts by relying solely on ahistorical theoretical models. It might be tempting, for example, to make use of Stanley Milgram's important arguments about people's capacity to "abandon humanity," when he observed the disturbing ease with which most people became obedient to authority. He did not see hatred, vindictiveness, or anger as driving people's infliction of pain on others. In his experiments, the capacity to inflict large amounts of pain to another person happened when an individual merged his personality into a larger institutional structure of authority.[107] Yet the forms of insurgent torture and killing were not simply the result of a commander giving fighters orders to cause pain. Unlike the participants in Milgram's experiments, the insurgents' violent actions had a deeply historical component—that is, many of them had recently been subjected to extreme acts of violence, and had seen their neighbors and relatives killed. The role of the historical context here in helping us account for the manifestation and methods of insurgent retaliatory violence cannot be overstated. And this is a factor that Milgram's important psychological research did not pay sufficient attention to. Prior feelings of hatred and anger may not always be necessary for people to commit violence. People who harbor such feelings may not ever be in a position to act on them, especially if forces of restraint are present. But such historically contingent feelings played a crucial role in fueling the wave of insurgent revenge killing that exploded in the Kulen Vakuf region that summer.

What this killing also demonstrated was what could be called both "selective" and "indiscriminate" forms of violence, to use the distinction of the political scientist Stathis Kalyvas. But here both forms were practiced simultaneously.[108] The insurgents chose specific targets, such as the local Catholic priest in Krnjeuša, or the father of the local Ustaša leader in Vrtoče, whom they viewed as intimately connected to the Ustašas and as representatives of the local Croat community. They made a point of torturing, mutilating, and killing these individuals in cruel and public ways. Yet these selective acts of violence set the stage for what quickly became mass killings, in which the insurgents sought out their victims less because of their real and perceived role as Ustašas or key representatives of the community, and more because of who they understood their victims to be: "Catholic Croats." Both approaches converged toward realizing the objective of taking vengeance on the entire perceived Croat community.

Unlike the local Ustašas, who during July threw the bodies of their victims into pits or buried them in mass graves to hide the evidence of their killings, the insurgents tended to leave their victims' mutilated bodies in plain view. One of their objectives was to horrify and enrage those who later found the corpses. This is exactly what happened. When a regiment (*pukovnija*) of NDH soldiers made their way through the destroyed village of Krnjeuša a few days after the insurgent attack, they were aghast at the "heavy stench of decomposing bodies of people and animals," and the sight of mutilated and burned bodies, many of which could not be identified.[109] "No one could remain indifferent to the horrible sight," the report from the village indicated. "The soldiers could barely contain themselves from going out and killing every Serb."[110] News of these atrocities caused upper echelons within the NDH military to harshly criticize those officers "who were still in favor of merciful treatment toward the Serbs."[111]

But others who encountered such corpses, or heard about these and other killings, responded not merely with shock and criticism, but with another wave of retaliatory violence. After learning that insurgents had decapitated his father and mother in Vrtoče, the Ustaša leader in Kulen Vakuf, Miroslav Matijević, went immediately to the town's primary school where some prisoners were being held. With two other Ustašas he took nineteen of them to the nearby Serbian Orthodox Church and butchered them inside.[112] The church was a main repository of their history and community identity. In what was now becoming civil war, the intensity of the violence from both sides was ratcheting up, especially through revenge killings and corpse mutilation that were carried out in ways to be physically and symbolically destructive.

After the insurgency began, local Ustašas increased the frequency of their attacks on Orthodox villages near the town of Kulen Vakuf, such as Prkosi, Oraško Brdo, and Rajinovci, where they killed men, women, and children, and then stole vast quantities of their livestock and other property.[113] In addition, they continued to arrest Orthodox villagers in the wider region, whom they marched to Kulen Vakuf and its surrounding Muslim villages, where they killed most.[114] This wave of killing was directed at the entire Orthodox population, which was believed to be supplying the insurgents. Those villagers who still remained in their homes, most of whom were women, children, and the elderly, were easy targets. Killing them allowed the Ustašas to continue plundering, and it gave them a sense that they were fighting the insurgents, even though they were not directly engaging their guerilla opponents militarily.

The local Ustašas received official sanction to intensify their violence from the NDH's military, whose regional leadership in northwest Bosnia and Lika had launched a counter-insurgency campaign just days after the uprising began. As stated in a report written on July 29: "The army command has ordered that during operations forces should act *mercilessly* toward all those they find in this area regardless of whether they are armed or not. All military age men should be placed in front of a military court, and those who are found with arms, or wherever there is suspicion that individuals may have arms but have thrown them away, should be shot. The same goes for those, including women and children, who supply the rebels with food, weapons and ammunition."[115]

Other methods, or what the NDH military simply called "reprisals" (*represalije*), were to be implemented, including "the taking of hostages, confiscating livestock and food, and destroying settlements that are assisting rebel actions."[116] On the ground, these kinds of orders and policies could easily be interpreted as a green light to escalate patterns of Ustaša violence that had been ongoing in the region. Moreover, military orders explicitly mentioned the imperative to practice a policy of "cleansing the land" (*čišćenje zemljišta*), which for months had been understood in the localities as the euphemism for mass killing and other forms of "indiscriminate violence."[117]

As scholars of political violence have noted, these are military tactics that governments facing guerilla insurgencies have employed in many contexts, such as in Guatemala during the early 1980s.[118] The idea is to crush an insurgency not just by destroying fighters; their supporters must also be dealt with in the same way so as to remove the insurgents' base of support.[119] The result is usually a dramatic increase in the violence, especially against civilians perceived to be supporting guerilla fighters. Here, a state's military often takes an all or nothing approach to crushing an insurgency before the cost of fighting becomes too great, as the case not only of Guatemala, but also those of Algeria, Chechnya, Afghanistan, and Sri Lanka suggest to us.[120] Like the orders that the NDH military issued in late July 1941, such methods of counterinsurgency tend to be extremely brutal. Yet these tactics often quickly become counterproductive because they merely increase the violence that has usually caused a rebellion in the first place.[121]

The initial approach by the NDH military to combating the insurgency fit this pattern by sanctioning increased levels of violence against the Orthodox population. This resulted in some Ustašas, such as a group whom the NDH authorities decided to prosecute for killing unarmed Orthodox women, children and elderly in a village in Herzegovina, claiming that the killings they carried out were now legitimate reprisals taken in response to "Chetnik" killings of their relatives.[122] Quickly lost in discussions of these tit-for-tat murders was what originally triggered the insurgent violence in the first place: the Ustaša killings earlier in the summer. In short, the government's policies of a waging counter-insurgency now provided local Ustašas with a convenient pretext for more violence, which drove more men into the forests and into the ranks of the fighters resisting the NDH. None of this suggested that the insurgency would soon end.

As the violence intensified, each side used increasingly similar techniques for revenge. In the village of Krnjeuša, insurgents had burned down nearly every house, mutilated and killed the local Catholic priest, and killed hundreds of villagers. Not long after, the Ustašas returned and captured two Orthodox brothers. They took them to a nearby forest where they cut off their ears and noses, before throwing them in a vertical cave, all of which was similar to what the insurgents had done to the village's Catholic residents. And in their counterattack on the nearby village of Vrtoče, Ustašas herded Orthodox villagers, most of whom were women, children, and the elderly, into houses. They set them on fire, and watched their victims burn to death, just as the insurgents had done with the Catholic population in Krnjeuša. As for the few military age men they captured, they ripped off their mustaches and cut out their tongues, after which they demanded that the victims sing songs praising the supreme leader of the NDH, Ante Pavelić. And a child whom the Ustašas captured there met a similar fate as Josip Matijević, the father of local Ustaša leader Miroslav Matijević, whom insurgents had decapitated and whose head they placed on a stick. As an act of revenge, the Ustašas impaled the child and attached the pole to the wall of a house for the insurgents to later find.[123] This mimicking of violent techniques became a form of communication between the warring factions.

Under the leadership of Miroslav Matijević, the Ustašas tried to spread this wave of revenge-driven killing and mutilation to other nearby Orthodox villages, such as Prkosi and Rajinovci. But the insurgents launched immediate counterattacks and managed to prevent these attempted massacres.[124] Still, after the attack on Prkosi, the Ustašas managed to capture two women, Đura Zorić, age sixty, and Đuka Zorić, age sixteen. They forced them to help carry away what they stole from the village. About kilometer from Prkosi, they killed both by cutting off their heads, leaving the decapitated bodies on the road to be found later by the insurgents.[125]

These methods of execution, as opposed to the Ustašas' previous practice of mass killing and disposal of bodies in deep vertical caves, were not just employed as a means to crush the insurgency. They were also a way to graphically inform the insurgents that revenge would be taken in a brutal fashion, and it would be deeply humiliating to the fighters by mutilating the bodies of their women and children and others who remained in their villages. What was striking was the apparent way that local perpetrators learned and adopted behaviors from each other. This included not only methods of killing, but also those of corpse disposal. As one insurgent was said to have remarked after killing a group of Ustašas and at least one child: "Let's throw them in the pit over there with our [Serb] victims."[126]

Yet it would be a mistake to assume that all local Ustašas were of a single mind about enthusiastically fighting the insurgents, and taking revenge on their families and neighbors. Some Muslims and Catholics willingly joined with the Ustašas when plundering Orthodox property earlier in the summer was easy. But the outbreak of insurgency, and the fighters' brutal tactics, dampened the desire of some local Ustašas to continue participating in the ongoing violence. Once their victims began fighting back, at least twenty-five individuals considered to be local Ustašas, along with some of their families, fled from the town of Kulen Vakuf to Bihać during the first week of August. Thirteen from the village of Orašac were said to have quickly followed suit. Three male members of the Maričić family from Vrtoče, who had apparently been Ustašas during the early summer, also left their units just after the insurgency began. NDH documents suggest that the main reason they left was to look for assistance in Bihać in the fight against the insurgents.[127]

But their sudden departure in the face of the insurgent challenge sheds light on their reasons for having participated in the violence against their neighbors earlier in the summer. Once it became life threatening for them and their families to continue stealing and killing, these men quickly abandoned their role in the "cleansing operations" just as suddenly as they had decided to participate in them. This suggests strong situational roots of their violent behavior. For them, joining the Ustašas appears to have been based more on the ease through which they could momentarily benefit, rather than a deep commitment to any larger ideological objective, such as creating an ethnically pure Croatian nation state.

The departure of some local Ustašas reflected a growing distinction that some NDH leaders were attempting to make among such men, especially as the violence intensified after the outbreak of the insurgency during early August. The men who had plundered the property of Orthodox villagers and tortured and killed them in sadistic ways earlier in the summer were now increasingly referred to as "wild Ustašas" (*divlje ustaše*). They were said to not respect the authority of NDH leaders. Their violence, in the words of one official in the Derventa region, "was damaging the honor of the entire Croat nation."[128] These individuals apparently had nothing to do with "real Ustašas" (*prave ustaše*), who were considered to be national fighters for the NDH and were ready to defend the state from the insurgents. The uprising was causing an internal fissure among the NDH authorities. Among them, support for an independent Croatian state was widespread. But there were different views about the use of violence by that state, especially given the security crisis that the Ustaša killings had triggered. As one official put it:

> These crimes [against the Serb population] by irresponsible types have brought about a general feeling of insecurity to the detriment and appearance of the state authorities. The Croat people are, in essence, brave, moral, and honorable. They can understand that the enemy is killed on the battlefield, and that a person can be killed in a fight because of a moment of personal weakness. They can understand that the state authorities, through their lawful military and gendarmerie forces, use force to protect state interests. But it is far outside the moral understanding of our people to allow irresponsible elements, who do not acknowledge any recognized authority, to torture and kill those who have surrendered and asked for mercy, even those who are enemy.[129]

Whatever negative feelings may have existed among the greater population about their neighbors whom they perceived to be non-Croats, the violence of the Ustašas, and especially the response in kind by the insurgents, had now provoked serious doubts about the behavior of the Ustašas. As the NDH gendarmerie in Lika put it in mid-August report:

> Criticisms are being heard about the actions of the Ustaša organizations from all those who are serious and level-headed Croats. The organizations, through their so-called "cleansings"—i.e., killing, burning, and stealing from the population of the Greek-Eastern faith ["Serbs"]—have made it so that today, after four months of the existence of our state, conditions have not normalized, but rather are worsening each day. There is fear, and especially fear about the future, and especially the near future—i.e., tomorrow—so long as no energetic effort is taken to stop the anarchy and independent usurpation of authority by the Ustaša organizations and especially those among them known as the "wild Ustašas."[130]

The insurgents' ferocious response to the Ustaša violence, which was now affecting even so-called "level-headed Croats," provided a real reason for such fear. Each insurgent advance fueled retaliatory violence. And few on either side seemed capable of containing the spiral of killing.

The insurgent attack on the village of Boričevac illustrated the mounting difficulties. On August 2, the fighters overran this center of Ustaša activity, which was located near the pit where hundreds of Orthodox villagers had been killed earlier in the summer.[131] Many fighters had heard hair-raising stories about this deep vertical cave. So a group of them quickly left the village in search of the place where they believed many of their relatives and neighbors had been killed. A man who had escaped one of the killings there led them toward it. According to a witness, around its entrance they found several severed heads; the eyes had been poked out, and ears and noses cut off. There were pools of semi-dried blood all around, and some bodies and heads had been hung from nearby trees.[132] While contemplating this scene of horror, the group began inching toward the edge of the vertical cave. As one fighter recalled: "It was difficult to approach the pit due to the stench on the hot day. We came to the opening and yelled down, asking if anyone was alive. But no one answered. We yelled down again, saying that we had started an uprising, that we had overrun and taken over Boričevac, and that we had expelled the Ustaša evildoers [*zlikovci*] to Kulen Vakuf. Then we heard a voice: 'Brother, save me!'"[133]

The insurgents lowered an improvised rope and eventually managed to pull out two men. One was Vladimir Tankosić, who had been shot in the head, but had somehow managed to survive. The other, Mile Pilipović, had jumped in after watching the Ustaša leader Miroslav Matijević kill his son, two brothers, and three uncles. They had both managed to survive among the corpses for nine days and nights, licking the rocks to quench their thirst.[134] Exhausted, filthy, and blood-soaked, the two survivors recounted in graphic detail what they had endured. Tankosić told how he survived among the corpses for three days before Pilipović threw himself in. They explained how the pit was full of the bodies of men and women and children, and that the Ustašas even threw babies still in their cradles to their deaths. Those listening were deeply shaken. Several later noted that the experience of finding these two survivors and listening to their stories instilled in them a desire for revenge that was, as one put it, "all consuming."[135]

Several insurgents recalled that some of their commanders had given them explicit orders not to act on such feelings. They were not to set the village of Boričevac on fire nor harm its Catholic residents. "Innocent people," said these commanders, "were not to be held responsible for the crimes of the Ustašas."[136] Stevan Pilipović Maćuka was one of these would-be leaders. He made a point of giving his fighters a short speech just before they launched their attack during which he stressed that women, children, and others from the village were not guilty for what the Ustašas had done.[137] His comrade, Gojko Polovina, recalled in his memoirs that earlier revenge killings, such as the executions of the extended Ivezić family in Brotnja,

> were a serious warning about the danger of the bloody revenge of our fighters against the innocent part of the Croat population in Boričevac. . . . The danger of revenge there was even greater because it was known that a group of peasant Ustašas from that village under the command of Grco Pavičić and his wife Marija had participated in the brutal killings of Serb families in the neighboring Serbian village of Bubanj [on July 3] and that a certain number of Croats from Boričevac had participated in the plundering of property in the nearby Serbian villages.
>
> For us, the tragedy [of the killing of the Ivezić clan in Brotnja] was a warning of the danger of the wild revenge in which innocent men, women, and children were the victims, and so [prior to the attack on Boričevac] we immediately took measures under the greatest difficulties to make sure that something like that would not be repeated.[138]

Polovina claims that as he and his like-minded commanders began to plan the attack on Boričevac he sent a message to the village in which he implored its residents to flee to Kulen Vakuf. "I would not have been able to save their lives if they remained in their homes." He and the others gave the order for the attack to begin once they received word that the village was empty.[139]

However, as another local fighter recalled: "It wasn't just the leaders of the insurgency who decided such things, but also the survivors of the [Ustaša] attacks whose families and neighbors had been killed. They were looking for revenge without mercy."[140] Another insurgent noted that the desire by some to take vengeance even overpowered the appeal of plundering the village's houses and stores, many of which were full of the property that local Ustašas had stolen from Orthodox villagers during the preceding weeks. "The individuals who came to Boričevac with the intention to destroying everything that was Croat were even faster than the thieves."[141]

The desire for revenge among many surged even more after a group of fighters left the area around Boričevac and came across freshly destroyed houses in the nearby village of Kalati, which the local Ustašas had recently ransacked and burned after they had fled from Boričevac. Under the hot summer sun, the corpses of massacred women, children, and the elderly lay inside their still smoldering houses, and strewn throughout their yards and gardens.[142] The methods of torture and mutilation prior to killing were clearly visible: the bodies of women and girls showed signs of having been raped; some children were missing eyes, while others had been stabbed with pitchforks and leaned up against fences and walls around houses.[143] "What we saw there," one insurgent later wrote, "was very difficult for us, and we could barely wait to find the Ustašas."[144] This dynamic—in which a traumatic encounter with victim corpses, especially those perceived to be part of one's community, triggers a sudden rush to commit retaliatory violence—is something that scholars have noted in other contexts. As Wendy Lower has shown in her research on mass violence in Ukraine during 1941, one Ukrainian nationalist fighter recalled: "During our march, we saw with our own eyes the victims of the Jewish-Bolshevik terror, which strengthened our hatred of the Jews, and so, after that, we shot the Jews we encountered in two villages."[145] Here, what matters is not whether those targeted are actually guilty of anything, but rather how an experience with corpses can trigger revenge killings of those perceived as enemies.

After pulling the two survivors out of the pit, and then seeing the mutilated bodies in Kalati, the insurgents had no outlet for their rush to commit this kind of retaliation. The entire population of Boričevac, including the local Ustašas, had fled not long before to Kulen Vakuf. So the fighters returned to the empty village. Joining them were local Orthodox peasants, including many women, who arrived after hearing that the insurgents had overrun Boričevac. Some had come to search for their stolen property. But many more were looking for their Catholics neighbors who had killed their relatives and fellow villagers during the July 1–3 attacks on the Serbian villages of Suvaja, Bubanj, and Osredci. "The desire for revenge," as one insurgent remembered, "became wild and uncontrollable [*neobuzdana i nesavladiva*]."[146] With no one left in the village, the mob of fighters and peasants quickly set every building on fire, including the Catholic Church. Within an hour the whole village had nearly burned to the ground. While the fires raged, some of Boričevac's former residents were still fleeing to Kulen Vakuf, about ten kilometers away. A few turned around, looked toward the distant hills, and watched smoke billowing into the sky as flames consumed their homes and village.[147]

The destruction of Boričevac in early August brought several crucial dynamics into focus. First, the Ustaša violence had not only victimized the "Serb" population; now, by triggering processes of antagonistic collective categorization and the insurgency, it transformed all those perceived as "Croats"—all Catholics and Muslims—into potential victims of retaliatory violence. This dynamic suggests a broader set of micro transformations at work with regard to "ethnicity." Each wave of killing reconfigured people's

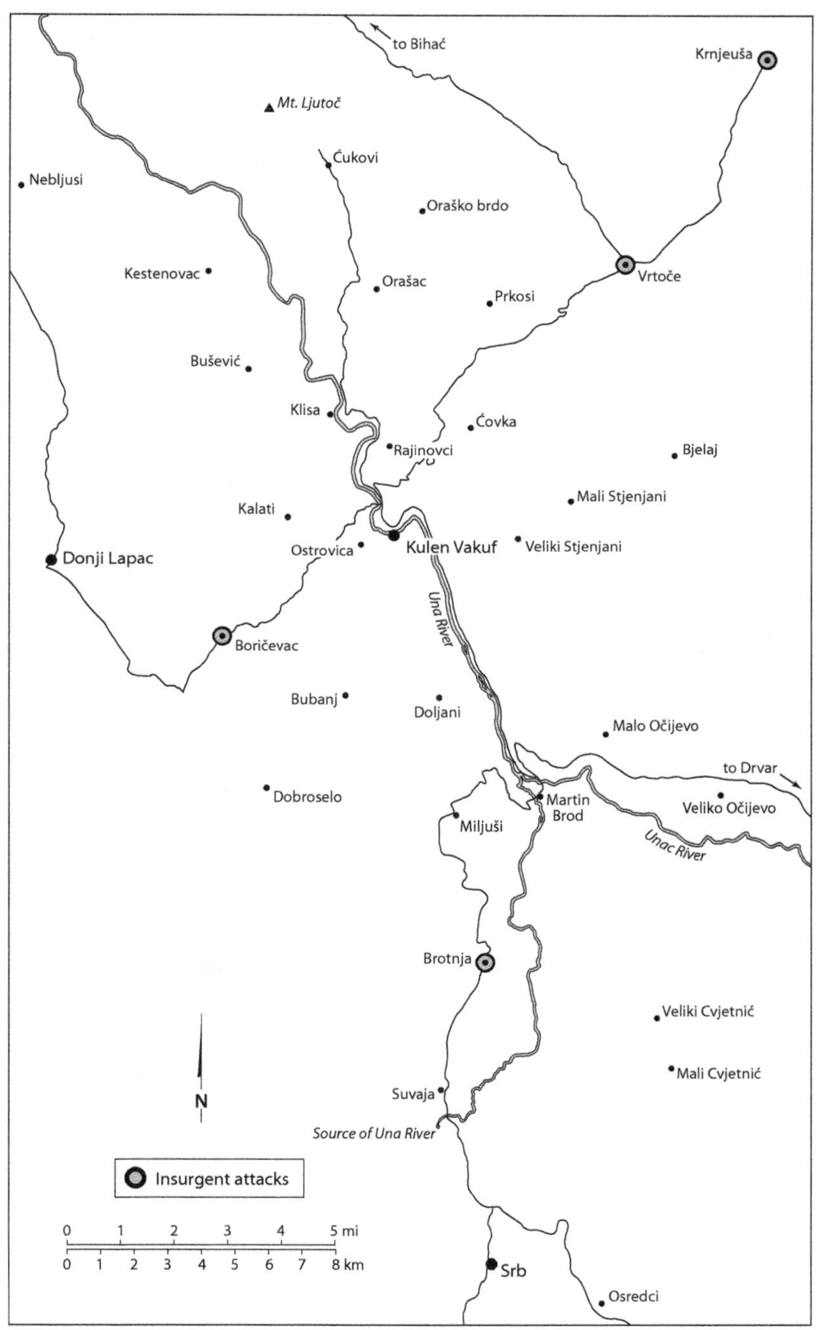

MAP 10. Insurgent attacks, late July–August 1941

self-perceptions and that of others. The initial blast of Ustaša violence was the trigger. But the insurgency, and then counter-insurgency, propelled it still further and faster. People became perpetrators and turned others into victims. Some saw themselves as victims and categorized others as enemies, including their "own" people who refused to be swept up in collective categorization. There was an element of agency in these spiraling processes, but also a dimension of powerlessness, as those committing violence possessed immense power to sweep people into categories over which they had no control. These rapidly unfolding dynamics of violence deeply affected perceptions of ethnicity. Killing on an ethnic axis made survivors conscious of their "ethnicity" in new and terrifying ways. And many now had little choice but to quickly sort their neighbors into categories of potential allies and enemies through the new salience of ethnicity, which now could determine survival or death. What emerges in the aftermath of the attack on Boričevac, as well as those on Brotnja, Vrtoče, and Krnjeuša, is the profoundly situational nature of ethnic identification of both self and others in contexts of extreme violence. On the ground in these villages, killing in large part determined the salience of "ethnicity."

Second, these attacks created a profound crisis for the would-be leaders of the insurgency who opposed collective revenge, most of whom were pre-1941 communists, or their sympathizers. The increasing frequency of traumatic encounters between their fighters and the bodies of their relatives and neighbors, as well as with survivors of Ustaša killings, had the effect of radically intensifying their desire to commit more retaliatory violence. These would-be commanders faced the enormous challenge of somehow restraining the surging tendency among many fighters to pursue the end result of antagonistic collective categorization: the complete destruction of groups of neighbors based on their perceived belonging to an ethnic category.

The insurgent commanders who opposed this revenge, such as Stevan Pilipović Maćuka, issued stern criticisms to their fighters after the attack on Boričevac. "What kind of fighters for freedom are we when we burn and steal?" he asked. "If we continue in this way, we'll become just like the Ustašas. We have to take the most severe measures to punish those who act this way."[148] Another like-minded commander, Gojko Polovina, also condemned the destruction of Boričevac in a speech he gave to a crowd of insurgents and local peasants during a gathering held in the town of Donji Lapac. According to a contemporary present that day, he denounced the chaos and plunder that ensued after the insurgents entered the village. He declared that all Croats were not guilty for the crimes of the Ustašas. And he emphasized the need for fighters of all ethnicities to join together in the fight against the Ustašas. Yet during his speech, some insurgents were noted yelling out words of opposition to his exhortations.[149] It was not clear how Polovina, and the few others like him, could change the attitudes of such individuals.

Some commanders felt that establishing an effective authority structure among the insurgents, which was largely absent in the Kulen Vakuf region, as well as in most localities nearby, was essential if their violence was to be curtailed. Toward this end, regional commanders in northwest Bosnia and Lika began issuing orders by mid-August "for a unified command," and for local units to be placed in closer contact with each other. It was hoped that this would make it possible for insurgent actions to be better coordinated, and thus increase the likelihood of them being used to achieve political objectives, such as widening the insurgency to include non-Serbs, rather than for acts of revenge against them.[150]

But frequently, the harsh reality of encountering the effects of Ustaša violence made realizing these lofty objectives difficult and frequently impossible. Graphically exemplifying this dynamic was what one of the handful of non-Serb insurgents in the region, Ivica Bodnaruk (who was nominally "Croat"), experienced after he and the fighters he was with tried to stop the Ustašas from attacking an Orthodox village. Bodnaruk was a proponent of the "brotherhood" (*bratstvo*) of all insurgents, regardless of their perceived ethnicity. Earlier on this day he had given this group of insurgents a speech about their need to fight against the Ustašas, but not to assign collective guilt to all Muslims and Croats for their crimes. When they arrived to the village they found burning houses and the bodies of several men and seven children. As Bodnaruk remembered: "The sight was horrifying. I wasn't sure that if in that moment I too wasn't ready to carry out slaughter and all other kinds of acts of revenge [on the Ustašas]. Then I heard the voice of an insurgent, who was now aiming his rifle at me: 'Does what you were saying earlier, about us not slaughtering all Muslims and Croats, now still stand?' I didn't have any idea how to answer his question."[151] Not even Bodnaruk's active commitment to the insurgency was a guarantee that he would be protected from the process of collective categorization, which surged in such traumatic moments. The mental template—that all "Croats" were guilty—formed a seemingly impermeable way of thinking in certain moments. Bodnaruk was an insurgent, and believed strongly in intercommunal collaboration among fighters. He was actively trying to inculcate this sentiment in other fighters. Yet in the eyes of some, while they stood together over the slain bodies of Orthodox villagers, he could be nothing else except a "Croat," and thus an "Ustaša."

The great challenge for insurgent leaders like Bodnaruk was to find a way to transform the now seemingly impermeable mind-set of collective categorization. Ljubo Babić, the commander of a large group of fighters based in the nearby town of Drvar (known as the "Drvar brigade"), characterized this struggle as one over establishing greater discipline among the insurgents. For him, the greatest difficulty was a chronic lack of capable Communist Party members to carry out this task, which he outlined in a report to the District Committee (Oblasni komitet) of the Communist Party for northwest Bosnia:

> As far as the state of our units is concerned: the greatest failure thus far has been the lack of discipline. We are exerting every possible effort to discipline the units. It is proceeding with great difficulty, especially in certain areas, and the main reason is the weak political consciousness of the fighters. So the most important task in front of us, and in front of the whole [Communist] Party, is the political education of the masses. But we can't carry out this task in the manner necessary because we lack a sufficient number of [Communist] Party cadres, and those we do have are not sufficiently capable. I have looked for help from all sides . . . including from the Central Committee [of the Communist Party]. I received a few people, but this is still not sufficient. The main help that you can offer us is indeed in connection with the question of cadres. In some units there are a number of Chetnik elements [Serb nationalists], which we have managed to control up to now, but difficulties are emerging.
>
> Because of these weaknesses several very difficult shocks have shaken our movement and struggle: chauvinistically inclined people have attacked innocent people in certain areas . . . and have carried out large-scale burning (such as in the village of Boričevac in Lika). This happened especially in the first moments of the insurgency; we are taking all possible measures to stop these crimes. Our success in stopping this evil will depend on the strength of our political work.[152]

Toward these ends, communist-oriented commanders organized meetings in villages under their control, during which they articulated a vision for the behavior of their units that they hoped the fighters would adopt. During one on August 10 in the village of Bastasi, located near the town of Drvar, Ljubo Babić declared to the nearly five-hundred people gathered: "Our army is not the army of the Ustašas, of thieves and robbers. It has to be based on discipline. It has to stop anarchy, stealing, and violence against the peaceful population, regardless of their religion and nationality, and it has to be worthy and capable from the beginning of establishing order based on the justice and freedom of the people."[153]

Other commanders found ways to print leaflets that they distributed in villages. "If we wish to liberate ourselves and win this struggle," read one poster, "then we cannot allow ourselves to be like the Ustašas, our struggle cannot be one for revenge." They were often specific about behaviors that needed to cease: "We cannot burn and destroy the property of Croats who have fled or surrendered . . . we cannot kill innocent men, women, and children . . . we cannot allow ourselves to kill for revenge." Attempts were made to differentiate the non-Serb population from the violence of the Ustašas: "The entire Croat people are not responsible for the slaughter of Serbs."[154] Or another: "Not every Croat is our enemy . . . there are respectable Croats who have not slaughtered Serbs, their wives, and children."[155]

Such texts also addressed the terrified non-Serb population, seeking to portray the insurgents in positive terms: "The Croat people must realize that we are not seeking revenge, but rather that we are their brothers, who are fighting for all of our freedom."[156] Other insurgent commanders issued orders to their units about the special importance of "explaining to people the need for unity and friendship with all respectable Muslims and Croats" and the imperative "to never dare allow the killing of prisoners, of those soldiers who have surrendered and who do not wish to fight against us."[157] Such calls for restraint and increased discipline were present in communist propaganda materials and internal communications in other regions, such as Herzegovina. There, as was the case in northwest Bosnia and Lika, insurgents were using violence not only for self-defense and resistance to the Ustašas, but also for taking revenge against their Muslim and Catholic neighbors.[158]

This urgency to create a centralized ideational framework for the insurgency was rooted in the bottom-up way that the uprising had begun. For the most part, it was the local peasant fighters who took the initiative to wage an armed insurgency, with the few would-be communist commanders scrambling to keep up with their activities and establish themselves as their leaders. The intensifying drive to centralize the outlook and behavior of the armed men they purported to command was rooted in their striking lack of control, which the revenge killings and destruction of whole villages vividly demonstrated. As scholars of rebellion have noted in other contexts, such as Africa and Latin America, a push toward centralizing discipline under a single authority is often a reflection of the weakness of a guerrilla movement's leadership, and the chaotic behavior of insurgents.[159] Less than a month into the insurgency, the central challenge facing communist-oriented commanders in northwest Bosnia and Lika was not how to compel local men to engage in violence and achieve military success. Rather, it was whether their desire to kill their neighbors according to their perceived ethnicity could be somehow restrained.

Chapter 5

The Challenge of Restraint

The scope and nature of the insurgents' killings suggests that a powerful desire to retaliate was their main motive, and thus should be seen as the primary cause for their violence. The locally executed Ustaša killings triggered a process of antagonistic collective categorization, and this resulted in insurgents carrying out mass killings of those whom they viewed as non-Serbs. While the revenge motive does seem like a compelling explanation, the existence of "negative cases"—that is, instances in which retaliatory killing did not occur despite previous Ustaša persecution—in the same region and during the same period should give us pause. The Ustaša violence did have its own geographical and temporal variations during the summer of 1941, which are under researched; nonetheless, it had profoundly destructive effects on most Orthodox communities in northwest Bosnia and Lika. Yet large-scale retaliatory violence, such as what occurred in some villages in the Kulen Vakuf region, did not happen everywhere.

There were instances in this same region when insurgent commanders managed to prevent or restrain this violence. During an ambush of several hundred NDH soldiers who were making their way to Kulen Vakuf, commanders stopped their fighters from executing the prisoners, even though several were brandishing knives and loudly expressing a desire "to fuck their Ustaša mothers." In the Muslim villages of Rašinovac and Bjelaj, commanders prevented revenge-seeking insurgents from joining the attacks, and when such individuals still managed to take part, they succeeded in stopping them from killing civilians and burning their property. And near the town Bosanska Dubica, located northeast of the Kulen Vakuf region, commanders managed to stop a column of nearly a thousand embittered peasants, armed mostly with axes and other farm tools, from entering the town where they intended to slaughter those whom they saw as Croats and Muslims.

How can we account for the success of restraint in these cases? What explains this striking variation in insurgent behavior in a region where Ustašas had subjected the Orthodox population to similar forms of persecution? The literature in the field of genocide studies has been focused for the most part during the past several decades on explaining the origins, causes, and macro dynamics of large-scale, usually state-directed violence against civilians. But this work has had little to say about instances in which mass violence seems likely, yet does not occur.[1] Scholarship on political violence and civil war has been much more attentive to the question of variation in levels of violence, including that against civilians, as well as the reasons for their persecution and rescue. But generally, this literature has yet to investigate the micro-dynamics of restraint.[2] In moments of rapidly escalating tension, how do insurgent leaderships succeed in answering the question—"to kill or not to kill?"—in the negative? Empirically rich and especially micro-oriented studies on this subject are hard to come by.[3] This overall lack of attention to "negative cases" is especially striking given that mass violence is a rare phenomenon; its non-occurrence or low-level intensity, despite the existence of factors that scholars have noted are central for its escalation, is actually much more common.[4] So when examining the microhistory of the Kulen Vakuf region during the summer of 1941, we are left with a macro theoretical puzzle: What explains why retaliatory violence does not always occur in contexts in which it seems over determined to take place?

Answering this question holds the promise of better illuminating not only the under-researched dynamics of restraint, but also those widely debated mechanisms that drive the escalation of violence. After all, we will be in a better position to support our hypotheses about what made violence possible in a given village if we can also account for why it did not happen in a nearby village. Identifying and analyzing these factors will be of use to scholars of genocide and political violence because they promise to tell us more about what elements must be absent or overcome for mass killing to happen. The Kulen Vakuf region, with its history during the summer of 1941 of both the explosive escalation and puzzling restraint of insurgent violence, provides an ideal site for exploring the question of what micro mechanisms make restraint possible. In doing so, we can open up new ways to better answer two fundamental, yet still perplexing questions: Why does intercommunal killing happen, or not happen, in local communities?

This investigation of the dynamics of restraint first takes us to August 19, 1941. On that day, just over two weeks after the assault on the village of Boričevac, and the subsequent encounter with the corpses of victims and survivors at the nearby pit in the village of Kalati, a column of about 250 NDH soldiers was making its way toward the embattled Ustašas in Kulen Vakuf. Less than five kilometers from their destination, in an area called Pištalska Draga, the group approached a stretch of road where hundreds of insurgents were hidden in the forest. One was Rade Obradović, who was sitting behind a machine gun watching the soldiers approach. Among them he recognized a friend named Tomo. Just a few months earlier the two had fought together in the army of the Kingdom of Yugoslavia against the invading German army. Obradović demanded that his comrades hold off their ambush so that he could approach his friend and convince him and the others to surrender. They told him that they would shoot him if he left, but he went anyway. "Whose army is this?" he asked several of the officers at the head of the column. They replied that they were not Ustašas, but rather the "Croatian Army," which was coming to establish order. They promised that there would not be any more slaughters by the Ustašas, and that the insurgents should surrender their weapons. They asked to speak with the leaders of the insurgency. Obradović returned to the forest with their message. The column waited for about a half hour to see what would happen, but no answer came. The NDH officers gave the order to move forward, but a few moments later one remembered hearing a voice from the trees yell out: "Chetniks! Let's get to work!" And then the insurgents opened fire.[5]

The shooting lasted about ten minutes, but it was enough time for a large massacre. According to insurgent sources, they shot to death 126 NDH soldiers, wounded twenty-six, and took the rest (about ninety men) prisoner; NDH sources suggest that five were killed, 181 were "missing," and twenty-six wounded. For many insurgents, the real victory was taking revenge. One fighter who participated in the ambush said later how he and his comrades had been thinking constantly about the mutilated bodies of the women, children, and elderly that they had discovered sixteen days earlier in the village of Kalati. They had been daydreaming about taking revenge ever since. With the soldiers' bodies now laid out on the road "like matches," their dream had suddenly become a reality.[6]

For some, it seems that the encounter with the corpses of their enemy gave them a feeling of satisfaction; and so their desire to kill quickly dissipated.

For others, however, the massacre compelled them to want to finish off the prisoners. An argument soon erupted between those who wished to send the prisoners on to the main insurgent command in the nearby town of Drvar, and those who wished to report to their commanders that "they had taken no prisoners," which meant they would immediately execute them.[7] Some fighters pulled out long knives while standing near the prisoners. "Give them to us and we'll take care of them," they declared. "We'll fuck their Ustaša mothers."[8] But other insurgents placed themselves in-between the prisoners and those who now wanted to kill them. "You won't be taking care of anyone," they loudly declared. The standoff continued until those who wished to protect the prisoners raised their rifles, after which the would-be executioners relented.[9]

In the end, the group prevailed that wished to send the prisoners on to a main insurgent camp in Drvar for questioning and subsequent release. Among them were those insurgents, like Rade Obradović, who did not see the NDH soldiers as "Ustašas" or other collectivities such as "Muslims" or "Croats," whom they categorized as collectively guilty for killing their relatives and neighbors. Rather, they recognized among them former comrades from the Yugoslav army, whom they felt deserved the chance to join the insurgents.[10] A similar process worked in the opposite direction: some of the prisoners recognized friends and colleagues among the insurgents, such as Dušan Vojvodić, from various facets of prewar political life. Witnesses noted that recalling these positive connections between insurgents and prisoners during these moments helped to diffuse the tense situation.[11] There were those who were aware that most NDH soldiers were not guilty of having participated in the mass killing of Orthodox villagers, whose deaths local Ustašas were overwhelmingly responsible for.[12] These were all factors that appear to have tipped the scales in favor of not killing the prisoners. In short, not all the fighters here were swept up in the process of antagonistic collective categorization.

The advocates of restraint benefitted from two other important situational factors. First, no insurgents were killed during the ambush, which meant that no vacuum in leadership suddenly opened up into which advocates of escalating violence could decisively assert themselves. Second, the insurgents did not find any corpses or survivors of previous Ustaša attacks. This further reduced the possibility of the emotional destabilization that played such a key role during some of the instances in which insurgents committed widespread revenge killings in other locations. Here, the advocates of restraint carried the day not only because of their presence and commitment to using selective violence, but also because situational factors that were largely out of their control happened to work in their favor.

This delicate and unstable balance among insurgents in favor of restraint was clear to see in another instance that occurred in the region during August. The fight against the Ustašas brought them to Rašinovac, a village in which Muslim and Orthodox residents lived, with the latter constituting the majority.[13] A refugee remembered that "local muslim Ustašas" had arrested about thirty-five Orthodox men between mid-July and early August. Most were killed later in the town of Bosanski Petrovac. The Muslim villagers who carried out the arrests, many of whom appear to have been members of several extended families, plundered nearly every Orthodox home in the village and then set about sixty-five of them on fire. Evidence suggests that the Ustašas raped several women, whom they later killed, and whose bodies they then doused with petrol and set on fire. Between forty-five and fifty women and children were also killed during the first week of the insurgency, many of whom the Ustašas burned alive inside houses.[14]

The few insurgent leaders with communist sympathies who approached the village had no intention of harming any non-Ustaša Muslim residents, or plundering and destroying their property. Most villagers did not appear to have joined Ustašas. But these insurgents had great difficulty exerting influence over the large group of fighters that was following them. Some carried rifles, some axes, while others were simply known as "the house burners" (*palikuće*), because of their previous behavior during such attacks. Many wanted revenge for killings that local Ustašas had committed, and were intent on destroying all Muslim parts of Rašinovac. Persuading them to abandon this desire was not easy. As one fighter later remembered: "There was no other way for our commander to stop people from burning houses and the mosque except to threaten them with death."[15] This stopped most, but several insurgents still had to physically intervene to stop a group of peasants who were about to burn down the village mosque. They also had to restrain a woman who wanted to burn a house where she believed an Ustaša lived. The local insurgent commander, Đuro Đurekan Pećanac, then made explicit whom he believed the insurgents were fighting against, and those whom they were not. He knocked on the door of a local Muslim man. With other fighters and peasants closely watching what he would do next, he greeted the terrified man who emerged by kissing him on his cheeks. He then told him that the insurgents were not fighting against all Muslims and Croats, but rather only against "Ustaša evildoers" (*ustaški zlikovci*).[16] In this case, no killings occurred in the village after this episode. The faction among the insurgents that sought a restrained approach to using violence, and that wished to build intercommunal alliances, prevailed.

In the most basic sense, the success in restraining violence in Rašinovac was due to the presence, numbers, and strength of insurgent commanders who believed in this strategy. Just as important, however, were those specific acts they took to protect individuals and their property, and to stop those who sought to take revenge on the entire Muslim community for crimes that individual Ustašas had committed. What was striking was the refusal by insurgent leaders to succumb to the real pressures of dehumanization, which others were attempting to bring about. Threatening to kill and physically restraining those who joined the attack from committing retaliatory violence against the whole Muslim community because of the acts of individual Ustašas; embracing a Muslim man at his doorstep, which presented him to the rest of the insurgents not as a member of an abstract "ethnic group," but as an individual—these risky acts helped to preserve the individual human qualities of those living in Rašinovac. This significantly reduced the space for this volatile situation to transform into a process of dehumanization, which could have resulted in the rapid transformation of the residents of Rašinovac into "Ustašas," thus making retaliatory violence much more likely.[17]

In other cases, these tense and unstable moments when insurgents had to choose between escalation and restraint could trigger intra-insurgent violence. At the end of June or early July in Herzegovina, where Ustaša killings had caused a rebellion that emerged more than a month earlier than the insurgency in northwest Bosnia, a group of embittered Orthodox peasants made the decision to take revenge on a neighboring Muslim village. But one local Orthodox man whose last name was Popadić demanded that they avert their plans to destroy their Muslim neighbors. In response to his protests, one of the insurgent leaders from the Kašiković clan picked up a rifle and shot him to death. The dead man's son immediately raised his rifle and killed the insurgent leader, and in process wounded another insurgent. This intra-ethnic, and most likely intra-insurgent violence, that occurred just before the attack on the Muslim village had the effect of aborting the planned retaliation.[18] This was most likely the case because the violence resulted in a draw. Had the son of the man who was shot for protesting the decision to attack the nearby Muslim village not decided to immediately avenge his father's death, those in favor of retaliation would have likely carried out their plans. Restraint or escalation thus could depend on a handful of gunshots in a given moment, and the ways that these acts of violence could rapidly sway emotions in volatile situations.

Vividly illustrating how such a momentary decision could determine whether retaliatory violence would take place, or not, is an encounter that local communist Gojko Polovina had immediately after the fall of Boričevac:

> I found myself in the middle of the village in front of the sawmill and store of the Ustaša murderers Grco Pavičić and [his wife] Marica.

> Two armed fighters [insurgents], one of whom was a distant relative of mine, came toward me with lit shingles from the roof of a peasant's house. I asked where they were going, and they answered with complete indifference: "To set [Pavičić's] sawmill and store on fire . . . so that no one ever again eats polenta from that dog's mill . . ." I drew my pistol, pointed at them, and yelled out in a threatening voice: "I forbid the burning of anything . . . I'll kill you if you do this." In response, they calmly pulled their rifles off their shoulders, and then set them on the ground in front of me. My relative then said: "Comrade commander, you can kill us with our rifles . . . but if you don't then we're going to set the mill and store on fire." I put my pistol back in my pocket. They picked up their rifles and went off to start the fire.[19]

Here, although Polovina raised his weapon and made threats, he was unprepared to take the step of shooting his own fighters, including one whom he was related to. His hesitation meant that the opportunity to prevent the insurgents' retaliatory violence was lost. The difference between escalation and restraint was thus also linked to the capacity and willingness of a would-be authority figure to risk committing violence against the fighters whom he apparently commanded.

The loss of nerve in such tense moments could have enormously destructive consequences that went far beyond the burning of property. During the August 25 insurgent attack on the village of Berkovići in Herzegovina, where local Ustašas had murdered scores of Orthodox villagers earlier in the summer, the commander Savo Belović encountered a large group of Muslim women and children. They were so terrified of what the insurgents might do to them that none could speak. Belović attempted to calm them, explaining that no one would harm them, and that they should come with him. At this moment, another group of fighters appeared, under the leadership of Vlado Radan. He approached Belović. While looking at the women and children, he yelled out: "Wait a minute, who are you? And where are you taking these Ustašas?!" He demanded that Belović hand them over so that he and his fighters could determine if they were guilty. Belović stood directly in front of the women and children and answered: "You can shoot at me, but not at innocent women and children!" Radan then shoved him out of the way. Along with his fighters, he opened fire on the group, killing them all.[20] Belović's inability to shoot first at these fellow fighters left the door open for them to take the initiative. The result was a large massacre of unarmed civilians.

A week later in the same region, a group of residents from the village of Fatnica, most of whom were elderly, women, and children, sought assistance from local insurgents to protect them from other fighters who were killing Muslims. They planned to flee to a nearby town, and reached an agreement with several local insurgents who promised to provide them with an armed escort. They set off together, with a small group of insurgents guarding perhaps as many as 400 unarmed Muslim civilians. However, along the way they were stopped by local revenge-seekers. It was clear that engaging them with force was the only way to prevent another massacre. However, according to memoir accounts, because of "their small numbers and for other reasons, they would not have been able to engage in a fight against the bandits . . . and so they abandoned the column of defenseless civilians and went home."[21] The "other reasons" appear to have been a struggle that occurred among those who had been protecting the villagers. A handful wanted to use their weapons against the men now poised to attack the column, while the majority were not prepared to open fire, nor did they wish to turn against the Muslims whom they were protecting. So instead they abandoned them.[22] Not long after, "the bandits" took all the Muslims to a pit, where they bludgeoned each and then dropped their bodies into the vertical cave. One woman survived in it for some time before being pulled out by local residents.[23]

Such an instance makes clear that failing to use force against revenge-seekers, or merely by daring them to kill other insurgents who favored a restrained approach to violence, were generally ineffective strategies. In such critical moments, the desire and capability to use physical force against fellow insurgents was critical for preventing violence against civilian non-combatants. Doing so, however, was a step that many insurgents who favored restraint seemed to struggle with greatly. The price for their hesitation and ambivalence would be paid in the lives of unarmed civilians.

The very real possibility of intra-insurgent violence breaking out over whether to take revenge on the entire non-Serb population was a dilemma that insurgent leaders faced with nearly every village they contemplated attacking. Those in favor of restraint sometimes went to sizable lengths prior to launching an operation to ascertain how their fighters might behave, and then formulated their military plans accordingly in order to prevent retaliatory killings. What happened in the predominately Muslim village of Bjelaj, located east of Kulen Vakuf, illustrates this dynamic. There were no more than three Ustašas in the village, who were Catholics from other localities. They had mobilized approximately ten to fifteen local Muslim men to defend the village. Because of their small numbers, the Ustašas had not engaged in mass killings in the village's immediate vicinity before the insurgency, but had subjected some local people to beatings, and had plundered property. Some, such as Rustan Ibrahimpašić, had participated in killings of Orthodox neighbors in other villages in the region. There appear to have been about seven villagers in Bjelaj who were sympathetic to the insurgency, most of whom had participated in Communist Party youth organizations prior to 1941. Memoirs suggest that strong traditions of intercommunal friendship existed prior to the war between villagers in Bjelaj and neighbors in nearby villages. These connections grew stronger after the establishment of the NDH and attempts by local Ustašas to persecute the Orthodox population. The villagers who supported the insurgency had been in contact with local commanders at the end of July and during the first half of August about collaborating to overthrow the Ustašas in their village.[24]

However, by mid-August, these commanders were aware of the revenge killings that had occurred in the region. Even though most of the Ustašas in Bjelaj had not engaged in mass violence, others in the immediate region had destroyed the families and homes of many of the fighters who were now preparing to attack the village. The process of collective categorization, whereby people in the region who happened to be nominally Muslim or Catholic were transformed into "Ustašas," was widespread among many local insurgents because, as one commander later recalled, "the Ustaša killings of the Orthodox had been done in the name of Catholics and Muslims." As such, insurgent commanders knew that "preventing a slaughter of the muslim population [in Bjelaj] by fanatical elements had to be accomplished at all costs."[25]

To realize this objective, they decided that those who would carry out the attack had to be "sympathizers of the [Communist] Party and those who had already been directly involved with the Party's work." As dusk fell one evening, the commanders held a meeting in a village not far from Bjelaj; 400–500 people attended. A handful had rifles, but many more stood with axes, pitchforks, and other farm tools that they were using as weapons. The commanders explained that plans were being made to attack Bjelaj, and that local Muslim youth there who were affiliated with the communists would provide assistance from within the village. They declared that no one was to harm the Muslim population. There was immediate disagreement, hesitation, and doubt among those in the crowd. Some argued that help would not come from the village, and that the supposed assistance waiting for them from the Muslim youth was a trap. Several communist-oriented commanders argued that a distinction had to be made between the Ustašas and the rest of the Muslim and Croat population. They recalled the work of several Muslims in Bjelaj with the communist movement prior to and during 1941. But the majority of the crowd remained unmoved by these arguments, and so the tension grew. As one commander recalled: "The meeting showed [us] that it would be difficult to quickly change the attitude of the mass of people, and that this was dangerous because it would be impossible to control so many people and succeed in getting them to behave appropriately." So the commanders decided to select a much smaller group of insurgents to carry out the attack, whom they believed would not be inclined to take revenge. They received help from local Muslim residents in Bjelaj who did not support the Ustašas, and who were aware of the efforts that the insurgent commanders were making to "eliminate hatred" among their fighters. Together, they disarmed the local Ustašas. As one commander recalled after the war: "There was not a single instance of violence during the liberation of Bjelaj."[26]

It was possible to avoid retaliatory violence in this case because insurgent commanders understood the specific ways that the Ustaša violence had affected the mental outlook of their fighters. They were also aware of their own weaknesses. "The Ustašas," one recalled, "who were recruited from the Croat and Muslim population, committed atrocities against the Serb population in the name of Croats and Muslims. This provoked hatred . . . , and the mass participation [of Serbs] in the insurgency, along with the lack of party cadres, threatened to give the fight the character of a fratricidal war."[27] Because they lacked sufficient numbers and authority, and because they were propagating a vision of restrained, selective violence that many insurgents did not accept, these commanders took special measures to prevent intercommunal killing. Before launching any attack, they assessed the mood of their fighters during the meeting. They concluded that revenge killings were likely and so they developed a new strategy of sending fewer, but more politically reliable fighters to Bjelaj. They also forged an alliance with some of the village's Muslims, which was based on the previous existence of intercommunal activism in Communist Party youth organizations. As one insurgent remembered, this strategy made it possible "for the Muslims [in Bjelaj] to wait for the insurgents in their homes," and for "the insurgents to show their honor and demonstrate that they were not revenge-seekers."[28] This not only helped to prevent violence, it also created a basis for future intercommunal cooperation. It was possible that embittered insurgents might make Bjelaj into another site for mass revenge. But the local insurgent leaders' understanding of the dynamics of collective categorization; an awareness of their own limitations; their efforts to assess the mood of the fighters; the existence of a tradition of intercommunal activism; and the decision to change their strategy of attack—these factors helped make restraint the order of the day.

Farther away to the northeast, examining the insurgency in and around the town of Bosanska Dubica further illuminates the micro-dynamics of successfully exercising restraint. As was the case in the Kulen Vakuf region, a relatively small number of Muslims and Catholics joined the Ustašas after the sudden change in government in April. Memoir accounts suggest that some of these men had prewar criminal histories, and took advantage of the new situation to steal.[29] While some appear to have come from outside the region, local witnesses reported that others were "our neighbors."[30] Persecution of those considered to be Serbs appears to have begun already in May with restrictions placed on their movement, resettlement of key community figures such as Orthodox priests, forced labor of men, plunder of private property, beatings, and selective killings. It appears that these repressive measures increased in intensity during July, and were followed at the end of that month with the transfer and subsequent killing of about 110 men.[31]

In the predominately Orthodox villages that surrounded the town, feelings of terror and fear were dominant because nearly every man who ventured to town never returned. In these villages, there were incidents of Ustašas raping Orthodox women who remained in their homes. For many, it had become commonplace to live part of the time in their villages, and the other part in the nearby forests, to which they would flee whenever word would spread of Ustašas on patrol in the vicinity.[32] As was the case in many other local communities in northwest Bosnia, these dynamics of persecution set in motion rapid, antagonistic collective categorization because, as one witness recalled, "the people saw that, in general, it was the Serb population that was persecuted, while muslims and Croats still had some rights."[33] In short, the nature of Ustaša violence established a mental template in which it was over determined that revenge, if it came, would likely unfold along an ethnic axis.

Yet what was striking in the Bosanska Dubica region was that retaliatory killing along ethnic lines did not occur once the insurgency began at the end of July. Instead, commanders made the decision to restrain their fighters once they took up arms and began massing on the town of Bosanska Dubica, and managed to succeed in accomplishing this objective. The question is how? Part of the answer can be found in the specific social and political conditions in the town and its immediate region in the years prior to the war. Unlike many other areas in Bosnia, such as the Kulen Vakuf region, the Bosanska Dubica region had an active, local workers' movement, which had its nucleus in the sawmills along the Una River, whose origins dated to the 1920s. This organization provided the basis for the growth of a regional, underground Communist Party. Its activists also included students and teachers. Like the workers, they came from all ethnic backgrounds. In the years immediately prior the war, these groups deepened their bonds by participating in strike activities, sports organizations, and through collecting funds to assist unemployed workers. There was, therefore, a decades-long history in the region of intercommunal socialization, political activism, and mutual aid among a part of the population.[34]

The establishment of the NDH did not destroy these social and political networks. On the contrary, under the leadership of prominent communist activists, such as Boško Šiljegović, they deepened. This happened through the creation of more formal Communist Party structures whose main objective was to determine how to successfully resist the NDH.[35] Local communists in the town of Bosanska Dubica—the vast majority of whom were young Muslims and Catholics—along with their Orthodox counterparts in the nearby villages, attempted to establish local leadership structures, discussed plans for armed resistance, and held meetings during which they attempted to mobilize support for their cause.[36] Accounts from those expelled from Bihać in June, and who ended up Bosanska Dubica as refugees by July, attest to the atmosphere of intercommunal cooperation among some in the town. "We want to mention," said three teenage students, "that the majority of the muslim population in Bosanska Dubica behaved very well toward Serbs during our time there [July 1941–June 1942]. Some local Croats also behaved just as well." These individuals gave the refugees money and food. Some received beatings from local Ustašas for having done so, while others were killed.[37]

Nonetheless, those in favor of intercommunal solidarity faced sizable obstacles. In his memoirs, local communist Boško Šiljegović acknowledged that the Ustaša violence "was not without success" in engendering hatred among many Orthodox villagers toward their Muslim and Catholic neighbors. As plans for an armed uprising became more concrete, he and his comrades were aware that "there existed great and serious danger that an insurgency would begin as a struggle of Serbs against Muslims and Croats, and that it would begin with bloodshed and a settling of scores."[38]

On July 30, insurgents under the command of men such as Šiljegović quickly overran several NDH posts in the villages near Bosanska Dubica. They were joined by a steadily increasing number of local peasants who heard the shooting, as well as the church bells ringing in the nearby Orthodox villages, which signaled to them that an uprising had begun. Their numbers quickly swelled to nearly a thousand, and they began chasing the survivors of the attacks as they fled to the town. The idea suddenly crystalized among some in the crowd that they would "take Dubica." If successful, the town's fall to the insurgents would almost certainly be followed by the "settling of scores" along an ethnic axis, which local communists feared. But they were not prepared to simply stand by and watch this happen. As Šiljegović recalled:

> However understandable and "heroic," the thought [of taking Dubica] had to be rejected and stopped, even at the price of one's life. In fact, an attack on Dubica would not only have been unorganized. It would have been even worse because this would have given various chauvinists and other similar types the opportunity to "drink from the cup of revenge as much as they wanted" [*napiju osvete do mile volje*] and "to return what was taken from them" [*povrate ono što im je oteto*]. Because of this, the party leadership made the decision to stop the column that was on its way to town. The majority of the peasants accepted this decision, or better said, they accepted this order from the communists. Aside from the grumbling of individuals and groups, the whole column stopped. One part remained in the villages by the road, while another part went home.[39]

Here, several long- and short-term factors made restraint possible. A multi-ethnic workers' organization, and later, underground Communist Party, existed in the region since the 1920s. Its members were active before the war, and had worked hard to create organizational structures after the establishment of the NDH through which they endeavored to spread the message that they would lead an armed uprising. This enabled the communists to establish their embryonic authority among a sizable section of the population in the Orthodox villages. Even though the Ustaša violence had unfolded along an ethnic axis, the communists here had not succumbed to collective categorization of Muslims and Catholics as enemies. When speaking of the Ustašas, local communists called them "not only the enemy of us Serbs, but also the enemy of every honorable Croat and Muslim in the world."[40] In letters that they sent to their non-Serb neighbors, they were emphatic about this: "We are raising our fists against the source of the evil that had befallen us, and this is not you, Croats, but rather . . . [Ante] Pavelić and his dogs, the fascist Ustašas."[41] This message was also what they preached to their peasant fighters, and they made efforts to mobilize non-Serbs to join them.[42] In short, the existence of a multi-ethnic group of politically active communists; their organizational work in 1941 and commitment to launching an armed uprising; their establishment of a certain level of authority in the Serbian villages; and their belief that one's guilt depended on one's actions, not ethnic background—these were the factors that help us account for why most of the armed peasants on their way to

Bosanska Dubica stopped when the communists told them to. When this order came, it is likely a majority perceived it as coming from a legitimate authority.

This is not to say that the fighters who sought revenge were suddenly freed from the process of antagonistic collective categorization that the Ustaša violence had triggered and fueled. Rather, the work of the communists, and the limited authority they established because of it, combined with their willingness to risk intervening in a moment of great tension, was just enough to dissuade most from following through with their desire for retaliatory violence. This was a moment of profound contingency, the specific dynamics of which allowed the communists to momentarily realize their delicate agenda of "waging military actions and avoiding bloody revenge against the Muslim and Croat population in towns and villages."[43]

Recalling the period when these successful instances of restraint took place in northwest Bosnia and Lika, one of the region's communist-oriented commanders noted: "The question arose as to whether the [Communist] Party needed to put the brakes on the insurgency, and to ensure that its development went hand-in-hand with the development of cadres. We decided that it was not necessary."[44] The gamble was that they could continue to enforce restraint and the selective use of violence, even though they were few in number, and those who favored escalation and retaliatory killing were far from marginalized. What this microanalysis makes clear is that a cluster of factors would be necessary for this gamble to pay off. First, the restraint advocates needed to be on the ground with their fighters, and ready to intervene at any moment; their disappearance or death could make the difference between restraint and mass killing. Second, their task of avoiding revenge killing was much easier when their fighters were not suddenly destabilized through the discovery of the mutilated corpses of their relatives and neighbors. Third, commanders needed to find ways to counteract the processes of antagonistic collective categorization and dehumanization. Fourth, an awareness of the limitations of their authority was crucial, as was a willingness to quickly adjust military strategy accordingly. Finally, the existence of strong intercommunal organizational activity—both before the establishment of the NDH and especially during the summer of 1941—was crucial to acquiring embryonic authority and legitimacy among their fighters.

In a region where mass killing had rapidly become a feature of daily life, these factors made it possible in certain instances to save lives rather than violently end them. Teasing them out helps us explain why the strong desire for revenge—which was present in most villages where the Orthodox community was subjected to Ustaša persecution—did not automatically lead to retaliatory killing in all locations where insurgents launched attacks. If that was a key factor for escalation of violence in Brotnja, Vrtoče, Krnjeuša, and Boričevac, then these killings were also contingent on the absence of the advocates of restraint that we see present in the cases of Pištalska Draga, Rašinovac, Bjelaj, and Bosanka Dubica.

One might be inclined to take a less situational approach in accounting for the escalation or restraint of violence by examining the longer-term political history of the Kulen Vakuf region. One method could be to analyze interwar voting patterns to discern regional variations in social solidarity and division, an approach that several political scientists have recently employed in various contexts with illuminating results.[45] The successful intervention in Bosanska Dubica, as well as events in Bjelaj, does indeed suggest that prewar communist organizational activities played an important role in helping insurgent leaders establish an embryonic level of authority. However, analysis of prewar voting behavior in the wider Kulen Vakuf region does not suggest clear linkages to wartime behavior. In the 1920s, local residents often voted for the political parties that claimed to speak on behalf of "nations" and religious groups, aside from during the years of royal dictatorship from 1929 until 1934 when such parties were effectively banned. This finding varies little at the level of municipality and village. The Communist Party was outlawed from competing in elections in 1921 (as well as from that point forward), and its underground membership in northwest Bosnia and Lika was small, especially in the countryside. In the Kulen Vakuf region, the election results in some villages suggest that significant intra-ethnic splits existed (among Orthodox and Muslim residents, for example), but more qualitative, micro-level research would be needed to determine whether these intra-communal voting differences were of significance with regard to local intercommunal relations and, if so, how. In short, prewar voting patterns do not suggest along which regional variations violence, or the restraint of it, would unfold if it did break out—or that violence was likely to occur at all.[46]

Instead, what emerges from a "thick description" of killing and restraint in the Kulen Vakuf region during the summer of 1941 is the need to better appreciate the power of violence itself as a generative force in radically shaping the limits and possibilities for human behavior.[47] The establishment of the NDH suddenly empowered opportunists and a few extremists to plunder and kill on an ethnic axis. This violence triggered a rapid process of antagonistic collective categorization, whereby many former neighbors suddenly viewed one another as dehumanized parts of abstract collectivities. Brutal retaliation by insurgents, and an equally brutal counterinsurgency by the NDH authorities, resulted in waves of cascading group-selective violence, which further intensified intercommunal polarization. Yet these revenge killings were also what provided the main impetus for restraint. Communist-oriented commanders and their sympathizers quickly realized that the initial success of the insurgency would mean nothing if the fighters whom they attempted to command continued to kill all "Croats." Because of the counterproductive nature of insurgent retaliatory violence, these commanders and their followers increasingly sought to make restraint a central part of their military strategy wherever their numbers, authority, and luck allowed them to do so.

What created a context in which restraint would be possible were some longer-term factors, such as decades-long political activities of the small number of local communists and their sympathizers. This helped to forge a group of individuals who shared a common ideational framework in which restraint of violence on an ethnic axis was of crucial importance. It also created a small, embryonic network of intercommunal connections based on solidarity and reciprocal assistance, which rapidly took on greater importance after the establishment of the NDH, and its accompanying policies of persecution. While these factors helped make restraint a possible avenue of action, it was certainly not a necessary result given the cascading intercommunal violence, which polarized local life and made escalation of retaliatory killings more likely.

Of decisive importance were situational factors and a capacity to take risky decisions within the new context of civil war. The presence of a commander during a military action, or his sudden absence; the willingness to risk kissing the cheeks of a terrified Muslim man in front of one's revenge-seeking fighters, or instead issuing the order to kill him; the recognition in captured NDH soldiers of former comrades from the former Yugoslav army, or a decision "to take no prisoners"; the refusal to allow vengeance-driven fighters to take part in attacks, or the handing over to them of defenseless civilian prisoners; threatening revenge-seekers with death who managed to join attacks, or refusing to use force against them and then walking away—all of these momentary decisions and actions comprised the mechanisms of successful restraint, or could open the door for the sudden escalation of violence. When the former were in greater concentration, killing tended not to happen. Reference to prewar structural factors, such as political cleavages based on pre-conflict voting patterns, may help less than we might expect in explaining such moments. This is because the dynamics of violence and events on the ground could quickly assume a much greater level of importance. Key advocates of restraint could be killed or called away, with the result being the explosion of violence. Ideational frameworks and organizational networks in favor of restraint were crucial; yet they meant nothing if those who believed in such ideas and participated in such organizations could not—for whatever reason—take decisive action in moments of great tension and risk. From an analytical perspective, what emerges is a need to pay greater attention to endogenous dynamics of conflict, and to be cautious of explaining the ebb and flow of violence—or restraint of it—primarily through analysis of pre-conflict macro-cleavages, ideologies, and political processes.[48]

By identifying and analyzing the factors and processes that lead to restraint, we can then better understand the overarching dynamics that cause and drive violence. Perhaps most important, one's momentary disposition in favor of killing—such as a strong desire for revenge—emerges as an insufficient factor to explain why violence escalates in a given instance. Rather, a host of situational factors—from the incitement to killing by leaders to the unexpected discovery of corpses, from processes of dehumanization to the sudden absence of advocates of restraint—must coalesce in a particular moment for this disposition to be transformed into violent action. The insurgent violence in the Kulen Vakuf region during the summer of 1941 shows us that powerful dispositions in favor of escalating violence are contingent on the absence of advocates of restraint, which can still be successful even in moments when the point of no return seems terrifyingly close.

Perhaps surprisingly, this push during August to restrain the region's spiraling violence was not limited to a fraction among the insurgents. It also appeared among a part of the NDH authorities, although for different reasons, particularly among some within the NDH military. This created a split between some in the army, who wished to contain the cascading violence and establish order, and many of the local Ustašas, who wanted to intensify their killing, expulsion, and plunder of the Orthodox population, particularly after the uprising began. The impetus toward restraint can be seen in a frank assessment of the situation in northwest Bosnia that a Lieutenant Colonel named Stjepan Najberger wrote less than a week into the insurgency:

> If one believes that the evacuation [of the Orthodox population] will be accomplished by first sending the Serbs to concentration camps, then a very long time and enormous military forces will be needed to gather up these peasants, who under no circumstances will allow themselves to be taken away without resistance. And that resistance will be so great that our losses will be incomparably larger to anything we have thus far experienced. Because of this, a different solution to this problem needs to be found.

> I recommend the following: First, send reasonable people to villages, and not blood thirsty murderers. Second, guarantee the security of the [Orthodox] peasants in their villages and protect them from any interference from unauthorized members of different organizations [i.e., the Ustašas] who would take peasants away from the [NDH] military and send them to the political authorities to have them transferred to concentration camps, cut into pieces, their eyes gouged out, their limps hacked off, or thrown into the water to drown. The Serbs who have remained in the villages are aware that all this is happening, and so it is completely understandable that they are defending their lives at any price.[49]

Lt. Col. Najberger concluded that "cleansing the terrain," a euphemism that the NDH military used to refer to mass killings, expulsions, and the burning of houses, would do nothing but further fuel the insurgency. For him, the only viable option would be to "withdraw all blood thirsty murderers [i.e., Ustašas] from the field."[50]

Implementing such recommendations, even if a strong desire existed to do so, would be neither simple nor easy. We can return to the town of Bosanska Dubica to appreciate the difficulties that men like Lt. Col. Najberger faced in containing the violence among "their people." In the days following the outbreak of the insurgency, a large group of fighters began closing in on the town. A contingent of NDH soldiers was sent to help the local Ustašas in their defense. Local NDH leaders and Ustašas requested permission from the army to burn and kill everything that was "Vlah" (a derogatory word for "Serb"). Military commanders told them not to touch a single house or hurt any local Serb resident. With the insurgents just outside the town, an NDH military commander began to hear shooting. But he quickly determined that it was not coming from insurgents, but rather from local Ustašas who had on their own volition decided to attack several nearby Orthodox villages. They killed everyone they found, including a sizable number of women. This set the stage for the mass plunder of these houses. Joining the Ustašas were local Muslims, who stole everything that they could carry, including doors and windows. Fights broke out among them over who would take what. The Ustašas discovered in some homes several hundred liters of homemade brandy, which they proceeded to drink throughout the night, often firing their guns into the air while doing so. This caused the army units to believe that the insurgents were once again launching an attack. On August 1, the main NDH military commander in Bosanska Dubica issued a second order prohibiting the burning of Serbian houses and the killing of Serb civilians. According to an NDH military report that a first lieutenant wrote, one local

Ustaša commander indicated that, "he didn't have to listen to my orders if it meant that he wasn't allowed to do whatever he wanted." Many of the other Ustašas, who apparently wanted only to steal, and burn, and kill, now simply abandoned the town rather than assist the army in its fight again the insurgents.[51]

This struggle between regional NDH army commanders and local Ustašas who were intent on intensifying "cleansing operations" continued unabated in northwest Bosnia during the beginning of August, and even worsened in some localities. In the towns of Bosanski Novi and Bosanska Krupa, Commander Lt. Col. Najberger took several large groups of Orthodox villagers prisoner as a strategy to contain and stop the insurgency. He declared that if the insurgents ceased their attacks, then he would release all of them in a day's time. This tactic worked in Bosanski Novi. But local Ustašas derailed Najberger's plans in Bosanska Krupa. He awoke the day after taking the prisoners into custody to see their bodies floating down the Una River; local Ustašas had slaughtered them during the night. Rather than contain or stop the insurgency, the fear was now that the disturbing sight of the corpses in the river would set off insurgent revenge killings. NDH army commanders were incensed: "The Ustaša system of radical cleansing is not only failing to stop the insurgency, but is actually provoking more resistance, especially in those areas where things are already most difficult for the army."[52] For them, total control over all military operations needed to be given immediately to the army. "For now," the commanders insisted, "all [Ustaša] cleansing actions must be stopped."[53]

The conflict between the NDH military and the Ustašas was not just rooted in the deteriorating security situation and the cascading violence; it was also connected to wider self-perceptions about what each party saw as its role. "The relationship of the army and the Ustaša organizations has turned negative," a military commander in the Gospić region remarked in mid-August, "because the army feels that a nation cannot become cultured through the 'cleansings' of Serbs in the way that the Ustašas are carrying them out. The Ustaša organizations, however, are of the opinion that their work is correct and that the army's actions are a form of sabotage, which instead work in favor of Yugoslavism and Serbdom."[54] Another concluded: "The Ustašas have pulled out, but are offended and have criticisms. They maintain that everyone who is of the Greek-Eastern faith [i.e., Serb], and who is alive and walking, should be killed, and they now believe that if they do not carry out the so-called 'cleansing,' then the state will collapse. In fact, it is this position, and especially their stealing, which have led in large part to this Chetnik action, that is, the rebellion."[55] This perception that the Ustašas were guilty of causing the insurgency, which the army now needed to devote all of its resources to putting down, was increasingly widespread among NDH soldiers and had already started to emerge with the June uprising in Herzegovina.[56]

More and more, it appeared to some in the NDH military that the key to stopping the insurgency lay in establishing control over the local Ustašas. Yet army commanders worried that the ongoing violence, especially the tit-for-tat killings among the warring factions that were fueling what appeared to be endless cycles of retaliation, would not easily be de-escalated. As an NDH general in the field in Herzegovina put it: "I personally believe that establishing order will be very difficult. Local residents, regardless of their religion and nationality, are equally shocked. They are trying to protect themselves from the burning, stealing, disorder, and arbitrariness that are occurring. Inside everyone has arisen a desire for revenge that is being carried from one generation to the next."[57]

By the first week of August, the rapidly deteriorating security situation, fueled by the interactive effects of Ustaša and insurgent violence, helped to compel the highest military and political authorities in the NDH to order the de-escalation of violence among the Ustašas. With directives from supreme leader Ante Pavelić and the NDH's supreme gendarmerie command (*vrhovno oružničko zapovjedništvo*), it was ordered that "local Ustaša organizations immediately cease every action" and that those "formations that have come from Zagreb and other locations are also to cease every cleansing action." Indirectly acknowledging that many Ustaša units had been essentially operating outside of any authority except their own, they were now permitted to engage only in the protection of their own territory and "only at the request of the district leader [*kotarski predstojnik*] for the purpose that he determines."[58] By August 12, another order was issued to "remove all armed Ustašas from the field." Once again demonstrating that the NDH government had, in fact, empowered such units, which had previously enjoyed wide authority in their localities, the order announced: "the Ustašas will no longer hold executive authority" because "the Poglavnik [Ante Pavelić] no longer allows the use of Ustaša units in the field or in decision making."[59] Pavelić himself appears to have begun issuing orders during the second half of August to "stop all plunder, self-will, and violence, and whoever commits such acts, whether it's the *Domobrani* [NDH soldiers], the Ustašas, or the population, will be sent to stand trial." His threats against his own supposed armed units continued: "I warn all Croats who have armed themselves without authorization and who enter other people's villages, that they will be considered as thieves, and that the harshest measures will be taken against them."[60]

This striking retreat from mass violence was an attempt to exert control over the Ustašas, whose violence had triggered the insurgency. It did not, however, suggest a major ideological retreat among the NDH elite with regard to solving the "Serb question." Rather, these orders represented an acknowledgement of the uprising's success, and in particular how the insurgent violence was rapidly destabilizing the NDH. This was a sea change in tactics from the initial strategy of employing harsh counterinsurgency methods to crush the rebellion. The NDH leadership was now trying to defuse support for the insurgents by creating an environment in which the Orthodox population would have security and could soon return home, which would hopefully stop the insurgency from spreading.[61] Like their communist-oriented insurgent opponents, some of the NDH authorities were realizing that restraint—not violent escalation—was now a preferable strategy, at least during this time of crisis.

Yet implementing directives for de-escalation and the establishment of law and order was not easy. Calls by some in the NDH military to encourage Serbs to return to their homes were met with mixed reactions from local and regional police commanders who saw such a policy as fraught with difficulties. As one in northwest Bosnia put it on August 21:

> It is very unpleasant that the military authorities are allowing the Greek-Eastern peasants, who are returning from the forests without weapons, to be permitted to immediately enter their villages. There are not enough [police] forces available—or in most cases, any forces at all—to keep an eye on the movements and actions of the Vlah [i.e., Serb] population. It has happened that some have turned themselves in without weapons, gone home, and then the next day are killed with rifles in their hands. These types carry food and bring livestock to their people in the forest, and in that way bring significant harm to our army. They spy on the numbers and positions of our soldiers, which they inform the Chetnik commanders about. It would therefore be necessary to throw the returnees into concentration camps, and make their movement impossible until our main military operations have concluded.[62]

With the insurgency still very much in full force, initial attempts at de-escalation thus quickly created unexpected problems for NDH officials in the localities, where it was often difficult, if not impossible, to distinguish returnees from fighters.

In other cases, orders to allow Orthodox villagers to return home and to ensure their subsequent safety fell on deaf ears because local Ustašas had their own ideas about how the returnees should be dealt with. As one military commander reported with dismay from Herzegovina in mid-August: "They [Serbs] were called by [NDH military] officers for discussions, and were told to return to their homes. They were told that no one would do anything to them, that they were free to work in their fields, and that they didn't need to be afraid of anyone. But every time after this they were attacked, with the elderly, women, and children seized, and then killed or thrown into pits."[63] Ensuring the safety of the returnees was made difficult by the fact that in many localities, the NDH's civil and military authorities remained fearful of the local Ustašas. As one gendarme described it: "I—like all the gendarmes, in general—was completely powerless. Everything was done [by the Ustašas] without our knowledge and with great mistrust toward us. If I were to say anything to the Ustašas, even something insignificant, I would endanger my life."[64] Many Catholic and Muslim residents shared these sentiments, and demanded protection, as exemplified by a letter that a group of terrified Catholic villagers sent to the regional NDH authorities in late August: "Where we reside the government has lost its head—all citizens are at the mercy of irresponsible people (i.e., the Ustašas), who have been given weapons and are doing whatever they want. . . . Save our souls, if you have the strength, while it is still not too late."[65]

Yet it was not clear who could intervene to dislodge the Ustašas from what was frequently their stranglehold on power at the local level. The NDH military was aware of this, as can be seen in its assessment of the political situation in mid-August: "The relationship between the Ustaša organization and the civil authorities is not normal. This is because the Ustaša organization has taken all power and authority, and has even impinged on the authority of the courts. Today, one does not feel that there exists any authority except the Ustaša organization because all other forms of authority are not functioning."[66]

These dynamics were also present in the town of Kulen Vakuf, the main NDH stronghold in the region. During the second half of August, the military commander stationed there, Captain Vladimir Veber, received orders from his superiors in Bosanski Petrovac to stop the local Ustašas from killing Serb prisoners whom they had captured and were holding in the school. Yet several days after he issued the orders, he received a letter from the mother of a young female prisoner in which she indicated that the Ustašas were continuing to come to the school every night with flashlights. They chose their victims, killed them, and dumped their bodies in nearby canals. Witnesses have suggested that Capt. Veber continued to challenge the authority of the local Ustašas, led by Miroslav Matijević, but was also increasingly afraid that they would kill him.[67]

So in the Kulen Vakuf region, the orders from the highest authorities in the NDH for the immediate de-escalation of violence against the Orthodox community had little to no effect. Promises of ensuring the safety of the returnees were impossible to fulfill because almost no one was powerful enough to enforce them. Even many Catholics and Muslims felt endangered from the Ustašas. Civil and military leaders frequently held their positions only in name. Particularly in the countryside and smaller towns, authority still remained largely in the hands of the Ustašas. For this situation to change, it would have to be wrestled from them through force.

These difficulties that NDH political and military leaders experienced in instituting policies of de-escalation and restraint have wider implications for the study of mass violence. Some scholars have suggested that top-down macro factors, such as the capacity of powerful leaders and states to create and institute violent policies, are among the most important in explaining why mass violence happens.[68] Yet when examining these attempts by the NDH authorities to exercise restraint over the violence that they unleashed several months earlier, one sees leaders and a state stymied by weaknesses. If the power of state authority is so crucial to explaining the causes of mass violence, then how can the same authority prove so incapable of stopping the violence that it unleashes?

By analyzing the under-researched dynamics of restraint, particularly at the local level, we see that while a certain amount of power is necessary to initiate mass violence, perhaps even more is needed to de-escalate, especially in a context of civil war. What appears to have emerged in the Kulen Vakuf region, along with many other parts of the NDH, is a dynamic in which those who were suddenly empowered to commit acts of violence—that is, the Ustašas—quickly amassed a striking degree of power and authority through the process of engaging in violence. They did not usurp this power from other NDH authorities; rather, they created it through their acts of killing, torture, and plunder. This suggests a need to conceptualize violence not just as a destructive force, but also as a highly generative one that can quickly establish new sources and configurations of power, sometimes even to the detriment of a state authority ideologically committed to policies of persecution.

Our analysis of restraint on the NDH side reveals that the Ustašas' capacity to use violence endangered the authority of the state, whose non-Ustaša representatives did not have the numbers and authority to dislodge them from power, particularly at the local level. In this weak state, what emerged was the unexpected imperative of using force against one's own violent factions in order to institute restraint. Like their opponents—the insurgents—NDH military leaders seemed to be unwilling to attack the most violent faction on their own side—the Ustašas—in order to accomplish this objective. And so the violence continued to spiral in the localities, with every round of killing further destabilizing the NDH. Examining the difficulties of instituting restraint on the NDH side thus reveals a striking paradox: the state's central authorities actually created the very forces of violence in the localities that were now contributing to their creators' rapid undoing.

During late August, in the aftermath of the insurgent attacks and massacres in the region's Catholic villages of Brotnja, Vrtoče, Krnjeuša, and Boričevac, and the ambush of the column of NDH soldiers at Pištalska Draga, the NDH authorities in Kulen Vakuf realized they were in great danger. About 500 people had been killed during these attacks. During the preceding month, the insurgents had forced their opponents to flee from their command posts in Donji Lapac and Boričevac. Several thousand Catholic villagers followed them. All sought refuge in Kulen Vakuf, which was now the last remaining NDH stronghold in the region.[69] With the encirclement of the town tightening day-by-day through a non-stop siege, the NDH authorities there knew that if the insurgents launched a major attack, they would be unable to hold their position, as well as defend the local Muslim population in several nearby villages.

The insurgents had amassed a considerable amount of weapons and ammunition after their attacks on the Catholic villages during the preceding weeks. They were now nearly a thousand armed men, which was many times more than their opponents in the region. They had encircled this part of the Una River valley, which meant that neither supplies nor reinforcements could easily reach the Ustašas, NDH military, and Catholic and Muslim civilian population in the Kulen Vakuf region.[70] The evidence suggests that only one shipment of about 200 rifles managed to reach the town of Kulen Vakuf in mid-August, where about 100–150 men were defending the town. While the arrival of the weapons increased morale, it also fueled tension. Some local residents, suffering due to shortages, promptly used them to attack nearby Orthodox villages to steal wheat and other sources of food. Witnesses reported that Muslim and Catholic refugees were taking horses to nearby Orthodox villages, such as Prkosi, and returning with sacks of wheat, livestock, and household items stolen from Orthodox houses. While such actions may have been rooted more in hunger than a desire to persecute their neighbors, the forays increased animosity among the Orthodox villagers and insurgents in the forests.

A report by an NDH official who managed to visit Kulen Vakuf on August 12 reflected the unrelenting tension in the region, noting that scores of unburied bodies littered the area surrounding the town. It is likely that these were corpses of Orthodox villagers murdered by local Ustašas, although some may have been of Catholics and Muslims who had ventured into Orthodox villages to steal.[71] By the end of the month, according to the regional NDH authorities, the town was "completely cut off."[72] The various insurgents groups in the surrounding hills had organized themselves by their respective home villages. Thus, they were largely composed of men who had survived, or escaped from, horrific acts of violence that the local Ustašas had committed earlier in the summer.[73] They cut all the telegraph lines in the region, which meant that no one in Kulen Vakuf could easily communicate with the regional NDH authorities to request assistance, as well as to receive intelligence reports about insurgent movements in the wider area.[74] The insurgents' increasing proximity to the region's Muslim villages during late August can be appreciated through the recollection of a child who lived in the village of Ćukovi: "Every chicken can be seen from these hills [around our village]. Whenever any of us would move they [the insurgents] would shoot. They would throw stones at us from the hills and would yell out that they were sending us 'packages.'"[75]

By the last days of August, the local Ustašas and NDH soldiers in Kulen Vakuf were, in the words of a regional military commander, "exhausted due to the constant fighting, bad weather, illness, poor equipment" and especially the non-stop insurgent encirclement that had now lasted for more than thirty days.[76] The regional NDH military command wrote to its superiors in Zagreb that food shortages were growing worse. Muslim and Catholic refugees continued to flood the town. Dysentery was becoming widespread and typhus was breaking out.[77] The situation, in the words of one regional official, had become "hopeless."[78] Others made equally bleak and pessimistic assessments: "Kulen Vakuf is in the greatest danger."[79] And from another: "The worst could happen at any moment."[80]

The nature of the insurgent violence during the previous month had left many NDH military commanders in an untenable position. Their army units and the local Catholic and Muslim population were encircled and under siege. Reports from the region make clear that they understood what was likely to happen if the insurgents overran their positions: "If it is not possible to deal with the communist-Chetnik bands [the insurgents], then what's coming is slaughter, killing, burning—the taking of revenge—on the unarmed Croat population."[81] This was not mere speculation; when the municipality of Berkovići in Herzegovina fell to the insurgents on August 25, what immediately followed was the killing of about 450 Muslim civilians—including women and children—along with a handful of the local NDH authorities.[82]

With no possibility of sending reinforcements, more than a few commanders were coming to the conclusion that, as one in the Gospić region put it, "it was better to withdraw everyone from these places because the Chetniks are going to kill them all." Some were remarkably candid in their internal reports about the root cause for this potential fate of their soldiers and the civilian population: "It should be mentioned that today's situation in this command's territory is a reaction of what our people have done, i.e., now the Chetniks and the rest of the population of the Greek-Eastern faith are taking revenge against Croats for the injustice done and the killings committed of their dearest."[83] The situation was identical in the Kulen Vakuf region.

On August 23, the entire population—nearly 2,700 people—of the Catholic village of Boričevac, which had fled to Kulen Vakuf at the end of July, was sent on foot and in horse-drawn carts to Bihać. Insurgents appear not to have been aware of their movements until late in the day. They eventually attacked part of the column along the way, managing to kill four and wound eight. With the refugees came a report from Capt. Veber, the embattled NDH military commander in Kulen Vakuf. "There are still thousands of Muslim refugees in Kulen Vakuf [from the nearby villages] and there is fear that an eventual breakthrough of the Chetniks [into the town] will result in a huge, catastrophic slaughter of the entire population."[84] In addition to these fears, Veber expressed concern about the potential political consequences of a possible massacre of so many Muslim civilians. While revenge killings had already taken place in northwest Bosnia, as well as in Herzegovina, the number of potential victims in the Kulen Vakuf region—over 5,000 civilians—dwarfed anything that had occurred so far.[85] Veber voiced specific concern that any mass slaughter "would have especially painful reverberations in circles of Muslims throughout all of Bosnia." The evidence suggests that the NDH authorities in Bihać agreed with this assessment.[86]

An enormous massacre of Muslim civilians would graphically demonstrate that the NDH government and military was incapable of protecting the lives of its Muslim citizens. This would likely lead to an erosion of their support for the state, which would be a major blow to the government given that only by claiming that Muslims were "Croats of the Islamic faith" was it able to purport to govern on behalf of a (slim) majority of the population. Mass killing of Muslim civilians needed to be avoided at all costs. The potentially destabilizing political effects of a large-scale loss in Muslim lives was yet another reason that abandoning the NDH position in Kulen Vakuf and evacuating the Muslim population to safety was becoming the only tenable option.

The insurgents provided the trigger that transformed this option into reality. On September 4, fighters with the communist-oriented commander

Stevan Pilipović Maćuka descended from the hills surrounding village of Ćukovi and began a furious assault. The handful of Ustašas there fled shortly after the first shots were heard.[87] But the village's approximately fifteen armed residents refused to surrender. They yelled out of the windows of their houses: "We're not Ustašas! Ćukovi has never surrendered, no one has ever conquered the village, and you won't either!"[88] A fierce battle ensued. The villagers fired at the insurgents from their windows for much of the afternoon. As the communist commander Gojko Polovina later recalled: "Our fighters were not able to take a single one of their houses without first setting it on fire. Only when they saw that it was burning would they leave the house and go to the next, which they would not leave until it too began to burn."[89] After about five hours of fighting, the insurgents had set nearly every house in the village on fire. It was only then that Ćukovi's defenders fled south to the neighboring village of Orašac.[90]

What then happened illustrates the difficulties that advocates of restraint, such as commander Stevan Pilipović Maćuka, faced in such moments. Munira Dedić had remained in Ćukovi with her three sons while the battle raged. As one of the last homes burst into flames, she finally decided to flee with her children to Orašac. Not far outside of Ćukovi several insurgents caught up to them. Without hesitation, they murdered all four on the spot. Two more women from Ćukovi had fled just before Munira and her children. The insurgents could see them just ahead and quickly chased them down. Once again, they executed their prisoners on the spot. Hadžera Lipovača, who had fled even earlier, was doing everything she could to escape, but running with her five children meant she could move only slowly. Yet again the insurgents caught up. But by this time the communist-oriented fighter Stevo Ovuka had managed to join them. He jumped in between the insurgents and Hadžera and her children. He raised his weapon toward his fellow fighters and prevented them from committing another set of killings.[91] In such moments, the only way for the advocates of restraint to succeed was to be on the ground and be ready—without hesitation—to intervene with physical force against their opponents (on their own side) who favored violent escalation.

The terrified residents of Ćukovi came streaming into the village of Orašac over the course of the evening. "The Chetniks are coming!" they called out to their neighbors. "And they are slaughtering everyone!"[92] News of the attack on Ćukovi, and the killing of women and children, spread like wildfire throughout Orašac, filling its residents with panic. They quickly gathered as many of their belongings as they could and raced with the refugees from Ćukovi to the edge of the Una River. On the other side was the village of Klisa. They yelled across to their neighbors that the Chetniks were coming to kill them. For the rest of the evening, and throughout much of the night, the residents of Klisa rowed small boats back and forth across the river's frigid waters, shuttling their neighbors to temporary safety.[93]

While this rescue effort unfolded, the insurgents arrived to the recently abandoned village of Orašac. Rather than push on toward Kulen Vakuf to attack the region's main center of Ustaša power, a large number of them suddenly stopped. Now they turned their attention to plundering whatever was left in the Muslim houses.[94] After ransacking the village, they set all structures on fire, and were assisted by some local Orthodox peasants who had descended from the hills, including women.[95] According to NDH military reports, Ćukovi and Orašac were "completely destroyed," and the families who did not escape "have been slaughtered." With the insurgent noose tighter than ever on this part of the Una River valley, the region's NDH military leaders concluded that it was impossible to send help to their embattled counterparts in Kulen Vakuf.[96] The scene that an insurgent would later describe of Klisa—the last village destroyed on September 5—applied equally to Ćukovi and Orašac: "It was a complete wasteland. There were only ruins, without life or people. The Una River flowed in silence through the gentle cornfields, as if it had almost come to a stop in this lifeless place, where the scent of things rotting and burning was still strong. Not even the clay and wicker foundations of the Muslim houses remained standing."[97]

As smoke from burning homes in Ćukovi and Orašac billowed into the sky, the villages' former residents began making their way from Klisa to Kulen Vakuf, two kilometers away. As they set out, cornfields lined the left side of the road. They climbed a short hill and descended toward the Una, arriving at Kulen Vakuf's gendarmerie station, which stood above the river's rushing waters. Here was a fork in the road. Some may have turned right, and followed a road along the railroad lines built by local men during the late 1930s. They would have eventually passed by Kulen Vakuf's primary school, where during the previous months Orthodox villagers had been held prisoner, tortured, and often killed. Others may have turned left at the fork, crossing the bridge spanning the Una at the small gorge called the *buk*. They would have passed by the house and tavern of Ustaša leader Miroslav Matijević, and after another kilometer or so would have arrived at the second larger bridge. There, they would have turned right and crossed toward the center of Kulen Vakuf, where the mosque's white minaret could be seen directly ahead, reaching for the sky.

Regardless of which route they took, the town was their final stop; there was nowhere else left in valley to go. The vast majority arrived by around 4:00 p.m. on September 5—slightly more than twenty-four hours after the

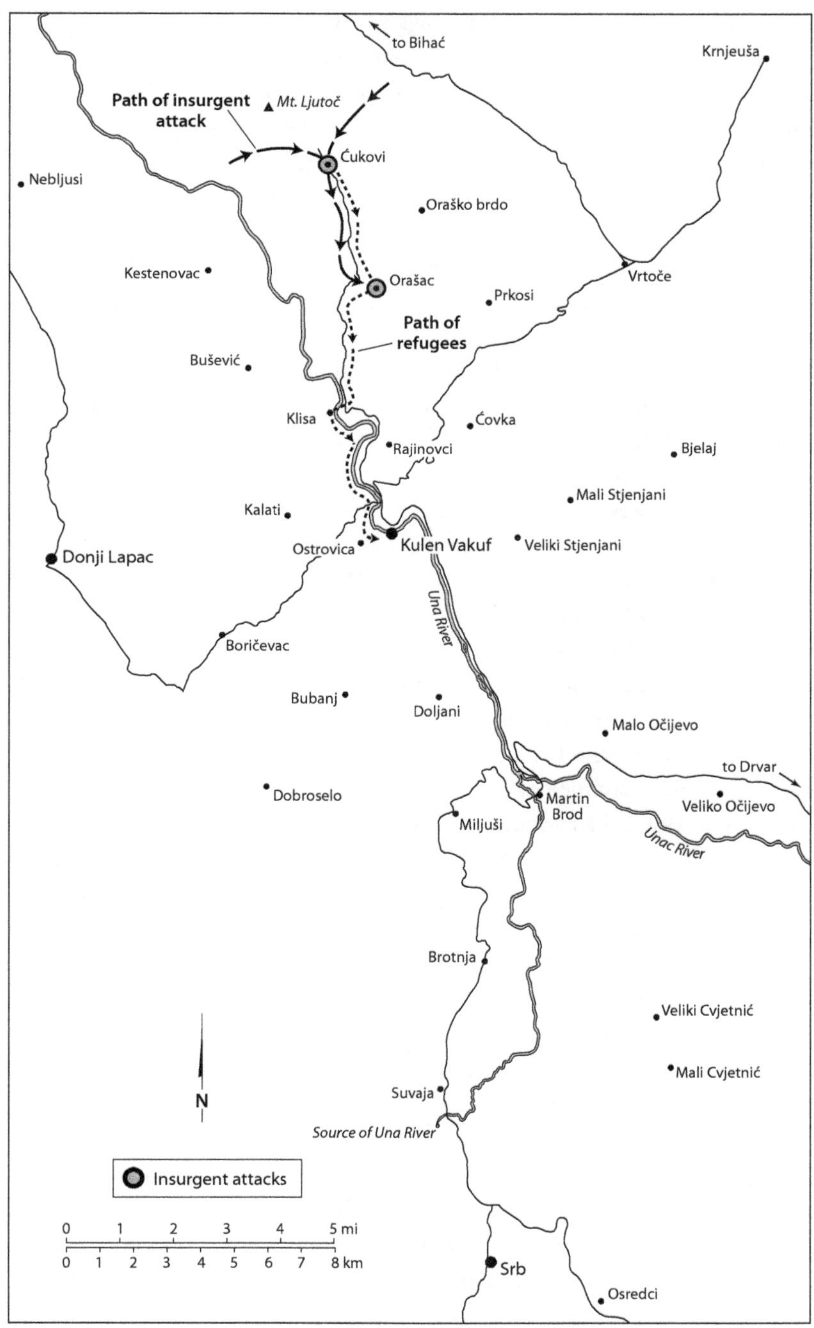

MAP 11. Insurgent attacks on Ćukovi and Orašac, September 4–5, 1941

attack on Ćukovi began. The town was by now bursting with refugees. Nearly 3,700 refugees joined Kulen Vakuf's population of about 2,000. The town's population had almost tripled in the space of a single day. The thousands of exhausted newcomers found whatever space they could for their few belongings and whatever livestock they had managed to bring with them.[98]

By early evening, Capt. Veber summoned all the men to Kulen Vakuf's main square located next to the mosque. He now revealed his plan for saving their lives and those of their families. On the next day, September 6, everyone was to assemble at dawn. In order to avoid "complete destruction," they would depart together and travel to the city of Bihać, approximately fifty kilometers away. Everyone was ordered to leave; there were to be no exceptions.[99] Only three men intended to disobey Veber's order: Esad Bibanović, his brother Ibrahim, and Džafer Demirović, all of whom comprised the town's small, underground cohort of communists. They intended to wait for the arrival of the insurgents—whom they had yet to meet—so they could finally join them in what they hoped would be their collective struggle against "fascism."[100]

Capt. Veber planned to take a route to Bihać that led through the village of Vrtoče, which had already been a site of insurgent killing and mutilations in early August. Because of his lack of communication with the regional authorities, he had no idea that the insurgents had overrun this village again on September 1, after cutting off food supplies to the NDH soldiers stationed there. The NDH military reported that the insurgent attack "was so violent that no resistance was possible, and that the two companies had to withdraw to Bosanski Petrovac during which seven officers and 120 soldiers went missing."[101] Many of the rest fled in such panic and haste that they arrived to Bosanski Petrovac without their coats and walking barefoot.[102] The insurgents had not only liberated another village from their enemies; their victory also gave them machine guns, rifles, and a large amount of ammunition that the NDH soldiers had left behind.[103] Capt. Veber and his soldiers, along with the remaining Ustašas, and the rest of the region's non-Serb civilian population—nearly 5,600 people—were now unwittingly poised to escape from the Una River valley by travelling through Vrtoče. They were heading straight toward their enemies.

As night fell on September 5, Kulen Vakuf's residents and the thousands of refugees packed up their remaining belongings. Adults spoke quietly among themselves about the coming day. The children were scared and nervous. One young boy named Abas Mušeta, whose father Mehmed "Meho" had been recognized by a survivor of one of the killings in July as an Ustaša, pondered his grandmother's recent advice. If the "Vlahs" (a derogatory word for "Serbs") attacked them, she said, the best way for him to save himself would be to jump into the frigid waters of the Una River. He was to make his way to one of the small islands near the confluence of that river with the Ostrovica. According to the old woman, none of their Orthodox neighbors would able to harm him there because none apparently knew how to swim.[104]

High in the hills surrounding Kulen Vakuf on that evening were a handful of men who understood that they now stood at a crossroads. As those in the valley readied themselves for the next day's journey to Bihać, the local communist commander, Gojko Polovina, wrote an urgent letter to his superiors in the Party: "The situation in this region," his first sentence began, "is very serious." In his view, the main problem was the way in which the cascading intercommunal violence of the previous weeks was transforming the insurgency: "The painful reality is that each day our struggle becomes more and more a vicious fratricidal war between Serbs, on one side, and Croats [and Muslims], on the other. All of our actions and struggles will fall into dust and ashes [*pašće u prah i pepeo*], and we will all become victims of the occupiers, if we don't succeed in transforming this fratricidal war into a struggle against our collective enemy: the occupiers and their collaborators."[105]

Polovina's admission of the great difficulty in bringing about this transformation reflected the concerns of other key communist insurgent leaders in the wider region, such as Marko Orešković-Krntija.[106] He also realized that gaining control over the fighters, and especially stamping out the desire of many for revenge on whole ethnic groups, was a central challenge, perhaps as much or even more so than mobilizing men to fight. In a remarkable document that he wrote in early September called "The role and tasks of Partisan units (*Uloga i zadaci partizanskih odreda*), he minced no words about the urgency of the tasks ahead. As a major clash between the insurgents and the whole non-Serb population of the Kulen Vakuf region seemed imminent, he forcefully discussed the imperative to establish greater discipline among the fighters (whom he now referred to as "Partisans" [*partizani*]), to cease their retaliatory violence against innocent civilians, and to transform them into a fighting force for the liberation of all people:

> The tasks and difficulties before us demand that we unconditionally create a level of exemplary discipline, without which all of our actions are impossible, to not even speak about us achieving success! We will mention several examples that took a bitter revenge on us because of the lack of discipline. The burning of Boričevac—this was not only a huge material loss to us, but it could be easily said that the real damage we suffered was moral. The town of Kulen Vakuf has held out for so

> long because the people there are terrified of suffering the same fate as Boričevac . . .
>
> The town of Glamoč [located southeast of Kulen Vakuf] was cleansed by the Ustašas, but instead of pursuing the enemy until its destruction our Partisans stopped and turned their attention to getting drunk. This allowed the enemy to regroup its forces and then push our Partisans out of Glamoč. Let's also take the example from Čorci. There, Croat peasants voluntarily handed their weapons over to the Partisans and waited for them as brothers and expected brotherly understanding. But instead they encountered irresponsible elements in our ranks who later went through the village with their guns and terrorized these peaceful peasants and women. Because of the danger that this posed to their lives, they left the village and fled into the forests to once again seek weapons from the Ustašas to protect themselves. There have been instances in which elements from our forces have carried out violence against women, and there have instances in which they have slaughtered women, children and everyone else whom they found in a house. It is not necessary to explain the consequences of this kind of behavior. In such cases we are no different than the Ustaša hordes, even though we took up arms to win an honorable and free life for all respectable Serbs, Croats, Slovenes, Muslims, and others. All of this is the result of the lack of discipline and necessary responsibility that stands in front of us. The members of the Partisan units must be conscious that they are NATIONAL LIBERATION FIGHTERS. Theirs is an army of the people, and they must always be ready to fight against every injustice, against every instance of violence, and for the freedom of the entire people.
>
> In a word, if we don't create discipline (self-conscious and voluntary discipline), the danger exists that our struggle will transform into the most horrible violence and thievery. That is something that none of us wants, that is, that we will carry on the work of our most hated enemies—the Ustašas. To avoid that, we need discipline. And I say once again: discipline.[107]

Insurgent commanders in northwest Bosnia and Lika, such as Polovina and Orešković-Krntija, were not the only ones who faced this challenge of creating discipline among their fighters and restraining their violence. In Herzegovina, others had been struggling with the same problems for at least a month, and even longer. There, fear of enormous retaliatory violence by insurgents for the Ustaša killings earlier in the summer led some commanders to take the radical step of evacuating Muslim civilians from certain villages where they believed mass killings were likely to occur, and where they knew they had neither the manpower nor influence to control local, revenge-seeking fighters. In a report written on or about September 8, they described their situation in stark terms: "Here it is absolutely impossible to avoid a slaughter [by the insurgents of the local population] on the basis of religion, since the Ustašas have committed horrendous violence . . . and our influence is very weak. For the moment we are going to avoid all military actions until we can strengthen discipline in the army, and until we can politically prepare the masses so that the fighting in Herzegovina will not end up unfolding along anti-Muslim lines."[108]

Closer to the Kulen Vakuf region, in other parts of northwest Bosnia, the capacity to exercise restraint by avoiding military actions and engaging in political work was precarious, and in some cases insurgent commanders were unable to prevent retaliatory violence. On August 12, commanders in the vicinity of the town of Sanski Most wrote a blunt assessment about their limitations: "Our influence in that region is very weak, and because of this there have been battles with the Ustašas and [NDH] army, as well as an entire massacre, which have taken place on a completely Chetnik line. The insurgents have killed Muslim and Croat peasants, and even their families—women and children."[109]

As the sun set behind the hills surrounding Kulen Vakuf on the evening of September 5, the local advocates of restraint, such as Gojko Polovina, Đoko Jovanić, Stevan Pilipović Maćuka, and Stojan Matić, faced these challenges and dilemmas. Thousands of largely unarmed civilians whom many of the insurgents saw antagonistically as "Croats"—and thus as "Ustašas"—were poised to travel the next morning into their path. In the likely event of a battle, all the insurgents would need to decide what kind of struggle they wanted to wage. Would it continue to cascade, as Polovina feared, into an ever more "vicious fratricidal war" of neighbors against neighbors, with fates decided by one's association with an ethnicity? Or could it be redirected into a multi-ethnic liberation struggle, in which neighbors joined together to resist foreign occupiers and their local proxies, as communists like Polovina and others so desperately wanted?

There were several reasons to suggest that the first option might prevail. The amount of intercommunal killing during the previous two months was enormous, and so the desire for revenge was strong among most local insurgents. The advocates of restraint were few in number, and had little influence over many of the embittered fighters in the forests. There was no time to engage in the kind of political work that some felt would be necessary to transform the consciousness of those seeking to avenge the brutal deaths of their relatives and neighbors. And there were few intercommunal links left given the town's position as both a center in the region of Ustaša power and a site of mass killing. Men like Polovina sensed these dynamics. "We were avoiding the final attack [on Kulen Vakuf]," he recalled, "because under such circumstances the innocent Muslim population would perish in huge numbers."[110]

Like the other outnumbered advocates of restraint in the region, Polovina attempted to find a way to avoid a violent confrontation that he knew he would most likely not be able to control. Through residents in the village of Demirovo Brdo, he sent a message to Capt. Veber in Kulen Vakuf. He implored him to surrender the town's weapons and hand over the Ustašas. Veber's reply was to demand that the Ustašas, NDH soldiers, and civilian population be allowed to leave with their weapons. The empty town would then be handed over to the insurgents. Polovina answered that without handing over the Ustašas, he would be unable to protect anyone who would attempt to reach Bihać. So Veber asked Polovina to send a list of the Ustašas whom the insurgents wanted. "We sent a list of about sixty Ustaša-murderers, whom we wanted to be handed over," Polovina recalled. "But we received no answer to that request."[111] Capt. Veber would have most likely lost his life had he tried to hand over men like local Ustaša strongman Miroslav Matijević, or some of the others who had killed scores of Orthodox villagers since the beginning of July. Neither he nor Polovina could find a way to defuse the coming confrontation.

As night slowly turned to dawn on the morning of September 6, the stage was thus set for a dual showdown. It was a near certainty that a major clash was going to take place later in the day between the NDH forces (and the civilians associated with them), and the insurgents in the forests. But an equally crucial battle would be between those insurgents—the advocates of escalation and those of restraint. To kill or not to kill? Whichever was to prevail would determine the fate of thousands of people in the coming hours.

CHAPTER 6

Forty-Eight Hours

The sun rose on the morning of September 6 into an intensely blue, cloudless sky. Shortly after daybreak, the residents of Kulen Vakuf, along with the newly arrived refugees, set free most of their livestock into the nearby meadows. Many unleashed their dogs, which began wandering around town. At around 6:30 a.m., Capt. Veber gave the order to begin the trek to Bihać. A column of nearly 5,600 people began making its way up the small hill leading toward Klisa, Orašac, and Ćukovi, villages where the remains of most of the houses and mosques were still smoldering from being burned the previous two days. Men drove at least ninety horse-drawn carts packed with clothing, food, and possessions. The women sat next to them or in back while holding babies at their chests and the hands of older children. The elderly and sick lay in back. Many more, especially the refugees from Ćukovi, Orašac, and Klisa had no choice but to walk. A cloud of fine dust arose and hung in the air along the road. The forests lining the narrow road were silent. Testimonies suggest that sadness and especially fear were the dominant feelings among most of those in the column.[1]

The atmosphere on this September 6 contrasted strikingly with what took place in Kulen Vakuf on the same date just three years earlier—in 1938. That day was the annual birthday celebration of Yugoslavia's king, Petar II. The two leaders of the municipality, Adem Kulenović and Vlado Milanović, gave short speeches about the importance of the King and his dynasty, which were followed by applause from a large crowd of townspeople and their neighbors from the region's villages. Adem Kulenović was known as a moderate politician, and for his thorny relations with fellow Muslims. Vlado Milanović was the son of Father Vukosav Milanović, the local Orthodox priest who had intervened decisively in 1918 to stop fellow Orthodox villagers from attacking the Muslim population in Kulen Vakuf during the period of agrarian reform.[2] Now, three years later, local Ustašas such as Miroslav Matijević and Husein Zelić—the tavern owner and the notoriously unsuccessful merchant who had existed on the margins of society—had removed Adem Kulenović from his position. And, with their like-minded associates, they killed Vlado Milanović, his older brother Vojo, and their father Vukosav.[3] They were just three among the hundreds who perished in the many instances of nightly torture and killing in the town during July and August, with victims buried in mass graves near the school and Orthodox Church, or dumped into the darkness of the Boričevac pit. Along with them, many of the town's advocates of moderation had been silenced and destroyed during this short period, in which some of their neighbors seized upon sudden, unexpected opportunities to use violence to take over—and create—positions of power.

These local Ustašas were at the head of the long column of people as they climbed up the hill leading out of Kulen Vakuf. Those who glanced left could still see the gurgling, emerald green waters of the Una River shimmering in the morning sunlight. Not far from town, the column turned right, and began climbing along a winding road that led through the village of Ćojluk toward the well-known spring on the road called Milota from which pure, icy water gushed. It was located near the villages of Ćovka and Prkosi, which from Kulen Vakuf were about two hours away up the road. After climbing up the switchbacks through the dense forest to this point, the trip would be easier along the grassy plateau, which would lead them to Vrtoče. Capt. Veber promised that lunch would be waiting for them in that village.[4] There, they would rest and eat in the same place where the Ustaša Miroslav Matijević was born, and where in early August insurgents had decapitated his parents, placed their heads on sticks, and killed many of their Catholic neighbors.

Shortly after the column departed, the three young communists who had chosen to defy Capt. Veber's orders to abandon Kulen Vakuf—the brothers Esad and Ibrahim Bibanović, along with their friend Džafer Demirović—walked to the center of town. They managed to open a shop, where they searched for a large piece of red cloth. This was to be the flag they intended to fly in order to show the insurgents in the hills that now only fellow communists remained in Kulen Vakuf. They were excited and impatient to meet their comrades and join them in the fight against fascism. They cut the material into a large rectangle and then set off through the town's empty streets and abandoned homes toward the mosque. The three entered the building and climbed the steep spiral staircase of the white minaret until they emerged into the sunlight at the top. They unfurled the flag into the breeze. Kulen Vakuf was now in communist hands, they thought. Waiting for the insurgents to arrive, they stared out at the hills as the sun beamed down.[5]

As the column climbed slowly out of the Una River valley, and the three young communists waited at the top of the mosque with their flag, insurgents in the forests would soon need to decide how to treat both groups when they made contact. Restraint or escalation of violence? The analysis here thus far of the challenge of restraint suggests that powerful dispositions in favor of escalating violence are in fact highly contingent on the absence of advocates of restraint, which can still be successful even when the point of no return seems very close. Yet their absence is not the only factor required; as some of the evidence has shown, both forces can be at play simultaneously in a given situation. What is missing from the analysis thus far is an exploration of a critical question that can help us better account for the often-bewildering ebb and flow of local violence: In a direct clash between the advocates of escalation and restraint, how does one overcome the other?

Framing the analysis in this way can help us restore a necessary level of contingency to our examination of the causes of local violence. When we know that a large massacre took place in a given location, a strong tendency exists to retroactively explain it as almost inevitable because of macro factors, such as long-term polarized political conditions, supposedly deep "ethnic" cleavages, utopian ideologies of cleansing, extremist political leaders, or even a supposedly widespread desire for revenge among perpetrators. While these factors may frequently be necessary causes of violence, they cannot be seen as sufficient because they do not tell us why killing occurs when and where it does—or does not. Relying on such factors can blind us to carefully analyzing how advocates of escalation actually manage to overcome those of restraint on the ground, or vice versa. Yet examining this generally local-level clash in greater detail is exactly what can help us better illuminate and theorize the path toward violence—and non-violence—in more productive ways. It is through analyzing the interaction of these forces, and especially what causes one to fail and the other to gain strength and seize the initiative, that we can better identify what transforms a context conducive to violence into actual killing—or prevents it from happening. We can undertake the challenge of teasing apart this inter-dependent relationship between the advocates of escalation and restraint by following the column as it climbed the switchbacks leading from Kulen Vakuf toward Vrtoče, unwittingly on its way toward contact with the insurgents.

Witnesses in the column recall that their first indication they were not alone on that winding dirt road was the popping sound of isolated gunshots after about two hours of travel. They were heard with increasing frequency as the column approached Milota, the spring on the right side of the road near the footpath that led toward the village of Ćovka, home of insurgent commander Nikola Karanović. Whizzing over their heads, and occasionally splintering the wood of their carts, it quickly became clear that the shots were being aimed at them.[6] It appears that insurgents from Ćovka, nominally under Karanović's command, as well as others under the authority of Stevan Pilipović Maćuka, were taken by surprise that the entire population from this part of the Una River valley was now on the road fleeing the region. A number of fighters grabbed their weapons and scrambled to the thick woods that lined the road, and began firing. One witness account based on insurgent testimonies, noted that during this shooting "no differentiation was made among the muslim population."[7] Another confirmed this description: "From the nearby hills, the insurgents shot at everything that moved."[8]

It appears that most of the armed men from Kulen Vakuf—the Ustašas, Veber's contingent of NDH soldiers, and a number of other men with rifles—were positioned near the head of the column. When the shooting began they returned fire, which ignited a fierce battle. This firefight seems to have engulfed about the first third of the column. As the shooting intensified, scores of civilians were killed in the crossfire. The forces in the column fought relentlessly, and eventually managed to break through the hastily improvised insurgent ambush after several hours. Pressing on toward Vrtoče, they managed to bring with them about 3,100 of the refugees.[9]

Left behind in the chaos were nearly 2,500 others. Some were stranded on the section of road between the Milota spring and the fork in the road that led to the village of Prkosi. Others had made it a kilometer or so farther, where the right side of the road was lined with a thick forest, while the left opened up to large meadows, with no place to take cover. Men tried to drive their carts forward, but their horses were nervous and unsteady because of the gunshots; women tried to protect their terrified children; the elderly could barely move. It was in these areas that a vast massacre began. More and more insurgents arrived, who hid in the forests lining the road. They trained their weapons on the civilians now trapped on the road and opened fire. Bodies fell in all directions. People were killed as they ran for cover. Most were forced to leave their dead and injured relatives and neighbors behind.

Children were separated from their parents.[10] Witnesses recall small children sitting on the side of the road next to their dead or dying mothers, screaming and crying, but unable to move while bullets flew near their heads. In other instances, babies shrieked while still somehow being held by their now lifeless mothers.[11] In the midst of the fire of rifles and machine guns, some of the children could hear insurgents yelling: "Fuck your Turkish mothers!"[12]

The scene along this approximately two-kilometer stretch of dirt road quickly filled with carnage.[13] Mujo Dervišević, from the village of Klisa, had been at the rear of the column when it left Kulen Vakuf. He recalled what he saw when he arrived at the place of the killings: "For an entire kilometer I saw only dead bodies on the road . . . you could barely find a place to step where there were no bodies. Most were elderly. And there were children who had been thrown into the canal. I remember one dead woman. A child was lying on her and was trying to nurse from her breast. There was a young boy, maybe fifteen or sixteen. His throat had been cut. Under it, they [the insurgents] had shoved a washbowl. It was filled with blood that was spilling out on to the road."[14] The number killed by the insurgents on the road is difficult to determine due the chaotic nature the violence. But all sources suggest that the number was large. In reference to the battle with the NDH forces in the column, one subsequent insurgent report stated: "Our forces attacked and inflicted enormous losses. Our losses in these battles were not large. We lost five comrades and four were injured. The enemy lost so many that it was impossible to determine the exact number of dead and wounded. The battles were difficult and bloody as none that can be remembered."[15] Several insurgents who were present indicated that about 300 civilians were killed.[16] Other sources suggest that the number was 350–500, with many more wounded.[17]

Among the insurgents, the advocates of restraint, such as Gojko Polovina and others, were aware of the potential for an enormous loss of life if revenge-seekers made contact with those in the column. So we have to ask: What allowed the advocates of escalation to so rapidly gain the initiative along the road? It appears that no one among the insurgents expected the entire population of this part of the Una River valley to suddenly leave. The unexpected arrival of the column of thousands of people surprised the insurgents—both the advocates of restraint and escalation. Those seeking to restrain and prevent insurgent violence had no time to prepare. Unlike in other successful instances of restraint, such as in Bjelaj, they had no time to make a careful selection of fighters prior to the attack whom they trusted and could exert authority over. Instead, the atmosphere was chaotic. Word spread among those in the forests, which quickly travelled to those in nearby villages, that the "Ustašas" of Kulen Vakuf were coming. Fighters grabbed their weapons and raced toward the road with the intent of taking revenge. There appeared to be few authority figures involved in their mobilization.

However, as the case of successful restraint in Bosanska Dubica shows us, an embittered group of revenge-seeking fighters could still be contained even while on the way to commit violence if key authority figures arrived on the scene and took action. We can recall that their success was more likely if they had engaged in previous organizational activities, and established embryonic authority. There were a handful of such men in the hills with the insurgents as many began shooting at the column. One was the respected local commander Stevan Pilipović Maćuka. He was known for constantly reminding his fighters that they were to kill only Ustašas—not any of the civilian Catholic and Muslim population. But Maćuka was killed during the firefight with the NDH forces at the head of the column. While the fighting raged, he somehow became separated from his fighters. Just before local Ustašas were about to capture him, he pulled the pin from a grenade and then held it to his chest. His sudden death, as one local insurgent recalled, triggered "confusion and uncertainty" among the fighters with him.[18] For Gojko Polovina, Maćuka's death was a turning point: "After his fall, there was total chaos in the battalion that he was commanding."[19] Here was one of the "within-war," or endogenous dynamics, that suddenly and dramatically tipped the scales toward the escalation of violence. The sudden loss of one of the few local leaders who advocated restraint, and who had a semblance of authority over some of the fighters, created an unexpected opportunity for those who wished to take revenge. With no one present to forcefully demand and compel restraint, the shooting intensified. Evidence suggests that insurgents continued to fire at the unarmed civilians in the column even after the battle with the NDH forces ended.[20]

Taking advantage of this sudden weakness among the advocates of restraint, one group of insurgents immediately took prisoner about seventy men from the column. Leading them was a commander named Mane Rokvić, who had helped organize the massacres of Catholics in the village of Krnjeuša a month earlier. Some evidence suggests that Rokvić was joined by the local commander Nikola Karanović, who was from the nearby village of Ćovka, located about a kilometer from where most of the shooting took place. Karanović was one of the few men from that village with military training from before the war. His status gave him a certain level of authority among the local fighters, many of whom were from his village and others nearby.[21] When such influential individuals gave orders, their neighbors tended to follow. Without making any attempt to determine if the men whom they captured had been Ustašas, these commanders ordered their prisoners to march away from the road to a nearby place called Dulidba. Bećo Šiljdedić was among them:

> The insurgents immediately divided the men on one side and the women and children on the other side. They tied our hands with rope and then took us [the men] toward Vrtoče. Along the way I could not dream of what was waiting for us. I started praying [out loud] to God to rescue us. Hearing me, one insurgent struck me in the head so hard with the butt of his rifle that my head still hurts me today.[22] They brought us to some pit at Dugopolje. Then they made us take our clothes off. It was only at that point that I understood what was in store for us. They started shooting men and throwing them into the pit. Then my turn came. They fired a bullet at me. It went through my shoulder and part of my head but I could tell that it wasn't enough to kill me. I fell into the pit. When I hit the bottom I could hear screams for help. One of the voices was familiar to me. It was Huse Galijašević from Kulen Vakuf. He begged me to take a knife and slit his throat because he couldn't take the pain anymore. Beside his wounds from the gunshot, both of his legs were broken. More dead people fell around us as we spoke, many of whom I recognized. More than seventy people in my group were shot and thrown into the pit.[23]

The shift into more organized mass killing was closely connected to the preceding incapacity and subsequent absence of key advocates of restraint. Because the desire for revenge was strong among many insurgents, any sudden weakness or disappearance of those in favor of restraint—even one key individual such as the commander Steven Pilipović Maćuka—could quickly tip the scales toward mass killing. But it bears repeating that the desire for revenge was not enough to cause the killing; the advocates of restraint first had to be marginalized, absent, or killed in order for the killing to go forward. Once those intent on taking revenge no longer faced any resistance, their killing proceeded unabated.

Further illustrating this inter-play between escalation of violence and the weakness or strength of advocates of restraint was what happened when several communist-oriented commanders eventually arrived. They quickly undertook forceful interventions to stop fighters from attacking those still stranded on or near the road.[24] One of the most active was Stojan Matić from the village of Nebljusi, whose mother the Ustašas had killed earlier in the summer along with scores of his neighbors. Defying any easy assumption we might have that those who suffered from Ustaša violence were automatically those most committed to taking revenge, Matić demanded that the insurgents immediately stop their violence.[25] As one fighter who was present recalled: "Stojan was extremely severe with those who were coming to steal from [the horse-drawn] carts [of those in the column]. He was shooting his pistol, taking away the plundered property from those who were stealing, and giving them orders. The fighters knew Stojan as a quiet and peaceful man, as an individual with knowledge about military culture. But this time he was ready to shoot at anyone who was stealing or abusing innocent people, especially women and children."[26] Such forceful and armed confrontations with the advocates of escalation—with guns drawn and shots fired—appear to have been enough to stop the killing and stealing on the road, at least where individuals such as Matić were present and willing to undertake this kind of risky intervention. The desire for revenge was present among many fighters, but it was not inevitable that they would be able act on this impulse. Again, the advocates of restraint would first have to be marginalized to the extent that their interventions were ineffective. Matić's actions suggest that room can still exist for successful confrontation with advocates of violence, even when killings are still taking place.

Men like Matić and others managed to stop the shooting on and near the road. As many as 2,000–2,200 people from the column were left with him. Some were wounded. Many had already lost scores of relatives and neighbors in the morning's massacre of 300–500 people. Several commanders who had intervened to stop the killing now climbed up a small hillside and began giving speeches to the shell-shocked survivors, who were also now prisoners. Smajo Vojić, from the village of Orašac, was in the crowd: "They invited us to return peacefully to our houses and to continue our daily work. Some of those captured [villagers from Ćukovi and Orašac] said that they had nowhere to return to since their houses had already been burned. The insurgents replied that they would build them new and better houses. They reassured us that they were not [Ante] Pavelić's Ustašas, but instead were a people's army [*narodna vojska*] that was fighting for the freedom of all peoples."[27]

Here was an attempt by the advocates of restraint to put forth their vision of hoped-for intercommunal collaboration, and even harmony. Yet the current context vividly exemplified the enormous struggle that lay in front of those who wished to transform such words into reality. A group of communist-oriented commanders was now telling the shell-shocked survivors of a massacre—which was committed by fighters nominally under the authority of these very same commanders—that they should return to their homes. Many of those houses had been plundered and burned to the ground during the previous days by some of these same fighters. As many as 500 relatives and neighbors of those listening to this speech lay dead in the immediate vicinity. It is likely that few of those in the crowd believed that the commanders on the hill actually wished to rebuild their homes, let alone had the capacity and desire to both protect their lives and fight "for the freedom of all peoples."

As the terrified survivors digested these strange words, another set of incidents took place that further exemplified the tenuous position of the advocates of restraint. Back in Kulen Vakuf, the three young communists—Esad and Ibrahim Bibanović, along with Džafer Demirović—were still perched high in the minaret of the town's mosque, with their red flag flying in the breeze. They were anxiously waiting for the insurgents to arrive so they could join them as comrades in the fight against fascism. The fighters could be heard in the nearby hills. On several occasions the three called out to them to enter the town.[28] Soon shooting started. As the three climbed down the spiral staircase, they could hear the bullets hitting the mosque's walls. Then the sounds stopped. They concluded that the insurgents had entered the town. And so they emerged from the mosque to greet them.[29]

Approaching them were three fighters from the village of Kalati, where Ustašas had committed a number of massacres during the previous month. They were dressed in black clothing and wore the caps of the former Yugoslav Army. Bandoliers crisscrossed their chests. They demanded to know why the three young men had stayed in Kulen Vakuf. Holding rifles, the young communists exclaimed: "To join you and to fight together against fascism!"[30] In a matter of minutes many more insurgents arrived. While the Bibanovićes and Demirović tried to make small talk with the three fighters from Kalati, a number of the others lunged at them. While punching the young communists, several yelled out: "Fuck your Turkish mothers!" It appeared that these fighters would kill the three would-be insurgents whom they saw not as potential comrades, but rather antagonistically as "Turks" from an "Ustaša" town.

Just before the Bibanović brothers and Demirović lost their lives, the commander Gojko Polovina arrived with several other insurgents who appeared loyal to him. Immediately, they intervened and broke up the fight. Polovina ordered that the three men be sent under trusted armed guard to an insurgent headquarters in Donji Lapac. As Esad Bibanović recalled, had these commanders not appeared and intervened, he and his brother and Demirović would have been executed in front the mosque by the very insurgents with whom they wished to join.[31] The incident illustrates the shaky ground on which the advocates of restraint stood in Kulen Vakuf. Unlike in the case of Bjelaj, where they successfully collaborated with local Muslims in overthrowing the village's Ustašas, in Kulen Vakuf they barely prevented revenge-seekers from murdering the handful of Muslims who wanted to join and fight with them. Like Maćuka's death on the road and Matić's intervention there, the intervention in front of Kulen Vakuf's mosque showed how restraint was extremely tenuous. If its advocates—even a single individual—were not present and ready to forcefully intervene, killing was much more likely. With perhaps as many as 2,000–2,200 prisoners from the column now under the insurgents' authority, preventing further loss of life in the coming hours would be a challenge fraught with difficulty.

More and more insurgents streamed into Kulen Vakuf, while shots could still be heard in the hills from the road. Among them was the communist-oriented commander Đoko Jovanić. Seeing the recently abandoned houses, taverns, and stores—which were still full of belongings and in clean, orderly condition—he ordered a temporary command to be set up, which included approximately sixteen men. Their orders were to stop other fighters from entering Kulen Vakuf and plundering the town, and to prevent Orthodox peasants from nearby villages from doing the same. Jovanić was not familiar with the fighters now milling about in the town. He had spent most of his life outside the region. Unlike in the case of Bjelaj, it appears that he had little way, and no time, to assess the reliability of those whom he now selected to carry out these orders. He placed Petar "Pero" Đilas in charge of the guards, a thirty-one-year-old former Yugoslav gendarme from the village of Krško Brdo.[32] Đilas was not a prewar communist, and the evidence does not suggest that he became a sympathizer of the communist movement during the weeks following the outbreak of the insurgency. According to those from the village of Martin Brod who knew him, he was prone to violence and considered arrogant. It appears that he had been in conflict on several occasions with fellow insurgents from the villages of Veliki and Mali Cvjetnić. He wished to be their commander, while others opposed him. He was said to have viewed the residents of Kulen Vakuf as collectively responsible for the Ustaša killings of the previous months.[33]

Having never met Đilas before, Đoko Jovanić was unaware of the history and sensibilities of the individual whom he now selected to guard Kulen Vakuf. In such conditions, he had neither the time nor capacity to quickly gather more complete information about Đilas. He simply needed a fighter to be in charge of a group of guards who would protect the town. Đilas happened to be among those present when this decision had to be taken, and his status as a former gendarme most likely made him appear to Jovanić as a logical choice as leader. But as we have seen, in this kind of tense atmosphere, the presence, absence, and behavior of a single individual could exert a decisive effect on prospects for violence and non-violence.

Jovanić roamed around the abandoned town. He soon had an encounter that strongly suggested that the qualities of those fighters now milling about Kulen Vakuf would matter greatly in determining which direction subsequent events were to unfold.

> While I was walking through the town, all of a sudden Đorđe Pilipović from the village of Begluk appeared. He had just come from the village in his [former] gendarme jacket, and had his rifle on his shoulder. He snapped at me: "Are you the one who set up these guards?" I said yes. He then loaded his rifle, pointed the barrel at my chest, and while cocking the trigger said to me: "Remove them immediately if your life means anything to you." I answered: "I'm not removing the guards, and you should point your rifle at the enemy," and I motioned him toward the hills leading to the village of Prkosi [where the battles with the Ustašas were still taking place]. He stared angrily at me for a while longer, and then lowered his gun and left. But he did not go in the direction toward the enemy.[34]

With such armed individuals now in the town, preventing them from ransacking the place would be difficult. It would require a sizable number of individuals who would be ready to answer any provocation with forceful intervention. Jovanić had no way of knowing if the sixteen or so men whom he charged with this task, with the former gendarme Petar Đilas at their helm, were committed to carrying it out. He made his decision on the basis of incomplete information, which should not surprise us given the chaotic conditions and ongoing violence. What was already clear, however, was that intra-insurgent tension was running high over how to behave not only toward the property left in Kulen Vakuf, but especially toward the town's former inhabitants—perhaps more than 2,000 of whom were now the insurgents' prisoners.

All of these micro-level encounters—Stojan Matić firing his pistol on the road; the near execution of the three young communists in front of the mosque; the rifle pressed to Đoko Jovanić's chest and then cocked—suggest the striking degree to which authority remained up for grabs. In each of these situations, enforcing restraint was a dangerous endeavor: it required nothing less than putting one's life on the line and being prepared to use violence against fellow insurgents. The result of each encounter was not predetermined—no matter how strong the desire for revenge and plunder may have been among the advocates of escalation. To carry out killing and plunder, they first had to defeat their opponents, who faced the risky and difficult task of enforcing restraint with threats of death.

Back on the road, the advocates of restraint, such as Stojan Matić and others, ordered that those from the column whom had been captured were to be returned to Kulen Vakuf. They instructed their fighters to escort them back the way they had come in the morning. Broken into smaller groups, the 2,000–2,200 people began slowly returning during the late afternoon and early evening under armed guard. Near the bridge that crossed the Una River about a kilometer from town, at the spot known as the *buk*, the insurgents directed their prisoners toward different locations. All males aged twelve and older—about 400–420—were separated and taken to the center of Kulen Vakuf, and held near a tavern on the town square next to the mosque. About 400–500 women and children were taken across the bridge at the buk toward the gendarmerie station and held in a nearby meadow. The remaining 900–1,000 women and children were marched back toward the town, and then around a kilometer past it in the direction of Martin Brod. The insurgents directed them to the right from the road to a large meadow that ended at the bank of the Una River. Their orders were to guard these groups until the next day when they would be escorted out of valley, most likely toward the safety of Bihać.[35]

A fragile stability ensued as the prisoners returned to Kulen Vakuf and were split into these groups. Among those guarding them were some fighters who shared Stojan Matić's attitude that none among them should be harmed unless they were Ustašas. But given the size of the groups, these advocates of restraint could not be in all places at all times. Where they were absent, witnesses recall that a number of killings began to take place. Several fighters discovered Stipan Kovačević and Jakov Markovinović, whom they believed were Ustašas. They immediately took both away and killed them, along with Kovačević's wife and children.[36] Upon arriving to Kulen Vakuf, several witnesses recognized the body of Bećo Mehadžić lying in a ditch by the side of the road. A few approached, and noticed that his head had been cut off. It appears that at least ten male prisoners were taken to the bridge at the buk. There, a group of insurgents slit their throats in rapid succession, and then dumped their bodies into the Una River whose waters quickly washed them downstream. Among those who carried out these executions appears to have been Jovica Medić from the village of Bubanj, which local Ustašas attacked on July 3, along with a group of his neighbors. Just over two months after the destruction of their village, they now took revenge on those whom they perceived as guilty.[37] A number of other prisoners were still in the hills, near the Milota spring, where similar executions began to take place. Smajo Vojić was among them: "Night began to fall at Ćovka, near Milota, and that's where we were told to sleep. As soon as dusk fell, I sensed how our armed escorts [the insurgents] began taking men away from my group into the forest and not long after that shooting could be heard. Because of that I concluded they were killing people. It was then that I decided to run."[38] In all these instances, wherever the advocates of restraint were not on the ground, those intent on taking revenge began to seize the opportunity to kill. Their opponents faced the challenge of preventing these murders, which began to take place more or less simultaneously in multiple locations. As afternoon turned to evening, it became increasingly critical for those opposed to the killing to find a way to marshal their forces in order to intervene to stop this shift toward violence.

But around this point, word reached the commanders who would need to meet this challenge that the NDH authorities had dispatched a battalion of soldiers and Ustašas to assist those from Kulen Vakuf who had made it through the insurgent ambush earlier that day. At the village of Drenovača these forces attacked a group of insurgents, as well as the villagers there. When news of these developments reached commanders in Kulen Vakuf, most decided that the situation near that village was more pressing. If it fell, some felt that the NDH forces would then advance on the village of Nebljusi and the town of Donji Lapac, which were insurgent strongholds. And so they decided to leave Kulen Vakuf to help stop the battalion from advancing any further. Among them was Stojan Matić and Đoko Jovanić, two of the key advocates of restraint. They took with them a majority of their best and most reliable fighters.[39] This constituted a sizable number of those who were opposed to the taking of revenge against the prisoners.

Why was this important? Like the sudden death of Stevan Pilipović Maćuka on the road earlier that day, the departure of this group critically weakened the capacity of those remaining who wished to prevent further violence. What made possible the instances of successful restraint in August, such as Pištalska Draga, Bjelaj, and Rašinovac, was the on-the-ground presence of key individuals. They were of decisive importance in preventing killings, or stopping those underway from cascading further. Now, several of the key advocates of restraint had left. It was an open question whether events and personalities would tip the scale of violence in a different direction. These commanders who left Kulen Vakuf had unwittingly placed responsibility for protecting the prisoners in the hands of local fighters about whom they knew little. Before their attack on Bjelaj in August, they had time to hold a meeting during which they determined they could not rely on the vast majority of their fighters whom they believed would engage in revenge killings if given the opportunity. Thus, they adopted a different strategy. In Kulen Vakuf on the late afternoon and early evening of September 6 there was no time for such a meeting, and a subsequent reorientation in tactics.

Gojko Polovina was in the area around this time. He instructed the guards whom Đoko Jovanić had organized to prohibit all entry into Kulen Vakuf, and to protect the three large groups of prisoners. Yet again, unexpected "within war," endogenous dynamics had dramatically altered the prospects for potential violence. The bulk of the advocates of restraint intended to protect the lives of the 2,000 or so people from the column now under their authority. They did not expect a battle at Drenovača or the prospect of having to leave Kulen Vakuf at this moment. But responding to this contingency, and the threat that they believed it posed to the insurgency, led them to delegate the delicate task of protecting the prisoners to a group of fighters about whom they knew next to nothing. Their behavior would now in large part determine the fate of the prisoners.

Once most of the advocates of restraint left, those favoring escalation quickly took over. With the apparent encouragement of Petar Đilas, the former gendarme whom Đoko Jovanić placed in charge of the guards in Kulen Vakuf, some of the insurgents began breaking into shops and homes. They plundered whatever they could carry. Others focused their attention on the town's many taverns. Smashing them open, they found bottles of wine and brandy, which they began drinking. They paid no attention to their orders to prevent other insurgents and local peasants from entering the town, who began steadily arriving during the early evening. As Gojko Polovina recalled:

> These were the surviving fathers and mothers, brothers and sisters, relatives, friends and neighbors of the Serbs whom the Ustašas had brutally murdered. . . . They were coming with the desire to take revenge for the death of their dearest, and to search for something of their stolen property, or to take something from the Muslim houses as "compensation." Others came with these Serbs, whose relatives and neighbors had not been killed, and whose property had not been stolen, but came to take revenge anyway because of the fear that they had been forced to endure, as well as to steal.[40]

More than a few arrived carrying axes, pitchforks, and other farm tools, and joined in the plunder of the town. While they stole, armed fighters were seen in increasing numbers roaming around drinking bottles of alcohol.[41] Soon, plumes of smoke appeared billowing into the evening sky, as insurgents and peasants set fire to ransacked houses and stores. At some point the flames reached the town's mosque where, earlier that day, three local communists had hung a red flag from the minaret to signal the insurgents that they wished to join them in the fight against fascism. The site of their attempt to forge an intercommunal alliance quickly went up in smoke.[42]

Any semblance of order was rapidly disintegrating in this atmosphere charged with plunder, fire, and drunkenness. A key turning point that would trigger a surge in the tension came when a group of insurgents approached several of the male prisoners being held in the center of town. They demanded to be shown the location of the mass graves of Orthodox villagers whom the Ustašas had killed in Kulen Vakuf. The prisoners took them up the hill toward the school and pointed to a shallow mass grave where local Ustašas under the command of Miroslav Matijević had committed many of their killings.[43] The corpses had not been buried very well; the smell of decomposing flesh emanating from the site was overpowering. Apparently under the orders of Petar Đilas, the insurgents returned to the larger group of male prisoners and then ordered a number to begin unearthing the corpses. As they dragged each filthy, mutilated corpse out of the hole, the insurgents inspected each, trying to identify their relatives and neighbors. Joining them were other local peasants, who were arriving from their villages and hiding places in the forests as word spread that Kulen Vakuf had fallen to the insurgents.[44]

Seeing the mutilated corpses was traumatic for relatives and neighbors even when it occurred in a controlled, non-violent context. For example, Italian military forces organized an exhumation in October 1941 of Orthodox villagers whom the Ustašas had killed during the summer in the Glamoč region of western Bosnia. There, it was noted that the display of mutilated corpses created a situation in which "the souls [of the dead] cannot rest." The local NDH authorities braced themselves for what they saw as the inevitable negative effects on intercommunal relations: "The already deep chasm that exists between Croats and Serbs will [now] only be deeper."[45]

In Kulen Vakuf on the evening of September 6, the potential for an exhumation to worsen intercommunal relations was exponentially greater due to the radically different context in which it was occurring. Here, some of the people dragging the corpses out of the mass grave had almost certainly killed earlier on the same day (e.g., along the road). There was no central authority figure present to supervise the action, and calm those searching desperately among the corpses for relatives and neighbors. Very few, if any figures were present who could restrain whatever retaliatory action they might feel compelled to take. On the contrary, the only designated authority figure present—the insurgent commander Petar Đilas—was the individual who ordered the exhumation to be undertaken, and who had encouraged the plunder and burning of the town.

About 2,000–2,200 prisoners were being held in the immediate vicinity. Traumatic emotions surged among those now trying to identify corpses. As a consequence, perceptions of the prisoners from Kulen Vakuf—the town that many searching for corpses had come to think of as an "Ustaša place" during the previous months of violence—now transformed as well. A new wave of collective categorization now welled up, and began to crest. For many who were pulling the corpses out of the mass grave, and the others who examined and touched them in search of their relatives and neighbors, the prisoners from this "Ustaša place" now merged together; they collectively embodied the "Ustašas." They all somehow appeared responsible for the deaths of these relatives and neighbors, whose mutilated corpses were now being unearthed and put on display for identification. The combination of emotional forces at play was extremely destabilizing.

The exhumation marked a turning point. According to one insurgent, the fact that some of the corpses still seemed almost "warm" suggested that the Ustašas had continued to kill their Orthodox prisoners until just before leaving Kulen Vakuf. This contributed to a sense among some that all the Muslim prisoners deserved to be sentenced to death.[46] In the words of a fighter who was present, what was rapidly taking hold was "a psychosis of revenge."[47] Another described the atmosphere as producing "a wild and uncontrollable desire for revenge."[48] The presence of the corpses was crucial in creating this surging psychological frenzy, and compulsion to commit retaliatory violence: "This inflamed the rage of the mass of people even more," remembered Gojko Polovina. "That fury, combined with the town burning, created together a terrible chaos."[49]

This dynamic of escalation—when an exhumation takes place and relatives and friends of the victims immediately have the opportunity to retaliate against those whom they perceive as guilty—was present in other parts of Europe in 1941. Scholars of the Holocaust in Ukraine have shown that in numerous cases, the invasion by the German army led to the discovery of hastily buried corpses of local men whom the Soviets had executed in prisons just before retreating. Local residents often believed that Jews, whom many associated with the generally hated Soviet rule, were somehow responsible for these killings. Like the prisoners in Kulen Vakuf, Jews were sometimes forced to exhume these corpses, which often revealed signs of torture. This highly destabilizing encounter around corpses between grief-stricken local residents and those whom they perceived as guilty for the death of their loved ones was often the spark that triggered pogroms against the local Jewish population.[50]

A similar dynamic was unfolding in Kulen Vakuf, as fire spread from house to house. A group of insurgents and a number of local villagers left the mass grave once darkness had fallen. They walked back to the center of town where the men and boys were being held prisoner. Distraught and enraged, some entered the group and began circulating within it. They cursed the prisoners, while stealing their clothing, watches, rings, and money.[51] Every so often a voice could be heard yelling out: "This one is an Ustaša!" Another voice would offer confirmation: "He killed my brother and father!"[52] The individual would be dragged out of the group and led away into the night. Soon after, a gunshot would be heard, or the gurgling sound after a throat was cut. Among those seized and taken away were those who helped exhume the corpses from the mass grave, including Smajo Kurtagić, Šefkija Bojčić, and Bajro Demirović. None returned.[53]

Sometime in the middle of the night, Petar Đilas, the commander whom Đoko Jovanić placed in charge of guarding the prisoners and preventing the plunder of Kulen Vakuf, ordered that the 400–420 or so men and boys be taken to the nearby village of Martin Brod. No attempt was made to separate out those suspected of being Ustašas; all were ordered to leave. There, he indicated they would await some kind of improvised trial to determine their fate. The insurgents assembled these prisoners in a long column, two men across. At approximately 4:00 a.m., a group of fighters began marching them south along the road leading out of town. They stopped briefly near the meadow a kilometer outside of Kulen Vakuf where about 900–1,000 women and children were being held. None dared to call out to their wives, mothers, sisters, and children. Shortly thereafter, the insurgents ordered them to begin marching. As night slowly turned to dawn, the men and boys began their fifteen or so kilometer trek toward Martin Brod.[54] Left behind in Kulen Vakuf were groups of insurgents and local peasants. Some were armed with rifles and machine guns. But many more were roaming around the burning town with axes, pitchforks, and improvised clubs. Nearby were 1,400–1,500 unarmed women, children, and elderly, whom many of these armed fighters and peasants saw collectively as "Ustašas."

The surge in tension appears remarkably similar to what the sociologist of violence, Randall Collins, has described as what comes before a "forward panic." This is violence that explodes in a certain moment after a buildup, and for a time remains unstoppable: "Persons who have fallen off the point of tension into a forward panic situation have gone down into a tunnel and cannot stop their momentum . . . they not only kill, but destroy everything in sight."[55] Those with a monopoly over the means of violence enter into an altered state of consciousness in which moral constraints vanish for a time. An ideology may in many cases be a necessary factor in creating a context for this violence, but it is not sufficient to trigger actual violence; the situational dynamics are most crucial. In Kulen Vakuf, it was the sudden rush of taking over the town and capturing a large number of its inhabitants. It was the rapid growth of an embittered crowd that arrived to look for the bodies of their relatives and neighbors, to steal what had been stolen from them, to take revenge for everything they had lost—in short, to "get even."

Yet "getting even" may not have even been the primary desire at this point. As psychologist Nico Frijda has suggested, escaping pain that the "other" has inflicted is central to vengeful acts. This helps explain why revenge, if unleashed, tends to be immoderate. The main task is to get rid of pain—not to "get even." Retaliating against those who have caused one to feel dominated, powerless, and humiliated does not neutralize this pain. Rather, obliteration of its causes appears much more effective. For the insurgents and the local villagers in Kulen Vakuf, it was not possible to undo the damage the Ustašas and their perceived followers had done. But for those in such situations, Frijda has noted that, "what one can do is remove every trace of his or her gains, every recollection of it, and everything that might remind one of the offense. The nearest one can come to terminating the pain, perhaps, is to secure the object's total destruction, removing him or her from the face of the earth, erasing him or her from the records of history."[56]

The victors in Kulen Vakuf were clearly ecstatic with the fall of the town, and their overwhelming domination over their prisoners, who until that moment many had seen as their tormentors who had benefitted from their immense suffering. The sudden, unexpected, and complete helplessness of the prisoners most likely emboldened the insurgents and local peasants even more, who were already emotionally pumped up in destabilizing ways by the rush produced during the exhumation of their relatives and neighbors. This traumatic experience helped to focus their perception of the residents of Kulen Vakuf as nothing else except "Ustašas." Like others during the tense buildup before the explosion of a riot, pogrom, or lynching, they were now poised to begin "roaring down into a tunnel."[57]

It seems that one of the few remaining advocates of restraint, Gojko Polovina, was by now very much aware of the grave danger that the women and children faced. He gave an order to those fighters who still appeared willing to listen for them to be taken to the nearby village of Bjelaj.[58] But he had great difficulty in obtaining horses and carts with which to transport such a large number of people. Local peasants had already stolen those that these families had used the previous day in their attempt to flee the valley. Polovina requested assistance from peasants in nearby villages. But instead of their horses and carts, he received this response: "When the Ustašas forced out the remaining Serb people from the villages around Slunj, Bihać and Kulen Vakuf toward us in free territory, those who were not able to move were immediately killed. And you are [now] asking us to help transport the women and children of those murderers in our carts . . . !?"[59]

In this moment of great tension, the process of antagonistic collective categorization had reached an extreme level. The Ustaša violence of the previous months had resulted in even the unarmed women and children in Kulen Vakuf now being seen as basically no different than "those murderers" (i.e., the Ustašas) who had killed Orthodox villagers. With little support and no resources, Polovina attempted to remove the women and children from this dangerous situation. But as a single individual—and now without several of the key advocates of restraint who had suddenly left the night before—he simply was not powerful enough to counteract the tension that had built up during the months of violence, and especially during the previous day, in order to secure support for their rapid evacuation. He had no choice but to send the terrified women and children on foot toward Bjelaj.

To reach that village they would first have to pass through a large crowd of insurgents and peasants. Some held rifles. Many more carried axes, scythes, and improvised clubs. Many were drunk and by now had set nearly every structure in Kulen Vakuf on fire after plundering the town. Some were extremely distraught after spending hours trying to identify the mutilated corpses of their relatives and neighbors among those recently exhumed from the mass grave near the town's school. More than a few had already committed killings during the previous twenty-four hours. Hana Štrkljević and her three children were among the hundreds of women and children as they departed for Bjelaj, with no choice but to try and walk past this group:

> Just as we were setting out we came across a group of about 200 insurgents and peasants who were armed with different kinds of weapons . . . rifles, axes, scythes, pitchforks, sticks. They were screaming and swearing at us. It was chaos. It was impossible to make sense of anything through the shooting, yelling, swearing, beating, and the crying of the children and the screaming of the women. Terrified of death, people ran in every direction. I went with a group of women and children toward the Una [River].

> Ten insurgents and peasants ran after us, cursing our Ustaša mothers, and yelling that all of us needed to be killed. When I heard that, I jumped into the river with my three children. So too did Zlata Kosović-Demirović with her two children. I don't know how, but Zlata was somehow able to save herself, and she took me by the hand and pulled me out onto dry land, while one of my little girls was holding on to a branch in the water. When we found ourselves on the riverbank it was only then that we saw that [the rest of] our children were not there, that is, my other two, and her two.
>
> Zlata then lost her mind. With her soul broken, she got a running start and jumped once again into the water. She was on the surface of the river for only a few seconds [before drowning]. I stayed with my daughter in the same place, not moving anywhere. I was completely out of my mind. I didn't know what to do. Maybe I would have gone and done the same as Zlata had the insurgents and peasants not begun to chase me again.[60]

The night before, as the residents of Kulen Vakuf and their neighbors from the nearby destroyed Muslim villages prepared to leave for Bihać, the young boy Abas Mušeta recalled his grandmother's recent advice. If the insurgents attacked the next day, he should jump into the Una River and swim through the icy water to a nearby island. He would be safe there because she believed that none of his Orthodox neighbors could swim. The self-inflicted drownings that now began to occur in increasing numbers made her advice seem perverse.

The banks of the Una River, and the two bridges that spanned its emerald green waters, quickly transformed into a site of mass death. Armed with axes and scythes and clubs, peasants and insurgents chased the women and children in all directions throughout the meadows near the river. They sliced the throats and stabbed the stomachs of those whom they caught. They plunged their axes into necks and backs. Mothers, such as Ajša Galijašević, fell to the ground bleeding with their throats slit. Sometimes their babies and small children, some of whom the insurgents and peasants had neglected to kill in the chaos, crawled slowly around their now, or soon-to-be, lifeless bodies.[61] More and more distraught women, with nowhere else to go, ran toward the Una with their children. Many converged at the bridge over the buk, where they found themselves trapped on both sides by advancing groups of peasants and insurgents. They turned frantically left, and right, and left again, searching for an escape. Yet the only way off the bridge that did not lead toward the furious mob was over its edge, and straight down into the rushing water. Like Hana Štrkljević and Zlata Kosović-Demirović, they readied themselves to jump into the river with their children, rather than fall into the hands of those intent on killing them.[62] Mothers picked their children and threw them over the edge, and then jumped into the water. None could swim. Their bodies bobbed on the surface for a few seconds before the frigid, rushing water sucked them under, disappearing without a trace.[63]

Other women ran to the river's edge, but stopped and stood paralyzed, unable to bring themselves to throw their children into the water and then jump in on their own. Local peasants caught up to them, and pushed them from their frozen positions into the water to drown like the rest.[64] Some of these peasants pummeled their victims wildly with sticks and clubs, as well as with rocks found near the riverbank.[65] The handful of young men and boys somehow still left in the town also began jumping into the river. Some did so after having broken free from insurgents and peasants who had caught them and were attempting to beat them to death. Like the women and children, they too drowned in the river's frigid waters.[66] Some women and children tried to hide in cornfields near the river, but insurgents and peasants methodically combed through the stalks, discovering most and killing them. Evidence suggests that rapes took place during these hunts.[67] In this frenzy of killing by the Una, "drunk and furious people acted savagely," according to Gojko Polovina.[68]

FIGURE 9. The view of the Una River from the bridge over the buk, from which women threw their children and then themselves rather than be killed by insurgents and peasants; most quickly drowned. Image taken by the author.

Although this level of cruelty is shocking, we should resist the urge to see it as incomprehensible, and instead rise to the challenge of discerning its internal logic. At work were powerful desires for revenge, which were unleashed like a torrent due to the unique set of situational factors that transformed the urge to retaliate into acts of extreme violence. The failure of the advocates of restraint was crucial. Too many had left Kulen Vakuf on the evening of September 6. Thus there were not enough of them available to stop the chain-reaction of events—the entry into the town of large number of insurgents and peasants; their plunder and burning of it; the consumption of alcohol; and the traumatic exhumation—all of which made this explosion of vengeance possible. As Nico Frijda has suggested, if unleashed, revenge tends to be immoderate because the primary objective is not merely "getting even" by spreading previously inflicted pain to the offending party; rather, obliteration of its causes is more effective in counteracting this pain and profound sense of powerlessness previously felt by the revenge-seekers.[69]

The disturbing behavior of the peasants and insurgents who perpetrated this killing "makes sense" if we view it as intimately connected to fulfilling this desire. Taking vengeance and making sure to cause immense suffering and ultimate obliteration was, in fact, a frighteningly effective way to restore a sense of power. One can almost see the yearning to achieve this objective in some survivor testimony and other evidence. Mujo Dervišević recalled hearing peasants, who had chased women and children to the bank of the Una, express outrage at the idea that the women might survive after jumping into the river's icy waters, where they would almost surely drown. They cried out: "Don't let the Muslims jump, don't let them save themselves!"[70] A child who survived these killings noticed insurgents watching people throwing themselves into the water in an attempt to put an end to their suffering. "But the Chetniks pulled them out and continued to chase them because, as they said, the [Muslims] had not paid enough of a price."[71] Bećo Duračković was one such individual. He jumped from the bridge into the Una River, yet those chasing him were not prepared to watch him swim away or drown. They shot and wounded him, and then managed to pull him out of the water. Rather than finish him off quickly with another gunshot, they turned their rifles around and pummeled him to death with the butts of their weapons, one bone-shattering swing at a time.[72]

Such evidence suggests that killing was not the only objective; rather, there was a powerful desire among the perpetrators for their victims' deaths to be as torturous as possible. This was a way of settling scores or "getting even." But it also helped bring about the obliteration that Frijda suggests is central to taking revenge in ways that bring relief to its perpetrators. This sense of experiencing feelings of relief in causing extreme pain to those perceived as prior inflictors of suffering—as disturbing as that might seem—can even be seen in the evidence. Đoko Jovanić returned to Kulen Vakuf on September 7, and was shocked that "the peaceful and clean houses that I had walked around in the day before were burning before my eyes." Yet even more shocking was what one of the fighters who had been in the town during the previous twenty-four hours said to him: "Last night we destroyed and ruined them, and this is real joy," while pointing toward the burning town.[73] With a similar sense of satisfaction, another later noted: "We razed Kulen Vakuf to the ground."[74] It might be tempting to simply interpret such comments as evidence of these insurgents' inhumanity. But when taking into account that obliteration may be the most effective form of revenge, which is committed to relieve oneself of pain, then we may need to consider that feelings of relief, satisfaction, and even "joy" at having wrought such destruction are, in fact, chillingly understandable. Broad comparative evidence from a wide array of cases across temporal and geographical boundaries suggests similar feelings among perpetrators of extremely cruel acts of violence. Linking instances of lynchings in the United States, mass killings in Indonesia, and riots in Kyrgyzstan and India, is evidence of laughter, and even manifestations of "joy," which seem strikingly similar to the comments of some insurgents in Kulen Vakuf. Whether such feelings in these other cases were rooted in a sense of relief and happiness in having taken vengeance remains to be determined. But if shown to be the case, we would need to appreciate their "logic" just as much as we should when considering the insurgent violence in Kulen Vakuf.[75]

The killing in and around that town from the evening of September 6 through the next day does indeed resemble "the tunnel" that Randall Collins has described in his work on violence. Entering it after a sudden surge in tension, which is broken by a victory over, and the complete helplessness of the victims, perpetrators emerge only after committing an enormous amount of violence.[76] In Kulen Vakuf, the insurgents and local peasants exited their tunnel only after they had killed everyone they could catch, obliterating in the process whole extended families in a frenzy of revenge-driven violence.[77] As the afternoon sun began to descend behind the hills surrounding the valley on September 7—approximately twenty-four hours after the prisoners began returning to Kulen Vakuf—the results of their vengeance were coming into focus. Of the approximately 1,400–1,500 women and children who were brought back after the massacre that began on the road near the Milota spring on September 6, the sources suggest that as many as 900 had now been killed in and around the town. Their bodies lay in the cornfields and meadows near the Una River; many others were already swept away in its frigid, rushing waters.[78]

And what of the 400–500 who were still alive? While the killing raged, the few remaining advocates of restraint attempted to save lives. These insurgents ran into the meadows and physically intervened in an attempt to stop others from murdering women and children.[79] Some who took action did so because they owed their lives to certain prisoners and their families, who had taken risks earlier in the summer to save them from the Ustašas. Sprinting toward insurgents and peasants who were swinging axes and clubs at their victims, they demanded that the prisoners been seen as individuals, and made reference to their past behavior. As one cried out: "Listen! Let him go. This is a good person—he saved me!"[80]

In other cases, witnesses and their children noted that long-standing, prewar connections compelled insurgents, peasants, and local merchants to save their neighbors. During the chaos and killing, those who could took women and children to safety, or showed them where they could run. Ilija Majstorović was a peasant and seasonal worker from the village of Bubanj who had several close friends in Kulen Vakuf. Local Ustašas killed his mother, wife, and two children during the July 3 attack on his village. Yet on September 7, he ran into a burning house to rescue a child of one of these friends who had been left behind.[81] Dušan Polovina from the village of Dobroselo, who was related through the practice of *kumstvo* (godfatherhood) to Abas Mušeta, intervened to save him and a number of his family members.[82]

Here, too, among those saving lives were individuals who had themselves been saved during the preceding months by those whose lives, or those of their families, were now in mortal danger.[83] Hana Štrkljević, who had jumped into the Una River with Zlata Kosović-Demirović and their children, was one such individual. After emerging from the water with only one of her three children, furious peasants began chasing her once again:

> Running from them for the second time, I somehow managed to get to the road after running through a cornfield, and then went in the direction of Martin Brod. At the Šolić house I came across a peasant who began beating me on my back with a stick. If Milan Karanović from Očijevo had not arrived at that point, the peasant would have killed me for sure. He protected me and took me to Martin Brod. He put me in Marko Vladetić's house. Even though the Ustašas had killed two of his sons, he and his daughter treated my daughter and I as if they were our father and sister.[84]

As one of the most prominent merchants in the region, Vladetić had several longstanding friends from Kulen Vakuf. Apparently, they assisted him while he was being held in the town's prison in August. It seems they also tried to help his two sons, but ultimately failed in preventing their deaths. These earlier connections, and recent interventions, almost certainly contributed to his decision to protect Hana Štrkljević and her daughter in this critical moment. As for Milan Karanović, he appears to have been willing to risk such interventions out of a sense of obligation for what others did to help him and his family escape the Ustašas. After Hana Štrkljević spent a brief time in Marko Vladetić's house, Karanović personally took her and her daughter to the village of Bjelaj. His desire to return the assistance that he had previously received only appeared to grow with each rescue: "Along the way," Štrkljević recalled, "he asked about the family of Ibro Muranović so he could save them because Ibro had saved six members of Karanović's family."[85]

Through these examples we see the counter-intuitive dynamic in which violence on a nominally ethnic axis can actually produce stronger inter-ethnic ties through acts of rescue. While waves of killing can rapidly create antagonistic collective categorization along the lines of ethnicity, they can also produce their opposite: waves of inter-ethnic rescue and a sense that one's behavior—not ethnicity—is paramount in distinguishing enemies from friends. In short, violence can generate a dual cascading effect in multi-ethnic communities. Massacres can cause inter-ethnic retaliatory killings and increased polarization; yet inter-ethnic rescue prior to, and during such violence, can lead to more such rescues and increased solidarity. Perception of ethnic boundaries can simultaneously harden and soften in such contexts.

Vastly outnumbered by those who were intent on killing, many advocates of restraint appeared to find each other during the mayhem. Some converged near the gendarmerie station, located just beyond the bridge over the buk, where women were throwing their children, and then themselves, into the water. From this location, they somehow managed to gather together several hundred women and children. Located on a steep hill that led directly into the Una River, the station was reachable only from the road that passed in front of it. Here was Ilija Majstorović from Bubanj, who had already run into a burning house to save a child of his friends in Kulen Vakuf. Here was Uroš Ljiljak from Bušević, whose neighbor Muharem Dervišević of Klisa had warned his village about an impending Ustaša attack in July, and in so doing saved many lives. These insurgents directed the women and children into the building, and others who would not fit to the small clearing immediately next to it.[86] They could see smoke all around from the burning town.

They could hear other insurgents only 150 meters or so away on the bridge at the buk as they cursed the women and children trapped there before they jumped or were thrown to their deaths. They could hear screams coming from the nearby cornfields from the women and children whom insurgents and peasants killed, after discovering them hiding in the tall stalks.

But at the station's entrance and by the road, these advocates of restraint stood guard and refused to let any revenge-seekers past.[87] On several occasions furious insurgents and peasants demanded that they leave immediately so that they could set the building on fire in order to kill everyone inside. The insurgents at the entrance refused.[88] Both sides shouted at each other in a tense standoff. As one witness recalled, "those who opposed the taking of revenge were called traitors of the Serb people."[89] Fighters aimed at each other and cocked their weapons. It seemed that fighting would break out at any moment. Yet neither side took the step of firing a shot, nor physically attacked their opponents.

So enforcing restraint could be achieved without resort to intra-insurgent violence. What was necessary, however, was a commitment to stand one's ground with weapons at the ready, and a refusal to back down in the face of threats and verbal attacks. Frenzied mass murder was taking place all around within a 200-meter radius of the gendarmerie station; yet inside its walls and immediately next to the building, the advocates of restraint managed to save several hundred lives. A relatively small group of committed fighters (perhaps ten or so) was enough to prevent the killing frenzy from engulfing the women and children. In the midst of a full-blown massacre, it was too late for the other methods of restraint that insurgents had employed in the previous weeks—organizational activities; political work to counter dehumanization and collective categorization; and meetings with fighters and a subsequent reorientation in tactics. Saving lives at this point was only possible where the advocates of restraint had both the numbers and especially the will to risk their own lives by being ready to use violence against fellow fighters to prevent or stop killing. Of the 400–500 women and children who survived the killings by the Una River, insurgents and others who risked these interventions managed to save perhaps 250–300.[90]

A group of about 80–130 somehow managed to escape on their own. They fled up the steep hill on the east bank of the river. Less than a kilometer above the town were the remains of an old Ottoman fortress called Havala. Its location afforded a semblance of protection, and a direct view into the town where the massacres were taking place. Without any armed protection, they huddled together and hoped that no one would discover them. On the morning of September 8—nearly forty-eight hours after they had attempted to flee

FIGURE 10. The remains of the gendarmerie station in Kulen Vakuf, where a small number of insurgents protected several hundred women and children from other fighters who wished to kill them. Image taken by the author.

Kulen Vakuf—a group of insurgents found them. The fighters calmly said that they would escort them to the village of Bjelaj. The terrified women and children agreed to go. Fata Hodžić-Selimović was among the prisoners as they walked on the same road they traveled while fleeing from Kulen Vakuf two days earlier on the morning of September 6:

> I saw lots of dead men, women, and children [whom had been killed on September 6] when we passed through Prkosi. The peasants had gathered them together, most likely to bury them somewhere. At the Ešanović forest, we turned right from the road. When we had walked around two kilometers from the road into the forest, the insurgents stopped us at a pit. Then they took out axes. They started smashing heads [of the women and children], and throwing their bodies into the pit. Children screamed for help at the top of their lungs. Women shrieked. It was terrible! A girl from Kulen Vakuf and I were among the last [to be attacked]. They cut us just above our eyes with the edge of the axe, but we came back to consciousness relatively quickly [after falling into the pit]. I spent three days in the pit and then somehow I managed to pull myself out.[91]

When the advocates of restraint were absent, the killing proceeded swiftly. A large number of advocates of escalation was not necessary to cause another enormous loss of life, just as a large number of their opponents was not required to save lives, as the successful intervention at the gendarmerie station shows us. What was crucial in these moments when lives hung in the balance was, first, the presence or absence of one side, and second, whether one had the capacity to put up unwavering resistance to realize its objective. At this pit two kilometers from the road in a dense forest, no such confrontation could take place. While the advocates of restraint successfully protected the several hundred women and children by the station, they had no idea that this other group was being marched to their deaths.

The 900 or so women and children already killed near the Una River now became more than a thousand by the morning of September 8. Their corpses were added to the 350–500 shot two days earlier on the road, which Fata Hodžić-Selimović saw on her way to the pit in the Ešanović forest. The total body count was now somewhere between 1,500 and 1,600. And the insurgents had yet to decide what to do with the over 400 men and boys whom they had marched to Martin Brod, where they were now being held prisoner, awaiting some kind of trial to determine their fate.

FIGURE 11. The road from Kulen Vakuf to Martin Brod, along which insurgents marched about 400–420 men and boys, whose fate they would soon determine. Image taken by the author.

By the morning of September 8, it appeared that the advocates of escalation—driven by a desire for vengeance—had decisively gained the upper hand, having killed many times the number of those whom the advocates of restraint had managed to save. Yet if our analysis of violence during the summer of 1941 tells us anything, it is that we must always strive to explain the contingency of killing—or its prevention. Powerful desires for one result or the other may be necessary causes for one side to prevail, but they cannot be seen as sufficient; we have already seen evidence in which a host of other factors have made it possible for lives to be saved or brutally ended, in spite of strong urges for restraint or revenge. If we wish to explain why the potential for violence or its prevention leads to killing or rescue, then we have to continue to deal head-on with the question of how one side—escalation and restraint—actually manages to overcome the resistance of the other in a direct confrontation. In doing so, we can better understand how desire transforms into action—or not. Exploring the fate of the men and boys whom the insurgents had marched to Martin Brod provides us with an opportunity to explore this question.

The men and boys were among the last still alive of those captured from the column that left Kulen Vakuf on September 6. Now in the insurgent stronghold of Martin Brod, they were being held near the village's train station. Several insurgents guarding the prisoners selected three—Džafer Mušeta, Hamdija Kulenović-Bajbutović, and Hamdija Kulenović-Ćouvka—to help them establish which men were Ustašas. They determined that eleven were guilty, among them Džafer's father—the merchant Mehmed Mušeta—whom survivors of Ustaša killings had seen at the Boričevac pit in July. Several insurgents declared that these men should be sentenced to death. Around this time the commander Petar Đilas, who had helped trigger the massacres the previous day in Kulen Vakuf by ordering the exhumations, arrived on a horse. He gazed out at the prisoners for a moment, and then turned toward the insurgents who were guarding them. "They should all be killed!" he yelled out. "No one should be left alive. They are all Ustašas!"[92]

A twenty-four year-old local communist from the nearby village of Veliko Očijevo, Ranko Šipka, immediately condemned Đilas's order and demanded that the insurgents ignore it. Šipka had spent time during the second half of the 1930s in larger urban centers, such as Banja Luka, and later in Zagreb, where he was a student, not unlike his compatriot Stojan Matić. It was there that he became involved in the communist movement, and became a member of the underground party in 1937. His instant and forceful rebuttal to Đilas's incitement to mass killing seemed to catch the group of fighters off guard; there was a pause.[93]

Breaking the silence was Marko Vladetić, who stood. He was the village's most prominent merchant. He had been robbed several times during the preceding months, both by Ustašas and local Orthodox villagers who impersonated Ustašas in order to seize the opportunity to enrich themselves at his expense. His two sons, Stevo and Dušan—who had played on the soccer team Mladost with local Muslim friends in Kulen Vakuf prior to 1941—had been recently killed in the town's makeshift prison by Miroslav Matijević and his gang of Ustašas. So too had his daughter's husband. In Vladetić's house, he, along with his wife and their daughter-in-law, were sheltering Hana Štrkljević and her daughter, both of whom the previous day had nearly drowned in the Una River, and then narrowly escaped being beaten to death by local peasants. He stepped up on to a crate so that people could see him and better hear his voice:

> My brothers! A black flag has been hoisted above my house. It flies there not just because of the horrible deaths of my two sons and son-in-law, but also because of the death of a man whom we all loved: our [Stevan Pilipović] Maćuka [the insurgent commander who killed himself with a grenade on the road on the morning of September 6 rather than be captured].
>
> Permit me to tell you of my only wish in this sad hour. Look there at those men with bound hands who were brought from Kulen Vakuf. Among them are three of my friends. Spare their lives for me. My debt to Maćuka and the blood of my slaughtered sons obligates me to ask you for mercy toward them.[94]

But before he could finish his sentence, shouting erupted. A number of fighters rejected his plea to save the lives of these men. Vladetić was known for his close friendship with a number of merchants and others from Kulen Vakuf prior to 1941.[95] Some of them were now among the prisoners in Martin Brod. It is likely that the three men whom he pointed toward had recently assisted Vladetić, who had been in the same jail as his sons in Kulen Vakuf. Vladetić confirmed this when he shouted back to those now denouncing him: "Listen to me! That man there, Ibrahim Šiljević. Let him go . . . he is a respectable man. He saved me."[96]

But more angry shouts from the crowd quickly drowned out his voice. Increasing numbers of fighters joined in denouncing the call by Vladetić, as well as that by Šipka, for a selective approach in dealing with the prisoners. Witnesses recall hearing the voice of one of Vladetić's own daughters. Ustašas in Kulen Vakuf had killed her husband and two brothers—Stevo and Dušan. "Daddy, don't ask for mercy for anyone!" she cried out. "Where are your

[sons] Stevo and Dušan?"[97] Her exhortation that the recent Ustaša killing of her two brothers meant that none of the men and boys should be freed mimicked what Đilas has just declared from his horse. Not just the "Ustašas" needed to be killed; rather, all the prisoners needed die because all were, in fact, "Ustašas."

A handful of others, however, gave their approval for sparing the lives of at least some of the prisoners. Perhaps emboldened by this modest display of support, Vladetić, along with his wife and their daughter-in-law, attempted to lead away some of the prisoners toward the safety of their house.[98] But their opponents did not stand by and watch. Unlike the standoff in Kulen Vakuf at the gendarmerie station, these advocates of escalation now took the step of attacking the advocates of restraint. As fists and the butts of rifles began to swing, fighting now broke among the insurgents. Witnesses remember that after being attacked, Vladetić and his family, along with their small group of supporters, quickly retreated. They fled to his house to protect themselves from most of the rest of the insurgents, who not only wished to kill the prisoners, but also them.[99]

Here was a direct clash between the advocates of restraint and those of escalation. Why did Šipka and Vladetić, and the others who shared their desire to save at least some of the prisoners, fail in their attempted intervention? It is tempting to conclude that the revenge motive was so strong in Martin Brod that retaliatory killing was simply impossible to avoid. Yet the evidence from other instances in the region suggests that mass killing could still be prevented, even at such a late moment. After all, in August, commanders had managed to stop the large crowd marching toward Bosanska Dubica, as well as those who wanted to burn and kill after they had entered the village of Rašinovac. And just the previous day, fighters managed to hold off a group of revenge-seekers at the gendarmerie station under tense circumstances, with killing and burning taking place all around. So why did the words of the insurgent commander Pero Đilas—"They are all Ustašas and should all be killed!"—resonate more strongly with a majority of insurgents than Vladetić's and Šipka's plea to distinguish friends from enemies, and the guilty from not guilty?

Research by social psychologists, such as that by Stanley Milgram, suggests that when people are given contradictory commands by multiple authority figures, further action will tend to become paralyzed because a clearly defined authority no longer exists. And so a person subsequently has difficulty determining what course of action to take.[100] Yet this did not happen in Martin Brod. From the evidence, it is clear that a majority of insurgents were far from paralyzed after hearing the diametrically opposed orders. They shouted down Šipka and beat those who gave approval for Vladetić's plea, and seemed poised to carry out Đilas's order to kill all the prisoners. They were thus capable of deciding which command, in their view, was legitimate.

Here, the question of what constitutes legitimate authority becomes crucial. So too does the need to seek our explanation not only from psychological, but also—and especially—from historical factors.[101] While it may be frequently true that contradictory commands make further action less likely in experimental settings, one must keep in mind the historical context within which subjects in non-staged situations interpret incompatible orders. In Martin Brod, many insurgents could not easily view the prisoners as individuals whose guilt needed to be determined on a one-by-one basis; rather, they appeared more as an undifferentiated mass of "Ustašas," who had killed members of the insurgents' families and communities, and destroyed and plundered their property. This way of thinking was a result of the previous months of violence and the way that the killing had produced a psychological template of antagonistic collective categorization. While perhaps strange to us, it could be seen as an entirely logical response to the context during the preceding weeks in which violence on an ethnic axis—along with cascading revenge killings—had become a central part of daily life. This was not a permanent mental template, but rather was generated by acts of mass violence, and thus historically contingent.

Vladetić attempted to counteract this situational mentality by suggesting that several of his friends were among the prisoners; for him, they were not a mass of enemies, but rather individuals, some of whom were innocent. But his attempt to stop the process of dehumanization fell largely on deaf ears. Why? Here, one must keep in mind that the incident in Martin Brod occurred after the previous forty-eight hours of sustained mass killing. There was no longer any psychological barrier to cross for many insurgents when it came to engaging in large-scale violence. Indeed, it is a near certainty that among those insurgents in the village were men who had already committed multiple killings during the previous two days. These killings were generally intimate and face-to-face: victims were shot at close range in the head and then dumped into vertical caves; their throats were cut and heads sliced off; women and children were seized while screaming and crying and thrown into the Una River to drown; people were beaten wildly with clubs, rocks, and rifle butts. There was already little distance—both psychological and especially physical—between perpetrator and victim. Convincing these insurgents to commit more violence was significantly less fraught with psychological strain than it would have been had many of them not already committed intimate acts of violence during the previous two days. Conversely, convincing them at this moment to suddenly take a selective, restrained approach to violence after a two-day frenzy of hands-on killing should be seen as a task significantly more difficult—and perhaps nearly impossible—than most of the other instances in the region in which advocates of restraint managed to succeed.[102]

The earlier cases of successful restraint—Bosanska Dubica and Rašinovac—are instructive. If acting forcibly to rein in the twin processes of antagonistic collective categorization and dehumanization is essential to successfully exercising restraint, then doing so *before* intimate mass killing begins, and perpetrators "enter the tunnel," seems equally crucial. This was not possible in Martin Brod, and thus the advocates of restraint were in a weakened position. Like the fighters who successfully held off revenge-seekers the previous day at the gendarmerie station, their only remaining option also carried the most risk: threatening their opponents with death, and being capable of carrying out such threats. But in Martin Brod, they had neither the numbers nor the capacity to take this path; the advocates of escalation, who were more numerous, physically attacked them first for suggesting restraint, and they fled.

During the previous five weeks of the insurgency, regular disputes among insurgents and their leaders had flared non-stop, which NDH military analysts had begun to note in their intelligence reports.[103] As a result, many fighters had grown accustomed to operating in a context in which authority was often unclear, could be questioned on a regular basis, and overturned in certain situations. We need only recall the many instances in which fighters, supposedly under the command of the local communists Gojko Polovina and Đoko Jovanić, successfully challenged their orders. During the attack on Boričevac a month earlier, Polovina demanded that fighters stop burning houses. In response, they placed their weapons on the ground in front of him and dared him to pick them up and shoot them, which he did not; and so they continued setting fires. Just two days earlier on September 6, a fighter pulled out his rifle, cocked it, and put the barrel on Jovanić's chest, before ignoring his order to leave Kulen Vakuf. Authority thus remained up for grabs. It could be taken by those willing to stand their ground and threaten violence against other fighters. This factor ensured that many insurgents were far from paralyzed in a moment of contradictory orders, and were capable of speaking out in favor of a position that reflected their own sentiments, especially revenge.

So events during the previous weeks and days had over-determined that at this particular moment many insurgents would perceive Đilas's order—"They should all be killed!"—as legitimate. This was because the already shaky authority of the advocates of restraint had been compromised by their failure to prevent most of the previous two days of killing, which was due in large part to the absence of many of these commanders from Kulen Vakuf and its vicinity at critical moments. By not being present, they could not attempt to prevent dehumanization or exercise physical force to restrain those seeking revenge. The severe erosion of their authority was most evident in the fact that several, such as Ranko Šipka, were nearly killed by their *own* fighters in Martin Brod for suggesting the selective use of violence and restraint.

As evidence from the summer of 1941 in the region demonstrates, key individuals—not unlike Šipka and Vladetić—could still sway these extremely tense situations in the direction of restraint. However, the insurgents were not like the subjects in Milgram's experiments, who were unclear about who was the discernible authority and, more importantly, did not have any antagonistic historical relationship with those whom they were in a position to harm. For many insurgents, their traumatic experiences during the summer of 1941 preconditioned them to be receptive to the order to kill. If Đilas had not called for the mass executions of the prisoners, and if Šipka and Vladetić had more support, and especially armed support, the result might have been different. Yet a conflict of some kind would have still been likely. But given the extreme violence of the previous two days, and the failure of the advocates of restraint to contain it early on, the odds were already heavily stacked against intervention and rescue in Martin Brod. In short, the analysis here of the failed attempt at restraint helps us understand a central dynamic driving this final stage of escalation: once a killing frenzy was unleashed, and the advocates of restraint had lost their legitimacy and capacity to use force, the violence tended to escalate until no victim remained alive.

This micro examination of the clash in Martin Brod suggests our need to be more conscious about analyzing the path toward violence—and attempts at its prevention—with a sufficient level of contingency. As we have seen repeatedly, a powerful desire to kill can certainly create a context that is highly conducive to killing. But relying on this desire as a primary explanatory factor does not get us very far when we encounter situations in which advocates of violence sometimes succeed, and sometimes fail, yet with both occurring in close geographical and temporal proximity to one another. This suggests that the path toward killing is not as clear as we might think, even when examining contexts such as Kulen Vakuf, in which the advocates of escalation are numerous and their desire to commit violence seems overwhelming. We cannot be blinded by the shock of body counts and torturous methods of violence when we attempt to explain how such violence comes to pass, and conclude that strong desires to kill are sufficient causes for mass violence. Rather, the challenge is to disaggregate the violence into its various components, and then zoom our analytical lens in as much as possible in order to discern how and why advocates of killing or restraint succeed or fail in critical moments.

What emerges when we examine these forty-eight hours in this way is a striking level of contingency, not simply a linear path toward mass killing. A series of events critically weakened the advocates of restraint, and empowered those in favor of escalation, which tipped the scales toward violence. But the potential for a much less violent result was present throughout, and even became a reality in certain moments, such as in front of the gendarmerie station, and in other smaller individual interventions. Some local fighters were conscious that a different result could have been possible. As one put it, when reflecting on the death of Stevan Pilipović Maćuka, the key advocate of restraint who pulled a pin out of a grenade on the road during the firefight on the morning of September 6, and held it to his chest rather than be captured by the Ustašas: "This was an irrecoverable loss for the insurgency, which was especially visible after his death. Had he remained alive, perhaps the treatment and errors in dealing with the Muslim population after the occupation of Kulen Vakuf would not have come to pass."[104]

Had this key commander not been killed that morning, or had others like him and their most reliable fighters not suddenly left Kulen Vakuf on the late afternoon and evening of that day; had Đoko Jovanić had more information about Petar Đilas and chosen not to place him in charge of the guards in Kulen Vakuf; had insurgents and peasants been prevented from entering the town; had they not found alcohol in the many taverns; and had the traumatic exhumation been avoided—it is entirely possible that the story of Kulen Vakuf would be told alongside that of Bosanska Dubica: as one in which the advocates of restraint faced a major challenge to stop the advocates of escalation, and managed to prevail. The stunning escalation of violence in and around Kulen Vakuf during September 6–8 was not simply caused by a desire for revenge. In fact, it was contingent on the failure of the advocates of restraint. It is only through a detailed analysis of their mistakes, unexpected problems, lack of information, and structural weaknesses that we can explain why the killing continued to cascade during these two days. This is the analytical payoff of carefully reconstructing what took place during these forty-eight hours: the vivid exposure of how the escalation of violence can be locked in a highly inter-dependent relationship with the restraint of violence. We better understand the success of one by examining how its advocates faced off and defeated their opponents, and what caused the losers to fail.

In Martin Brod, with those opposed to killing the prisoners now silenced, a group of insurgents bound the hands of the 400–420 men and boys behind their backs with wire. They proceeded to march them in small groups up into the hills to the west, toward a place known only to local villagers: Golubnjača, or "the pigeon cave."[105] As they walked, the insurgents demanded that their prisoners sing Serbian songs. They were told to repeatedly shout "Long Live King Petar!," the monarch of the recently disintegrated Kingdom of Yugoslavia, whose birthday the region's residents had celebrated together each September 6 since the assassination of his father King Aleksandar in 1934. Their shouts and singing echoed through the valley as the groups climbed along the switchback dirt road, passing orchards of plum trees.[106] Approximately three kilometers from Martin Brod, just before the road turns sharply to the left toward the village of Miljuši, in an area where there were open meadows along a plateau, the insurgents directed their prisoners to turn right off the road. They passed through plum trees, walking about thirty-five meters down a grassy slope toward a depression in the ground, which led toward the edge of a forest. Just beyond the first trees, there was the opening of a deep vertical cave. A stone tossed in it would hit the walls, bounce from side to side, and then hit the bottom a few seconds later, which suggested considerable depth.

Local villagers believed that this cave was home to witches, vampires, and devils. They said that the pigeons often seen around its entrance—which were what gave the cave its local name—were actually angels that God had sent in order to prevent the evil spirits inside from leaving and attacking villagers. Having grown up in the nearby village of Dobroselo, Gojko Polovina recalled: "As children, for every mischievous act we feared the words: 'If you're not good, we'll throw you into Golubnjača.'"[107] He once asked his grandfather if the stories about the evil spirits were true. The answer he received helps us better understand why the local insurgents chose this place to take the prisoners: "What kinds of devils and what kinds of witches?" his grandfather responded. "In Golubnjača lay the bones of rebels who were killed without trial and outside the law. They were thrown into the pit so no one would know where their graves are."[108] The fighters who were leading the prisoners toward the cave were almost entirely local men, from the villages Martin Brod, Veliki and Mali Cvjetnić, Veliko and Malo Očijevo, Begluk, Doljani, and Brotnja.[109] It is likely that, like Gojko Polovina, they too had grown up listening to similar stories about Golubnjača's real use. This mystical place of angels, witches, and pigeons, now served a useful purpose for the local men who had defeated the advocates of restraint, and were now intent on taking vengeance. The cave provided them an ideal site for the obliteration of their enemies—their lives and corpses, and thus any memory of them.

Among the groups of prisoners walking toward the cave was Mujo Dervišević from the village of Klisa, a father of six children:

> They led us in groups of around sixteen to twenty. Around seven to eight groups went before mine. None of us had any idea where we were going. When my group's turn came, and when we arrived at the Golubnjača pit, it was only then that we realized what was happening. They killed people with axes, butcher's knives, short scythes, and then threw them half-alive into the pit. About five to six men carried out the killings, while around ten stood guard.[110]
>
> I came to the edge of the pit. One of them asked me if I had anything on me. "Fuck your Turkish mother!" he said to me [after seeing that I had nothing], "they already took everything from you!"[111]
>
> When it came time for me to be killed, I managed to get my hands free from the wire and then I ran with all of my strength.[112] One of them, whose voice was familiar to me, yelled out: "Mujo is running away, fuck his mother!" And they started shooting at me. They chased me on the steep slope, but by then I was already in the thick forest. I heard them say: "He's wounded, let's go back, he'll die soon."[113]
>
> From that spot, which was around one hundred meters from Golubnjača, I watched as they continued to bring men, kill them, and then throw them into the pit. I could hear their screams loudly and clearly. This lasted for an hour and a half after my escape. After the last group had been killed, I heard some of the killers say loudly, "Let's go, we've finished our job!" They then left for Martin Brod, singing as they walked.[114]

Out of the 400–420 men and boys whom the insurgents brought from Kulen Vakuf to Martin Brod, Mujo Dervišević was the only one who escaped. If anyone was in the houses or fields in the village of Miljuši, located just a few hundred meters away from the cave, it is likely they heard the screams of those being killed. After walking through the forest for several kilometers, a group of insurgents captured Dervišević. They turned him over to their commander, Đuro Rašeta, who sent him on with several guards to their headquarters in Drvar. There, he met several communist-oriented fighters. They implored him to join them and fight. Having just witnessed the mass murder of hundreds of his neighbors, his main concern was whether his wife and six children were still alive. He first needed to search for them, he told the fighters. Just before he left, one motioned him to come closer: "Don't go to [Kulen] Vakuf," he said. "Everything there has been burned to the ground. Not even a cat has been left alive."[115]

FIGURE 12. The charred remains of Kulen Vakuf after it was burned during September 6–8, 1941 by insurgents and local peasants, as photographed by NDH military forces in October 1941. The pieces of wood in the lower left are the remnants of the bridge over the Una River. Image courtesy of the Military Archive, Belgrade.

In the end, of the approximately 5,600 people who left Kulen Vakuf on the morning of September 6, 1941, 3,124 arrived to Bihać, according to the NDH authorities there, who conducted a precise count of the refugees by village, gender, and age. It seems among them were many—if not most—of the local Ustašas, whose violence and plunder had triggered the successive waves of mass killing in the region.[116] Of the remaining 2,500 or so, it appears that the advocates of restraint managed to save as many as 400–500 lives.[117] According to both insurgent and NDH sources, the remaining 2,000 or so people, a majority of whom were women and children, disappeared during the forty-eight hours that passed between the morning of September 6 and that of September 8, 1941. Their bodies lay riddled with bullets on roadsides; strewn throughout meadows with throats slashed; drowned in the frigid, emerald green waters of the Una River and then washed downstream; and in piles in the darkness of deep vertical caves.[118] These massacres, which took the lives of about 35 percent of those who attempted to flee Kulen Vakuf on September 6, abruptly brought to a close the cascading waves of collective ethnic categorization and local revenge killings along such lines. In a final, convulsive shockwave of mass killing and population displacement, which was the culmination of these processes of violent antagonistic categorization, one entire side in the region's conflict suddenly vanished.

Taking a step back, we can see that the rough estimate of the total death count for the Kulen Vakuf region since the establishment of the NDH in April 1941 until the massacres of September 6–8 was approximately 3,300, which includes victims of Ustašas and insurgents, as well as others. This figure constitutes just over 20 percent of region's total estimated population in 1941 of about 16,000. In just five months, two out of every ten people had lost their lives. Such a death rate deserves our attention because, aside from the levels of destruction during the Holocaust of European Jewry and Roma, it falls among the highest suffered by local communities during World War II, especially among those in which outsiders were not responsible for the killing.

Yet there is another reason that this high death rate from a largely unknown region of Europe should attract our attention. This has to do with our methodological choices for both how we research mass violence, and choose to tell its history. There is no evidence to suggest that any foreign soldier committed even a single one of these killings; rather, they were a local affair, with many perpetrators having previously known their victims. Those caught up in this explosion of locally executed mass violence were, in a word, "neighbors," to use the title of Jan Gross's study of the destruction of the Jewish community in Jedwabne, Poland.[119] These findings should give us pause in a moment when macro-level studies of mass violence during World War II, such as *Bloodlands* by Timothy Snyder, have received much scholarly and popular attention.[120] It is indisputable—if not also obvious—that the ideologies, policies, and plans of key leaders, such as Hitler, Stalin, and in our case, Pavelić, deserve serious attention and analysis in any attempt to explain such high levels of violence. But in communities where we see nearly exclusive local participation and involvement in mass killing, such as the Kulen Vakuf region, we cannot reconstruct and analyze this history without devoting sizable attention to local agency—to the acts of those who lived and killed and died in those communities. Often, the most perplexing dimension of those parts of the world that some might wish to call the "bloodlands," is less the machinations of faraway leaders, and more the immense destruction that local people inflict on each other and themselves.[121] The ideologies, plans, and policies of key leaders can, and usually do, decisively shape their incentives for violence; yet we can only hope to explain their seemingly unspeakable acts by taking up the challenge of carefully telling the history that they have made.

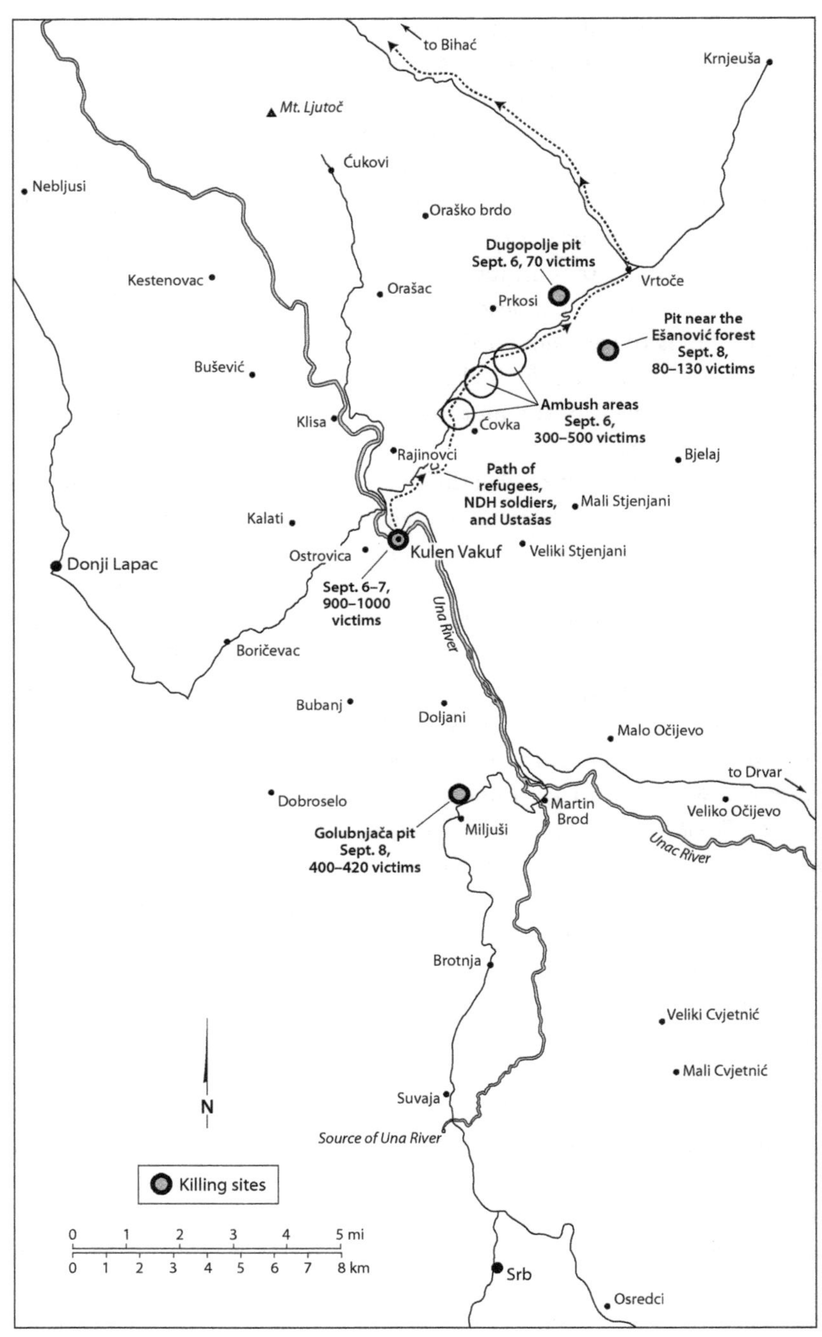
to Bihać
Krnjeuša
Mt. Ljutoč
Ćukovi
Nebljusi
Oraško brdo
Dugopolje pit
Sept. 6, 70 victims
Kestenovac
Orašac
Prkosi
Vrtoče
Pit near the
Ešanović forest
Sept. 8,
80–130 victims
Bušević
Ambush areas
Sept. 6,
300–500 victims
Klisa
Ćovka
Rajinovci
Bjelaj
Path of
refugees,
NDH soldiers,
and Ustašas
Mali Stjenjani
Kalati
Ostrovica
Kulen Vakuf
Veliki Stjenjani
Donji Lapac
Sept. 6–7,
900–1000
victims
Una River
Boričevac
Bubanj
Doljani
Malo Očijevo
to Drvar
Dobroselo
Martin
Brod
Veliko Očijevo
Golubnjača pit
Sept. 8,
400–420 victims
Miljuši
Unac River
Brotnja
Veliki Cvjetnić
Mali Cvjetnić
N
Suvaja
Source of Una River
Killing sites
0 1 2 3 4 5 mi
0 1 2 3 4 5 6 7 8 km
Srb
Osredci

Map 12. Main killing sites, September 6–8, 1941

In the days that followed the killings of September 6–8, the region's communist-oriented commanders sent a flurry of letters to local commanders, demanding explanations and "a detailed report about which units participated in the fighting, and the stealing and burning."[122] It appears that Gojko Polovina was the principal author of at least one of these reports. He noted that the insurgent entry into Kulen Vakuf brought with it "horrible chaos and many innocent victims."[123] Others told of the mass plunder, openly compared the insurgents' violent behavior with that of the Ustašas, and warned of even greater damage if action was not taken to change course:

> After taking over and liberating Kulen Vakuf, Orašac, and Ćukovi, there then began merciless plundering and pillaging, unfortunately by those among our guerillas who lack [political] consciousness. Their behavior has surpassed that of even the Ustaša bands. The robbery of our own property, including livestock and everything else, has gone beyond every boundary of comprehension. Because of this, we are requesting that the command endeavor to stop the crimes of our guerillas. If this does not happen, then we can expect from such acts even greater destruction that what we have experienced from the Ustašas.[124]

Even Petar Đilas, who had played a key role in triggering the killings, sent a short report. Not surprisingly, he downplayed the scale of the violence: "The truth is that there was stealing," he began. Yet "there was no slaughter of women and children," although he acknowledged that, "there was a slaughter of men at the end of the battles." Nowhere did he indicate who was responsible for the violence, nor did he criticize the killings.[125]

Communist-oriented leaders in Drvar were incensed at what happened in and around Kulen Vakuf; they sent out terse rejoinders to these reports demanding that every effort be taken to prevent such acts from ever occurring again:

> We received your exhaustive report about the battles around Kulen Vakuf and Dulidba and about the results of those battles. The history of Boričevac has been repeated. Our units—which went into battle with the will and excitement to fight for the freedom of their lands, their towns and villages—are burning those same towns and villages. These same units, which have fought against the bloody terror of Pavelić's bands [the Ustašas], . . . have shown themselves to be weak in preventing irresponsible elements from plundering and burning Kulen Vakuf.
>
> We trust that every one of our honorable guerillas will condemn the burning and plunder of Kulen Vakuf, and the killing of innocent men, women and children. We also trust that in our future battles our honorable guerillas will prevent these crimes at all costs.[126]

Despite the shock and disgust of these communist-oriented commanders, there is no evidence to suggest that they made any effort to determine who exactly was responsible for the killings, nor to punish the perpetrators, such as Petar Đilas and others. As the massacres vividly demonstrated, these commanders—the advocates of restraint—suffered from a sizable lack of authority over many of the fighters who committed the killings. And so beyond issuing angry letters and calls for change, they took little further action against these individuals. In fact, the evidence shows their willingness to tolerate the ongoing presence in leadership positions of several individuals who had played a major role in the killings of September 6–8. The names of two of the men most responsible—Mane Rokvić and Petar Đilas—appear in insurgent documents for weeks after the massacres as insurgent leaders.[127]

Several NDH soldiers, whom insurgents had held prisoner, confirmed the continued presence of these men in leadership positions. Some mentioned that Rokvić, who helped orchestrate the mass execution of about seventy men at the Dugopolje pit, was still in command of a battalion of insurgents.[128] Đilas, who ordered the exhumation of corpses in Kulen Vakuf and helped incite the killing of the men and boys at the Golubnjača pit, felt secure enough to make a series of written requests of his commanders about a week after the killings. In one, he asked for contributions to be made to the families of four "of our fallen brothers," who had been killed during the previous weeks.[129] In another, he requested fresh supplies of bullets since "our people spent their ammunition due to the occupation of Kulen Vakuf and its surrounding villages."[130] Some of those "fallen brothers" whom he mentioned had been killed in the attacks on Kulen Vakuf, specifically during the firefight along the road on the morning of September 6, where hundreds of unarmed civilians were killed. Most of the shooting that had occurred during "the occupation of Kulen Vakuf," aside from the battle along the road between Prkosi and Vrtoče, was due to the execution-style killing of unarmed civilians. Now, a week later, Đilas felt comfortable enough to ask the main insurgent command to replace his fighters' ammunition spent during these killings.

What explains Đilas's ongoing presence in a leadership position and his bold, nonchalant requests, is that he had genuine support from many of his fighters. A remarkable hand-written document sent from his battalion to the main insurgent command in Drvar on September 10—two days after the massacres that Đilas ordered at the Golubnjača pit—shows that "he was chosen to be the commander of our battalion by a majority of the men."[131] These fighters saw Đilas as their leader, which suggests that few were concerned about his central role in the killings, stealing, and burning that occurred in and around Kulen Vakuf. It is likely that many participated alongside him in these acts of violence.

Đilas and Rokvić were not the only individuals active in the September 6–8 killings who would continue to play a role in the insurgency. Another local commander, Nikola Karanović, remained popular with his fighters. He participated in the attack on the column on the morning of September 6, and evidence suggests that he played some part, along with Rokvić, in the execution of about seventy men shortly thereafter at the Dugopolje pit. "A part of the responsibility for the burning of Kulen Vakuf rested with his units," the communist Kosta Nađ recalled, "and with Karanović himself." Others noted: "He did not know how to explain to his fighters . . . that it was not possible to equate Ustaša-ism [*ustaštvo*] with all Croats and Muslims." He wore a beard until others warned him that doing so made him look like a "Chetnik," or Serb nationalist guerrilla fighter. After the fall of Kulen Vakuf, his units' next military objective was to attack the village of Ripač located near Bihać. A senior commander gave a speech in which he warned that under no circumstances could there be a repeat of what happened in Kulen Vakuf. It made no difference. Once again, Karanović and his men played a major role in the attack on Ripač and burned nearly the entire village to the ground.[132]

In short, the struggle between the advocates of escalation and those of restraint within the insurgency continued in the weeks and months after the mass killings in and around Kulen Vakuf. An article published in the NDH newspaper *Novi list* on September 10 in the aftermath of insurgent killings of Muslims in Herzegovina correctly grasped these dynamics:

> On one hand, they [the insurgents] do not spare a single muslim. They kill the defenseless and powerless—the elderly, women, girls, and small children who are still in cradle—all of whom they throw into the flames while still alive. They are destroying muslim villages and homes down to their foundations, as well as everything else that falls into their hands. On the other hand, they are spreading leaflets in which they write about their friendship toward muslim Croats, about their desire to work together, about justice, about a happy future that awaits them if they join their bandit movement.[133]

The depiction was hardly flattering. Yet, in the aftermath of the fall of Kulen Vakuf, the text grasped the tension among the insurgents. The advocates of restraint did desire some version of the "happy future" described here. But they continued to struggle in asserting authority over those who favored mass killing on an ethnic axis. In leaflets distributed throughout villages in northwest Bosnia, communist oriented-commanders attempted to counter such claims by acknowledging the violence that characterized the early months of the insurgency, but also claiming that such behavior was now a thing of the past: "Don't believe the lies that the Ustašas and Croatian newspapers are spreading, that we are allegedly torturing people, putting them on sticks, killing women and children, etc. In the beginning of the insurgency there were unpleasant things that our people did, but that is all behind us. Now there is order and discipline in our army, and not one of our soldiers dares to do anything like that."[134]

But the intra-insurgent tension would not magically dissipate. It would soon explode into open civil war among the fighters during the autumn of 1941. The communist oriented-commanders and their advocates of restraint eventually crystalized into "the Partisan Movement"; some of the advocates of escalation joined the nationalist "Chetnik Movement," whose leaders based themselves some distance away from the Kulen Vakuf region, in other parts of Lika and in Dalmatia.[135] By the end of 1941 and into 1942, the fighting between these two factions grew increasingly bitter. In some locations it became fiercer than the conflict between both elements of the insurgency with the NDH forces.[136]

In the autumn of 1941, two of the insurgent commanders most responsible for the massacres in and around Kulen Vakuf—Rokvić and Đilas—abandoned the communist-oriented units, now increasingly called the "Partisans," and joined others who had become "Chetniks."[137] Their subsequent activities illuminate how civil war created a context in which violence had become a key tool through which individuals sought to resolve problems. And, depending on the situation, factors such as "ethnicity," which might appear to us to be of decisive importance in explaining the nature of local killing during 1941, could quickly assume little to no relevance. On January 21, 1944, Đilas—who played such a key role in the mass killings of Muslims in and around Kulen Vakuf—arrived with a group of Chetnik fighters to a Serbian village in the region called Begluk. They gathered together about twenty men and two women, and then placed machine guns in front of them. According to witnesses, "Đilas then gave a speech in which he said that he would shoot everyone if they did not accept weapons and join the Chetniks." None came forward to volunteer. In response, he and his fighters took the terrified villagers to a hill where the winter wind was blowing fiercely. In the freezing air, they were made to take their clothes off and then lie down. Đilas and his fighters beat them until they fell unconscious; then they tortured several to death. In subsequent months, these armed men regularly returned to the village and "committed plunder and terror," killing at least seven residents, beating nearly all the rest on multiple occasions, destroying nine houses, and stealing large quantities of their limited food supply and livestock.[138]

Begluk was located not far from Suvaja, the village where on July 1, 1941 local Ustašas had committed one of the region's first large massacres of Orthodox villagers, during which they killed as many as 300 villagers. Đilas and his fighters had supposedly taken up arms to defend themselves and their communities from this violence, and to avenge their Orthodox brethren who had been killed. Now, a handful of years later, they had become the tormentors of the very same people they had earlier fought to defend. What this example reveals is how little permanent connection the region's violence could have with ethnic categories. In Begluk, there was no nominal difference in the ethnicity of the victims and perpetrators. As the nature of local conflicts changed, so too did the salience of ethnic categories within such conflicts. In one moment, such as early September 1941, killing Muslims made sense; just over three years later, killing Orthodox villagers, in whose name the Muslims had been murdered earlier, became equally logical—yet the perpetrators in each instance of violence were the same. "Ethnicity" or "ethnic categories" did not retain any kind of permanent salience in who would be categorized as victims. Rather, the shifting, endogenous dynamics of local conflict caused the selection of victim groups to change—from inter-ethnic to intra-ethnic—according to the fluctuating needs of those with a monopoly over the means of violence.

Regardless of the armed faction we examine, the primacy of these local dynamics—rather than solely macro factors such as supposed ethnic affinity or nationalist and communist ideology—emerges as critical to better understanding the region's ongoing violence. We have seen that in Begluk, Serb nationalist Chetniks had no qualms about torturing and killing "Serb" villagers who did not wish to join their units. But the departure for the Chetniks of a handful of insurgents, such as Rokvić and Đilas, who were directly involved in the massacres of September 6–8, 1941, did not mean that the region's communist-led, and therefore supposedly anti-nationalist, Partisan units were cleansed of those who sought out their victims according to ethnicity. More than a year after the killings, many—if not most—of the likely several hundred insurgents who had participated in those massacres were with the Partisans. Among them, for example, was Mile Pilipović, the man who stood poised to cut Mujo Dervišević's throat at the edge of the Golubnjača pit, just before he managed to get his hands free and escape. Prior to Dervišević's arrival, he had murdered scores of other men and boys. He was now a Partisan captain.[139]

Well before and especially since the massacres of September 6–8, local communist activists engaged in ever more intensive political work among their fighters. They endeavored to transform the mind-set of those who wished to continue to use ethnicity as a lens through which to distinguish comrades from enemies. They constantly stressed the importance of a new ideology called "Brotherhood and Unity" (*bratstvo i jedinstvo*) among people seen to be of different nationalities, such as "Serbs, Croats, and Muslims." This ideology—which recognized ethnic difference but demanded the enforcement of ethnic equality—was to be one of the communists' cornerstones for building a new postwar Yugoslav state.[140] Yet a year after the September 6–8 massacres, this multi-ethnic mind-set still had shallow roots among many fighters in the region.

In November 1942, Partisans defeated the NDH forces in the city of Bihać. But the presence of those who favored killing on an ethnic axis was still felt. After the liberation of the city, a Partisan from the Kulen Vakuf region came upon Huso Šabić, who was a teenager and communist sympathizer. His first question was to ask where the boy came from. Šabić replied that he was a refugee from the town of Kulen Vakuf, having fled on September 6, 1941. Upon hearing "Kulen Vakuf," this Partisan immediately drew his weapon and executed him. In another instance, several Partisans arrested Halil Omanović, who was from the village of Orašac in the Kulen Vakuf region. The first from the group to approach him was a Partisan from Oraško Brdo, an Orthodox village in the hills just above the Muslim village of Orašac, whose population suffered at the hands of local Ustašas during the summer of 1941. Omanović asked his former neighbor why his hands had been bound. The Partisan from Oraško Brdo stared at him for a moment. "I personally killed seven members of the Omanović family [during the massacres in September 1941]," he said. "And now I'm going to kill you!" He raised his weapon, but several other Partisans nearby heard this exchange and intervened to save Omanović's life.[141]

Such interventions, however, were not always possible. As this locally rooted settling of scores advanced, torture and executions of suspected "Ustašas" took place in various makeshift jails in Bihać. After NDH forces pushed the Partisans out of the city in 1943, they exhumed the corpses from these killings and found that victims had often been repeatedly stabbed and their throats cut. Many victims were identified as having been refugees from the town of Kulen Vakuf and the nearby villages of Orašac and Ćukovi.[142] It is likely that those who carried out the killings made a point of seeking out their victims based on their ethnicity, place of origin, and the wartime associations from 1941 that they attached to such individuals. A powerful perception of the Kulen Vakuf region as an "Ustaša place" (*ustaško mjesto*), and that those from this area were "Ustašas," remained among some local Partisans. This sensibility was rooted in the violence of the summer of 1941, and its effects continued to fuel revenge-driven killings along ethnic lines whenever the opportunity presented itself. As a result, the local Partisan units, whose leaders were generally committed to waging war in the name of a future multi-ethnic society based on "Brotherhood and Unity," contained fighters who remained ready to kill—and continued to kill—along an ethnic axis whenever memories of past Ustaša violence were triggered.[143]

The trajectory of these two instances of violence in Bihać in 1942 by Partisans and in Belguk in 1944 by Chetniks is of interest to us because of the primacy of their local and endogenous dynamics—those shaped by the course of violence. Supposedly Serb nationalist Chetnik fighters, who had killed large numbers of Muslims in 1941, had no qualms about killing Orthodox villagers in Begluk in 1944; Partisans supposedly under the command of communists, who were intent on building a multi-ethnic socialist state, did not hesitate to kill Muslims from the Kulen Vakuf region. In both cases, memories of past violence and immediate military concerns trumped nationalist or communist ideology in how local fighters chose to employ violence. Depending on the momentary circumstances, ethnic categories could matter greatly—or not. Ethnicized mental templates were fluid and highly contingent. They were capable of undergoing rapid change based on new needs in the present, as well as how present experiences could trigger the surfacing of ethnicized ways of seeing shaped by earlier wartime experiences. Their importance and unimportance was never frozen; they were shaped by violence, and constantly reshaped by it as time unfolded.

Illuminating these dynamics helps us to better understand the difficulties Partisan leaders faced as they took on the challenge of forging a multi-ethnic resistance movement that would hopefully form the basis of a new Yugoslav state based on ethnic equality. The intimate, and often highly ethnicized memory of local violence, which manifested in revenge killings such as those in Bihać, was a constant threat to these larger goals. As the Partisans approached victory in the late spring of 1945, the key challenge for communists in local communities, such as the Kulen Vakuf region, would be to find ways to manage the immense social transformations that the locally executed mass violence had wrought.

Key among them was that so much of the killing radically reduced the space to be "nationally indifferent." The nature of much of the local violence, especially during 1941, meant that one's life frequently depended on what ethnicity one was perceived to be. The violence powerfully inscribed ethnic forms of identification and self-identification, often without one's consent, in ways that were far reaching. This is not to say that forms of ethnic belonging did not exist prior to 1941; rather, the killing imbued them with a degree of unprecedented salience. Not even the multi-ethnic Partisans were immune from this transformative force of the war's violence. The communists' ideology of "Brotherhood and Unity," which was expressly anti-nationalist, was nonetheless firmly embedded in the clear acknowledgement that each individual belonged to an ethnic category. It too reflected the immense ethnicization of social relations and intercommunal perceptions driven to a great extent by wartime killing along ethnic lines. The new postwar society was indeed to be one of "brothers"—that is, of distinct national groups, united and equal in one family, which would take the form of a new Yugoslav state and its recognized "nations." But to achieve this objective, the public knowledge that many of these same "brothers" had transformed their "brothers" into profoundly antagonistic "others" through acts of extreme violence during the war would have to be suppressed, and ultimately silenced.

Managing the legacy of such intimate violence, in a new world characterized by state-enforced "Brotherhood and Unity," would not erase nationalism, or what many communists referred to by the war's end as "chauvinism." Instead, the experience of intercommunal killing, the traumatic memories of it, and the imperative not to speak about any of this, ensured that its dynamics would function differently. As people began to try to live together again, everyday incidents would trigger memories of the collective ethnic categorization that the killing had scarred into people's memories. In such moments, antagonistic nationalism would momentarily surge in outbursts of tension before dissipating just as quickly—at least from public view—under the pressure of the new anti-nationalist authorities. This was the new dynamic of nationalism that would emerge after the Partisan victory in 1945. It was the result of both the war's massive local violence, and the silence about it that the proponents of "Brotherhood and Unity" sought to impose after the killing finally stopped.

Part III

After Intercommunal Violence

Chapter 7

Sudden Nationhood

The Una River's emerald green waters that gurgle through Kulen Vakuf, which had been transformed into a site of mass death during September 6–8, 1941, flowed peacefully in the war years that followed. Most of the refugees who survived the massacres were dispersed throughout the NDH. Some eventually joined the Partisans.[1] Barely anyone saw Kulen Vakuf's charred remains, aside from various soldiers passing through the region, on the way to and from battles. The forests covering the nearby hills and mountains grew thicker from lack of cutting. With no one left to fish, the river's trout thrived in the cold water. The old fortress on the ridge overlooking the town stood in silence. The only sustained human activity was a handful of communist youth activists who cultivated corn in the abandoned fields in the village of Orašac, which insurgents burned on September 4–5, 1941.[2]

The refugees who had fled this part of the Una River valley during those days began returning following the Partisans' victory in the summer and autumn of 1945. Many were women and children. As small groups trickled back, others searched for family members—especially children—many of whom had been scattered throughout the NDH during the war. In some cases, reunions did not take place for many years; when the killings happened in 1941, there were children who were so young that they could not recall exactly where they were from. With few resources, the returnees built improvised shelters, often using the remains of burned houses.[3] Multiple families lived cramped in flimsy dwellings, which the new communist authorities described as "ruins."[4] This situation persisted for years: in 1957, a local newspaper indicated that "nowhere else in the region are there as many burned down houses as in Kulen Vakuf."[5]

Yet oral testimonies suggest that existing alongside difficult material conditions was a sense of happiness among many returnees. As Mustafa Dervišević of Klisa, who at the time was a teenager, recalled: "There was barely any food, but people were in a good mood. We were all so glad that we had come home to our land."[6] Derviš Dervišević, who had been found as a four-year-old sitting next to his mother's body after the insurgents killed her in September 1941, remembered "a sense of happiness [immediately] after the war . . . people loved and hugged each other."[7] Many would gather in the evenings to sing songs and dance while men played accordions. A report by the new communist authorities during the first postwar years reflected this mood: "The people seem alive and engaged."[8] Fueling this positive atmosphere was a push by the government to rebuild the region's railroad lines, which provided work for many local men.[9] By the late 1940s, there was an equal demand for workers in the forestry industry, especially in the sawmills in the nearby town of Drvar.[10]

The local communist authorities were composed exclusively of men who had become Partisans during the war years. According to archival documents, they were classified overwhelmingly as "Serbs." For example, during the second half of the 1940s in Kulen Vakuf and Orašac, nearly all holders of key leadership positions—such as the secretaries of the local committees (*osnovni komiteti*) of the Communist Party—were described in party documents as "Serb." This was the case even though more than 95 percent of the population in this town and village was described as "Muslim."[11] This composition of the local committees of the Communist Party (renamed the League of Communists [Savez komunista] in 1952) would remain more or less unchanged throughout the early postwar decades.[12]

Most party members were of peasant origin, with little to no formal education.[13] Many were said to prefer drinking in taverns to political discussions in party meetings.[14] Regional leaders described more than a few as ideologically "weak elements," who had joined the Partisans late in the war, and who still maintained ties to "Chetniks" during the early postwar years.[15] Most of the handful of communist activists, who in 1941 had played key roles as advocates of restraint and in fostering multi-ethnic resistance, had left the region by 1945. Gojko Polovina had been ejected from the party for making critical remarks about its wartime strategies, and would spend most of the rest of his life in anonymity in Belgrade; Stojan Matić and Stevan Pilipović Maćuka had been killed in the war; Đoko Jovanić was now a high-ranking officer in the Yugoslav People's Army.[16]

With the assistance of reliable, local party members, the new communist authorities sought to settle scores with the remnants of their wartime enemies. In some cases, they hunted down and executed the few remaining Chetniks and Ustašas who were still hiding in the mountains.[17] In many others, however, the government formed war crimes commissions, often while the war was still ongoing, whose local staff collected testimonies from survivors and other witnesses. Their official task was to "determine the responsibility of all individuals, whether with the occupiers or their collaborators, who are responsible for war crimes committed against the people."[18] In practice, this generally meant prosecuting those who had posed the greatest threat to the Partisans during the war, and in the Kulen Vakuf region the obvious target was former Ustašas. Perhaps as many as ten men from the town of Kulen Vakuf and its nearby villages were captured during the early postwar years and sentenced either to long jail terms or to death.[19] Other investigations and trials were conducted for Ustašas from villages such as Boričevac.[20] Yet many key organizers and executioners of their violence in 1941, like tavern owner Miroslav Matijević, escaped the region and were never captured.

The question of what to do with former insurgents and local peasants who had participated in some way in the massacres of September 6–8, 1941 was an extremely sensitive one for the local authorities. Some participants who had joined the Chetniks, such as Petar Đilas, had been killed during the war. Others thought to have played some role, however, had gone on to become Partisan commanders and then important figures in the postwar Yugoslav People's Army, such as Nikola Karanović, who rose to the rank of general. A majority of the region's insurgents who took up arms during the summer of 1941 joined the Partisans at some point during the war years, and more than a few now occupied regional and local leadership positions. It was thus politically impossible for these individuals to be held accountable by the war crimes commissions for the killings of September 6–8.

So what crystallized among the local authorities during the first postwar years was a specific telling of the history of 1941 that sought to erase any negative connection between the killings and those who later joined the Partisans. The local war crimes commissions were among the first who drafted the raw materials for this version of history. As an internal report from August 1946 put it when narrating the events of September 6–8, 1941: "On the hill near Ćovka [about six kilometers from Kulen Vakuf], severe and violent battles broke out between the insurgents and the Domobrani [the NDH military forces]. About 2,000 souls were killed, the majority of whom were Muslims. The insurgents captured a large number of people, and killed many of them. These insurgents were of a 'Chetnik disposition' [*četnički nastrojeni*]."[21] Key here was the formulation "Chetnik disposition," which was something of an anachronism given that the local commissions themselves produced little documentation on Chetnik war crimes in the Kulen Vakuf region, and none on the killings of September 6–8.[22] Employing this rubric, however, was an effective way of creating a clear distinction among the insurgents in 1941: between those who had committed killings in Kulen Vakuf (who could now be thought of essentially as "Chetniks") and those who had not—even though fighters from both groups had actually gone on to join the Partisans.

Such distinctions became more pronounced as Communist Party members began writing more formalized local histories of 1941. According to a group that drafted materials for such a history in 1951: In and around Kulen Vakuf "there was a lot of stealing, burning, and killing of the innocent population by Chetnik elements . . . and there were rapes. This was the result of the desire for revenge for the burning and violence that the Ustašas had carried out earlier in Serbian villages. But later these thieving elements fell out of our [Partisan] ranks and became Chetniks, and the struggle was then taken up against them in the same way as against the Ustašas."[23] There was some truth here, as a handful of these men, such as Petar Đilas and Mane Rokvić, did in fact become formal Chetniks. But many others did not. Instead, they became "Partisans," and some were now in leadership positions in the Kulen Vakuf region. This was a troubling truth that the war crimes commissions and party historians distorted and ultimately buried in their selective telling of 1941.

Yet this history was widely known in the area among those who experienced the violence of that year. But this was a truth that local people soon learned not to speak of, at least publicly, due to the postwar political context. As a result, at the local level—in the town of Kulen Vakuf and its surrounding villages—what characterized daily life after 1945 was a strange silence about much of the worst intercommunal violence of 1941. It was made even more deafening by the fact that perpetrators and survivors were now living in close proximity to one another, sometimes encountering each other in weekly markets, on dusty village roads, and in their places of work.

So what did it mean for local perpetrators and survivors—the identities of which, as we have seen, could easily be held by the same person and group—to try to live together again after intercommunal killing? How did neighbors who committed and experienced atrocities find ways to rebuild their communities, while still living cheek by jowl? And in what ways did people speak—or not speak—the language of nationalism in the shadow of interethnic killing, yet now under a communist government committed to eradicating ethnic antagonisms? Our best means through which to search for answers to these perplexing questions is to continue our local-level analysis, and elucidate what social relations may have been like in such a tension-filled context.

A scene from a community far from the Kulen Vakuf region can help us identify more precisely the puzzle we need to reckon with in order to analyze the new dynamics of social relations that crystallized after intercommunal killing. The place is Višegrad, the town in eastern Bosnia that the Nobel laureate Ivo Andrić made famous in his novel *The Bridge on the Drina* (1945). On a day in 1962, a fight occurred in which one man killed another. While the dead man was described as "Muslim" and his fellow combatant "Serb," when the local communist authorities put the latter on trial for murder, it was not clear whether the incident had a basis in "ethnic conflict." Violence among local men, sometimes resulting in death, was not uncommon in the region, but such altercations were often rooted in ongoing personal disputes, especially when alcohol was involved, and did not necessarily have anything to do with the ethnic identities of those who took part. Moreover, this killing occurred during the heyday of the communist government's promotion of the ideology of "Brotherhood and Unity," which stressed interethnic solidarity while strongly sanctioning expressions of nationalism, both of which led to a dramatic decrease in the everyday use of ethnic categories after World War II. Nevertheless, at one point the nearly fifty Muslims who had come to watch the trial began shouting "Fuck your Serb-Chetnik mother!" toward the accused, making reference not only to his ethnicity, but also to the mostly Serb guerrilla fighters, known as Chetniks, who had murdered thousands of Muslims in the Višegrad region during World War II. They demanded that the court sentence the man to death, or else they would take matters into their own hands. Things got so out of control that at least ten police officers had to intervene to restore order. After the incident, local Muslims were reported to have told each other that the accused "will not be punished the way he deserves because his Serb friends in the government are protecting him. If he were Muslim, he would have been sentenced to death."[24]

What explains this rapid crystallization of an antagonistic sense of "us" and "them," especially before the court had the chance to establish whether the ethnicities of the victim and the accused had anything to do with the killing? How can such a powerful sense of nationhood suddenly appear at such moments? Influential scholars of nationalism, including Ernest Gellner, Eric Hobsbawm, Benedict Anderson, and Miroslav Hroch, have proposed various developmental explanations of nationhood, arguing that a strong sense of it evolves gradually over a long period of time, mostly in response to significant economic, political, and cultural transformations.[25] Others, such as historians Pieter Judson, Jeremy King, James Bjork, and Tara Zahra, have questioned this developmental paradigm by showing that ordinary people often remain indifferent when elites attempt to promote a sense of nationhood.[26] Some political scientists and anthropologists have also pointed to the supposed national indifference of the masses, highlighting instead the role of the political elite in fomenting conflicts along ethnic lines when widespread feelings of interethnic animosity apparently do not exist.[27]

While these approaches certainly have their merits, they offer little in the way of answers to the questions that arise from the account of the fight near Višegrad. How are we to make sense of situations in which, like a train switching tracks, an abrupt shift takes place, leading to the emergence of a sense of "sudden nationhood," marked by an antagonistic form of intensely felt collective solidarity and a simultaneous collective categorization of others as enemies? Despite the booming interest in the study of ethnicity and nationhood—and conflict along such lines—this phenomenon remains curiously understudied, especially at the micro level. As the sociologist Rogers Brubaker observed, "I know of no sustained analytical discussions of nationness as an event, as something that suddenly crystallizes rather than gradually develops, as a contingent, conjuncturally fluctuating, and precarious frame of vision and basis for individual and collective action."[28] Some scholars have responded to his observation by producing macro-level studies of the role played by large-scale, contingent events in the success and failure of nationalist movements.[29] Yet few have taken up the challenge of investigating and explaining how nationhood can suddenly surface at the micro level—in small communities and among neighbors. This is a subject that demands attention if we wish to better understand how ordinary people practice nationhood, and how their actions affect local intercommunal relations.[30]

A newly available source base, containing reports on local intercommunal relations in post–World War II Bosnia-Herzegovina, has made such a micro-level examination possible. These documents, compiled during the 1950s and 1960s by municipal committees (*opštinski komiteti*) of the League of Communists of Bosnia-Herzegovina (Savez komunista Bosne i Hercegovine) and only recently released by the State Archive of Bosnia-Herzegovina in Sarajevo and the Archive of the Una-Sana Canton in Bihać, were originally produced for internal use only. The purpose of their creation was to help the League's Central Committee conduct surveillance on local intercommunal relations and, most importantly, to aid in finding ways to eradicate any manifestations of "national chauvinism" among the residents in local communities who were now living together in the shadow of a civil war and intercommunal violence. By examining the reports from the Kulen Vakuf region, along with others nearby, and supplementing those documents with the views of some local residents, we can undertake an eventful analysis of local incidents of conflict, thereby shedding new light on the micro-dynamics of nationhood and the power of contingent and unexpected events to radically and suddenly transform social relations.[31] By analyzing how local incidents can trigger mental schemas of collective categorization that are based in traumatic memories and experiences of intercommunal violence, we can better understand how nationhood can suddenly become such a powerful lens through which ordinary people interpret their world.[32] More broadly, we can open up new ways for historians and others to explain how nationalism works.

In the postwar period, there were three main mental schemas that structured people's thinking about intercommunal relations in the Kulen Vakuf region. The first was harmony. Given the amount of violence during the war, it is perhaps surprising that relations among some residents were more positive after it ended. A key element was the lengths to which some neighbors had gone to save each other during the peak of the violence (July–September 1941). More than a few took great risks to rescue their neighbors, sometimes paying with their lives.[33] Those whose lives were saved in one round of massacres might then go on to save those who had previously saved them. This dynamic ensured that deep feelings of admiration and gratitude existed after 1945. For example, the wife of Mujo Dervišević, who narrowly escaped being murdered at the Golubnjača pit where insurgents executed more than four hundred men and boys, always praised the insurgent who saved her family, inviting him for coffee and referring to him as "my brother."[34] Other Muslims fondly recalled their Orthodox neighbors who had saved their lives during the war, making it a point to remind others who had not experienced the same treatment that "the Serbs are not all the same."[35] Those who were rescued by their neighbors during the war apparently came to believe that it was a person's character and behavior that mattered most, not his or her ethnicity.[36]

The positive postwar relations between some who considered themselves Serbs and Muslims in the region were visible once they began rebuilding their houses of worship in Kulen Vakuf during the mid-to-late 1950s. When the Serbs were rebuilding their Orthodox church, they received assistance from some Muslim neighbors, who donated materials and money.[37] In 1962, the local communist authorities were surprised to discover that the man who had made the largest contribution, for the church's bell and tower, was a Muslim.[38] This generosity went both ways: when the Muslims began rebuilding their mosque, some of their Serb neighbors gave donations.[39] It is impossible to know exactly what motivated these individuals, but it seems likely that the violence of 1941—specifically, surviving the mass killings because of what their neighbors did to save them—had the paradoxical effect of strengthening intercommunal relations. This made postwar social harmony a reality for some.

A second mental schema, which at least gave the appearance of harmony, was state-enforced "Brotherhood and Unity." As a local Partisan remembered, "[National] relations were good, but they had to be good. Brotherhood and Unity was the law."[40] Or in the words of Mujo Dervišević's daughter: "It was Brotherhood and Unity and 'goodbye,' that's it. Everyone is now equal, everyone is now the same. What happened during the war is what happened, and that's the end of it."[41] Toward this end, the local authorities staged various celebrations, memorializing such events as President Josip Broz Tito's birthday on May 25 and the day that the authorities decided marked the outbreak of the communist insurgency, July 27, 1941.[42] These were engineered, in part, to provide citizens considered to be of different ethnicities with common holidays.[43] Another method that was used to unify the multiethnic population was to selectively remember the war dead in non-ethnic ways, such as through the public ritual of carrying wreaths to the graves of "Fallen Fighters" (*pali borci*) and "Victims of Fascist Terror" (*žrtve fašističkog terora*) on July 4, "The Day of the Fighter" (*Dan borca*), and other commemorative days related to the war.[44] The authorities also organized "work actions" (*radne akcije*), such as building roads and rail lines.[45] Not only were these activities geared toward rebuilding and expanding the existing infrastructure, they were also designed to encourage people perceived to be of different ethnicities who were now living together after a civil war to work together toward common objectives.

This is not to say that the Yugoslav communists sought to transform their multiethnic population into a new monoethnic "Yugoslav nation." Like their Soviet counterparts, they generally supported the national principle and often encouraged nationally defined territories, languages, and cultures. But all such expressions had to take place within the framework of "Brotherhood and Unity," which could be loosely compared to the concept of "the Friendship of Peoples" in the Soviet Union. In both cases, "nations" could be national in form, but they had to be socialist in content and united as "brothers." Antagonistic nationalism was not tolerated.[46]

A central element in the cultivation and enforcement of "Brotherhood and Unity" was the local authorities' monitoring of intercommunal relations. They conducted such surveillance not only to gather information, but also to find ways of molding the population's behavior in accordance with the desire for true "Brotherhood and Unity."[47] Following the war, the Central Committee of the Communist Party instructed its local committees to amass information on "national" or "intercommunal relations" (*međunacionalni odnosi*) in the localities. It was primarily interested in finding out whether "Brotherhood and Unity" existed, or was coming into existence, and if not, then who were the individuals, groups, or "elements" standing in the way.[48] This information gathering remained a top priority for decades.[49]

A report on intercommunal relations in the Kulen Vakuf municipality produced in December 1958 provides examples of the types of behaviors that concerned the authorities. A Muslim named Omer Kulenović referred to Kulen Vakuf as having been "Turkish" until 1918, after which it fell into Serb hands; he criticized the Serbian monarchy during the interwar period and the dominance of Serbs in the Partisan movement during the war and in the Communist Party after 1945. At a gathering organized by the Serbian Orthodox church in the village of Mali Cvjetnić, a Serb named Miloš Knežević was said to have yelled to the crowd: "Here are the Serbs of Cvjetnić! Where are the Turks of [Kulen] Vakuf? Fuck their Turkish mothers!" The report contained several other examples of behavior that the authorities classified as "chauvinism," acts deemed threatening to individuals of a different ethnicity, and thus damaging to "Brotherhood and Unity."[50]

Having gathered this information, the authorities then dealt with the offenders. They instructed the Socialist Association of Working People (Socijalistički savez radnog naroda), a large sociopolitical organization to which most citizens belonged, to organize public meetings for all local residents regarding "Some chauvinist expressions in our municipality and the work of the organization of the Socialist Association on this question."[51] Prior to the meetings, local communists spoke privately with each of the offenders and advised them that they would have to attend and apologize to the entire community. Later, most stood up at the meetings and expressed regret for their comments.[52]

Such public events provided a forum for the authorities to communicate to the local population that insulting their neighbors on the basis of ethnicity would not be tolerated.[53] This practice provided local residents with powerful incentives to get along, at least on the surface, irrespective of their true feelings. People knew that they were being watched, and that they would be reprimanded if they acted in ways damaging to "Brotherhood and Unity." These anti-nationalist practices had two additional effects, one intentional and one not. First, the use of surveillance and discipline taught the population to speak the language of "Brotherhood and Unity," an element of which was learning how to criticize in non-ethnic ways.[54] Second, the official punishment meted out for such infractions showed them that by accusing local enemies of being "national chauvinists," they could potentially leverage the state against their opponents. This dynamic was similar to what Jan Gross has called "the privatization of politics" in his study of the Sovietization of parts of Eastern Europe between 1939 and 1941.[55] It may have unintentionally encouraged people to view everyday incidents and personal conflicts as possible manifestations of "chauvinism" that could be brought to the attention of the authorities as a way to settle local disputes.[56] In this sense, the state's enforcement of the anti-nationalist ideology of "Brotherhood and Unity" may have resulted in people thinking more—not less—about using nationalism and ethnic categories in their interpretations of everyday experiences.

Another way that the enforcement of "Brotherhood and Unity" may have paradoxically increased the salience of ethnic categories had to do with how the charge of "chauvinism" could be invoked when discussion of wartime violence was in question. A 1959 report on "chauvinistic fights and incidents" noted that residents in Kulen Vakuf discussed how monuments for "Serb victims" of the Ustašas were built without problems. However, they complained that nothing had been built for Muslim victims of the insurgents. The regional committee of the League characterized those who criticized this apparent inequality as "chauvinistically oriented Muslims."[57] Here, we can see that while "Brotherhood and Unity" was indeed an ideology of ethnic equality, it was also one that contained strict limits, which were rooted in the specific local dynamics of wartime violence. Some members of the League foreshadowed the rationale for this inequality years earlier, commenting in a closed meeting: "Since people did not participate equally in the war, then all things cannot be looked at equally now."[58] The charge of "chauvinism" in this case thus illuminates how the enforcement of "Brotherhood and Unity" could actually increase awareness of antagonistic ethnicity. At the local level, it was clear that certain groups, which were defined by ethnic categories, enjoyed preferential treatment due to the specific dynamics of intercommunal killing, and whether they fit with the postwar political imperatives of the communist authorities. In the Kulen Vakuf region, victims of the Ustašas could have monuments because they could be classified as "Victims of Fascist Terror"; those killed by insurgents could not because their killers—the insurgents, some of whom had become Partisans by the war's end—could not be categorized as fascists. Wartime violence thus decisively structured the limits and possibilities of building postwar ethnic equality.

The enforcement of "Brotherhood and Unity" was therefore not only about monitoring nationalistically minded individuals and disciplining them; nor was it characterized only by how individuals might use the charge of "chauvinism" in an attempt to leverage the authorities against opponents in local conflicts; it was also a means whereby the authorities silenced politically indigestible aspects of the local intercommunal killing. Because of the nature of that violence, engineering ethnic equality after 1945 paradoxically required an unequal treatment of part of the population on an ethnic axis.

Returning to the day-to-day policing of "Brotherhood and Unity," when individuals who had insulted others on the basis of ethnicity chose not to apologize at public meetings, or when the offenses were considered egregious enough that a public apology would not suffice, the authorities employed other methods. Local communists had no qualms about instructing the local police and courts to arrest, prosecute, and punish the offenders, usually through expulsion from sociopolitical organizations, fines, and in some cases imprisonment. In January 1957, for example, Milka Grubiša, described as a Serb member of the League of Communists from the municipality of Kulen Vakuf, got into a "chauvinistic fight" with a Muslim schoolteacher. The incident was serious enough that those present called the police. When the officers, who appeared to be Muslims, arrived, Grubiša insulted them as well. The regional committee of the League of Communists in Bihać, to which Grubiša belonged, recommended that she be expelled from the organization because of this incident, as well as several other occasions on which she had exhibited behavior considered unacceptable for a member of the League.[59]

In another instance, in 1958, a man described as a Serb named Branko Altagić tried to persuade a group of Serbs from the village of Prkosi to leave their municipality and join the future municipality of Vrtoče, promising that if they did so, they would be given a store in their village. They responded by saying that they already had one. It happened to be operated by the trading firm "Ostrovica," which was based in Kulen Vakuf and run by Muslims. The firm also employed a mostly Muslim workforce. Altagić exploded in anger, yelling out to the other Serbs: "The store in Prkosi is Ustaša! We Serbs from Vrtoče liberated you Serbs in Prkosi and Oraško Brdo from the Ustašas whose municipality you now love being part of. The time will come again when they will slaughter you, and so let them slaughter you . . . we won't defend you from them." The Ministry of Internal Affairs recommended that he be prosecuted and punished for this chauvinistic verbal assault.[60]

The enforcement of "Brotherhood and Unity" through vigorous policing consumed a significant amount of the attention of the authorities in the region, and in fact throughout Bosnia-Herzegovina, during the late 1950s and early 1960s. In the Bihać region (in which the municipality of Kulen Vakuf was located), the Secretariat of Internal Affairs (Sekretarijat unutrašnjih poslova) prosecuted 110 cases in 1961 against individuals who had acted in ways that were considered to be "chauvinistic," and thus damaging to "Brotherhood and Unity."[61] The number of people who were arrested and warned but not prosecuted was likely much higher. Throughout Bosnia-Herzegovina, thousands of individuals were disciplined by the authorities for "chauvinism" during the same period. Between January 1958 and September 1961, local police counted 329 serious physical altercations that had started because of chauvinistic comments, involving more than 2,500 individuals.[62] From late 1959 or early 1960 until mid-1962, 7,433 individual acts of "chauvinism" were reported across the republic, an average of 8 per day. It is not clear whether all the offending individuals were formally charged and prosecuted, although the existence of such precise statistical information strongly suggests the involvement of the police in some way, and a high probability of some kind of punishment.[63] The large number of reported incidents and the extensive involvement of the police and courts illustrate the importance that the communist authorities placed on rigorously policing "Brotherhood and Unity." If anyone was perceived to be wavering in supporting this ideology, the government's readiness to enforce positive ethnic relations was a compelling incentive for people to get along in their everyday affairs.

A third mental schema affected intercommunal relations among a smaller number of people: discord. The evidence suggests that their attitudes were rooted in the mass killings of 1941 and other instances of wartime violence. Some of those who actively spread these views were religious leaders. Father Branislav Branić, an Orthodox priest from the Kulen Vakuf region, was known to refer to Muslims as "dogs." Alluding to the fact that some Muslims had murdered Serbs during the war, he warned Serbs that they should protect themselves from their Muslim neighbors, because "the dog that bit you last year will bite you again this year."[64] Several Muslim clerics in the wider region reportedly warned local Muslims that they were in danger from former Serb Partisans, whom they sometimes called "Chetnik-Communists"—a reference to the Partisans' absorption during the war of many Serb fighters who had previously murdered Muslims.[65] Such examples suggest the importance of wartime events in structuring the negative attitudes toward Muslims and Serbs that were espoused by some Orthodox and Islamic clerics after the war.

Even some of those who were in the vanguard of promoting "Brotherhood and Unity"—communist officials and members of the military—held negative views about their neighbors of different nationalities.[66] Some individuals described as Serbs, including a handful of members of the League of Communists, were noted during 1958 to have referred to Muslims in the area in a derogatory way as "Turks" and to have cursed their "Turkish mothers," especially while drinking.[67] Some Serb members of the League of Communists in the region were noted for complaining during meetings that it was difficult to enlarge the membership of their organization beyond fellow Serbs because "the Muslims are Ustašas."[68]

Such comments could cause fights, as was the case in 1958 when a Serb who was an active major in the Yugoslav People's Army was drinking heavily in a hotel at a table with several other Serbs. At one point he turned toward a Muslim sitting nearby and shouted that he was an Ustaša. The Muslim and the others he was sitting with shouted back that the major and his company were Chetniks. The two men stood up and faced off against each other, with the major drawing his pistol. Approximately twenty Serbs gathered around the major, and sixty to seventy Muslims assembled opposite them. Some pulled out knives, while others picked up chairs. At the last moment, a Muslim former Partisan managed to calm the Serbs down, and a mass brawl was avoided.[69] This example suggests that wartime experiences and categories, which often overlapped with ethnic categories (e.g., Ustašas as Muslims and Chetniks as Serbs), continued to exert a strong influence on some individuals after the war, even among communists and members of the military, despite their mandate to promote "Brotherhood and Unity."[70]

There were similar occurrences in other parts of the wider region during the late 1950s and early 1960s. In 1962, a group of Serb youth crept into a Croatian village one night and began singing Serbian songs and yelling "Fuck your Ustaša mothers!" to the Croats. Some Croat youth came out of their houses to confront them, and a brawl started, involving thirty to forty people. In a report about the incident, the League of Communists identified the legacy of the war as a direct cause, noting that many of the Croats' parents were Ustašas who had murdered the parents of the Serbs in 1941.[71] On other occasions, no physical altercations occurred, but the legacy of the war in structuring perceptions was clearly evident. Some Serbs criticized the installation of electricity and the construction of water and sewage systems in Muslim villages and towns, arguing that these were "Ustaša places" that did not deserve infrastructure.[72]

In 1963, the regional League of Communists indicated that a special problem with regard to "chauvinism" was that some individuals who had lost relatives in the wartime mass killings were expressing a desire to take revenge.[73] As one was heard in a tavern in 1962: "If I stay alive, I will avenge my parents. I'm not rolling up my sleeves for nothing. I pray to God that none of the Turks will say anything to me, because I'll show them who slaughtered my parents—I'll fuck their Turkish mothers."[74] Or, during the same year, another yelled out to a group after they attended the unveiling of a war monument: "You are all Ustašas, and you'll remember whose mothers you killed in 1941. I'll fuck your Turkish mothers!"[75] The situation was similar in other regions of Bosnia-Herzegovina. In some Orthodox and Muslim villages in the Zenica region, many residents had been either Chetniks or Ustašas during the war. The League noted that conflicts between several individuals that were rooted in wartime mass killings had stretched on into the 1960s.[76] In the commune of Lukavac, two men—described as a Muslim and a Serb—got into a fight in a tavern, and the Muslim yelled out: "What happened to your father [in 1941] will happen to you . . . you need to be slaughtered just like your father . . . your time will come!"[77] These examples lend support to a claim made by the League of Communists in a 1962 report: "Aside from economic and cultural issues, the war has had the biggest impact on contemporary national relations."[78] For some, the traumas that they endured during the war had left them with seemingly unchangeable negative views of their neighbors of different perceived nationalities. And this attitude sometimes permeated perceptions not only of the past, but also of the future. A former Chetnik in the Kakanj region was reported to have said to his Serb neighbors in 1961: "Hold on to your weapons because there will come a time when you will need them."[79] At the end of the 1960s in eastern Bosnia, where there had been widespread mass killings of Muslim civilians by Chetniks during the war, a local Muslim man predicted that war would soon return: "Things are difficult for us Muslims. The Serbs will slaughter us once again."[80]

These three mental schemas—harmony, state-enforced "Brotherhood and Unity," and discord—offer a window into the complex nature of local postwar intercommunal relations in smaller communities, such as those in the Kulen Vakuf region. But the suggestion of a neat distinction among them, while useful for the sake of analysis, presents a somewhat static portrait of social relations that obscures a much more fluid and volatile dynamic. Previously unavailable documents suggest that high levels of antagonistic "groupness" could rapidly crystallize in response to incidents that were perceived to be based in "ethnic conflict." At such moments, some people would experience an abrupt shift, quickly interpreting the cause of an incident as being rooted in a participant's ethnicity, and especially the wartime associations they attached to whole ethnicities. These interpretations did not merely describe such incidents as "ethnically based"; they actually constituted them in such terms.[81] As a result, often-mundane incidents between individuals were rapidly transformed into conflicts between collectivities, between an "us" and a "them." In the process, some people would suddenly experience a powerful sense of antagonistic nationhood.

Two further points are relevant in conceptualizing this dynamic of "sudden nationhood." First, the fact that ethnic categories retained their salience for some people after the war should not lead us to conclude that such categories and wartime associations were dominant among a majority of people on an everyday basis. The evidence suggests that they were not, especially because of the authorities' vigorous policing of "Brotherhood and Unity." Rather, they could surface at times when emotions became volatile, usually in response to incidents of conflict. The second point is that the reactions to incidents that produced sudden nationhood were not necessarily driven by a calculated desire to instrumentalize ethnicity for a particular objective, such as to leverage the state against individuals in a personal dispute; rather, individuals suddenly adopted a highly ethnicized interpretation of incidents in a much more un-self-conscious and quasi-automatic way after threats or acts of violence triggered ethnic ways of seeing, which had roots in experiences and memories of wartime violence.[82] Sudden nationhood was thus a rapid shift from a generally non-ethnicized to a highly ethnicized way of seeing the world, and it was more an automatic emotional response than a rational, instrumental decision.

Among the incidents that tended to give rise to sudden nationhood were verbal assaults, physical altercations, and murders, many of which appear to have had linkages to wartime events. In a 1963 report, the regional League of Communists demonstrated its awareness of how rapidly such incidents could transform intercommunal relations: "Chauvinism remains an ongoing problem . . . its danger is latently alive. Every improper gesture or action has the potential to awaken and initiate political problems."[83] Several examples from the 1950s and 1960s illustrate how sudden nationhood could crystallize in the aftermath of local incidents. During the late 1950s, the League of Communists did not characterize intercommunal relations in the wider region as negative. But when several men described as "Serbs" murdered "a Muslim" who was walking through their village in the municipality of Bužim one night, some local Muslims suddenly lost whatever illusions they might have had about the communist authorities' support of "Brotherhood and Unity." It was not clear whether the murder was rooted in "ethnic conflict."

Yet as one Muslim later summed up the general sentiment: "If a Serb had been killed, then the government would have killed fifty Muslims, but if fifty Muslims were killed, they wouldn't kill a single Serb."[84] This killing not only inflamed tensions between local Serbs and Muslims, it also revealed an underlying sense among some Muslims that the authorities were heavily biased against them. The killing showed how quickly such an incident could be interpreted and constituted entirely through the lens of ethnic conflict, as well as the government's potentially disappointing response. It was no longer a murder that involved several individuals, some of whom happened to be nominally Serb and one of whom happened to be nominally Muslim; it was now an incident between "Serbs" and "Muslims" more generally.

Other cases show how incidents of conflict exposed some people's implicit belief that their neighbors were guilty of causing problems not because of their individual behaviors, but rather because they were perceived to be of a different ethnicity. Sometime during 1958 in a village located near Kulen Vakuf, a Muslim named Salih Hadžić showed up at his Serb neighbor Branko Rokvić's house in a state of intoxication. He invited himself in, then struck Rokvić for no apparent reason. The police investigation did not conclude that Hadžić had assaulted Rokvić because he hated Serbs; drunkenness and some kind of ongoing personal dispute between the two appeared to be the causes of the incident. But Rokvić's family nevertheless insisted that it be treated as an act of "national chauvinism," and began spreading the rumor that "Muslims" were responsible for all acts of chauvinism.[85] In this case, the family's immediate perception that the fight was about ethnic hatred was a more important factor in their interpretation of the incident than whatever information the police investigation uncovered. The "ethnic" quality of "ethnic conflict" was not self-evident and intrinsic in this case, even though the incident occurred between individuals described as a "Serb" and "Muslim"; rather, relatives of the victim attempted to constitute it as "ethnic conflict" through their post-incident interpretive claims.[86] In so doing, they were the central actors in producing sudden nationhood.

These sorts of incidents sometimes led people to demand that all those perceived to be members of a particular ethnicity be punished, even though the incident in question may have had nothing to do with "ethnic conflict," and the guilty party may have been only a single individual. For example, in the late 1950s or early 1960s, a Muslim boy raped an elderly Serb woman in the village of Bušević, near Kulen Vakuf. Even though the police determined that the boy had committed the crime for reasons other than "national chauvinism," Serbs in the village began to talk about the need to take revenge on the "Muslims" for the incident. In a similar local occurrence, two boys, one described as "Serb" and the other "Muslim," got into a fight, with the Muslim killing the Serb. The reasons for the fight did not appear to have anything do to with ethnic conflict; it apparently was a personal dispute that had spiraled out of control. Nevertheless, local Serbs spoke about the need to avenge the boy's death by dealing not only with the Muslim boy who was guilty of the killing, but also with all the "Muslims" in the region, whom they saw as collectively guilty.[87] In similar cases, some Serbs refused to speak about the murder of one of their own as the act of an individual. In one such case, a Muslim named Haso had killed a Serb boy. Local Serbs, however, quickly jumped from saying "Haso killed the boy" to "The Turks killed the boy," which was a derogatory way of referring to Muslims, and could also mean "Ustašas."[88] Such examples illuminate how some people interpreted conflicts that were nominally interethnic exclusively through the lens of "ethnic conflict." This perspective then framed their calls for revenge along the lines of ethnicity. But their interpretive claims and their subsequent calls for revenge were *constitutive* acts, geared toward making incidents "ethnic," with the effect of producing sudden nationhood.

The Central Committee of the League of Communists of Bosnia-Herzegovina noted in 1959 that it was often small, everyday incidents that ended up snowballing into "ethnic conflicts"—or, perhaps more accurately, conflicts that people perceived as ethnic. A Muslim's livestock wandering onto a Serb's property, or a Serb walking through a Muslim village singing a Serbian song—such incidents could provoke Muslims to curse the "Serb," "Vlah," or "Chetnik" mothers of the Serbs, or the Serbs to curse the "Turkish," "Ustaša," or "balijska" mothers of the Muslims, all of which were highly offensive to those on the receiving end.[89] These curses, which almost always categorized the recipient in ethnic and/or wartime terms and included a declaration to sexually assault the recipient's mother, suggest that there was a close intersection between memories of wartime violence, gender, and instances of sudden nationhood. Hurling such insults may have been a means for men—who appear to have been the vast majority of those who yelled these curses—to regain their sense of power and masculinity, which had been so profoundly damaged during the war through acts of mass violence, frequently including instances of mass sexual assault against their women.[90] Scholars of South Asia have noted a similar dynamic in local forms of nationalism in which overcoming a sense of effeminization at the hands of the "ethnic other" is a central driving force in instances of local conflict, particularly among young men.[91]

Thus it is hardly surprising that these verbal assaults, which could readily be construed as making reference to the intimate, traumatic histories of violence against a community's women during the war, could easily lead to small fights, which could rapidly escalate into mass brawls. On some occasions, entire villages that normally enjoyed a peaceful coexistence suddenly found themselves facing off against each other after a relatively minor incident, often with no clear basis in "ethnic conflict," sparked a fight between individuals of nominally different ethnicities.[92] The degree to which individuals would suddenly align themselves exclusively with their perceived co-ethnics during and after such incidents was evident when the authorities tried to prosecute the guilty parties. More often than not, only Muslim witnesses would come forward to help Muslims accused of having participated in such fights, and only Serbs would come forward to help Serbs.[93]

Sometimes it was not even necessary for an incident to occur for interpretations that could lead to intercommunal violence to instantly emerge and rapidly spread. Rumors were often all it took to cause a major disturbance, as historians and anthropologists of a number of parts of Europe and South Asia have noted in other contexts.[94] The Central Committee reported with dismay about a brawl between the Serb and Muslim residents of a village in the Sarajevo region during the late 1950s. The cause of the fight was a report that had quickly circulated among local Serbs that their Muslim neighbors had damaged their Orthodox church and cemetery. A huge fight ensued. The report, however, was false; it had simply been a rumor: the Muslims had done nothing.[95]

In a similar occurrence in 1964 from the Velika Kladuša region, a Muslim boy herding livestock near an Orthodox cemetery threw a rock and damaged a picture on a gravestone. The family of the deceased was incensed and immediately demanded that the local police arrest the boy for a nationalist attack. His family quickly apologized, but the Serb family continued to insist that the League of Communists treat the incident as a chauvinistic act. Wild rumors then began to circulate through the Serbian villages in the area that Muslims were removing corpses from the cemetery and that they planned to build a new mosque next to the Orthodox church.[96] Even a child's simple act of throwing a stone could quickly escalate into an "ethnic conflict."

These examples do not suggest that communities in which the residents are perceived, and perceived themselves to be of different ethnicities are somehow more prone to conflict and violence than mono-cultural communities. It was not an intrinsic sense of antagonistic cultural difference among the local residents that produced the reactions to these incidents. Rather, it was the specific historical dynamics of local intercommunal relations that predisposed certain individuals to interpret conflicts in a particularly antagonistic way. In many cases, the evidence suggests that the shadow of wartime violence was in the background, structuring and giving amplification to the ways in which certain people interpreted rumors and actual incidents of conflict. Because of this, they were predisposed to quickly believe stories about the supposed hostile intentions of certain individuals and groups that often rapidly materialized during and after incidents. As Donald Horowitz has noted in his study of riots in many other contexts, "a rumor will not take hold unless there is a market for it."[97] In the Kulen Vakuf region, the experience and memory of wartime intercommunal violence in large part created that market.

For example, in 1961, a Serb worker was killed on a jobsite in the Bosanski Petrovac region, near Kulen Vakuf, when some heavy materials accidentally fell on him. Only Muslim workers had been loading such materials that day. Several Serb workers—whom the League of Communists later referred to as "Serb nationalist elements" because they had served time in prison for having been Chetniks during the war—then started a rumor that the Muslim workers had intentionally killed the Serb. After hearing this story, the rest of the Serb workers prepared to engage in a brawl with their Muslim co-workers. The presence of the police averted what would surely have been a serious fight. It appears that the wartime experiences of the Serbs who spread the rumor had conditioned them to instantly interpret such an accident through the prism of ethnic conflict.[98]

Wartime events also played a role in structuring reactions to incidents of interethnic conflict in other regions. In the Foča region of eastern Bosnia, a fight occurred in 1963 between two co-workers, one described as Muslim and the other Serb, at the region's thermoelectric plant. Reports by the League of Communists did not suggest that the two men had a direct history of interethnic conflict that dated to World War II. In fact, it appears that both had been children during the war. Nonetheless, their fight caused the Muslim, Hajrudin Hasanbegović, who was a member of the League, to yell at his Serb co-worker, Anđelko Pavlović, that "people like him" (i.e., Serbs) had cut his brother's throat during the war, then stolen everything from their house, and now they were building themselves a new house with what they had plundered. Pavlović responded that the Muslim men of the Hasanbegović family had all been Ustašas during the war, and that Hajrudin would have been one as well had he been old enough.[99] A key factor here was how the fight triggered a mental schema of wartime experiences and/or memories, perhaps transmitted by relatives, that structured the way each man categorized and disparaged the other. This fight between two co-workers who happened to be nominally of different ethnicities was thus transformed into an "ethnic conflict" with strong wartime associations.

That relatives at home and in the village could be the main transmitters of traumatic historical memories about intercommunal violence to the children who would participate in such fights years later can be seen in evidence from the League's local committees. In 1961, a committee visiting several Orthodox villages in the Kulen Vakuf region discovered that many children made no distinction between the category "Muslim" and "Turk," despite the fact that "Turk" was not used by the government or in schools and, moreover, carried with it derogatory overtones. More often than not, the children declared matter-of-factly: "The Turks live in different parts of our region."[100] When asked for an example of violence between their people and the "Turks," the committee expected the children to reference the days of Ottoman rule over the region; instead, about 60 percent responded that 1941 was such an example.[101] In another case, several committees of the League in northwest Bosnia noted in 1959 that school children in Orthodox villages sometimes answered the question, "Who was the enemy of our people during the war?" not with "fascists" or "Ustašas," but rather: "Our Croat neighbors."[102] Such evidence suggests that the mental template for interpreting fights and other conflicts through wartime categories, and their association with local acts of intercommunal violence, had formative roots at the micro level—at home and in one's village. These were among the primary places where children learned "who was what" in terms of ethnic categories, and "what they did to us" during the war. Such ethnicized ways of seeing could be suddenly activated as an interpretive grid in making sense of moments of local conflict, especially in determining causes of fights and other disputes.

A government report compiled in 1961 on "chauvinistic fights and incidents" in the wider region in which the municipality of Kulen Vakuf was located confirmed this tendency on the part of certain individuals to quickly give fights, killings, rapes, and other incidents of violence a "chauvinistic color." It appears that their automatic response was to interpret a given incident as a "chauvinistic attack," or as a manifestation of ethnic conflict, simply because the victim and the perpetrator were perceived to be of different ethnicities.[103] The League of Communists noted that wartime experiences played a crucial role in some people's interpretations of such incidents.[104]

The archival evidence for who, exactly, the main actors were in fueling instances of sudden nationhood is frequently thin, and contemporary ethnographic research can yield frustratingly few insights given the degree to which the most recent war in Bosnia-Herzegovina (1992–1995) devastated local communities through mass killing, expulsion, and emigration. There often are few survivors who can provide further insights about specific local conflicts noted in archival documents written in the 1950s and 1960s.

Nonetheless, it is still possible to sketch a social profile of those who initiated and fed the flames of sudden nationhood.

A majority appear to have been from rural regions and small towns where the wartime intercommunal violence was often most severe and intimate. Many were middle-aged and said to have participated in "Chetnik" and "Ustaša" formations during the war. Others were the children of such individuals, described by communists as having been imbued with the views of their parents.[105] The family members of a victim in a given incident often played the most active role in creating and propagating an ethnicized interpretation of a conflict.[106] One group that appears prominently is men who were released early from prison during the 1950s and 1960s after serving time for participating in mass killings and other war crimes. In some cases, they returned to their villages and received a hero's welcome, with celebrations lasting for days and guns being fired into the air, all of which unnerved the residents of the neighboring villages where the survivors of their wartime violence lived.[107] These individuals appear to have often been the key "strong men," to use Sudhir Kakar's evocative term from his work on leaders of communal violence in India, in launching attempts to frame incidents in ethnic terms.[108] According to the authorities, they had more success in mobilizing others to adopt their interpretations when they evoked painful wartime memories. As the League stated in 1962: "A special form of chauvinistic activity relates to evoking events from the war. This influences youth and encourages them to hate other nationalities and to engage in chauvinistic activities. It is expressed especially in regions where there were mass slaughters during the war. Under the influence of such individuals, it is not uncommon for people to express a desire to avenge their loved ones who were killed during the war."[109]

Sometimes it was communists who initiated incidents of sudden nationhood, rather than those whom the communists had fought against and imprisoned for wartime interethnic killings.[110] Their participation, while perhaps surprising to us, was not to their neighbors, as party documents from eastern Bosnia suggest: "There are many people who committed crimes during the war who today live camouflaged . . . [but] people know what others did during the war, including those who are now [communist] party members."[111] Archival evidence shows that there were many instances in which local police officers and members of the League of Communists played the leading role, contradicting the authorities' argument that it was usually wartime "enemies of the people" who were responsible for triggering and escalating incidents of "national chauvinism."[112] Thus whether the instigator was inside or outside the communist government was not a primary determining factor. Rather, it was the direct experience of extreme intercommunal violence, or a memory of it transmitted by relatives and neighbors, that resulted in a mental schema in which wartime perpetrator categories and whole "ethnic groups" could easily be conflated during and after highly charged moments of conflict.[113]

The evidence, however, *does not* suggest that such a schema was dominant in most people's everyday lives. It usually had to be triggered by an incident, often something mundane, in order to provide the fuel for the outbreak and escalation of sudden nationhood. This was a dynamic that was widespread throughout Bosnia-Herzegovina. In 1962 in the Jajce region, located southeast of Kulen Vakuf, the League of Communists noted that the "mass liquidation of the population on the basis of nationality" during the war had established a postwar template for "personal conflicts" to rapidly take on "a chauvinistic character." Disputes among neighbors over the borders of their fields and the use of water, or quarrels between sheep herders in the hills who happened to nominally be of different ethnicities, could immediately be framed as a "ethnic conflict." This framing in collective ethnic terms could activate local memories of intercommunal violence from the war, which sometimes swept two villages into a mass brawl. At such moments, local communists lamented that because of a simple fight between two shepherds in a field, a mind-set rooted in wartime violence had suddenly become paramount: "Every Croat and Muslim is called an Ustaša, and every Serb a Chetnik."[114] Identical explosions of wartime-based collective categorization were part of such everyday conflicts in the Kulen Vakuf region too. In 1958, local tavern owner Nikola Filipović, while intoxicated, yelled out to his patrons in a moment of anger: "All you Muslims from [Kulen] Vakuf are Ustašas! And I know you from 1941."[115]

The importance of wartime experiences in conditioning some people to interpret postwar incidents between individuals of different nominal ethnicities as "ethnic conflict" can be further seen by examining reactions to intra-ethnic murders—those that occurred only between "Serbs" or only between "Muslims." On such occasions, people paid dramatically less attention. For the most part, there were no wild rumors about the reason for the murder. People did not invoke events from the war to explain why the killing had taken place; nor did they use their wartime experiences to justify the need for any kind of punishment or revenge to be taken against the guilty parties.[116]

When the victim and the perpetrator were considered to be of the same ethnicity, people saw the incident as tragic, but they generally did not characterize it as connected to the war, and they did not demand that punishment be extended to everyone perceived to be of the perpetrator's ethnicity.[117] This suggests that interethnic incidents of conflict, or rumors of such incidents, had a special power to quickly evoke memories of the extreme violence of the war, especially in regions where the killing had unfolded along ethnic lines and created mental schemas of collective categorization. These emotional responses, rooted in traumatic experiences and memories, appear to have been a critical factor in some people's near-instant interpretation of such incidents exclusively through the prism of ethnic conflict.

Of course, memories of wartime violence were slow to fade in many communities. They were triggered on a regular basis because perpetrators and survivors continued to live in close proximity. In the Kulen Vakuf region, there were men who worked on the railroad every day alongside the very men who had murdered their parents.[118] At the weekly Thursday market, women silently passed by others who had tried to beat them to death in 1941 by the Una River.[119] Mujo Dervišević, the sole survivor of the massacre of the men and boys at the Golubnjača pit, sometimes encountered Mile Pilipović, who had stood poised to slit his throat just before he managed to escape. As he recalled about one such meeting: "The war was over . . . so I employed myself in construction. One day I was mixing the mortar, and I looked down the road. I saw some captain [in the Yugoslav People's Army] who was walking toward me and smiling. He yelled out: 'Hello Mujo!' And then he offered me his hand. I stared and stared at him [and then realized who he was] . . . 'Why are you offering me that hand!? Have you forgotten that you wanted to use that hand to kill me and push me into the pit?!'"[120]

Family members of victims endured similar experiences. A former insurgent named Jovo Medić was said to have entered a tailor shop in Kulen Vakuf some years after the war. The shop owner's son had been killed during the September massacres of 1941. While speaking with Medić, the owner recognized his son's watch on Medić's wrist. He said nothing, but began to cry. Medić quickly left, never to return.[121] Fathers of sons killed at the Golubnjača pit sometimes attempted to visit the site, but local peasants—some of whom may have participated in the wartime killings—often harassed them and chased them away.[122] One father who did manage to locate Golubnjača began praying near the cave's opening, but was interrupted by a former insurgent who threw stones at him. "If you are a man, then continue on your way," the father cried out, "Allah will protect my son's grave from the devil."[123] These everyday encounters that triggered traumatic wartime memories continued as the postwar years ticked by. A former insurgent who later joined the Partisans and worked after the war as a census-taker was said to have once knocked on a door to ask how many people lived in the house, only to be told coldly: "You should know; you killed many of them during the war."[124]

Such meetings ensured that the local, intimate traumas of the war did not easily dissipate. And they meant that, at the village and town level, perpetrators were not merely described with the abstract categories of "insurgents," "Chetniks," or "Ustašas," which most historians employ; rather, they were known by their names—"the Kurtagićes, the Kadićes, and the Mašinovićes," as two residents in Martin Brod could still instantly recall many decades after the war—and by their individual wartime deeds.[125]

This region was something of an exception in this regard in comparison with much of the rest of Europe, where a great "unmixing" of peoples—and thus perpetrators and survivors—took place along ethnic lines during and after the war. This made the kinds of daily encounters that caused memories of wartime intercommunal violence to resurface less likely.[126] In this corner of Yugoslavia, by contrast, the victory of the communist-led Partisans preserved a multi-ethnic community in postwar Europe's dramatically ethnically homogenized landscape. But the victory of the multiethnic principle came with a price: survivors and perpetrators, as well as their offspring, remained neighbors, and their daily encounters, especially incidents of conflict, regularly sparked sudden nationhood. Postwar intercommunal relations thus were often exceptionally fluid and highly dependent on the extent to which contemporary incidents of conflict activated forms of collective categorization rooted in wartime experiences and memories. It was in these highly charged moments that a near-instant coding of incidents as "ethnic" rapidly gave rise to a surging, antagonistic sense of "us" and "them" among some people, which they then tried to spread.

We began with a story from the town of Višegrad in which a man accused of murder suddenly lost his individuality in the courtroom and became a "Serb" and a "Chetnik." What explains this rapid transformation in which people are relegated to collective and antagonistic categories? How does nationhood abruptly happen in these moments? What role, if any, does violence play in this process? And what can an eventful analysis of the micro-dynamics of nationhood contribute more generally to the study of nationalism? After the war, we can see the emergence of three primary mental schemas of intercommunal relations: harmony, state-enforced "Brotherhood and Unity," and discord. For some, the fact that neighbors saved neighbors of a different perceived ethnicity during the war drove home the importance of interethnic friendship, and this helped to produce a genuine sense of harmonious postwar intercommunal relations. The intensive work by the communist authorities in enforcing "Brotherhood and Unity" was central in creating and policing social harmony, which was genuine for many, but for others could be seen more as a form of "counterfeit courtesy."[127] For yet others, the losses they had experienced during the war locked them into a mind-set in which perceived ethnic differences, and their association with wartime atrocities, were primary in distinguishing postwar friends from enemies.

While these mental schemas capture an important reality, new local-level evidence reveals the volatile dynamic of sudden nationhood. After the war's extreme intercommunal violence, certain people tended to rapidly code local incidents between individuals of different perceived ethnicities in terms of "ethnic conflict," even if the subsequent police investigations, as well as local interpretations among many residents, did not attribute such motivations to the participants themselves. In this way, they attempted to produce and spread a sense of "ethnic conflict" in their communities, as well as a sense of hard, antagonistic group boundaries, even though prior to these incidents those boundaries may have been soft and unimportant in daily life for many people. In short, it was the after-the-fact coding of incidents as "ethnic conflict," due in large part to wartime-created mental templates—not a preexisting, widespread sense of antagonistic nationhood—that often led to their being more broadly interpreted as "ethnic conflict."

The discovery of this dynamic is significant because it enables us to better understand the micro-mechanisms of nationalism among ordinary people, an often-elusive group whose behavior scholars often speculate about but less frequently closely research. Some analysts, for example, claim that nationalism and "ethnic conflict" are elite-created phenomena, which in some cases can overwhelm ordinary people's sense of national indifference, or demobilize them from seeking non-nationalist alternatives.[128] This argument captures an important dynamic of nationalism in many cases, but it also leaves unanswered the question of why certain individuals in small communities almost instantly interpret incidents of conflict through an "ethnic" lens even when there is evidence to the contrary. Accounting for local agency is crucial because micro-level behavior is often of decisive importance for the success or failure of any elite-generated attempt to spread an antagonistic sense of groupness. The notion of sudden nationhood—with an emphasis on the role of mental schemas produced by experiences and memories of mass violence—provides a means of analyzing this agency. It shows us, and allows us to grasp, the process whereby ordinary people make local incidents of conflict into "ethnic conflict," and how their actions can contribute to a dramatic shift in the salience of ethnic categories at the micro level.

Conversely, in recognizing and analyzing sudden nationhood, we are reminded that moments of intensely felt collective solidarity and the antagonistic collective categorization of others are *not* constant and enduring features of local life. Unfortunately, source limitations make it difficult to extend this focus beyond incidents in which particular individuals attempted to produce a powerful sense of antagonistic groupness. The communist authorities, who were highly concerned with policing "Brotherhood and Unity," devoted much more time to writing internal reports about local incidents of conflict that had snowballed into "national chauvinism" than to recording examples of interethnic incidents in which this escalation did not take place.

Yet there were most likely interethnic incidents in which a sense of antagonistic groupness did not suddenly happen. A 1962 report on manifestations of "national chauvinism" by one local committee of the League of Communists concluded that such incidents "frequently did not find support or approval from the local population."[129] Thus far, however, the available evidence has not allowed for much analysis of this dynamic. Further research on interethnic incidents of conflict that did not result in sudden nationhood would help us to better explain why it emerges in other instances. For example, it would be important to better determine whether the legacy of the intercommunal violence of World War II was, in fact, the primary contributor to some people's tendency to interpret events through the lens of "us" and "them." Perhaps there were interethnic incidents of conflict that took place in regions with a history of wartime interethnic violence but did not produce sudden nationhood. What other factors would explain this?

One possible hypothesis, which is supported by archival evidence in western Bosnia, concerns the behavior of the local political leadership. Many communists from areas that experienced severe intercommunal violence during the war believed strongly in reacting quickly and decisively to ensure that postwar incidents of interethnic conflict did not escalate.[130] Their position was often rooted in their own wartime experiences of witnessing acts of extreme violence, which they wished never to see repeated. The presence of such individuals in positions of power was most likely critical in preventing the appearance of sudden nationhood. After all, the same structural factors—a mixed ethnic makeup, a wartime history of intercommunal violence, and regular postwar incidents of conflict—were common in many communities in Bosnia. But a key factor in whether incidents escalated was the postwar behavior of local leaders: some vigorously intervened to prevent or stop incidents; others remained indifferent or tacitly approved; while a minority actively initiated and/or participated in incidents, which rapidly fueled sudden nationhood.[131]

Another hypothesis is that wartime experiences of interethnic rescue or other forms of solidarity forged during those years may have produced a mental schema that exerted a powerful restraint on sudden nationhood, just as experiences of interethnic persecution might create a schema that could be activated for its escalation.[132] The case of Rajko Srdić is suggestive. As a nine-year-old Serb, he escaped a mass execution in the Kulen Vakuf region during the summer of 1941 and survived thanks to a Muslim family who hid him for more than a month. On September 6, they fled the region together with the rest of the refugees from Kulen Vakuf, but were soon captured by Serb insurgents. "For most [of the insurgents]," Srdić recalled, "it was enough to be a Muslim or a Croat to lose one's head."[133] By perfectly reciting several Orthodox prayers, he convinced the insurgents that he was a fellow "Serb," and thereby saved himself and the Muslim family who had saved him. Such an experience could create an unforgettable sense of interethnic solidarity. As Srdić emphatically stated more than forty years after the war, "If not for the Muslims, I wouldn't be alive."[134]

A local postwar incident can perhaps illuminate how such wartime experiences of interethnic solidarity could act as a restraint on sudden nationhood, even in the Kulen Vakuf region where intercommunal violence had been severe. In the spring of 1958, two candidates faced off in a local election over who would represent the region in the parliament of Bosnia-Herzegovina. One was Vaso Trikić, a former member of the Central Committee of the League of Communists of Bosnia-Herzegovina; the other was Milan Zorić, a general in the Yugoslav People's Army.[135] On March 6, 1958, Trikić came to Kulen Vakuf and, in the words of a witness, claimed that the Muslims in the region "are Ustašas and that Kulen Vakuf is an Ustaša place."[136] His comments set off a wave of rage, with a local resident rushing off to find a knife in order to kill Trikić, which the local militia intervened to prevent. Others quickly mobilized neighbors to make sure that none would vote for him in the upcoming election. It seemed likely that the incident, which triggered wartime memories, would set off a more general sense that the "Serbs" were against the "Muslims." Yet what could have spiraled into the antagonistic collective categorization that was typical of incidents of sudden nationhood *did not.* One local resident, who was active in convincing his neighbors not to vote for Trikić, was nevertheless overheard around the same time in a tavern enthusiastically declaring: "We'll vote for General Zorić!"[137] Both candidates were nominally "Serb," yet the derogatory comments by Trikić did not cause at least some local residents to leap to the conclusion that "Serbs" were the source of tension. Why?

Reference to wartime behavior, particularly during 1941, appears to have been crucial here in their thought process. General Zorić, who had been a local insurgent that year, was said to have enjoyed the wide respect of local Muslims. While the tensions in the spring of 1958 mounted, some Muslims from the village of Bjelaj came to the village of Orašac and told a story about him. In 1941, General Zorić had come to a house in their village. He was wearing a torn shirt. A local man with whom he spoke immediately offered him two fresh shirts. Zorić told him that he could not accept anything if the man did not first seek permission from the village elders. And so the man immediately went off to consult with them. Only after they agreed to give Zorić the shirts did he accept them. Because of such behavior, the villagers from Bjelaj told their neighbors in Orašac that General Zorić is "the most just and righteous man in the world."[138] In this case, the tension diffused as rapidly as it had mounted, due in large part to the villagers from Bjelaj who reminded their neighbors that one's behavior—and not ethnicity—was paramount. What allowed them to do so was the creation during the war of a mental schema that could be activated in moments of tension to exert a powerful restraint on sudden nationhood.

These kinds of recollections from 1941—of interethnic solidarity and rescue—appear to have left such individuals significantly less inclined after the war to engage in, or respond positively to, antagonistic ethnic categorization after local interethnic incidents. Still, more systematic micro-comparative research on several regions will be needed if we are to better answer this important question about the relationship between the effects of wartime persecution and rescue and the postwar escalation and restraint of sudden nationhood. It will be especially important to investigate cases in which interethnic conflict did not evoke an antagonistic sense of "us vs. them." The study of such cases is thus a future subject for research that holds great potential to better illuminate why certain people in specific communities are more susceptible to initiating and responding to sudden nationhood than others.

But regardless of which cases one examines, the findings of this micro-level analysis provide a cautionary note for scholars who would too easily accept the label "ethnic conflict" in characterizing incidents between individuals considered to be nominally of different ethnicities.[139] Many of the incidents noted by local committees of the League of Communists were indeed nominally interethnic, but the evidence suggests that this ethnic difference often had little or nothing to do with the actual cause of conflict. What matters is that others chose to ignore the drunkenness and personal disputes that often set off these incidents, and instead decided to turn them into an "ethnic conflict" by invoking the language of nationhood (along with its wartime associations) as a primary cause. Scholars who uncritically adopt such labels make the mistake of conflating the descriptions of incidents given by contemporary historical actors with their causes. In so doing, they replicate the claims of those who would seek to transform interethnic incidents into "ethnic conflict." In uncritically accepting this description, we short-circuit the task of determining how and why an incident comes to be understood by some people in this way. The challenge, for historians and others, is to uncover the kinds of micro-level evidence that will enable us to look deeply into the process that leads some people to react to interethnic incidents by using "ethnic" to modify "conflict." Analyzing the specific mechanisms that produce sudden nationhood not only provides scholars with a way to examine how and why historical actors choose to join these two words together; it also pushes us to ask whether the label actually reflects the dynamics of local conflicts, or instead tells us more about how and why some people wish to shape perceptions of them.

Despite scholars' increasing recognition that nationhood is something that can "happen," few have attempted to explain the moments when at the local level it suddenly becomes the dominant and antagonistic lens of social categorization. As Rogers Brubaker has written, "We know well from a variety of appalling testimony that this has happened; but we know too little about how it happened."[140] The concept of sudden nationhood offers a concrete way to uncover some of the micro-mechanisms of eventful nationhood, especially in wartime and post–civil war local communities. Specifically, it highlights the analytical leverage we can gain by focusing on how incidents of conflict can trigger moments of collective ethnic categorization based in experiences and memories of intercommunal violence. Thinking about these linkages suggests a need to reflect more broadly on how ordinary people practice nationhood. It can be something that people adopt gradually over time in response to structural economic, societal, and cultural transformations. It can be something that people remain stubbornly indifferent to, or use instrumentally.[141] Yet it can also be a way of seeing the world that ordinary people quickly adopt in response to events that trigger ethnicized forms of collective categorization with real roots in their traumatic experiences and memories of violence. This understanding of nationhood helps to explain the complex dynamics of intercommunal relations in the Kulen Vakuf region during and after World War II. But it also has the potential to shed light on other instances of rapid, antagonistic collective categorization, such as during the pogroms in Eastern Europe in 1941, the genocide in Rwanda in 1994, and riots in South Asia at various times.[142] The concept of sudden nationhood, with an emphasis on the linkages among violence, memory, and local incidents of conflict, thus offers a promising way to provide new answers to a crucial yet vexing question of interest to many scholars: How do ordinary people come to speak the language of nationalism?

Finally, taking account of, and accounting for, sudden nationhood matters if we want to be able to better explain the relationship between nationalism and violence. Interethnic incidents of conflict are not, in and of themselves, sufficient triggers for the eruption of more widespread violence. Rather, it is the coding of such incidents, and especially the choice to spread such interpretations, that seems to hold the potential to rapidly poison intercommunal relations. It was a relatively small number of individuals in postwar Bosnia-Herzegovina who initiated and escalated instances of sudden nationhood. But a majority of the communist authorities were deeply committed to policing such individuals and devoted significant time and resources to containing their actions through the intensive enforcement of "Brotherhood and Unity."

The most fertile ground for the rapid spread of sudden nationhood, however, would be in a context in which the minority of individuals who practice it would no longer face much resistance from the authorities, and where the specific historical factors that make some people momentarily receptive to it, such as the legacy of intercommunal violence, are front and center in politics and the mass media. This is exactly what happened in this part of the former Yugoslavia during the late 1980s and early 1990s, a period that witnessed the sudden disappearance of the League of Communists and the rise of nationalist political parties, some of which sought to mobilize their constituencies by drawing linkages between contemporary instances of inter-ethnic incidents (or merely rumors of them) and memories of World War II–era intercommunal violence.[143]

While studying the phenomenon of sudden nationhood can help us to better understand the dynamics of intercommunal relations in the immediate post–World War II decades, it potentially has a larger role to play. It may well prove to be crucial in helping to explain the poorly understood processes before and during the wars of the 1990s that ensued during Yugoslavia's dissolution—a time when, for many, neighbors suddenly lost their individuality and became of antagonistic ethnic categories, with thousands killed as a result. Micro-level research on these critical moments when nationhood suddenly happened can yield important new insights about how the most recent wave of violence took hold in the region on the most intimate level.

Taking up this challenge—and others like it in conflict zones throughout the world—requires us to rethink whatever conscious or unconscious preconceptions we might have about the relationship between nationalism and violence. Evidence from the Kulen Vakuf region shows us that nationalism does not simply produce violence. Rather, as we have seen repeatedly, violence can produce immensely forceful waves of nationalism, the experience of which can leave those swept up in them susceptible to sudden nationhood (or opposed to it). This can create a context for future violence, or solidarity. But in this hard-to-discern process—visible almost entirely at the local level—violence is not merely a result; it is a generative force.

Epilogue

Violence as a Generative Force

To appreciate the challenge of telling this story of Kulen Vakuf, and to better grasp its broader significance, it is worth considering three portraits from the region's more recent history. They can illuminate the extent to which events from the 1980s through the present have created a sense of historical consciousness that obscures and conceals—rather than explains—the causes and effects of the violence in 1941. Before we can conclude the main threads of that story, we need to take into account how the recent past has shaped—and continues to shape—basic assumptions and perceptions about how to tell this violent history. And we need to be aware of how they impair our capacity for historical comprehension.

The first portrait takes us to an autumn day in 1981, when the local communist authorities unveiled the first-ever war monument in Kulen Vakuf. The second takes us to June 1992, when the most recent wave of violence in the region—the 1992–1995 war in Bosnia-Herzegovina—reached this part of the Una River valley. The third brings into focus the present-day landscape of war memory.

November 3, 1981: Kulen Vakuf looked strikingly different compared to autumn 1941. Then the town was little more than a skeleton of burned down structures, with only the charred remnants of the wooden bridge once spanning the Una River protruding from the rushing water. Now everything was clean and orderly. The facades of the many new buildings and homes were in near perfect condition. The streets were swept clean. Brightly colored flowers filled the boxes on balconies. Lampposts lined the new steel and asphalt bridge that spanned the emerald green waters of the Una gurgling beneath, which sparkled under the sun. And the mosque's minaret once again reached for the sky. November 3, 1981 marked the unveiling by the local communist authorities of the town's first ever war monument.[1] For decades, Kulen Vakuf was an exception in the region, and throughout Yugoslavia, where thousands of war monuments had been constructed for many of those killed between 1941 and 1945, often at a frenzied pace. But here, as was the case in local communities with similar wartime histories, publicly remembering war victims was fraught with tension. The prospect of recalling one group instantly raised the question of others, which led directly back to the intercommunal killings of 1941 and their postwar political indigestibility. Instead of public memory, what reigned was a decades-long silence about much of that violence.[2]

At one o'clock in the afternoon, several thousand people assembled at the new monument next to the primary school. Holding wreaths, a group of Partisan veterans dressed in suits stood opposite a podium. The crowd behind them was filled with people of all ages. Dressed in folk costumes, children danced the *kolo*, a circle dance, spinning around the monument while holding hands. Young men and teenagers climbed to the rooftops of nearby buildings to get a better view.[3] The monument's site was round. At its center was a large, closed stone flower, which represented Yugoslavia. Surrounding it were eight smaller flowers, each representing the six republics and two autonomous provinces of the Yugoslav federation.[4] There were four plaques on the ground. Inscribed on them were the names of 147 of the region's "Fallen Fighters" (i.e., Partisans killed during war).[5]

The first speaker was Hajro Kulenović, a retired general who was originally from the region and namesake of the man who gave Kulen Vakuf its name centuries earlier. "Our sons and daughters," he declared, "along with fighters from other regions of the country, wrote the most celebrated pages of our history with their blood and forged the greatest legacy of our revolution: the Brotherhood and Unity of our nations and nationalities."[6] Then another retired general walked to podium. It was Nikola Karanović from the nearby village of Ćovka. He was a "People's Hero" (*narodni heroj*), the most prestigious designation given to former Partisans.[7] He had been among the insurgents who attacked the column of refugees on September 6, 1941 as they fled Kulen Vakuf. He may have even participated that day in a massacre of about seventy men who were shot and thrown into the Dugopolje pit.

A photograph taken at the ceremony shows Gen. Karanović at the podium. Among those gathered in the crowd on that sunny fall afternoon were hundreds of survivors of the massacres of September 6–8, 1941 and their children. Quietly they stood opposite the short general with graying hair and a mustache, who had been one of those in command of insurgents responsible for the killing of about 2,000 of their relatives and neighbors. Neither Karanović nor anyone in the crowd said a word about that violence, or the mass killings of Orthodox peasants earlier in the summer of 1941 that triggered it. Instead, he praised the bravery of the "Fallen Fighters" whose names appeared on the plaques. Those in the crowd listened, and then applauded.[8] Several approached the monument later to examine the names. Many were familiar to older residents. It was said that among them were names of some insurgents who had participated in the September 6–8 massacres.[9]

June 12, 1992: At a spot on the Una River called *Štrbački buk*, not far from the villages of Orašac and Ćukovi, the river's waters descend over a set of spectacular waterfalls, cascading downwards over several steps, and then rushing toward a canyon. A footbridge of wooden planks once spanned the

Figure 13. Retired General Nikola Karanović speaking during the unveiling of the first-ever war monument in Kulen Vakuf on November 3, 1981, which was for local fallen Partisan Fighters. In the crowd were survivors of the killings that he and the insurgents whom he commanded played a role in committing during September 6–8, 1941. He did not mention those killings in his speech. Image courtesy of Sadeta Ibrahimpašić.

river just before these falls. On this June day, its eastern bank was filled with nearly 6,000 refugees from Kulen Vakuf, Klisa, Orašac, and Ćukovi. Since June 10, they had been under attack and on the run from Bosnian Serb forces. Three men among those fleeing had set off for Donji Lapac, where a contingent of French soldiers from the United Nations Protection Force (UNPROFOR) were stationed, a result of the war that began in the newly independent country of Croatia in 1991.[10] After crossing the Una's frigid waters and then hiking to Donji Lapac, they implored the peacekeepers to meet the refugees on the western side of the bridge and place them under their protection.

The French soldiers arrived at the bridge, but so too did a contingent from the newly formed Bosnian Serb Army, which joined Croatian Serb forces already there. Each side stated its intentions: the UNPROFOR soldiers indicated they intended to take the refugees to their camp. But the commanders of the Serb forces balked; they had a list of wanted men whom they believed were among the refugees. They would first need to be identified, taken into custody, and interrogated. The UNPROFOR soldiers discussed the matter; the Bosnian Serb commanders cursed them in their local language. The exhausted refugees watched nervously having fled their homes and spent the previous night in a cold rain. The UNPROFOR soldiers decided to stand aside and allow the Serb forces to carry out a detailed selection among the male refugees.[11]

One at a time, each male refugee had to approach a contingent of soldiers holding the lists, some wearing black facemasks. The lists contained the names of men whom the Serb forces believed had been active in the newly formed the Party of Democratic Action (Stranka demokratske akcije [SDA]). There were names of supposed members of a paramilitary group, the so-called Green Berets, which the Serb forces believed existed in the region, as well as members of the local police and their reserves. Over 200 men and teenage boys were led away.[12] Among those who assisted in the selections were former local bus drivers and police officers, men who had known the refugees—their neighbors—for years.[13] The prisoners were loaded on to trucks. As they were driven off, Hilmo Kozlica from Orašac heard a voice yell out: "*Balije* (a derogatory word for "Muslims"), get your heads down! Fuck your Turkish mothers, we're going to kill you!"[14] Reserve policeman Đulaga Dervišević from Klisa, recalled his subsequent interrogation: "Fuck your Ustaša mother! Where did you get these Serbian army boots?" yelled former member of the regional police force, Ilija Majstorović. Dervišević's father, he insisted, had once been an Ustaša.[15] The self-justification for such aggression would be later discovered in internal

Bosnian Serb security documents, written in 1993: "The Serbian people in this municipality instinctively felt the danger from Ustaša-ism [*ustaštvo*] because of the war in Croatia [in 1991] and began to organize themselves. The most significant conclusion was for the Serb people to organize for self-defense, and to prepare to acquire arms."[16]

Those not selected on June 12 were permitted to cross the wooden footbridge spanning the Una. They were loaded into white UN trucks and taken to Donji Lapac, where they were temporarily housed in an open-air warehouse, before being transported to Bihać. They would live there as refugees for more than three years, while the city was under near constant siege.[17] A group of mostly women formed soon after their arrival and demanded news about the prisoners. They advocated relentlessly for their release, but as the months passed their fears grew. "[Kulen Vakuf] was once full of youth and music," wrote a refugee from that town named Nataša Kadić, a mother of two. "Now so many are no longer with us. 210 are missing . . . could they have they been killed?"[18] Seventy-two prisoners were exchanged later in 1992. But fate of the rest remained unknown. A group of women continued to demand news of their fate during the next several years while the war dragged on. They had no way of knowing that many, including Nataša's husband Ahmet, had already been executed by late summer 1992, with most of their bodies dumped into two vertical caves. The search for their remains, and the attempt to identify those found, continues today.[19]

Summer, 2014: A stone plaque was bolted into a large rock in 2004 near the bridge in Kulen Vakuf that spans the *buk*, from which women threw their children and then themselves to their deaths in September 1941 rather than be butchered by insurgents and local peasants. Its inscription reads: "In September 1941, the insurgents committed genocide against the Bosniaks [Muslims] on this bridge, and in 1992 the Chetniks destroyed it." No one would learn today that local Ustaša strongman Miroslav Matijević once ran a tavern within shouting distance of this bridge, from which he helped organize the mass killing of hundreds of local Orthodox peasants in 1941. And no one would know that a hundred meters or so up the newly paved road beyond the plaque once stood the gendarmerie station where local insurgents raised and cocked their rifles to prevent their fellow fighters from murdering hundreds of Muslim women and children hiding inside. The ruins of the building, overgrown with trees during the postwar decades, stood until 2013 when a local man, who was found as a small child sitting next to his murdered mother in September 1941, ordered that the site be

FIGURE 14. The site of the former gendarmerie station in Kulen Vakuf, where a small group of insurgents protected women and children in September 1941. It was razed in 2013. Image taken by the author.

razed. The space is now empty, a few old bricks here and there bulldozed into the ground.

In Kulen Vakuf, the monument unveiled on November 3, 1981 to the 147 "Fallen Fighters," and the "Brotherhood and Unity" for which they supposedly fought, was crushed and removed with heavy machinery several years after the 1992–1995 war. This was done apparently under the orders of a former director of the town's primary school who, along with other local residents, was said to have felt that it preserved the memory of some men who had committed mass killings of their neighbors and relatives in September 1941. No trace of the site exists today. In its place now stands a home for orphaned children. A new monument was unveiled in December 2008 in a small park next to the town's bus stop. At its center is a large black plaque cut into the shape of a unified Bosnia-Herzegovina. On it are etched the faces of seventy-eight local men killed during the 1992–1995 war. Islamic motifs surround the site, and a stone copy of the Koran, with a page open, stands to the right of the plaque. The recovered and identified remains of some of these men have been buried just north of the village of Ćukovi in the Cemetery of Holy Martyrs (Šehidsko mezarje), a burial site built exclusively for them. In the aftermath of their violent deaths, they have in memory been ethnicized and harnessed to propagate a vision of a unified state.

On July 27, 2011, in Boričevac (present-day Croatia), a plaque was unveiled on the restored walls of the Catholic Church. The village had been burned to the ground by insurgents in early August 1941, and was nearly empty for decades after 1945. Its inscription reads: "Around this parish church of the Nativity of Mary lived the villagers of Boričevac until Saturday, August 2, 1941, when insurgents (*ustanici*) expelled them, plundered their village, and set their houses on fire (with some residents inside their homes). Their descendants have placed this plaque in memory of the banished and murdered villagers of Boričevac." No one would learn that here once lived local Ustaša strongman Grga Pavičić and his followers among more than a few villagers in Boričevac, such as several from the Markovinović clan. No one would learn about their killings of their Orthodox neighbors in villages such as Suvaja, Osredci, and Bubanj, and the mass plunder of their property during the summer of 1941—all of which preceded and triggered the insurgent attack on Boričevac. Today, Boričevac's former residents are to be remembered solely as innocent victims, as if the attack on them materialized out of thin air. The church with its plaque is a place to commemorate exclusively ethnicized suffering, and to erase any responsibility of the village for contributing to the region's history of violence.

Just up the road to the north, in the village of Neljubsi, the monument to the village's nearly 270 victims of the Ustašas—categorized by the communist authorities as "Victims of Fascist Terror"—still stands. Each victim's name can be read on the seven plaques. Many belonged to the same extended families: twenty from the Repac clan; eleven Škorićes; six Smrzlićes; and many more—men, women, children, and the elderly. Just before the last plaque on the far left side stands a monument to local insurgent Stojan Matić, whom the postwar communist authorities designated as a "People's Hero." Matić was twenty-six-years-old when, on September 6, 1941, he fired his pistol several times in an attempt to stop the killing and plunder by his fellow insurgents of the refugees who were fleeing Kulen Vakuf. From a distance, the bust of his head still appears intact. Upon closer inspection, however, one sees that five bullets have been fired into its right side: one through the temple, another through the chin, and two through the neck, all of which exited through larger holes on the left side of his head. One round is still lodged in Matić's face at its entry point, halfway between his ear and chin.

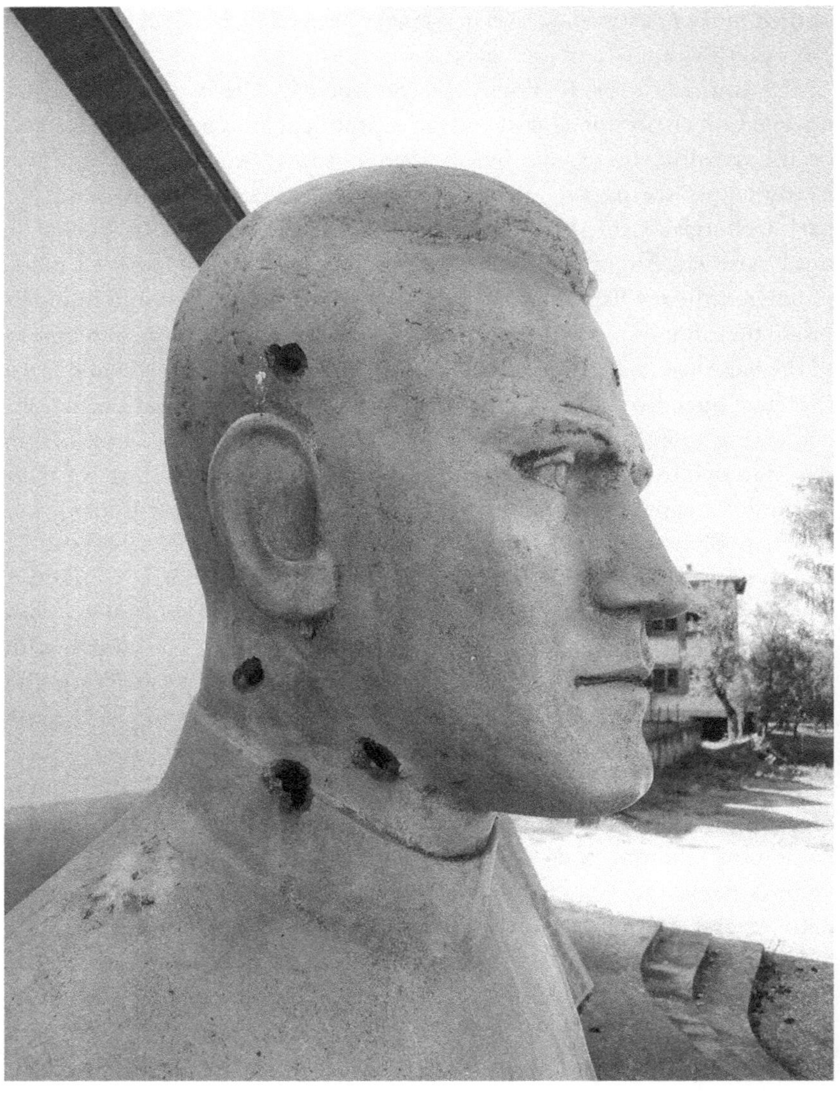

FIGURE 15. Exit holes of the bullets fired into the statue of Stojan Matić in the village of Nebljusi. Image taken by the author

In the village of Malo Očijevo, high on the ridge above Martin Brod where the rushing waters of the Una and Unac rivers meet, the monument built in memory of local communist Ranko Šipka lays on the ground in his now depopulated village. On September 8, 1941, Šipka was to the first to stand up and demand that the insurgents in Martin Brod ignore Petar Đilas's order that all the Muslim prisoners brought the night before from Kulen Vakuf should be killed because all were supposedly Ustašas. The monument built in his memory was about six feet tall: there was a bust of his head, and a plaque with his name and the date of his birth and death. Today, it can be seen that the monument was forcibly pulled out of the ground; the bust of Šipka's head is gone; the plaque had been smashed; and the year of Šipka's birth is missing. Like the shot-up head of Stojan Matić in Nebljusi, the shattered remains of Šipka's monument speak volumes about the desire of some to physically erase and forget a history that includes any memory of intercommunal solidarity.

Below in the valley, in the village of Martin Brod, the stone remains of Marko Vladetić's house are surrounded with a rusty barbed-wire fence and overgrown with trees and bushes. It was here that he sheltered Hana Štrkljević and her daughter after they escaped the mass killing of hundreds of women and children by the Una in Kulen Vakuf on September 7, 1941. There is nothing to remind anyone passing by that he was the second individual who attempted to save the lives of some of the prisoners in Martin Brod on September 8. He did this despite having been robbed by Ustašas (as well as insurgents impersonating them), and despite the fact that Miroslav Matijević and his gang of Ustašas had recently murdered his sons Stevo and Dušan.

FIGURE 16. The remains of Marko Vladetić's house in Martin Brod, as seen in 2014. Image taken by the author.

Just over three kilometers from Martin Brod, across the border with Croatia, and up the winding switch-backed dirt road, the Golubnjača cave remained hidden to the outside world until as recently as July 2014. It was then that a local policeman managed to locate the site, making use of documents given to him by the author of this book, and an old classified military map from the former Yugoslav People's Army. He immediately recognized the abandoned plum orchards near the sharp turn on the road leading toward the nearby village of Miljuši, which Gojko Polovina noted in his memoirs when he described finding the site the day after the massacres on September 8, 1941. There is no fence around the cave's opening. Neither is there any monument in memory of the victims killed and thrown into it, nor any mention of who killed them. A stone tossed into the darkness falls for several seconds, with increasingly faint sounds heard as it bounces from side to side, before hitting the bottom. Somewhere there are the remains of over 400 men and boys. If pigeons ever did flock around its entrance, as legend has it, in order to protect local villagers from evil spirits, they are long gone, leaving the place in an eerie silence. The only sound one hears is the swirling mountain wind rushing through the nearby meadows and rustling the leaves of the long abandoned plum orchards.

These three portraits help us bring this region's history up to the present: the 1981 unveiling of the monument in Kulen Vakuf; the selection of men and teenage boys at the footbridge by the Una in 1992; and a view of the current landscape of war memory. What emerges when contemplating them is the immense degree to which past and recent violence has shaped, and continues to shape, perceptions of identities in this part of the world. To the present day, forms of self-identification, and that of others, have been re-forged during and after acts of violence with (or into) totalizing categories. These include explicit and implicit "ethnic groups" as clearly bounded, mutually antagonistic actors; certain "groups" as either martyrs or villains, as either perpetrators or victims; and strikingly selective public memories propped up with deafening silences. These stark conceptualizations of the human landscape continue to exert a profound influence on how histories of this part of the world are told: they are frequently Manichean, deeply ethnicized, and highly selective. These ways of seeing the past (and present) are understandable if we imagine what it might be like to walk in the shoes of those who have lived through this traumatic history. But if our objective is to *explain* the causes, dynamics, and consequences of violence, adopting these ways of seeing ultimately obscures much more than they illuminate.

Our challenge, then, is formidable: to uncover and explain a past that has been both profoundly ethnicized and selectively silenced as a consequence of extreme violence, by people of all political persuasions and walks of life—from communists to nationalists, from taxi-cab drivers to historians. The nuances and complexities of history have been continuously blurred, obscured, hidden, and physically destroyed. These grey areas—where historians are (or should be) most at home—have, especially in the region today, been reduced to largely antagonistic black and white categories and explanations. We thus face enormous challenges in telling this history because episodes of violence, and their reverberations, have helped to conceal the contingencies and multiple possibilities that the people whom we wish to analyze, and whose behavior we seek to explain, actually faced in the past. Instead, we are tempted today to adopt "ethnicities" as our collective actors; to identify overly simplified, bi-polar categories of perpetrators and victims; to assume their supposed long-term histories of committing mass killings; or to accept a past composed solely of their having endured repeated massacres at the hands of ethnic others.

Especially because of the shadow of the most recent violence in the region during the 1990s, it thus seems irresistible not to observe: "history repeats itself" (*istorija/povijest se ponavlja*). This is something one often hears in the region today when people try to account for why one's supposed "ethnic group" has suffered at the hands of "another." And so it might seem reasonable for us to begin our writing of this history of violence by simply asking: "Why has ethnic group x perpetrated killings of ethnic group y?" But it should be clear by now that this kind of seemingly straightforward question is, in fact, perilous; it is actually geared toward selectively assembling information in order to advance an identity politics agenda—not toward increasing our understanding of the causes, dynamics, and effects of violence. As such, that question should be left to those who wish to create and maintain a sense of ethnic identities and communities based on perceptions of ethnicized suffering. We would do well to phrase our questions in ways that allow us to immediately problematize the linkage between "ethnicity" and "violence" in order to keep our eyes focused squarely on the task of explaining, and leave identity politics to ethnic entrepreneurs.

Posing two simple, yet globally significant questions can help us rise to this challenge of differentiating our categories of historical analysis from categories of popular (as well as some scholarly) practice. They are, in fact, what have framed the path of our detailed journey into the history of the Kulen Vakuf region: What causes mass violence among neighbors in multi-ethnic communities? And how does this violence affect their identities and relations? We can now gaze back at the twists and turns that we have navigated, and identify the main promontories that have jutted forth along the way, which deserve attention when considering these questions, and the broader dynamics among violence, nationalism, and historical memory.

We began our story long before the pivotal year of 1941. Rather than compose this history primarily with the secondary literature devoted to this part of the Balkans, much of which has a macro-level political focus, uncovering under-utilized archival documents allowed us to enter the largely unknown world of the localities. Using a single community in the rural hinterland as the primary analytical lens, our first task was to reconstruct the poorly understood local dynamics of social identification, cohesion, and conflict. The sources reveal a world in which the language of antagonistic ethnicity did come to exist as an available vocabulary. It was a mental template and language that people could employ to make sense of events, relationships, problems, and conflicts. Yet it co-existed with other available vocabularies, which functioned on non-ethnic and intra-ethnic axes. Contrary to the views of many scholars, who tend to assume that a sense of elite-level, ethnic cleavages extended out to the localities, our evidence suggests that the language of antagonistic ethnicity was present—but not dominant—in the local community during the years immediately prior to 1941.[20]

These findings allow us to restore a much-needed sense of contingency to our study of local intercommunal relations. By using a local lens of analysis, we can avoid assuming that "ethnic conflict" was the primary lens through which people viewed their relationships, and that this would naturally be the central axis around which they would seek to resolve future conflicts in the event of any upheaval. Instead, uncovering the contingency of local social relations challenges us to ask what must happen to imbue "ethnicity" with greater political salience, rather than assume that this salience was already at a high level. In this way, conducting a local history does not simply provide us a view "from below," which can complement a history "from above," and provide a more complete, but fundamentally unchanged historical portrait from what historians already claim to know. Rather, the local perspective provides us with a critical means through which to question a central assumption at the heart of so many studies of this part of the world—that ethnicity is a deeply rooted and central category of practice, and thus a central axis for conflict. So when faced with the challenge of explaining what appears as a dramatic rise in "ethnic conflict," such as what took place in 1941, the key question we must pose is: Are there concrete incentives that emerge for people in local communities to frame their problems, and initiate or act out pre-existing conflicts, on an ethnic axis?

When we examine the local dynamics of change during the first critical months of the NDH's existence, we note that "ethnic conflict" did not, in fact, "explode" among neighbors who were already supposedly constituted into clearly defined, mutually antagonistic "groups." Rather, it had to be consciously made through sizable effort at the macro, meso, and micro levels of social and political life. The role of nationalist ideology (i.e., an ethnicized view of humanity and a commitment to remaking the human landscape by including and excluding people according to their perceived ethnicity) in fueling change was crucial among actors at the macro and meso levels. But it was far less important among those at the micro level. There, we discovered that concrete, everyday incentives—especially material gain and the opportunity to resolve long-standing inter-personal conflicts—were far more important in motivating some people to engage in local persecution on an ethnic axis. There were clear, tangible incentives at the local level for those who fit into the new government's ethnicized categories of inclusion to gain economically from their participation, and in so doing to resolve long-festering conflicts in their communities.

There is nothing mysterious here about what drove local mobilization; in fact, the rationality at work is what stands out. There were unprecedented benefits to be obtained by joining the persecution of those now marked for exclusion according to redefined ethnic categories, and their newly politicized salience. Some local residents quickly perceived these opportunities, and took advantage of them. This dynamic driving local mobilization into micro-level persecution on an ethnic axis, as we have noted, has broad parallels to a host of other contexts throughout the world, including communities in Africa, Asia, Eastern Europe, and Latin America. Our story thus demonstrates that high levels of persecution and violence can proceed even if a sizable disjuncture exists among actors' motivations at the macro, meso, and micro levels. Widespread ideological indoctrination with the ideas of the nationalist elite is not, in fact, a necessary precondition at all levels of society. Nor is the existence of widespread, deeply rooted "ethnic" cleavages at the local level. Rather, a convergence of differing agendas and mutually beneficial incentives can be sufficient to compel a certain number of people toward persecuting and committing violence against their neighbors.

"Ethnic conflict" thus quickly became a dominant axis for local conflict during the spring and summer of 1941 because the new NDH authorities offered clear incentives—which were especially attractive to local residents previously at the margins of economic, social, and political life—to act out pre-existing social conflicts, and to initiate new ones, through an ethnic key. Why is this finding important? Our local story suggests more broadly that conflicts actually crystalize as "ethnic" in response to highly situational incentives. We should not confuse, conflate, or mistake these powerful incentives of a contingent political situation with supposed mutually antagonistic "ethnic" affinities that some might assume to be long-standing, widespread, and deeply rooted. Here, at the local level, the evidence suggests that pre-conflict political dispositions along an ethnic axis were far less important in driving behavior than one might assume. "Ethnic conflicts," therefore, have to be *made* at the micro level through vigorous work in the present; they do simply reflect macro level cleavages, or emerge logically and naturally from pre-existing cultural differences, or even antagonisms along such lines. They are, in short, highly contingent, even in societies in which many people are perceived to be nominally of different ethnicities.

Just how contingent comes vividly clear once we are confronted with the local level evidence that those who respond to the incentives to engage in inter-ethnic persecution often simultaneously engage in intra-ethnic plunder and violence. Our evidence suggests that this dynamic existed among nearly all the main protagonists of our story, regardless of an actor's nominal ethnicity. As such, it further supports a notion of "ethnic conflict" as fluid and tenuous, rather than fixed and enduring. It thus follows that any investigation of a conflict in a region depicted as "multi-ethnic" should not proceed with the assumption that ethnicity must be a key social fault line, even if evidence suggests that persecution and violence have occurred, or is occurring, on an ethnic axis. Rather, how a conflict comes to be "ethnicized" has to be carefully explained—not assumed, even when the actors appears to be nominally "ethnic." By conducting our analysis at the local level, we can illuminate the specific process, and discern the logic, of how an environment potentially conducive to "ethnic conflict" actually crystallizes on the ground.

The local lens brings into sharp focus another puzzle that challenges us to engage further with the subject of contingency in "ethnic conflict." If, as many might assume on first glance, the initial wave of violence in this region was supposedly driven by deeply rooted and widespread ethnic cleavages, then what accounts for its high level of variation across time and place? During the past decade, scholars have devoted attention to this puzzle of variation in local violence, producing illuminating studies, especially by engaging in subnational comparative analysis.[21] Rather than provide analysis of several different regions, we maintained our focus on a single region, but dug deeper into it—down to the village level—in order to better discern when and why violence occurred in certain villages, but not in others. A central issue of broader significance stands out, which can contribute to this debate about variation in the occurrence of violence. Mutually reinforcing fears at the meso and micro levels, which crystalize at different times and places according to local conditions, can compel multiple levels of state authority into undertaking "self-defensive" mass violence. Appreciating the role of fear—both real and especially imagined—allows us to better understand why armed groups may choose to initiate mass violence in certain moments and locations, even against civilians who may pose little real threat.[22]

Fear of potential attack from those whom the perpetrators are already persecuting can trigger a dramatic "defensive" escalation of violence among perpetrators. This is especially likely once such fear of victim resistance reaches a tipping point, which is usually triggered by incidents, or merely rumors of them. In terms of explaining the temporal and geographical variation of violence, we noted that this defensive violence tends to occur according to where a state's armed groups perceive security threats to be most acute. The macro and meso levels of authority are often crucial here in setting a context for this dramatic escalation; certain actors at these levels may be key decision makers about taking the step toward mass violence. But again, our story strongly suggests that the local level matters greatly. An initial blast of mass killing, while often explained by a broad perception of a security threat in a given locality, can then generate its own endogenous dynamics that can trigger further escalation of violence at the micro level, which the macro and meso levels may not want. Analysis of these two levels may not reveal what actually drives the continued escalation of violence on the ground (or its cessation), which can vary greatly according to time and place due to the often highly varied behavior of micro-level actors.

This endogenous dynamic of violence, in which local level actors take the initiative in ways that can diverge from the wishes of their superiors, further helps us clarify why instances of local violence can vary so dramatically across time and place. The evidence vividly demonstrates that violent organizations can enjoy significant local autonomy, especially in weak states, such as the NDH. The Ustaša units were not simply the last chain of obedient actors carrying out a conveyor belt of commands that the central authorities sent down to the localities. Once constituted, these units quickly became a power unto themselves due to the overall weakness of the NDH, and the lack of armed authority (i.e., the army and gendarmerie) over them. They attacked and killed wherever they perceived security threats. Yet they plundered, arrested, and tortured—but often did not kill—wherever extracting resources and wealth was easier by employing a less violent approach. And when this plunder was no longer feasible without resort to greater levels of violence, they often shifted once again to killing. The evidence reveals their striking level of autonomy and near total control over violent activity in the rural localities, such as the Kulen Vakuf region. This dynamic helps us to better explain the puzzling level of temporal and geographical variation in their local violence. While constituted from above, and certainly under orders to execute policies of their superiors, the Ustaša units nonetheless often acted in response to their local concerns, and deployed violence accordingly. More broadly, our evidence suggests that in such contexts where central authority is weak, orders for the escalation of violence can come from both above and below.

So, in response to the question, "What causes mass violence among neighbors in multi-ethnic communities?" When strong situational incentives appear in a local community to decisively solve economic and inter-personal problems in an ethnic key, some neighbors will engage in violence on an ethnic axis; this violence will tend to occur in locations where, and at times when, perceived security threats of those neighbors targeted for persecution are highest; and, while this violence can be instituted "from above," it can also be driven "from below," especially in contexts where state control is weak, and local autonomy over violence is strong. These findings provide us with ways of accounting for why, as well as when and where, neighbors in local communities who have been peaceful, if not entirely conflict-free, for long periods, might attack their neighbors in certain moments. In doing so, we do not have to adopt a conception of "ethnic groups" as our collective historical actors, nor assume a sense of long-term conflict among such actors, or accept notions of a group's traumatic history of suffering somehow mystically repeating itself. What is perhaps most striking in these findings is the clear logic and rationality that drives some neighbors to attack each other on an ethnic axis.

Our story has been about more than just the search to better understand the causes of, and variation in, "ethnic violence." Missing here is reflection about the second major question that we have taken up, but for which answers are far less voluminous: How do identities and social relations change in the midst of such violent conflict? Lack of attention to this subject, particularly through detailed empirical investigation, remains a striking gap in the literature on ethnic violence and nationalism. This is surprising because recent, influential work on civil war has shown that violence can, in fact, profoundly shape and reshape identities in unexpected ways, often producing far-reaching transformations in social relations, forms of categorization, and configurations of power, particular at the micro level.[23] Of importance here are the poorly understood endogenous dynamics of violence, and their capacity to rapidly transform social and political identification in ways that diverge significantly from what exists prior to violent conflict. The literature on ethnic violence and nationalism, however, has been slow to pick up on these insights from scholars of political violence. As a result, while we are learning more than ever about what factors might cause "ethnic violence," as well as the reasons for its geographical and temporal variation, we continue to know comparatively little about how this violence then affects ethnic identification, nationalism, and social relations after violent conflict begins.[24]

This local study provides us with a rich set of empirics to take up the challenge of shedding theoretical light on this vital subject. To begin with, how does violence transform the meaning of ethnic categories? Our story vividly demonstrates that violence can rapidly and dramatically alter people's perceptions of their neighbors on an ethnic axis. Persecution and violence in an ethnic key can significantly enhance the saliency of "ethnicity," which helps create a basis for "ethnic conflict." In this context, violence does not so much represent the culmination of widespread, deeply rooted ethnic antagonisms; rather, it is often a trigger that can set off the rapid ethnicization of social identities and relations.

Once killing according to a perception of a victim's ethnicity begins, ethnic categories matter much more because what one is perceived to be can determine whether one lives or dies. By inscribing ethnicized identities and boundaries through the act of killing, perpetrators rapidly create perceptions of extremely polarized, antagonistic group identities. The result appears to produce something similar to what has been called "the collective categorization of the other."[25] The specific individuals who trigger this group-making process often quickly fade into the periphery. The perpetrators of violence—and all those ethnically associated with them—now quickly come to be seen by the victims solely as antagonistic "ethnic others."

Yet when examined closely at the local level, our story reveals that violence-driven collective categorization is actually a process that simultaneously reverberates in *multiple* directions. It not only fuels a sense of the local multi-ethnic community as now antagonistically divided between "ethnic others." A similar process often takes place within these newly hardened group boundaries among supposed "ethnic brothers," some of whom may have not conformed to the newly transformed social order. For example, survivors of massacres may demand ethnicization among their perceived "brothers" in response to their collective ethnic persecution. Our story thus reveals an inter-related cluster of ethnicization processes that commence with violence on an ethnic axis in a multi-ethnic community: perpetrators inscribe ethnicity on victims; victims, in turn, can both internalize this externally imposed ethnic categorization and, through acts of revenge, can inscribe ethnicity on the initial perpetrators. Yet ethnicization can also spread rapidly within perpetrator/victim groups through acts of violence and threats—against both ethnic "others" and "brothers."

In a context of civil war in a multi-ethnic community, each subsequent wave of cascading retaliatory killings propels these identity and boundary-making processes faster and deeper. As perceptions of antagonistic ethnic boundaries harden in response to spiraling violence, a clear distinction between perpetrators and victims often begins to fade. Waves of retaliatory killing can merge these two identities into one. Those with no desire to be involved in the violence and its accompanying processes of ethnicization are often powerless to resist. They may now be increasingly viewed as ethnic enemies merely by their association with perpetrators. And if this happens, they may then be exposed to retaliatory violence on an ethnic axis, despite the fact they are not guilty of having committed any violence, and perhaps have little strong ethnic feeling about themselves and others. In this context, the space to be "nationally indifferent" narrows quickly and dramatically. Those who still might wish to downplay the importance of ethnicity in daily life are quickly made conscious of its critical importance because perceptions of ethnicity can now determine life and death.

When we disaggregate and examine the instances of violence that trigger and fuel these dynamics, examining their build up, unfolding, and aftermath, what stands out is the prevalence of surges as a primary characteristic of identity salience. Crucial here are the flood of emotions unleashed by killings; the discovery of mutilated corpses of relatives and neighbors; and the encounter with ransacked and burned homes, as well as entire villages. These traumatic experiences can set off a rapid and dramatic re-orientation in identification of self and others. This notion of a "surge" fueling ethnic identification helps us better capture the micro-dynamics whereby self-identification on an ethnic axis—of both "others" and "brothers"—actually happens on the ground. As we have seen in our discussion of what is required to produce "ethnic conflict," these surges in antagonistic ethnicization are not the result of deeply rooted historical forces that somehow sweep people along into "groups." Rather, they have to be consciously made through concrete human acts, through forceful community-building work at the local level, which often happens on an intra-ethnic axis. One way this happens is through the telling of atrocity stories to promote a sense of intra-ethnic homogenization. Intra-ethnic threats, and even acts of violence against perceived "brothers," is another method such actors employ to separate their own perceived people into a coherent group opposed to others. Taken together, these acts help to create a broader, antagonistic sense of "us" and "them."

Yet something counter-intuitive emerged from our local story: inter-ethnic persecution and killing, and the accompanying waves of antagonistic ethnicization, can also produce inter-ethnic solidarity. Segments of multi-ethnic communities can actually forge stronger intercommunal ties under the pressure of inter-ethnic violence. Pre-violence ties matter to some extent in creating the potential for acts of intercommunal solidarity during violence. But contingent opportunity to act on such connections to protect neighbors ultimately determines whether intervention will take place. Among the key factors can be whether community members perceive the perpetrators' authority as legitimate, and whether they knew them previously. If their authority is seen as illegitimate, and if they are well known but not respected, acts of intervention tend to be more frequent. In contexts where this occurs, what can emerge is an increased sense that a person's behavior in the past, and especially in the present, matters most in determining whether one is seen as a "brother" or "other"—and not reference to a person's perceived ethnicity or association with an "ethnic group." Warnings to flee, interventions to release prisoners, sheltering survivors of killings, and outright rescues during acts of killing—all of these behaviors help make inter-ethnic solidarity a reality on the ground during inter-ethnic violence.

These solidarities, and the resulting blurring of ethnic boundaries, often crystalize in surges just like the antagonisms and their concomitant hardening of boundaries. Violence is frequently the fire in which both are dramatically forged, generating these rapid transformations in practices and perceptions of ethnicity. They become visible to us when we question *how* people see and do not see themselves as "ethnic," instead of assuming that people exist with distinct ethnic identities, and that they engage in violence in certain moments as coherent "groups."

This brings us to a second major finding about how violence affects identities and social relations: the forging of profound antagonisms and solidarities during periods of violence *creates* new forms of communities. Killing on an ethnic axis is, of course, destructive to peaceful intercommunal relations and communities in multi-ethnic milieus. But violence is not simply a set of behaviors whereby pre-existing, mutually antagonistic ethnic communities engage in destructive physical conflict. Rather, violence creates new configurations of local communities. As we have seen from our story, these can be composed of a) those who commit violence; b) those who are subjected to it, survive, and seek revenge; c) those who witness it, but do not participate; d) and those who attempt to intervene and stop it and save neighbors. As a consequence, the pre-conflict local community quickly becomes suffused with powerful new forms of self and group identification. Some people identify with several at once, such as with those who are victims and then become perpetrators (and vice versa), or those who have been rescued and then choose to rescue (and vice versa). These new communities can align with ethnic categories (e.g., Ustašas as "Croats" or "Muslims;" insurgents as "Serbs"), but can also cut across them (e.g., neighbors of all perceived ethnicities as "rescuers").

The experience of mass violence creates the context for the creation of the new mental templates that serve as a basis for constituting these communities. They may include a sense of antagonistic collective categorization or that of solidarity. Those able to exercise agency, particularly through acts of violence or those of rescue/intervention, are the key actors who drive the formation of these templates, and the communities that emerge from them. But the crystallization of these new forms of identification reminds us of the profound powerlessness of many others. They may have no wish to be a part of any of these communities. But the community-making power contained within the act of killing in the name of groups quickly assumes an overwhelming force, which can sweep people into the newly perceived "groups."

These violence-created communities crystalize in highly contingent and situational ways. But memories of the traumatic experiences that constitute them can remain as a potent community-making tool to be invoked for mobilization in the future. If victims are sought out on an ethnic axis, and tortured and killed in profoundly humiliating ways, then such acts can help constitute distinct, antagonistic perceptions of ethnic communities, the memory of which is not easily dissolved. Conversely, if people are targeted for death on the same axis, but their neighbors of a different nominal ethnicity save them, such acts can provide the basis for profoundly grateful, warm, and friendly perceptions of supposed ethnic "others," which do not easily dissipate.

Such mental templates forged during experiences of extreme violence can be drawn on repeatedly for making sense of subsequent unfolding reality, and specifically for determining friends and enemies. Of course, perceptions of communities generated by local intercommunal violence may not be constant and enduring. The post-conflict authorities may work hard to promote the prominence of some, while downplaying others, as did the communist authorities in the Kulen Vakuf region, especially with regard to repressing public expression from antagonistically created communities. But other local actors, such as parents, religious leaders, and local participants in violence, may work just as hard to keep alive non-official forms of antagonistic group identification. The divergence in these agendas can remain an ongoing struggle, and may have a significant effect on the dynamics of local politics and everyday life in the future. These conflicts are difficult, if not impossible to discern through macro-level analysis; yet they emerge vividly when we shift our analytical focus to the meso and especially micro level. It is at that level of analysis that we can appreciate how experiences of intercommunal violence, and memories of it, constitute an exceptionally powerful force in community building.

Appreciating the power of violence in creating new forms of social identification leads us to a third finding. Not only can inter-ethnic killing help generate "anti-nationalist" communities, but ongoing violence can also compel their members to develop concrete strategies to restrain, avoid, and stop inter-ethnic killing. As we have noted, those who adopt the new mental templates of antagonistic collective categorization do not fuel waves of inter-ethnic killing in a vacuum. Their violence can result in attempts by others, whom we have referred to as "the advocates of restraint," to distinguish people by behavior—not ethnicity. The deeply polarizing effects of intercommunal violence thus can help generate among those opposed to it specific methods of restraint.

In accounting for the emergence of these advocates of restraint, pre-conflict factors (i.e., demographics, economic development, prior political conflicts and activities, etc.) can matter significantly because they may create a context with greater or lesser potential for the formation of such a group.[26] But our story suggests that endogenous dynamics of violence are crucial in the crystallization of advocates of restraint on the ground in particular times and places. This is because in contexts of civil war such forces are often highly mobile (i.e., guerrilla forces), which may significantly reduce the importance of the pre-conflict factors that often tend to be rooted in a constellation of factors in a given location. The local lens allows us to discern the formation and actions of these forces.

Specifically, by examining the dynamics of restraint, and the interaction of its advocates with those of escalation, we learn more about what drives killing at the local level. Restraint tends to fail when a) its advocates have no time to prepare their military actions, that is, to make a careful selection of fighters committed to restraint; b) there is little to no experience of previous organizational activity by its forces, and thus little basis exists for establishing authority among local fighters; and c) when key advocates of restraint are absent or killed. In such contexts, escalation of violence will tend to proceed not simply because of the desires of its advocates (e.g., for revenge, to achieve military objectives, etc.), but also because they successfully defeat the advocates of restraint, or these forces contribute in some way to marginalizing themselves.

It follows that for those interested in explaining the dynamics of mass violence, analyzing the ideologies, plans, and actions of perpetrators can be insufficient in certain contexts. We have to also consider why those opposed to them—the advocates of restraint, which may be nominally "on the same side"—prove incapable of mounting successful resistance, either through strategic mistakes, their situational absence, lack of force, or other factors. A better overall understanding of violence emerges when we devote attention to analyzing what are often simultaneous attempts to restrain and escalate violence. In a broader sense, we arrive at this new methodological horizon by seeing that intercommunal violence can create forces of restraint; and where they emerge and clash, the result will decisively determine whether killing will escalate—or not.

When we shift our examination of restraint away from non-state actors, such as guerilla groups, and devote attention to attempts by state authorities to restrain or stop violence, we note a fourth significant finding: Violence can create new forms and configurations of power, especially at the local level. Our story presents us with a puzzle: If powerful state-level actors in favor of persecution are central in most explanations for why mass violence happens, then why in some contexts, such as the NDH, are these same central authorities seemingly incapable of restraining or stopping the violence that they unleash? The structure of a state, especially a weak one such as the NDH, can quickly place a tremendous amount of autonomy—and thus power—in the hands of local leaders and their followers. Better understanding the subsequent dynamics of persecution and violence will be difficult without paying close attention to this particular distribution of power toward regime supporters in the local community.

What does our story reveal more generally about the relationship between violence and power? Violence can be conceptualized as a form of behavior that the already powerful undertake to achieve specific ideological, military, and political objectives. Alternatively, violence may be the result of rebels or non-state actors who resort to armed conflict in an attempt to take pre-existing power from the state authorities into their hands. But our local study suggests a different dynamic: new forms of local power can be rapidly amassed through the act of committing violence. Killing and plundering creates new sources of power, and therefore new configurations of power. The state elite can empower actors and groups at the meso and micro levels to engage in violence. But in so doing, these actors may quickly create new forms of local power, especially in weak states. Moreover, they may escalate violence in ways that diverge from elite interests. In this way, a macro-level shift to violence in a weak state may quickly become a costly and highly destabilizing policy choice.

This is not simply because mass violence may trigger resistance from the victim population. Such a state can also quickly lose a strong capacity to control its own instruments of violence in the localities because once empowered, they may quickly amass unexpected levels of power through their acts of violence. This dynamic can help us account for the variation in local violence. In weak states, it is not always so simple for the central and regional authorities to quickly stop violence at the local level once unleashed. This violence can bring about unintended consequences, such as massacres, which may occur at times and in locations that the central authorities have not ordered, and can lead to the further destabilization of the already weak state. The point to remember, however, is that these kinds of cracks in a state's authority are self-created. Victim groups may fight back successfully, which may bring about awareness of these weaknesses. But local state actors may continue to pursue counter-productive local killings and plunder. In doing so, they accumulate more power in their communities, which may further embolden them to ignore orders from above for restraint.

Finally, our story vividly demonstrates how intercommunal violence can generate the dynamics for the emergence of a new form of local level, post-conflict nationalism; what is called here "sudden nationhood." The basis for an antagonistic sense of ethnicity, and for its sudden increased salience in certain moments, can have roots in previous experiences and memories of local violence. An approach taken here is "eventful analysis," whereby we examine local conflicts to discern how contingent and unexpected events might radically and suddenly transform social relations. By noting how local incidents can trigger mental templates or schemas of collective ethnic categorization based in traumatic memories and experiences of violence, we can better understand how nationhood can rapidly become a primary lens through which people make sense of unfolding reality. Whether those who seek to fuel instances of sudden nationhood are successful depends on a host of factors, such as receptivity of relatives and neighbors, and the threat of sanctions from the authorities. But regardless of the result, what remains striking is the degree to which memories of local intercommunal violence, when triggered during moments of conflict, can maintain the capacity to generate sudden nationhood for decades. These concrete micro-dynamics of how people in local communities actually practice nationalism, which are characterized by high levels of fluidity, have heretofore been understudied and thus underappreciated in the voluminous literature on nationalism.

Scholars have recently devoted significant attention to what makes some people indifferent or disinterested in nationalism, such as in Poland and parts of the former Austro-Hungarian Empire.[27] But few have taken up the challenge of explaining how and why such indifference, and especially resistance, to nationalism can also crystalize at the local level in communities living in the shadow of immense levels of intercommunal violence. Why do we see indifference and anti-nationalist forces in contexts in which neighbors have committed and experienced atrocities on an ethnic axis? Our detailed story has repeatedly suggested a counter-intuitive answer: moments of extreme intercommunal violence can, in fact, forge inter-ethnic solidarity, which can then create the basis for the resistance to sudden nationhood. This violence, then, generates the mental templates not only for sudden nationhood, but also for its restraint, either through indifference or through outright resistance. The experience of locally executed killing, and the interaction with others during this experience, often decisively determines whether people will fuel escalation or restraint of violence. And this can also be the case after the killing stops, and whether people will fuel or resist sudden nationhood in response to incidents of local conflict. The experience of violence, in short, generates the proponents of both positions.

We can now answer the second and final question that has framed our long journey into the history of the Kulen Vakuf region: How does violence affect identities and social relations in local multi-ethnic communities? Violence propels multiple, simultaneous transformations in the meaning of ethnic categories and boundaries in profound surges, and in so doing creates new forms of local communities. It helps create forces that seek to restrain killing, while creating new forms of power that seek to escalate killing. And violence creates new micro-dynamics of nationalism that last long after the killing stops, in which incidents trigger traumatic memories that lead to momentary eruptions of "sudden nationhood." Taken together, these findings suggest a single, overarching argument: local intercommunal violence is not merely destructive in a host of ways; rather, it can be *an immensely generative force* for the creation of social identities and configurations of power.

This argument provides us with new ways to tell the history of multi-ethnic communities wracked with violence, both in this part of the world and beyond. The three portraits at the beginning of this epilogue—the silences and selective public memory during the 1981 unveiling of the monument in Kulen Vakuf; the selections at the bridge by the Una in 1992; and today's profoundly ethnicized landscape of memory—suggest on first glance three ways of thinking about the past: that "ethnic groups" should be our primary historical actors; that people are either perpetrators or victims/martyrs; and that instances of violence are arranged, and sometimes erased, in order to create histories of either victimhood or persecution. At the end of our journey, we now have ways to transcend these assumptions. Instead of treating "ethnic groups" as primary actors in acts of violence, we should ask: "How do such acts make, unmake, and remake ethnicized perceptions of these 'groups'?" Instead of dividing humanity into perpetrators and victims/martyrs, we should ask: "What attracts certain people in particular moments and places to persecute their neighbors on an ethnic axis?" Instead of viewing and arranging the past in Manichean terms, in which ethnic group x has "always" targeted ethnic group y (or vice versa), we should ask: "How do those who employ violence to achieve various objectives end up producing a widespread perception of 'ethnic violence'?"

Ultimately, the history uncovered here shows us that conflict and violence in multi-ethnic communities are often *not* what they appear to be on the surface. The notion of *violence as a generative force*—which this story has repeatedly and vividly revealed to us—is not just a historical argument about the dynamics of conflict in the Kulen Vakuf region, a largely unknown zone straddling the border between Bosnia-Herzegovina and Croatia. It is, in fact, a way to move forward past an ongoing impasse that profoundly shapes scholarship, politics, and everyday life in many parts of the world: the continued prevalence of ethnic categories in daily practice and a general inability to formulate new categories for historical analysis. In our story, identity, nationalism, and memory are often *not* what caused violence to wreck the lives of so many; instead, far fewer people chose to perpetrate violence, and in so doing created and recreated highly antagonistic forms of identity, nationalism, and memory. And today, they loom large in many people's lives in this part of the world, and others like it, making an ethnically divided present and future seem almost unavoidable. A lack of comprehension of how this fractured sense of historical consciousness comes to be places huge limits on the possibilities for change in the present—and future.

To move forward may require first looking back and reconsidering how we tell the story of the violent past. Local intercommunal violence is the result of human choice at many levels of life, from the extremist elite to our neighbors with whom we share our bread and quarrel. The story of Kulen Vakuf challenges us to see such violence not simply as the result of "nationalism," "ethnic groups," or "ethnic conflict"—to which many may wish to assign causation. Rather, this story confronts us with the notion that it is actually the violence that largely generates these concepts, enhances their salience, and makes them matter in certain moments. In the end, facing the history of this Balkan community—or that of others throughout the world with violent pasts—entails wrestling with a much larger and unsettling question: Could such intimate violence, and the history of it we tell, ultimately be a choice that we all hold in our hands?

Notes

Introduction

1. Arhiv Bosne i Hercegovine [hereafter ABiH], Fond Saveza udruženja boraca Narodnooslobodilačkog rata Bosne i Hercegovine [hereafter SUBNOR BiH], Republički odbor, Pov. br. 05-7/83, June 20, 1983, 1–2; Pregled stratišta i žrtava terora u Bosni i Hercegovini, September 1985, 1.

2. Ibid., Osvrt na pregled stratišta i žrtava fašističkog terora i njihove obilježenosti u Bosni i Hercegovini, November 1986, 4; Pregled stratišta i žrtava terora u Bosni i Hercegovini, September 1985, 2, 4–5; Obrazloženje tabele (undated document, most likely from June 1985), 5.

3. Esad Bibanović, "Kulenvakufski komunisti u radničkom pokretu i ustanku," in *Bihać u novijoj istoriji (1918–1945): Zbornik radova sa Naučnog skupa održanog u Bihaću 9. i 10. oktobra 1986. godine*, ed. Galib Šljivo, 2 vols. (Banjaluka: Institut za istoriju u Banjaluci, 1987), 1: 419–466; Dušan Lukač, *Ustanak u Bosanskoj Krajini* (Belgrade: Vojnoizdavački zavod, 1967), 191–192.

4. For an exception, which is a journalistic and memoir piece, and not based on extensive archival research, see Slavko Goldstein, *1941., godina koja se vraća* (Zagreb: Novi Liber, 2007); in English translation: *1941: The Year That Keeps Returning*, trans. Michael Gable and Nikola Djuretic (New York: New York Review of Books, 2013).

5. On violence in the NDH more generally, see, for example, Savo Skoko, *Pokolji hecegovačkih Srba '41.* (Belgrade: Stručna knjiga, 1991); Nikola Živković & Petar Kačavenda, *Srbi u Nezavisnoj Državi Hrvatskoj: izabrana dokumenta* (Belgrade: Institut za savremenu istoriju, 1998); Vladimir Dedijer & Antun Miletić, eds., *Genocid nad Muslimanima, 1941–1945: zbornik dokumenata i svjedočenja* (Sarajevo: Svjetlost, 1990); idem, *Proterivanje Srba sa ognjišta, 1941–1944: svjedočanstva* (Belgrade: Prosveta, 1989); Smail Čekić, *Genocid nad Bošnjacima u Drugom svjetskom ratu: dokumenti* (Sarajevo: Udruženje Muslimana za antigenocidne aktivnosti, 1996); Šemso Tucaković, *Srpski zločini nad Bošnjacima-Muslimanima 1941–1945* (Sarajevo: El-Kalem, 1995); Zdravko Dizdar i Mihael Sobolevski, *Prešućivani četnički zločini u Hrvatskoj i Bosni i Hercegovini 1941.–1945.* (Zagreb: Hrvatski institut za povijest, 1999); Slavko Vukčević, ed., *Zločini na jugoslovenskim prostorima u Prvom i Drugom svetskom ratu. Zbornik dokumenata* [hereafter *Zločini*] (Belgrade: Vojno-istorijski institut, 1993); on the violence in the region of the NDH that this book examines, see, for example, Milan Vukmanović, *Ustaški zločini na području Bihaća u ljeto 1941. godine* (Banja Luka: Institut za istoriju u Banjaluci, 1987); Josip Jurjević, *Pogrom u Krnjeuši 9. i 10. kolovoza 1941. godine* (Zagreb: Vikarijat Banjalučke biskupije, 1999); Milan Obradović, "Zločini na kotaru Donji Lapac od 1941. do 1945.," in *Kotar Donji Lapac u Narodnooslobodilačkom ratu 1941–1945*, ed. Gojko Vezmar & Đuro Zatezalo (Karlovac: Historijski arhiv u Karlovcu, 1985); Josip

Pavičić, ed., *Dossier Boričevac* (Zagreb: Naklada Pavičić, 2012); Milan Štikavac, "Krvavo lapačko ljeto," in *Ratna sjećanja iz NOB, knjiga I*, ed. Esad Tihić & Momčilo Kalem (Belgrade: Vojno-izdavački zavod, 1981), 599–616; Ilija Rašeta, *Kazivanje pobjednika smrti* (Zagreb: Grafički zavod Hrvatske, 1988).

6. Timothy Snyder, *Bloodlands: Europe between Hitler and Stalin* (New York: Basic Books, 2010).

7. See, for example, Mark Mazower, "Timothy Snyder's *Bloodlands*," *Contemporary European History*, 21, no. 2 (2012): 117–123; Omer Bartov, "Bloodlands: Europe between Hitler and Stalin (Book Review)," *Slavic Review* 70, no. 2 (2011): 424–428; Christian Gerlach, "Bloodlands: Europe between Hitler and Stalin (Book Review)," *American Historical Review* 116, no. 5 (2011): 1594–1595.

8. See, for example, Živković & Kačavenda, *Srbi u Nezavisnoj Državi Hrvatskoj.*

9. With regard to the Kulen Vakuf region, see Ana Došen, *Krnjeuša u srcu i sjećanju* (Rijeka: Matica hrvatska, 1994); idem, *To je bilo onda* (Zagreb: Došen, self-published, 2006); Jurjević, *Pogrom u Krnjeuši*; Pavičić, ed., *Dossier Boričevac*; Mujo Begić, *Zločini ustanika u Ljutočkoj dolini 1941. godine* (Sarajevo: Institut za istraživanje zločina protiv čovječnosti i međunarodnog prava Univerziteta u Sarajevu, 2013).

10. See, for example, Dizdar & Sobolevski, *Prešućivani četnički zločini u Hrvatskoj i Bosni i Hercegovini*; Skoko, *Pokolji hecegovačkih Srba '41.*; Živković & Kačavenda, *Srbi u Nezavisnoj Državi Hrvatskoj*; Čekić, *Genocid nad Bošnjacima u Drugom svjetskom ratu*; Tucaković, *Srpski zločini nad Bošnjacima-Muslimanima*; Došen, *Krnjeuša u srcu i sjećanju*; idem, *To je bilo onda*; Jurjević, *Pogrom u Krnjeuši*; Pavičić, ed., *Dossier Boričevac.*

11. Dizdar & Sobolevski, *Prešućivani četnički zločini u Hrvatskoj i Bosni i Hercegovini*, 104.

12. There are important studies of the NDH in the South Slavic languages that do not share these characteristics; however, they focus more generally on the creation of that state, the history of its leaders, and their ideology and policies, but not very much on the subject of violence. See, for example, Fikreta Jelić-Butić, *Ustaše i Nezavisna Država Hrvatska, 1941–1945.* (Zagreb: Sveučilišna naklada Liber i Školska knjiga, 1977); Bogdan Krizman, *Ante Pavelić i Ustaše* (Zagreb: Globus, 1978).

13. Donald Horowitz, *The Deadly Ethnic Riot* (Berkeley: University of California Press, 2001), 2–3.

14. See Tara Zahra, "Going West," *East European Politics and Societies* 25, no. 4 (2011): 785–791.

15. On wartime life in Sarajevo, see Emily Greble, *Sarajevo, 1941–1945: Muslims, Christians, and Jews in Hitler's Europe* (Ithaca, NY: Cornell University Press, 2011); on the policies and practices of the Ustašas and Chetniks, see Tomislav Dulić, *Utopias of Nation. Local Mass Killing in Bosnia-Herzegovina, 1941–1942* (Uppsala: Uppsala University, 2005); Alexander Korb, "Understanding Ustaša Violence," *Journal of Genocide Research* 12, nos. 1–2 (2010): 1–18; a more detailed analysis of Korb's arguments about violence in the NDH can be found in idem, *Im Schatten des Weltkriegs. Massengewalt der Ustaša gegen Serben, Juden und Roma in Kroatien 1941–1945* (Hamburg: Hamburger Edition, 2013); on the Partisans and the Chetniks, see Marko Atilla Hoare, *Genocide and Resistance in Hitler's Bosnia: The Partisans and the Chetniks* (Oxford: Oxford University Press, 2006); on the cultural politics of the NDH regime, see Rory Yeomans, *Visions of Annihilation: The Ustasha Regime and the Cultural Politics of Fascism, 1941–1945* (Pittsburgh: University of Pittsburgh Press, 2013).

16. Stathis Kalyvas, "The Urban Bias in Research on Civil Wars," *Security Studies* 13, no. 3 (2004), 160–190, here 166.

17. See, for example, Yang Su, *Collective Killings in Rural China during the Cultural Revolution* (Cambridge: Cambridge University Press, 2011); Lee Ann Fujii, *Killing Neighbors: Webs of Violence in Rwanda* (Ithaca, NY: Cornell University Press, 2009); Séverine Autesserre, *The Trouble with the Congo: Local Violence and the Failure of International Peace Building* (Cambridge: Cambridge University Press, 2010); Omar Shahabudin McDoom, "Who Killed in Rwanda's Genocide? Micro-Space, Social Influence and Individual Participation in Intergroup Violence," *Journal of Peace Research* 50, no. 4 (2013): 453–467; idem, "Antisocial Capital: A Profile of Rwandan Genocide Perpetrators' Social Networks," *Journal of Conflict Resolution* 58, no. 5 (2014): 866–894.

18. See Jan T. Gross, *Neighbors: The Destruction of the Jewish Community in Jedwabne, Poland* (Princeton, NJ: Princeton University Press, 2001); on Eastern Galicia, see Shimon Redlich, *Together and Apart in Brzezany: Poles, Jews, and Ukrainians, 1919–1945* (Bloomington and Indianapolis: Indiana University Press, 2002); Omer Bartov, "Communal Genocide: Personal Accounts of the Destruction of Buczacz, Eastern Galicia, 1941–1944," in Omer Bartov and Eric D. Weitz, *Shatterzone of Empires: Coexistence and Violence in the German, Habsburg, Russian, and Ottoman Borderlands* (Bloomington and Indianapolis: Indiana University Press, 2013), 399–420.

19. See Goldstein, *1941*, which is the only comparable book on the NDH, but also one not based on extensive archival research.

20. See, for example, Dulić, *Utopias of Nation*; Korb, "Understanding Ustaša Violence."

21. An important exception here is the work of Mark Biondich, who while not dealing with the subject of killing (he instead analyzes NDH policies and practices of religious conversion) demonstrates the significant autonomy that local leaders enjoyed in the rural localities to craft policies according to their needs. See Mark Biondich, "Religion and Nation in Wartime Croatia: Reflections on the Ustaša Policy of Forced Religious Conversions, 1941–1942," *Slavonic and East European Review* 83, no. 1 (2005), 71–116.

22. Vojni arhiv [hereafter VA], Fond Nezavisne Države Hrvatske [hereafter NDH], kut. 85, f. 11, dok. 45, Zapovjedništvo vojne krajine Zapovjedništvu bosanskog divijskog područja, Situacija u Jajcu, September 30, 1941, 1.

23. Hrvatski državni arhiv [hereafter HDA], Fond 306, Zemaljska komisija za utvrđivanje zločina okupatora i njihovih pomagača [hereafter ZKUZ] (Hrvatska), kut. 245, Zh. br. 11639–11651, Okružna komisija za utvrđivanje zločina okupatora i njihovih pomagača [hereafter OKUZ] za Liku, Zapovjedništvo posade Bihać Zapovjedniku Gospićkog oružničkog krila, Izvještaj o događajima na teritoriji kotara Donji Lapac, July 5, 1941, 1.

24. Omer Bartov, "Eastern Europe as the Site of Genocide," *Journal of Modern History* 80, no. 3 (2008): 557–593; idem, "Seeking the Roots of Modern Genocide: On the Macro- and Microhistory of Mass Murder," in *The Specter of Genocide: Mass Murder in Historical Perspective*, ed. Robert Gellately and Ben Kiernan (Cambridge: Cambridge University Press, 2003), 75–96.

25. See Dulić, *Utopias of Nation*; Marko Atilla Hoare, "Genocide in the Former Yugoslavia before and after Communism," *Europe-Asia Studies* 62, no. 7

(2010): 1193–1214; idem, *The Bosnian Muslims in the Second World War: A History* (London: Hurst, 2013); idem, *Genocide and Resistance in Hitler's Bosnia*; Greble, *Sarajevo*.

26. For recent overviews of this literature, see Benjamin Valentino, "Why We Kill: The Political Science of Political Violence against Civilians," *Annual Review of Political Science* 17 (2014): 89–103; Charles King, "Can There Be a Political Science of the Holocaust?" *Perspectives on Politics* 10, no. 2 (2012): 323–341; for an overview with greater focus on genocide studies, see Peter B. Owens, Yang Su, David A. Snow, "Social Scientific Inquiry Into Genocide and Mass Killing: From Unitary Outcome to Complex Processes," *Annual Review of Sociology* 39, no. 4 (2013): 4.1–4.16.

27. The key work here is Stathis Kalyvas, *The Logic of Violence in Civil War* (Cambridge: Cambridge University Press, 2006).

28. See, for example, Diana Dumitru and Carter Johnson, "Constructing Interethnic Conflict and Cooperation: Why Some People Harmed Jews and Others Helped Them during the Holocaust in Romania," *World Politics* 63, no. 1 (2011), 1–42; Jeffrey Kopstein and Jason Wittenberg, "Deadly Communities: Local Political Milieus and the Persecution of Jews in Occupied Poland," *Comparative Political Studies* 44, no. 3 (2011), 259–283; Su, *Collective Killings in Rural China*.

29. Scott Straus, "Retreating from the Brink: Theorizing Mass Violence and the Dynamics of Restraint," *Perspectives on Politics* 10, no. 2 (2012), 343–362; idem, *Making and Unmaking Nations. War, Leadership, and Genocide in Modern Africa* (Ithaca, NY: Cornell University Press, 2015), especially chap. 2.

30. Laia Balcells, "Rivalry and Revenge: Violence against Civilians in Conventional Civil Wars," *International Studies Quarterly* 54, no. 2 (2010), 291–313; Horowitz, *The Deadly Ethnic Riot*, 15.

31. See, for example, Veena Das, "Collective Violence and the Shifting Categories of Communal Riots, Ethnic Cleansing, and Genocide," in *The Historiography of Genocide*, ed. Dan Stone (New York: Palgrave Macmillan, 2008), 93–127; Glenn Bowman, "The Violence in Identity," in Bettina E. Schmidt and Ingo W. Schröder, *Anthropology of Violence and Conflict* (London: Routledge, 2001): 25–46; Stephen C. Lubkemann, *Culture in Chaos. An Anthropology of the Social Conditions in War* (Chicago: University of Chicago Press, 2008); Elisabeth Jean Wood, "The Social Processes of Civil War: The Wartime Transformation of Social Networks," *Annual Review of Political Science* 11 (2008): 539–561; Kalyvas, *The Logic of Violence in Civil War*; idem, "Ethnic Defection in Civil War," *Comparative Political Studies* 41, no. 8 (2008): 1043–1068; Nicholas Sambanis & Moses Shayo, "Social Identification and Ethnic Conflict," *American Political Science Review* 107, no. 2 (May 2013): 294–325.

32. See, for example, Scott Straus, "The Historiography of the Rwandan Genocide," in *The Historiography of Genocide*, ed. Stone, 527–528.

33. Rogers Brubaker, *Nationalism Reframed: Nationhood and the National Question in the New Europe* (Cambridge: Cambridge University Press, 1996), 13–22.

34. Marshall Sahlins, "The Return of the Event, Again," in Marshall Sahlins, *Culture in Practice. Selected Essays* (New York: Zone Books, 2000), 293–352; William H. Sewell Jr., "Three Temporalities: Towards an Eventful Sociology," in *The Historic Turn in the Human Sciences*, ed. Terrence J. McDonald (Ann Arbor: University of Michigan Press, 1996), 245–280.

Chapter 1. Vocabularies of Community

1. Sir Arthur J. Evans, *Illyrian Letters. A Revised Selection of Correspondence From the Illyrian Provinces of Bosnia, Herzegovina, Montenegro, Albania, Dalmatia, Croatia, and Slavonia, Addressed to the "Manchester Guardian" during the Year 1877* (New York: Cosimo Classics, [1878] 2007), 114.

2. Lični arhiv Esada Bibanovića [hereafter LAEB], Esad Bibanović, "Kulen Vakuf. Svjedočanstvo jednog vremena" (unpub. ms., private collection, Sarajevo), 3–6, 19–20; *Krajina: list Saveza socijalističkog radnog naroda bihaćkog sreza*, "Kulen Vakuf," June 18, 1964, 4; Nijazija Maslak, et al., *Turističke informacije. Stari gradovi općine Bihać* (Bihać: Općina Bihać, 2008), 26. On the importance of the vakuf in Islamic life in Bosnia and Herzegovina, see Muhamed Hadžijahić et al., *Islam i Muslimani u Bosni i Hercegovini* (Sarajevo: Svjetlost, 1977), 66–68.

3. On the history of the kapetanije, see Hamdija Kreševljaković, *Kapetanije u Bosni i Hercegovini* (Sarajevo: Svjetlost, [1953] 1980).

4. Kreševljaković, *Kapetanije u Bosni i Hercegovini*, 180–182; on the reputation of the Kulenović family as allegedly one of the oldest, largest, and most wealthy in Bosnia, see Slavoljub Bošnjak [Ivan Franjo Jukić], *Zemljopis i poviestnica Bosne* (Zagreb: Bèrzotiskom narodne tiskarnice dra. Ljudevit Gaja, 1851), 93; Ivan Kukuljević Sakcinski, *Putovanje po Bosni* (Zagreb: Narodna tiskarnica dr. Ljudevit Gaja, 1858), 32; Husnija Kamberović, *Begovski zemljišni posjedi u Bosni i Hercegovini od 1878. do 1918. godine* (Zagreb: Hrvatski institut za povijest-Zagreb; Institut za istoriju-Sarajevo, 2003), 398–409; LAEB, Bibanović, "Kulen Vakuf," 8–13.

5. On the role played by powerholders in the Ottoman Empire's peripheries in dictating local policy, see, for example, Suraiya Faroqhi, "Coping with the Central State, Coping with Local Power: The Ottoman Regions and Notables from the Sixteenth to the Early Nineteenth Century," in *The Ottomans and the Balkans: A Discussion of Historiography*, ed. Fikret Adanir and Suraiya Faroqhi (Leiden: Brill, 2002), 351–382; Frederick Anscombe, ed., *The Ottoman Balkans, 1750–1830* (Princeton, NJ: Markus Wiener, 2006); Metin Heper, "Center and Periphery in the Ottoman Empire: With Special Reference to the Nineteenth Century," *International Political Science Review* 1, no. 1 (1980): 81–105.

6. On how events along the western borderlands fueled these practices more generally, see Edin Hajdarpašić, "Whose Bosnia? National Movements, Imperial Reforms, and the Political Re-Ordering of the Late Ottoman Balkans, 1840–1875" (PhD diss., University of Michigan, 2008), 97.

7. Ibid., 99–100.

8. Evans, *Illyrian Letters*, 104–105.

9. On how the word previously did not refer to a single religious community, see Ćiro Truhelka, *Historička podloga agrarnog pitanja u Bosni* (Sarajevo: Zemaljska štamparija, 1915), 30–31; on the history of the agrarian question in Bosnia, with special focus on transformations during the middle of the nineteenth century, see Vasilj Popović, *Agrarno pitanje u Bosni i turski neredi za vreme reformnog režima Abdul-Medžida (1839–1861)* (Belgrade: Srpska akademija nauka, 1949).

10. Hajdarpašić, "Whose Bosnia?," 108, 122.

11. Matija Mažuranić, *A Glance into Ottoman Bosnia or a Short Journey into That Land by a Native in 1839–1840* (London: Saqi, [1842] 2007), 63.

12. On these campaigns in Bosnia, see Galib Šljivo, *Omer-paša Latas u Bosni i Hercegovini, 1850–1852* (Sarajevo: Svjetlost, 1977), 48–71.

13. LAEB, Bibanović, "Kulen Vakuf," 3–6, 19–20; *Krajina*, "Kulen Vakuf," June 18, 1964, 4.

14. Husejn Altić, "Lički muslimani," *Kalendar Narodna uzdanica za godinu 1941.*, godina IX (Sarajevo: Narodna uzdanica, 1941), 97–100; on the region's history up to the Ottoman conquest, see Branimir Gušić, "Naseljenje Like do Turaka," in *Lika u prošlosti i sadašnosti, zbornik 5*, ed. Branimir Gušić (Karlovac: Historijski arhiv u Karlovcu, 1973), 13–61.

15. Evans, *Illyrian Letters*, 65; LAEB, Esad Bibanović, "Stanovništvo Kulen-Vakufa i okoline kroz istoriju" (unpub. ms., private collection, Sarajevo, 1980), 9, 15–16; on the blurring of lines in local practices between "Christian" and "Muslim" communities under the Ottomans, see the important work of F.W. Hasluck, *Christianity and Islam under the Sultans*, 2 vols. (New York: Octagon Books, [1929] 1973).

16. On the history of Klisa and Orašac, which, like Kulen Vakuf, generally developed in response to nearby Ottoman military fortifications located on the ridges next to the international border, see Hamdija Kreševljaković, *Kulen Vakuf* (Sarajevo: Islamska dionička štamparija, 1935), 9–10.

17. Evans, *Illyrian Letters*, 53.

18. See, for example, Kreševljaković, *Kapetanije u Bosni i Hercegovini*, 186. See also LAEB, Bibanović, "Kulen Vakuf," 34.

19. Evans, *Illyrian Letters*, 104.

20. Ibid., 30.

21. Alessandro Portelli, "The Peculiarities of Oral History," *History Workshop* 12, no. 1 (Autumn 1981): 96–107, here 100.

22. For a claim by a local scholar that local, intercommunal violence occurred in 1873, but for which no verifiable evidence is presented, see Mujo Demirović, *Bosna i Bošnjaci u srpskoj politici* (Bihać: Ekonomski fakultet, 1999), 270–271.

23. On the origins of the 1875 rebellion in Bosnia, see Milorad Ekmečić, *Ustanak u Bosni, 1875–1878., treće, izmenjeno izdanje* (Belgrade: Službeni list SRJ, [1960] 1996), 23, 25–26, 28, 44–45; Vasa Čubrilović, *Bosanski ustanak, 1875–1878., Drugo izdanje* (Belgrade: Novinsko-izdavačka ustanova Službeni list SRJ, [1930] 1996), 22.

24. Čubrilović, *Bosanski ustanak*, 72–73.

25. See, for example, Evans, *Illyrian Letters*, 21, 98–99; Bibanović cites the "Životopis" by insurgent Pero Kreco in which he describes cutting off the heads of "Turks" and sending them to the insurgent commander Golub Babić. See LAEB, Bibanović, "Kulen Vakuf," 26.

26. Evans, *Illyrian Letters*, 3–4, 16.

27. Ibid., 39; accounts written decades later by historians, who made use of archival material, do not differ from Evans's eyewitness reports, as can be seen in Ekmečić, *Ustanak u Bosni*, 101, 121; Čubrilović, *Bosanski ustanak*, 82.

28. Evans, *Illyrian Letters*, 53.

29. Ibid., 77–78.

30. Ibid., 77.

31. Ibid., 104.

32. Ibid., 106.

33. Ibid., 118–119.

34. Ekmečić, *Ustanak u Bosni*, 120.

35. Ibid., 93, 98–99.

36. Ibid., 111.

37. Edin Hajdarpašić, *Whose Bosnia? Nationalism and Political Imagination in the Balkans, 1840–1914* (Ithaca, NY: Cornell University Press, 2015).

38. On the general resentment of the Muslim elite to the Austro-Hungarian occupation, see Ekmečić, *Ustanak u Bosni*, 102; on the overall absence of widespread violence in response to the occupation in the Kulen Vakuf region, during which it appears that two Muslims were killed, see Kreševljaković, *Kulen* Vakuf, 24.

39. LAEB, Bibanović, "Kulen Vakuf," 30–31; *Krajina*, "Kulen Vakuf," June 18, 1964, 4. On the maintenance by the Austro-Hungarian authorities of the existing patterns of land ownership as established under the Ottoman authorities, see Mustafa Imamović, *Pravni položaj i unutrašnjo-politički razvitak Bosne i Hercegovine od 1878–1914* (Sarajevo: Bosanski kulturni centar, [1976] 1997), 49–59.

40. See, for example, ABiH, Fond Zemaljske Vlade Sarajevo, kut. 522, fas. 171–193 (1912–1914).

41. The 1903 fire destroyed ninety-six houses as well as the entire market area (i.e., what was called the *čaršija*). For a report on the 1903 fire, see ABiH, Fond Zajedničkog ministarstva finansija za Bosnu i Hercegovinu, dok. br. 9784, August 10, 1903, 1–8.

42. Kreševljaković, *Kulen Vakuf*, 3–4.

43. On Habsburg perceptions of the Serb community in Bosnia in the aftermath of the June assassination, and methods of repression taken against it, see Jonathan Gumz, *The Resurrection and Collapse of Empire in Habsburg Serbia, 1914–1918* (Cambridge: Cambridge University Press, 2009), 34–43. For a brief account of the persecution of the perceived Serb population in Bosnia in the wake of the Sarajevo assassination, especially members of the intelligentsia and the political elite, see Vladimir Ćorović, *Bosna i Hercegovina* (Banja Luka: Glas srpski, [1940] 1999), 235–236.

44. On the intercommunal violence that took place in Bosnia-Herzegovina during the first few years of World War I, see Atif Purivatra, *Jugoslavenska muslimanska organizacija u političkom životu Kraljevine Srba, Hrvata i Slovenaca* (Sarajevo: Bosanski kulturni centar, [1974] 1999), 16–17, 47, note 124. On debates over the ethnic composition of the "Schutzkorps," see Ivo Banac, *The National Question in Yugoslavia. Origins, History, Politics* (Ithaca: Cornell University Press, 1984), 367, note 18.

45. A main reason for the government's decision to institute agrarian reform appears to have been fear that the revolutionary ideas emerging from post-1917 Russia would fuse with the already agitated mood of the peasantry and trigger a major social and political revolution. See Purivatra, *Jugoslavenska muslimanska organizacija*, 32.

46. On the government's decrees on agrarian reform, see Jozo Tomasevich, *Peasants, Politics, and Economic Change in Yugoslavia* (Stanford: Stanford University Press, 1955), 345–347; on the subject of agrarian reform in Yugoslavia more generally, see Milivoje Erić, *Agrarna reforma u Jugoslaviji 1918–1941* (Trebinje: Kultura, 1958); see also Đorđo Krstić, *Agrarna politika u Bosni i Hercegovini* (Sarajevo: Štamparija "Bosanka pošta," 1938).

47. ABiH, Fond Agrarne direkcije u Sarajevu, kut. 18, Mile i Lazo Tintor Njegovom kraljevskom Visočanstvu Regentu Aleksandru Karađorđeviću u Beogradu, October 12, 1919, 1.

48. Ibid., 14846/20, Agrarna direkcija, Ministarstvu za agrarnu reformu u Beogradu (undated handwritten letter, most likely from October 1919), 1.

49. Ibid., Alajbeg Kulenović Kotarskom uredu u Bosanskom Petrovcu, October 14, 1919, 1.

50. On the chaos and violence against Muslims—both former landlords and others—in the wake of the declaration for agrarian reform, see Atif Purivatra, "Političke partije prema agrarnoj reformi u Bosni i Hercegovini neposredno poslije 1918. godine," in Atif Purivatra, *Nacionalni i politički razvitak Muslimana. Rasprave i članci* (Sarajevo: Svjetlost, 1969), 220–224, 226.

51. For these interpretations of the violence against the Muslim community, see Šaćir Filandra, *Bošnjačka politika u XX. stoljeću* (Sarajevo: Sejtarija, 1998), 57; Safet Bandžović, *Iseljavanje Bošnjaka u Tursku* (Sarajevo: Institut za istraživanje zločina protiv čovječnosti i međunarnodnog prava, 2006), 325; Kemal Hrelja, "Proizvodni odnosi u poljoprivredi Bosne i Hercegovini, 1918–1941," in Kemal Hrelja and Atif Purivatra, *Ekonomski genocid nad bosanskim muslimanima* (Sarajevo: MAG—Udruženje Muslimana za antigenocidne aktivnosti, 1992), 46.

52. Banac, *The National Question in Yugoslavia*, 367–368.

53. Purivatra, *Jugoslavenska muslimanska organizacija*, 33.

54. Ibid., 33–34, 39–40.

55. LAEB, Bibanović, "Kulen Vakuf," 32. Father Vukosav Milanović was born in 1866 (in the village of Suvaja, it seems), and was the father of five children. See Arhiv Srpske pravoslavne crkve, Ministarstvo vere, Pravoslavno odeljenje, Personalna knjiga pravoslavnog sveštenstva I.

56. LAEB, Bibanović, "Stanovništvo Kulen-Vakufa," 115.

57. LAEB, Bibanović, "Kulen Vakuf," 34.

58. Arhiv Jugoslavije [hereafter AJ], Fond 14, Ministarstvo unutrašnjih poslova [hereafter MUP] Kraljevine Jugoslavije, f. 4, Pitanje gospodinu ministru unutrašnjih dela, September 15, 1920, 1 (lowercase "muslim" in the original).

59. See, for example, ibid., f. 179, Okružno načelstvo Bihać Ministarstvu unutrašnjih dela, Odeljenje za javnu bezbednost, Odeljenje za Bosnu i Hercegovinu, Politička situacija u okrugu, izvještaj za mjesec oktobar 1921., November 9, 1921, 2.

60. Ibid., Okružno načelstvo Bihać Ministarstvu unutrašnjih dela, Odeljenje za javnu bezbednost, Politička situacija u okrugu, izvještaj za mjesec avgust 1921., September 8, 1921, 1.

61. Ibid., Okružno načelstvo Bihać Ministarstvu unutrašnjih dela, Odeljenje za javnu bezbednost, Politička situacija u okrugu bihaćkom, izvještaj za mjesec septembar 1921., October 7, 1921, 4.

62. For an example of one of these killings, see Arhiv Unsko-sanskog kantona [hereafter AUSK], Fond Okružnog inspektorata Vrbaske Banovine [hereafter OIVB] Bihać, kut. 11, Okružni inspektor Vrbaske Banovine Bihać Kraljevskoj banskoj upravi, Upravnom odeljenju Banja Luka, April 15, 1930, 1; see also LAEB, Bibanović, "Stanovništvo Kulen-Vakufa," 114.

63. See, for example, AUSK, Fond Okružne oblasti Bihać, kut. 4, Zapisnik poveden u Kestenovcu sa Đurom Tišom netijakom Jandrije Majstorovića sa Kestenovca, July 7, 1920, 1–4; Tužba Jandrije Majstorović iz Kestenovca, Kotar Bos. Petrovca, June 1, 1920, 1; ibid., Fond Velikog župana Bihaćke oblasti, kut. 7, Zapisnik o glavnoj raspravi, June 13, 1922, 1–7.

64. Stevan Obradović "Langa" and his band of followers had apparently been arrested by this time. See AJ, Fond 14, MUP Kraljevine Jugoslavije, f. 179, Ispostava Sreza bosanskog-petrovačkog u Kulen Vakufu Velikom županu bihaćke oblasti u Bihaću, Izveštaj o političkoj situaciji za mesec decembar 1925. godine, December 31, 1925, 1.

65. AJ, Fond 14, MUP Kraljevine Jugoslavije, f. 179, Okružno načelstvo Bihać Ministarstvu unutrašnjih dela, Odeljenje za javnu bezbednost, Politička situacija u okrugu bihaćkom, izvještaj za mjesec septembar 1921, October 7, 1921, 7.

66. See, for example, AJ, Fond 14, MUP Kraljevine Jugoslavije, f. 179, Poglavar Sreza cazinskog Velikom županu bihaćke oblasti u Bihaću, Politički izveštaj za mjesec mart 1924, April 6, 1924, 3.

67. AJ, Fond 14, MUP Kraljevine Jugoslavije, f. 179, Veliki župan bihaćke oblasti u Bihaću Ministarstvu unutrašnjih dela, Odeljenju za javnu bezbednost, Izveštaj o situaciji za mjesec novembar 1923., December 29, 1923, 2.

68. See, for example, Arhiv Republike Srpske Banja Luka [hereafter ARSBL], Fond 9, Kraljevska banska uprava Vrbaske Banovine [hereafter KBUVB], Poljoprivredno odeljenje, arhivska jedinica [hereafter aj.] 30, Kulenović-Vođenica Omerbeg i drug iz Bos. Petrovca, agr. spor-žalba, 1936.

69. On the frequent changes in the laws on agrarian reform, and how the internal reorganization of the state, which was a result of the establishment of royal dictatorship, affected the implementation of the reforms and resolution of local conflicts over land, see Samija Sarić, "Prilog pregledu provođenja agrarne reforme u Bosni i Hercegovine 1918–1941. godine," *Glasnik arhiva i društva arhivskih radnika Bosne i Hercegovine*, godina XVIII–XIX, knjiga XVIII–XIX (Sarajevo, 1978–1979), 213–223.

70. LAEB, Bibanović, "Kulen Vakuf," 34; Derviš Kurtagić, *Zapisi o Kulen-Vakufu* (Bihać: Kurtagić, 2005), 10–11.

71. See, for example ARSBL, Fond 9, KBUVB, Poljoprivredno odeljenje III, aj. 31, Prijava Ajiše Kulenović umrl. Jasimbega Mehmeda Kulenovića umrl. Sulejmanbega iz Kulen Vakufa za isplatu šuma šikara u bivšim kmetskim selištima, October 19, 1936, 1–3.

72. See, for example, Hrelja and Purivatra, *Ekonomski genocid nad bosanskim muslimanima*; Marko Atilla Hoare, *The History of Bosnia: From the Middle Ages to the Present Day* (London and Beirut: Saqi, 2007), 108; Dulić, *Utopias of Nation*, 66–67.

73. Tomasevich, *Peasants, Politics, and Economic Change in Yugoslavia*, 345–355. For a short summary of the agrarian question in Bosnia-Herzegovina according to the views of the authorities of the Kingdom of Yugoslavia in northwest Bosnia in 1933, see ARSBL, Fond KBUVB, Poljoprivredno odeljenje III, aj. 33, Historijat agrarnog pitanja u B. i H. za vreme od okupacije u B. i H. po austro-ugarskoj do oslobođenja i poslije oslobođenja (1933), 1–3.

74. AJ, Fond 14, MUP Kraljevine Jugoslavije, f. 63, Pravila trgovačkog udruženja u Kulen Vakufu, February 26, 1930, 1–7.

75. On the economic difficulties in the town up to this point due to the lack of transportation links, see ARSBL, Fond KBUVB, Opšte odeljenje I, aj. 13, Ispostava Sreza bosanskog-petrovačkog u Kulen Vakufu Kraljevskoj banskoj upravi Vrbaske Banovine, Otsek za trgovinu, obrt i industriju Banja Luka, Predmet: izveštaj o stanju obrta i trgovine za mesec novembar 1930. na teritoriji sreske ispostave Kulen Vakuf, November 30, 1930, 1.

76. LAEB, Bibanović, "Kulen Vakuf," 36. Local historians, such as Bibanović, claim that the market was held each Thursday. However, archival evidence suggests that it was actually held each Tuesday. See ARSBL, Fond 9, KBUVB, Opšte odeljenje I, aj. 18, Spisak o godišnjim sajmovima (panaćurima) i nedeljnim pazarnim danima, 1.

77. Kajmak is a homemade dairy product, which is made by slowly boiling milk, and then by simmering it for several hours. After cooling, the cream is skimmed off, chilled, and then eaten.

78. Jovica Keča, "Ustanički dani u okolini Kulen Vakufa," in *Bosanski Petrovac u NOB. Zbornik sjećanja. Knjiga IV*, ed. Vladimir Čerkez (Bosanski Petrovac: Opštinski odbor SUBNOR-a Bosanski Petrovac, 1974), 199–200.

79. Mara Kecman-Hodak, "Sjećanja na Bušević, Kestenovac, Bosanske Štrpce i Kalate," in *Bosanski Petrovac u NOB. Zbornik sjećanja. Knjiga III*, ed. Vladimir Čerkez (Bosanski Petrovac: Opštinski odbor SUBNOR-a Bosanski Petrovac, 1974), 150.

80. On Kulen Vakuf's designation as a headquarters for construction of a section of the rail lines, see HDA, f. 1352, Grupa V, inv. br. 316, Predmet: Štrajk radnika na unskoj pruzi, proveravanje navoda izveštaja g. Pomoćnika Ministra saobraćaja, June 26, 1937, 1; on the economic stimulus caused by the railroad construction, see LAEB, Bibanović, "Kulen Vakuf," 36.

81. Ibid., f. 1363, Grupa XXI, inv. br. 2645, Sresko načelstvo u Donjem Lapcu, Predmet: Tromjesečni izvještaj o radu opće uprave, March 28, 1932, 1.

82. AUSK, Fond OIVB Bihać, kut. 9, Načelnik Sreza bosanskog-petrovačkog Okružnom inspektoratu Bihać, Predmet: ekonomska i socijalna situacija u Srezu Bosanski Petrovac, November 22, 1929, 1. It was not until the 1930s that a number of new schools would be built in villages such as Prkosi, Orašac, and Kestenovac. On their construction, see ARSBL, Fond 9, KBUVB, Prosvjetno odeljenje IV, aj. 10, Sresko načelstvo u Bosanskom Petrovcu Kraljevskoj banskoj upravi, Prosvetnom odeljenju u Banjoj Luci, Predmet: podaci o novootvorenim i novosagrađenim školama, March 13, 1933, 1.

83. See, for example, ARSBL, Fond 9, KBUVB, Poljoprivredno odeljenje III, aj. 6, Sresko načelstvo Sreske ispostave u Kulen Vakufu Kraljevskoj banskoj upravi III, Poljoprivredno odeljenje, Banja Luka, Izveštaji o stanju poljoprivrede, September 30, 1933; September 30, 1935, May 20, 1937.

84. AUSK, Fond OIVB Bihać, kut. 14, Sreska ispostava u Drvaru Kraljevskoj banskoj upravi, Odeljenje za socijalnu politiku i narodno zdravlje Banja Luka, Predmet: ishrana naroda, January 15, 1932, 1.

85. Milan Obradović, "Selo Bubanj u plamenu," in *1941–1942. u svedočenjima učesnika narodnooslobodilačke borbe, knjiga* 7, ed. Radomir Petković (Belgrade: Vojnoizdavački zavod, 1975), 434.

86. AJ, Fond 14, MUP Kraljevine Jugoslavije, f. 179, Ispostava Sreza bosanskog-petrovačkog u Drvaru Velikom županu bihaćke oblasti, Izveštaj o političkoj situaciji za mesec novembar 1923., December 2, 1923, 3.

87. In April 1924, local officials indicated that the workers' movement in the region existed solely in Drvar. See AJ, Fond 14, MUP Kraljevine Jugoslavije, f. 179, Veliki župan bihaćke oblasti u Bihaću Ministarstvu unutrašnjih dela, Odeljenje javne bezbednost, Izveštaj o situaciji za mesec mart 1924., April 30, 1924, 2.

88. HDA, f. 1352, Grupa V, inv. br. 316, Kraljevina Jugoslavije, Ministarstvo unutrašnjih poslova, Odeljenje za državnu zaštitu, Predmet: Štrajk radnika zaposlenih na izgradnji unske pruge, June 12, 1937, 1; on the smaller strikes, see ibid., Kraljevska banska uprava Vrbaske banovine, June 23, 1937, 1; Sresko načelstvo u Donjem Lapcu, Predmet: Štrajk radnika na izgradnji Unske pruge, June 23, 1937, 1; ibid., Sresko načelstvo u Donjem Lapcu, Predmet: Unska pruga—stanje štrajka, June 28, 1937, 1.

89. On the local authorities' characterization of the workers' demands, see ibid; on the workers' demands, see ibid., Savez građevinskih radnika Jugoslavije—podružnica Kulen Vakuf, June 27, 1937, 1.

90. On Josip Hodak's role in organizing the strikes, see ibid., Kraljevina Jugoslavije, Ministarstvo unutrašnjih poslova, Odeljenje za državnu zaštitu, Predmet: Štrajk radnika zaposlenih na izgradnji Unske pruge, June 12, 1937, 1; ibid., Predmet: Izazivanje nereda i nemira među radnicima zaposlenim na Unskoj pruzi od strane raznih agitatora, June 21, 1938, 1; ibid., Predmet: Spremanje štrajka na Unskoj pruzi, June 27, 1938, 1.

91. Ibid., Sresko načelstvo u Donjem Lapcu, Predmet: Unska pruga pripremanje štrajka, June 27, 1938, 1.

92. Ibid., Kraljevina Jugoslavije, Ministarstvo unutrašnjih poslova, Odeljenje za državnu zaštitu, Predmet: Hodak, Josip, Sekretar građevinskih radnika u Kulen Vakufu—nadzor, July 2, 1938, 1.

93. See, for example, HDA Državni arhiv Karlovac [hereafter DAKA], Fond Radnog materijala Zbornik Donji Lapac [hereafter RMZDL], Likovi (kut. bez broja), Mićo Medić, "Hvatao je za cijevi četničkih pušaka," 1; ibid., Milan Obradović, "Politički komsar Dušan Obradović," 1; ibid., kut. 3, Milan Majstorović i Mićo Medić, "Formiranje i borbena dejstva doljanske partizanske čete," 3; ibid., Radovi za hronike sela (neobjavljeno), Rade Grbić, "Osredci u prošlosti i sadašnjosti. Put osredačkog odreda od 27.07.1941–28.03.1942. god.," 8; ibid., Radica Popović, "Donjolapački kotar: omladina Nebljusa i okolnih sela u Narodno-oslobodilačkoj borbi," 5; "Bušević u Narodnooslobodilačkoj borbi," 6–8.

94. For the view of a local historian, see LAEB, Bibanović, "Kulen Vakuf," 39. For the most comprehensive, macro-level study of the complex political landscape of Yugoslavia at the national level from 1918 to 1921, see Banac, *The National Question in Yugoslavia*; on the country's political situation during the 1930s, see Dejan Djokić, *Elusive Compromise: A History of Interwar Yugoslavia* (New York: Columbia University Press, 2007); on the Croat Peasant Party, see Mark Biondich, *Stjepan Radić, the Croat Peasant Party, and the Politics of Mass Mobilization, 1904–1928* (Toronto: University of Toronto Press, 2000); on the Yugoslav Muslim Organization, see Purivatra, *Jugoslavenska muslimanska organizacija*; Zlatko Hasanbegović, *Jugoslavenska muslimanska organizacija 1929–1941. U ratu i revoluciji 1941.–1945.* (Zagreb: Bošnjačka nacionalna zajednica za grad Zagreb i Zagrebačku županiju, 2012).

95. ARSBL, Fond 9, KBUVB, Opšte odeljenje I, aj. 24–25, Izborni okrug broj 11 (izborni srezovi: petrovački, sanski, cazinski).

96. AJ, Fond 14, MUP Kraljevine Jugoslavije, f. 179, Ispostava Sreza bosanskog-petrovačkog u Kulen Vakufu Velikom županu bihaćke oblasti, Izveštaj o političkoj situaciji za mesec mart 1924. godine, April 1, 1924, 1.

97. See, for example, HDA, f. 1353, Grupa VI, inv. br. 277, Sresko načelstvo Donji Lapac Velikom županu primorsko-krajiške oblasti, Karlovac, September 11,

1929, 1, in which villagers from Boričevac, who were said to have been supporters of the Croat Peasant Party, had "forgotten about politics and are only concerned with their livelihoods and economic questions."

98. VA, Fond Narodnooslobodilačke vojske [hereafter NOV], kut. 1997, f. 8, dok. 4, Drago Đukić, "Pripreme ustanka, ustanak i borbe 1941 godine u bosansko-petrovačkom srezu," (undated document, most likely written in the early 1950s), 2; HDA DAKA, Fond RMZDL, kut. 3, Originali, Milan Majstorović i Milan Medić, "Formiranje i borbna dejstva doljanske partizanske čete" (undated), 4.

99. HDA, f. 1361, Grupa XVII, inv. br. 1411, Sresko načelstvo Donji Lapac Kraljevskoj Banskoj upravi Savske Banovine, Otsek za državnu zaštitu, Širenje letaka, October 25, 1935, 1; ibid., inv. br. 1753, Sresko načelstvo u Donjem Lapcu Kraljevskoj Banskoj upravi Savske Banovine, Odeljku za državnu zaštitu, Ubacivanje komunističke literature iz inostranstva u našu državu, September 25, 1937, 1.

100. Ibid., f. 1363, Grupa XXI, inv. br. 5499, Sresko načelstvo u Donjem Lapcu, Predmet: Izvještaj o političkim prilikama i događajima u mjesecu maju 1939. godine, June 3, 1939, 1.

101. On Mile Budak, see Darko Stuparić, ed., *Tko je tko u NDH. Hrvatska 1941.–1945.* (Zagreb: Minerva, 1997), 53–55.

102. HDA, f. 1355, Grupa VIII, inv. br. 236, Načelstvo sreza Donjolapačkog Kraljevskoj banskoj upravi Savske banovine, Odeljak za državnu zaštitu, Predmet: Pavičić, Juko, veze sa hrvatskim emigrantima, November 3, 1933, 1; on the continued surveillance of these individuals by the local authorities, and the lack of political activity by them, see ibid., f. 1363, Grupa XXI, inv. br. 3470, Načelstvo sreza Donjolapačkog, Predmet: Političke prilike i događaji u mjesecu aprilu 1934. god.—izvještaj, May 1, 1934, 1; ibid., inv. br. 5006, Sresko načelstvo u Donjem Lapcu, Predmet: Političke prilike, podaci, June 23, 1937, 1.

103. See, for example, VA, Fond Sekretarijata unutrašnjih poslova Bosne i Hercegovine [hereafter SUP BiH], Film 3, Predmet: Elaborat o izvršenoj rekonstrukciji ustaške nadzorne službe na terenu srezu Bihaća, 1959, 1–2; ibid., Elaborat ustaškog pokreta Bihać (undated), 1; ibid., Ustaški elaborat Banja Luka (undated), 1–2; ARSBL, Fond 9, KBUVB, Upravno odeljenje II, aj. 5, Ispostava Sreza bosanskog-petrovačkog, October 5, 1932, 1; ibid., Sreska ispostava u Drvaru, "Ustaška organizacija": sprečavanje širenja antidržavnih lektira," October 4, 1932, 1; on the lack of Ustašas from the region who were in exile in Italy during the 1930s, see AJ, Fond 14, MUP Kraljevine Jugoslavije, f. 27 Odeljenje za državnu zaštitu, Delatnost ekstremnih političkih organizacija, Spisak ustaša u Italiji, 1–13.

104. On the Chetnik associations in Bosnia-Herzegovina, see Nusret Šehić, *Četništvo u Bosni i Hercegovini, 1918–1941. Politička uloga i oblici djelatnosti četničkih udruženja* (Sarajevo: Akademija nauke i umjetnosti Bosne i Hercegovine, 1971).

105. ARSBL, Fond 9, KBUVB, Upravno odeljenje II, aj. 5, Predmet: Rad četničkih udruženja, August 9, 1937, 1; on the lack of Chetnik societies in the Srez of Bosanski Petrovac in 1938, see ibid., Opšte odeljenje I, aj. 45, Društva i udruženja na teritoriji Vrbaske Banovine, 1938., November 1939, 1.

106. See, for example, ARSBL, Fond 9, KBUVB, Upravno odeljenje II, aj. 11, Sresko načelstvo u Bosanskom Petrovcu Kraljevskoj banskoj upravi, Upravno odeljenje, Predmet: izvještaj o političkoj situaciji za mjesec april 1936. god., April 30,

1936, 1; ibid., Predmet: izvještaj o političkoj situaciji za mjesec juli 1938. god., August 2, 1938, 1.

107. ARSBL, Fond KBUVB, Upravno odeljenje II, aj. 11, Ispostava Sreza bosanskog-petrovačkog u Kulen Vakufu Kraljevskoj banskoj upravi, Upravno odeljenje, Predmet: izveštaj o političkoj situaciji za mesec juli 1938. god., 1; ibid., Predmet: izveštaj o političkoj situaciji za mesec juli 1939. god., 1; ibid., Predmet: izveštaj o političkoj situaciji za mesec avgust 1939. god., 1

108. AUSK, Fond OIVB Bihać, kut. 16, Okružni inspektor Vrbaske Banovine Bihać Kraljevskoj banskoj upravi Vrbaske Banovine, Upravno odeljenje, October 1, 1932, 1; on what the nature of these "hatreds" may have been with regard to Ivan Topalović, see ibid., kut. 15, Opština kulen vakufska Okružnom inspektoratu bihaćke oblasti u Bihaću, Žalba: protiv zapljene opštinskog namještaja po g. Ivanu Topaloviću star. sreske ispostave u Kulen Vakufu, June 27, 1932, 1.

109. AUSK, Fond OIVB Bihać, kut. 16, Žandarmerijska stanica Drvar Sreskom sudu u Bosanskom Petrovcu, Predmet: Đurđević Jovan pok. Đurđa iz Drvara radi izvršenja krivičnog dela, September 14, 1932, 1.

110. ARSBL, Fond 9, KBUVB, Opšte odeljenje I, aj. 42, Statistički pregled kriminaliteta, 1935–1936.

111. AJ, Fond 14, MUP Kraljevine Jugoslavije, f. 179, Okružno načelstvo Bihać Ministarstvu unutrašnjih dela, Odeljenje za javnu bezbednost, Odeljenje za Bosnu i Hercegovinu, Politička situacija u okrugu, izvještaj za mjesec oktobar, November 9, 1921, 1.

112. Ibid., Ispostava Sreza bosanskog-petrovačkog u Kulen Vakufu Velikom županu bihaćke oblasti u Bihaću, Izveštaj o političkoj situaciji za mesec novembar 1925., 1; on intra-ethnic murders among the Orthodox population, see also HDA, f. 1364, Grupa XXI, inv. 2191, Sresko načelstvo u Donjem Lapcu, Predmet: Javne uprave stanje za mesec januar i februar 1931, I. Javna bezbednost, February 28, 1931, 1.

113. Ibid., f. 1363, Grupa XXI, inv. br. 5500, Sresko načelstvo u Donjem Lapcu, Predmet: Izvještaj o radu opšte uprave za tromjesečje januar, februar i mart 1939, I. Javna bezbednost, April 3, 1939, 1.

114. On the case of the Kečas of Suvaja, see HDA, f. 1363, Grupa XXI, inv. br. 2191, Sresko načelstvo Donji Lapac, Predmet: Izvještaj o stanju javne uprave za mjesec maj i juni 1931, I. Javna bezbednost, July 1, 1931, 1; on the Obradovićes of the municipality of Donji Lapac, see ibid., inv. br. 2645, Sresko načelstvo Donji Lapac, Predmet: Tromjesečni izvještaj o stanju opće uprave / april–juni 1932. god., July 1, 1932, 1; on a case among those living in the same household in the village of Osredci, see ibid., inv. br. 5162, Sresko načelstvo u Donjem Lapcu, Predmet: Izvještaj o radu opšte uprave za tromjesečje juli, avgust i septembar 1938. god., October 3, 1938, 1.

115. See, for example, Marvin Wolfgang, *Patterns in Criminal Homicide* (Philadelphia: University of Pennsylvania Press, 1958).

116. HDA, f. 1363, Grupa XXI, inv. br. 1819, Sresko načelstvo Donji Lapac, Predmet: Izvještaj o stanju javne uprave za mjesec maj i juni 1930, I. Javna bezbednost, July 2, 1930, 1.

117. Ibid., Sresko načelstvo Donji Lapac, Predmet: Javne uprave stanje izveštaj za mesec septembar i oktobar 1930, IX. Elementarne nepogode, October 31, 1930, 1.

118. See, for example, AUSK, Fond OIVB Bihać, kut. 12, Opštinsko poglavarstvo u Kulen Vakufu, Izvadak iz sjedničkog zaključka opštinskog vijeća u Kulen Vakufu, March 10, 1930, 1–3; ibid., May 18, 1930, 1–5; on lectures held by doctors and veterinarians in the region, see, for example, ARSBL, Fond 9, KBUVB, Upravno odeljenje II, aj. 30, Ispostava Sreza bosanskog-petrovačkog u Kulen Vakufu, Narodni univerzitet u Kulen Vakufu, Izveštaj za avgust 1930. godine, August 30, 1930; on the concerns of the local authorities with economic development, public health, and social problems associated with unemployment, see ARSBL, Fond 9, KBUVB, Upravno odeljenje II, aj. 27, Ispostava Sreza bosanskog-petrovačkog u Kulen Vakufu Kraljevskoj banskoj upravi Vrbaske Banovine, Upravnom odeljenju Banja Luka, Održavanje konferencija sa opštinskim načelnicima kod sreskih načelnika, April 30, 1930, 1–2.

119. ARSBL, Fond 9, KBUVB, Upravno odeljenje II, aj. 11, Ispostava Sreza bosanskog-petrovačkog u Kulen Vakufu Kraljevskoj banskoj upravi, II odeljenja Banja Luka, Predmet: proslava rođendana nj. v. Kralja, September 7, 1938, 1.

120. For an overview of these meetings and the participants' resolutions, see HDA, f. 1363, Grupa XXI, inv. broj. 6129, Banska vlast Banovine Hrvatske, Odjeljak za državnu zaštitu, Predmet: Ocjepljenje i odvajanje pojednih srezova od banovine Hrvatske u vezi sa pokretom "Srbi na okup," April 26, 1940, 1–10; on the movement more generally in the Croatian Banovina, see Djokić, *Elusive Compromise*, especially chaps. 5–6.

121. On Stevo Rađenovic, see ibid., 3; on the movement's absence in the Kulen Vakuf region, see ibid., Sresko načelstvo u Donjem Lapcu, Predmet: Pokret "Srbi na okup," ocjepljenje i odvajanje pojedinih srezova sa područja banovine Hrvatske, March 15, 1940, 1.

122. For examples of the rhetoric, as well as incidents of conflict, see ibid., Rezolucija prestavnika srpskih nacionalnih i kulturnih ustanova i Srba građana Tuzle, November 14, 1939, 1; Ispostava banske vlasti u Splitu, Predmet: Pokret "Srbi na okup," otcijepljenje i odvajanje pojedinih srezova iz područja banovine Hrvatske, April 16, 1940, 1; Gospodinu Dr. Ivi Subašiću, Banu Banovine Hrvatske u Zagrebu, U ime Srba daruvarskog sreza, July 10, 1940, 1–2; Akcioni odbor savjetovanja u Vrhovinama, Srbi Like i Korduna, November 20, 1939, 1.

123. LAEB, Bibanović, "Kulen Vakuf," 38–39.

124. Interviews with Murat Mušeta, September 27, 2008, Kulen Vakuf; Abas Mušeta, July 7, 2012, Crikvenica; Smajo Hodžić, June 23, 2013, Ćukovi.

125. Jurjević, *Pogrom u Krnjeuši*, 64.

126. AUSK, Fond OIVB Bihać, kut. 11, Okružni inspektor Vrbaske Banovine Bihać Kraljevskoj banskoj upravi Upravnom odeljenju Banja Luka, br. 657/30, April 15, 1930, 2–3.

127. Ibid., Okružni inspektor Vrbaske Banovine Bihać Kraljevskoj banskoj upravi Upravnom odeljenju Banja Luka, br. 466/30, April 15, 1930, 2.

128. Ibid., Okružni inspektor Vrbaske Banovine Bihać Kraljevskoj banskoj upravi Upravnom odeljenju Banja Luka, br. 657/30, April 15, 1930, 1.

129. Ibid., Okružni inspektor Vrbaske Banovine Bihać Kraljevskoj banskoj upravi Upravnom odeljenju Banja Luka, br. 466/30, April 15, 1930, 2.

130. Evans, *Illyrian Letters*, 130.

131. See, for example, Banac, *The National Question in Yugoslavia*; for an alternative perspective, which highlights dynamics other than conflict, see Djokić, *Elusive Compromise*.

Chapter 2. A World Upended

1. With no census from 1941, and the last one conducted in 1931, we can only estimate the size and structure of the population. According to Hamdija Kreševljaković, the approximate population structure of the Kulen Vakuf region in the mid-1930s was: 5,600 "Muslims," 8,600 "Serb Orthodox," and 1,600 "Croat Catholic." On these numbers, see Kreševljaković, *Kulen Vakuf*, 17–23; see also, LAEB, Bibanović, "Stanovništvo Kulen-Vakufa," 36–59.

2. See Jozo Tomasevich, *War and Revolution in Yugoslavia, 1941–1945: Occupation and Collaboration* (Stanford: Stanford University Press, 2001), chap. 2.

3. On the German advance into northwest Bosnia in April, see Slavko Odić, "Okupacija Bosne u aprilskom ratu 1941. godine," in *Srednja Bosna u NOB-u: srednja Bosna do ustanka i u ustanku 1941., članci i sjećanja, knjiga prva*, ed. Slavko Odić (Belgrade: Vojnoizdavački zavod, 1976), 163–170.

4. On the attempted rebellion, see Todor Stojkov, "O takozvanom Ličkom ustanku 1932.," *Časopis za suvremenu povijest*, godina II, broj 2 (1970): 167–180.

5. On the formation and activities of the Ustašas prior to 1941, see Fikreta Jelić-Butić, "Prilog proučavanju djelatnosti ustaša do 1941.," *Časopis za suvremenu povijest*, godina I, broj 1–2 (1969): 55–91; idem, *Ustaše i Nezavisna Država Hrvatska*, 54–55.

6. Ivo Andrić, *The Bridge on the Drina*, trans. Lovett F. Edwards (Chicago: University of Chicago Press, [1945] 1977), 227.

7. On these decrees on the NDH leadership's formulation of categories of "racial belonging" (*rasna pripadnost*), see HDA, Fond 223, Ministarstvo unutarnjih poslova (MUP) NDH, kut. 99, 1126, IIA, 11648/41, Zakonska odredba o rasnoj pripadnosti, 1–2; ARSBL, Fond 631, Ustaški stožer i povjereništvo za bivšu Vrbasku banovinu Banja Luka [hereafter USPBVBBL], kut. 3, Uputa za sastav izjave o rasnoj pripadnosti, 1–2. Fikreta Jelić-Butić cites an interview that Pavelić gave on April 15, 1941 to an Italian newspaper in which he used racial concepts to differentiate between "Serbs" and "Croats." Yet such comments do not appear to have structured very much—if at all—the officially sanctioned categories and laws, and especially the state practices that delineated the boundaries of these "groups." See Jelić-Butić, *Ustaše i Nezavisna Država Hrvatska*, 139–140.

8. *Hrvatski narod: Gasilo hrvatskog ustaškog pokreta*, "Bošnjački muslimani jesu krv naše krvi, oni su cvijet naše hrvatske narodnosti," April 24, 1941, 5 (lowercase "muslim" in the original).

9. *Hrvatski Narod*, "Poglavnik je uvijek imao pravo, on će urediti ovu državu," June 16, 1941, 1. Just after the establishment of the NDH, Budak was appointed minister of Religion and Education (ministar bogoštovlja i nastave). For Budak's biographical information, see Stuparić, ed., *Tko je tko u NDH*, 53–55 (lowercase "muslim" in the original).

10. On NDH intellectual articulations about the "Croatianness" of Bosnian-Herzegovinian Muslims, see VA, Fond NDH, kut. 284, f. 1, dok. 19, Nezavisna Država Hrvatska, Hrvatska izvještajna služba, "Hrvatstvo bosansko-hercegovačkih muslimana," undated document, 1–4; ibid., kut. 284, f. 1, dok. 20, Muhamed Hadžijahić, "Narodnosna pripadnost i opredjeljenje bosansko-hercegovačkih muslimana," undated document, 1–9, here 8; ibid., kut. 284, f. 2, dok. 7, Dr. Mehmed

Alajbegović, "Islam i njegovi sljedbenici u Nezavisnoj Državi Hrvatskoj," undated document, 1–8, here 1; see also the text by Ahmed Muradbegović in *Hrvatski Narod*, "Hrvati i muslimanske vjere," April 28, 1941, 5 (lowercase "muslim" in the original).

11. VA, Fond NDH, kut. 284, f. 2, dok. 7, Dr. Mehmed Alajbegović, "Islam i njegovi sljedbenici u Nezavisnoj Državi Hrvatskoj," undated document, 1–8, 1. For Alajbegović's biographical information, see Stuparić, ed., *Tko je tko u NDH*, 4–5 (lowercase "muslim" in the original).

12. VA, Fond NDH, kut. 284, f. 1, dok. 20, Muhamed Hadžijahić, "Narodnosna pripadnost i opredjeljenje bosansko-hercegovačkih muslimana," undated document, 1–9, here 8 (lowercase "muslim" in the original); on the subject of "Muslims," the NDH, and Croatian nationalism, see also Nada Kisić Kolanović, *Muslimani i hrvatski nacionalizam, 1941.–1945.* (Zagreb: Hrvatski institut za povijest; Školska knjiga, 2009).

13. For portraits of persecution during World War I, see *Hrvatski Narod*, "Srbi su htjeli uništiti muslimanske Hrvate," May 30, 1941, 12.

14. See, for example, HDA, f. 246, Zavod za kolonizaciju NDH, kut. 111, Problem agrarne reforme u Bosni i Hercegovini, Korektura nepravde učinjene muslimanima (undated document, most likely from May or June 1941), 1–4 (lowercase "muslim" in the original); ibid., Referat o stanju kmetskog, beglučkog i erarskog zemljišta u Bosni i Hercegovini, May 24, 1941, 1–12; Vukčević, ed., *Zločini*, br. 150, Predlog poglavnikovog povjerenika u Sarajevu od 23. jula 1941. Ministarstvu unutrašnjih poslova za naseljavanje istočne granice NDH muslimanskim i katoličkim življem, July 23, 1941, 369–372.

15. See, for example, *Hrvatski Narod*, "Kako su nas ubijali 'braća' Srbi—Djelomičan popis poubijanih Hrvata u Velikosrpskoj Jugoslaviji," June 20, 1941, 4.

16. *Hrvatska Krajina*, "Proglas Hrvatskim Muslimanima," April 20, 1941, 2.

17. Interestingly, those considered to be "Montenegrins" were afforded full rights and protection by the NDH authorities, despite their close cultural connections (e.g., as Orthodox Christians) with those perceived to be members of the Serb community. See ARSBL, Fond 631, USPBVBBL, kut. 1, 1661/41, Ravnateljstvo za javni red i sigurnost za Nezavisnu Državu Hrvatsku, Predmet: Postupak s Crnogorcima, July 16, 1941; the same was true with individuals categorized as "Romanians" and "Ukrainians"; ibid., Fond 74, Velika Župa Sana i Luka, 54/41, Nezavisna Država Hrvatska, Ministarstvo vanjskih poslova Zagreb, Predmet: Postupak s Rumunjima, July 24, 1941; ibid., 57/41, Nezavisna Država Hrvatska, Ministarstvo vanjskih poslova Zagreb, Predmet: Postupak s Ukrajincima, June 30, 1941.

18. On these numbers, and the maps that show how NDH leaders viewed the spatial distribution of these preceived populations in Bosnia-Herzegovina, see VA, Fond NDH, kut. 284, f. 1, dok. 24, Propagandne etnografske karte Bosne i Hercegovine (undated maps).

19. *Hrvatski Narod*, "Doglavnik Mile Budak o dužnostima svakog Hrvata," July 7, 1941, 3. For a collection of similar quotations that the postwar communist war crimes commission compiled from NDH newspapers, see AJ, Fond 110, Državna komisija za utvrđivanje zločina okupatora i njihovih pomagača (hereafter DKUZ), f. 131, F. br. 6017, Kvaternik Ljubomir (undated document, most likely written in 1946 or 1947), 1–2. For Puk's biographical information, see Stuparić, ed., *Tko je tko u NDH*, 333–334.

20. On Viktor Gutić's prewar activities, see VA, Fond SUP BiH, Film 3, Ustaški elaborat Banja Luka (undated), 1–2; *Glas Socijalističkog saveza radnog naroda banjalučkog sreza*, "Ko je bio Viktor Gutić. Gutić postaje i ustaša," July 26, 1965, 4; ARSBL, Fond Zbirka varia, 330, Optužnica Viktora Gutića, Javno tužioštvo okruga Banja Luka Okružnom sudu Banja Luka, December 25, 1946, 21–22, 49; see also Stuparić, ed., *Tko je tko u NDH*, 145.

21. AJ, Fond 110, DKUZ, f. 121, F. br. 4536, Gutić Dr. Viktor, October 9, 1945, 4.

22. The locations where he played a key role in establishing Ustaša power included Banja Luka, Bosanski Novi, Bosanska Krupa, Kotar Varoš, Sanski Most, Bosanska Gradiška, Mrkonjić Grad, Bosanski Petrovac, Bosansko Grahovo, and Derventa. On Gutić's detailed knowledge of Ustašas in northwest Bosnia and his key role in installing them in power, see VA, Fond SUP BiH, Film 3, Ustaški elaborat Banja Luka (undated), 15, 19; ARSBL, Fond Zbirka varia, 330, Optužnica Viktora Gutića, Javno tužioštvo okruga Banja Luka Okružnom sudu Banja Luka, December 25, 1946, 4–5, 25, 49; ARSBL, Lični fond Milan Vukmanović (1928–1993), 559, Ispis o Viktoru Gutiću, 5, 13. The latter document is a collection of transcribed materials (the originals still remain largely classified) from various branches of communist state security in Banja Luka about Gutić's postwar arrest in 1946 and interrogation. See also, AJ, Fond 110, Inv. br. 56127, Zapisnik sastavljen u Bihaću po Zemaljskoj komisiji za utvrđivanje zločina okupatora i njihovih pomagača [hereafter ZKUZ], August 7, 1946, 1.

23. On the economic incentives that Gutić used to build the Ustaša movement and NDH state apparatus in northwest Bosnia, see VA, Fond SUP BiH, Film 3, Ustaški elaborat Banja Luka (undated), 17–18; *Glas Socijalističkog saveza radnog naroda banjalučkog sreza*, "Ko je bio Viktor Gutić. Prvi dani 'mira, reda i rada,'" August 16, 1965, 4–5; AJ, Fond 110, DKUZ, f. 121, F. br. 4536, Gutić Dr. Viktor, October 9, 1945, 1; ARSBL, Fond Zbirka varia, 330, Optužnica Viktora Gutića, Javno tužioštvo okruga Banja Luka Okružnom sudu Banja Luka, December 25, 1946, 27.

24. *Hrvatska Krajina*, "G. Suljo Hadžidedić imenovan za komesara," April 29, 1941, 2; see also in ibid., "Poziv stanarima u zgradama grčko-istočnjaka," August 10, 1941, 4.

25. *Hrvatska Krajina*, "Proglas," July 11, 1941, 4. It appears that these laws were frequently violated, as the government was forced to issue calls for people to report the property they received or purchased from those defined as "Serbs and "Jews," and to threaten punishment for those who did not. See *Hrvatska Krajina*, "Građani su pozvani da prijave sve što su kupili ili dobili od Srba i Židova," September 26, 1941, 3.

26. On the history of NDH's military, see Nikica Barić, *Ustroj kopnene vojske domobranstva Nezavisne Države Hrvatske 1941.–1945.* (Zagreb: Hrvatski institut za povijest, 2003).

27. On the command structure of the Ustašas, see *Hrvatski Narod*, "Ustav ustaše hrvatskoga oslobodilačkoga pokreta," May 31, 1941, 17.

28. On the structure and authority of regional and local Ustaša organizations in northwest Bosnia, see VA, SUP BiH, Film 3, Ustaški elaborat Banja Luka (undated document), 22–27.

29. *Hrvatska Krajina*, "Dr Viktor Gutić imenovan je Stožernikom Bosanske Hrvatske," April 20, 1941, 2. See also VA, Fond SUP BiH, Film 3, Ustaški elaborat

Banja Luka (undated), 15. On June 28, 1941 Pavelić appointed Gutić as the "liquidator" (*likvidator*) of the former Vrbaska banovina, which was done once the "great counties" (*velike župe*) were created as the largest administrative units within the NDH. See *Hrvatska Krajina*, "Odredbom Poglavnika Dr. Ante Pavelića Stožernik Dr. Gutić postavljen je likvidatorom bivše Vrbaske banovine," June 22, 1941, 1; ibid., "Ustaški Stožer za Bosansku Hrvatsku i Likvidator Vrbaske Banovine," July 2, 1941, 6.

30. For one of the earliest uses of this designation, see *Hrvatska Krajina*, "Oglas za predaju radio i fotografskih aparata te dalekozora (durbina)," April 26, 1941, 4.

31. *Hrvatska Krajina*, "Put Stožernika i Povjerenika Dra Viktora Gutića u Zagreb i posjet kod Poglavnika Dra Pavelića i Hrvatskih ministara," April 24, 1941, 1.

32. *Hrvatska Krajina*, "Čišćenje Hrvatske Krajine od nepoželjnih," May 28, 1941, 1.

33. *Hrvatska Krajina*, "Brišu se srpski i balkanski natpisi," April 23, 1941, 2. Gutić appears to have issued this order to ban all writing in Cyrillic several days in advance of the central authorities in Zagreb, and more than a month ahead of NDH officials in Sarajevo, or at least before they issued orders to enforce the order. See VA, Fond NDH, kut. 171a, f. 1, dok. 16, Povjereništvo Sarajevo, Predmet: Zabrana ćirilice, May 29, 1941, 1.

34. *Hrvatska Krajina*, "Raspis svima ustanovama," April 23, 1941, 4.

35. *Hrvatska Krajina*, "Novi nazivi ulica," June 4, 1941, 3.

36. *Hrvatska Krajina*, "Naredba," April 24, 1941, 4. This order later went through a number of modifications, such as requiring those considered to be "Serbs" from Serbia who settled in the NDH after January 1, 1900, along with their "descendants," to register with the local authorities in their place of residence. It seems that this order was part of a larger NDH plan for the resettlement of many of those considered to be "Serbs." See ibid., "Naredba o dužnosti prijave Srbijanaca," June 15, 1941, 3.

37. *Hrvatska Krajina*, "Muslimani i katolici ne trebaju seliti," April 26, 1941, 1; ibid., "Dodatak," April 26, 1941, 4.

38. *Hrvatska Krajina*, "Odredba," May 14, 1941, 3; ibid., "O ograničenju kretanja Srba i Židova na području grada Banje Luke, May 18, 1941, 4.

39. *Hrvatska Krajina*, "Službeni dio, Odpušteni su iz banovinske službe slijedeći činovnici i službenici," May 30, 1941, 3; ibid., "Otpušteno je 26 Srba namještenika Gradske općine," June 29, 1941, 3.

40. *Hrvatska Krajina*, "Odredba," May 28, 1941, 4.

41. *Hrvatska Krajina*, "Neka se zna . . . ," May 25, 1941, 3.

42. Exceptions existed, however. Jews working in the public administration who had not yet been replaced were not required to the wear the patch. See *Hrvatski Narod*, "Koji Židovi ne moraju iznimno nositi znaka," May 28, 1941, 11. On the statewide law, see *Hrvatska Narod*, "Židovi moraju nositi židovski znak," May 23, 1941, 5. On Gutić's implementation in northwest Bosnia, see Hrvatska *Krajina*, "Židovi u Banjoj Luci dobili su znakovi," June 18, 1941, 3; ibid., "Ustaško Redarstvo," July 9, 1941, 6; VA, Fond SUP BiH, Film 3, Ustaški elaborat Banja Luka (undated), 17. On Jews ignoring this law in Banja Luka, see *Hrvatska Krajina*, "Židovi moraju nositi znakove 'Ž,'" October 5, 1941, 3.

43. ARSBL, Fond Zbirka varia, 330, Optužnica Viktora Gutića, Javno tužioštvo okruga Banja Luka Okružnom sudu Banja Luka, December 25, 1946, 5. For Gutić's May 17 order that instituted this change, see ARSBL, Fond 631, USPBVBBL, dok. br.

499, Ustaški stožer za Bosansku Hrvatsku i povjereništvo za bivšu vrbasku banovinu, Naredba, May 17, 1941, 1; see also Slavko Odić, "Ustaški pokret i katolička crkva u Hrvatskoj, Bosni i Hercegovini," in *Srednja Bosna u NOB-u: srednja Bosna do ustanka i u ustanku 1941., članci i sjećanja, knjiga prva*, ed. Slavko Odić (Belgrade: Vojnoizdavački zavod, 1976), 259–260. It appears that the central NDH authorities officially sanctioned this shift from the designation "Serb-Orthodox faith" to "Greek-Eastern faith" on July 18, 1941. See Živković & Kačavenda, *Srbi u Nezavisnoj Državi Hrvatskoj*, 103, Ministarska naredba o nazivu "grčko-istočne vjere," July 18, 1941.

44. See, for example, Odić, "Ustaški pokret i katolička crkva u Hrvatskoj i Bosni i Hercegovini," 256–257.

45. Among the newer studies see, for example, Greble, *Sarajevo*; Dulić, *Utopias of Nation*; Korb, "Understanding Ustaša Violence"; Hoare, *Genocide and Resistance in Hitler's Bosnia*; Yeomans, *Visions of Annihilation.*

46. HDA, f. 1355, Grupa VIII, Emigracija, Načelstvo sreza Donjolapačkog Kraljevskoj banskoj upravi savske banovine, Odeljak za državnu zaštitu, Predmet: Pavičić, Juko, veze sa hrvatskim emigrantima, November 3, 1933, 1.

47. AJ, Fond 110, DKUZ, dos. br. 5361, Zapisnik br. 22, Mjesni odbor: Kulen Vakuf, August 9, 1946, 1; ibid., f. 230, F. broj 24047, Matijević, Miro, April 29, 1947, 2.

48. AJ, Fond 110, DKUZ, f. 230, F. broj 24047, Matijević, Miro, April 29, 1947, 1; for a brief character sketch and physical description of Matijević, see Nikica Pilipović, *Romori vrtočke prošlosti* (Bihać: Mjesna zajednica Vrtoče, 1989), 136–138.

49. Došen, *To je bilo onda*, 10–15, photograph on 10.

50. For some details about possible connections between Matijević, as well as his father, and the Ustašas prior to the German invasion, see Nikica Pilipović, "Vrtočani u danima ustanka, požara i otpora," in *Bosanski Petrovac u NOB, Knjiga I*, ed. Vladimir Čerkez (Bosanski Petrovac: Opštinski odbor SUBNOR-a Bosanski Petrovac, 1974), 541–542; Došen, *To je bilo onda*, 190.

51. LAEB, Bibanović, "Kulen Vakuf," 43.

52. Ibid., 43–44.

53. See, for example, AJ, Fond 110, DKUZ, kut. 817, Okružni sud Bihać, Pojedinačne optužnice i presude, 1946, dos. br. 817–320, Javno tužioštvo za Okrug Bihać, Krivični predmet protiv Burzić, Avde, May 27, 1946; ibid., dos. br. 817–376, Javno tužioštvo za Okrug Bihać, Krivični predmet protiv Kadić Bege, September 23, 1946; ibid., dos. br. 817–403, Javno tužioštvo za Okrug Bihać, Krivični predmet protiv Kozlice Agana, October 12, 1946; ibid., dos. br. 817–421, Javno tužioštvo za Okrug Bihać, Krivični predmet protiv Kulenović Mahmuta, August 26, 1946; ibid., dos. br. 817–469, Javno tužioštvo za Okrug Bihać, Krivični predmet protiv Pehlivanović Ibrahim, May 30, 1946; ibid., dos. br. 817–534, Javno tužioštvo za Okrug Bihać, Krivični predmet protiv Sušnjar-Vukalić Mujaga, October 15, 1946; AJ, Fond 110, DKUZ, kut. 531, dos. broj. 5361, Zapisnik br. 14, Mjesni odbor: Vrtoče, July 31, 1946; ibid., Zapisnik br. 10, Mjesni odbor: Kalati, August 5, 1946; Zapisnik br. 20, Mjesni odbor: Rajinovci, August 7,1946; Zapisnik br. 21, Mjesni odbor: Veliki Stjenjani, August 8, 1946; Zapisnik br. 22, Mjesni odbor: Kulen Vakuf, August 9, 1946; ABiH, Fond Zemaljske komisije za utvrđivanje zločina okupatora i njegovih pomagača Bosne i Hercegovine [hereafter ZKUZ BiH], kut. 91, Zapisnik br. 22, Mjesni odbor: Malo Očijevo, August 9, 1946; ibid., kut. 68, Srez Bosanski

Petrovac, Zapisnik br. 18, Mjesni odbor: Prkosi, August 4, 1946; kut. 14, Srez Bihać, Zapisnik br. 21, Mjesni odbor: Veliki Stjenjani, August 8, 1946.

54. In 1941, the population of the town of Kulen Vakuf was around 2,100, of which 1,975 could be considered to have been nominally Muslim. In the rest of the Muslim villages in this part of the Una River valley (i.e., Klisa, Orašac and Ćukovi) the total number residents was around 3,700. To these 5,675 Muslims should be added around 2,500 or so Catholic residents, who were perceived as "Croats," who lived for the most part in the nearby villages of Boričevac, Kalati, and Vrtoče.

55. On the outsiders sent to work in Donji Lapac and their difficulties in mobilizing local men into the Ustašas, see HDA DAKA, Fond RMZDL, Nikola Vidaković, "Partijska organizacija u Donjem Lapcu od osnivanja do početka ustanka 1941. godine," 18; on the non-indigenous origins of most of the Ustašas, see also ibid., Đoko Jovanić, "Kotar donjolapački u ustanku 1941. godine," 11–12.

56. HDA, f. 1355, Grupa VIII, inv. br. 236, Načelstvo sreza Donjolapačkog Kraljevskoj banskoj upravi Savske banovine, Odeljak za državnu zaštitu, Predmet: Pavičić, Juko, veze sa hrvatskim emigrantima, November 3, 1933, 1.

57. On Mehmed Mušeta's involvement with the Ustašas, see his wife's request for state assistance from the NDH authorities in 1944: ARSBL, Fond 76, Rizičko upraviteljstvo Banja Luka (NDH), dok. br. 7248, Mehmed Mušeta (1944), Predmet: Đula Mušeta, molba za obiteljsku državnu pomoć, January 23, 1944, 1–3; see also AJ, Fond 110, dos. br. 5361, Zapisnik broj 20, Mjesni odbor: Rajinovci, August 7, 1946, 1; on his participation in the municipal council of Kulen Vakuf prior to 1941, see AUSK, Fond Okružnog inspektorata Vrbaske Banovine Bihać, kut. 14, Članovi opštinkog vijeća Kulen Vakuf, October 25, 1931.

58. Interview with Abas Mušeta, July 8, 2012, Crikvenica; Abas Mušeta, "Kulen Vakuf: Tragedija od 10.04 do 06–18.09 1941. godine" (unpub. ms., private collection), 21.

59. On Husein "Huća" Zelić's involvement with the Ustašas, see HDA DAKA, Fond RMZDL, Radovi za hronike sela (neobjavljeno), Bušević u Narodnooslobodilačkoj borbi, 1941–1945 (1980), 24; Bibanović, "Kulenvakufski komunisti u radničkom pokretu i ustanku," 430; AJ, Fond 110, DK dos. br. 5361, Zapisnik broj 20, Mjesni odbor: Rajinovci, August 7, 1946, 1; ibid., dos. br. 5361, Zapisnik br. 22, Mjesni odbor: Kulen Vakuf, August 9, 1946, 1.

60. Obradović, "Zločini na kotaru Donji Lapac od 1941. do 1945.," 827.

61. The merchant in question named "Mehmed" may have been Mehmed Altić. On these examples, see Đuro Karanović, "Napad na žandarmerijsku stanicu u Martin Brodu," in *Drvar 1941–1945. Sjećanja učesnika, knjiga 2*, ed. Pero Morača (Drvar: Skupština opštine, 1972), 425.

62. M.J. Akbar, *Riot after Riot: Reports on Caste and Communal Violence in India* (New Delhi: Penguin Books, 1988), 23.

63. On the Pehlivanovićes of Ostrovica, see Obradović, "Zločini na kotaru Donji Lapac od 1941. do 1945.," 824; on the widespread tendency of local villagers to illegally cut trees in such areas during the decades prior to 1941, see also HDA, f. 1363, Grupa XXI, inv. br. 1819, Sresko načelstvo Donji Lapac, Predmet: Izvještaj o stanju javne uprave za mjesec mart i april 1930, I. Javna bezbednost, May 1, 1930, 1–2; ibid., inv. br. 2191, Sresko načelstvo Donji Lapac, Predmet: Izvještaj o stanju javne uprave za mjesec januar i februar 1931, IV. Poljoprivreda, February 28, 1931, 1; inv.

br. 2645, Sresko načelstvo u Donjem Lapcu, Predmet: Tromjesečni izvještaj po struci šumarskoj, July 1, 1932, 1–2.

64. See, for example, Stevo Trikić, "Upostavljanje vlasti NDH i ustaški terror u Drvaru," in *Drvar, 1941–1945. Sjećanja učesnika, knjiga 1*, ed. Pero Morača (Drvar: Skupština opštine Drvar, 1972), 219.

65. On similarities with eastern Bosnia, see Vukčević, ed., *Zločini*, br. 128, Izvještaj Krilnog oružničkog zapovjedništva Tuzla od 14. jula Zapovjedniku 4. Hrvatske oružničke pukovnije o vojno-političkoj situaciji na svojoj teritoriji i zlostavljanju pravoslavaca od ustaša, naročito u kotaru vlaseničkom, July 14, 1941, 328.

66. See McDoom, "Who Killed in Rwanda's Genocide?"; idem., "Antisocial Capital."

67. On NDH officials who suggested a connection between the negative effects of the agrarian reforms on the former Muslim landlords and Muslim support for the NDH, see Vukčević, ed., *Zločini*, br. 327, Izveštaj Ministarstva unutrašnjih poslova od 4. novembra Ministarstvu domobranstva o prilikama u Bosni sa podacima o odnosu Hrvata, Muslimana i Srba, November 14, 1941, 814; ibid., br. 150, Predlog Poglavnikovog povjerenika u Sarajevu od 23. jula 1941. Ministarstvu unutrašnjih poslova za naseljavanje istočne granice NDH muslimanskim i katoličkim življem, July 23, 1941, 369–370.

68. Obradović, "Zločini na kotaru Donji Lapac od 1941. do 1945.," 824.

69. On the similiarities between the Kulen Vakuf region's Ustašas and those in Herzegovina, See Vukčević, ed., *Zločini*, br. 101, Izvještaj posebnog opunomoćenika podmaršala Lakse od 5. jula 1941. Zapovjedniku kopnene vojske o divljačkim i neljudskim postupcima ustaša u Hercegovini, July 5, 1941, 208.

70. VA, Fond SUP BiH, Film 3, Ustaški elaborat Banja Luka, 2; on this prewar social profile of Ustašas in parts of Lika, see Stojkov, "O takozvanom Ličkom ustanku 1932.," 171.

71. Pilipović, "Vrtočani u danima ustanka, požara i otpora," 545.

72. On Miroslav Matijević, see Pilipović, "Vrtočani u danima ustanka, požara i otpora," 545; LAEB, Bibanović, "Stanovništvo Kulen-Vakufa," 129; AJ, Fond 110, DKUZ, f. 230, F. broj 24047, Matijević, Miro, April 29, 1947, 2; on Mehmed Mušeta and Husein "Huća" Zelić, see AJ, Fond 110, dos. br. 5361, Zapisnik broj 20, Mjesni odbor: Rajinovci, August 7, 1946, 1; ARSBL, Fond 76, Rizičko upraviteljstvo Banja Luka (NDH), dok. br. 7248, Mehmed Mušeta (1944), Predmet: Đula Mušeta, molba za obiteljsku državnu pomoć, January 23, 1944, 1–3; on Zelić, see also HDA, f. 1355, Grupa VIII, Emigracija, Načelstvo sreza Donjolapačkog Kraljevskoj banskoj upravi savske banovine, Odeljak za državnu zaštitu, Predmet: Pavičić, Juko, veze sa hrvatskim emigrantima, November 3, 1933, 1; on Vinko Marinković and Grga Pavičić, see Milan Šijan, "Nastanak i djelovanje KPJ na teritoriji kotara do oslobođenja Donjeg Lapca februara 1942. godine," in *Kotar Donji Lapac u Narodnooslobodilačkom ratu*, ed. Vezmar & Zatezalo, 41; Obradović, "Zločini na kotaru Donji Lapac od 1941. do 1945.," 827; Rašeta, *Kazivanje pobjednika smrti*, 14, 22.

73. On violent attempts by Muslims in the Cazin region of Bosnia to convert Orthodox Serbs to Islam, which caused them to flee to the town of Slunj where they expressed their desire to become Catholics, see Arhiv Muzeja Unsko-sanskog kantona [hereafter AMUSK], Prijepisi originalnih dokumenata iz Arhiva za historiju radničkog pokreta [hereafter AHRP], 1941–1945., Nezavisna Država Hrvatska, Ured Poglavnika, Predmet: Izvještaj Ravnateljstva za javni red i sigurnosti, September 6, 1941.

74. VA, Fond NDH, kut. 170, f. 12, dok. 18, Državno ravnateljstvo za ponovu Svim kotarskim oblastima, Svim ispostavama, Svim redarstvenim ravnateljstvima, Svim Velikim Županima, Svim gradskim poglavarstvima, Svim izseljeničkim logorima, Predmet: Uhićenje popova, postupak sa Rumunjima, Makedoncima i Rusima, August 9, 1941, 1.

75. *Hrvatska Krajina*, "Objašnjenje: kako se imade postupati sa onim grkoistočnjacima koji su prešli na katoličku vjeru," June 22, 1941, 4.

76. On the evolution of Ustaša policies of forced religious conversions, and especially on their subnational variation, see the important article by Biondich, "Religion and Nation in Wartime Croatia," 71–116.

77. Vukčević, ed., *Zločini*, br. 169, Oružnica Ministarstva pravosuđa i bogoštovlja od 30. jula 1941. sa uputstvima za prevođenje pravoslavaca u katoličku veru, July 30, 1941, 412–413; see also ibid., br. 282, Okružnica Predsjedništva vlade NDH od 15. septembra 1941. Ministarstvu unutrašnjih poslova o nadležnostima i poslovima u vezi sa prelaskom iz jedne vere u drugu, September 15, 1941, 702–703.

78. Gutić seems to have been especially concerned with the fate of Serb schoolteachers, as seen in his attempt on June 9 to compile precise lists of such individuals in the former Vrbaska banovina. See ARSBL, Fond 631, USPBVBBL, 1656/41, Ustaški stožer za Bosansku Hrvatsku, Spiskovi učitelja i učiteljica grko-istočne vjere na teritoriji bivše Vrbaske banovine, June 9, 1941, 1.

79. For a study that stresses the importance of racial ideas in the NDH (and especially in the Croat lands prior to 1941), but which pays little attention to actual policies and governmental practices, see Nevenko Bartulin, *The Racial Idea in the Independent State of Croatia: Origins and Theory* (Leiden: Brill, 2014).

80. Yet even with a seemingly clear conception of "Jews" and "Gyspies" as immutable racial categories, the NDH authorities issued exceptions and qualifications, such as with the "White Gypsies," who were said to be "Aryans" because "they adhere to Islam, their women marry other muslim Croats, they have their own houses, and are in general craftsmen." As was the case with NDH conceptions of "Serbs," here behavior seems to have often been the deciding factor about one's supposed danger, and not abstract, immutable categories of "race" or "nation." See VA, Fond NDH, kut. 200B, f. 1, dok. 23, Ministarstvo unutarnjih poslova, Predmet: Cigana bijelih—rasna pripadnost, August 30, 1941, 1 (lowercase "muslim" in the original). On NDH proclamations that used the language of "race," which dealt with definitions of "Jews" and "Gypsies"—and not "Serbs"—see *Hrvatska Krajina*, "Zakonska odredba o rasnoj pripadnosti" and "Zakonska odredba o zaštiti arijske krvi i časti hrvatskog naroda," May 4, 1941, 4; *Hrvatski Narod*, "Krv i cast hrvatskog naroda zaštićeni posebnim odredima," May 1, 1941, 1.

81. Vukčević, ed., *Zločini*, br. 169, Oružnica Ministarstva pravosuđa i bogoštovlja od 30. jula 1941. sa uputstvima za prevođenje pravoslavaca u katoličku veru, July 30, 1941, 413.

82. HDA DAKA, Fond 143, Memoarsko gradivo o NOR-u, 31/2010, Sjećanja Lika (LI-3), Podaci za dvadeset sela s područja kotara Donji Lapac, Popis učesnika aprilskog rata sela D. Lapca, 6.

83. Vukčević, ed., *Zločini*, br. 169, Oružnica Ministarstva pravosuđa i bogoštovlja od 30. jula 1941. sa uputstvima za prevođenje pravoslavaca u katoličku veru, July 30, 1941, 413.

84. Jelić-Butić, *Ustaše i Nezavisna Država Hrvatska*, 174.

85. On the Romanian case, see Vladimir Solonari, *Purifying the Nation. Population Exchange and Ethnic Cleansing in Nazi-Allied Romania* (Washington, DC: Woodrow Wilson Center Press; Baltimore: Johns Hopkins University Press, 2010); on Nazi Germany, see Mark Mazower, *Hitler's Empire: How the Nazis Ruled Europe* (New York: Penguin Books, 2008); on Eastern Europe more generally, see Alexander V. Prusin, *The Lands Between: Conflict in the East Europen Borderlands, 1870–1992* (Oxford: Oxford University Press, 2010), espec. chaps. 6–7.

86. Plans were originally drawn up, in conjuction with the German army, to resettle several hundred thousand Serbs to Serbia, and to replace them with an equal number of Catholic Slovenes. Attempts were made to realize these plans in June and July, but were later abandoned. See, for example, HDA, Fond 306, ZKUZ (Hrvatska) za Liku, kut. 70, inv. br. 4790, Ministarstvo prometa i javnih radova—Odio za željeznički promet, Predmet: Transporti Slovenaca u Slavonsku Požegu i Srba iz Hrvatske u Srbiju, July 10, 1941, 1–2. For a study of these policies, see Tone Ferenc, *Nacistička politika denacionalizacije u Sloveniji u godinama od 1941 do 1945* (Ljubljana: Partizanska knjiga, 1979).

87. On the creation of the State Office for Renewal, see *Hrvatski Narod*, "Osniva se Državno Ravnateljstvo za Ponovu," June 25, 1941, 19; *Hrvatska Krajina*, "Osnovano Državno ravnateljstvo za ponovu," June 27, 1941, 2.

88. VA, Fond NDH, kut. 170, f. 12, dok. 18, Državno ravnateljstvo za ponovu Svima kotarskim oblastima, Svima redarstvenim ravnateljstvima, Predmet: Upute za iseljavanje obitelji dviju vjera, July 24, 1941, 1.

89. HDA DAKA, Fond 141, Razni spisi iz razdoblja NDH, kut. 3, Ministarstvo Hrvatskog Domobranstva, II. Odjel, I. Odsjek Domobranskom popunitbenom zapovjedništvu, Tko se smatra Srbin, November 4, 1941, 1.

90. See, for example, VA, Fond NDH, kut. 143a, f. 10, dok. 14, Zapovjedništvo 3. Hrvatske oružničke pukovnije Zapovjedništvu 4. Hrvatske oružničke pukovnije, Izvještaj o obavještajnoj službi dostavlja, July 16, 1941, 2–3. The transcribed records of the postwar interrogation of Viktor Gutić suggest that a special conference was held in Zagreb to discuss the resettlement of Serbs from the region. In attendance were many of the key political elite in the NDH, including Slavko and Eugen Kvaternik, as well as Dr. Rožanković, the director of the State Office for Renewal. See ARSBL, Lični fond Milan Vukmanović (1928–1993), 559, Ispis o Viktoru Gutiću, Saslušanje, June 7, 1946, 9; on state wide orders, see Vukčević, ed., *Zločini*, br. 93, "Okružnica Državnog ravnateljstva za ponovu od 2. srpnja 1941. svim Kotarskim predstojništvima o osnivanju ureda za iseljavanje, njegovoj organizaciji i zadacima," July 2, 1941, 183–188.

91. On these instructions, see VA, Fond NDH, kut. 170, f. 12, dok. 2, Državno ravnateljstvo za ponovu Svima kotarskim predstojništvnima, July 2, 1941, 1–6.

92. VA, Fond NDH, kut. 170, f. 13, dok. 3, Raspis Velikim županima (undated documents, mostly likely from mid-July 1941), 1.

93. The sudden departure of the non-Croat population usually prompted a large number of requests from local Muslim and Catholic residents for their apartments, belongings, and businesses. Most justified their requests by emphasizing that they were "Croats" or "Croats of the Islamic faith," that they had suffered prior to the establishment of the NDH because of their non-Croat neighbors and the Yugoslav state authorities, that they were poor, and thus deserved the Serb and Jewish property. See,

for example, the large number of requests for Serb and Jewish property in ARSBL, Fond 631, USPBVBBL, Ustaški stožer i povjereništva za bivšu Vrbasku banovinu, Ravnateljstvo za ponovu (unnumbered).

94. ARSBL, Fond Zbirka varia, 330, Optužnica Viktora Gutića, Javno tužioštvo okruga Banja Luka Okružnom sudu Banja Luka, December 25, 1946, 7–8.

95. VA, Fond NDH, kut. 170, f. 12, dok. 17, Državno ravnateljstvo za ponovu Svima općinskim poglavarstvima, Predmet: Čuvanje pokretne i nepokretne imovine ispražnjenih posjeda trgovina, industrija, obrta, te kuće izseljenih i nestalih Srba, July 24, 1941, 1.

96. *Hrvatski Narod*, "Židovi su dužni prijaviti svoju imovinu," June 6, 1941, 14.

97. Izvještaj Gradskog poglavarstva u Banjoj Luci Povjerenstvu za upostavu javnoga reda i poretka, November 22, 1941, as ctied in ARSBL, Fond Zbirka varia, 330, Optužnica Viktora Gutića, Javno tužioštvo okruga Banja Luka Okružnom sudu Banja Luka, December 25, 1946, 29.

98. This wide variation caught the attention of the Italian vice consul in Banja Luka, who mentioned it in a report he wrote at the end of July 1941: "The expulsion of the Orthodox population from the territory of the former Vrbaska banovina is taking place most frequently on the basis of personal criteria, on the understanding of the stožernik (Viktor Gutić) and the Veliki župan (Ljubomir Kvaternik). Indeed, while in Bihać not a single Orthodox (Serb) remains, and where all were forced out in a matter of hours, in Banja Luka there are still about 2,000 families. Some of those who had to leave have been given time to pack their luggage and take appropriate care of their property, while others have been forced to leave suddenly." See Vukčević, ed., *Zločini*, br. 162, Izveštaj Italijanskog vicekonzula u Banjaluci od 26. jula 1941. Italijanskom poslanstvu u Zagrebu o proterivanju Srba i Jevreja sa teritorije bivše Vrbaske banovine, July 26, 1941, 397. On the first resettlements of "Serbs" from Banja Luka, see also *Hrvatska Krajina*, "Prvi transport iseljenih srba napustio je Banju Luku," July 23, 1941, 3.

99. On the NDH military's awareness of this dynamic, see VA, Fond NDH, kut. 143a, f. 10, dok. 14, Zapovjedništvo 3. Hrvatske oružničke pukovnije Zapovjedništvu 4. Hrvatske oružničke pukovnije, Izvještaj o obavještajnoj službi dostavlja, July 16, 1941, 2–3.

100. See, for example, VA, Fond NDH, kut. 169, f. 6, dok. 3, Ravnateljstvo ustaškog redarstva (Banja Luka) Ustaškom redarstvenom ravnateljstvu u Banja Luci, Izvještaj izaslanika Josipa Knopa, July 16, 1941, 1.

101. Vukčević, ed., *Zločini*, br. 209, Dopis Državnog ravnateljstva za ponovu od 13. avgusta 1941. Ministarstvu vanjskih poslova o intervenciji nemačkog vojnog zapovednika Srbije povodom masovnog hapšenja i smeštaja Srba u sabirne logore i preseljavanja u Srbiju, August 13, 1941, 497–498. On the agreement, see Jelić-Butić, *Ustaše i Nezavisna Država Hrvatska*, 169; Ferenc, *Nacistička politika denacionalizacije.*

102. On Kvaternik's order for Serbs to leave Bihać and to not come within fifteen kilometers of city unless given special permission from the authorities, see VA, Fond NDH, kut. 195, f. 20, dok. 14, Veliki Župan Velike Župe Krbava i Psat, Proglas, June 20, 1941; see also *Zbornik dokumenata i podataka o Narodnooslobodilačkom ratu jugoslovenskih naroda* [hereafter *Zbornik NOR-a*], *tom IV, knjiga 1, Borbe u Bosni i Hercegovini 1941. god.* (Belgrade: Vojno-istoriski institut Jugoslovenske Armije, 1951), br. 235,

"Izvještaj Zapovjedništva bosanskog divizijskog područja od 10. srpnja o pripremama naroda za ustanak i raseljavanju srpskog stanovništva u Bosanskog Krajini," 523–524.

103. VA, Fond NDH, kut. 85, f. 8, dok. 14, Zapovjedništvo 4. Hrvatske oružničke pukovnije Zapovjedništvu hrvatskog oružništva, Prebacivanje pravoslavnog življa, July 12, 1941, 1. For recollections of citizens of Bihać of the deportations, see AJ, Fond 110, DKUZ, f. 735, Okrug Bihać, Inv. br. 56127, Zapisnik sastavljen 7. avgusta 1946. god. u Bihaću, srez Bihać, po ZKUZ, August 7, 1946, 2–3.

104. For vivid testimonies about the circular path of these expulsions and the suffering that the expellees endured, see ARSBL, Fond 209, Memoarske građe, sig. 209-017-008, Anka Toman (rođena Radaković), "Interniranje moje porodice iz Bihaća 1941 godine," October 7, 1988, 1–9; AJ, Fond 110, DKUZ, Dos. br. 3136, Zapisnik sastavljen u Ministarstvu unutrašnjih poslova (Beograd), Izjava od Božidarke Vojvodića, July 2, 1941, 1–2; ibid., f. 588, Inv. br. 14398, Zapisnik od 2. jula 1941. godine sastavljen u Ministarstvu unutrašnjih poslova (Izjava od Božidarke Vojvodića iz Bihaća), July 2, 1941, 2; ibid., Inv. br. 14399, Zapisnik od 20. aprila 1941. godine sastavljen u Komesarijatu za izbeglice i preseljenike u Beogradu, April 20, 1942, 1–6.

105. On the supposed ban on "Serbs" coming within five kilometers of Bosanski Petrovac, see VA, Fond NOV, kut. 1997, f. 8, dok. 2, Podgrupa Bosanski Petrovac, Stenografske beleške, June 8, 1951, 2.

106. VA, Fond NDH, kut. 153a, f. 5, dok. 13, Talijanski vicekonzulat, Banja Luka, Predmet: Mjere za protjerivanje Srba, July 16, 1941, 1.

107. Ibid., Zapovjedništvo Hrvatskog oružništva Zapovjedništvu vojske i Ministarstvu domobranstva, July 14, 1941, 1. On the improvisation involved in the resettlements, see also AJ, Fond 110, Inv. br. 56127, Zapisnik sastavljen u Bihaću po ZKUZ, August 7, 1946, 7–8.

108. VA, Fond NDH, kut. 85, f. 6, dok. 12, Izvještaj o vanjskoj i unutarnjoj situaciji za prvu deseticu (1.-10.) srpnja (undated document, but most likely from mid-July 1941), 8–9. On the difficult conditions that the deportees from Bihać faced, see also ibid., kut. 312, f. 1, dok. 55, Kratak pregled masovnih zločina ustaša u 1941. godini, bihaćki okrug, 1.

109. VA, Fond NDH, kut. 84, f. 4, dok. 24, Zapovjedništvo kopnene vojske, Izvještaj o vanjskoj i unutarnjoj situaciji za drugu deseticu (10.-20.) sprnja 1941, July 21, 1941, 9, 12.

110. VA, Fond NDH, kut. 84, f. 4, dok. 24, Stožer Vrbaskog divijskog područja Zapovjedništvu kopnene vojske, Izvještaj o vanjskoj i unutarnjoj situaciji za drugu deseticu (10.–20.) sprnja 1941, July 18, 1941, 2.

111. AJ, Fond 110, DKUZ, f. 230, F. broj 24047, Matijević, Miro, April 29, 1947, 1–2.

112. HDA, Fond 223, MUP NDH, kut. 32, Ustaša—Hrvatski oslobodilački pokret—Ustaški stožer u Bihaću Ravnateljstvu za ponovu u Zagrebu, September 6, 1941, 1. In postwar investigative reports that the communist war crimes commission produced, witnesses from Croatian villages in northwest Bosnia (e.g., Zavalje) recalled that Kvaternik and others supposedly made promises that they would receive the property of Serbs if they participated in cleansing actions against them. See AJ, Fond 110, DKUZ, Inv. br. 56136, Mjesni narodni odbor Zavalje, Zapisnik sastavljen u Sreskom narodnom odboru po ZKUZ, July 21, 1946, 1.

113. Vukčević, ed., *Zločini*, br. 305, Izveštaj Zapovjedništva Vojne krajine od 1. oktobra 1941. Doglavniku—Vojskovođi o izvršenom pokolju pravoslavnog življa u Jajcu i okolini, October 1, 1941, 768.

114. On the *Janjaweed* in Darfur, for example, see Gérard Prunier, *Darfur: A 21st Century Genocide*, 3rd ed. (Ithaca, NY: Cornell University Press, 2008), 122.

115. Vukčević, ed., *Zločini*, br. 98, Izvještaj predstojnika kotarske oblasti Bileća Ravnateljstva za javni red i sigurnosti o situaciji na području kotara i čitave Hercegovine za period 11. juni–4. juli 1941. god. sa podacima o pravoslavnom stanovništvu, međusobnim odnosima naroda, zločinima ustaša i uzrocima takvog stanja, 202; see also VA, Fond NDH, kut 135i, f. 8, dok. 4, Zapovjednik trusinskog odreda, Izvještaj o događajima u selu Berkovićima, August 29, 1941, 1, which suggests that, in the words of NDH military commanders who were stationed in villages in Herzegovina, local Muslims who joined the Ustašas "took advantage of the newly created conditions to engage in plunder and rapidly enrich themselves."

116. On this point, see Philip Zimbardo, *The Lucifer Effect: Understanding How Good People Turn Evil* (New York: Random House, 2007), 449–451.

117. VA, Fond NDH, kut. 150a, f. 2, dok. 40, Krilno oružničko zapovjedništvo Gospić Zapovjedništvu I. Hrvatske oružničke pukovnije, Rezultat izviđaja po ucjeni oružnika postaje Doljane, July 12, 1941, 1–2.

118. Ilija Rašeta, "Pripremanje i početak ustanka u Donjem Lapcu," in *1941–1942. u svedočenjima učesnika narodnooslobodilačke borbe, knjiga 4*, ed. Radomir Petković (Belgrade: Vojnoizdavački zavod, 1975), 218.

119. VA, Fond NDH, kut. 179, f. 1, dok. 15, Kotarska oblast u Vlasenici Velikoj Župi Vrhbosna, Izvještaj o nezakonitom radu pojedinih ustaških organa, July 19, 1941, 1–2; ibid., kut. 180, f. 1, dok. 24, Kotarska oblast u Rogatici Velikoj Župi Vrhbosna, July 17, 1941, 1–2.

120. VA, Fond NDH, kut. 84, f. 6, dok. 15, Zapovjedništvo kopnene vojske, Vojni ured, Izvještaj o vanjskoj i unutarnoj situaciji za treću desetice, May 31, 1941, 6.

121. Ibid., kut. 84, f. 5, dok. 25, Zapovjedništvo kopnene vojske, Izvještaj o vanjskoj i unutarnjoj situaciji za treću (20–31.) srpnja 1941, August 1, 1941, 10.

122. Ibid., kut. 179, f. 1, dok. 15, Kotarska oblast u Vlasenici Velikoj Župi Vrhbosna, Izvještaj o nezakonitom radu pojedinih ustaških organa, July 19, 1941, 1–2; ibid., kut. 180, f. 1, dok. 24, Kotarska oblast u Rogatici Velikoj Župi Vrhbosna, July 17, 1941, 1–2.

123. Ibid., kut. 85, f. 7, dok. 14, Zapovjedništvo III. hrvatske oružničke pukovnije Zapovjedništvu hrvatskog oružništva, Ćubrilo Ilija i dr. pljačke za račun ustaša vršili, July 16, 1941, 1.

124. On the *Interahamwe* in Rwanda and *Janjaweed* in Darfur, see Prunier, *Darfur: A 21st Century Genocide*, 97; idem., *The Rwanda Crisis: A History of a Genocide* (London: Hurst & Company, [1995] 2010), 135–144, 231.

125. Trial documents suggest that Gutić made this statement while visting a monastery in mid-May. See ARSBL, Fond Zbirka varia, 330, Optužnica Viktora Gutića, Javno tužioštvo okruga Banja Luka Okružnom sudu Banja Luka, December 25, 1946, 31.

126. Included in the Velika Župa Krbava i Psat were the following municipalities: Bihać, Bosanska Krupa, Bosanski Petrovac, Bosansko Grahovo, Cazin, the city

of Bihać, Donji Lapac, and Korenica. See AJ, Fond 110, DKUZ, f. 131, F. br. 6017, Kvaternik Ljubomir (undated document, most likely written in 1946 or 1947), 1.

127. VA, Fond NOV, kut. 2000, f. 2, dok. 2, Podgrupa za Bihać, Period od 27. marta do okupacije, Stenografske beleške, May 22, 1951, 4.

128. On Pavelić's decision, see See AJ, Fond 110, DKUZ, f. 131, F. br. 6017, Kvaternik Ljubomir (undated document, most likely from 1946 or 1947), 1. For a short biography of Kvaternik, see *Hrvatski narod*, "Ljubomir Kvaternik, Veliki Župan Velike Župe Krbava i Psat," June 9, 1941, 4.

129. HDA, Fond 223, MUP NDH, Personalni podaci službenika NDH, br. 2539, Ljubomir Kvaternik, Velika župa Krbava i Psat Ministarstvu unutarnjih poslova, June 19, 1941, 1.

130. VA, Fond NOV, kut. 2000, f. 2, dok. 2, Podgrupa za Bihać, Period od 27. marta do okupacije, Stenografske beleške, May 22, 1951, 4; AJ, Fond 110, DKUZ, f. 735, Okrug Bihać, Inv. br. 56127, Zapisnik sastavljen 7. avgusta 1946. god. u Bihaću, srez Bihać, po ZKUZ, August 7, 1946, 1.

131. VA, Fond NDH, kut. 195, f. 10, dok. 61, Veliki Župan Velike Župe Krbave i Psat, Proglas, June 23, 1941, 1.

132. Arhiv Srbije [hereafter AS], Fond G-2, Komesarijat za izbeglice [hereafter KI], f. 5, Okrug bihaćki srez, br. 3, Teror Hrvata (ustaša) u Bihaću i okolini (1941–1944), undated document, 1, 3. While politically marginalized, Ibrahimpašić and his supporters continued to speak out against the NDH authorities in Bihać through 1941 and into 1942, apparently often doing so in taverns by trying to pay for drinks with currency from the interwar Kingdom of Yugoslavia, and by publicly accusing certain individuals of persecuting Serbs. On these acts, see VA, Fond NDH, kut. 195, f. 10, dok. 33, Velika župa Krbava i Psat, Predmet: Doglasni izvještaj, March 1, 1942, 1–2.

133. Slavko Odić, "Radnički pokret Bihaća i okoline do ustanka 1941. godine," in *Podgrmeč u NOB: Podgrmeč do ustanka i u ustanku 1941. Zbornik sjećanja, knjiga prva*, ed. Dušan Pejanović (Belgrade: Vojnoizdavački zavod, 1972), 81.

134. VA, Fond NDH, kut. 201, f. 21, dok. 12, Veliki župan Velike Župe Krbava i Psat Kotarskim oblastima—svima, Kotarskim ispostavama—svima, Gradskom poglavarstvu—Bišće, July 12, 1941, 1.

135. Ibid., kut. 195, f. 5, dok. 3, Velika župa Bribir i Sidraga, Predmet: izvještaj o događajima u župi za vrijeme od 7. kolovoza do 16. kolovoza, August 16, 1941, 7–8.

136. VA, Fond NOV, kut. 1997, f. 8, dok. 6, Jovo Kecman, "Podaci o organizacionom stanju Partijske organizacije prije rata na srezu Bosanskom Petrovačkom," May 24, 1951, 6.

137. AJ, Fond 110, DKUZ, f. 588, Inv. br. 14437, Zapisnik od 25. januara 1944. sastavljen u Komesarijatu za izbeglice i preseljenike u Beogradu (Nikolić Natalija iz Drvara), January 25, 1944, 3; VA, Fond NDH, kut. 169, f. 6, dok. 3, Ravnateljstvo ustaškog redarstva (Banja Luka) Ustaškom redarstvenom ravnateljstvu u Banja Luci, Izvještaj izaslanika Josipa Knopa, July 16, 1941, 1–2; ibid., SUP BiH, Film 3, Ustaški elaborat Drvar, March 10, 1953, 2.

138. See, for example, AJ, Fond 110, DKUZ, f. 588, Inv. br. 14437, Zapisnik od 25. januara 1944. sastavljen u Komesarijatu za izbeglice i preseljenike u Beogradu (Nikolić Natalija iz Drvara), January 25, 1944, 3

139. On the importance of removing moderates among the NDH authorities in Bihać, and their replacement with advocates of radicalization, in order to pave the way for more radical policies of presecution against the region's non-Croat population, see Vukčević, ed., *Zločini*, br. 373, Pregled masovnih zločina ustaša u 1941. godini na teritoriji bihaćkog i travničkog okruga (undated document), 981. The removal of several of these individuals later in the 1941 was also a key reason for the de-escalation of the violence. On this point, see ibid., 985.

140. See, for example, Scott Straus, *The Order of Genocide: Race, Power, and War in Rwanda* (Ithaca, NY: Cornell University Press, 2006), especially chap. 3.

141. AJ, Fond 110, DKUZ, dos. br. 5361, Zapisnik br. 22, Mjesni odbor: Kulen Vakuf, August 9, 1946, 1; ibid., f. 230, F. broj 24047, Matijević, Miro, April 29, 1947, 2.

142. On Zelić, see HDA DAKA, Fond RMZDL, Radovi za hronike sela (neobjavljeno), Bušević u Narodnooslobodilačkoj borbi, 1941–1945 (1980), 24.

143. The depth of his understanding of Nazi ideology remains an open question. See Bibanović, "Kulenvakufski komunisti u radničkom pokretu i ustanku," 430.

Chapter 3. Killing and Rescue

1. For evidence on what appears to have been one of the first killings in the region, which took place on or about June 5 in the village of Gajina (northwest of Kulen Vakuf), see HDA, Fond 306, ZKUZ (Hrvatska), kut. 244, OKUZ za Liku, Zh. br. 11479–11500, Odluke i izjave, May 1945, 1–24; on others during the second half of June, see ibid., kut. 244, OKUZ za Liku, Zh. br. 11754–11759, Zapisnik sastavljen pred komisijom u Bubnju, May 13, 1945, 1–2; ibid., inv. br. 42206–42211, Zapisnik sastavljen pred komisijom u Doljanima, July 15, 1945, 1–2.

2. On these killings, see, for example, Skoko, *Pokolji hecegovačkih Srba '41.*; Živković & Kačavenda, *Srbi u Nezavisnoj Državi Hrvatskoj*; Jelić-Butić, *Ustaše i Nezavisna Država Hrvatska*, 165.

3. On the importance of such ideologies in creating a context conducive to mass violence, see Eric Weitz, *A Century of Genocide. Utopias of Race and Nation* (Princeton, NJ: Princeton University Press, 2003).

4. Barbara Herff, "Genocide as State Terrorism," in *Government Violence and Repression: An Agenda for Research*, ed. Michael Stohl and George A. Lopez (Westport, CT: Greenwood Press, 1986), 165–187, here 182.

5. See, for example, Su, *Collective Killings in Rural China*; Fujii, *Killing Neighbors*; Autesserre, *The Trouble with the Congo*; McDoom, "Who Killed in Rwanda's Genocide?"; idem, "Antisocial Capital"; Gross, *Neighbors*; Redlich, *Together and Apart in Brzezany*; and Bartov, "Communal Genocide."

6. VA, Fond NDH, kut. 84, f. 6, dok. 19, Zapovjedništvo cjelokupne hrvatske kopnene vojske, V.T. Naredba br. 21, April 30, 1941, 1–3.

7. *Hrvatska Krajina*, "Proglas," April 24, 1941, 1.

8. VA, Fond NDH, kut. 84, f. 7, dok. 58, Stožer Vrbaskog divizijskog područja, Izvještaj po naredbi V.T-br. 2, toč. XIII. Zapovjedništvu hrvatske kopnene vojske, May 9, 1941, 1–2.

9. On these numbers, see ABiH, Fond ZKUZ BiH, kut. 7, Referati, inv. br. 80, Referat o geopolitičkim i etnografskim razmatranjima u Bosni i Herzegovini

(undated document, although the population figures appear to have been formulated with numbers gathered in 1940), 5–7.

10. On this point, see Rašeta, "Pripremanje i početak ustanka u Donjem Lapcu," 200; Obradović, "Selo Bubanj u plamenu," 435.

11. On the low numbers of weapons that the Ustašas in the region were able to collect, see Rašeta, "Pripremanje i početak ustanka u Donjem Lapcu," 205.

12. VA, Fond NDH, kut. 85, f. 3, dok. 9, Zapovjedništvo kopnene vojske (Vojni ured), Izvještaj, June 21, 1941, 2.

13. VA, Fond NOV, kut. 2000, f. 2, dok. 4, Srez Bihać, Period od okupacije do kraja 1941. godine, Stenografske beleške, June 9, 1951, 1; HDA DAKA, Fond 143, Memoarsko gradivo o NOR-u, 31/2010, Sjećanja Lika (LI-3), Učešće naroda i razvoj NOR-a na teritoriji Dobrosela, 5–7; ibid., Podaci za dvadeset sela s područja kotara Donji Lapac, Popis učesnika u aprilskom ratu 1941. godine koji su se zatekli kao vojnici na odsluženju kadrovskog roka ili bili pozvani kao rezervisti iz sela Osredaka, 1–2.

14. HDA DAKA, Fond 143, Memoarsko gradivo o NOR-u, 31/2010, Sjećanja Lika (LI-3), Podaci za dvadeset sela s područja kotara Donji Lapac, Popis učesnika u aprilskom ratu 1941. koji su se zatekli kao vojnici na odsluženju kadrovskog roka ili bili pozvani kao rezervisti iz sela Osredaka, 1–2; ibid., Fond RMZDL, Radovi za hronike sela (neobjavljeno), Rade Grbić, "Osredci u prošlosti i sadašnjosti—Put osredačkog odreda od 27.07.1941.–28.03.1942. godine," (1980), 9; ibid., kut. 3 (originali), Milan Majstorović i Mićo Medić, "Formiranje i borbena dejstva doljanske partizanske čete" (undated, most likely written in the late 1970s or early 1980s), 1–2.

15. VA, Fond NDH, kut. 84, f. 6, dok. 15, Zapovjedništvo kopnene vojske, Vojni ured, Izvještaj o vanjskoj i unutarnjoj situaciji za treću deseticu, May 31, 1941, 3; ibid., kut. 84, f. 1, dok. 58, Stožer Vrbaskog divizijskog područja, Zapovjedniku kopnene vojske (Vojni ured), Doglasni izvještaj, June 9, 1941, 1–2.

16. Đoko Jovanić, *Ratna sjećanja* (Belgrade: Vojnoizdavački i novinski centar, 1988), 37.

17. HDA DAKA, Fond 143, Memoarsko gradivo o NOR-u, LI-1, Izjave s područja Like, Sastanak ličke grupe, March 23, 1951, 16–17.

18. On fears within the NDH military that Serbs in the wider region had fled to the forests to prepare for some kind of rebel action, see VA, Fond NDH, kut. 85, f. 8, dok. 14, Zapovjedništvo 4. Hrvatske oružničke pukovnije Zapovjedništvu hrvatskog oružništva, Prebacivanje pravoslavnog življa, July 12, 1941, 1; ibid., kut. 84, f. 1, dok. 58, Stožer Vrbaskog divizijskog područja, Zapovjedniku kopnene vojske (Vojni ured), Doglasni izvještaj, June 9, 1941, 1.

19. HDA DAKA, Fond 143, Memoarsko gradivo o NOR-u, LI-1, Izjave s područja Like, Sastanak ličke grupe, March 23, 1951, 16–17.

20. For an analysis of Ustaša surveillance in the Bihać region, see VA, Fond SUP BiH, Film 3, Predmet: Elaborat o izvršenoj rekonstrukciji ustaške nadzorne službe na terenu srezu Bihaća, 1959, 5–8; on such activities at the village level, see HDA DAKA, Fond 143, Memoarsko gradivo o NOR-u, 31/2010, Sjećanja Lika (LI-3), Učešće naroda i razvoj NOR-a na teritoriji Dobrosela, 11; see also the testimonies of Milan Filipović and Stevo Inđić (both from Kalati) in Gojko Polovina, *Svedočenje: prva godina ustanka u Lici* (Belgrade: Izdavačka radna organizacija "Rad," 1988), 58.

21. For views in which a state's elite appears as the key driver of violent escalation, see, for example, Benjamin Valentino, *Final Solutions: Mass Killing and Genocide in the*

Twentieth Century (Ithaca, NY: Cornell University Press, 2004); Geoffrey Robinson, *The Dark Side of Paradise:. Political Violence in Bali* (Ithaca, NY: Cornell University Press, 1995).

22. VA, Fond NDH, kut. 84, f. 1, dok. 37, Stožer Vrbaskog divizijskog područja Zapovjedništvu Hrvatske kopnene vojske (Vojni odsjek), Prilike i političko stanje na području, May 31, 1941, 1.

23. On the rebellion in Herzegovina, see Savo Skoko and Milan Grahovac, "Junski ustanak," in *Hercegovina u NOB, april 1941.–juni 1942, tom 2*, ed. Sveta Kovačević and Slavko Stijačić-Slavo (Belgrade i Mostar: Vojnoidavački i novinski centar i Istorijski arhiv Hercegovina, 1986), 409–439; Uglješa Danilović, "Ustanak u Hercegovini, jun 1941—jun 1942," in *Hercegovina u NOB. Pišu učesnici*, ed. Milisav Perović (Belgrade: Vojnoizdavački zavod JNA "Vojno delo," 1961), 25–39; Davor Marijan, "Lipanjski ustanak u istočnoj Hercegovini 1941. godine," *Časopis za suvremenu povijest* 35, no. 2 (2003): 545–576.

24. VA, Fond NDH, kut. 84, f. 3, dok. 21, Zapovjedništvo kopnene vojske Zapovjedništvu vojske i Ministarstvu Domobranstva, Izvještaj o vanjskoj i unutarnjoj situaciji za treću deseticu (20.–30. lipnja 1941), July 1, 1941, 2, 4–5.

25. For the quotation, see VA, Fond NDH, kut. 84, f. 2, dok. 28, Stožer vrbaskog divizijskog područja Zapovjedništvu kopnene vojske, Izvješće, June 19, 1941, 1; on the threats and plans for these military operations, see ibid., VA, f. 3, dok. 24, Zapovjedništvo kopnene vojske u Zagrebu (Tajništvo) Vojnom uredu zapovjedništvu, July 1, 1941, 1; ibid., kut. 85, f. 8, dok. 11, Zapovjedništvo I. Hrvatske oružničke pukovnije Zapovjedništvu Hrvatskog oružništva, Pojava četnika u Srbu, July 6, 1941, 1; ibid., Fond NOV, kut. 2006, f. 5, dok. 1, Historijat Kotar Donji Lapac, Razvoj Narodno-oslobodilačke borbe u donjolapačkom kotaru, July 7, 1952, 4.

26. *Hrvatski Narod*, "Poglavnikova izvanredna zakonska odredba i zapovijed," June 27, 1941, 1; ibid., "Izvanredna zakonska odredba i zapovijed Poglavnika Nezavisne Države Hrvatske," June 28, 1941, 1; see also VA, Fond NDH, kut. 86, f. 1 dok. 1–20, Izvanredna zakonska odredba i zapovijed, June 28, 1941, 1.

27. HDA DAKA, Fond RMZDL, kut. 4, Originali, Milan Obradović, "Zločini na kotaru Donji Lapac od 1941. do 1945. godine," 30; VA, Fond NDH, kut. 85, f. 8, dok. 11, Zapovjedništvo I. Hrvatske oružničke pukovnije Zapovjedništvu Hrvatskog oružništva, Pojava četnika u Srbu, July 6, 1941, 1.

28. *Hrvatska Krajina*, "Najstrožije mjere biti će primijenjene za napadaje protiv Hrvata," June 18, 1941, 5.

29. Ibid., "Prema ubojicama ne smije biti obzira," July 9, 1941, 1.

30. Mile Labus, "Sjećanja i zapisi," in *Bosanski Petrovac u NOB, Knjiga II*, ed. Vladimir Čerkez (Bosanski Petrovac: Opštinski odbor SUBNOR-a Bosanski Petrovac, 1974), 518.

31. Horowitz, *The Deadly Ethnic Riot*, 87.

32. Jonathan Spencer, "Popular Perceptions of the Violence: A Provincial View," in *Sri Lanka in Change and Crisis*, ed. James Manor (London & Sydney: Croom Helm, 1984), 187–195, here 192–193; on the importance of rumors in creating a context for violence, see also Valery Tishkov, "'Don't Kill Me, I'm a Kyrgyz!': An Anthropological Analysis of Violence in the Osh Ethnic Conflict," *Journal of Peace Research* 32, no. 2 (1995): 133–149.

33. *Zbornik dokumenata i podataka o Narodnooslobodilačkom ratu jugoslovenskih naroda* [hereafter *Zbornik NOR-a*], *tom V, knjiga 1, Borbe u Hrvatskoj 1941. god.* (Belgrade: Vojno-istoriski institut Jugoslovenske Armije, 1952), Br. 229, "Izvještaj Grupe kraljevskih karabinjera iz Zadra iz 15. srpnja 1941. o zločinima ustaša u Lici," July 15, 1941, 511–512.

34. For a testimony of a survivor who saw the mutilated corpse of Ljubica Lavrnje and fetus of her unborn child, see HDA DAKA, Fond RMZDL, kut. 4, Originali, Milan Obradović, "Zločini na kotaru Donji Lapac od 1941. do 1945. godine," 27; on these killings and mutilations, see also HDA, Fond 306, ZKUZ (Hrvatska), kut. 245, Zh. br. 11639–11640, OKUZ za Liku, Zapisnik sastavljen pred komisijom u Donjoj Suvaji, May 11, 1945, 1–2.

35. On lynchings in the U.S., see Orlando Patterson, *Rituals of Blood. Consequences of Slavery in Two American Centuries* (New York: Basic Books, 1998), 179–180; on Rwanda, see Prunier, *The Rwandan Crisis*, 256–257.

36. *Zbornik NOR-a, tom V, knjiga 1, Borbe u Hrvatskoj 1941. god.*, br. 229, "Izvještaj Grupe kraljevskih karabinjera iz Zadra iz 15. srpnja 1941. o zločinima ustaša u Lici," July 15, 1941, 511–512.

37. Rade Dubajić Čkaljac, "Tragično djetinjstvo," in *Kotar Donji Lapac u Narodnooslobodilačkom ratu*, ed. Vezmar and Zatezalo, 862–863.

38. *Zbornik NOR-a, tom V, knjiga 1, Borbe u Hrvatskoj 1941. god.*, br. 229, "Izvještaj Grupe kraljevskih karabinjera iz Zadra iz 15. srpnja 1941. o zločinima ustaša u Lici," July 15, 1941, 511–512; on the supposed presence of "Chetniks" in the region as the reason for the attacks, see also AS, Fond G-2, KI, f. 16, Srez Donji Lapac, Medić Milica, student medicine, daje sledeće podatke o stradanju Srba u njenom kraju, July 3, 1941, 1.

39. VA, Fond NDH, kut. 84, f. 3, dok. 48, Stožer Vrbaskog divizijskog područja Zapovjedništvu kopnene vojske (Glavaru Vojnog ureda—za III Odsjek), 10—dnevno izvješće o stanju na području, July 12, 1941, 2.

40. VA, Fond NDH, kut. 85, f. 8, dok. 11, Zapovjedništvo I. Hrvatske oružničke pukovnije Zapovjedništvu Hrvatskog oružništva, Pojava četnika u Srbu, July 6, 1941, 1.

41. HDA, Fond 1450, Ministarstvo oružanih snaga Nezavisne Države Hrvatske [hereafter MINORS NDH], D-2230, Izvještaj o vanjskoj i unutarnjoj situaciji za prvu deseticu (1.–10) srpnja 1941., 4–5.

42. For the quotation, see VA, Fond NDH, kut. 84, f. 3, dok. 54, Zapovjedništvo kopnene vojske, Izvještaj o vanjskoj i unutarnjoj situaciji za prvu deseticu (1.–10.) srpnja 1941., July 11, 1941, 5; see also ibid., kut. 84, fas. 3, dok. 48, Stožer vrbaskog divizijskog područja 10-dnevno izvješće o stanju na području Zapovjedništvu kopene vojske (Glavaru Vojnog ureda—za III odsjek), July 12, 1941, 2; ibid., kut. 85, f. 6, dok. 12, Izvještaj o vanjskoj i unutarnjij situaciji za prvu deseticu (1.–10) srpnja 1941 (undated document, mostly likely from mid-July 1941), 4–5.

43. VA, Fond NDH, kut. 84, f. 3, dok. 48, Stožer Vrbaskog divizijskog područja Zapovjedništvu kopnene vojske (Glavaru Vojnog ureda—za III Odsjek), 10—dnevno izvješće o stanju na području, July 12, 1941, 1; see also VA, Fond NDH, kut. 84, f. 3, dok. 51, Stožer Vrbaskog divizijskog područja Zapovjedništvu kopnene vojske (Vojni ured V. odsjek), Obavještajni izvještaj, July 9, 1941, 1.

44. *Zbornik NOR-a, tom V, knjiga 1,* br. 132, Izvještaj Zapovjedništva Prve hrvatske oružničke pukovnije od 16. kolovoza 1941. god. o zločinima ustaša i akcijama partizana u Kordunu, August 16, 1941, 340.

45. On the exaggerations about the number of insurgents, see HDA, Fond 1450, MINORS NDH, D-2189, Zapovjedništvo kopnene vojske (veomo žurno tajno), August 2, 1941, 1.

46. VA, Fond NDH, kut. 84, f. 3, dok. 54, Zapovjedništvo kopnene vojske, Izvještaj o vanjskoj i unutarnjoj situaciji za prvu deseticu (1.–10.) srpnja 1941., July 11, 1941, 5

47. HDA DAKA, Fond RMZDL, kut. 4, Originali, Milan Obradović, "Zločini na kotaru Donji Lapac od 1941. do 1945. godine," 30–31.

48. Vukčević, ed., *Zločini,* br. 133, Izvještaj Territorijalne legije karabinjera u ankoni grupa Zadra od 15. jula 1941. kr. Guvernatoratu Dalmacije kabineta u Zadru o represalijama ustaša nad pravoslavcima na teritoriji Srba, July 15, 1941, 341.

49. HDA DAKA, Fond RMZDL, kut. 4, Originali, Milan Obradović, "Zločini na kotaru Donji Lapac od 1941. do 1945. godine," 31–32.

50. VA, Fond NDH, kut. 84, f. 3, dok. 48, Stožer Vrbaskog divizijskog područja Zapovjedništvu kopnene vojske (Glavaru Vojnog ureda—za III Odsjek), 10—dnevno izvješće o stanju na području, July 12, 1941, 2.

51. Milica Dubajić-Damjanović, "Omladina sela Zalužja 1941. godine," in *Lika u NOB. Zbornik. Pišu učesnici,* ed. Đoko Jovanić (Novi Sad: Budućnost, 1963), 590; on similar dynamics in other parts of the wider region, such as in the village of Krnjeuša, see Arhiv Srbije, Fond G-2, KI, f. 5, Bosanski Petrovac, br. 98, Srez Bosanski Petrovac, Dalmatinska eparhija Arhijerejskom namjesniku sreza moravskog, August 4, 1941, 1; ibid., br. 103, Srez Bosanski Petrovac, Dalmatinska eparhija V. preč. srpsko prav. arh. nam. Ljubićkom u Preljini, March 30, 1942, 1–2.

52. *Zbornik NOR-a, tom IV, knjiga 1,* br. 249, Izvještaj Kotarske oblasti u Vlasenici od 7. avgusta 1941. god. o širenju narodnog ustanka u Vlaseničkom srezu, August 7, 1941, 555.

53. *Zbornik NOR-a, tom V, knjiga 1,* br. 132, Izvještaj Zapovjedništva Prve hrvatske oružničke pukovnije od 16. kolovoza 1941. god. o zločinima ustaša i akcijama partizana u Kordunu, August 16, 1941, 343.

54. Vukčević, ed., *Zločini,* br. 123, Izvještaj Krilnog oružničkog zapovjedništva Gospić od 12. jula 1941. Zapovjedniku 1. Hrvatske oružničke pukovnije o klanju, ubijanju, paljenju i plački srpskog življa u selu Bubanj, July 12, 1941, 319.

55. VA, Fond NDH, kut. 143, f. 1, dok. 19, Zapovjedništvo 3. Hrvatske oružničke pukovnije Zapovjedništvu 4. Oružničke pukovnije, Izvješće doglasne službe, June 26, 1941, 1.

56. On the "collective categorization of the other" in Rwanda during 1994, see Straus, *The Order of Genocide.* For a more theoretical treatment, see James Waller, *Becoming Evil: How Ordinary People Commit Genocide and Mass Killing* (New York: Oxford University Press, 2002). On the notion of "soft" and "hard" boundaries in people's perceptions of groups, and the fluid and historically contingent nature of these boundaries, see Prasenjit Duara, "Historicizing National Identity, or Who Imagines What and When," in *Becoming National. A Reader,* ed. Geoff Eley and Ronald Grigor Suny (New York: Oxford University Press, 1996), 168–169.

57. For other examples of the rapid emergence of this sensibility in the aftermath of the mass killings in the Kulen Vakuf region during the summer of 1941, see LAEB, Bibanović, "Kulen Vakuf," 54–55; Vukmanović, *Ustaški zločini na području Bihaća u ljeto 1941. godine*, 130; Kecman-Hodak, "Sjećanje na Bušević, Kestenovac, Bosanske Strpče i Kalate," 199–200; Nikola Karanović, "Sadjejstvo sa ličkim ustanicima," in *Drvar, 1941–1945. Sjećanja učesnika, knjiga 2*, ed. Pero Morača (Drvar: Skupština opštine Drvar, 1972), 410.

58. For Greece, see Kalyvas, *The Logic of Violence in Civil War*; for South Asia, see Das, "Collective Violence and the Shifting Categories of Communal Riots, Ethnic Cleansing and Genocide," 93–127; on this dynamic more generally, see Bowman, "The Violence in Identity," 25–46.

59. For an example of a study that advances this theoretical proposition, but which provides little empirical evidence to illustrate it, see İpek Yosmaoğlou, *Blood Ties: Religion, Violence and the Politics of Nationhood in Ottoman Macedonia, 1878–1908* (Ithaca, NY: Cornell University Press, 2013).

60. VA, Fond NDH, kut. 150a, f. 2, dok. 39, Krilno oružničko zapovjedništvo Gospić Zapovjedniku I. Hrvatske oružničke pukovnije, Rezultat izviđaja o događajima u selu Bubnju, July 12, 1941, 2.

61. HDA, Fond 306, ZKUZ (Hrvatska), kut. 245, Zh. br. 11647, Odluka, Marinković dr. Vinko (ustaški politički povjerenik iz Donjeg Lapca), May 1945, 2; ibid., OKUZ za Liku, Zapisnik sastavljen pred komisijom u Bubnju, May 12, 1945, 1. According to the archival documentation that the postwar communist war crimes commission produced, among the villagers from Boričevac were: Antić Markovinović, Mile Markovinović, Nikola Markovinović, Joso Markovinović, Marko Markovinović, Jure Markovinović, Ivan Markovinović, Juko Gužvina, Dane Brkić, Grga "Grco" Pavičić, and others.

62. Vukčević, ed., *Zločini*, br. 123, Izvještaj Krilnog oružničkog zapovjedništva Gospić od 12. jula 1941. Zapovjedniku 1. Hrvatske oružničke pukovnije o klanju, ubijanju, paljenju i plački srpskog življa u selu Bubanj, July 12, 1941, 319–322.

63. HDA, Fond 306, ZKUZ (Hrvatska), kut. 235, Zh. br. 10278–10287, OKUZ za Liku, Zapisnik sastavljen pred komisijom u Malom Bubnju, May 13, 1945, 1–2.

64. HDA DAKA, Fond RMZDL, kut. 1, Đoko Jovanić, "Kotar donjolapački u ustanku 1941. godine," 13.

65. Vukčević, ed., *Zločini*, br. 116, Izvještaj Zapovjedništva kopnene vojske zapovjedništva vojske i Ministarstvu domobranstva o vojno-političkoj situaciji NDH od 1. do 10. jula 1941. sa podacima o raspoloženju naroda i posebno o odnosu prema pravoslavnom življu, iseljavanju, paljevinama čitavih sela i ubistvima, 304.

66. See ARSBL, Fond 330, Zbirka dokumenata VII JNA, 817/10, MUP, Ravnateljstvo za javni red i sigurnost [hereafter RAVSIGUR] NDH, Izvještaj o stanju do 19.VII. u 8 sati, July 19, 1941, 1.

67. VA, Fond NDH, kut. 85, f. 8, dok. 49, Uredovni zapisnik, June 21, 1941, 1.

68. Ibid., Krilno oružničko zapovjedništvo Zapovjedniku 3. oružničke pukovnije, June 22, 1941, 1.

69. For further evidence suggesting directives to engage in mass violence were often given on the telephone, which in this case refers to Ljubomir Kvaternik's supposed order on July 31, 1941 to the civil authorities in Cazin to begin killing Serbs,

see Vukčević, ed., *Zločini*, br. 373, Pregled masovnih zločina ustaša u 1941. godini na teritoriji bihaćkog i travničkog okruga (undated document), 986; VA, Fond NDH, kut. 312, f. 1, dok. 55, Kratak pregled masovnih zločina ustaša u 1941. godini, bihaćki okrug, 4; AJ, Fond 110, DKUZ, f. 131, F. br. 6017, Kvaternik Ljubomir (undated document, most likely from 1946 or 1947), 4; ibid., Inv. br. 55967, Zapisnik sastavljen u Cazinu po ZKUZ, July 12, 1946, 2. Postwar communist investigations of the key Ustaša leader in northwest Bosnia, Viktor Gutić, also suggest that he frequently gave orders over the telephone to his charges in smaller towns to engage in mass violence. See ARSBL, Fond Zbirka varia, 330, Optužnica Viktora Gutića, Javno tužioštvo okruga Banja Luka Okružnom sudu Banja Luka, December 25, 1946, 44–45.

70. AJ, Fond 110, DKUZ, f. 131, F. br. 6017, Kvaternik Ljubomir (undated document, most likely written in 1946 or 1947), 1.

71. VA, Fond NDH, kut. 85, f. 2, dok. 7, Zapovjedništvo I. hrvatske oružničke pukovnije Zapovjedništvu hrvatskog oružništva, Iskaz o prilikama na području oružničkog krila u Gospiću, May 10, 1941, 1.

72. HDA, Fond 306, ZKUZ (Hrvatska), kut. 245, Zh. br. 11639–11651, OKUZ za Liku, Zapovjedništvo posade Bihać Zapovjedniku Gospićskog oružničkog krila, Izvještaj o događajima na teritoriji kotara Donji Lapac, July 5, 1941, 1.

73. Robert W. Hefner, *The Political Economy of Mountain Java. An Interpretative History* (Berkeley: University of California Press, 1990), 211.

74. On the number of dead as determined by the NDH authorities, see Vukčević, ed., *Zločini*, br. 142, Izveštaj Ravnateljstva za javni red i sigurnosti od 19. jula 1941. o stanju na teritoriji NDH, zločinima ustaša u selu Bubnju i iseljavanju Srba, July 19, 1941, 357.

75. See AS, Fond G-2, KI, f. 16, Srez Donji Lapac, Medić Milica, student medicine, daje sledeće podatke o stradanju Srba u njenom kraju 3. jula 1941. god. (undated document, most likely written during the late summer 1941), 1.

76. Some of these individuals had already participated in a much smaller attack on Bubanj on June 19, 1941, during which they arrested approximately six men, tortured them in jail in the village of Boričevac during several days, and then took them to a pit and shot them. Vlado Drča was the only survivor. See AJ, Fond 110, DKUZ, dos. br. 2758, OKUZ za Liku (Medić Smilja iz Bubnja; Vlado Drča iz Dobrosela), May 13, 1945, 1–2.

77. AS, Fond G-2, KI, f. 16, Srez Donji Lapac, Medić Milica, student medicine, daje sledeće podatke o stradanju Srba u njenom kraju 3. jula 1941. god, 2; on the participation of Muslims from Kulen Vakuf and its surroundings in the attack on Bubanj, see also Obradović, "Selo Bubanj u plamenu," 437, 439; VA, Fond NDH, kut. 67, f. 2, dok. 8, Zapisnik sastavljen po izjavi pričuvnog nadporučnika Sabati Dragutina prilikom borbe kod sela Ostrovice (undated document, most likely from late August 1941), 2.

78. Vukčević, ed., *Zločini*, br. 123, Izvještaj Krilnog oružničkog zapovjedništva Gospić od 12. jula 1941. Zapovjedniku 1. Hrvatske oružničke pukovnije o klanju, ubijanju, paljenju i pljački srpskog življa u selu Bubanj, July 12, 1941, 319–322. The testimonies of survivors confirmed these observations, noting local Muslims from the Kulen Vakuf area, such as Suljo Pehlivanović from the village of Ostrovica, came to steal their property. See AS, Fond G-2, KI, f. 16, Srez Donji Lapac, Medić Milica, student medicine, daje sledeće podatke o stradanju Srba u njenom

kraju, July 3, 1941, 1; on Pehlivanović's presence in Bubanj, see also Obradović, "Selo Bubanj u plamenu," 437, which is based on interviews conducted in 1969 with eyewitnesses who survived the attack. Another local Muslim who apparently participated was Meho Kumalić. See LAEB, Esad Bibanović, Radni materijal za knjigu "Kulen Vakuf i okolina kroz istoriju," Civili ubice, saradnici ustaša i UDB-e (unnumbered pages); also participating was Ibrahim Pehlivanović, whose participation in the attack is discussed in AJ, Fond 110, kut. 817, Okružni sud Bihać, Pojedinačne optužnice i presude, 1946, dos. br. 817-469, Javno tužioštvo za Okrug Bihać, Javno tužioštvo za Okrug Bihać, Optužnica Pehlivanović Ibrahima (iz Ostrovice), May 30, 1946, 1.

79. HDA DAKA, Fond RMZDL, kut. 1, Đoko Jovanić, "Kotar donjolapački u ustanku 1941. godine," 15.

80. Ibid., kut. 4, Originali, Milan Obradović, "Zločini na kotaru Donji Lapac od 1941. do 1945. godine," 7.

81. HDA, Fond 306, ZKUZ (Hrvatska), kut. 245, OKUZ za Liku, Zapisnik sastavljen pred komisijom u Bubnju, May 12, 1945, 1. According to the commission's documentation, among the men from Markovinović clan were Antić Markovinović, Mile Markovinović, Nikola Markovinović, Joso Markovinović, Marko Markovinović, Jure Markovinović, and Ivan Markovinović.

82. VA, Fond NDH, kut. 143a, f. 9, dok. 36, Krilno Zapovjedništvo Blieće Zapovjedništvu 4. Hrvatske oružničke pukovnije, June 25, 1941, 2.

83. Testimony of Nikola Vučković in Rašeta, *Kazivanje pobjednika smrti*, 190.

84. See, for example, HDA, Fond 306, ZKUZ (Hrvatska), kut. 235, Zh. br. 1027, Odluka, Markovinović Antić (komandant ustaša iz Boričevca), May 1945, 2.

85. See, example, Beth Roy, *Some Trouble with Cows: Making Sense of Social Conflict* (New Delhi: Vistaar Publications, 1994).

86. Vukčević, ed., *Zločini*, br. 137, Izvještaj 3. Hrvatske oružničke pukovnije od 16. jula 1941. Zapovjedništvu 4. hrvatske oružničke pukovnije o situaciji na svojoj teritoriji, iseljavanju i hapšenju Srba i Jevreja, July 16, 1941, 347.

87. ABiH, Fond ZKUZ, Presude, Okružni sud Bihać, 1946, kut. 3 (Vojić Avdo, Vojić Sulejman, Vojić Ahmet—svi iz Orašca), June 27, 1946, 2–3.

88. See, for example, Jack Katz, *Seductions of Crime: A Chilling Exploration of the Criminal Mind—from Juvenile Delinquency to Cold-Blooded Murder* (New York: Basic Books, 1988); Wolfgang, *Patterns in Criminal Homicide*; see also Lewis A. Coser, *The Functions of Social Conflict* (New York: Free Press, 1956).

89. See, for example, Sudhir Kakar, *The Colours of Violence: Cultural Identities, Religion, and Conflict* (Chicago: University of Chicago Press, 1996); Fujii, *Killing Neighbors*; see also Stanley Milgram, *Obedience to Authority: An Experimental View* (New York: HarperPerennial, [1974] 2009), who suggested that the less distance that exists between victimizer and victim, the greater the likelihood of reducing obedience-driven violence.

90. Testimony of Jovo Radaković from Bubanj in Rašeta, *Kazivanje pobjednika smrti*, 163.

91. Testimony of Rade Radaković from Bubanj in ibid., 156.

92. HDA, Fond 306, ZKUZ (Hrvatska), kut. 245, Zh. br. 11639–11651, OKUZ za Liku, Zapovjedništvo posade Bihać Zapovjedniku Gospićskog oružničkog krila, Izvještaj o događajima na teritoriji kotara Donji Lapac, July 5, 1941, 1.

93. For another example of fights among "Croats" over who should get "Serb property" after an attack on an Orthodox village, see *Zbornik NOR-a, tom V, knjiga 1*, br. 132, Izvještaj Zapovjedništva prve hrvatske oružničke pukovnije od 16. kolovoza 1941. god. o zločinima ustaša i akcijama partizana u Kordunu, 340.

94. See, for example, Jan Grabowski, *Hunt for the Jews: Betrayal and Murder in German-Occupied Poland* (Bloomington: Indiana University Press, 2013), 53; Timothy Longman, *Christianity and Genocide in Rwanda* (Cambridge: Cambridge University Press, 2010), 295.

95. On this point in the Rwandan context, see Aliza Luft, "Toward a Dynamic Theory of Action at the Micro Level of Genocide: Killing, Desistance, and Saving in 1994 Rwanda," *Sociological Theory* 33, no. 2 (2015): 148–172.

96. HDA DAKA, Fond RMZDL, kut. 1, Đoko Jovanić, "Kotar donjolapački u ustanku 1941. godine," 15.

97. See Nico Frijda, "The Lex Talionis: On Vengeance," in *Emotions: Essays on Emotion Theory*, ed. Stephanie van Goozen, Nanne van de Poll, and Joseph Sergeant (Hillsdale, New Jersey: Lawrence Erlbaum, 1994), 263–289, here 267; see also Wolfgang, *Patterns in Criminal Homicide.*

98. Veena Das, *Life and Words: Violence and the Descent into the Ordinary* (Berkeley: University of California Press, 2007), 157; on the role of "past affronts" in driving intercommunal conflicts at the local level in South Asia, see also Roy, *Some Trouble with Cows.*

99. Longman, *Christianity and Genocide in Rwanda*, 295.

100. Victor Montejo, *Testimony: Death of a Guatemalan Village*, trans. Victor Perera (Willimantic, CT: Curbstone Press, 1987), 35–36.

101. Michael Fellman, *Inside War. The Guerrilla Conflict in Missouri during the American Civil War* (New York: Oxford University Press, 1989), 62.

102. Leslie Dwyer and Degung Santikarma, "'When the World Turned to Chaos': 1965 and Its Aftermath in Bali, Indonesia," in *The Spectre of Genocide*, ed. Gellately and Kiernan, 293–294.

103. See Jan T. Gross, *Revolution from Abroad: The Soviet Conquest of Poland's Western Ukraine and Western Belorussia* (Princeton, NJ: Princeton University Press, [1988] 2002).

104. For more evidence on how prewar local conflicts played a role motivating perpetrators and determining victim selection in the violence in 1941, see Arhiv Srpske pravoslavne crkve [hereafter ASPC], Prepisi iz Komisije za prikupljanje podataka o zločinima nad Srbima u NDH, 1941–42., Zapisnik sastavljen u Komesarijatu za izbeglice i preseljenike u Beogradu, Čajkanović Rajko (Bosanski Petrovac), April 21, 1943, 2, 5; on the large quantities of livestock and household goods that the Ustašas stole during their attacks on Suvaja and Bubanj, see AS, Fond G-2, KI, f. 16, Srez Donji Lapac, Zapisnik od 2. juna 1942. godine sastavljen u Komesarijatu za izbeglice i preseljenika u Beogradu, Obradović Jovo, Krtinić Božo, 2; Obradović, "Selo Bubanj u plamenu," 441.

105. Srđan Brujić and Đuro Stanisavljević, "Razvoj organizacija KP u Lici i njihova uloga u ustanku 1941.," in *Lika u NOB, 1941. Zbornik, knjiga prva*, ed. Đoko Jovanić (Belgrade: Vojno izdavački zavod JNA "Vojno delo," 1963), 30.

106. On this dynamic in the American Southwest, see Philip Deloria, *Indians in Unexpected Places* (Lawrence: University Press of Kansas, 2004), 15–21; on Rwanda, see Straus, *The Order of Genocide*, 172; on Sri Lanka, see Jonathan Spencer, "Violence

and Everyday Practice in Sri Lanka," *Modern Asian Studies* 24, no. 3 (July 1999): 603–623, here 618–619; for a more general theoretical reflection, see Scott Straus, "'Destroy Them to Save Us': Theories of Genocide and Logics of Political Violence," *Terrorism and Political Violence* 24, no. 4 (2012): 544–560.

107. See, for example, Mika Haritos-Fatouros, *The Psychological Origins of Institutionalized Torture* (London: Routledge, 2003), 88–89; on "violence workers," see Martha Huggins, Mika Haritos-Fatouros, and Philip Zimbardo, *Violence Workers: Police Torturers and Murderers Reconstruct Brazilian Atrocities* (Berkeley: University of California Press, 2002).

108. HDA DAKA, Fond RMZDL, kut. 4, Razna pisma, Rade Radaković, "U raljama smrti," 1–2; on the stories that survivors told to those in the forests, see Obradović, "Selo Bubanj u plamenu," 439–440; idem, "Zločini na kotaru Donji Lapac od 1941. do 1945.," 836.

109. HDA DAKA, Fond RMZDL, kut. 1, Đoko Jovanić, "Kotar donjolapački u ustanku 1941. godine," 18.

110. Keča, "Ustanički dani u okolini Kulen Vakufa," 200.

111. On the rapid spread of news about the mass killings, see HDA DAKA, Fond RMZDL, Radovi za hronike sela (neobjavljeno), "Bušević u Narodnooslobodilačkoj borbi," 1941–1945 (1980), 27.

112. Obradović, "Selo Bubanj u plamenu," 445.

113. HDA DAKA, Fond 143, Memoarsko gradivo o NOR-u, 31/2010, Sjećanja Lika (LI-3), Učešće naroda i razvoj NOR-a na teritoriji Dobrosela, 17.

114. HDA, Fond 306, ZKUZ (Hrvatska), kut. 43, OKUZ za Liku, Popis žrtava lišenih života, Mjesto: Donja Suvaja, Kotar: Donji Lapac, Okrug: Lika, 1–12.

115. Jovanić, *Ratna sjećanja*, 41–42.

116. On the killings of the extended Keča family in Suvaja, see HDA DAKA, Fond RMZDL, kut. 4, Originali, Milan Obradović, "Zločini na kotaru Donji Lapac od 1941. do 1945. godine," 28–29.

117. Obradović, "Selo Bubanj u plamenu," 446.

118. AS, Fond G-2, KI, f. 16, Srez Donji Lapac, Medić Milica, student medicine, daje sledeće podatke o stradanju Srba u njenom kraju, July 3, 1941, 2.

119. HDA DAKA, Fond RMZDL, Radovi za hronike sela (neobjavljeno), Bušević u Narodnooslobodilačkoj borbi, 1941–1945 (1980), 27; for other examples in the region of how instances of killings severed intercommunal ties, see Kecman-Hodak, "Sjećanja na Bušević, Kestenovac, Bosanske Štrpce i Kalate," 150; Keča, "Ustanički dani u okolini Kulen Vakufa," 199–200.

120. Vukčević, ed., *Zločini*, br. 123, Izvještaj Krilnog oružničkog zapovjedništva Gospić od 12. jula 1941. Zapovjedniku 1. Hrvatske oružničke pukovnije o klanju, ubijanju, paljenju i plački srpskog življa u selu Bubanj, July 12, 1941, 321.

121. Barry Posen, "The Security Dilemma and Ethnic Conflict," *Survival* 35, no. 1 (Spring 1993): 27–47, here 28.

122. On how such violence abolishes the concept of transgression, see Stathis Kalyvas, "The Paradox of Terrorism in Civil War," *Journal of Ethics* 1, no. 1 (2004): 97–138, here 104.

123. These villages included: Stjenjani, Rajinovci, Kalati, Palučci, Rmanj Manastir (Martin Brod), Veliko and Malo Očijevo, Kestenovac, Bušević, Prkosi, Oraško Brdo, and Vrtoče.

124. AJ, Fond 110, DKUZ, dos. br. 4670, Inv. br. 56146, M.N.O. Kestenovac, Zapisnik sastavljen 1. avgusta 1946. u Bihaću, August 1, 1946, 1; ibid., Inv. br. 56808, Zapisnik Br. 14, Mjesni odbor: Vrtoče, July 31, 1946, 1; ibid., Inv. br. 55905, Zapisnik br. 21, Mjesni odbor: Veliki Stjenjani, August 8, 1946, 1; HDA DAKA, Fond 143, Memoarsko gradivo o NOR-u, Zbirka o zločinima, Presuda Vojnog suda II Korpusa s područja Lika, 55/2010, Presuda Okružnog suda za Liku u Gospiću optuženom Vidaković Ivanu iz Donjeg Lapca, February 21, 1946, 1–3.

125. AJ, Fond 110, DKUZ, Inv. br. 56901, Zapisnik br. 19, Mjesni odbor: Kalati, August 5, 1946, 1–2.

126. Đoko Jovanić, "Ustanak u južnoj lici 1941. godine (Neki podaci i sjećanje)," in *Lika u NOB, 1941. Zbornik, Knjiga prva*, ed. Jovanić, 105.

127. AJ, Fond 110, DKUZ, Inv. br. 56902, Zapisnik broj 20, Mjesni odbor: Rajinovci, August 7, 1946, 1–2; ibid., Inv. br. 56904, Zapisnik Br. 22, Mjesni odbor: Kulen Vakuf, August 9, 1946, 2–3.

128. Vukčević, ed., *Zločini*, br. 123, Izvještaj Krilnog oružničkog zapovjedništva Gospić od 12. jula 1941. Zapovjedniku 1. Hrvatske oružničke pukovnije o klanju, ubijanju, paljenju i plački srpskog življa u selu Bubanj, July 12, 1941, 320; see also VA, Fond NDH, kut. 150a, f. 2, dok. 39, Krilno oružničko zapovjedništvo Gospić Zapovjedniku I. Hrvatske oružničke pukovnije, Rezultat izviđaja o događajima u selu Bubnju, July 12, 1941, 2.

129. VA, Fond NDH, kut. 150a, f. 2, dok. 39, Krilno oružničko zapovjedništvo Gospić Zapovjedniku I. Hrvatske oružničke pukovnije, Rezultat izviđaja o događajima u selu Bubnju, July 12, 1941, 2.

130. Testimony of Nikica Medić in Obradović, "Zločini na kotaru Donji Lapac od 1941. do 1945.," 843–844; see also HDA DAKA, Fond RMZDL, kut. 4, Originali, Milan Obradović, "Zločini na kotaru Donji Lapac od 1941. do 1945. godine," 49–50.

131. Obradović, "Zločini na kotaru Donji Lapac od 1941. do 1945.," 844.

132. Vukčević, ed., *Zločini*, br. 123, Izvještaj Krilnog oružničkog zapovjedništva Gospić od 12. jula 1941. Zapovjedniku 1. Hrvatske oružničke pukovnije o klanju, ubijanju, paljenju i plački srpskog življa u selu Bubanj, July 12, 1941, 320–321.

133. AJ, Fond 110, DKUZ, Inv. br. 56140, M.N.O. Kestenovac, Zapisnik sastavljen 1. avgusta 1946. u Bihaću, August 1, 1946, 2; Inv. br. 56901, Zapisnik br. 19, Mjesni odbor: Kalati, August 5, 1946, 3; HDA, Fond 306, ZKUZ (Hrvatska), kut. 247, Zh. br. 11865–11868, OKUZ za Liku, Zapisnik sastavljen pred komisijom u Dobroselu, May 13, 1945, 1–2; testimony of Milan Filipović and Stevo Inđić (both from Kalati) in Polovina, *Svedočenje*, 58–59.

134. AJ, Fond 110, DKUZ, Inv. br. 56902, Zapisnik broj 20, Mjesni odbor: Rajinovci, August 7, 1946, 2–4.

135. According to some accounts, the mass killing at pits near Boričevac began early in the month of July, perhaps on or around July 2–3, 1941, see Bogdan Čučak, *Nebljusi u Narodnooslobodilačkom ratu i revoluciji, 1941.–1945.* (Belgrade: Savez boraca NOR-a Nebljusi i Skupština opštine Donji Lapac, 1981), 35–39.

136. HDA DAKA, Fond RMZDL, kut. 4, Originali, Milan Obradović, "Zločini na kotaru Donji Lapac od 1941. do 1945. godine," 22; see also Čučak, *Nebljusi u Narodnooslobodilačkom ratu i revoluciji*, 35–39.

137. ABiH, Fond ZKUZ BiH, kut. 88, Srez Drvar, Selo Boričevac, Zapisnik sastavljen kod Sreskog suda u Drvaru, December 12, 1945, 1–3; ibid., Zapisnik sastavljen u kancelariji okružnog organa ZFM-KOM-e za okrug Drvar, Saslušanje Vladimira Tankosića po masovnom ubistvu u selu Boričevac dana 24.VII.1941, March 28, 1945, 1–2; on the postwar trial of the Ustaša Hilmija Altić, and his supposed confession of having committed crimes against the Serb population, see *Glas: organ Oblasnog odbora Narodno-oslobodilačkog fronta za Bosansku Krajinu*, "Veliko javno suđenje u Sanskom Mostu: izdajnici i ratni zločinici pred sudom," October 28, 1944, 3–4.

138. See, for example, Milan Majstorović and Mićo Medić, *Prve iskre: Doljani u NOB* (Zagreb: Lykos, 1961), 11–12.

139. Obradović, "Zločini na kotaru Donji Lapac od 1941. do 1945.," 831. An exception was Draginja Matić, a young woman from Nebljusi. According the testimony of survivor Dara Škorić Popović, she physically fought the Ustašas at the edge of the Boričavac pit who were attempting to kill her. They eventually stabbed her with bayonets and then threw her into the pit while still alive. See Rašeta, *Kazivanje pobjednika smrti*, 133; Čučak, *Nebljusi u Narodnooslobodilačkom ratu i revoluciji*, 35–39.

140. LAEB, Bibanović, "Kulen Vakuf," 50.

141. ABiH, Fond ZKUZ BiH, kut. 88, Zapisnik sastavljen u kancelariji okružnog organa ZFM-KOM-e za okrug Drvar, Saslušanje Vladimira Tankosića po masovnom ubistvu u selu Boričevac dana 24.VII.1941, March 28, 1945, 1–2.

142. ABiH, Fond ZKUZ BiH, kut. 88, Zapisnik sastavljen u kancelariji okružnog organa ZEM-KOM-e za okrug Drvar, Saslušanje Vladimira Tankosića po masovnom ubistvu u selu Boričevac dana 24.VII.1941, March 28, 1945, 2; AJ, Fond 110, DKUZ, dos. br. 4670, Inv. br. 40740, Zapisnik sastavljen u kancelariji okružnog organa ZEM-KOM za okrug Drvar 23. marta 1945. god., March 23, 1945, 1–2; a somewhat different version of how Mile Pilipović fell into the pit appears in AJ, Fond 110, DKUZ, dos. br. 5361, Mesni odbor: Rajinovci, August 7, 1946, 3.

143. For examples of mass killings that took place at the Boričevac pit, see AJ, Fond 110, DKUZ, kut. 531, dos. br. 5361, Zapisnik br. 20, Mjesni odbor: Rajinovci, August 7, 1946, 1–3; ibid., Zapisnik br. 21, Mjesni odbor: Veliki Stjenjani, 1; ABiH, Fond ZKUZ BiH, kut. 91, Zapisnik br. 22, Mjesni odbor: Malo Očijevo, August 9, 1946, 1. For another firsthand account by an individual who survived the mass killings at Boričevac, see the testimony of Dara Škorić in Čučak, *Nebljusi u Narodnooslobodilačkom ratu i revoluciji*, 36–39; on these killings, see also Rade Repac, "Nebljuški kraj u NOB-u," in *Kotar Donji Lapac u Narodnooslobodilačkom ratu*, ed. Vezmar and Zatezalo, 209.

144. Franjo Odić, "Julski dani 1941. na unskoj pruzi," in *Podgrmeč u NOB. Podgrmeč do ustanka i u ustanku 1941. Zbornik sjećanja, knjiga prva*, ed. Dušan Pejanović (Belgrade: Vojnoizdavački zavod, 1972), 212–213; see also AJ, Fond 110, DKUZ, dos. br. 4670, Inv. br. 55919, Zapisnik sastavljen dana 9. avgusta 1946. god. u Drvaru, August 9, 1946, 1–2; ibid., Inv. br. 56904, Zapisnik br. 22, Kulen Vakuf, August 9, 1946, 2.

145. Nikola Vidaković, "Sjećanje na osnivanje i rad partijske organizacije do početka ustanka 1941.," in *Kotar Donji Lapac u Narodnooslobodilačkom ratu*, ed. Vezmar and Zatezalo, 31.

146. See Gross, *Neighbors*. See also Jan T. Gross, with Irena Grudzinska Gross, *Golden Harvest. Events at the Periphery of the Holocaust* (Oxford: Oxford University Press, 2012).

147. On these dynamics of killing and plunder of the corpses, see Savo Novaković, "Tuk Dževar—Dobro selo u zla vremena," in *Bosanski Petrovac u NOB, Knjiga II*, ed. Čerkez, 483.

148. HDA, Fond 1450, MINORS NDH, D-2175, Izvještaj o vanjskoj i unutarnjoj situaciji za treću deseticu (19–29) kolovoza 1941, 1.

149. VA, Fond NDH, kut. 84, f. 4, dok. 24, Stožer Vrbaskog divizijskog područja Zapovjedništvu kopnene vojske, Izvještaj o vanjskoj i unutarnjoj situaciji za drugu deseticu (10.–20.) srpnja 1941, July 18, 1941, 1.

150. AJ, Fond 110, DKUZ, f. 588, Inv. br. 14400, Zapisnik na 15. januara 1944. godine sastavljen u Komesarijatu za izbeglice i preseljenike u Beogradu (izjave od Turudije Sminje, Turudije Vere, Turudije Branka), January 15, 1944, 4 (lowercase "muslim" in the original).

151. *Zbornik NOR-a, tom V, knjiga 1*, br. 132, Izvještaj Zapovjedništva prve hrvatske oružničke pukovnije od 16. kolovoza 1941. god. o zločinima ustaša i akcijama partizana u Kordunu, August 16, 1941, 343.

152. HDA DAKA, Fond RMZDL, kut. 4, Originali, Milan Obradović, "Zločini na kotaru Donji Lapac od 1941. do 1945. godine," 24–25.

153. Ibid., Radovi za hronike sela (neobjavljeno), "Bušević u Narodnooslobodilačkoj borbi 1941–1945 (1980)," 46; Mićo Medić, "Obavještajna služba na području donjolapačkog kotara," in *Kotar Donji Lapac u Narodnooslobodilačkom ratu*, ed. Vezmar and Zatezalo, 889.

154. Polovina, *Svedočenje*, 62.

155. LAEB, Bibanović, "Stanovništvo Kulen-Vakufa," 236–241.

156. ABiH, Fond ZKUZ BiH, Presude, Okružni sud Bihać, 1945, kut. 2, Presuda Dervišević Muharema, February 7, 1946, 4.

157. LAEB, Bibanović, "Stanovništvo Kulen-Vakufa," 208.

158. For an example from Herzegovina of a Muslim who was mobilized into an Ustaša unit, but who refused to kill his Serb neighbor, and was then killed by an Ustaša for resisting orders, see Mahmud Konjhodžić, *Kronika o ljubuškom kraju* (Sarajevo: Oslobođenje; Opštinski odbora SUBNOR-a ljubuški, 1974), 291–292; see also Skoko, *Pokolji hercegovačkih Srba '41.*, 164.

159. On this dynamic in Rwanda, see Straus, *The Order of Genocide*, chap. 5.

160. Rašeta, "Pripremanje i početak ustanka u Donjem Lapcu," 211.

161. HDA DAKA, Fond RMZDL, Nikola Vidaković, "Partijska organizacija u Donjem Lapcu od osnivanja do početka ustanka 1941. godine," 21.

162. Ibid., 27. See also ibid., kut. 1, Đoko Jovanić, "Kotar donjolapački u ustanku 1941. godine," 16.

163. Testimony of Nikola Vučković in Rašeta, *Kazivanje pobjednika smrti*, 190.

164. Vidaković, "Sjećanje na osnivanje i rad partijske organizacije do početka ustanka 1941.," 30.

165. Testimony of Rajko Srdić in Rašeta, *Kazivanje pobjednika smrti*, 179.

166. Testimony of Milica Pilipović in ibid., 141.

167. See, for example, Đoko Jovanić, "Ustanak u donjolapačkom kotaru 1941. godine," in *Kotar Donji Lapac u Narodnooslobodilačkom ratu*, ed. Vezmar and Zatezalo,

105; Šijan, "Nastanak i djelovanje KPJ na teritoriji kotara do oslobođenja Donjeg Lapca februara 1942. godine," 41, 43; Obradović, "Zločini na kotaru Donji Lapac od 1941. do 1945.," in ibid., 824, 831–832; Medić, "Obavještajna služba na području donjolapačkog kotara," in ibid., 889; HDA DAKA, Fond RMZDL, kut. 4, Originali, Milan Obradović, "Zločini na kotaru Donji Lapac od 1941. do 1945. godine," 6–7, 14, 24–25.

168. LAEB, Bibanović, "Kulen Vakuf," 48–50; ibid., "Stanovništvo Kulen-Vakufa," 120–124; idem, "Kulenvakufski komunisti u radničkom pokretu i ustanku," 432–434; for the identity cards of what appear to have been thirty-five of these victims, of whom nine were children and thirteen women, see AMUSK, Doprinos u NOB, 1941–1945 (informacije o poginulim borcima i žrtvama fašističkog terora—Kulen Vakuf, Klisa, Kalati), Kulen Vakuf—žrtve fašističkog terora (the data on these civilian victims appears to have been compiled in 1967).

169. See, for example, Rogers Brubaker and David Laitin, "Ethnic and Nationalist Violence," *Annual Review of Sociology* 24, no. 4 (1998): 423–452; Das, "Collective Violence and the Shifting Categories of Communal Riots, Ethnic Cleansing, and Genocide," 93–127; Chaim Kaufmann, "Possible and Impossible Solutions to Ethnic Civil Wars," *International Security* 20, no. 4 (1996): 136–175.

170. Rašeta, "Pripremanje i početak ustanka u Donjem Lapcu," 215–216.

171. See, for example, Straus, *The Order of Genocide*, 127–128.

172. See Milgram, *Obedience to Authority*.

173. VA, Fond NDH, kut. 150a, f. 2, dok. 40, Krilno oružničko zapovjedništvo Gospić Zapovjedništvu I. Hrvatske oružničke pukovnije, Rezultat izviđaja po ucjeni oružnika postaje Doljane, July 12, 1941, 2.

174. Rašeta, *Kazivanje pobjenika smrti*, 20; on the appointment on May 29, 1941 of Tomo Ivaniš to the position of the Ustaša logornik in Kulen Vakuf, see *Narodne novine*, br. 44/1941, June 5, 1941, 7.

175. See, for example, the testimonies of Milan Filipović and Stevo Inđić (both from Kalati) in Polovina, *Svedočenje*, 58–60.

176. HDA DAKA, Fond RMZDL, kut. 4, Originali, Milan Obradović, "Zločini na kotaru Donji Lapac od 1941. do 1945. godine," 24–25; VA, Fond NDH, kut. 84, f. 1, dok. 58, Stožer Vrbaskog divizijskog područja, Zapovjedniku kopnene vojske (Vojni ured), Doglasni izvještaj, June 9, 1941, 1; Vukčević, ed., *Zločini*, br. 305, Izveštaj Zapovjedništva vojne krajine od 1. oktobra 1941. Doglavniku—Vojskovođi o izvršenom pokolju pravoslavnog življa u Jajcu i okolini, October 1, 1941, 768; ibid., br. 101, Izvještaj posebnog opunomoćenika podmaršala Lakse od 5. jula 1941. Zapovjedniku kopnene vojske o divljačkim i neljudskim postupcima ustaša u Hercegovini, July 5, 1941, 208.

177. VA, Fond NDH, kut. 152, f. 4, dok. 55, Priepis pisma, "Braći hrvatski seljacima," August 29, 1941, 1.

178. Milgram, *Obedience to Authority*, 97.

179. LAEB, Bibanović, "Kulen Vakuf," 63.

180. Vukčević, ed., *Zločini*, br. 289, Izveštaj Zapovjedništva vojne krajine od 20. septembra 1941. Zapovjedništvu bosanskog divizijskog područja o zlodelima hercegovačkih ustaša u Jajcu i okolini i pokolju u pravoslavnoj crkvi u Jajcu, September 20, 1941, 718–719; see also the account in Zorić, *Drvar u ustanku 1941.*, 242–243, which is based on NDH documents.

181. Vukčević, ed., *Zločini*, br. 305, Izveštaj Zapovjedništva vojne krajine od 1. oktobra 1941. Doglavniku—Vojskovođi o izvršenom pokolju pravoslavnog življa u Jajcu i okolini, October 1, 1941, 770.

182. HDA, Fond 1450, MINORS NDH, D-2177, Zapovjedništvo vojne krajine, Pokolj u Jajcu, October 1, 1941, 2; see also the collection of testimonies by residents in the region during 1941, Pero Morača, ed., *Jajačko područje u oslobodilačkom ratu i revoluciji 1941–1945. Zbornik sjećanja, Knjiga I* (Novi Sad: "Budućnost"; Skupština opštine Donji Vakuf, Jajce i Šipovo, 1981).

183. VA, Fond NDH, kut. 150a, f. 2, dok. 41, Zapovjedništvo 3. Hrvatske oružničke pukovnije Zapovjedništvu 1. Hrvatske oružničke pukovnije, Izvješće o stanju na području krila u vezi sa izvještajnom službom, August 16, 1941, 1.

184. Vukčević, ed., *Zločini*, br. 101, Izvještaj posebnog opunomoćenika podmaršala Lakse od 5. jula 1941. Zapovjedniku kopnene vojske o divljačkim i neljudskim postupcima ustaša u Hercegovini, July 5, 1941, 208.

185. VA, Fond NDH, kut. 85, f. 11, dok. 45, Zapovjedništvo vojne krajine Zapovjedništvu Bosanskog divizijskog područja, Situacija u Jajcu, September 30, 1941, 1.

186. See Grabowski, *Hunt for the Jews*, 70–71. Of course, we must not forget that this participation was also due to the desire of local peasants to steal from Jews, which means that fear of German reprisals was not the only motivating factor.

187. On the dynamics of rescue in Rwanda, see Scott Straus, "From 'Rescue' to Violence: Overcoming Local Opposition to Genocide in Rwanda," in *Resisting Genocide: The Multiple Forms of Rescue*, ed. Jacques Semelin, Claire Andrieu, and Sarah Gensburger, trans. Emma Bently and Cynthia Schoch (New York: Columbia University Press, 2011), 331–343.

188. See, for example, Kristen Renwich Monroe, *Ethics in an Age of Terrorism and Genocide: Identity and Moral Choice* (Princeton, NJ: Princeton University Press, 2011); Nechama Tec, *When Light Pierced the Darkness: Christian Rescuers of Jews in Nazi-Occupied Poland* (Oxford: Oxford University Press, 1986); Samuel P. and Pearl M. Oliner, *The Altruistic Personality: Rescuers of Jews in Nazi-Europe* (New York: Free Press, 1988); for a nuanced, albeit limited analysis of the role of morality in explaining rescue, see Perry London, "The Rescuers: Motivational Hypotheses about Christians Who Saved Jews From the Nazis," in *Altruism and Helping Behavior: Social Psychological Studies of Some Antecedents and Consequences*, ed. Jacqueline Macaulay and Leonard Berkowitz (New York: Academic Press, 1970), 241–250; for a critique of the role of morality in explaining acts of intervention, see Milgram, *Obedience to Authority*, 153.

189. Polovina, *Svedočenje*, 42.

190. Rašeta, "Pripremanje i početak ustanka u Donjem Lapcu," 219.

191. VA, Fond NDH, kut. 84, f. 5, dok. 28, Stožer vrbaskog divizijskog područja, Izvještaj o vanjskoj i unutarnjoj situaciji za treću deseticu (20–31.) srpnja, July 31, 1941, 1; VA, Fond NDH, kut. 84, f. 5, dok. 25, Zapovjedništvo kopnene vojske, Izvještaj o vanjskoj i unutarnjoj situaciji za treću deseticu (20–31.) srpnja, August 1, 1941, 10.

192. Rašeta, "Pripremanje i početak ustanka u Donjem Lapcu," 220.

193. VA, Fond NOV, kut. 2000, f. 2, dok. 9, Savo Popović, "O borbi i radu partijske organizacije na bihaćkom srezu 1941. i 1942. godine" (undated document, most likely written during the early 1950s), 3 (lowercase "muslim" in the original).

194. VA, Fond NDH, kut 135i, f. 8, dok. 4, Zapovjednik trusinskog odreda, Izvještaj o događajima u selu Berkovićima, August 29, 1941, 2.

195. HDA, Fond 1450, MINORS NDH, D-2175, Izvještaj o vanjskoj i unutarnjoj situaciji za treću deseticu (19–29) kolovoza 1941, 1.

196. VA, Fond NDH, kut. 85, f. 9, dok. 6, Vrhovno oružničko zapovjedništvo Zapovjedništvu kopnene vojske i Ministarstvu Domobranstva, July 22, 1941, 1.

197. *Zbornik NOR-a, tom V, knjiga 1*, br. 132, "Izvještaj Zapovjedništva prve hrvatske okružičke pukovnjie od 16. kolovoza 1941. o zločinima ustaša i akcijama partizana u Kordunu," August 16, 1941, 343.

198. Dubajić Čkaljac, "Tragično djetinjstvo," 862–863.

199. HDA, Fond 1450, MINORS NDH, D-2229, Izvještaj o vanjskoj i unutarnjoj situaciji za treću desetice (19.–29. srpnja 1941.), 1.

200. VA, Fond NDH, kut. 84, f. 3, dok. 55, Posebni opunomoćenik poglavnika Zapovjedniku kopnene vojske na ruke pukovniku gospodinu Luliću, July 5, 1941, 1.

201. VA, Fond NDH, kut. 85, f. 6, dok. 12, Izvještaj o vanjskoj i unutarnjij situaciji za prvu desetice (1.–10) srpnja 1941 (undated document, mostly likely from mid-July 1941), 5.

Chapter 4. Rebellion and Revenge

1. NDH military reports show that "Chetniks" (the term that the authorities used to refer to armed Orthodox rebels), along with local peasants, attacked the command post in the village of Nebljusi on July 24, and then others in the following days in the wider Kulen Vakuf region. See VA, Fond NDH, kut. 85, f. 9, dok 52, Vrhovno oružničko zapovjedništvo Zapovjedništvu vojske i Ministarstvu Domobranstva, July 30, 1941, 1.

2. HDA DAKA, Fond RMZDL, Radovi za hronike sela (neobjavljeno), Štikovac, "Krvavo lapačko ljeto" (undated), 2.

3. On the history of planning the insurgency in the region, according to oral testimonies of participants recorded in the 1950s, see VA, Fond NOV, kut. 2006, f. 5, dok. 1–8, Historijat kotar Donji Lapac, Razvoj Narodno-oslobodilačke borbe u donjolapačkom kotaru, July 7, 1952, 5–6; VA, Fond NOV, kut. 1997, f. 8, dok. 4, Pripreme ustanka, ustanak i borbe 1941. godine u bosansko-petrovačkom srezu (undated, written most likely during the early 1950s), 6–8.

4. HDA DAKA, Fond RMZDL, kut. 1, Đoko Jovanić, "Kotar donjolapački u ustanku 1941. godine," 22.

5. Kosta Nađ, *Ustanak: ratne uspomene Koste Nađa* (Zagreb: Spektar, 1981), 123.

6. HDA DAKA, Fond RMZDL, kut. 1, Đoko Jovanić, "Kotar donjolapački u ustanku 1941. godine," 22–23; idem, *Ratna sjećanja*, 29.

7. Karanović, "Sadjejstvo sa ličkim ustanicima," 410; for additional biographical information on Karanović, see *Krajina*, "Likovi boraca iz revolucije. Nikola Karanović," June 1, 1961, 5; Olga Đurđević-Đukić, ed., *Narodni heroji Jugoslavije, Knjiga prva A-M* (Belgrade: Mladost, 1975), 346–347.

8. AS, Fond G-2, KI, f. 16, Srez Donji Lapac, Zapisnik od 2. juna 1942. godine sastavljen u Komesarijatu za izbeglice i preseljenika u Beogradu, Obradović Jovo, Krtinić Božo, 2; see also Jovanić, "Ustanak u južnoj lici 1941. godine," 116–119.

9. These villages and towns included: Oštrelj, Drvar, Rmanj Manastir (Martin Brod), Srb, and Grkovac. For NDH reports about these attacks, see HDA, Fond 1450, MINORS NDH, D-2229, Vrhovno oružničko zapovjedništvo Zapovjedništvu

kopnene vojske, July 28, 1941; see also ibid., Izvještaj o vanskoj i unutarnjoj situaciji za treću deseticu (20.–31.) srpnja 1941., 6–7; ibid., D-2121, Telefonska bavjest primijena 27.VII.1941, 1; on the killing of Ustašas during some of these attacks, see VA, Fond NDH, kut. 85, f. 10, dok. 31, Zapovjedništvo I. Hrvatske oružničke pukovnije Vrhovnom oružničkom zapovjedništvu, Napad na oružničku postaju Doljani, razoružanje i ubistvo oružnika i ustaša, July 31, 1941, 1.

10. VA, Fond NDH, kut. 169, f. 6, dok. 3, Ravnateljstvo ustaškog redarstva (Banja Luka) Ustaškom redarstvenom ravnateljstvu u Banja Luci, Izvještaj izaslanika Josipa Knopa, July 16, 1941, 1.

11. These villages included Doljani, Nebljusi, Palanka, and Drenovo Tijesno. For NDH sources on these attacks, see HDA, Fond 1450, MINORS NDH, D-2121, Situacija, 30. srpnja 1941. godine prije podne, Bihać u 12.05 časova, 1; see also VA, Fond NDH, kut. 85, f. 9, dok. 53, Vrhovno oružničko zapovjedništvo Zapovjedništvu vojske i ministarstvu domobranstvu, Izviješće o borbama sa četnicima, July 30, 1941, 1–2; ibid., kut. 143, f. 2, dok. 1, Zapovjedništvo 3. Hrvatske oružničke pukovnije Zapovjedniku 4. oružničke pukovnije, Doglasno izvješće dostavlja, August 8, 1941, 1–2.

12. VA, Fond NDH, kut. 1i, f. 1, dok. 27–1, Sarajevo u 23 sata 30 časaka, July 27, 1941, 1; Knin u 23.50 sati, July 27, 1941, 1; Bihać u 2.40 sati, July 28, 1941, 2; ibid., k. 1i, f. 1, dok. 31–1, Rezime situacije, July 30 and July 30–31, 1941, 1–2.

13. VA, Fond NDH, kut. 152a, f. 11, dok. 58, Kotarska oblast u Udbini Velikoj župi Gacka i Like, Predmet: Izvješće o izvanrednoj situaciji, August 2, 1941, 1.

14. On the mixed appearance of the insurgents, from their clothing to their flags, see the testimony of Hamid Agfan, a former NDH official in the town of Drvar, whom the insurgents held prisoner for several weeks, ARSBL, Fond 330, Zbirka dokumenata VII JNA, Izjava g. Agfana Hamida, zakupnika činovničkog doma u Drvaru, sada nastanjenog u Banjoj Luci, October 20, 1941, 1–2. On the insurgents who waved red flags, but also called for the resurrection of Serbia and the disappearance of Croatia, see VA, Fond NDH, kut. 85, f. 14, dok. 3, Izvješće, August 20, 1941, 3; on the presence of red flags, see also ibid., f. 9, 45, Zapovjedništvo I. Hrvatske oružničke pukovnije Vrhovnom oružničkom zapovjedništvu, Rezanje brzojavno-brzoglasnih žica u Gračacu i pojava četnika sa crvenim zastavama, July 28, 1941, 1.

15. *Zbornik NOR-a, tom V, knjiga 1*, br. 116, "Izvještaj Zapovjedništva I hrvatske oružničke pukovnije o akcijama partizana u južnoj lici u vremenu od 27. srpnja do 4. kolovoza 1941. godine, August 9, 1941, 315.

16. Dušan Vojvodić, "Sjećanje na događaje u kotaru Donji Lapac od 1940. do 1942. godine," in *Kotar Donji Lapac u Narodnooslobodilačkom ratu*, ed. Vezmar and Zatezalo, 170.

17. For biographical information on Jovanić, see Đurđević-Đukić, ed., *Narodni heroji Jugoslavije, Knjiga prva A-M*, 316–317.

18. On the origins of the insurgency in the region see, Jovo Reljić, "Martin Brod 1941. godine," in *Drvar, 1941–1945., knjiga 2*, ed. Morača, 393–394; Karanović, "Sadjejstvo sa ličkim ustanicima," 410; Jovanić, *Ratna sjećanja*, 119; idem, "Ustanak u južnoj lici 1941. godine," 105–116; Nikola Majstorović, "Kulen Vakuf opština u NOR-u," in *Bosanski Petrovac u NOB. Knjiga III*, ed. Čerkez, 379; Keča, "Ustanički

dani u okolini Kulen Vakufa," 201; Majstorović and Medić, *Prve iskre*, 59; on the weakness of the communists in Herzegovina, as well as throughout much of the rest of Bosnia-Herzegovina in asserting control over the insurgents, see Rasim Hurem, *Kriza Narodnooslobodilačkog pokreta u Bosni i Hercegovini krajem 1941. i početkom 1942. godine* (Sarajevo: Svjetlost, 1972), 33–71; see also Danilović, "Ustanak u Hercegovini," 29.

19. HDA DAKA, Fond RMZDL, Nikola Vidaković, "Partijska organizacija u Donjem Lapcu od osnivanja do početka ustanka 1941. godine," 7, 47; HDA DAKA, Fond 143, Memoarsko gradivo o NOR-u, LI-1, Izjave s područja Like, Sastanak ličke grupe, March 23, 1951, 3.

20. Jovanić, "Ustanak u južnoj lici 1941. godine," 124.

21. VA, Fond CK HRV, 11/320–321, Okružni komitet Komunističke partije Hrvatske, Politička situacija i stanje partiskih organizacija, September 11, 1941, 2.

22. VA, Fond NOV, kut. 2000, f. 2, dok. 9, Savo Popović, "O borbi i radu partijske organizacije na bihaćkom srezu 1941. i 1942. godine" (undated, most likely written during the early 1950s), 3.

23. Gojko Polovina, "Sjećanja na početni period narodnog ustanka u Lici godine 1941," in *Zbornik 3: Prva godina Narodnooslobodilačkog rata na području Karlovca, Korduna, Gline, Like, Gorskog kotara, Pokuplja i Žumberka*, ed. Đuro Zatezalo (Karlovac: Historijski arhiv u Karlovcu, 1971), 779.

24. On how the June insurgency in Herzegovina was characterized by "a spontaneous rebellion by the Serb population against Ustaša killings and the burning of property," which local communists struggled greatly to control, see Danilović, "Ustanak u Hercegovini," 25.

25. Reljić, "Martin Brod 1941. godine," 398; idem, "Martin Brod—Partizanska baza," in *Ustanak naroda Jugoslavije 1941. Pišu učesnici, Zbornik, knjiga šesta*, ed. Svetislav Savković (Belgrade: Vojnoizdavački zavod JNA "Vojno delo," 1964), 396; on Štikovac's pre-1941 position as treasurer in Dobroselo, see HDA, f. 1353, Grupa VI, inv. br. 1412, Sresko načelstvo u Donjem Lapcu Banskoj vlasti Banovine Hrvatske, Predmet: Mesnih odbora SDS osnivanje u Doljanima i Dobroselu, March 6, 1940, 1.

26. Sava Mileusnić, "Donji Lapac u ustanku," in Jovanić, ed., *Lika u NOB. Zbornik. Pišu učesnici*, 392; HDA DAKA, Fond 143, Memoarsko gradivo o NOR-u, Lika 2 (LI-2), 30/2010, Sava Mileusnić, "Organizacija i djelatnost KPJ u uslovima Drugog svjetskog rata na kotaru Donji Lapac," 1963, 14.

27. See, for example, Lutvo Džubur, "Poslednje školsko zvono," in *Hercegovina u NOB*, ed. Kovačević & Stijačić-Slavo, 396, 400; on the continuation of this intra-ethnic plunder into September, see *Zbornik NOR-a, tom IV, knjiga 1*, br. 204, Izvještaj Uglješe Danilović od 17. septembra 1941. god. Svetozaru Vukmanoviću-Tempu o vojno-političkoj situaciji u istočnoj Hercegovini, September 17, 1941, 446.

28. Mao Tse-tung, *On Guerrilla Warfare*, trans. Samuel B. Griffith (Mineola, NY: Dover Publications, [1937] 2005), 44–45.

29. VA, Fond NDH, kut. 85, f. 7, dok. 14, Zapovjedništvo III. hrvatske oružničke pukovnije Zapovjedništvu hrvatskog oružništva, Ćubrilo Ilija i dr. pljačke za račun ustaša vršili, July 16, 1941, 1.

30. HDA DAKA, Fond RMZDL, kut. 1, Đoko Jovanić, "Kotar donjolapački u ustanku 1941. godine," 50.

31. VA, Fond NDH, kut. 152a, f. 11a, dok. 28, Zapisnik nad Himzom Aganovićem i Alija Vučkovićem o njihovom zarobljivanju u Drvaru od strane Četnika, September 2, 1941, 2.

32. VA, Fond NDH, kut. 213, f. 2, dok. 48, Iz saslušanja domobrana koji su bili zarobljeni u Drvaru i koji su se vratili 22. rujna, October 7, 1941, 1.

33. On this mental outlook, see Jovanić, "Ustanak u donjolapačkom kotaru 1941. godine," 122, 128; HDA DAKA, Fond RMZDL, kut. 4, Originali, Simo Lukić, "Četnici u kotaru Donji Lapac," 9.

34. HDA DAKA, Fond RMZDL, kut. 1, Duško Vojvodić, "Sjećanje na političke i ostale događaje u kotaru Donji Lapac od 1940. do 1942. godine," 29.

35. Rašeta, "Pripremanje i početak ustanka u Donjem Lapcu," 222.

36. Ibid., 223.

37. VA, Fond NDH, kut. 67, f. 1, dok. 26, Saslušanje pokusnog oružnika Mate Bijondića, sa službom na oružničkoj postaji Doljani, August 8, 1941, 1.

38. Polovina, "Sjećanja na početni period narodnog ustanka u Lici," 798.

39. Jovanić, *Ratna sjećanja*, 107–108.

40. HDA DAKA, Fond RMZDL, Milan Šijan, "Nastanak i djelovanje KPJ na teritoriji donjolapačkog kotara" (undated document, most likely written in 1979 or 1980), 36.

41. The word "balija" originally referred to a Muslim peasant, but it eventually became a derogatory term for Muslims. See Abdulah Škaljić, *Turcizmi u srpskohrvatskom jeziku* (Sarajevo: Svjetlost, 1966), 118.

42. Branko Popadić, "Na prostoru Stoca i Bileće," in *Hercegovina u NOB*, ed. Kovačević and Stijačić-Slavo, 638; on the anti-Muslim tendencies among many fighters during the initial stages of the insurgency, see also Danilović, "Ustanak u Hercegovini," 27–29.

43. Asim Pervan, "Ljudi i događaji fatničkog kraja," in *Hercegovina u NOB*, ed. Kovačević and Stijačić-Slavo, 766.

44. On how many local fighters in northwest Bosnia perceived the insurgency as "a war against the Turks," see also Nađ, *Ustanak*, 179; Svetozar Vukmanović Tempo, *Revolucija koja teče. Memoari* (Belgrade: Komunist, 1971), 217, 223.

45. *Zbornik NOR-a, tom IV, knjiga 1*, br. 222, Izvještaj Štaba NOP odreda za Bosansku krajinu od septembra 1941. god. Štabu NOP odreda Bosne i Hercegovine o vojno-političkoj situaciji i borbama protiv okupatora i domaćih izdajnika na području Bos. krajine, 489.

46. VA, Fond NDH, kut. 67, f. 1, dok. 45, Saslušanje oružničkog vodnika, na službi kod krilnog oružničkog zapovjedništva u Gospiću Frkovića Jakova, August 11, 1941, 1.

47. HDA, Fond 1450, MINORS NDH, D-2174, Sadržaj: Rašeta Boško major Jugoslavenske vojske sa majkom Milkom i služavkom Maricom i Rašeta Jandre sa ženom Anđom i bratom Milom svi iz Donjega Lapca—vrijedni priznanja, October 24, 1941, 2.

48. Ivica Bodnaruk, "Sjećanje na dane ustanka u Drvaru i Petrovcu," in *Bosanski Petrovac u NOB, Knjiga II*, ed. Čerkez, 45.

49. Vladimir Veber, the military commander of the NDH army forces (i.e., the homeguards [*domobrani*]) in Kulen Vakuf, was said to have found a "Chetnik" document

in which all "Serb fighters" were called on to join the insurgency. See ARSBL, Fond 328, Zbirka dokumenata VII JNA (Bosanska Krajina), MUP NDH, RAVSIGUR, Izvješće o stanju do 30.VIII.1941. godine u 8 sati, August 30, 1941, 2.

50. HDA, Fond 1450, MINORS NDH, D-2251, Prijepis pisma u Svračkovom selu, August 28, 1941.

51. On the effects of atrocity stories among insurgents, see Milkan Pilipović, "Dramatična borba na vrtočkoj gradini," in *Bosanski Petrovac u NOB. Knjiga II*, ed. Čerkez, 305.

52. Rašeta, "Pripremanje i početak ustanka u Donjem Lapcu," 226–227; idem, *Kazivanje pobjednika smrti*, 22–23.

53. VA, Fond NDH, kut. 67, f. 1, dok. 26, Saslušanje pokusnog oružnika Tome Crnković, sa službom na oružničkoj postaji Srb, August 8, 1941, 1. Some insurgents also had no qualms about taking Orthodox villagers prisoner when they elected not to offer support for the fight against NDH. See, for example, VA, Fond NDH, kut. 213, f. 2, dok. 48, Iz saslušanja domobrana koji su bili zarobljeni u Drvaru i koji su se vratili 22. rujna, October 7, 1941, 1.

54. On such dynamics in Guatemala, see David Stoll, *Rigoberta Menchú and the Story of All Poor Guatemalans* (Boulder, CO: Westview Press, 1999), 58–61; in Latin America more generally, see Timothy Wickman-Crowley, "Terror and Guerrilla Warfare in Latin America, 1956–1970," *Comparative Studies in Society and History* 32, no. 2 (1990): 201–237; in Algeria, see Alistair Horne, *A Savage War of Peace. Algeria 1954–1962* (New York: New York Review of Books, [1977] 2006), 134; and in a host of other contexts, see Kalyvas, *The Logic of Violence in Civil War.*

55. Polovina, *Svedočenje*, 67.

56. HDA, Fond 1450, MINORS NDH, D-2229, Zapovjedništvo kopnene vojske, Vojni ured, July 30, 1941, 1.

57. Živković & Kačavenda, *Srbi u Nezavisnoj Državi Hrvatskoj*, br. 111, Izvještaj oficira za transport pri nemačkom generalu u Zagrebu od 27. avgusta 1941. Ispostavi Abvera u Zagrebu o vojno-političkoj situaciji i zločinima ustaša nad srpskim stanovništvom u NDH, August 27, 1941, 200.

58. Dušan Balaban, "Vrtoče u prvim danima ustanka," in *Bosanski Petrovac u NOB, Knjiga II*, ed. Čerkez, 49–73, here 64.

59. HDA DAKA, Fond 143, Memoarsko gradivo o NOR-u, Lika 2 (LI-2), 30/2010, Sava Mileusnić, "Organizacija i djelatnost KPJ u uslovima Drugog svjetskog rata na kotaru Donji Lapac," 1963, 21; ibid., Fond RMZDL, Radovi za hronike sela (neobjavljeno), "Bušević u Narodnooslobodilačkoj borbi 1941–1945," 1980, 44; Đuro Stanisavljević, "Narodni heroj, Matić Ilije Stojan," in *Kotar Donji Lapac u Narodnooslobodilačkom ratu*, ed. Vezmar and Zatezalo, 974; see also Đurđević-Đukić, ed., *Narodni heroji Jugoslavije, Knjiga prva A-M*, 497–498.

60. Dušan Grbić, "Cvjetnićka četa," in *Drvar, 1941–1945., knjiga 2*, ed. Morača, 358.

61. *Zbornik NOR-a, tom IV, knjiga 1*, br. 66, Izvještaj o savjetovanju i rezolucija delegata narodnooslobodilačkih gerilskih odreda za zapadnu Bosnu i Liku od 31. avgusta 1941. godine, August 31, 1941, 147.

62. On Polovina's prewar political activism in the region, see HDA, f. 1353, Grupa VI, inv. br. 1267, Sresko načelstvo u Donjem Lapcu Ministarstvu unutrašnjih poslova,

Odeljenje javne bezbednost, Predmet: Političkih konferencija UO na području sreza D. Lapac—održavanje, November 25, 1938, 1–2.

63. *Zbornik NOR-a, tom V, knjiga 1*, br. 7, "Poziv Privremenog glavnog štaba gerilskih odreda za Liku početkom kolovozom 1941. godine srpskom i hrvatskom narodu protiv okupatora i ustaša," 29–31.

64. Vukčević, ed., *Zločini*, br. 248, Pismo seljaka iz Donjih Ploča od 31. avgusta 1941. Hrvatima i komšijama iz Vraničana sa pozivom da ne ubijaju više Srbe podsećajući na raniju slogu i ljubav, August 31, 1941, 592–593.

65. ARSBL, Fond 74, Velika Župa Sana i Luka, 3005/41, Pozdrav Narodnooslobodilačke vojske iz Grmeča (undated document but most likely written in mid to late September 1941).

66. Rašeta, "Pripremanje i početak ustanka u Donjem Lapcu," 211. For more examples of Catholics in the Donji Lapac region, who had taken steps to save their Orthodox neighbors, or who at least had not participated in any Ustaša actions, but were nevertheless killed by insurgents because they saw them as "Croats," see ibid., 226–227.

67. Balaban, "Vrtoče u prvim danima ustanka," 67.

68. Lazo Radošević, "Vrtoče u ustanku," in *Bosanski Petrovac u NOB, Knjiga II*, ed. Čerkez, 470.

69. Dane Ivezić, "Brotnja: ustanici istrijebili Iveziće," in *Dossier Boričevac*, ed. Pavičić, 343–352; HDA DAKA, Fond RMZDL, kut. 4, Originali, Simo Lukić, "Četnici u kotaru Donji Lapac," 9; for what appears to be only a partial list of the victims, whom are said to have been killed by "pro-Chetnik elements" who were responding to the killings that local Ustašas from the village committed earlier in July 1941, see *Kotar Donji Lapac u Narodnooslobodilačkom ratu*, ed. Vezmar and Zatezalo, 1126–1127; for a list of the victims (as well as an account of these events that does not mention the Ustaša violence in the region as having anything to do with the killings in Brotnja), see Luka Pavičić, *Kronika stradanja Hrvata južne Like* (Zagreb: D-GRAF, 1996), 245–252.

70. HDA, Fond 306, ZKUZ (Hrvatska), kut. 2243, Zh. br. 11379–11380, OKUZ za Liku, Zapisnici sastavljeni pred komisijom u Brotnji, May 11, 1945, 1–9; ibid., kut. 535, Zh. br. 42195, OKUZ za Liku, Zapisnici sastavljeni pred komisijom u Brotnji, July 18, 1945, 1–2.

71. Polovina, *Svedočenje*, 44; idem, "Sjećanja na početni period narodnog ustanka u Lici," 785; on Jocina Keča's participation in the killings, see also Simo Lukić, "Četnici u kotaru Donji Lapac od 1941. do 1945.," in *Kotar Donji Lapac u Narodnooslobodilačkom ratu*, ed. Vezmar and Zatezalo, 867.

72. HDA DAKA, Fond RMZDL, kut. 1, Đoko Jovanić, "Kotar donjolapački u ustanku 1941. godine," 42.

73. Pavičić, *Kronika stradanja Hrvata južne Like*, 249–252.

74. *Zbornik NOR-a, tom IV, knjiga 1*, br. 204, Izvještaj Uglješe Danilović od 17. septembra 1941. god. Svetozaru Vukmanović-Tempu o vojno-političkoj situaciji u istočnoj Hercegovini, 445; Džubur, "Poslednje školsko zvono," 395–397.

75. Frijda, "The Lex Talionis," 277.

76. Dane Ivezić, "Srbi su pobili cijeli rod Ivezića u selu Brotnja," *Vila Velebita*, br. 31, March 17, 1995, 10.

77. For another example of a successful escape from the insurgents, during which two Muslim refugees in the region managed to present themselves as Orthodox Serbs, see VA, Fond NDH, kut. 61a, f. 15, dok. 42, Dnevno izvješće o važnijim događajima, prema podatcima oružništva za dan 10. rujna 1941. godine, September 10, 1941, 2.

78. Jovanić, *Ratna sjećanja*, 86.

79. Jurjević, *Pogrom u Krnjeuši*, 64.

80. On this claim, which lacks confirmation in NDH archival sources, see Milan Zorić, *Drvar u ustanku 1941.* (Belgrade: Sloboda, 1984), 120.

81. On Father Krešimir Barišić, see Anto Orlovac, *Palme im rukama. Život i mučeništvo župnika Krešimir Barišić i uništenje župe Krnjeuša 1941. godine* (Banja Luka and Zagreb: Biskupski ordinarijat Banja Luka; Ekološki glasnik d.o.o., 2008), 83–106.

82. *Novi list*, "Užasna zvjerstva četničko-komunističkih banda nad hrvatskim življem u Bosni i Lici," September 21, 1941, 5; *Hrvatski narod*, "Zločinstva četničko-komunističkih družbi u Pounju," August 27, 1941, 6

83. VA, Fond NDH, kut. 67, f. 2, dok. 8, Zapisnik sastavljen po izjavi pričuvnog nadporučnika Sabati Dragutina prilikom borbe kod sela Ostrovice (undated document, most likely from late August 1941), 1.

84. For NDH reports on the killings of Catholics in Krnjeuša, see VA, Fond NDH, kut. 1j, f. 2, dok. 14, Situacija, August 14–15, 1941, 1, 6; ibid., kut. 85, f. 14, dok. 13, Izvješće, August 20, 1941, 1–11; HDA, Fond 1450, MINORS NDH, D-2121, Izvještaj o selu Krnjeuša, 14.VIII.1941 u 20.50 sati, August 14, 1941; *Novi list*, "Strašna zlodjela i pustošenja najgorih bandita u povijesti čovječanstva," August 20, 1941, 5; ibid., "Nevine žrtve četničko-komunističkih banda u Pounju," August 28, 1941, 5. The attempt by insurgents to destroy the village's entire Catholic population was also noted in reports compiled by the Commissariat for Refugees in Serbia, which took depositions from refugees who fled from the region in 1943. See AS, Fond G-2, KI, f. 5, Srez Bosanski Petrovac, 1943, 5. For a reconstruction of the violence in Krnjeuša, see Jurjević, *Pogrom u Krnjeuši*.

85. *Novi list*, "Nedužne žrtve strahovitih četničkih zločina pričaju o svojim užasnim doživljajima," September 14, 1941, 11.

86. Pilipović, *Romori vrtočke prošlosti*, 169.

87. HDA, Fond 1450, MINORS NDH, D-2232, Izvješće Aleksandra Seitza Poglavniku, August 20, 1941. See also Ministarstvo vanjskih poslova Nezavisne Države Hrvatske, *Odmetnička zvjerstva pustošenja u Nezavisnoj državi Hrvatskoj u prvim mjesecima života Hrvatske Narodne Države* (Zagreb: Ministarstvo vanjskih poslova, 1942), 38–42; *Hrvatski narod*, "Četnička krvološtva i brojni težki zločini u Hrvatskoj," August 20, 1941, 6; *Novi list*, "Strašna zlodjela i pustošenja najgorih bandita u povijesti čovječanstva," August 20, 1941, 5; ibid., "Nevine žrtve četničko-komunističkih banda u Pounju," August 28, 1941, 5.

88. VA, Fond NDH, kut. 1j, f. 2, dok. 13, Događaji i stanje, August 13–14, 1941, 2. On the killings and stealing that local Ustašas committed in Vrtoče on August 2–3, 1941, which was most likely the immediate trigger for the insurgent attack on the village, see AJ, Fond 110, DKUZ, dos. br. 4670, Zapisnik br. 14, Mjesni odbor: Vrtoče, July 31, 1946, 2. For a memoir by a former insurgent that downplays the reports by the NDH military about the extent and severity of the killings and mutilations in Vrtoče, see Pilipović, *Romori vrtočke prošlosti*, 151.

89. See Simon Schama, *Citizens: A Chronicle of the French Revolution* (New York: Albert Knopf, 1989), chap. 17; Karl Jacoby, *Shadows at Dawn: An Apache Massacre and the Violence of History* (New York: Penguin Books, 2008), 113–114, 156–157; Dwyer and Santikarma, "'When the World Turned to Chaos,'" 300.

90. On this point more generally, see Nathan Leites and Charles Wolf Jr., *Rebellion and Authority: An Analytic Essay on Insurgent Conflicts* (Chicago: Markham, 1970), 106–107.

91. See, for example, Kalyvas, *The Logic of Violence in Civil War*, 26, who argues that "violence is intended to shape the behavior of the targeted audience by altering the expected value of particular attitudes. Put otherwise, violence performs a communicative function with a clear deterrent dimension."

92. LAEB, Hamdija Kreševljaković, *Kulen Vakuf* (Sarajevo: Islamska dionička štamparija, 1935), 15.

93. In this sense, it is debatable whether these violent practices could be labeled with the recent social science concept of "extra-lethal violence," which has been defined as "physical acts committed face-to-face that transgress shared norms and beliefs about appropriate treatment of the living as well as the dead." Here, the style of the beheadings did, in fact, reflect a shared history of norms and beliefs about appropriate forms of execution. See Lee Ann Fujii, "The Puzzle of Extra-Lethal Violence," *Perspectives on Politics* 11, no. 2 (June 2013): 410–426, here 411.

94. Nikola Plećaš-Nitonja, *Požar u Krajini* (Chicago: Plećas-Nitonja, 1975), 36. Other evidence suggests that the impaling of live victims—also an Ottoman era practice—was another technique of violence that some insurgents practiced in northwest Bosnia. See, for example, *Novi list*, "Strašna zlodjela srbskih četnika nad hrvatskim muslimanima," September 6, 1941, 7.

95. *Novi list*, "Zvjerska krvoločnost četničko-komunističkih banda," September 19, 1941, 6.

96. See, for example, Dulić, *Utopias of Nation*, 356–357.

97. On the notion that killing by cutting of throats, rather than shooting, can be a way of placing victims on the level of animals, see John Allcock, *Explaining Yugoslavia* (New York: Columbia University Press, 2000), 398.

98. See, for example, VA, Fond NDH, kut. 61a, f. 11, dok. 12, Zapovjedništvo jadranskog divizijskog područja Ministarstvu hrvatskog domobranstva (Glavni stožer, Očevidni odjel), October 30, 1941, 1, which describes methods that insurgents used to mutilate and kill Muslim villagers in Avtovac in late June 1941.

99. See *Novi list*, "Strašna zlodjela srbskih četnika nad hrvatskim muslimanima," September 6, 1941, 7; see also ibid., "Grozna nedjela razbješnjelih četničko-komunističkih banda nad mirnim i golorukim Hrvatima muslimanima u stolačkom kotaru," September 10, 1941 5; ibid., "Nedužne žrtve strahovitih četničkih zločina pričaju o svojim užasnim doživljajima," September 14, 1941, 11.

100. On Algeria, see Horne, *A Savage War of Peace*, 112; on Guatemala, see Montejo, *Testimony*, 83–85.

101. The insurgents later attempted to kill this prisoner by throwing him into a pit, but he managed to climb out several days later. See VA, Fond NDH, kut. 135i, f. 8, dok. 4, Saslušanje svjedoka Ćastović Mahmuta, iz Milanića kotar Bileća, po napadu četnika na selu Berkoviće (rađeno u ambulanti), August 27, 1941, 1.

102. *Hrvatska Krajina*, "Jedno grozno zvjerstvo," June 20, 1941, 1.

103. On such methods of torture of Armenian Christians, see Peter Balakian, *Black Dog of Fate. A Memoir* (New York: Basic Books, 1997), 213–214; on the desecration of victims' bodies in other instances of mass violence during the twentieth century, see Weitz, *A Century of Genocide*, 180.

104. See Alon Confino, "Why Did the Nazis Burn the Hebrew Bible? Nazi Germany, Representations of the Past, and the Holocaust," *Journal of Modern History* 84, no. 2 (2012): 369–400; idem, *A World without Jews: The Nazi Imagination from Persecution to Genocide* (New Haven: Yale University Press, 2014), 161–162.

105. Fellman, *Inside War*, 188–189.

106. My attempts here to explain the insurgents' violent acts draw on Frijda, "The Lex Talionis," 280–281.

107. See Milgram, *Obedience to Authority*, 188.

108. On the notion of selective and indiscriminate violence, see Kalyvas, *The Logic of Violence in Civil War*, esp. 141–145.

109. VA, Fond NDH, kut. 85, f. 14, dok. 13, Izvješće, August 20, 1941, 10.

110. HDA, Fond 1450, MINORS, D-2121, Izvještaj o selu Krnjeuša, 14.VIII.1941 u 20.50 sati, August 14, 1941; on reactions to the killings in Krnjeuša, see also ibid., Glavni stožer, Stanje 14, August 14–15, 1941, 1; on the difficulty of identifying the bodies, see *Hrvatski narod*, "Zločinstva četničko-komunističkih družbi u Pounju," August 27, 1941, 6.

111. VA, Fond NDH, kut. 1j, f. 2, dok. 14, Situacija, August 14–15, 1941, 7.

112. LAEB, Bibanović, "Kulen Vakuf," 65; ibid., "Stanovništvo Kulen-Vakufa," 210.

113. AJ, Fond 110, DKUZ, dos. br. 5361, Zapisnik br. 18, Mjesni odbor: Prkosi, August 4, 1946, 1–2; Zapisnik br. 19, Mjesni odbor: Kalati, August 5, 1946, 1–2; Zapisnik br. 20, Mjesni odbor: Rajinovci, August 7, 1946, 2.

114. On a group of Orthodox villagers marched from the village of Pritoka to Kulen Vakuf in August, where most were later killed, see Jovanka Rudić, "Na prekopanoj cesti," in *Bosanski Petrovac u NOB, Knjiga I*, ed. Čerkez, 349–355.

115. VA, Fond NDH, kut. 84, fas. 5, dok. 20, Stožer vrbaskog divizijskog područja Zapovjedništvu kopnene vojske (Vojni ured), Akcija protiv pobunjenika, July 29, 1941, 1.

116. VA, Fond NDH, kut. 84, f. 6, dok. 9, Zapovjedništvo kopnene vojske, Zapovijed za akciju oko savlađivanja pobune u Bosni, July 31, 1941, 2; see also ARSBL, Dokumenti iz AVII, F-NDH, fas. 14, Vrhovno oružničko zapovjedništvo Zapovjedništvu 4. Hrvatske oružničke pukovnije, Zapovijed za akciju oko savlađivanja pobune u Bosni u svhu daljeg rada oko savlađivanja pobune u Bosni, August 1, 1941, 1–2.

117. HDA Fond 1450, MINORS NDH, D-2178, Zapovjedništvo kopnene vojske, Zapovijed za akciju oko savlađivanja pobune u Bosni (veoma žurno tajno), July 31, 1941, 2.

118. On the counter-insurgency in Guatemala, see Jennifer Schirmer, *The Guatemalan Military Project: A Violence Called Democracy* (Philadelphia: University of Pennsylvania Press, 1998); Stoll, *Rigoberta Menchú and the Story of All Poor Guatemalans*; idem, *Between Two Armies in the Ixil Towns of Guatemala* (New York: Columbia University Press, 1993).

119. For an analysis of this dynamic across many contexts, see Benjamin Valentino, Paul Huth, and Dylan Balch-Lindsay, "Draining the Sea: Mass Killing and Guerrilla Warfare," *International Organization* 58 (Spring 2004): 375–407.

120. On Algeria, see Horne, *A Savage War of Peace*; on Chechnya, see Sebastian Smith, *Allah's Mountains: The Battle for Chechnya* (New York: I.B. Tauris, 2006); Anna Politkovskaya, *A Small Corner of Hell: Dispatches from Chechnya* (Chicago: University of Chicago Press, 2003); on Afghanistan, see Lester Grau, *The Soviet-Afghan War: How a Superpower Fought and Lost* (Lawrence: University Press of Kansas, 2002); on Sri Lanka, see Manor, ed., *Sri Lanka in Change and Crisis.*

121. On this point, see Jeff Goodwin, *No Other Way Out: States and Revolutionary Movements, 1945–1991* (Cambridge: Cambridge University Press, 2001), 123; see also Kalyvas, *The Logic of Violence in Civil War*, 151–153.

122. On this dynamic, see Vukčević, ed., *Zločini*, br. 288, Telegram Predsjednika prijekog suda Mostara od 19. septembra 1941. Ministarstvu pravosuđa i bogoštovlja da se molba za pomilovanje dva ustaška zločinca osuđena na smrt ne prihvati, zbog teških zločina u selu Poplata, September 19, 1941, 717.

123. Petar Radošević, "Teror ustaša u Vrtoču," in *Bosanski Petrovac u NOB, Knjiga I*, ed. Čerkez, 648.

124. AMUSK, Fond Sjećanja boraca iz Narodnooslobodilačkog rata, 1941–1945, Razgovor sa drugovima Sajom Grbićem, Savom Popovićem i Slobodanom Pilipovićem o ustanku na području Bihaća 1941. godine, December 24, 1961, 10–11.

125. ABiH, Fond ZKUZ BiH, kut. 68, Zapisnici, Srez Bosanski Petrovac, Zapisnik br. 18, Inv. br. 56900, Mjesni odbor: Prkosi, August 4, 1946, 2.

126. VA, Fond NDH, kut. 67, f. 1, dok. 26, Saslušanje pokusnog oružnika Mate Bijondića, sa službom na oružničkoj postaji Doljani, August 8, 1941, 1.

127. For the NDH documents, see AMUSK, Prijepisi originalnih dokumenata iz AHRP, Izvještaj o situaciji na područjima pobune, Izvještaj iz Bihaća u 23 sata, August 4, 1941, 10; VA, Fond NDH, kut. 67, f. 1, dok. 26, Saslušanje pokusnog oružnika Mate Bijondića, sa službom na oružničkoj postaji Doljani, August 8, 1941, 2; ibid., dok. 45, Saslušanje oružničkog vodnika, na službi kod krilnog oružničkog zapovjedništva u Gospiću Frković Jakov, 2; on the departure of some of the Ustašas and their families, see also the recollections of local insurgents in HDA DAKA, Fond RMZDL, Radovi za hronike sela (neobjavljeno), "Bušević u Narodnooslobodilačkoj borbi 1941–1945 (1980)," 43–44; Pilipović, *Romori vrtočke prošlosti*, 138–139.

128. ARSBL, Fond 330, Zbirka "Varia," dok. br. 330-004-036, "Zločinstva i nasilja tako zvanih 'divljih ustaša' i njihovih pomoćnika u Derventi i okolici" (undated document), 2. On the appearance of the term "wild Ustašas" in NDH documents, see Vukčević, ed., *Zločini*, br. 315, Izveštaj Zapovjedništva oružničkog voda Metković od 9. oktobra 1941. Zapovjedništvu jadranskog divizijskog područja o bekstvu pravoslavaca sa područja Čapljine od ustaških zločina sa podatkom o 800 ubijenih Srba u selu Prebilovci, 793–794; VA, Fond NDH, kut. 150a, f. 2, kut. 41, Zapovjedništvo 3. Hrvatske oružničke pukovnije Zaovjedništvu 1. Hrvatske oružničke pukovnije, Izvješće o stanju na području krila u vezi sa izvještajnom službom, August 16, 1941, 1; ibid., kut. 152, f. 4, dok. 22, Zapovjedništvo 3. Hrvatske oružničke pukovnije Ravnateljstvu za javni red i sigurnost, Izvješće o stanju komunističko-četničke akcije na području krila, Gospić, August 19, 1941, 1.

129. ARSBL, Fond 330, Zbirka "Varia," dok. br. 330-004-036, "Zločinstva i nasilja tako zvanih 'divljih ustaša' i njihovih pomoćnika u Derventi i okolici," 6.

130. Vukčević, ed., *Zločini*, br. 219, Izveštaj Krilnog oružničkog zapovjedništva Gospić od 16. avgusta 1941. Zapovjedništvu 1. Hrvatske oružničke pukovnije o prilikama na području krila sa podacima o ubijanju, paljenju i pljački srpskog življa od strane ustaša, August 16, 1941, 524. For similar criticisms of the violence of the Ustašas from different regions of the NDH, see ibid., br. 243, Izveštaj Zapovjedništva 2. hrvatske oružničke pukovnije od 28. avgusta 1941. Vrhovnom oružničkom zapovjedništvu o situaciji sa podacima o pljački imovine Srba od strane ustaše na području kotara Stolac, August 28, 1941, 578.

131. For a brief NDH report on the insurgent attack on Boričevac, and the exodus of the village's entire population, see VA, Fond NDH, kut. 143, f. 1, dok. 1–2, Zapovjedništvo 3. Hrvatske oružničke pukovnije Zapovjedniku 4. oružničke pukovnije, Doglasno izvješće dostavlja, August 8, 1941, 3.

132. Plećaš-Nitonja, *Požar u Krajini*, 78–79; HDA, Fond 306, ZKUZ (Hrvatska), kut. 244, Zh. br. 11479–11500, OKUZ za Liku, Niko Vlatković i Nikola Rašeta (izjave), May 14, 1945, 2.

133. Pero Pilipović, "Borba Cvjetnićana na petrovačkom području, in *Bosanski Petrovac u NOB, Knjiga I*, ed. Čerkez, 589.

134. Ibid.; for Tankosić's testimonies about his experiences written in the 1970s, see Vlado Tankosić, "Kako sam strijeljan i bačen u jamu," in *Drvar, 1941–1945., knjiga 1*, ed. Morača, 250–252; for the testimony that he gave before the war was over, see ABiH, Fond ZKUZ BiH, kut. 88, Zapisnik sastavljen u kancelariji okružnog organa ZEM-KOM-e za okrug Drvar, Saslušanje Vladimira Tankosića po masovnom ubistvu u selu Boričevac dana 24.VII.1941, March 28, 1945, 2; AJ, Fond 110, DKUZ, dos. br. 4670, Inv. br. 40740, Zapisnik sastavljen u kancelariji okružnog organa ZEM-KOM za okrug Drvar 23. marta 1945. god., March 23, 1945, 1–2.

135. Štikavac, "Krvavo lapačko ljeto," 616; see also Karanović, "Sadjejstvo sa ličkim ustanicima," 410.

136. Nikola Knežević, "Cvjetnićani u akciji," in *Drvar, 1941–1945., knjiga 2*, ed. Morača, 457.

137. Nikola Knežević Niko, "Maćuka," in *Drvar, 1941–1945. Sjećanja učesnika, knjiga 3*, ed. Pero Morača (Drvar: Skupština opštine Drvar, 1978), 88.

138. Polovina, "Sjećanja na početni period narodnog ustanka u Lici," 785–786.

139. Polovina, *Svedočenje*, 42.

140. Karanović, "Napad na žandarmerijsku stanicu u Martin Brodu," 429.

141. Rašeta, "Pripremanje i početak ustanka u Donjem Lapcu," 226.

142. Majstorović and Medić, *Prve iskre*, 41; on the Ustaša attacks on Kalati more generally, see AJ, Fond 110, DKUZ, dos. br. 5361, Zapisnik br. 19, Mjesni odbor: Kalati, August 5, 1946, 1–5; the precise number of victims in this particular attack is difficult to determine, although data collected in the mid-1960s suggests that there were at least 158 killed. On these numbers, see AMUSK, Doprinos u NOB, 1941–1945 (informacije o poginulim borcima i žrtvama fašističkog terror—Kulen Vakuf, Klisa, Kalati), Kalati—žrtve fašističkog terora (the data appears to have been collected in 1967).

143. Danilo Damjanović Danić, *Ustanak naroda Hrvatske 1941 u Srbu i okolini* (Zagreb: IP "Progres," 1972), 121–122; Mileusnić, "Donji Lapac u ustanku," 390;

see also the testimonies of Milan Filipović and Stevo Inđić (both from Kalati) in Polovina, *Svedočenje*, 60–61.

144. Majstorović and Medić, *Prve iskre*, 41.

145. "Jewish-Bolshevik terror" was the formulation that such nationalist fighters used to conflate "Jews" and "communists." See Wendy Lower, "Pogroms, mob violence and genocide in western Ukraine, summer 1941: varied histories, explanations, and comparisons," *Journal of Genocide Research* 13, no. 3 (2011): 226.

146. Polovina, *Svedočenje*, 340.

147. Knežević, "Cvjetnićani u akciji," 457; for NDH newpaper accounts of the burning of Boričevac, see *Novi list*, "Kuće su palili, crkve opljačkali . . . Zvjerstva četnika u selima kotara Gračac i Donji Lapac," August 31, 1941, 5; ibid., "Jedan čas s postradalima iz Bihaća," September 22, 1941, 5; see also HDA, Fond 1450, MINORS NDH, D-2188, Saslušanje oružničkog narednika Antona Leševića, sa službom na oružničkoj postaji Donji Lapac, krilnog oružničkog zapovjedništva Gospić, povodom četničke akcije u području kotara Donji Lapac, August 28, 1941, 1–2.

148. Knežević Niko, "Maćuka," 88.

149. HDA DAKA, Fond RMZDL, kut. 1, Đoko Jovanić, "Kotar donjolapački u ustanku 1941. godine," 44.

150. VA, Fond CK HRV, 1/50–52, Štab brigade gerilskih odreda za oslobođenje krajeva Bosne i Like Svim dosadašnjim rukovodiocima gerilskih odreda i komandirima pojedinih odreda, Opšta naredba, August 16, 1941, 1.

151. Bodnaruk, "Sjećanje na dane ustanka u Drvaru i Petrovcu," 48. On the presence of a small number of men among the insurgents who viewed themselves as Croats, see VA, Fond NDH, kut. 213, f. 2, dok. 48, Iz saslušanja domobrana koji su bili zarobljeni u Drvaru i koji su se vratili 22. rujna, October 7, 1941, 1.

152. *Zbornik NOR-a, tom IV, knjiga 1*, br. 77, Izvještaj komandanta drvarske brigade od 2. septembra 1941. god. Oblasnom komitetu KPJ za Bosansku krajinu o razvoju ustanka na području brigade, September 2, 1941, 170–173.

153. Ibid., br. 18, Članak iz "Gerilca" br. 5 o narodnom zboru održanom u selu Bastasima 10. avgusta 1941. god., August 10, 1941, 51.

154. HDA, Fond 1450, MINORS NDH, D-2188, Štab gerilskih odreda za Liku (letak), undated document, most likely from August 1941, 1.

155. Ibid., Prepis proglasa Štaba gerilskih odreda za Liku, August 29, 1941, 1.

156. Ibid., Štab gerilskih odreda za Liku (letak), undated document, most likely from August 1941, 1.

157. *Zbornik NOR-a, tom IV, knjiga 1*, br. 25, Uputstvo Štaba Prvog bataljona "Sloboda" od 20. avgusta 1941 god. političkim komesarima odreda za politički rad u jedinicama, August 20, 1941, 65.

158. See, for example, Skoko, *Pokolji hercegovačkih Srba '41.*, 290–291.

159. On this point, see Jeremy Weinstein, *Inside Rebellion: The Politics of Insurgent Violence* (Cambridge: Cambridge University Press, 2007), chap. 4.

Chapter 5. The Challenge of Restraint

1. For earlier studies along these lines, see Helen Fein, *Accounting for Genocide: National Responses and Jewish Victimization during the Holocaust* (New York: Free Press, 1979); Leo Kuper, *Genocide: Its Political Use in the Twentieth Century* (New Haven: Yale University

Press, 1981); for a critique of newer literature, see Scott Straus, "Second-Generation Comparative Research on Genocide," *World Politics* 59, no. 3 (2007): 476–501. For an exception, which takes some account of instances in which mass violence was likely, but did not occur, see Manus Midlarsky, *The Killing Trap: Genocide in the Twentieth Century* (Cambridge: Cambridge University Press, 2005).

2. See, for example, Kalyvas, *The Logic of Violence in Civil War*; Alexander Downes, *Targeting Civilians in War* (Ithaca, NY: Cornell University Press, 2008); James Ron, *Frontiers and Ghettos: State Violence in Serbia and Israel* (Berkeley: University of California Press, 2004); Weinstein, *Inside Rebellion*; Su, *Collective Killings in Rural China*; Dumitru and Johnson, "Constructing Interethnic Conflict and Cooperation"; Kopstein and Wittenberg, "Deadly Communities."

3. For a critique of the literature along these lines, which is also an important attempt to formulate a research agenda on the restraint of violence, see Straus, "Retreating from the Brink." For an early anticipation of a research agenda that recognizes the importance studying why mass violence occurs and does not in cases with similar characteristics, see Herff, "Genocide as State Terrorism," especially 184.

4. On this point, see Straus, *Making and Unmaking Nations*; see also Daniel Chirot and Clark McCauley, *Why Not Kill Them All? The Logic and Prevention of Mass Political Murder* (Princeton, NJ: Princeton University Press, 2006), 8; David Laitin, *Nations, States, and Violence* (Oxford: Oxford University Press, 2007), 11; James Fearon and David Laitin, "Explaining Interethnic Cooperation," *American Political Science Review* 90, no. 4 (1996): 715–735.

5. For insurgent sources on these events, see Majstorović and Medić, *Prve iskre*, 47; Jovanić, "Ustanak u južnoj lici 1941. godine," 130; Mileusnić, "Donji Lapac u ustanku," 394; Milan Majstorović and Mićo Medić, "Doljani u narodnom ustanku," in *Ustanak naroda Jugoslavije 1941. Pišu učesnici, Zbornik, knjiga peta*, ed. Koča Popović (Belgrade: Vojnoizdavački zavod JNA "Vojno delo," 1964), 459–460; for NDH sources, see VA, Fond NDH, kut. 67, f. 2, dok. 8, Zapisnik sastavljen po izjavi pričuvnog nadporučnika Sabati Dragutina prilikom borbe kod sela Ostrovice (undated document, most likely from late August 1941), 2–4.

6. Majstorović and Medić, *Prve iskre*, 48; for NDH sources on the numbers of dead, missing, and wounded, see VA, Fond NDH, kut. 67, f. 2, dok. 8, Izkaz poginulih, ranjenih i nestalih časnika, dočasnika i momaka u borbama 18–20. VIII o.g. (undated document, most likely from late August 1941), 1.

7. Majstorović and Medić, *Prve iskre*, 50–51.

8. Vojvodić, "Sjećanje na događaje u kotaru Donji Lapac od 1940. do 1942. godine," 171.

9. HDA DAKA, Fond RMZDL, kut. 1, Dušan Vojvodić, "Sjećanje na političke i ostale događaje u kotaru Donji Lapac od 1940. do 1942. godine," 29.

10. Damjanović Danić, *Ustanak naroda Hrvatske 1941 u Srbu i okolini*, 202–203.

11. HDA DAKA, Fond RMZDL, kut. 1, Dušan Vojvodić, "Sjećanje na političke i ostale događaje u kotaru Donji Lapac od 1940. do 1942. godine," 29.

12. Damjanović Danić, *Ustanak naroda Hrvatske 1941 u Srbu i okolini*, 202–203.

13. Documents from the interwar period indicate that there were two official names for the village: Serbian Rašinovac [*Rašinovac srpski*] and Turkish Rašinovac [*Rašinovac turski*]. See AUSK, Fond Okružnog inspektorata Vrbaske Banovine Bihać, kut. 11, Poglavarstvo Sreza petrovačkog, Spisak svih sela na području ovoga sreza,

March 15, 1930, 1. Population statistics collected from what appears to have been the late 1930s suggest that Serbian Rašinovac had 611 residents, and Turkish Rašinovac had 252. See ARSBL, Fond 9, KBUVB, Opšte odeljenje, aj. 24–25, podaci o selima, 32.

14. AJ, Fond 110, DKUZ, f. 588, Inv. br. 14440, Zapisnik sastavljen u Komesarijatu za izbeglice i preseljenike u Beogradu, Latinović Luka iz Rašinovca, June 11, 1943, 1–2 (lowercase "muslim" in the original). On the Ustaša violence in Rašinovac before the insurgency began, see also VA, Fond NDH, kut. 312, f. 1, dok. 55, Kratak pregled masovnih zločina ustaša u 1941. godini, bihaćki okrug, 8; on killings and stealing in the village after the insurgency broke out, see ABiH, ZKUZ BiH, Srez Bosanski Petrovac, kut. 68, Inv. broj 37012–37017, Prijave, February 10, 1945; ibid., Inv. br. 5712, Zapisnik sastavljen kod NOO Rašinovac, srez Petrovac, okrug Drvar, January 17, 1946, 1; AJ, Fond 110, DKUZ, dos. br. 5105, Srez Bosanski Petrovac, Selo Rašinovac, Inv. br. 56884, Zapisnik sastavljen dana 19. jula 1941. godine u mjestu B. Petrovac, July 19, 1946, 1–2; ibid., Zapisnik br. 2, Mjesni odbor: Tuk Dževar, July 19, 1946, 1–5; for a list of seventeen men from the village whom the postwar communist war crimes commission considered to have been Ustašas, see AJ, Fond 110, DKUZ, f. 131, F. br. 6017, Odluka za Ljubomira Kvaternika, Prilog 3, Saučesnici (undated document, most likely written in 1946 or 1947), 5.

15. Milanko Pećanac, "Suvaja i njeni ljudi u ustaničkim danima," in *Bosanski Petrovac u NOB, Knjiga II*, ed. Čerkez, 86.

16. Ibid.

17. On the role of dehumanization in facilitating violence, see Zimbardo, *The Lucifer Effect*, 14–16, 298–313.

18. Vukčević, ed., *Zločini*, br. 98, Izvještaj predstojnika kotarske oblasti Bileća Ravnateljstva za javni red i sigurnosti o situaciji na području kotara i čitave Hercegovine za period 11. juni–4. juli 1941. god. sa podacima o pravoslavnom stanovništvu, međusobnim odnosima naroda, zločinima ustaša i uzrocima takvog stanja, 201. For an account of what appears to be this same incident, see Popadić, "Na prostoru Stoca i Bileće," 635.

19. Polovina, "Sjećanja na početni period narodnog ustanka u Lici," 788.

20. Popadić, "Na prostoru Stoca i Bileće," 639–640.

21. Ibid., 644.

22. Pervan, "Ljudi i događaji fatničkog kraja," 776.

23. On these killings, see Tahir Pervan, *Čavkarica. Vrata pakla* (Sarajevo: Behar, 2007); see also Danilović, "Ustanak u Hercegovini," 28.

24. On prewar intercommunal relations in Bjelaj and the actions of local Muslim youth in establishing links with insurgent commanders in the region, see Ahmet Hromađić, "Selo Bjelaj," in *Bosanski Petrovac u NOB, Knjiga II*, ed. Čerkez, 494–497; Filip Đukić-Pilja, "Bjelajčani u ustanku," in ibid., 502–504; Rade Kovačević, "Na zajedničkom djelu," in ibid., 573–578; Mićo Rakić, "Rad SKOJ-a u Bosanskom Petrovcu," in *Ustanak naroda Jugoslavije 1941. Pišu učesnici, knjiga treća*, ed. Koča Popović (Belgrade: Vojnoizdavački zavod JNA "Vojno delo," 1963), 368; on the local Ustašas, see ABiH, Fond ZKUZ BiH, Srez Bosanski Petrovac, kut. 65, Zapisnik br. 15, Mjesni odbor: Bjelaj, 1.

25. VA, Fond NOV, kut. 1997, f. 8, dok. 4, Drago Đukić, "Pripreme ustanka, ustanak i borbe 1941. godine u bosansko-petrovačkom srezu" (undated document, but most likely written in the early 1950s), 12 (lowercase "muslim" in the original).

26. For the quotations, see ibid., 13; on the meeting, see also Rakić, "Rad SKOJ-a u Bosanskom Petrovcu," 374; on the local Muslim residents in Bjelaj who were affiliated with the Communist Party before the war, see VA, Fond NOV, kut. 1997, f. 8, dok. 6, Jovo Kecman, "Podaci o organizacionom stanju Partijske organizacije prije rata na srezu Bosansko Petrovačkom," May 24, 1951, 3. One of these youth activists, Mahmut Ibrahimpašić, was eventually apprehended by the NDH authorities and put on trial for "spreading communism, anarchy, terrorism," as well as for being affiliated with groups (i.e., the Communist Party) that sought to overthrow the state. See HDA, Fond 493, Sudovi oružanih snaga Nezavisne Države Hrvatske, Optužnica Ibrahimpašić Mahmuta, October 16, 1941, 1–4.

27. VA, Fond NOV, kut. 1997, f. 8, dok. 4, Drago Đukić, "Pripreme ustanka, ustanak i borbe 1941. godine u bosansko-petrovačkom srezu" (undated document, but most likely written in the early 1950s), 36.

28. Pilipović, *Romori vrtočke prošlosti*, 168; on the alliance between villagers in Bjelaj and the insurgents, see also Zorić, *Drvar u ustanku 1941.*, 120–121.

29. Postwar investigations by communist state security concluded that there were less than seventy Ustašas in the Bosanska Dubica region. See VA, Fond SUP BiH, Film 3, Predmet: istorijat ustaškog pokreta na terenu sreza Bosanska Dubica, 2. On Ustaša violence in the region, see VA, Fond NOV, kut. 1997, f. 1, dok. 3, Bosanska Dubica, Stenografske beleške, July 4, 1951, 3–4; kut. 1997, f. 1, dok. 7, Bosanska Dubica, Podaci o radu i razvitku partiskih organizacija i narodne vlasti na terenu sreza Bosanska Dubica u periodu od 1941. do 1944. godine, 2. For a letter that a group of the region's Orthodox residents sent to the NDH authorities about the men with "very suspect and well-known histories" who "were misusing the Ustaša authority" to steal, kill, and rape, see VA, Fond NDH, kut. 1j, f. 2, dok. 15, Pismo Kotarskom predstojništvu u Bosanskoj Dubici, August 8, 1941, 1.

30. ABiH, Fond ZKUZ BiH, Srez Bosanska Dubica, kut. 26, Inv. br. 55899, Zapisnik sastavljen 25. jula 1946. godine u MNO Johova po ZKUZ, July 25, 1946, 1.

31. AJ, Fond 110, DKUZ, f. 487, dos. br. 4673, Bosanska Dubica, Zapisnik 19. jula 1946. godine u Bosanskoj Dubici po ZKUZ, July 19, 1946, 1–2; ABiH, Fond ZKUZ BiH, Srez Bosanska Dubica, kut. 24, Inv. br. 55889, Zapisnik sastavljen 22. jula 1946. godine u Bosanskoj Dubici po ZKUZ, July 22, 1946, 1; ibid., inv. br. 55886, Zapisnik sastavljen 18. jula 1946. godine u Bosanskoj Dubici po ZKUZ, July 22, 1946, 1.

32. ABiH, Fond ZKUZ BiH, Srez Bosanska Dubica, kut. 31, inv. br. 55901, Zapisnik sastavljen 24. jula 1946. godine u kancelariji mjesnog narodnog odbora u Sključanima po ZKUZ, July 24, 1946, 1; ibid., inv. br. 55898, Zapisnik sastavljen 23. jula 1946. godine, u selu Slabinji po ZKUZ, July 23, 1946, 1.

33. Ibid., inv. br. 55898, Zapisnik sastavljen 23. jula 1946. godine, u selu Slabinji po ZKUZ, July 23, 1946, 1 (lowercase "muslim" in the original).

34. On the history of the workers' and communist movement in the Bosanska Dubica region before 1941, see Ahmet Ćelam, "Sindikalna organizacija kožarskih radnika u Bosanskoj Dubici," in *Kozara u Narodnooslobodilačkom ratu. Zapisi i sjećanja, knjiga prva*, ed. Radomir Petković (Belgrade: Vojnoizdavački zavod, 1971), 100–104; Dušan D. Samardžija, *Bosanskodubičko područje u NOR-u i socijalističkoj revoluciji 1941–1945* (Bosanska Dubica: Društveno-političke organizacije i Skupština opštine Bosanska Dubica, 1984), 27–49; VA, Fond NOV, kut. 1997, f. 1, dok. 3, Bosanska Dubica, Stenografske beleške, July 4, 1951, 1.

35. Ahmet Ćelam, "U Dubici poslije okupacije," in *Kozara u Narodnooslobodilačkom ratu*, ed. Petković, 193–197.

36. On the organizational activities of local communists after the establishment of the NDH and prior to the insurgency, see VA, Fond NOV, kut. 1997, f. 1, dok. 1, Grupa za Bosansku Dubicu, O pripremama za ustanak, prikupljanju oružja i o prvim frontovima prema neprijatelju, Stenografske beleške, May 10, 1951, 1–3; ibid., kut. 1997, f. 1, dok. 3, Bosanska Dubica, Stenografske beleške, July 4, 1951, 4–7. For NDH reports about these groups, see VA, Fond NDH, kut. 1j, f. 2, dok. 15, 4. Satnija lakog odjela Hrvatske Legije Zapovjedništvu cijele kupne Kopnene vojske, August 14, 1941, 1.

37. AJ, Fond 110, DKUZ, f. 588, Inv. br. 14400, Zapisnik na 15. januara 1944. godine sastavljen u Komesarijatu za izbeglice i preseljenike u Beogradu (izjave od Turudije Sminje, Turudije Vere, Turudije Branka), January 15, 1944, 7–8 (lowercase "muslim" in the original).

38. Boško Šiljegović, "Pripremanje ustanka u dubičkim selima," in *Ratna sećanja aktivista jugoslovenskog revolucionarnog radničkog pokreta, knjiga prva: 1941–1945*, ed. Pero Morača (Belgrade: Kultura, 1961), 350–351. For biographical information on Šiljegović, see ARSBL, Kartoteka ličnosti iz NOR-a; Olga Đurđević-Đukić, ed., *Narodni heroji Jugoslavije, Knjiga druga N-Ž* (Belgrade: Mladost, 1975), 234–235.

39. Boško Šiljegović, "Kako se pripremio ustanak u dubičkim selima," in *Krajiške brigade* (Ljubljana: Ljudske pravice, 1954), 69–74, here 73–74. On the rapid formation of this column, see also VA, Fond NOV, kut. 1997, f. 1, dok. 4, Bosanska Dubica, Stenografske beleške, July 7, 1951, 2.

40. VA, Fond NDH, kut. 1j, f. 2, dok. 15, Ustašama sela Baćina (undated document, mostly likely from late July or early August 1941), 1.

41. Ibid., Pismo Srba seljaka i radnika radnom narodu Hrvatske (undated document, mostly likely from late July or early August 1941), 1.

42. On communist efforts to mobilize non-Serbs in the region to fight with them, see ibid., Zapisnik sastavljen u kancelariji Kotarske Oblasti u Bosanskoj Dubici, sa Bićanićem Petrom iz sela Maglajaca, August 11, 1941, 1.

43. VA, Fond NOV, kut. 1997, f. 1, dok. 6, Bosanska Dubica, Organizaciono stanje komunističke Partije na terenu sreza Bosanske Dubice—pre propasti stare Jugoslavije, posle propasti i u samom narodnom ustanku na ovom srezu (undated document, most likely from the early 1950s), 5.

44. VA, Fond NOV, kut. 1997, f. 8, dok, 4, Drago Đukić, "Pripreme ustanka, ustanak i borbe 1941. godine u bosansko-petrovačkom srezu," 37.

45. See, for example, Kopstein and Wittenberg, "Deadly Communities."

46. For an analysis of interwar election results in northwest Bosnia, see Đorđe Mikić, *Političke stranke i izbori u Bosanskoj Krajini, 1918–1941* (Banja Luka: Institut za istoriju, 1997). For the election results, see *Statistički pregled izbora narodnih poslanika za ustavotvornu skupštinu Kraljevine Srba, Hrvata i Slovenaca, izvršenih na dan 28. novembra 1920. god.* (Belgrade: Deliška tiskarna, 1921); *Statistika izbora narodnih poslanika Kraljevine Srba, Hrvata i Slovenaca 1923* (Belgrade: Državna štamparija Kraljevine Srba, Hrvata i Slovenaca, 1924); *Statistika izbora narodnih poslanika Kraljevine Srba, Hrvata i Slovenaca 1925* (Belgrade: Državna štamparija Kraljevine Srba, Hrvata i Slovenaca, 1926); *Statistika izbora narodnih poslanika Kraljevine Srba, Hrvata i Slovenaca 1927* (Belgrade: Štamparija Vladete Janićijevića, 1928); *Statistika izbora narodnih poslanika za*

Prvu Jugoslovensku Narodnu Skupštinu održanih 8. novembra 1931. god. (Belgrade, 1935); *Statistika izbora narodnih poslanika za Narodnu Skupštinu Kraljevine Jugoslavije izvršenih 5. maja 1935. godine* (Belgrade: Štampa državne štamparije Kraljevine Jugoslavije, 1938).

47. On the role of violence in rapidly reshaping human behavior and identities, see Das, "Collective Violence and the Shifting Categories of Communal Riots, Ethnic Cleansing, and Genocide," 108–109.

48. On the importance of "within-war dynamics," see Bacells, "Rivalry and Revenge," 308; Wood, "The Social Processes of Civil War."

49. HDA, Fond 1450, MINORS, D-2121, Stožer Hrvatske Legije Zapovjedniku Hrvatske kopnene vojske, Izvještaj o stanju, August 5, 1941, 1.

50. Ibid.

51. Ibid., 3 Satnije 3 Pješačke Pukovnije, Podnosi detaljan izvještaj o radu 3 Satnije u Bosanskoj Dubici, August 2, 1941, 1–4 (quote is from 3); see also VA, kut. 169, f. 6, dok. 19, Ravnateljstvo Ustaškog Redarstva Banja Luka Ravnateljstvu Ustaškog Redarstva, Detaljni izvještaj o radu III Satnije u Bosanskoj Dubici, August 10, 1941, 1–2.

52. AMUSK, Prijepisi originalnih dokumenata iz AHRP, Glavni Stožer Vojskovođe Vojskovođi i Ministru Domobranstva, Predmet: ugušenje pobune u Bosni i Lici, Veoma žurno-tajno, August 6, 1941, 1–3.

53. Ibid., 3.

54. Vukčević, ed., *Zločini*, br. 219, Izveštaj Krilnog oružničkog zapovjedništva Gospić od 16. avgusta 1941. Zapovjedništvu 1. Hrvatske oružničke pukovnije o prilikama na području krila sa podacima o ubijanju, paljenju i pljački srpskog življa od strane ustaša, August 16, 1941, 526.

55. VA, Fond NDH, kut. 152, f. 4, dok. 22, Zapovjedništvo 3. Hrvatske oružničke pukovnije Ravnateljstvu za javni red i sigurnost, Izvješće o stanju komunističko-četničke akcije na području krila, Gospić, August 19, 1941, 2.

56. Ibid., kut. 84, f. 3, dok. 21, Zapovjedništvo kopnene vojske Zapovjedništvu vojske i Ministarstvu Domobranstva, Izvještaj o vanjskoj i unutarnjoj situaciji za treću deseticu (21.–30. lipnja 1941.), June 30, 1941, 9.

57. HDA, Fond 1450, MINORS NDH, D-2174, Ministarstvo hrvatskog domobranstva, Glavni stožer, September 18, 1941, 2.

58. The order was issued on August 7, 1941 from the Ministarstvo Hrvatskog domobranstva (Glavni stožer). See VA, Fond NDH, kut. 143a, f. 2, dok. 44, Vrhovno oružničko zapovjedništvo Zapovjedništvu 1., 2., 3. i 4. Hrvatske oružničke pukovnije, August 8, 1941.

59. Ibid., kut. 143a, f. 2, dok. 47, Zapovjedništvo Vojne krajine (Vojni odjel) Zapovjedništvu 4. oružničke pukovnije, August 12, 1941, 1.

60. Ibid., kut. 67, f. 2, dok. 20, Lički zdrug, Zapovied Poglavnika, August 23, 1941, 1.

61. Ibid., Fond NOV, kut. 2000, f. 2, dok. 4, Savo Popović, "O borbi i radu partijske organizacije na bihaćkom srezu 1941. i 1942. godine," (undated document, most likely written during the early 1950s), 8.

62. Ibid., Fond NDH, kut. 195, f. 10, dok. 28, Velika župa Krbava i Psat, Redarstveno ravnateljstvo (Bihać) Ravnateljstvu za javni mir i sigurnost (Zagreb), August 21, 1941, 2.

63. Vukčević, ed., *Zločini*, br. 220, Izveštaj Zapovjednika letećeg odreda u Humu od 16. avgusta 1941. Zapovjedniku jadranskog divizijskog područja o pokolju i bacanju u jame pravoslavaca u selima Čavaš, Poljice i Šurmanci, August 16, 1941, 530.

64. *Zbornik NOR-a, tom V, knjiga 1*, br. 132, Izvještaj Zapovjedništva Prve hrvatske oružničke pukovnije od 16. kolovoza 1941. god. o zločinima ustaša i akcijama partizana u Kordunu, August 16, 1941, 343.

65. Vukčević, ed., *Zločini*, br. 246, Pritužba Hrvata iz Bosanskog Broda od 28. avgusta 1941. Velikom županu Župe Posavje o zločinima ustaša nad nevinim ljudima u okolini Bosanskog Broda i molba da se tome stane na put, August 28, 1941, 587–588.

66. VA, Fond NDH, kut. 150a, f. 2, dok. 41, Zapovjedništvo 3. Hrvatske oružničke pukovnije Zapovjedništvu 1. Hrvatske oružničke pukovnije, Izvješće o stanju na području krila u vezi sa izvještajnom službom, August 16, 1941, 2.

67. Odić, "Julski dani 1941. na unskoj pruzi," 213–215.

68. See, for example, Valentino, *Final Solutions*; Weitz, *a Century of Genocide*; Jacques Sémelin, *Purify and Destroy: The Political Uses of Massacre and Genocide* (New York: Columbia University Press, 2007).

69. For the testimony of an NDH official who fled from Donji Lapac to Boričevac, then to Kulen Vakuf, and finally to Bihać during July and August 1941, see VA, Fond NDH, kut. 86, f. 4, dok. 3, Saslušanje Oružničkog narednika Antona Leševića, sa službom na oružničkoj postaji Donji Lapac, krilnog oružničkog zapovjedništva Gospić, povodom četničke akcije u području kotara Donji Lapac, August 28, 1941, 1–2.

70. On how the local insurgents better armed themselves after each of their attacks during July and August 1941, as well as on their numbers, see Pilipović, "Borba Cvjetnićana na petrovačkom području," 593; on NDH estimates of the numbers of insurgents who had surrounded Kulen Vakuf, see VA, Fond NDH, kut. 67, f. 2, dok. 8, Lički zdrug Ministarstvu domobranstvu—Glavni stožer, August 21, 1941, 2.

71. VA, Fond NDH, kut. 157, f. 16, dok. 6, Izvještaj Jura Pavičića na zahtjev Gosp. Velikog Župana Kvaternik, August 13, 1941, 1. On the forays into Serbian villages for food and other items, see Odić, "Julski dani 1941. na unskoj pruzi," 213.

72. HDA, Fond 1450, MINORS NDH, D-2122, Situacija na dan 4. rujna i u noći 4./5. rujna 1941. godine, September 5, 1941, 2.

73. Pero Pilipović, "Organizacija ustanka u Cvjetniću i okolnim selima," in *Drvar, 1941–1945., knjiga 2*, ed. Morača, 288.

74. ARSBL, Fond 328, Zbirka dokumenata VII JNA (Bosanska Krajina), MUP RAVSIGUR NDH, Izvješće o stanju do 1.IX.1941. godine u 8 sati, September 1, 1941, 1.

75. *Novi list*, "Jedan čas s postradalima iz Bihaća," September 22, 1941, 5.

76. VA, Fond NDH, kut. 2, f. 1, dok. 1, Brzojavka, Zapovjedništvo Vrbaskog divizijskog područja Bosanski Petrovac Ministarstvu domobranstva, Glavni Stožer, Zagreb, 1; on the poor conditions for the army in Kulen Vakuf, see also HDA, Fond 1450, MINORS NDH, D-2121, Situacija u toku 28. i u noći 28./29. kolovoza 1941. godine, August 29, 1941, 2.

77. HDA, Fond 1450, MINORS NDH, D-2121, Situacija na dan 22. kolovoza i u toku noći 22./23. kolovoza, August 23, 1941, 1.

78. HDA, Fond 248, MINORS NDH, kut. 7, Situacija na dan 20. kolovoza i u toku noći 20/21. kolovoza, August 21, 1941, 1.

79. HDA, Fond 1450, MINORS NDH, D-2122, Situacija na dan 5. rujna i u toku noći 5./6. rujna 1941. godine, September 7, 1941, 2.

80. VA, Fond NDH, kut. 157, f. 16, dok. 6, Izvještaj Jura Pavičića na zahtjev Gosp. Velikog Župana Kvaternika, August 13, 1941, 1.

81. Ibid., kut. 152, f. 4, dok. 55, Zapovjedništvo 3. Hrvatske oružničke pukovnije Ravnateljstvu za javni red i sigurnost, Izvješće o komunističko-četničkoj akciji na području krila Gospić, September 4, 1941, 2.

82. Ibid., kut. 152, f. 18, dok. 3, Velika Župa Dubrava Ministarstvu unutarnjih poslova (Upravni odjel); Obćem upravnom povjereništvu kod II armate talijanske vojske, Predmet: Podatci o četničkim stražama i o ponovnu odlasku građana u odmetništvo, October 9, 1941, 1.

83. Ibid., kut. 86, f. 4, dok. 13, Zapovjedništvo I. Hrvatske oružničke pukovnije Vrhovnom oružničkom zapovjedništvu, Izvješće o komunističko-četničkoj akciji na području krila Gospić, September 5, 1941, 2.

84. Ibid., kut. 152a, f. 4, dok. 53, Velika župa Krbava i Psat, Redarstveno ravnateljstvo Bihać Ravnateljstvu za javni red i sigurnost, August 29, 1941, 4.

85. On attempts by the NDH authorities in northwest Bosnia to collect donations to support the Muslim survivors of insurgent attacks in Herzegovina, see *Hrvatska Krajina*, "Banjalučki muslimani poveli su sabirnu akciju za hercegovačke muslimane koji su stradali od srpskih četnika," July 23, 1941, 4.

86. VA, Fond NDH, kut. 152a, f. 4, dok. 53, Velika župa Krbava i Psat, Redarstveno ravnateljstvo Bihać Ravnateljstvu za javni red i sigurnost, August 29, 1941, 4. For a report by an NDH gendarmerie sergeant who fled with the Catholic refugees from Boričevac to Kulen Vakuf, and eventually to Bihać, see HDA, Fond 1450, MINORS NDH, D-2188, Saslušanje oružničkog narednika Antona Leševića, sa službom na oružničkoj postaji Donji Lapac, krilnog oružničkog zapovjedništva Gospić, povodom četničke akcije u području kotara Donji Lapac, August 28, 1941, 1–2.

87. Polovina, *Svedočenje*, 84.

88. Ibid., 85; on non-Ustaša Muslims who defended their villages from insurgents, see Rasim Hurem, "Samo su branili svoja sela," *Ogledalo* 1, no. 2 (December 1990): 32.

89. Polovina, *Svedočenje*, 85.

90. Jovanić, *Ratna sjećanja*, 124. For general information on the fierce nature of the battle for Ćukovi, see Abdulah Sarajlić and Dragutin Strunjaš, "Prvi dani ustanka u Drvaru i okolini," in *Godišnjak istorijskog društva Bosne i Hercegovine*, Godina II, Sarajevo, 1950, 15; *Zbornik NOR-a, tom V, knjiga I*, br. 42, "Izvještaj štaba gerilskih odreda za Liku koncem rujna 1941. god. Štabu drvarske brigade o vojno-političkoj situaciji, undated, but appears to have been written on or about September 15, 1941, 132.

91. LAEB, Bibanović, "Kulen Vakuf," 85; for NDH reports on the insurgent killings of families in Ćukovi and Orašac, see HDA, MINORS, D-2177, Dnevno izvješće o važnijim događajima, prema podatcima oružništva za dan 10. rujna 1941. godine, September 10, 1941, 2.

92. LAEB, Bibanović, "Kulen Vakuf," 86.

93. Ibid., 86–87.

94. Lukač, *Ustanak u Bosanskoj Krajini*, 181.

95. *Zbornik NOR-a, tom V, knjiga 1*, br. 39, Zapisnik sa sastanka delegata Like od 21. rujna 1941. godine, September 21, 1941, 125.

96. VA, Fond NDH, kut. 2, f. 1, dok. 5, Situacija na dan 5. rujna i u toku noći 5./6. rujna 1941. godine, September 6, 1941, 4; see also ibid., kut. 61a, f. 15, dok.

42, Dnevno izvješće o važnijim događajima, prema podatcima oružništva za dan 10. rujna 1941. godine, September 10, 1941, 2.

97. HDA DAKA, Fond RMZDL, Radovi za hronike sela (neobjavljeno), Milan Štikovac, "Neki detalji iz NOB-e, Dobroselo," 2.

98. LAEB, Bibanović, "Kulen Vakuf," 87.

99. VA, Fond NDH, kut. 156, f. 1, dok. 11, Velika župa Sana i Luka Ravnateljstvu za javni red i sigurnost, September 25, 1941, 2.

100. LAEB, Bibanović, "Kulen Vakuf," 89.

101. VA, Fond NDH, kut. 143, f. 2, dok. 39, Zapovjedništvo 3. oružničke pukovnije Zapovjedništvu 4. oružničke pukovnije, September 8, 1941, 3.

102. Ibid., kut. 152a, f. 11a, dok. 27, Zapovjedništvo 3. Hrvatske oružničke pukovnije Ravnateljstvu za javni red i sigurnost, Izvješće o četničkoj akciji, September 3, 1941, 1.

103. Fond 248, MINORS NDH, kut. 7, Izvješće o stanju do 3.IX.1941. godine u 8 sati, September 3, 1941, 1; see also in ibid., Fond 1450, MINORS NDH, D-2251, Izvješće o četničkoj akciji Vrhovnom oružničkom zapovijedništvu, September 3, 1941; *Zbornik NOR-a, tom IV, knjiga 1*, br. 73, Izvještaj Štaba Prvog bataljona "Sloboda" od 1. septembra 1941. god. Štabu drvarske brigade o rezultatima borbi na sektoru Krnjeuša—Bos. Petrovac—Bravski Vaganac, September 1, 1941, 162; ibid., br. 79, Naredba Štaba Prvog bataljona "Sloboda" od 2. septembra 1941. god. komandama jelašinovačkog i trećeg gerilskog odreda o načinu raspodjele zaplijenjenog ratnog materijala i obavještenje o rezultatima borbi četvrtog i petog odreda, September 2, 1941, 182; ibid., br. 87, Članak iz "Gerilca" br. 6 od 6. septembra 1941. god. o uspješnom napadu na neprijateljski logor kod Vrtoča, September 6, 1941, 198; ibid., br. 301, Izvještaj Oružničkog krila Bosanski Petrovac od 2. septembra 1941. god. o napadu na domobranske garizone u Krnjeuši i Vrtoču, September 2, 1941, 664–667.

104. Mušeta, "Kulen Vakuf," 19; interview with Abas Mušeta, July 8, 2012, Crikvenica; for the testimony of a survivor who claimed to see Mehmed Mušeta at one of the sites of mass killing, see DAKA, Fond RMZDL, kut. 4, Originali, Milan Obradović, "Zločini na kotaru Donji Lapac od 1941. do 1945. godine," 22; see also Čučak, *Nebljusi u Narodnooslobodilačkom ratu i revoluciji*, 35–39.

105. HDA, Fond 1220, Centralni komitet (CK) Komunističke Partije Hrvatske (KPH), KP-3/8, 1.

106. For his biographical information, see Đurđević-Đukić, ed., *Narodni heroji Jugoslavije, Knjiga druga N-Ž*, 38–39.

107. *Zbornik NOR-a, tom V, knjiga 1*, br. 22, Uputstvo delegata Centralnog komiteta KPH početkom rujna 1941. god. o organizaciji i zadacima partizanskih odreda, 74–75. Oreskovic-Krntija was later killed by insurgents in October 1941 under circumstances that continue to remain unclear. On his death, see ibid., br. 77, Proglas Okružnog komiteta KPH za Liku koncem listopada 1941. god. povodom mučkog ubistva narodnog heroja Marka Orešković-Krntije, 233–235.

108. *Zbornik NOR-a, tom IV, knjiga 1*, br. 98, Izvještaj Oblasnog Štaba za Hercegovinu i Lepe Perović od septembra 1941. god. Štabu NOP odreda za Bosnu i Hercegovinu o vojno-političkoj situaciji u Hercegovini, September 1941, 222.

109. Ibid., 7, Izvještaj Sekretara Oblasnog komiteta KPJ za Bosansku krajinu od 12. avgusta 1941. god. Pokrajinskom komitetu KPJ za Bosnu i Hercegovinu o

borbama u Bosanskoj krajini i o stanju partiske organizacije u Banjoj Luci i drugim gradovima, August 12, 1941, 27.

110. Polovina, *Svedočenje*, 86.

111. Ibid; on attempts to surrender, see also *Zbornik NOR-a, tom V, knjiga 1*, br. 42, Izvještaj Štaba gerilskih odreda za Liku koncem rujna 1941. god. Štabu drvarske brigade o vojno-političkoj situaciji, 133.

Chapter 6. Forty-Eight Hours

1. Bibanović, "Kulenvakufski komunisti u radničkom pokretu i ustanku," 446; LAEB, Bibanović, "Kulen Vakuf," 90; interview with Abas Mušeta, July 8, 2012, Crikvenica; see also VA, Fond NDH, kut. 61a, f. 15, dok. 44, Dnevno izvješće o važnijim događajima, prema podatcima oružništva za dan 16. rujna 1941. godine, September 16, 1941, 1.

2. ARSBL, Fond 9, KBUVB, Upravno odeljenje II, aj. 11, Ispostava Sreza bosanskog-petrovačkog u Kulen Vakufu Kraljevskoj banskoj upravi, II odeljenja Banja Luka, Predmet: proslava rođendana nj. v. Kralja, September 7, 1938, 1.

3. AJ, Fond 110, DKUZ, f. 230, F. broj 24047, Matijević, Miro, April 29, 1947, 1.

4. LAEB, Esad Bibanović, "Kulen Vakuf i okolina kroz istoriju" (unpub. ms., private collection, Sarajevo), 264.

5. Ibid., Bibanović, "Kulen Vakuf," 91.

6. Interview with Abas Mušeta, July 8, 2012, Crikvenica.

7. VA, Fond NOV, kut. 2000, f. 2, dok. 4, Srez Bihać, Period od okupacije do kraja 1941. godine, Stenografske beleške, June 9, 1951, 13 (lowercase "muslim" in the original).

8. Pilipović, *Romori vrtočke prošlosti*, 188.

9. HDA, Fond 1450, MINORS NDH, D-2122, Situacija na dan 5. rujna i u toku noći 5./6. rujna 1941. godine, September 7, 1941, 4–5; LAEB, Bibanović, "Kulen Vakuf," 95–96. Initial reports by the NDH authorities in Bihać suggested that "about 3500 people were missing" who had left Kulen Vakuf, and that "their fate was unknown." See VA, Fond NDH, kut. 61a, f. 15, dok. 44, Dnevno izvješće o važnijim događajima, prema podatcima oružništva za dan 16. rujna 1941. godine, September 16, 1941, 1.

10. For testimonies of children who lost their parents on the road, see *Novi list*, "Plač i pjesma, krikovi i smijeh, izvijaju se iz grudi nejake dječice, koja su vidjela najveće zlo što ih je mogla stići," September 30, 1941, 8; *Hrvatski narod*, "Još dvije stotine djece žrtava komunističko-četničkih bandi," September 30, 1941, 9.

11. *Hrvatski narod*, "Djeca iz Bosne i Like o zločinima četnika i komunista," September 15, 1941, 5; LAEB, Bibanović, "Kulen Vakuf," 97; interview with Derviš Dervišević, October 1 and 5, 2008, Klisa.

12. Mušeta, "Kulen Vakuf," 46–47.

13. On these shootings along the road, see *Zbornik NOR-a, tom IV, knjiga 1*, br. 114, Izvještaj Štaba partizanskih odreda u Brdu Oraškom drvarske brigade od 9. septembra 1941. god. o borbama za oslobođenje Kulen Vakufa, September 9, 1941, 253–254; Dedijer and Miletić, *Genocid nad Muslimanima*, Komanda 3. Žandarmerijske pukovnije Banja Luka Vrhovnoj komandi Žandarmerije NDH Zagreb, September 12, 1941, 66; Nikica Pilipović, "Vrtoče u ustanku 1941.," in *Ustanak*

naroda Jugoslavije 1941. Pišu učesnici, Zbornik, knjiga četvrta, ed. Koča Popović (Belgrade: Vojnoizdavački zavod JNA "Vojno delo," 1964), 869.

14. Testimony of Mujo Dervišević in Ibrahim Kajan, "Pakao Vakuf Golubnjača," *Ogledalo*, godina 1, no. 2 (prosinac/decembar 1990): 26. Other survivors reported seeing babies who were still alive trying to nurse from the breasts of their dead mothers. Interview with Murat Mušeta, September 27, 2008, Kulen Vakuf. See also Mušeta, "Kulen Vakuf," 46–47.

15. *Zbornik NOR-a, tom IV, knjiga 1*, br. 114, Izvještaj Štaba partizanskih odreda u Brdu Oraškom drvarske brigade od 9. septembra 1941. god. o borbama za oslobođenje Kulen Vakufa, September 9, 1941, 253–254.

16. Pilipović, "Borba Cvjetnićana na petrovačkom području," 601.

17. See, for example, LAEB, Bibanović, "Kulen Vakuf," 97; for an NDH source, see Komanda 3. Žandarmerijske pukovnije Banja Luka o pokolju Muslimanima Kulen Vakufa, 12. rujna 1941., in Tucakovic, *Srpski zločini nad Bošnjacima-Muslimanima*, 194–196; for the names of twenty-five men, women and children from the villages of Klisa and Ostrovica who appear to have been killed on the road near Prkosi and Ćovka, see AJ, Fond 110, DKUZ, kut. 531, dos. br. 5361, Zapisnik br. 10, Mjesni odbor: Kalati, August 5, 1946, 7.

18. Sava Mileusnić, "Donji Lapac u ustanku," 396.

19. *Zbornik NOR-a, tom V, knjiga 1*, br. 42, Izvještaj Štaba gerilskih odreda za Liku koncem rujna 1941. god. Štabu drvarske brigade o vojno-političkoj situaciji, 133.

20. On the continuing shooting at the unarmed civilians after the battle ended, see Komanda 3. Žandarmerijske pukovnije Banja Luka Vrhovnoj komandi Žandarmerije NDH Zagreb, September 12, 1941, in Dedijer and Miletić, *Genocid nad Muslimanima*, 66.

21. On the participation of Nikola Karanović in ordering the executions, see LAEB, Bibanović, Radni materijal za knjigu "Kulen Vakuf i okolina," 187; on the role of his men, as well as those of commander Branko Rađenović, during the shootings on the road see, *Zbornik NOR-a, tom V, knjiga 1*, br. 42, Izvještaj Štaba gerilskih odreda za Liku koncem rujna 1941. god. Štabu drvarske brigade o vojno-političkoj situaciji, 133; on Mane Rokvić's presence near the village of Prkosi, and his role in taking away a group of Muslim men, who were later executed, see ABiH, Fond ZKUZ BiH, kut. 88, Srez Drvar, Selo Boričevac, Svjedokinja Kadić Zejna, Mjesni narodni odbor Kulen Vakuf (undated, handwritten document, most likely from 1946), 1.

22. Šiljdedić's testimony appears to have been recorded during the late 1970s or early 1980s by local historian Esad Bibanović.

23. Šiljdedić recounted the names of nearly thirty Muslims who were murdered at the Dugopolje pit, including fathers and sons whom the insurgents executed together. He eventually managed to pull himself out: "I spent two days and two nights there. Rain fell and I was wearing only my under shorts and shirt. I gathered my strength and with a great effort managed to pull myself out. I went towards Bihać. Not far from the pit I came across a [Orthodox] peasant who had a *rogulj* [a long metal rod for roasting meat]. To defend myself I picked up two rocks. He passed by me. He didn't say a word." See LAEB, Bibanović, "Kulen Vakuf," 97–98.

24. VA, Fond NOV, kut. 1997, f. 8, dok, 4, Drago Đukić, "Pripreme ustanka, ustanak i borbe 1941. godine u bosansko-petrovačkom srezu," 25.

25. On Stojan Matić's role, see HDA DAKA, Fond 143, Memoarsko gradivo o NOR-u, Lika 2 (LI-2), 30/2010, Sava Mileusnić, "Organizacija i djelatnost KPJ u uslovima Drugog svjetskog rata na kotaru Donji Lapac," 1963, 21.

26. HDA DAKA, Fond RMZDL, Radovi za hronike sela (neobjavljeno), "Bušević u Narodnooslobodilačkoj borbi 1941–1945," 1980, 44.

27. LAEB, Bibanović, "Kulen Vakuf," 98–99; ibid., "Stanovništvo Kulen-Vakufa," 189.

28. Bibanović, "Kulenvakufski komunisti u radničkom pokretu i ustanku," 447.

29. LAEB, Bibanović, "Kulen Vakuf," 91–92.

30. Ibid.

31. Bibanović, "Kulenvakufski komunisti u radničkom pokretu i ustanku," 447; on this incident, see also Kosta Nađ, "Iz ratnih dana," in *Četrdeset godina. Zbornik sećanja aktivista jugoslovenskog revolucionarnog radničkog pokreta, 1941–1945, knjiga 5*, ed. Pero Morača (Belgrade: Kultura, 1961), 318.

32. Jovanić, *Ratna sjećanja*, 125.

33. Grbić, "Cvjetnićka četa," 358; Reljić, "Martin Brod 1941. godine," 403; for biographical information about Petar Đilas, see VA, Sekretarijat unutarnjih poslova Socijalističke Republike Hrvatske [hereafter SUP SRH], Otsjek zaštite naroda za Liku I., br. 2, Četnička-vojno politička organizacija u Lici, January 9, 1945, 5.

34. Jovanić, *Ratna sjećanja*, 125.

35. LAEB, Bibanović, "Kulen Vakuf," 100.

36. On Stipan Kovačević's supposed involvement with the local Ustaša units, see AJ, Fond DKUZ, kut. 817, Okružni sud Bihać, Pojedinačne optužnice i presude, 1946, dos. br. 817-320, Javno tužioštvo za Okrug Bihać, Krivični predmet protiv Burzić Avde, May 27, 1946, 1; on his killing and that of Jakov Markovinović, see LAEB, Bibanović, "Kulen Vakuf," 100–101.

37. On the decapitation of Bećo Mehadžić, see LAEB, Bibanović, "Kulen Vakuf," 100–101; on the killings of the ten or so men on the bridge, ABiH, Fond ZKUZ BiH, kut. 88, Svjedočenje Altića Aijše i Kadića Zejne (undated and handwritten document, most likely from the summer of 1946).

38. LAEB, Bibanović, "Kulen Vakuf," 99.

39. HDA DAKA, Fond RMZDL, kut. 3 (originali), Marko Šašić, "Lapački bataljon Stojan Matić" (undated, most likely written in the late 1970s or early 1980s), 5; on Stojan Matić's departure, see ibid., Fond 143, Memoarsko gradivo o NOR-u, Lika 2 (LI-2), 30/2010, Sava Mileusnić, "Organizacija i djelatnost KPJ u uslovima Drugog svjetskog rata na kotaru Donji Lapac," 1963, 21; on Gojko Polovina's role in organizing a group of insurgents to leave Kulen Vakuf and attack the NDH forces near the village of Nebljusi, see Polovina, *Svedočenje*, 352–353.

40. Polovina, *Svedočenje*, 86–87.

41. On the insurgents forcing their way into taverns and stealing from stores on the evening of September 6, 1941, see *Zbornik NOR-a, tom V, knjiga 1*, br. 42, Izvještaj Štaba gerilskih odreda za Liku koncem rujna 1941. god. Štabu drvarske brigade o vojno-političkoj situaciji, undated but appears to have been written on or about September 15, 1941, 134; see also Danilo Damjanović-Danić, "Pad Kulen Vakufa," in *Bosanski Petrovac u NOB, Knjiga I*, ed. Čerkez, 666.

42. On the burning of the town, see *Zbornik NOR-a, tom IV, knjiga 1*, br. 106, Naređenje Štaba prvog bataljona "Sloboda" od 8. septembra 1941. god. Komandama

četvrtog odreda, odreda u Boboljuskama, Velikom i Malom Cvjetniću i Osredcima za raspored snaga, September 8, 1941, 237; ibid., br. 114, Izvještaj Štaba partizanskih odreda u Brdu Oraškom drvarske brigade od 9. septembra 1941. god. o borbama za oslobođenje Kulen Vakufa, September 9, 1941, 254.

43. On these killings in July, see Odić, "Julski dani 1941. na unskoj pruzi," 213–214.

44. Karanović, "Sadjejstvo sa ličkim ustanicima," 413. On the exhumation of these bodies, and the reactions to them, see Lukač, *Ustanak u Bosanskoj Krajini*, 191–192; *Zbornik NOR-a, tom V, knjiga 1*, br. 42, Izvještaj Štaba gerilskih odreda za Liku koncem rujna 1941. god. Štabu drvarske brigade o vojno-političkoj situaciji, undated but appears to have been written on or about September 15, 1941, 134; see also ibid., br. 39, Zapisnik sa sastanka vojnih delegata Like od 21. rujna 1941. godine, September 21, 1941, 125.

45. Vukčević, ed., *Zločini*, br. 332, Izveštaj Kotarske oblasti u Glamoču od 18. oktobra 1941. o pomoći italijanskih vojnih vlasti srpskom življu u prenošenju leševa ubijenih pravoslavaca bačenih u jame, October 16, 1941, 828–829.

46. Plećaš-Nitonja, *Požar u Krajini*, 87.

47. Radošević, "Vrtoče u ustanku," 472.

48. Karanović, "Sadjejstvo sa ličkim ustanicima," 413.

49. *Zbornik NOR-a, tom V, knjiga 1*, br. 42, Izvještaj Štaba gerilskih odreda za Liku koncem rujna 1941. god. Štabu drvarske brigade o vojno-političkoj situaciji, undated but appears to have been written on or about September 15, 1941, 134.

50. On this dynamic in Ukraine in 1941, see Redlich, *Together and Apart in Brzezany*, 105–107; Omer Bartov, "White Spaces and Black Holes," in *The Shoah in Ukraine: history, testimony, memorialization*, ed. Ray Brandon and Wendy Lower (Bloomington: Indiana University Press, 2008), 318–353; Timothy Snyder, "The Life and Death West Volhyinian Jewry, 1921–1945, in *The Shoah in Ukraine*, ed. Brandon and Lower, 91; Lower, "Pogroms, Mob Violence and Genocide in Western Ukraine, Summer 1941," 221.

51. LAEB, Bibanović, "Kulen Vakuf," 103.

52. Jovanić, *Ratna sjećanja*, 128.

53. On this phase of the killings, see LAEB, Bibanović, "Kulen Vakuf," 100–101; see also ABiH, Fond ZKUZ BiH, kut. 88, Svjedočenje Altića Aijše i Kadića Zejne (undated and hand-written document, most likely from the summer of 1946).

54. LAEB, Bibanović, "Kulen Vakuf," 103; ibid., "Stanovništvo Kulen-Vakufa," 195.

55. Randall Collins, *Violence: A Micro-sociological Theory* (Princeton, N.J.: Princeton University Press, 2008), 94.

56. Frijda, "The Lex Talionis," 279.

57. Collins, *Violence*, 121; on the dynamics of a "forward panic" more generally, see chapter 3 in ibid.

58. Polovina, *Svedočenje*, 91.

59. Ibid.

60. Testimony of Hana Štrkljević in LAEB, Bibanović, "Kulen Vakuf," 101.

61. Halil Puškar, *Krajiški pečat* (Istanbul, s.n., 1996), 97.

62. The act of killing one's own children and subsequent suicide, such as what took place by the Una River, was noted in other locations in the NDH, such as Herzegovina, that came under insurgent attack. See, for example, *Novi list*, "Grozna nedjela

razbješnjelih četničko-komunističkih bandi nad mirnim i golorukim Hrvatima muslimanima u stolačkom kotaru," September 10, 1941, 5.

63. Interview with Mujo Demirović, September 30, 2008, Bihać; Murat Mušeta on September 27, 2008, Kulen Vakuf; Mehmed Štrkljević, September 28, 2008, Kulen Vakuf; see also Demirović, *Bosna i Bošnjaci u srpskoj politici*, 274; for a partial list of thirteen women and children (between the ages of four and forty-nine) who died in these instances, see AJ, Fond 110, DKUZ, kut. 531, dos. br. 5361, Zapisnik br. 10, Mjesni odbor: Kalati, August 5, 1946, 7.

64. Interviews with Adil Kulenović, November 7, 2006, Sarajevo; anonymous informant, September 24, 2008.

65. Interview with Bećo Pehlivanović, October 3, 2008, Bihać.

66. *Hrvatski narod*, "Hrvatska se pobrinula za djecu čiji su roditelji postradali u borbi s četnicima," September 22, 1941, 4.

67. Kurtagić, *Zapisi o Kulen Vakufu*, 32; Mušeta, "Kulen Vakuf," 48. Some memoir evidence suggests that there were instances in which insurgents took girls, particularly those from the families of former Muslim landholders, and kept them prisoner for days while passing them around from insurgent to insurgent to be raped. See LAEB, Bibanović, "Stanovništvo Kulen-Vakufa," 290.

68. *Zbornik NOR-a, tom V, knjiga 1*, br. 42, Izvještaj Štaba gerilskih odreda za Liku koncem rujna 1941. god. Štabu drvarske brigade o vojno-političkoj situaciji, 134.

69. Frijda, "The Lex Talionis," 279.

70. Kajan, "Pakao Vakuf Golubnjača," 26.

71. *Novi list*, "Jedan čas s postradalima iz Bihaća," September 22, 1941, 5.

72. LAEB, Bibanović, "Stanovništvo Kulen-Vakufa," 195.

73. Jovanić, *Ratna sjećanja*, 127.

74. Plećaš-Nitonja, *Požar u Krajini*, 87.

75. On these cases, see Horowitz, *The Deadly Ethnic Riot*, 114–115; for instances in which experiencing pleasure and a sense of rejoicing were responses by fighters after having taking vengeance in guerrilla fighting during the American Civil War, see Fellman, *Inside War*, 186; on violence and effervescence, see Oskar Verkaaik, "Fun and Violence. Ethnocide and the effervescence of collective aggression," *Social Anthropology* 11, no. 1 (2003): 3–22.

76. See Collins, *Violence*, chap. 3.

77. For a partial list of such families, see Husejn Altić, "Bivši Kulen Vakuf," *Narodna uzdanica Književni zbornik za godinu 1943*, god. XI (Sarajevo: Narodna uzdanica, 1942), 15–19; for testimonies of child survivors who witnessed the near total destruction of their extended families, see *Novi list*, "Sinoć je u Zagreb stiglo daljnjih 200 siročadi—žrtava četničkih krvavih zlodjela," September 15, 1941, 9; see also *Hrvatski narod*, "Hrvatska se pobrinula za djecu čiji su roditelji postradali u borbi s četnicima," September 22, 1941, 4.

78. LAEB, Bibanović, "Stanovništvo Kulen-Vakufa," 195.

79. Interview with Đula Seferović, October 13, 2008, Ostrovica.

80. Kajan, "Pakao Vakuf Golubnjača," 26.

81. Polovina, "Sjećanja na početni period narodnog ustanka u Lici," 798.

82. Interview with Abas Mušeta, July 8, 2012, Crikvenica.

83. Interview with Sead Kadić, November 3, 2008, Bihać; Mehmed Štrkljević, September 28, 2008, Kulen Vakuf; Kemal Štrkljević, September 27, 2008, Kulen Vakuf;

Svetozar Tankosić, October 16, 2008, Martin Brod. See also Damjanović-Danić, "Pad Kulen Vakufa," 666.

84. Testimony of Hana Štrkljević in LAEB, Bibanović, "Kulen Vakuf," 101; on the story of Hana Štrkljević and the individuals who saved her life, see also Puškar, *Krajiški pečat*, 97.

85. Testimony of Hana Štrkljević in LAEB, Bibanović, "Stanovništvo Kulen-Vakufa," 193.

86. On their presence, see Mušeta, "Kulen Vakuf," 53–56; Begić, *Zločini ustanika*, 165, note 313.

87. Interview with Ale Galijašević, October 12, 2008, Kulen Vakuf.

88. Interview with Murat Mušeta, September 27, 2008, Kulen Vakuf.

89. Karanović, "Sadjejstvo sa ličkim ustanicima," 413.

90. It appears that most of those who risked these interventions were communist-oriented fighters. See, for example, VA, Fond NOV, kut. 1997, f. 8, dok, 4, Drago Đukić, "Pripreme ustanka, ustanak i borbe 1941. godine u bosansko-petrovačkom srezu," 25.

91. Testimony of Fata Hodžić-Selimović in LAEB, Bibanović, "Kulen Vakuf," 102.

92. Bibanović, "Kulenvakufski komunisti u radničkom pokretu i ustanku," 452; see also the testimony of Mujo Dervišević, who was among the prisoners when this order was given, in LAEB, Bibanović, "Stanovništvo Kulen-Vakufa," 287.

93. LAEB, Bibanović, "Kulen Vakuf," 105; ibid., "Stanovništvo Kulen-Vakufa," 35, note 91; for biographical information on Šipka, see Đurđević-Đukić, ed., *Narodni heroji Jugoslavije, Knjiga druga N-Ž*, 235–236.

94. Milka Pilipović Mandžuka, "Očeva smrt," in *Drvar, 1941–1945., knjiga 2*, ed. Morača, 517; on Vladetić's pre-1941 friendships with several of the prisoners in Martin Brod, see also Polovina, *Svedočenje*, 92.

95. Interview with Dimitar Reljić, June 22, 2013, Martin Brod.

96. Testimony of Mujo Dervišević in Kajan, "Pakao Vakuf Golubnjača," 27.

97. Ibid.

98. Polovina, *Svedočenje*, 92.

99. Pilipović Mandžuka, "Očeva smrti," 517–519; Polovina, *Svedočenje*, 92; in a conversation a few days later with the communist commander Gojko Polovina, Vladetić recalled that these arguments also concerned who among the insurgents would take the property stolen from the prisoners in Kulen Vakuf, much of which had been brought to Martin Brod on horse-drawn carts. See Polovina, *Svedočenje*, 92.

100. Milgram, *Obedience to Authority*, 111.

101. For an illuminating example of a work on mass violence that relies primarily on psychological explanations, particularly those related to "group dynamics," see Fujii, *Killing Neighbors*.

102. On notions of distance between killer and victim, and the differing levels of psychological strain involved, see Lt. Col. Dave Grossman, *On Killing: The Psychological Cost of Learning to Kill in War and Society* (New York: Black Bay Books, 1995), especially section III.

103. As one such report indicated: "In some areas unconfirmed stories are circulating that the rebels are fighting amongst themselves and with their leaders." See VA, Fond NDH, kut. 143, f. 2, dok. 50, Zapovjedništvo 3. oružničke pukovnije Zapovjedništvu 4. oružničke pukovnije, Doglasno izvješće dostavlja, September 18, 1941, 2.

104. Knežević, "Cvjetnićani u akciji," 462.

105. Polovina, *Svedočenje*, 91–92.
106. Kajan, "Pakao Vakuf Golubnjača," 27.
107. Polovina, *Svedočenje*, 91.
108. Ibid., 91–92.
109. Jovanić, "Ustanak u donjolapačkom kotaru 1941. godine," 154; Polovina, *Svedočenje*, 92.
110. Testimony of Mujo Dervišević in LAEB, Bibanović, "Kulen Vakuf," 103.
111. Kajan, "Pakao Vakuf Golubnjača," 27.
112. Testimony of Mujo Dervišević in LAEB, Bibanović, "Kulen Vakuf," 103.
113. Kajan, "Pakao Vakuf Golubnjača," 27.
114. Testimony of Mujo Dervišević in LAEB, Bibanović, "Kulen Vakuf," 103–104.
115. Kajan, "Pakao Vakuf Golubnjača," 27.
116. HDA, Fond 223, MUP NDH, kut. 32, Kotarsko poglavarstvo Bihać Ministarstvu unutarnjih poslova u Zagrebu, Predmet: izvješće o izbjeglicama, September 18, 1941, 1–2.
117. LAEB, Bibanović, "Stanovništvo Kulen-Vakufa," 195; on this estimate, see also Zorić, *Drvar u ustanku 1941.*, 212.
118. For an NDH account of the massacres in and around Kulen Vakuf, which was written less than a week after they occurred, see HDA, Fond 1450, MINORS NDH, D-2251, Zapovjedništvo 3. oružničke pukovnije Vrhovnom oružničkom zapovjedništvu, Izvješće o napadu četnika na Kulen Vakuf, September 12, 1941, 1–2; on the number of more than 2,000 "missing," whom NDH military officers considered "killed or captured," see VA, Fond NDH, kut. 143, f. 2, dok. 50, Zapovjedništvo 3. oružničke pukovnije Zapovjedništvu 4. oružničke pukovnije, Doglasno izvješće dostavlja, September 18, 1941, 2. A precise list of all the victims will most likely never be possible to compile, due to the lack of detailed information collected around the time of the killings. The NDH statistics on the number of refugees who arrived to Bihać appears to be our best tool to use in order to determine the number of dead. For a very partial list of victims complied by the Yugoslav communist authorities in the mid-1960s, which was part of a state-wide attempt to more accurately determine the numbers of war dead, see *Žrtve rata 1941.–1945. Popis iz 1964. godine, SR Bosna i Hercegovina (Banovići—Bosanski Novi)* (Belgrade: Savezni zavod za statistiku, 1992), 95–99, 119–127, 135–139. These numbers include victims from Kulen Vakuf, Klisa, Ćukovi, Orašac, and Ostrovica.
119. See Gross, *Neighbors.*
120. See Snyder, *Bloodlands.*
121. For a trenchant critique of Snyder's book *Bloodlands* along such lines, see Jan T. Gross, "A Colonial History of the Bloodlands," *Kritika: Explorations in Russian and Eurasian History* 15, no. 3 (2014): 591–596.
122. *Zbornik NOR-a, tom IV, knjiga 1*, br. 138, Naređenje Štaba drvarske brigade od 14. septembra 1941. god. Štabu bataljona ličkih NOP odreda za podnošenje izvještaja o stanju na području bataljona i za stezanje obručja oko Bihaća, i obavještenje o situaciji poslije četničke izdaje, September 14, 1941, 302.
123. *Zbornik NOR-a, tom V, knjiga 1*, br. 42, Izvještaj Štaba gerilskih odreda za Liku koncem rujna 1941. god. Štabu drvarske brigade o vojno-političkoj situaciji, undated but appears to have been written on or about September 15, 1941, 134; See also *Zbornik NOR-a, tom IV, knjiga 1*, br. 114, Izvještaj Štaba partizanskih odreda u Brdu

Oraškom drvarske brigade od 9. septembra 1941. god. o borbama za oslobođenje Kulen Vakufa, September 9, 1941, 253–254.

124. VA, Fond NOV, kut. 1701, f. 2/I, dok. 11, Štab risovačkog bataljona oslobodilačke vojske u Brdu Oraškom Štabu brigade nacionalno oslobodilačkih odreda Drvar, September 13, 1941, 1.

125. Ibid., f. 2/I, dok. 4, Štab II bataljona Štabu N.O.G.O Drvar, September 10, 1941, 1.

126. *Zbornik NOR-a, tom IV, knjiga 1*, br. 106, Naređenje Štaba prvog bataljona "Sloboda" od 8. septembra 1941. god. Komandama četvrtog odreda u Boboljuskama, Velikom i Malom Cvjetniću i Osredcima za raspored snaga, September 8, 1941, 237.

127. See, for example, VA, Fond NOV, kut. 1701, f. 23, dok. 3, Štab II Bataljona Gerilskih odreda za Veliki Cvjetnić i okolinu Komandantu brigade Drvar, September 16, 1941, 1; ibid., kut. 1701, f. 23, dok. 2, Štab II Bataljona Gerilskih odreda za Veliki Cvjetnić i okolinu Komandiru čete Bjelajske, September 10, 1941, 1; *Zbornik NOR-a, tom IV, knjiga 1*, br. 146, Naređenje Štaba Drvarske brigade od 15. septembra 1941. god. Štabu Drugog bataljona za raspored bataljona i način njegovog vođenja borbe, 326–327; ibid., br. 149, Izvještaj Operativnog oficira Štaba Prvog bataljona "Sloboda" od 15. septembra 1941. god. Štabu bataljona o izvršenom obilasku drugog, četvrtog i petog odreda, September 15, 1941, 335.

128. VA, Fond NDH, kut. 213, f. 2, dok. 48, Iz saslušanja domobrana koji su bili zarobljeni u Drvaru i koji su se vratili 22. rujna, October 7, 1941, 1.

129. VA, Fond NOV, kut. 1701, f. 2/I, dok. 18, Štab II Bataljona Gerilskog odreda za Veliki Cvjetnić i okolinu Komandantu brigade Drvar, Ubiranje dobrovoljnog priloga, September 15, 1941, 1.

130. Ibid., dok. 17, Štab II Bataljona Gerilskog odreda za Veliki Cvjetnić i okolinu Komadantu brigade Drvar, Moli da se dostavi izvesna količina municije, September 15, 1941, 1. Đilas had mentioned his units' lack of ammunition in a letter that he sent to the main command of the "Sloboda" battalion on September 13, but did not specifically identify "the occupation of Kulen Vakuf" as the reason for it. See VA, Fond NOV, kut. 1700, f. 4, dok. 1, Štab II Bataljona Gerilskog odreda za Veliki Cvjetnić i okolinu Komadantu brigade "Sloboda," September 13, 1941, 1.

131. VA, Fond NOV, kut. 1701, f. 2/I, dok. 4, Štab II bataljona Štabu N.O.G.O Drvar, September 10, 1941, 1.

132. Nađ, *Ustanak*, 208.

133. *Novi list*, "Grozna nedjela razbješnjelih četničko-komunističkih bandi nad mirnim i golorukim Hrvatima muslimanima u stolačkom kotaru," September 10, 1941, 5 (lowercase "muslim" in the original).

134. ARSBL, Fond 74, Velika Župa Sana i Luka, 3005/41, untitled and undated document (most likely from late summer or early autumn 1941), written by insurgents in the Banja Luka region.

135. See, for example, Fikreta Jelić-Butić, *Četnici u Hrvatskoj 1941.–1945.* (Zagreb: Globus, 1986); Đuro Stanisavljević, "Pojava i razvitak četničkog pokreta u Hrvatskoj," *Istorija XX veka—Zbornik radova* (Belgrade, 1962): 5–140.

136. See, for example, Hurem, *Kriza Narodnooslobodilačkog pokreta.*

137. On Rokvić, see VA, Fond NDH, kut. 202, f. 2, dok. 33, Kotarska oblast Bosanski Petrovac Velikoj Župi Krbava i Psat Bihać, Četnički vojvoda: o Mani Rokviću, August 2, 1943, 1; ibid., Velika Župa Krbava i Psat, Predmet: Mane

Rokvić—'Četnički vojvoda' u Bosanskom Petrovcu—podaci, August 2, 1943, 1; ABiH, Fond ZKUZ BiH, kut. 91, Zapisnik br. 22, Mjesni odbor: Malo Očijevo, August 9, 1946, 2; ibid., kut. 68, Srez Bosanski Petrovac, Zapisnik br. 18, Mjesni odbor: Prkosi, August 4, 1946, 3; ARSBL, Kartoteka ratnih zločinaca, Mane Rokvić; on Đilas, see Reljić, "Martin Brod 1941. godine," 404–405; Polovina, *Svedočenje*, 92–93; Pero Pilipović, "Istina o jednom zločinu," in *Bosanski Petrovac u NOB, Knjiga II*, ed. Čerkez, 605; *Zbornik NOR-a, tom V, knjiga 1*, br. 42, Izvještaj Štaba gerilskih odreda za Liku koncem rujna 1941. god. Štabu drvarske brigade o vojno-političkoj situaciji, undated but appears to have been written on or about September 15, 1941, 134.

138. AJ, Fond 110, DKUZ, dos. br. 3793, 5394, OKUZ za Liku, Zapisnik sastavljen pred komisijom u Beglucima, May 25, 1945, 1–2.

139. Testimony of Mujo Dervišević in Kajan, "Pakao Vakuf Golubnjača," 27.

140. For examples of this political work, see *Zbornik dokumenata i podataka o Narodnooslobodilačkom ratu jugoslovenskih naroda* [hereafter *Zbornik NOR-a*], *tom IV, knjiga 2, Borbe u Bosni i Hercegovini* (Belgrade: Vojno-istoriski institut Jugoslovenske Armije, 1951), br. 57, "Otvoreno pismo Glavnog štaba NOP Odreda za Bosnu i Hercegovinu od novembra 1941. god. Zavedenim četnicima o izdajničkom radu Majora Dangića," November 20, 1941, 143–144; AMUSK, Prijepisi originalnih dokumenata iz AHRP, 3 četa bataljona "Miloš Čavića" partizanskog odreda Banije Oružničkoj postaji Otoka, March 31, 1942, 1.

141. LAEB, Bibanović, "Stanovništvo Kulen-Vakufa," 331–332.

142. Among the victims were Hamdija Šimdedić of Kulen Vakuf and Muharem Stupac of Orašac, whose bodies showed signs of having been repeatedly stabbed, and whose throats has been cut. Other corpses were found in similar conditions, but were so badly deformed that they could not be identified. On the exhumations, see VA, Fond NDH, k. 281, f. 4, dok. 1–46, Zapisnik o izkopavanju lješeva poubijenih građana grada Bihaća za vrieme boravka partizana u Bihaću, March 2, 1943, 1; on the fact that many of these victims were from the Kulen Vakuf region, see ibid., kut. 281, f. 4, dok. 1–60, Zapisnik sastavljen u prostorijama ustaškog logora u Bihaću, February 16, 1943, 1.

143. For another example of the settling of scores that went on during the Partisan takeover of Bihać in 1942, during which fighters from the Kulen Vakuf region sought out former Muslim neighbors whom they believed had been Ustašas, see Kurtagić, *Zapisi o Kulen Vakufu*, 37; see also ABiH, Fond ZKUZ BiH, Zapisnici Srez Drvar, kut. 91, Zapisnik sastavljen kod NOO-a Malo Očijevo, Opština Martin Brod, Srez drvarski, January 28, 1945, 1, which suggests that two other men from Kulen Vakuf, Omer Kadić and Hilmija Altić, were killed during the Partisan victory in Bihać.

Chapter 7. Sudden Nationhood

1. On the refugees' experiences, see, for example, HDA, Fond 226, Ministarstvo zdravstva i udružbe NDH, kut. 7, Kotarska oblast u Kutini, Predmet: Molba izbeglica iz Orašca da ih se preseli, December 16, 1941, 1; Kotarska oblast Cazin, Predmet: Izbeglica iz Orašca preselenje iz Moslovačkog selišta, January 22, 1942, 1; for a list of local men who joined the Partisans, see AMUSK, Zbirka informacija o spomenicima NOB, fas. 47, Kulen Vakuf, Odbor za izgradnju spomenika palim borcima NOR-a

Kulen Vakuf, Predmet: Utvrđeni spisak palih boraca NOR-a od 1941. do 15. maja 1945. godine, April 3, 1981, 1–6.

2. Dušan Knežević, "Omladinska radna akcija u selu Orašcu," in *Bosanski Petrovac u NOB. Zbornik sjećanja. Knjiga IV*, ed. Vladimir Čerkez (Bosanski Petrovac: Opštinski odbor SUBNOR-a Bosanski Petrovac, 1974), 253.

3. Interview with Derviš Dervišević, October 1 and 5, 2008, Klisa; Smajo Hodžić, June 23, 2013, Ćukovi; Mujo Hasanagić, November 4, 2008, Kulen Vakuf; Ale Galijašević, October 12, 2008, Kulen Vakuf; Maho Vazović, September 24, 2008, Kulen Vakuf; anonymous informant, October 11, 2008; on instances of children who were separated in 1941, see Nurija Rošić, "Arena traži vaše najmilije. Sjetili se pljeska," *Arena*, 1978 (date and month unknown), 20, which discusses a brother and sister, Derviš Dervišević and his sister Šefika of Klisa, who did not reunite until the 1970s.

4. AUSK, Fond Sreskog komiteta Saveza komunista Bosne i Hercegovine Bihać [hereafter SK SK BiH Bihać], kut. 145, Neki problemi u Kulen Vakufu koji se moraju odmah riješiti, August 21, 1953, 3; see also ABiH, Fond Centralnog komiteta Saveza komunista Bosne i Hercegovine [hereafter CK SK BiH], kut. 175, Izvještaj za mjesec decembar 1947. godine o radu i stanju na terenu sreza Bosanski Petrovac, December 29, 1947, 1.

5. *Krajina*, "Kulenvakufske ruševine," November 3, 1957, 4.

6. Interview with Mustafa Dervišević, October 11, 2008, Klisa.

7. Interview with Derviš Dervišević, October 1, 2008, Klisa.

8. ABiH, Fond CK SK BiH, kut., 220, Mjesečni izvještaj o radu SK KPJ Bosanski Petrovac, March 30, 1948, 1.

9. Ibid., kut. 297, Izvještaj sa terena Srez Bosanski Petrovac, Bihać, Unska Pruga, Cazin, 1948, 29; ibid., kut. 318, Dnevne informacije Sreskih komiteta, 1949, Sreski komitet Bihać, May 11, 1949, 1.

10. Ibid., kut. 318, Dnevne informacije Sreskih komiteta, 1949, Sreski komitet Bihać, May 1, 1949, 1; May 28, 1949, 1; June 22, 1949, 1; June 28, 1949, 1; July 12, 1949, 1.

11. Đuro Kresoje was the secretary of the local committee of the Communist Party in Orašac and Mićo Radak held the same position in Kulen Vakuf. See ibid., kut. 327, Zapisnik sa sastanka Sreskog komiteta Komunističke Partije, Bosanski Petrovac, May 3, 1949, 1; during the first postwar decades, the communist authorities did not designate the category "Muslim" as an official "nation" (*narod*) or "nationality" (*nacionalnost*), but nonetheless still counted party members during this time according to whether it was perceived that they belonged to this category. See, for example, ibid., kut. bez broja, Ukupan broj Muslimana članova SK prema popisu 31.III.1958. i njihovo nacionalno opredeljenje, 1958. (It is unclear if the "M" in "Muslimana" was written in a capital or lowercase "m," as the entire title was typed in capital letters.)

12. In 1955, there were thirteen members in the local committee of the League of Communists for the municipality (*opština*) of Kulen Vakuf, with eleven described as "Serbs" and two as "Muslims." Leadership positions, such as party secretary, were almost always held by "Serbs," and this situation did not change through the 1950s. See AUSK, Fond SK SK BiH Bihać, kut. 147, Spisak rukovodećeg kadra u Savezu komunista i predsjednika NO opština na terenu sreza Bihać, September 27, 1955; ibid., kut, 152, Analiza o kadru u opštinskom komitetu i osnovnim organizacijama

Saveza komunista na području opštine Kulen Vakuf, January 10, 1956, 1; ibid., Spisak predsjednika NO opština i sekretara komiteta sreza bihaćkog, 1956, 1. By 1959, the imbalance was still striking. According to reports that the League of Communists compiled, the ethnic composition of the population of the municipality of Kulen Vakuf was described as 5,300 Serbs (57%), 270 Croats (2.9%) and 3,720 Muslims (40.1%); yet the composition of the League of Communists was 196 Serbs (76%), 7 Croats (2.7%), and 59 Muslims (23%). See ABiH, Fond CK SK BiH, kut. 7, Izvještaj o radu na brojnom jačanju organizacija Saveza komunista na opštinama Bihać, Bosanska Krupa, i Kulen Vakuf, June 15, 1959, 11.

13. More than ten years after the war, out the 230 members of the municipal committee of the League of Communists for Kulen Vakuf, 32 had no education whatsoever, while 162 had only finished some primary school. Nineteen had some kind of skilled training, and only thirteen had finished high school. None had finished university. See AUSK, Fond SK SK BiH Bihać, kut. 151, OK SK BiH Kulen Vakuf, Mjesečni izvještaj o godinama starosti članova Saveza komunista na terenu, April 5, 1956.

14. ABiH, Fond CK SK BiH, kut. 192, Analiza informacije iz mjesečnih izvještaja partijskih rukovodstava, December 16, 1947, 3.

15. Ibid., kut. 205, Mjesečni izvještaj o radu SK KPJ Bihać, January 31, 1948, 2.

16. On Polovina, see his memoir, *Svedočenje*; on Matić, see Stanisavljević, "Narodni heroj, Matić Ilije Stojan," in *Kotar Donji Lapac u Narodnooslobodilačkom ratu*, ed. Vezmar and Zatezalo, 974; see also Đurđević-Đukić, ed., *Narodni heroji Jugoslavije, Knjiga prva A-M*, 497–498; on Pilipović Maćuka, see Knežević Niko, "Maćuka," in *Drvar, 1941–1945.*, ed. Morača, 86–88; on Jovanić, see Đurđević-Đukić, ed., *Narodni heroji Jugoslavije, Knjiga prva A-M*, 316–317.

17. ABiH, Fond CK SK BiH, kut. N-4, Pitanje ustaško-četničkih bandi, January 3, 1947, 1–4; ibid., kut. 192, Analiza izvještaja od Sreskih komiteta o političkoj situaciji na terenu, Org.-instruktorsko odjeljenje, November 19, 1947, 1; on operations in the wider Kulen Vakuf region, see ibid., kut. 175, Stanje partijske organizacije Srez Bihać, December 1947; ibid., kut. 211, Podaci iz UDBE o čišćenju neprijateljskih bandova sa terena, 1948, Sreski komitet Bihać, February 14, 1948, 1; Sreski komitet Drvar, February 16, 1948,1; Sreski komitet Bosanski Petrovac, February 16, 1948, 1.

18. For a brief history on the formation of Yugoslavia's State Commission for Determining of the Crimes of the Occupiers and Their Collaborators (Državna komisija za utvrđivanje zločina okupatora i njihovih pomagača), and especially of its commission for Bosnia and Herzegovina, see Krunoslava Lovrenović, "Zemaljska komisija za utvrđivanje zločina okupatora i njegovih pomagača," *Glasnik arhiva i društva arhivskih radnika Bosne i Hercegovine*, godina 1968–1969., knjiga VIII–IX, Sarajevo, 1968–1968, 51–61, here 52.

19. On these cases, see AJ, Fond 110, DKUZ, kut. 817, Okružni sud Bihać, Pojedinačne optužnice i presude, 1946, dos. br. 817-320, Javno tužioštvo za Okrug Bihać, Krivični predmet protiv Burzić Avde, May 27, 1946; dos. br. 817-376, Javno tužioštvo za Okrug Bihać, Krivični predmet protiv Kadić Bege, September 23, 1946; dos. br. 817-403, Javno tužioštvo za Okrug Bihać, Krivični predmet protiv Kozlice Agana, October 12, 1946; dos. br. 817-421, Javno tužioštvo za Okrug Bihać, Krivični predmet protiv Kulenović Mahmut, August 26, 1946; dos. br. 817-469, Javno tužioštvo za Okrug Bihać, Krivični predmet protiv Pehlivanović Ibrahim,

May 30, 1946; dos. br. Javno tužioštvo za Okrug Bihać, Krivični predmet protiv Sušnjar-Vukalić Mujaga, October 15, 1946.

20. See, for example, HDA, Fond 306, ZKUZ (Hrvatska), kut. 245, Zh. br. 11647, Odluka, Marinković dr. Vinko (ustaški politički povjerenik iz Donjeg Lapca), May 1945, 2; ibid., OKUZ za Liku, Zapisnik sastavljen pred komisijom u Bubnju, May 12, 1945, 1; ibid., kut. 235, Zh. br. 1027, Odluka, Markovinović Antić (komandant ustaša iz Boričevca), May 1945, 2.

21. AJ, Fond 110, DKUZ, dos. br. 5361, Zapisnik br. 22, Mjesni odbor: Kulen Vakuf, August 9, 1946, 5.

22. On the war crimes commissions' documentation about crimes that Chetniks had committed in wider area surrounding Kulen Vakuf, see ibid., kut. 817, Okružni sud Bihać, Grupne optužnice i presude, 1946, dos. br. 817-622, Javno tužioštvo za Okrug Bihać, Krivični predmet protiv Mirković Koste i Mirković Rajka, September 30, 1946, 1; ABiH, Fond ZKUZ, kut. 91, Srez Bosanski Petrovac, Zapisnik br. 22, Mjesni odbor: Malo Očijevo, August 9, 1946, 2.

23. AUSK, Fond SK SK BiH Bihać, kut. 166, SK SK Bihać, Srez Bihać, stenografske bilješke, prisutni: Enver Redžić, Stevan Blanuša, Mirko Stanarević, Gojko Beslać, Pero Grbić, May 9, 1951, 11.

24. ABiH, Fond CK SK BiH, kut. 37, Aktuelni problemi u oblasti međunacionalnih odnosa, November 1962, 22–23.

25. Ernest Gellner, *Nations and Nationalism* (Ithaca, NY: Cornell University Press, 1983); E. J. Hobsbawm, *Nations and Nationalism since 1780: Programme, Myth, Reality* (Cambridge: Cambridge University Press, 1990); Benedict Anderson, *Imagined Communities: Reflections on the Origin and Spread of Nationalism* (London: Verso, 1983); Miroslav Hroch, *Social Preconditions of National Revival in Europe: A Comparative Analysis of the Social Composition of Patriotic Groups among the Smaller European Nations*, trans. Ben Fowkes (Cambridge: Cambridge University Press, 1985).

26. Pieter M. Judson, *Guardians of the Nation: Activists on the Language Frontiers of Imperial Austria* (Cambridge, MA: Harvard University Press, 2006); Jeremy King, *Budweisers into Czechs and Germans: A Local History of Bohemian Politics, 1848–1948* (Princeton, NJ: Princeton University Press, 2002); James E. Bjork, *Neither German nor Pole: Catholicism and National Indifference in a Central European Borderland* (Ann Arbor: University of Michigan Press, 2008); Tara Zahra, *Kidnapped Souls: National Indifference and the Battle for Children in the Bohemian Lands, 1900–1948* (Ithaca, NY: Cornell University Press, 2008). See also the contributions in *Austria History Yearbook* 43 (April 2012), edited by Pieter M. Judson and Tara Zahra, which are largely devoted to the subject of "national indifference" in East-Central Europe.

27. See, for example, Stanley Tambiah, *Levelling Crowds: Ethnonationalist Conflicts and Collective Violence in South Asia* (Berkeley: University of California Press, 1996); Paul Brass, *Theft of an Idol: Text and Context in the Representation of Collective Violence* (Princeton, NJ: Princeton University Press, 1997); V. P. Gagnon Jr., *The Myth of Ethnic War: Serbia and Croatia in the 1990s* (Ithaca, NY: Cornell University Press, 2004).

28. Brubaker, *Nationalism Reframed*, 19.

29. See, for example, Mark R. Beissinger, *Nationalist Mobilization and the Collapse of the Soviet State* (Cambridge: Cambridge University Press, 2002); Eric Lohr, *Nationalizing the Russian Empire: The Campaign against Enemy Aliens during World War I* (Cambridge, MA: Harvard University Press, 2003).

30. For an important study that devotes extensive attention to how ordinary people use (and especially how they do not use) the idiom of nationhood in everyday life, but which does not focus on accounting for sudden surges in a sense of antagonistic nationhood, see Rogers Brubaker, Margit Feischmidt, Jon Fox, and Liana Grancea, *Nationalist Politics and Everyday Ethnicity in a Transylvanian Town* (Princeton, NJ: Princeton University Press, 2006).

31. On the definition and merits of an eventful analysis, see Sewell, "Three Temporalities," 245–280.

32. On how events can activate existing cultural schemas, see Sahlins, "The Return of the Event, Again," 293–352.

33. For examples of intercommunal rescue during the summer of 1941, see LAEB, Bibanović, "Kulen Vakuf," 48–50; ibid., "Stanovništvo Kulen-Vakufa," 120–124; Bibanović, "Kulenvakufski komunisti u radničkom pokretu i ustanku," 432–434; Mušeta, "Kulen Vakuf," 36; Šijan, "Nastanak i djelovanje KPJ na teritoriji kotara do oslobođenja Donjeg Lapca februara 1942. godine," 41, 43; Jovanić, "Ustanak u donjolapačkom kotaru 1941. godine," 105; Obradović, "Zločini na kotaru Donji Lapac od 1941. do 1945," 824, 831–832; Medić, "Obavještajna služba na području donjolapačkog kotara," 889.

34. Interview with Đula Seferović, October 13, 2008, Ostrovica.

35. Interviews with Sead Kadić, November 3, 2008, Bihać; Adil Kulenović, November 7, 2006, Sarajevo; and Svetozar Tankosić, October 16, 2008, Martin Brod.

36. Interview with Branko Dobrac, October 1, 2008, Kulen Vakuf.

37. Interviews with Mujo Hasanagić, November 4, 2008, Kulen Vakuf; Ale Galijašević, October 12, 2008, Kulen Vakuf; and Sead Kadić, November 3, 2008, Bihać.

38. AUSK, Fond SK SK BiH Bihać, kut. 195, Informacija o nekim pitanjima ideološkog i političkog djelovanja osnovnih organizacija Saveza komunista na opštini Bihać, February 2, 1962, 5–6. On the reaction of the local authorities to the building of the Orthodox church in Kulen Vakuf, see ibid., kut. 196 I, Narodni odbor sreza Bihać, Komisija za vjerska pitanja, Informacija o stanju i nekim problemima u razvitku odnosa država-crkva (na srezu), 1962, 3.

39. Interview with Mujo Hasanagić, November 4, 2008, Kulen Vakuf.

40. Interview with Dimitar Reljić, October 10, 2008, Martin Brod.

41. Interview with Đula Sefervović, October 13, 2008, Ostrovica.

42. AUSK, Fond SK SK BiH Bihać, kut. 318, Dnevne informacije sreskih komiteta, 1949, Sreski komitet Bihać, May 3, 1949, 1; May 26, 1949, 1; ibid., kut. 139, Oblasni komitet KP BiH, Odjeljenje za propagandu i agitaciju, U vezi proslave dana ustanka 27. jula, July 8, 1950, 1.

43. By 1961, which was the twentieth anniversary of the insurgency, at least fifteen such holidays were to be celebrated in the Bihać region. For a complete list, see ibid., kut. 199, Program proslave 20-to godišnjice Ustanka naroda Jugoslavije na području opštine Bihać, February 9, 1961, 2–4.

44. See, for example, AUSK, Fond SK SK BiH Bihać, kut. 196, Opštinski odbor Saveza boraca Bihać, Pripreme proslave 4. jula, "Dana borca," pripremanje i polaganje vijenaca na grobove palih boraca i žrtve fašističkog terora, June 17, 1956. See also *Krajina*, "Svečano je proslavljen '4. juli' Dan borca," July 27, 1956, 1.

45. AUSK, Fond SK SK BiH Bihać, kut. 318, Dnevne informacije sreskih komiteta, 1949, Sreski komitet Bihać, May 3, 1949, 1; May 11, 1949, 1; May 14, 1949, 1; ibid., Sreski komitet Bosanski Petrovac, May 20, 1949, 1.

46. On the similarities and differences between Yugoslav and Soviet nationality policies, see Veljko Vujačić and Victor Zaslavsky, "The Causes of Disintegration in the USSR and Yugoslavia," *Telos* 1991, no. 88 (1991): 120–140; for a discussion of the cultural politics of "Brotherhood and Unity" in Yugoslavia, see Andrew Baruch Wachtel, *Making a Nation, Breaking a Nation: Literature and Cultural Politics in Yugoslavia* (Stanford: Stanford University Press, 1998), chap. 3; on the history of Soviet nationality policy, see Terry Martin, *The Affirmative Action Empire: Nations and Nationalism in the Soviet Union, 1923–1939* (Ithaca, NY: Cornell University Press, 2001); Ronald Grigor Suny and Terry Martin, ed., *A State of Nations: Empire and Nation-Making in the Age of Lenin and Stalin* (Oxford: Oxford University Press, 2001); Francine Hirsch, *Empire of Nations: Ethnographic Knowledge and the Making of the Soviet Union* (Ithaca, NY: Cornell University Press, 2005).

47. This understanding of surveillance carried out by the communist authorities is based on an analysis of scores of documents produced by various organs of the League of Communists on the state of national relations in Bosnia-Herzegovina between 1945 and the late 1960s. For an important discussion of surveillance as a method of social engineering, see Peter Holquist, "'Information Is the Alpha and Omega of Our Work': Bolshevik Surveillance in Its Pan-European Context," *Journal of Modern History* 69, no. 3 (1997): 415–450.

48. ABiH, Fond CK SK BiH, kut. 175, Izvještaj za mjesec decembar 1947. godine o radu i stanju na terenu sreza Bosanski Petrovac, December 29, 1947, 2; ibid., kut. 294, Razni izvještaji, Stanje po okruzima: Okrug Bihać, Političko stanje, 1948, 1.

49. For examples of the emphasis on monitoring intercommunal relations from the wider region during the 1950s, see AUSK, Fond SK SK BiH Bihać, kut. 140, Analiza o djelovanju klera na srezu bihaćkom, April 20, 1952, 1; ibid., Političko stanje i rad masovnih organizacija na terenu sreza Bihać, 1952, 7–8; ABiH, Fond CK SK BiH, kut. 56, O nekim negativnim pojavama u partiskim organizacijama, 1952, 11; ibid., kut. 6N-103, Iz informacije Sreskog komiteta Bihać o radu osnovnih organizacija i nekim negativnim pojavama, June 13, 1953, 2; ibid., Iz izvještaja Sreskog komiteta SK Bihać, December 25, 1953, 3; AUSK, Fond SK SK BiH Bihać, kut. 144, Materijali sa opštinske konferencije, August 4, 1955, 5; ibid., kut. 148, Zapisnik sa sastanka Sekretarijata Sreskog komiteta Saveza komunista BiH Bihać, June 6, 1956, 11; ibid., Sastanak Sreskog komiteta Saveza komunista u Bihaću, 1956, 5; ibid., kut. 159, Referat koji je podnesen na III Plenumu CK SK BiH, June 20, 1957, 19–23.

50. Ibid., kut. 161, Opštinski komitet Saveza komunista Bosne i Hercegovine [hereafter OK SK BiH] Kulen Vakuf, Informacija o oblicima ispoljavanja šovinizma na opštini Kulen Vakuf, December 28, 1958, 1–3.

51. AUSK, Fond SK SK BiH Bihać, kut. 168, Sastanci Opštinskog odbora Socijalističkog saveza radnog naroda Jugoslavije za opštinu Kulen Vakuf, dnevni redovi i datumi održanih sastanka, 1958, "Neke šovinističke pojave na našoj opštini i rad organizacije Socijalističkog saveza po ovom pitanju," November 10, 1958. For further information about the organization of these meetings on the problem of chauvinism, see ibid., kut. 167, Referat o radu Opštinskog komiteta i organizacije

Saveza komunista na opštini Kulen Vakuf u vremenu od III do IV opštinske konferencije Saveza komunista, January 5, 1958–February 8, 1959, 11.

52. Ibid., kut. 161, OK SK BiH Kulen Vakuf, Informacija o oblicima ispoljavanja šovinizma na opštini Kulen Vakuf, December 28, 1958, 1–3.

53. For examples from the wider region in which the municipality of Kulen Vakuf was located, see ibid., kut. 164, Informacija o nekim pojavama šovinizma na području opštine Velike Kladuše, December 26, 1958, 1–2; ibid., Informacija o nekim pojavama šovinizma na području opštine Bužim, December 26, 1958, 1–2; ibid., Informacije Opštinskog komiteta Saveza komunista Bosanska Krupa, Predmet: Pojave šovinizma, December 28, 1958, 1–2; ibid., Informacija o nekim pojavama šovinizma na terenu bihaćke opštine u 1958 godini, December 30, 1958, 1–2; ibid., Informacije o šovinističkim pojavama na terenu Bosanski Petrovac, 1958, 1; ibid., kut. 165, Informacija o nekim pojavama šovinizma na području sreza Bihać, December 31, 1958, 1–2.

54. My thinking about the notion of speaking the language of "Brotherhood and Unity" was influenced by Stephen Kotkin's work on "speaking Bolshevik" in the Soviet context. See Kotkin, *Magnetic Mountain: Stalinism as a Civilization* (Berkeley: University of California Press, 1995).

55. On "the privatization of politics," see Gross, *Revolution from Abroad.*

56. See, for example, ABiH, Fond CK SK BiH, kut. 37, Analiza o međunacionalnim odnosima na goraždanskom srezu, July 1962, 8–10.

57. AUSK, Fond SK SK BiH Bihać, kut. 184, Informacija o šovinističkim pojavama na terenu sreza Bihać, October 19, 1962, 5; see also ibid., kut. 187, Šovinistički istupi i tuče u 1961 godini, 1961, 9.

58. ABiH, Fond CK SK BiH, kut. 56, O nekim negativnim pojavama u partiskim organizacijama, 1952, 11. What an individual did during the war continued throughout the 1950s to be a crucial yardstick that would determine what was possible in postwar life for that individual, as well as for his or her children. For example, permission to join the League of Communists often turned on whether or not a parent of a prospective candidate had been an Ustaša or Chetnik during the war, or was perceived to have been related in some way to an Ustaša or Chetnik. On this point, see AUSK, Fond SK SK BiH Bihać, kut. 169, Zapisnik sa savjetovanja članova sekretarijata Sreskih komiteta, nekih članova Sreskog komiteta, sekretara opštinskih komiteta Saveza komunista i predsjednika NOO-e sa terena srezova Banja Luke, Prijedora i Bihaća, September 14, 1959, 4.

59. AUSK, SK SK BiH Bihać, kut. 196, Odluka Sreskog komiteta sa kojom se potvrđuje kazna "Isključenje iz SKJ" Grubiše Milke, January 12, 1957, 1.

60. Ibid., kut. 161, Sekretarijat za unutrašnje poslove Bihać, Predmet: Altagić, Branko—prijedlog za krivično gonjenje, December 13, 1958.

61. Ibid., kut. 187, Šovinistički istupci i tuče u 1961. godini, 1961. (This document contains no information about who was responsible for its production, but its style and form suggest that it was created by members of either the Secretariat of Internal Affairs [SUP] or State Security [UDBA].)

62. On prosecutions of individuals for chauvinistic behavior in other regions of Bosnia-Herzegovina, see ABiH, Fond CK SK BiH, kut. 9, Neke pojave i problemi u međunacionalnim i vjerskim odnosima u Bosni i Hercegovini, 1959, 57; ibid., kut. 37, Organizaciono-politička komisija CK SK BiH, Analiza o raznim vidovima

neprijateljske aktivnosti i djelovanja stihije i konzervatizma u današnjim uslovima, November 1961, 66.

63. Ibid., kut. 37, Aktuelni problemi u oblasti međunacionalnih odnosa, November 1962, 22. The data on the number of violations, arrests, and prosecutions for the 1960s is incomplete. However, the available documentation suggests that the police remained busy throughout the decade policing "Brotherhood and Unity." For example, during the first eight months of 1969, there were 220 criminal charges and around 1,600 more minor violations for chauvinism, nationalism, and acts against the communist leadership. On these numbers, see ibid., kut. bez broja, Razni napisi koji se odnose na neke aktuelne probleme nacionalnih odnosa u Jugoslaviji, 1969, Podaci, Sekretarijat unutrašnjih poslova, 1968.

64. AUSK, Fond SK SK BiH Bihać, kut. 140, Analiza o djelovanju klera na srezu bihaćkom, April 20, 1952, 1. The Orthodox priest Dragoljub Jovanović from the Bosanski Petrovac region was also apparently making anti-Muslim comments around the same time. On his acts, see ABiH, Fond CK SK BiH, kut. 6N-103, Iz izvještaja Sreskog komiteta SK Bihać, December 25, 1953, 3.

65. AUSK, Fond SK SK BiH Bihać, kut. 140, Političko stanje i rad masovnih organizacija na terenu sreza Bihać, 1952, 7–8.

66. On the involvement of some members of the League of Communists in chauvinistic incidents in the wider Bihać region, see ibid., kut. 169, Razni materijali vezani za rad Sreskog komiteta SKJ Bihać, March 20, 1959, 8; on a more general attitude among some high-ranking members of the League of Communists of Bosnia-Herzegovina that certain regions and villages in the republic were "Ustaša" or "Chetnik," see ABiH, Fond CK SK BiH, kut. 9, Neke pojave i problemi u međunacionalnim i vjerskim odnosima u Bosni i Hercegovini, 1959, 17; ibid., kut. 37, Organizaciono-politička komisija CK SK BiH, Analiza o raznim vidovima neprijateljske aktivnosti i djelovanja stihije i konzervatizma u današnjim uslovima, November 1961, 29.

67. AUSK, Fond SK SK BiH Bihać, kut. 161, OK SK BiH Kulen Vakuf, Informacija o oblicima ispoljavanja šovinizma na opštini Kulen Vakuf, December 28, 1958, 1–3.

68. ABiH, Fond CK SK BiH, kut. 7, Izvještaj o radu na brojnom jačanju organizacija Saveza komunista na opštinama Bihać, Bosanska Krupa, i Kulen Vakuf, June 15, 1959, 41.

69. AUSK, Fond SK SK BiH Bihać, kut. 164, Informacija o nekim pojavama šovinizma na području opštine Velike Kladuše, December 26, 1958, 1–2.

70. The Central Committee of the League of Communists of Bosnia and Herzegovina noted in a classified 1959 report on national relations throughout the republic that some members of the organization were guilty of holding extremely negative views of members of other nationalities, which were often based in wartime events. See ABiH, Fond CK SK BiH, kut. 9, Neke pojave i problemi u međunacionalnim i vjerskim odnosima u Bosni i Hercegovini, 1959, 31.

71. AUSK, Fond SK SK BiH Bihać, kut. 184, Informacija o šovinističkim pojavama na terenu Bihać, October 19, 1962, 6. Similar incidents occurred in other regions of Bosnia-Herzegovina. For example, during 1962, in the municipality of Duvno, some schoolchildren who had gotten into a fight quickly divided along the lines of nationality. They threw rocks at each other, and shouted that they would one day avenge their side's victims from the war. The authorities determined that

the incident was connected to a brawl the previous year between the parents of the children. That fight was also rooted to some extent in wartime events. See ABiH, Fond CK SK BiH, kut. 37, Aktuelni problemi u oblasti međunacionalnih odnosa, November 1962, 28.

72. AUSK, Fond SK SK BiH Bihać, kut. 165, Informacija o nekim pojavama šovinizma na području sreza Bihać, December 31, 1958, 2. On Serbs criticizing the building of infrastructure in Muslim towns and villages because they saw them as "Ustaša places," see ibid., kut. 164, Informacije Opštinskog komiteta Saveza komunista Bosanska Krupa, Predmet: Pojave šovinizma, December 28, 1958, 1. In other regions of Bosnia and Herzegovina, Muslims sometimes behaved the same way, and even worse, toward their Serb neighbors. For example, Muslims from the village of Turija (located in the Tuzla region) cut the power lines so that electricity would no longer flow from their village to a neighboring Serbian village. Muslim members of the local committee of the League of Communists were reported to have participated in this incident. It is not clear what compelled the Muslims to take such measures, but conflicts dating back to the war may have been a contributing factor. On this incident, see ABiH, Fond CK SK BiH, kut. 37, Aktuelni problemi u oblasti međunacionalnih odnosa, November 1962, 6.

73. ABiH, Fond CK SK BiH, kut. 11, Neki idejno-politički organi i organizacije Saveza komunista na selu bihaćkog sreza, September 1963, 11–12.

74. AUSK, Fond SK SK BiH Bihać, kut. 184, Informacija o šovinističkim pojavama na terenu sreza Bihać, October 19, 1962, 6.

75. Ibid.

76. ABiH, Fond CK SK BiH, kut. 37, Neki vidovi negativnih pojava na planu međunacionalnih odnosa na području zeničkog sreza, August 29, 1962, 3.

77. Ibid., Analiza o aktuelnim problemima međunacionalnim odnosa na području komune Lukavac, 1962, 3.

78. Ibid., Aktuelni problemi u oblasti međunacionalih odnosa u Bosni i Hercegovini, November 1962, 1. For more examples of problems in various regions of Bosnia-Herzegovina that illustrate how wartime experiences caused some people to hold on to very negative perceptions of their neighbors of different nationalities during the postwar years, see ibid., Analiza o problemima međunacionalnih odnosa na području živiničke komune, June 26, 1962, 2; ibid., Analiza o aktuelnim problemima međunacionalnih odnosa na području opštine Srebrenica, June 1962, 3; ibid., Informacija o aktuelnim idejnim problemima međunacionalnih odnosa i uticaja iz inostranstva na opštinama: Livno, Duvno, Kupres i Bugojno, July 7, 1962, 1, 5; ibid., Analiza o aktuelnim problemima međunacionalnih odnosa na području sreza Prijedora, July 15, 1962, 2; ibid., Analiza o međunacionalnim odnosima na području dobojskog sreza, July 21, 1962, 12–13, 23; ibid., Analiza o međunacionalnim odnosima na goraždanskom srezu, July 1962, 9–10; ibid., Analiza o nekim problemima međunacionalnih odnosa u srezu Brčko, July 1962, 3–6; ibid., Analiza o aktuelnim problemima međunacionalnih odnosa na srezu Banjaluka, July 28, 1962, 10, 14; ibid., Analiza o nekim problemima međunacionalnih odnosa na srezu Tuzla, August 3, 1962, 3, 5.

79. Ibid., kut. 37, Organizaciono-politička komisija CK SK BiH, Politička dokumentacija o metodama i formama neprijateljske aktivnosti ustaških, četničkih i mladomuslimanskih elemenata, djelovanje stihije i konzervatizma u današnjim uslovima, November 1961, 157.

80. Arhiv Republike Srpske [hereafter ARS], Područna jedinica Foča [hereafter PJF], Fond Sreskog komiteta Saveza komunista Bosne i Hercegovine Foča [hereafter SK SK BiH Foča], Zapisnik sa proširene sjednice Opštinskog komiteta Saveza komunista Foča, April 4, 1969, 12.

81. On this dynamic, see Rogers Brubaker, *Ethnicity without Groups* (Cambridge, MA: Harvard University Press, 2004), 16.

82. On how ethnic ways of seeing can be triggered in un-self-conscious ways, rather than being instrumental, see Rogers Brubaker, Mara Loveman, and Peter Stamatov, "Ethnicity as Cognition," *Theory and Society* 33, no. 1 (2004): 31–64; for a discussion of more instrumentalist interpretations, see Jonathan Y. Okamura, "Situational Ethnicity," *Ethnic and Racial Studies* 4, no. 4 (October 1981): 452–465.

83. ABiH, Fond CK SK BiH, kut. 11, Neki idejno-politički organi i organizacije Saveza komunista na selu bihaćkog sreza, September 1963, 12.

84. AUSK, Fond SK SK BiH Bihać, kut. 164, Informacija o nekim pojavama šovinizma na području opštine Bužim, December 26, 1958, 2.

85. Ibid., Informacije o šovinističkim pojavama na terenu Bosanski Petrovac, 1958, 1. On this incident, see also ibid., kut. 186, Analiza metoda i formi neprijateljske djelatnosti na području opštine Bosanski Petrovac, May 30, 1961, 7–8.

86. See Brubaker, "Ethnicity without Groups," 11.

87. AUSK, Fond SK SK BiH Bihać, kut. 184, Informacija o šovinističkim pojavama na terenu sreza Bihać, October 19, 1962, 3.

88. Ibid., kut. 234, Zapisnik sa zajedničke proširene sjednice Opštinskog komiteta Saveza komunista i Izvršnog odbora Opštinskog odbora Socijalističkog saveza radnog naroda Bosanska Krupa, February 3, 1965, 5.

89. The Bosnian word *balija* originally referred to a Muslim peasant, but it eventually became a derogatory term for Muslims. See Škaljić, *Turcizmi u srpskohrvatskom jeziku*, 118.

90. While it appears to have been mostly men who yelled such curses, evidence from eastern Bosnia suggests that women sometimes took part. See, for example, ARS, PJF, Fond SK SK BiH Foča, Preduzetni komitet Saveza komunista rudnika mrkog uglja Miljevina, Predmet: Informacija o nekim pojavama, May 21, 1961, 2.

91. For an analysis of this dynamic among Hindu and Muslim youth, see Thomas Blom Hansen, "Recuperating Masculinity: Hindu Nationalism, Violence, and the Exorcism of the Muslim 'Other,'" *Critique of Anthropology* 16, no. 2 (1996): 137–172; on Hindus and Sikhs, see Das, *Life and Words*, 110.

92. ABiH, Fond CK SK BiH, kut. 9, Neke pojave i problemi u međunacionalnim i vjerskim odnosima u Bosni i Hercegovini, 1959, 7–9.

93. AUSK, Fond SK SK BiH Bihać, kut. 186, Metod i forme neprijateljske aktivnosti ustaških, četničkih i mladomuslimanskih elemenata, djelovanje stihije i konzervatizma u današnjim uslovima, June 1961, 7.

94. For South Asia, see Tambiah, *Leveling Crowds*; Akbar, *Riot after Riot*; Ranajit Guha, *Elementary Aspects of Peasant Insurgency in Colonial India* (Delhi: Oxford University Press, 1983); for a classic study on France, see Georges Lefebvre, *The Great Fear of 1789: Rural Panic in Revolutionary France*, trans. Joan White (New York: Pantheon Books, 1973); see also George F. E. Rudé, *The Crowd in the French Revolution* (Oxford: Oxford University Press, 1959); for France and England, see Rudé, *The Crowd in History: A Study of Popular Disturbances in France and England, 1730–1848*

(New York: Wiley, 1964); for Russia, see Jerome Blum, *Lord and Peasant in Russia: From the Ninth to the Nineteenth Century* (Princeton, NJ: Princeton University Press, 1961); on the phenomenon of rumor more generally, see Peter Lienhardt, "The Interpretation of Rumour," in *Studies in Social Anthropology: Essays in Memory of E. E. Evans-Pritchard by His Former Oxford Colleagues*, ed. J. H. M. Beattie and R. G. Lienhardt (Oxford: Clarendon Press, 1975), 105–131; Gordon W. Allport and Leo Postman, *The Psychology of Rumor* (New York: H. Holt, 1947).

95. AUSK, Fond SK SK BiH Bihać, kut. 186, Metod i forme neprijateljske aktivnosti ustaških, četničkih i mladomuslimanskih elemenata, djelovanje stihije i konzervatizma u današnjim uslovima, June 1961, 46.

96. Ibid., kut. 219, Neke pojave nacionalne netrpeljivost i šovinističkih ispada na području velikokladuške opštine, 1964, 4.

97. Horowitz, *The Deadly Ethnic Riot*, 75.

98. AUSK, Fond SK SK BiH Bihać, kut. 186, Analiza metoda i formi neprijateljske djelatnosti na području opštine Bosanski Petrovac, May 30, 1961, 8.

99. ARS, PJF, Fond SK SK BiH Foča, Informacija o sprovođenju zaključaka i stavova Opštinskog komiteta Saveza komunista usvojenim na ranijim sastancima (undated document, but appears to have been written in late 1963 or early 1964), 11–12.

100. AUSK, Fond SK SK BiH Bihać, kut. 186, Metod i forme neprijateljske aktivnosti ustaških, četničkih i mladomuslimanskih elemenata, djelovanje stihije i konzervatizma u današnjim uslovima na području opštine Drvar, June 1961, 5.

101. Ibid., 4.

102. Ibid., kut. 169, Zapisnik sa savjetovanja članova sekretarijata Sreskih komiteta, nekih članova Sreskog komiteta, sekretara opštinskih komiteta Saveza komunista i predsjednika NOO-e sa terena srezova Banja Luke, Prijedora i Bihaća, September 14, 1959, 8.

103. Ibid., kut. 187, Šovinistički istupi i tuče u 1961. godini, 1961, 10.

104. Ibid., kut. 184, Informacija o šovinističkim pojavama na terenu sreza Bihać, October 19, 1962, 1–2.

105. ARS, PJF, Fond SK SK BiH Foča, Druga sreska konferencija Saveza komunista goraždanskog Sreza, April 1958, 16; ibid., Materijal sa Treće sreske konferencije Saveza komunista goraždanskog sreza, April 11–12, 1960, 18; ABiH, Fond CK SK BiH, kut. 9. Neke pojave i problemi u međunacionalnim i vjerskim odnosima u Bosni i Hercegovini, May 7, 1959, 23–24, 46.

106. AUSK, Fond SK SK BiH Bihać, kut. 164, Informacije o šovinističkim pojavama na terenu Bosanski Petrovac, 1958, 1.

107. ARS, PJF, Fond SK SK BiH Foča, Informacija o sprovođenju zaključaka i stavova Opštinskog komiteta Saveza komunista usvojenim na ranijim sastancima (undated document, but appears to have been written in late 1963 or early 1964), 12.

108. On the notion of "strong men," see Kakar, *The Colours of Violence*, 71. On how individuals released from prison after serving sentences for war crimes played a role in framing incidents in ethnic and wartime categories, see ABiH, Fond CK SK BiH, kut. 37, Informacija o aktuelnim problemima međunacionalnih odnosa na području sreza Prijedora, July 15, 1962, 3; ibid., Aktuelni problemi međunacionalnih odnosa na srezu Banjaluka, August 2, 1962, 14; ibid., Analiza o problemima međunacionalnih odnosa na području živiničke komune, June 26, 1962, 2; AUSK, Fond SK SK BiH Bihać, kut. 186, Analiza metoda i formi neprijateljske djelatnosti na području opštine Bosanski Petrovac, May 30, 1961, 8; on the role of those who fought during the

war with factions that the communists called "enemy elements" (Ustašas, Chetniks, etc.), see ABiH, Fond CK SK BiH, kut. 36, O nekim problemima međunacionalnih odnosa i pojavama šovinizma na srezu Sarajeva, November 24, 1962, 13, 24.

109. AUSK, Fond SK SK BiH Bihać, kut. 184, Informacija o šovinističkim pojavama na terenu srezu Bihać, October 19, 1962, 5.

110. See, for example, ibid., kut. 164, Informacija o nekim pojavama šovinizma na području opštine Velike Kladuše, December 26, 1958, 1–2.

111. ABiH, Fond CK SK BiH, kut. 294, Izvještaj instruktora sa terena, Srez Goražde, 1948, 1.

112. See, for example, ibid., kut. 37, Analiza o međunacionalnim odnosima na goraždanskom srezu, July 1962, 9–10; ibid., kut. 9, Neke pojave i problemi u međunacionalnim i vjerskim odnosima u Bosni i Hercegovini, May 7, 1959, 51; ARS, PJF, Fond SK SK BiH Foča, Zapisnik sa sastanka Opštinskog komiteta Saveza komunista Foča, February 29, 1960, 3; ibid., Zapisnik sa Druge sjednice Opštinskog komiteta Saveza komunista Foča, March 7, 1963, 1–3.

113. League reports on national relations written in the late 1950s stated that the local mass killings of Serbs, Muslims, and Croats during the war had "left a deep scar on people's consciousness, especially among the older generations, and most especially among the families who were directly affected by the consequences of the intercommunal violence," and that this was a major reason for "unhealthy national relations." See ABiH, Fond CK SK BiH, kut. 9, Neke pojave i problemi u međunacionalnim i vjerskim odnosima u Bosni i Hercegovini, May 7, 1959, 2.

114. Ibid., kut. 37, Informacija o međunacionalnim odnosima na terenu Narodnog odbora sreza Jajce, August 6, 1962, 1.

115. AUSK, Fond SK SK BiH Bihać, kut. 161, OK SK BiH Kulen Vakuf, Informacija o oblicima ispoljavanja šovinizma na opštini Kulen Vakuf, December 28, 1958, 1–2.

116. Ibid., kut. 234, Zapisnik sa zajedničke proširene sjednice Opštinskog komiteta Saveza komunista i Izvršnog odbora Opštinskog odbora Socijalističkog saveza radnog naroda Bosanska Krupa, February 3, 1965, 2, 6.

117. Ibid.

118. Interview with Sead Kadić, November 3, 2008, Bihać.

119. Interview with anonymous informant, September 24, 2008.

120. Testimony of Mujo Dervišević in Kajan, "Pakao Vakuf Golubnjača," 27.

121. Kurtagić, *Zapisi o Kulen Vakufu*, 47.

122. Interview with Đula Seferović, October 3, 2008, Ostrovica.

123. HDA DAKA, Fond RMZDL, Radovi za hronike sela (neobjavljeno), Štikovac, "Krvavo lapačko ljeto" (undated), 83.

124. Interview with Bećo Pehlivanović, October 3, 2008, Bihać.

125. Interview with anonymous informants, June 22, 2013, Martin Brod.

126. On the wartime and postwar "unmixing" of people in Europe, in which the forced separation along ethnic lines also tended to separate perpetrators and survivors of wartime mass violence, especially in much of Eastern Europe as well as parts of the Balkans, see Philipp Ther and Ana Siljak, ed., *Redrawing Nations: Ethnic Cleansing in East-Central Europe, 1944–1948* (Lanham, MD: Rowman & Littlefield, 2001); Timothy Snyder, "'To Resolve the Ukrainian Problem Once and For All': The Ethnic Cleansing of Ukrainians in Poland, 1943–1947," *Journal of Cold War Studies*

1, no. 2 (1999): 86–120; Snyder, "The Causes of Ukrainian-Polish Ethnic Cleansing, 1943," *Past and Present* 179, no. 1 (2003): 197–234; Steven Béla Várdy and T. Hunt Tooley, eds., *Ethnic Cleansing in Twentieth-Century Europe* (Boulder, CO: Social Science Monographs and Columbia University Press, 2003), especially pt. 2; Redlich, *Together and Apart in Brzezany*; Benjamin Lieberman, *Terrible Fate: Ethnic Cleansing in the Making of Modern Europe* (Chicago: Ivan R. Dee, 2006), especially chaps. 5 and 6; Norman M. Naimark, *Fires of Hatred: Ethnic Cleansing in Twentieth-Century Europe* (Cambridge, MA: Harvard University Press, 2001), chap. 4; Pertti Ahonen, Gustavo Corni, Jerzy Kochanowski, Rainer Schulze, Tamás Stark, and Barbara Stelzl-Marx, *People on the Move: Forced Population Movements in Europe in the Second World War and Its Aftermath* (Oxford: Berg, 2008).

127. I say "counterfeit courtesy" because while the policing of "Brotherhood and Unity" by the communist authorities provided most people with powerful incentives to get along—from commemorations and work actions to verbal warnings and imprisonment—it also papered over the existence of more antagonistic relations among some people. The phrase comes from Ivo Andrić's short story "A Letter from 1920." Andrić, *The Damned Yard and Other Stories*, ed. and trans. Celia Hawkesworth (London: Forest, 1992), 107–119, here 117.

128. See Gagnon, *The Myth of Ethnic War*; Brass, *Theft of an Idol*; Tambiah, *Levelling Crowds*.

129. ABiH, Fond CK SK BiH, kut. 37, Neki vidovi negativnih pojava na planu međunacionalnih odnosa na području zeničkog sreza, August 30, 1962, 14.

130. Ibid., Informacija o aktuelnim idejnim problemima međunacionalnih odnosa i uticaja iz inostranstva na opštinama: Livno, Duvno, Kupres i Bugojno, July 7, 1962, 7–8.

131. Ibid., 9–10. On the wide variation in the behavior of local political leaders in response to interethnic incidents, see ibid., Informacija o aktuelnim problemima međunacionalnih odnosa na prodručju sreza Mostara, October 1962, 7–8; ibid., Analiza o nekim problemima međunacionalnih odnosa u srezu Brčko, July 25, 1962, 6–7, 21; ibid., Analiza o aktuelnim problemima međunacionalnih odnosa na srezu Banjaluka, August 2, 1962, 15; ibid., Neki problemi međunacionalnih odnosa u srezu Tuzla, August 3, 1962, 5; ibid., Analiza o aktuelnim problemima međunacionalnih odnosa na području komune Lukavac, 1962, 5–6; ibid., Aktuelni problemi međunacionalnih odnosa na području opštine Srebrenica, June 1962, 7; ibid., Informacija o aktuelnim problemima međunacionalnih odnosa na području sreza Prijedor, July 15, 1962, 2; ibid., Analiza o aktuelnim problemima međunacionalnih odnosa na području opštine Livno, August 9, 1962, 3–4; ibid., Neki vidovi negativnih pojava na planu međunacionalnih odnosa na području zeničkog sreza, August 30, 1962, 13–14; ibid., Informacija o međunacionalnim odnosima na terenu Narodnog odbora sreza Jajce, August 6, 1962, 7; ibid., Neki aktuelni problemi međunacionalnih odnosa u Bosni i Hercegovini, April 10, 1962, 10, 40–42; ibid., kut. NN, Izvještaj grupe Centralnog komiteta SK BiH o nekim političkim i privrednim problemima Hercegovine, 1966, 35; ibid., kut. 36, O nekim problemima međunacionalnih odnosa i pojavama šovinizma na srezu Sarajeva, November 24, 1962, 61–72; ARS, PJF, Fond SK SK BiH Foča, Grupa Opštinkog komiteta Saveza komunista koja je ispitala primjedbe na rad SUP-a Foča, Izvještaj o radu, November 1966, 3–4; Informacija o nekim negativnim pojavama na terenu Foča, October 20, 1960, 2.

132. On notions of restraint and escalation, see Straus, "Retreating from the Brink."

133. Rašeta, *Kazivanje pobjednika smrti*, 180.

134. Ibid., 20–21.

135. For further biographical information on Vaso Trikić, see AUSK, Fond SK SK BiH Bihać., kut. bez broja, Prijedlog drugova za sastav novog SK SK BiH Bihać, 1956; for Milan Zorić, see Đurđević-Đukić, ed., *Narodni heroji Jugoslavije, Knjiga druga N-Ž*, 351–352. On the points of difference between the two candidates, see AUSK, Fond SK SK BiH Bihać, kut. 163, Zapisnik sa sjednice Opštinskog komiteta Saveza komunista Kulen Vakuf, March 17, 1958, 4.

136. Ibid., kut. 164, OK SK BiH Kulen Vakuf, Analiza nekih pojava u vezi sa sprovedenim izborima za Narodne poslanike, March 31, 1958, 6.

137. Ibid., 5.

138. Ibid., 6.

139. For an example of a study that adopts an uncritical view of how conflicts come to be understood as "ethnic," see Roger D. Peterson, *Understanding Ethnic Violence: Fear, Hatred, and Resentment in Twentieth Century Eastern Europe* (Cambridge: Cambridge University Press, 2002).

140. Brubaker, *Nationalism Reframed*, 21.

141. On how ordinary people deploy the language of nationhood in instrumental ways, see Theodora Dragostinova, *Between Two Motherlands: Nationality and Emigration among the Greeks of Bulgaria*, 1900–1949 (Ithaca, NY: Cornell University Press, 2011).

142. On pogroms in Eastern Europe in 1941, see Gross, *Neighbors*, and Andrezj Żbikowski, "Local Anti-Jewish Pogroms in the Occupied Territories of Eastern Poland, June–July 1941," in *The Holocaust in the Soviet Union: Studies and Sources on the Destruction of Jews in the Nazi-Occupied Territories of the USSR, 1941–1945*, ed. Lucjan Dobroszycki and Jeffrey Gurock (Armonk, NY: M.E. Sharpe, 1993), 173–179; on the genocide in Rwanda, see Straus, *The Order of Genocide*; on communal violence in South Asia, see Das, *Life and Words*, and Tambiah, *Leveling Crowds*.

143. The judgments released by the International Criminal Tribunal for the former Yugoslavia (ICTY) contain suggestive examples of how Bosnian Serb politicians during the 1990s drew on memories of World War II violence to create an atmosphere of fear and suspicion in local communities. There are also examples of how some local perpetrators used World War II–era categories while committing acts of violence. An important subject for future research would be the role of such memories in the polarization of intercommunal relations and in motivating perpetrators of violence at the micro level. See, for example, International Tribunal for the Prosecution of Persons Responsible for Serious Violations of International Humanitarian Law Committed in the Territory of Former Yugoslavia since 1991, Case no. IT-94-1-T, May 7, 1997, Prosecutor versus Duško Tadić, paragraphs 83, 87, 88, 91, 94, 130, 154; Case no. IT-00-39-T, September 27, 2006, Prosecutor versus Momčilo Krajišnik, paragraphs 43, 45, 47, 638, 802, 896, 923, 1031.

Epilogue: Violence as a Generative Force

1. *Krajina*, "Svečano u Kulen Vakufu," November 4, 1981, 3; ibid., "U Kulen Vakufu 3. novembra. Otkrivanje spomenika palim rodoljubima," October 30, 1981, 1.

2. On the frenzied construction of war monuments in Yugoslavia during the 1950s and 1960s, see Max Bergholz "Među rodoljubima, kupusom, svinjama i

varvarima: spomenici i grobovi NOR-a, 1947–1965 godine," *Godišnjak za društvenu istoriju* XIV, nos. 1–3 (2007), 61–82; on the post–World War II silence about the region's intercommunal killings in 1941, see idem, "The Strange Silence: Explaining the Absence of Monuments for Muslim Civilians Killed in Bosnia during the Second World War," *East European Politics & Societies* 24, no. 3 (2010): 408–434.

3. *Kulen Vakuf* (a photographic album of the construction and unveiling of the town's monument in the possession of the monument's architect, Sadeta Ibrahimpašić), unnumbered pages; *Krajina*, "Uz novembarske praznike u Kulen Vakufu. Spomen obilježje—simbol revolucije," November 13, 1981, 2. Interview with anonymous informant, September 24, 2008, Kulen Vakuf.

4. The six republics included Slovenia, Croatia, Bosnia and Herzegovina, Macedonia, Montenegro, and Serbia; the two autonomous provinces were Vojvodina and Kosovo.

5. Interview with the monument's architect, Sadeta Ibrahimpašić, September 29, 2008, Bihać; *Kulen Vakuf* (a photographic album of the construction and unveiling of the monument in the possession of Sadeta Ibrahimpašić), unnumbered pages; *Krajina*, "U Kulen Vakufu grade spomen obilježje palim borcima. Simbol neraskidivog zajedništva," September 4, 1981, 1; for the list of names, see AMUSK, Zbirka informacije o spomenicima NOB, fas. 47, Kulen Vakuf, Odbor za izgradnju spomenika palim borcima NOR-a Kulen Vakuf, Predmet: Utvrđeni spisak palih boraca NOR-a od 1941. do 15. maja 1945. godine, April 3, 1981, 1–6.

6. *Krajina*, "Uz novembarske praznike u Kulen Vakufu. Spomen obilježje—simbol revolucije," November 13, 1981, 2.

7. Đurđević-Đukić, ed., *Narodni heroji Jugoslavije, Knjiga prva A-M*, 346–347.

8. The text of Karanović's speech was not printed in the regional newspaper *Krajina*, and a copy was not preserved in the local archives. For some details about his participation and comments, see *Kulen Vakuf*, unnumbered pages.

9. Interview with Derviš Kurtagić, November 9, 2006 and October 26, 2008, Kulen Vakuf; Sead Kadić, November 3, 2008, Bihać; Derviš Dervišević, October 1, 2008, Klisa; Adem Dervišević, October 1, 2008, Klisa; Ibrahim Lepirica, November 8, 2008, Kulen Vakuf; Ale Galijašević, October 12, 2008, Kulen Vakuf.

10. On plans by Bosnian Serb nationalists for the perceived Serb population to leave the Republic of Bosnia-Herzegovina and join a new Yugoslav federation, or a Union of "Serbian Lands," see MUSK, Arhiv 5. Korpusa, "Bosanka Krajina. Konstitutivni činilac nove jugoslovenske federacije," December 31, 1991, 7.

11. *Informacija o zločinima počinjenim nad civilnim stanovništvom sa područja Ripač-Ćukovi-Orašac-Klisa-Kulen-Vakuf* (undated pamphlet [which appears to have been published during the spring of 1994] by Udruženje žena i roditelja zarobljenih civila s područja Ripča, Ćukova, Orašca, Klise i Kulen-Vakufa), 1–2; Mujo Begić, *Ljutočko dolino, nikad ne zaboravi. Sjećanja* (Bihać: Grafičar, 2004), 106, 94–95.

12. Hilmo Kozlica, *Put kroz pakao* (Sarajevo: Savez logoraša Bosne i Hercegovine; CID—Centar za istraživanje i dokumentaciju, 2009), 33–36; Begić, *Ljutočko dolino*, 104, 80–81.

13. Begić, *Ljutočko dolino*, 77–78, 81.

14. Kozlica, *Put kroz pakao*, 40.

15. Viši sud u Bihaću, Zapisnik sastavljen dana 04.08.1992. povodom postupka za utvrđivanje ratnih zločina počinjenih u Republici Bosne i Hercegovine, Iskaz Derviševića Đulage, August 4, 1992, 2–3.

16. Ministarstvo za unutrašnje poslove, Centar službe bezbjednosti Bihać, Podaci koji se odnose na učešće radnika Službe javne bezbjednosti Bihać na pripremama i organizaciji Srpskog naroda prije izbijanje ratnih sukoba, October 13, 1993, 1 (photocopy of original document included as an appendix in Begić, *Ljutočka dolino*, 201–209).

17. Begić, *Ljutočko dolino*, 77–78, 81.

18. Nataša Kadić, "Ja nisam borac u uniformi, ali sam borac u srcu," (unpublished manuscript located in the personal archive of Nataša Kadić), 1.

19. Viši sud u Bihaću, Zapisnik sastavljen dana 4.8.1992. povodom postupka za utvrđivanje ratnih zločina počinjenih u Republici Bosne i Hercegovine, Iskaz Derviševića Đulage, August 4, 1992, 5.

20. See, for example, Banac, *The National Question in Yugoslavia*; see also Christian Nielsen, *Making Yugoslavs: Identity in King Aleksandar's Yugoslavia* (Toronto: University of Toronto Press, 2014).

21. See, for example, Kalyvas, *The Logic of Violence in Civil* War; see also Ashutosh Varshney, *Ethnic Conflict and Civil Life. Hindus and Muslims in India* (New Haven: Yale University Press, 2002).

22. For a more macro-level discussion of this subject, see Straus, "'Destroy Them to Save Us'"; idem, *Making and Unmaking Nations.*

23. See, for example, Wood, "The Social Processes of Civil War"; Kalyvas, *The Logic of Violence in Civil* War; idem, "Ethnic Defection in Civil War"; Balcells, "Rivalry and Revenge"; Sambanis and Shayo, "Social Identification and Ethnic Conflict"; on the importance of studying conflict processes, see also Fotini Christia, *Alliance Formation in Civil War* (New York: Cambridge University Press, 2012).

24. For examples of influential studies on ethnic conflict that propose static conceptions of ethnic categories, see Peterson, *Understanding Ethnic Violence*; Naimark, *Fires of Hatred*; Andreas Wimmer, *Waves of War. Nationalism, State Formation, and Ethnic Exclusion in the Modern World* (Cambridge: Cambridge University Press, 2013).

25. See Straus, *The Order of Genocide*; see also Waller, *Becoming Evil.*

26. On the role of such factors in creating resistance to state repression, see Evgeny Finkel, "The Phoenix Effect of State Repression: Jewish Resistance during the Holocaust," *American Political Science Review* 109, no. 2 (2015): 339–353.

27. See, for example, Judson, *Guardians of the Nation*; King, *Budweisers into Czechs and Germans*; Bjork, *Neither German nor Pole*; Zahra, *Kidnapped Souls.*

Bibliography

Archives

Bosnia-Herzegovina

Arhiv Bosne i Hercegovine (ABiH) | Sarajevo

- Fond Agrarne direkcije u Sarajevu
- Fond Centralnog komiteta Saveza komunista Bosne i Hercegovine (CK SK BiH)
- Fond Saveza udruženja boraca Narodnooslobodilačkog rata Bosne i Hercegovine (SUBNOR BiH)
- Fond Zemaljske komisije za utvrđivanje zločina okupatora i njihovih pomagača Bosne i Hercegovine (ZKUZ BiH)
- Fond Zajedničkog ministarstva finansija za Bosnu i Hercegovinu
- Fond Zemaljske Vlade Sarajevo

Arhiv Republike Srpske Banja Luka (ARSBL) | Banja Luka

- Fond 9, Kraljevska banska uprava Vrbaske Banovine (KBUVB)
- Fond 74, Velika Župa Sana i Luka Nezavisne Države Hrvatske (NDH)
- Fond 76, Rizičko upraviteljstvo Banja Luka Nezavisne Države Hrvatske (NDH)
- Fond 209, Memoarska građa
- Fond 328, Zbirka dokumenata Vojno-istorijskog instituta Jugoslovenske narodne armije (VII JNA), Bosanska Krajina
- Fond 330, Zbirka varia
- Fond 631, Ustaški stožer i povjereništvo za bivšu Vrbasku banovinu Banja Luka (USPBVBBL)
- Fond 559, Lični fond Milana Vukmanovića (1928–1993)
- Kartoteka ličnosti iz NOR-a
- Kartoteka ratnih zločinaca

Arhiv Unsko-sanskog kantona (AUSK) | Bihać

- Fond Sreskog komiteta Saveza komunista Bosne i Hercegovine (SK SK BiH) Bihać
- Fond Okružnog inspektorata Vrbaske Banovine (OIVB) Bihać
- Fond Okružne oblasti Bihać

Arhiv Muzeja Unsko-sanskog kantona (AMUSK) | Bihać

- Arhiv 5. Korpusa (razni materijali iz 1991. godine)
- Fond Prijepisi originalnih dokumenata iz Arhiva za historiju radničkog pokreta (AHRP), 1941–1945., Nezavisna Država Hrvatska
- Fond Sjećanja boraca iz Narodnooslobodilačkog rata, 1941–1945
- Doprinos u NOB, 1941–1945
- Fond Zbirke informacija o spomenicima Narodnooslobodilačkog ratu na području opštine Bihać
- Fond Zbirke fotografija bivšeg sreza i opštine Bihać

Arhiv Republike Srpske, Područna jedinica Foča (ARS PJF) | Foča

- Fond Opštinskog komiteta Saveza komunista Bosne i Hercegovine (OK SK BiH) Foča

Lični arhiv Esada Bibanovića (LAEB) | Sarajevo

- Neobjavljeni rukopisi o istoriji Kulen-Vakufa:
  - "Kulen Vakuf. Svjedočanstvo jednog vremena." (Undated)
  - "Kulen Vakuf i okolina kroz istoriju." (Undated)
  - Radni materijal za knjigu "Kulen-Vakuf i okolina kroz istoriju." (Undated)
  - "Stanovništvo Kulen-Vakufa i okoline kroz istoriju." (1980)

Croatia

Hrvatski državni arhiv (HDA) | Zagreb

- Fond 306, Zemaljska komisija za utvrđivanje zločina okupatora i njihovih pomagača (ZKUZ) Hrvatska
- Fond 223, Ministarstvo unutarnjih poslova (MUP) Nezavisne Države Hrvatske (NDH)
- Fond 226, Ministarstvo zdravstva i udružbe Nezavisne Države Hrvatske (NDH)
- Fond 246, Zavod za kolonizaciju Nezavisne Države Hrvatske (NDH)
- Fond 248, Ministarstvo oružanih snaga Nezavisne Države Hrvatske (MINORS NDH)
- Fond 493, Sudovi oružanih snaga Nezavisne Države Hrvatske (NDH)
- Fond 1220, Centralni komitet (CK) Komunističke Partije Hrvatske (KPH)
- Fond 1352, Grupa V
- Fond 1353, Grupa VI
- Fond 1355, Grupa VIII
- Fond 1361, Grupa XVII
- Fond 1363, Grupa XXI

- Fond 1364, Grupa XXI
- Fond 1450, Ministarstvo oružanih snaga Nezavisne Države Hrvatske (MINORS NDH)

Hrvatski državni arhiv Karlovac (HDA DAKA) | Karlovac

- Fond 143, Memoarsko gradivo o NOR-u
- Fond 141, Razni spisi iz razdoblja NDH
- Fond Radnog materijala za Zbornik Donji Lapac (RMZDL)

Serbia

Arhiv Jugoslavije (AJ) | Belgrade

- Fond 14, Ministarstvo unutrašnjih poslova (MUP) Kraljevine Jugoslavije
- Fond 110, Državna komisija za utvrđivanje zločina okupatora i njihovih pomagača (DKUZ)

Arhiv Srbije (AS) | Belgrade

- Fond G-2, Komesarijat za izbeglice (KI)

Vojni arhiv (VA) | Belgrade

- Fond Centralnog komiteta Komunističke Partije Hrvatske (CK HRV)
- Fond Narodnooslobodilačke vojske Jugoslavije (NOV)
- Fond Nezavisne Države Hrvatske (NDH)
- Fond Sekretarijata unutarnjih poslova Socijalističke Republike Hrvatske (SUP SRH)
- Fond Sekretarijata unutrašnjih poslova Bosne i Hercegovine (SUP BiH)

Arhiv Srpske pravoslavne crkve (ASPC) | Belgrade

- Ministarstvo vere, Pravoslavno odeljenje
- Prepisi iz Komisije za prikupljanje podataka o zločinima nad Srbima u NDH, 1941–42

Published Documents

Čekić, Smail. *Genocid nad Bošnjacima u Drugom svjetskom ratu: dokumenti.* Sarajevo: Udruženje Muslimana za antigenocidne aktivnosti, 1996.

Dedijer, Vladimir, and Antun Miletić, eds. *Proterivanje Srba sa ognjišta, 1941–1944: svjedočanstva.* Belgrade: Prosveta, 1989.

Dedijer, Vladimir, and Antun Miletić, eds. *Genocid nad Muslimanima, 1941–1945: zbornik dokumenata i svjedočenja.* Sarajevo: Svjetlost, 1990.

Dizdar, Zdravko, and Mihael Sobolevski. *Prešućivani četnički zločini u Hrvatskoj i Bosni i Hercegovini 1941.–1945.* Zagreb: Hrvatski institut za povijest, 1999.

Informacija o zločinima počinjenim nad civilnim stanovništvom sa područja Ripač-Ćukovi-Orašac-Klisa-Kulen-Vakuf. Udruženje žena i roditelja zarobljenih civila s područja Ripča, Ćukova, Orašca, Klise i Kulen-Vakufa [appears to have been published in 1994].

International Tribunal for the Prosecution of Persons Responsible for Serious Violations of International Humanitarian Law Committed in the Territory of Former Yugoslavia since 1991. Case no. IT-94-1-T, May 7, 1997; Prosecutor versus Duško Tadić. Case no. IT-00-39-T, September 27, 2006; Prosecutor versus Momčilo Krajišnik.

Ministarstvo vanjskih poslova Nezavisne Države Hrvatske. *Odmetnička zvjerstva pustošenja u Nezavisnoj državi Hrvatskoj u prvim mjesecima života Hrvatske Narodne Države.* Zagreb: Ministarstvo vanjskih poslova, 1942.

Pavičić, Josip, ed. *Dossier Boričevac.* Zagreb: Naklada Pavičić, 2012.

Statistički pregled izbora narodnih poslanika za ustavotvornu skupštinu Kraljevine Srba, Hrvata i Slovenaca, izvršenih na dan 28. novembra 1920. god. Belgrade: Deliška tiskarna, 1921.

Statistika izbora narodnih poslanika Kraljevine Srba, Hrvata i Slovenaca 1923. Belgrade: Državna štamparija Kraljevine Srba, Hrvata i Slovenaca, 1924.

Statistika izbora narodnih poslanika Kraljevine Srba, Hrvata i Slovenaca 1925. Belgrade: Državna štamparija Kraljevine Srba, Hrvata i Slovenaca, 1926.

Statistika izbora narodnih poslanika Kraljevine Srba, Hrvata i Slovenaca 1927. Belgrade: Štamparija Vladete Janićijevića, 1928.

Statistika izbora narodnih poslanika za Prvu Jugoslovensku Narodnu Skupštinu održanih 8. novembra 1931. god. Belgrade, 1935.

Statistika izbora narodnih poslanika za Narodnu Skupštinu Kraljevine Jugoslavije izvršenih 5. maja 1935. godine. Belgrade: Štampa državne štamparije Kraljevine Jugoslavije, 1938.

Tucaković, Šemso. *Srpski zločini nad Bošnjacima-Muslimanima 1941–1945.* Sarajevo: El-Kalem, 1995.

Vukčević, Slavko, ed. *Zločini na jugoslovenskim prostorima u Prvom i Drugom svetskom ratu. Zbornik dokumenata.* Belgrade: Vojno-istorijski institut, 1993.

Zbornik dokumenata i podataka o Narodnooslobodilačkom ratu jugoslovenskih naroda, tom IV, knjiga 1, Borbe u Bosni i Hercegovini 1941. god. Belgrade: Vojno-istoriski institut Jugoslovenske Armije, 1951.

Zbornik dokumenata i podataka o Narodnooslobodilačkom ratu jugoslovenskih naroda, tom IV, knjiga 2, Borbe u Bosni i Hercegovini. Belgrade: Vojno-istoriski institut Jugoslovenske Armije, 1951.

Zbornik dokumenata i podataka o Narodnooslobodilačkom ratu jugoslovenskih naroda, tom V, knjiga 1, Borbe u Hrvatskoj 1941. godine. Belgrade: Vojno-istoriski institut Jugoslovenske Armije, 1952.

Živković, Nikola, and Petar Kačavenda. *Srbi u Nezavisnoj Državi Hrvatskoj: izabrana dokumenta.* Belgrade: Institut za savremenu istoriju, 1998.

Žrtve rata 1941.–1945. Popis iz 1964. godine, SR Bosna i Hercegovina (Banovići—Bosanski Novi). Belgrade: Savezni zavod za statistiku, 1992.

Unpublished Manscripts and Doctoral Dissertations

Hajdarpašić, Edin. "Whose Bosnia? National Movements, Imperial Reforms, and the Political Re-Ordering of the Late Ottoman Balkans, 1840–1875." PhD diss., University of Michigan, 2008.

Kulen Vakuf. Bihać, 1981; private collection.
Mušeta, Abas. "Kulen Vakuf: Tragedija od 10.04 do 06–18.09 1941. godine."

Newspapers

Glas: organ Oblasnog odbora Narodno-oslobodilačkog fronta za Bosansku Krajinu (1944)
Glas Socijalističkog saveza radnog naroda banjalučkog sreza (1965)
Hrvatska Krajina (1941)
Hrvatski narod: Gasilo hrvatskog ustaškog pokreta (1941)
Krajina: list Saveza socijalističkog radnog naroda bihaćkog sreza (1956–1957, 1961, 1964, 1981)
Novi list (1941)

Cited Interviews

Anonymous informant, September 24, 2008
Anonymous informant, October 11, 2008
Anonymous informants, June 22, 2013, Martin Brod
Mujo Demirović, September 30, 2008, Bihać
Adem Dervišević, October 1, 2008, Klisa
Derviš Dervišević, October 1 and 5, 2008, Klisa
Mustafa Dervišević, October 11, 2008, Klisa
Branko Dobrac, October 1, 2008, Kulen Vakuf
Ale Galijašević, October 12, 2008, Kulen Vakuf
Mujo Hasanagić, November 4, 2008, Kulen Vakuf
Smajo Hodžić, June 23, 2013, Ćukovi
Sadeta Ibrahimpašić, September 29, 2008, Bihać
Sead Kadić, November 3, 2008, Bihać
Adil Kulenović, November 7, 2006, Sarajevo
Ibrahim Lepirica, November 8, 2008, Kulen Vakuf
Abas Mušeta, July 7 and 8, 2012, Crikvenica
Murat Mušeta, September 27, 2008, Kulen Vakuf
Bećo Pehlivanović, October 3, 2008, Bihać
Dimitar Reljić, October 10, 2008 and June 22, 2013, Martin Brod
Đula Seferović, October 13, 2008, Ostrovica
Kemal Štrkljević, September 27, 2008, Kulen Vakuf
Mehmed Štrkljević, September 28, 2008, Kulen Vakuf
Svetozar Tankosić, October 16, 2008, Martin Brod
Maho Vazović, September 24, 2008, Kulen Vakuf

Memoirs and Novels

Andrić, Ivo. *The Bridge on the Drina.* Translated by Lovett F. Edwards. Chicago: University of Chicago Press, [1945] 1977.
Andrić, Ivo. "A Letter from 1920." In *The Damned Yard and Other Stories*, edited and translated by Celia Hawkesworth, 107–119. London: Forest, 1992.
Balakian, Peter. *Black Dog of Fate: A Memoir.* New York: Basic Books, 1997.

Balaban, Dušan. "Vrtoče u prvim danima ustanka." In *Bosanski Petrovac u NOB, Knjiga II*, edited by Vladimir Čerkez, 49–73. Bosanski Petrovac: Opštinski odbor SUBNOR-a Bosanski Petrovac, 1974.

Bibanović, Esad. "Kulenvakufski komunisti u radničkom pokretu i ustanku." In *Bihać u novijoj istoriji (1918–1945): Zbornik radova sa Naučnog skupa održanog u Bihaću 9. i 10. oktobra 1986. godine,* 2 vols, edited by Galib Šljivo, 1: 419–466. Banjaluka: Institut za istoriju u Banjaluci, 1987.

Bodnaruk, Ivica. "Sjećanje na dane ustanka u Drvaru i Petrovcu." In *Bosanski Petrovac u NOB, Knjiga II*, edited by Vladimir Čerkez, 41–48. Bosanski Petrovac: Opštinski odbor SUBNOR-a Bosanski Petrovac, 1974.

Ćelam, Ahmet. "Sindikalna organizacija kožarskih radnika u Bosanskoj Dubici." In *Kozara u Narodnooslobodilačkom ratu. Zapisi i sjećanja, knjiga prva*, edited by Radomir Petković, 100–104. Belgrade: Vojnoizdavački zavod, 1971.

Ćelam, Ahmet. "U Dubici poslije okupacije." In *Kozara u Narodnooslobodilačkom ratu. Zapisi i sjećanja, knjiga prva*, edited by Radomir Petković, 193–197. Belgrade: Vojnoizdavački zavod, 1971.

Čučak, Bogdan. *Nebljusi u Narodnooslobodilačkom ratu i revoluciji, 1941.–1945.* Belgrade: Savez boraca NOR-a Nebljusi i Skupština opštine Donji Lapac, 1981.

Damjanović Danić, Danilo. *Ustanak naroda Hrvatske 1941 u Srbu i okolini.* Zagreb: IP "Progres," 1972.

Damjanović-Danić, Danilo. "Pad Kulen Vakufa." In *Bosanski Petrovac u NOB. Zbornik sjećanja. Knjiga I*, edited by Vladimir Čerkez, 664–670. Bosanski Petrovac: Opštinski odbor SUBNOR-a Bosanski Petrovac, 1974.

Danilović, Uglješa. "Ustanak u Hercegovini, jun 1941–jun 1942." In *Hercegovina u NOB. Pišu učesnici*, edited by Milisav Perović, 25–39. Belgrade: Vojnoizdavački zavod JNA "Vojno delo," 1961.

Došen, Ana. *Krnjeuša u srcu i sjećanju.* Rijeka: Matica hrvatska, 1994.

Došen, Ana. *To je bilo onda.* Zagreb: Došen, self-published, 2006.

Dubajić Čkaljac, Rade. "Tragično djetinjstvo." In *Kotar Donji Lapac u Narodnooslobodilačkom ratu, 1941.–1945.*, edited by Gojko Vezmar and Đuro Zatezalo, 862–863. Karlovac: Historijski arhiv u Karlovcu, 1985.

Dubajić-Damjanović, Milica. "Omladina sela Zalužja 1941. godine." In *Lika u NOB. Zbornik. Pišu učesnici*, edited by Đoko Jovanić, 589–597. Novi Sad: Budućnost, 1963.

Đukić-Pilja, Filip. "Bjelajčani u ustanku." In *Bosanski Petrovac u NOB, Knjiga II*, edited by Vladimir Čerkez, 502–504. Bosanski Petrovac: Opštinski odbor SUBNOR-a Bosanski Petrovac, 1974.

Džubur, Lutvo. "Poslednje školsko zvono." In *Hercegovina u NOB, april 1941.–juni 1942, tom 2*, edited by Sveta Kovačević and Slavko Stijačić-Slavo, 344–402. Belgrade and Mostar: Vojnoizdavački i novinski centar i Istorijski arhiv Hercegovina, 1986.

Evans, Sir Arthur J. *Illyrian Letters. A Revised Selection of Correspondence From the Illyrian Provinces of Bosnia, Herzegovina, Montenegro, Albania, Dalmatia, Croatia, and Slavonia, Addressed to the "Manchester Guardian" during the Year 1877.* New York: Cosimo Classics, [1878] 2007.

Goldstein, Slavko. *1941., godina koja se vraća.* Zagreb: Novi Liber, 2007.

Goldstein, Slavko. *1941: The Year That Keeps Returning.* Translated by Michael Gable and Nikola Djuretic. New York: New York Review of Books, 2013.

Grbić, Dušan. "Cvjetnićka četa." In *Drvar, 1941–1945. Sjećanja učesnika, knjiga 2*, edited by Pero Morača, 356–363. Drvar: Skupština opštine Drvar, 1972.

Hromađić, Ahmet. "Selo Bjelaj." In *Bosanski Petrovac u NOB, Knjiga II*, edited by Vladimir Čerkez, 494–497. Bosanski Petrovac: Opštinski odbor SUBNOR-a Bosanski Petrovac, 1974.

Ivezić, Dane. "Srbi su pobili cijeli rod Ivezića u selu Brotnja." *Vila Velebita*, no. 31, March 17, 1995, 10.

Ivezić, Dane. "Brotnja: ustanici istrijebili Iveziće." In *Dossier Boričevac*, edited by Josip Pavičić, 343–352. Zagreb: Naklada Pavičić, 2012.

Jovanić, Đoko. "Ustanak u južnoj lici 1941. godine (Neki podaci i sjećanje)." In *Lika u NOB, 1941. Zbornik, Knjiga prva*, edited by Đoko Jovanić, 99–141. Belgrade: Vojno izdavački zavod JNA "Vojno delo," 1963.

Jovanić, Đoko. "Ustanak u donjolapačkom kotaru 1941. godine." In *Kotar Donji Lapac u Narodnooslobodilačkom ratu, 1941.–1945.*, edited by Gojko Vezmar and Đuro Zatezalo, 96–156. Karlovac: Historijski arhiv u Karlovcu, 1985.

Jovanić, Đoko. *Ratna sjećanja*. Belgrade: Vojnoizdavački i novinski centar, 1988.

Kajan, Ibrahim. "Pakao Vakuf Golubnjača." *Ogledalo* 1, no. 2 (prosinac/decembar 1990): 26–27.

Karanović, Đuro. "Napad na žandarmerijsku stanicu u Martin Brodu." In *Drvar 1941–1945., sjećanja učesnika, knjiga 2*, edited by Pero Morača, 424–432. Drvar: Skupština opštine Drvar, 1972.

Karanović, Nikola. "Sadjejstvo sa ličkim ustanicima." In *Drvar, 1941–1945. Sjećanja učesnika, knjiga 2*, edited by Pero Morača, 407–414. Drvar: Skupština opštine Drvar, 1972.

Kecman-Hodak, Mara. "Sjećanja na Bušević, Kestenovac, Bosanske Štrpce i Kalate." In *Bosanski Petrovac u NOB. Zbornik sjećanja. Knjiga III*, edited by Vladimir Čerkez, 150–159. Bosanski Petrovac: Opštinski odbor SUBNOR-a Bosanski Petrovac, 1974.

Keča, Jovica. "Ustanički dani u okolini Kulen Vakufa." In *Bosanski Petrovac u NOB. Zbornik sjećanja. Knjiga IV*, edited by Vladimir Čerkez, 199–203. Bosanski Petrovac: Opštinski odbor SUBNOR-a Bosanski Petrovac, 1974.

Knežević, Dušan. "Omladinska radna akcija u selu Orašcu." In *Bosanski Petrovac u NOB. Zbornik sjećanja. Knjiga IV*, edited by Vladimir Čerkez, 253–255. Bosanski Petrovac: Opštinski odbor SUBNOR-a Bosanski Petrovac, 1974.

Knežević, Nikola. "Cvjetnićani u akciji." In *Drvar, 1941–1945. Sjećanja učesnika, knjiga 2.*, edited by Pero Morača, 454–462. Drvar: Skupština opštine Drvar, 1972.

Knežević, Nikola. "Maćuka." In *Drvar, 1941–1945. Sjećanja učesnika, knjiga 3.*, edited by Pero Morača, 86–89. Drvar: Skupština opštine Drvar, 1978.

Konjhodžić, Mahmud. *Kronika o ljubuškom kraju*. Sarajevo: Oslobođenje; Opštinski odbor SUBNOR-a ljubuški, 1974.

Kovačević, Rade. "Na zajedničkom djelu." In *Bosanski Petrovac u NOB, Knjiga II*, edited by Vladimir Čerkez, 573–578. Bosanski Petrovac: Opštinski odbor SUBNOR-a Bosanski Petrovac, 1974.

Kozlica, Hilmo. *Put kroz pakao*. Sarajevo: Savez logoraša Bosne i Hercegovine; CID—Centar za istraživanje i dokumentaciju, 2009.

Kurtagić, Derviš. *Zapisi o Kulen-Vakufu*. Bihać: Kurtagić, 2005.

Labus, Mile. "Sjećanja i zapisi." In *Bosanski Petrovac u NOB, Knjiga druga*, edited by Vladimir Čerkez, 514–529. Bosanski Petrovac: Opštinski odbor SUBNOR-a Bosanski Petrovac, 1974.

Lukić, Simo. "Četnici u kotaru Donji Lapac od 1941. do 1945." In *Kotar Donji Lapac u Narodnooslobodilačkom ratu, 1941.–1945.*, edited by Gojko Vezmar and Đuro Zatezalo, 865–888. Karlovac: Historijski arhiv u Karlovcu, 1985.

Majstorović, Milan, and Mićo Medić. *Prve iskre: Doljani u NOB.* Zagreb: Lykos, 1961.

Majstorović, Milan, and Mićo Medić. "Doljani u narodnom ustanku." In *Ustanak naroda Jugoslavije 1941. Pišu učesnici, Zbornik, knjiga peta*, edited by Koča Popović, 456–470. Belgrade: Vojnoizdavački zavod JNA "Vojno delo," 1964.

Majstorović, Nikola. "Kulen Vakuf opština u NOR-u." In *Bosanski Petrovac u NOB. Knjiga III*, edited by Vladimir Čerkez, 374–380. Bosanski Petrovac: Opštinski odbor SUBNOR-a Bosanski Petrovac, 1974.

Mažuranić, Matija. *A Glance into Ottoman Bosnia or a Short Journey into that Land by a Native in 1839–1840.* London: Saqi, [1842] 2007.

Medić, Mićo. "Obavještajna služba na području donjolapačkog kotara." In *Kotar Donji Lapac u Narodnooslobodilačkom ratu, 1941.–1945.*, edited by Gojko Vezmar and Đuro Zatezalo, 888–926. Karlovac: Historijski arhiv u Karlovcu, 1985.

Mileusnić, Sava. "Donji Lapac u ustanku." In *Lika u NOB. Zbornik. Pišu učesnici*, edited by Đoko Jovanić, 385–412. Novi Sad: Budućnost, 1963.

Montejo, Victor. *Testimony: Death of a Guatemalan Village.* Translated by Victor Perera. Willimantic, CT: Curbstone Press, 1987.

Morača, Pero, ed. *Jajačko područje u oslobodilačkom ratu i revoluciji 1941–1945. Zbornik sjećanja, Knjiga I.* Novi Sad: "Budućnost"; Skupština opština Donji Vakuf, Jajce i Šipovo, 1981.

Nađ, Kosta. "Iz ratnih dana." In *Četrdeset godina. Zbornik sećanja aktivista jugoslovenskog revolucionarnog radničkog pokreta, 1941–1945, knjiga 5*, edited by Pero Morača, 314–339. Belgrade: Kultura, 1961.

Nađ, Kosta. *Ustanak: ratne uspomene Koste Nađa.* Zagreb: Spektar, 1981.

Novaković, Savo. "Tuk Dževar—Dobro selo u zla vremena." In *Bosanski Petrovac u NOB, zbornik sjećanja, knjiga II*, edited by Vladimir Čerkez, 471–486. Bosanski Petrovac: Opštinski odbor SUBNOR-a Bosanski Petrovac, 1974.

Obradović, Milan. "Selo Bubanj u plamenu." In *1941–1942. u svedočenjima učesnika narodnooslobodilačke borbe, knjiga 7*, edited by Radomir Petković, 433–463. Belgrade: Vojnoizdavački zavod, 1975.

Obradović, Milan. "Zločini na kotaru Donji Lapac od 1941. do 1945." In *Kotar Donji Lapac u Narodnooslobodilačkom ratu, 1941.–1945.*, edited by Gojko Vezmar and Đuro Zatezalo, 821–847. Karlovac: Historijski arhiv u Karlovcu, 1985.

Odić, Franjo. "Julski dani 1941. na unskoj pruzi." In *Podgrmeč u NOB. Podgrmeč do ustanka i u ustanku 1941. Zbornik sjećanja, knjiga prva*, edited by Dušan Pejanović, 211–215. Belgrade: Vojnoizdavački zavod, 1972.

Odić, Slavko. "Radnički pokret Bihaća i okoline do ustanka 1941. godine." In *Podgrmeč u NOB: Podgrmeč do ustanka i u ustanku 1941. Zbornik sjećanja, knjiga prva*, edited by Dušan Pejanović, 15–109. Belgrade: Vojnoizdavački zavod, 1972.

Odić, Slavko. "Okupacija Bosne u aprilskom ratu 1941. godine." In *Srednja Bosna u NOB-u: srednja Bosna do ustanka i u ustanku 1941., članci i sjećanja, knjiga prva*, edited by Slavko Odić, 163–170. Belgrade: Vojnoizdavački zavod, 1976.

Odić, Slavko. "Ustaški pokret i katolička crkva u Hrvatskoj i Bosni i Hercegovini." In *Srednja Bosna u NOB-u: srednja Bosna do ustanka i u ustanku 1941., članci i sjećanja, knjiga prva*, edited by Slavko Odić, 247–273. Belgrade: Vojnoizdavački zavod, 1976.

Pećanac, Milanko. "Suvaja i njeni ljudi u ustaničkim danima." In *Bosanski Petrovac u NOB. Zbornik sjećanja. Knjiga II*, edited by Vladimir Čerkez, 74–100. Bosanski Petrovac: Opštinski odbor SUBNOR-a Bosanski Petrovac, 1974.

Pervan, Asim. "Ljudi i događaji fatničkog kraja." In *Hercegovina u NOB, april 1941.–juni 1942., tom 2*, edited by Sveta Kovačević and Slavko Stijačić-Slavo, 749–790. Belgrade and Mostar: Vojnoidavački i novinski centar i Istorijski arhiv Hercegovina, 1986.

Pervan, Tahir. *Čavkarica. Vrata pakla.* Sarajevo: Behar, 2007.

Pilipović, Milkan. "Dramatična borba na vrtočkoj gradini." In *Bosanski Petrovac u NOB. Knjiga druga*, edited by Vladimir Čerkez, 300–313. Bosanski Petrovac: Opštinski odbor SUBNOR-a Bosanski Petrovac, 1974.

Pilipović, Nikica. "Vrtoče u ustanku 1941." In *Ustanak naroda Jugoslavije 1941. Pišu učesnici, Zbornik, knjiga četvrta*, edited by Koča Popović, 858–874. Belgrade: Vojnoizdavački zavod JNA "Vojno delo," 1964.

Pilipović, Nikica. "Vrtočani u danima ustanka, požara i otpora." In *Bosanski Petrovac u NOB, Knjiga I*, edited by Vladimir Čerkez, 540–584. Bosanski Petrovac: Opštinski odbor SUBNOR-a Bosanski Petrovac, 1974.

Pilipović, Nikica. *Romori vrtočke prošlosti.* Bihać: Mjesna zajednica Vrtoče, 1989.

Pilipović, Pero. "Organizacija ustanka u Cvjetniću i okolnim selima." In *Drvar, 1941–1945. Sjećanja učesnika, knjiga 2*, edited by Pero Morača, 280–289. Drvar: Skupština opštine Drvar, 1972.

Pilipović, Pero. "Borba Cvjetnićana na petrovačkom području." In *Bosanski Petrovac u NOB. Zbornik sjećanja. Knjiga I*, edited by Vladimir Čerkez, 585–602. Bosanski Petrovac: Opštinski odbor SUBNOR-a Bosanski Petrovac, 1974.

Pilipović, Pero. "Istina o jednom zločinu." In *Bosanski Petrovac u NOB. Zbornik sjećanja. Knjiga II*, edited by Vladimir Čerkez, 603–605. Bosanski Petrovac: Opštinski odbor SUBNOR-a Bosanski Petrovac, 1974.

Pilipović Mandžuka, Milka. "Očeva smrt." In *Drvar, 1941–1945. Sjećanja učesnika, knjiga 2*, edited by Pero Morača, 516–519. Drvar: Skupština opštine Drvar, 1972.

Plećaš-Nitonja, Nikola. *Požar u Krajini.* Chicago: Plećaš-Nitonja, 1975.

Polovina, Gojko. "Sjećanja na početni period narodnog ustanka u Lici godine 1941." In *Zbornik 3: Prva godina Narodnooslobodilačkog rata na području Karlovca, Korduna, Gline, Like, Gorskog kotara, Pokuplja i Žumberka*, edited by Đuro Zatezalo, 771–813. Karlovac: Historijski arhiv u Karlovcu, 1971.

Polovina, Gojko. *Svedočenje: prva godina ustanka u Lici.* Belgrade: Izdavačka radna organizacija "Rad," 1988.

Popadić, Branko. "Na prostoru Stoca i Bileće." In *Hercegovina u NOB, april 1941.–juni 1942., tom 2*, edited by Sveta Kovačević and Slavko Stijačić-Slavo, 631–651. Belgrade and Mostar: Vojnoidavački i novinski centar i Istorijski arhiv Hercegovina, 1986.

Puškar, Halil. *Krajiški pečat.* Istanbul: n.p., 1996.

Radošević, Lazo. "Vrtoče u ustanku." In *Bosanski Petrovac u NOB, Knjiga II*, edited by Vladimir Čerkez, 462–479. Bosanski Petrovac: Opštinski odbor SUBNOR-a Bosanski Petrovac, 1974.

Radošević, Petar. "Teror ustaša u Vrtoču." In *Bosanski Petrovac u NOB, Knjiga I*, edited by Vladimir Čerkez, 647–649. Bosanski Petrovac: Opštinski odbor SUBNOR-a Bosanski Petrovac, 1974.

Rakić, Mićo. "Rad SKOJ-a u Bosanskom Petrovcu." In *Ustanak naroda Jugoslavije 1941. Pišu učesnici, knjiga treća*, edited by Koča Popović, 369–385. Belgrade: Vojnoizdavački zavod JNA "Vojno delo," 1963.

Rašeta, Ilija. "Pripremanje i početak ustanka u Donjem Lapcu." In *1941–1942. u svedočenjima učesnika narodnooslobodilačke borbe, knjiga 4*, edited by Radomir Petković, 199–235. Belgrade: Vojnoizdavački zavod, 1975.

Rašeta, Ilija. *Kazivanje pobjednika smrti*. Zagreb: Grafički zavod Hrvatske, 1988.

Reljić, Jovo. "Martin Brod—Partizanska baza." In *Ustanak naroda Jugoslavije 1941. Pišu učesnici, Zbornik, knjiga šesta*, edited by Svetislav Savković, 391–407. Belgrade: Vojnoizdavački zavod JNA "Vojno delo," 1964.

Reljić, Jovo. "Martin Brod 1941. godine." In *Drvar, 1941–1945. Sjećanja učesnika, knjiga 2.*, edited by Pero Morača, 389–406. Drvar: Skupština opštine Drvar, 1972.

Repac, Rade. "Nebljuški kraj u NOB-u." In *Kotar Donji Lapac u Narodnooslobodilačkom ratu, 1941.–1945.*, edited by Gojko Vezmar and Đuro Zatezalo, 206–238. Karlovac: Historijski arhiv u Karlovcu, 1985.

Rudić, Jovanka. "Na prekopanoj cesti." In *Bosanski Petrovac u NOB. Zbornik sjećanja, knjiga I*, edited by Vladimir Čerkez, 349–355. Bosanski Petrovac: Opštinski odbor SUBNOR-a Bosanski Petrovac, 1974.

Šijan, Milan. "Nastanak i djelovanje KPJ na teritoriji kotara do oslobođenja Donjeg Lapca februara 1942. godine." In *Kotar Donji Lapac u Narodnooslobodilačkom ratu, 1941.–1945.*, edited by Gojko Vezmar and Đuro Zatezalo, 34–52. Karlovac: Historijski arhiv u Karlovcu, 1985.

Šiljegović, Boško. "Kako se pripremio ustanak u dubičkim selima." In *Krajiške brigade*, edited by Ljubo Babić, 69–74. Ljubljana: Ljudske pravice, 1954.

Šiljegović, Boško. "Pripremanje ustanka u dubičkim selima." In *Ratna sećanja aktivista jugoslovenskog revolucionarnog radničkog pokreta, knjiga prva: 1941–1945*, edited by Pero Morača, 348–353. Belgrade: Kultura, 1961.

Štikavac, Milan. "Krvavo lapačko ljeto." In *Ratna sjećanja iz NOB, knjiga I*, edited by Esad Tihić and Momčilo Kalem, 599–616. Belgrade: Vojno-izdavački zavod, 1981.

Tankosić, Vlado. "Kako sam strijeljan i bačen u jamu." In *Drvar, 1941–1945. Sjećanja učesnika, knjiga 1*, edited by Pero Morača, 250–252. Drvar: Skupština opštine Drvar, 1972.

Trikić, Stevo. "Upostavljanje vlasti NDH i ustaški teror u Drvaru." In *Drvar, 1941–1945. Sjećanja učesnika, knjiga 1*, edited by Pero Morača, 199–225. Drvar: Skupština opštine Drvar, 1972).

Vidaković, Nikola. "Sjećanje na osnivanje i rad partijske organizacije do početka ustanka 1941." In *Kotar Donji Lapac u Narodnooslobodilačkom ratu, 1941.–1945.*, edited by Gojko Vezmar and Đuro Zatezalo, 17–34. Karlovac: Historijski arhiv u Karlovcu, 1985.

Vojvodić, Dušan. "Sjećanje na događaje u kotaru Donji Lapac od 1940. do 1942. godine." In *Kotar Donji Lapac u Narodnooslobodilačkom ratu, 1941.–1945.*, edited by Gojko Vezmar and Đuro Zatezalo, 157–182. Karlovac: Historijski arhiv u Karlovcu, 1985.

Vukmanović Tempo, Svetozar. *Revolucija koja teče. Memoari*. Belgrade: Komunist, 1971.

Secondary Literature

Ahonen, Pertti, Gustavo Corni, Jerzy Kochanowski, Rainer Schulze, Tamás Stark, and Barbara Stelzl-Marx. *People on the Move: Forced Population Movements in Europe in the Second World War and Its Aftermath*. Oxford: Berg, 2008.

Akbar, M. J. *Riot after Riot. Reports on Caste and Communal Violence in India*. New Delhi: Penguin Books, 1988.

Allcock, John. *Explaining Yugoslavia*. New York: Columbia University Press, 2000.

Allport, Gordon W., and Leo Postman. *The Psychology of Rumor*. New York: H. Holt & Company, 1947.

Altić, Husejn. "Lički muslimani." *Kalendar Narodna uzdanica za godinu 1941*. godina IX. Sarajevo: Narodna uzdanica, 1941: 97–100.

Altić, Husejn. "Bivši Kulen Vakuf." *Narodna uzdanica Književni zbornik za godinu 1943*, god. XI. Sarajevo: Narodna uzdanica, 1942: 15–19.

Anderson, Benedict. *Imagined Communities: Reflections on the Origin and Spread of Nationalism*. London: Verso, 1983.

Anscombe, Frederick, ed. *The Ottoman Balkans, 1750–1830*. Princeton, NJ: Markus Wiener, 2006.

Autesserre, Séverine. *The Trouble with the Congo: Local Violence and the Failure of International Peace Building*. Cambridge: Cambridge University Press, 2010.

Balcells, Laia. "Rivalry and Revenge: Violence against Civilians in Conventional Civil Wars." *International Studies Quarterly* 54, no. 2 (2010): 291–313.

Banac, Ivo. *The National Question in Yugoslavia. Origins, History, Politics*. Ithaca, NY: Cornell University Press, 1984.

Bandžović, Safet. *Iseljavanje Bošnjaka u Tursku*. Sarajevo: Institut za istraživanje zločina protiv čovječnosti i međunarnodnog prava, 2006.

Barić, Nikica. *Ustroj kopnene vojske domobranstva Nezavisne Države Hrvatske 1941.–1945*. Zagreb: Hrvatski institut za povijest, 2003.

Bartov, Omer. "Seeking the Roots of Modern Genocide: On the Macro- and Microhistory of Mass Murder." In *The Specter of Genocide: Mass Murder in Historical Perspective*, edited by Robert Gellately and Ben Kiernan, 75–96. Cambridge: Cambridge University Press, 2003.

Bartov, Omer. "Eastern Europe as the Site of Genocide." *Journal of Modern History* 80, no. 3 (2008): 557–593.

Bartov, Omer. "White Spaces and Black Holes." In *The Shoah in Ukraine: history, testimony, memorialization*, edited by Ray Brandon and Wendy Lower, 318–353. Bloomington: Indiana University Press, 2008.

Bartov, Omer. "Bloodlands: Europe between Hitler and Stalin (Book Review)." *Slavic Review* 70, no. 2 (2011): 424–428.

Bartov, Omer. "Communal Genocide: Personal Accounts of the Destruction of Buczacz, Eastern Galicia, 1941–1944." In *Shatterzone of Empires: Coexistence and Violence in the German, Habsburg, Russian, and Ottoman Borderlands*, edited by Omer Bartov and Eric D. Weitz, 399–420. Bloomington and Indianapolis: Indiana University Press, 2013.

Bartulin, Nevenko. *The Racial Idea in the Independent State of Croatia: Origins and Theory*. Leiden: Brill, 2014.

Begić, Mujo. *Ljutočko dolino, nikad ne zaboravi. Sjećanja*. Bihać: Grafičar, 2004.

Begić, Mujo. *Zločini ustanika u Ljutočkoj dolini 1941. godine*. Sarajevo: Institut za istraživanje zločina protiv čovječnosti i međunarodnog prava Univerziteta u Sarajevu, 2013.

Beissinger, Mark R. *Nationalist Mobilization and the Collapse of the Soviet State*. Cambridge: Cambridge University Press, 2002.

Béla Várdy, Steven, and T. Hunt Tooley, eds. *Ethnic Cleansing in Twentieth-Century Europe*. Boulder, CO: Social Science Monographs and Columbia University Press, 2003.

Bergholz, Max. "Među rodoljubima, kupusom, svinjama i varvarima: spomenici i grobovi NOR-a, 1947–1965 godine." *Godišnjak za društvenu istoriju* XIV, nos. 1–3 (2007): 61–82.

Bergholz, Max. "The Strange Silence: Explaining the Absence of Monuments for Muslim Civilians Killed in Bosnia during the Second World War." *East European Politics & Societies* 24, no. 3 (2010): 408–434.

Biondich, Mark. *Stjepan Radić, the Croat Peasant Party, and the Politics of Mass Mobilization, 1904–1928*. Toronto: University of Toronto Press, 2000.

Biondich, Mark. "Religion and Nation in Wartime Croatia: Reflections on the Ustaša Policy of Forced Religious Conversions, 1941–1942." *Slavonic and East European Review* 83, no. 1 (2005): 71–116.

Bjork, James E. *Neither German nor Pole: Catholicism and National Indifference in a Central European Borderland*. Ann Arbor: University of Michigan Press, 2008.

Blum, Jerome. *Lord and Peasant in Russia: From the Ninth to the Nineteenth Century*. Princeton, NJ: Princeton University Press, 1961.

Bošnjak, Slavoljub [Ivan Franjo Jukić]. *Zemljopis i poviestnica Bosne*. Zagreb: Bèrzotiskom narodne tiskarnice dra. Ljudevit Gaja, 1851.

Bowman, Glenn. "The Violence in Identity." In Bettina E. Schmidt and Ingo W. Schröder, *Anthropology of Violence and Conflict*, 25–46. London: Routledge, 2001.

Brass, Paul. *Theft of an Idol: Text and Context in the Representation of Collective Violence*. Princeton, NJ: Princeton University Press, 1997.

Brubaker, Rogers. *Nationalism Reframed: Nationhood and the National Question in the New Europe*. Cambridge: Cambridge University Press, 1996.

Brubaker, Rogers. *Ethnicity without Groups*. Cambridge, MA: Harvard University Press, 2004.

Brubaker, Rogers, Margit Feischmidt, Jon Fox, and Liana Grancea. *Nationalist Politics and Everyday Ethnicity in a Transylvanian Town*. Princeton, NJ: Princeton University Press, 2006.

Brubaker, Rogers, and David Laitin. "Ethnic and Nationalist Violence." *Annual Review of Sociology* 24, no. 4 (1998): 423–452.

Brubaker, Rogers, Mara Loveman, and Peter Stamatov. "Ethnicity as Cognition." *Theory and Society* 33, no. 1 (2004): 31–64.

Brujić, Srđan, and Đuro Stanisavljević. "Razvoj organizacija KP u Lici i njihova uloga u ustanku 1941." In *Lika u NOB, 1941. Zbornik, knjiga prva*, edited by Đoko Jovanić, 7–38. Belgrade: Vojno izdavački zavod JNA "Vojno delo," 1963.

Chirot, Daniel, and Clark McCauley. *Why Not Kill Them All? The Logic and Prevention of Mass Political Murder*. Princeton, NJ: Princeton University Press, 2006.

Christia, Fotini. *Alliance Formation in Civil War.* New York: Cambridge University Press, 2012.

Collins, Randall. *Violence: A Micro-Sociological Theory.* Princeton, NJ: Princeton University Press, 2008.

Confino, Alon. "Why Did the Nazis Burn the Hebrew Bible? Nazi Germany, Representations of the past, and the Holocaust." *Journal of Modern History* 84, no. 2 (2012): 369–400.

Confino, Alon. *A World without Jews: The Nazi Imagination from Persecution to Genocide.* New Haven: Yale University Press, 2014.

Coser, Lewis A. *The Functions of Social Conflict.* New York: Free Press, 1956.

Ćorović, Vladimir. *Bosna i Hercegovina.* Banja Luka: Glas srpski, 1999 [1940].

Čubrilović, Vasa. *Bosanski ustanak, 1875–1878., Drugo izdanje.* Belgrade: Službeni list SRJ, [1930] 1996.

Das, Veena. *Life and Words: Violence and the Descent into the Ordinary.* Berkeley: University of California Press, 2007.

Das, Veena. "Collective Violence and the Shifting Categories of Communal Riots, Ethnic Cleansing, and Genocide." In *The Historiography of Genocide*, edited by Dan Stone, 93–127. New York: Palgrave Macmillan, 2008.

Deloria, Philip. *Indians in Unexpected Places.* Lawrence: University Press of Kansas, 2004.

Demirović, Mujo. *Bosna i Bošnjaci u srpskoj politici.* Bihać: Ekonomski fakultet, 1999.

Djokić, Dejan. *Elusive Compromise: A History of Interwar Yugoslavia.* New York: Columbia University Press, 2007.

Downes, Alexander. *Targeting Civilians in War.* Ithaca, NY: Cornell University Press, 2008.

Dragostinova, Theodora. *Between Two Motherlands: Nationality and Emigration among the Greeks of Bulgaria*, 1900–1949. Ithaca, NY: Cornell University Press, 2011.

Duara, Prasenjit. "Historicizing National Identity, or Who Imagines What and When." In *Becoming National. A Reader*, edited by Geoff Eley and Ronald Grigor Suny, 151–177. New York: Oxford University Press, 1996.

Dulić, Tomislav. *Utopias of Nation. Local Mass Killing in Bosnia-Herzegovina, 1941–1942.* Uppsala: Uppsala University, 2005.

Dumitru, Diana, and Carter Johnson. "Constructing Interethnic Conflict and Cooperation: Why Some People Harmed Jews and Others Helped Them during the Holocaust in Romania." *World Politics* 63, no. 1 (2011): 1–42.

Đurđević-Đukić, Olga, ed. *Narodni heroji Jugoslavije, Knjiga prva A-M.* Belgrade: Mladost, 1975.

Đurđević-Đukić, Olga, ed. *Narodni heroji Jugoslavije, Knjiga druga N-Ž.* Belgrade: Mladost, 1975.

Dwyer, Leslie, and Degung Santikarma. "'When the World Turned to Chaos': 1965 and Its Aftermath in Bali, Indonesia." In *The Spectre of Genocide*, edited by Robert Gellately and Ben Kiernan, 289–305. Cambridge: Cambridge University Press, 2003.

Ekmečić, Milorad. *Ustanak u Bosni, 1875–1878., treće, izmenjeno izdanje.* Belgrade: Službeni list SRJ, [1960] 1996.

Erić, Milivoje. *Agrarna reforma u Jugoslaviji 1918–1941.* Trebinje: Kultura, 1958.

Faroqhi, Suraiya. "Coping with the Central State, Coping with Local Power: The Ottoman Regions and Notables from the Sixteenth to the Early Nineteenth Century." In *The Ottomans and the Balkans: A Discussion of Historiography*, edited by Fikret Adanir and Suraiya Faroqhi, 351–382. Leiden: Brill, 2002.

Fearon, James, and David Laitin. "Explaining Interethnic Cooperation." *American Political Science Review* 90, no. 4 (1996): 715–735.

Ferenc, Tone. *Nacistička politika denacionalizacije u Sloveniji u godinama od 1941 do 1945.* Ljubljana: Partizanska knjiga, 1979.

Fein, Helen. *Accounting for Genocide: National Responses and Jewish Victimization during the Holocaust.* New York: Free Press, 1979.

Fellman, Michael. *Inside War. The Guerrilla Conflict in Missouri during the American Civil War.* New York: Oxford University Press, 1989.

Filandra, Šaćir. *Bošnjačka politika u XX. stoljeću.* Sarajevo: Sejtarija, 1998.

Finkel, Caroline. *Osman's Dream: The Story of the Ottoman Empire, 1300–1923.* London: John Murray, 2005.

Finkel, Evgeny. "The Phoenix Effect of State Repression: Jewish Resistance during the Holocaust." *American Political Science Review* 109, no. 2 (2015): 339–353.

Frijda, Nico. "The Lex Talionis: On Vengeance." In Stephanie van Goozen, Nanne van de Poll, and Joseph Sergeant, eds. *Emotions: Essays on Emotion Theory*, 263–289. Hillsdale, NJ: Lawrence Erlbaum, 1994.

Fujii, Lee Ann. *Killing Neighbors: Webs of Violence in Rwanda.* Ithaca, NY: Cornell University Press, 2009.

Fujii, Lee Ann. "The Puzzle of Extra-Lethal Violence." *Perspectives on Politics* 11, no. 2 (June 2013): 410–426.

Gagnon, V. P., Jr. *The Myth of Ethnic War: Serbia and Croatia in the 1990s.* Ithaca, NY: Cornell University Press, 2004.

Gellner, Ernest. *Nations and Nationalism.* Ithaca, NY: Cornell University Press, 1983.

Gerlach, Christian. "Bloodlands: Europe between Hitler and Stalin (Book Review)." *American Historical Review* 116, no. 5 (2011): 1594–1595.

Goodwin, Jeff. *No Other Way Out: States and Revolutionary Movements, 1945–1991.* Cambridge: Cambridge University Press, 2001.

Grabowski, Jan. *Hunt for the Jews: Betrayal and Murder in German-Occupied Poland.* Bloomington: Indiana University Press, 2013.

Grau, Lester. *The Soviet-Afghan War: How a Superpower Fought and Lost.* Lawrence: University Press of Kansas, 2002.

Greble, Emily. *Sarajevo, 1941–1945: Muslims, Christians, and Jews in Hitler's Europe.* Ithaca, NY: Cornell University Press, 2011.

Gross, Jan T. *Revolution from Abroad: The Soviet Conquest of Poland's Western Ukraine and Western Belorussia.* Princeton, NJ: Princeton University Press, [1988] 2002.

Gross, Jan T. *Neighbors: The Destruction of the Jewish Community in Jedwabne, Poland.* Princeton, NJ: Princeton University Press, 2001.

Gross, Jan T. "A Colonial History of the Bloodlands." *Kritika: Explorations in Russian and Eurasian History* 15, no. 3 (2014): 591–596.

Gross, Jan T., with Irena Grudzinska Gross. *Golden Harvest. Events at the Periphery of the Holocaust.* Oxford: Oxford University Press, 2012.

Grossman, Lt. Col. Dave. *On Killing: The Psychological Cost of Learning to Kill in War and Society.* New York: Black Bay Books, 1995.

Guha, Ranajit. *Elementary Aspects of Peasant Insurgency in Colonial India*. Delhi: Oxford University Press, 1983.

Gumz, Jonathan. *The Resurrection and Collapse of Empire in Habsburg Serbia, 1914–1918*. Cambridge: Cambridge University Press, 2009.

Gušić, Branimir. "Naseljenje Like do Turaka." In *Lika u prošlosti i sadašnosti, zbornik 5*, edited by Branimir Gušić, 13–61. Karlovac: Historijski arhiv u Karlovcu, 1973.

Hadžijahić, Muhamed, et al. *Islam i Muslimani u Bosni i Hercegovini*. Sarajevo: Svjetlost, 1977.

Hajdarpašić, Edin. *Whose Bosnia? Nationalism and Political Imagination in the Balkans, 1840–1914*. Ithaca, NY: Cornell University Press, 2015.

Hansen, Thomas Blom. "Recuperating Masculinity: Hindu Nationalism, Violence, and the Exorcism of the Muslim 'Other.'" *Critique of Anthropology* 16, no. 2 (1996): 137–172.

Haritos-Fatouros, Mika. *The Psychological Origins of Institutionalized Torture*. London: Routledge, 2003.

Hasanbegović, Zlatko. *Jugoslavenska muslimanska organizacija 1929–1941. U ratu i revoluciji 1941.–1945*. Zagreb: Bošnjačka nacionalna zajednica za grad Zagreb i Zagrebačku županiju, 2012.

Hasluck, F.W. *Christianity and Islam under the Sultans*, 2 vols. New York: Octagon Books, [1929] 1973.

Hefner, Robert W. *The Political Economy of Mountain Java: An Interpretative History*. Berkeley: University of California Press, 1990.

Heper, Metin. "Center and Periphery in the Ottoman Empire: With Special Reference to the Nineteenth Century." *International Political Science Review* 1, no. 1 (1980): 81–105.

Herff, Barbara. "Genocide as State Terrorism." In *Government Violence and Repression: An Agenda for Research*, edited by Michael Stohl and George A. Lopez, 165–187. Westport, CT: Greenwood Press, 1986.

Hirsch, Francine. *Empire of Nations: Ethnographic Knowledge and the Making of the Soviet Union*. Ithaca, NY: Cornell University Press, 2005.

Hoare, Marko Atilla. *Genocide and Resistance in Hitler's Bosnia: The Partisans and the Chetniks*. Oxford: Oxford University Press, 2006.

Hoare, Marko Atilla. *The History of Bosnia: From the Middle Ages to the Present Day*. London and Beirut: Saqi, 2007.

Hoare, Marko Atilla. "Genocide in the Former Yugoslavia before and after Communism." *Europe-Asia Studies* 62, no. 7 (2010): 1193–1214.

Hoare, Marko Atilla. *The Bosnian Muslims in the Second World War: A History*. London: Hurst, 2013.

Hobsbawm, E. J. *Nations and Nationalism since 1780: Programme, Myth, Reality*. Cambridge: Cambridge University Press, 1990.

Holquist, Peter. "'Information Is the Alpha and Omega of Our Work': Bolshevik Surveillance in Its Pan-European Context." *Journal of Modern History* 69, no. 3 (1997): 415–450.

Horne, Alistair. *A Savage War of Peace: Algeria, 1954–1962*. New York: New York Review of Books, [1977] 2006.

Horowitz, Donald. *The Deadly Ethnic Riot*. Berkeley: University of California Press, 2001.

Hrelja, Kemal. "Proizvodni odnosi u poljoprivredi Bosne i Hercegovini, 1918–1941." In *Ekonomski genocid nad bosanskim muslimanima*, edited by Kemal Hrelja and Atif Purivatra, 43–82. Sarajevo: MAG—Udruženje Muslimana za antigenocidne aktivnosti, 1992.

Hroch, Miroslav. *Social Preconditions of National Revival in Europe: A Comparative Analysis of the Social Composition of Patriotic Groups among the Smaller European Nations.* Translated by Ben Fowkes. Cambridge: Cambridge University Press, 1985.

Huggins, Martha, Mika Haritos-Fatouros, and Philip Zimbardo. *Violence Workers: Police Torturers and Murderers Reconstruct Brazilian Atrocities.* Berkeley: University of California Press, 2002.

Hurem, Rasim. *Kriza Narodnooslobodilačkog pokreta u Bosni i Hercegovini krajem 1941. i početkom 1942. godine.* Sarajevo: Svjetlost, 1972.

Hurem, Rasim. "Samo su branili svoja sela." *Ogledalo* 1, no. 2 (prosinac/decembar 1990): 32.

Imamović, Mustafa. *Pravni položaj i unutrašnjo-politički razvitak Bosne i Hercegovine od 1878–1914.* Sarajevo: Bosanski kulturni centar, [1976] 1997.

Jacoby, Karl. *Shadows at Dawn: An Apache Massacre and the Violence of History.* New York: Penguin Books, 2008.

Jelić-Butić, Fikreta. "Prilog proučavanju djelatnosti ustaša do 1941." *Časopis za suvremenu povijest* I, nos. 1–2 (1969): 55–91.

Jelić-Butić, Fikreta. *Ustaše i Nezavisna Država Hrvatska, 1941–1945.* Zagreb: Sveučilišna naklada Liber i Školska knjiga, 1977.

Jelić-Butić, Fikreta. *Četnici u Hrvatskoj 1941.–1945.* Zagreb: Globus, 1986.

Judson, Pieter M. *Guardians of the Nation: Activists on the Language Frontiers of Imperial Austria.* Cambridge, MA: Harvard University Press, 2006.

Jurjević, Josip. *Pogrom u Krnjeuši 9. i 10. kolovoza 1941. godine.* Zagreb: Vikarijat Banjalučke biskupije, 1999.

Kakar, Sudhir. *The Colours of Violence: Cultural Identities, Religion, and Conflict.* Chicago: University of Chicago Press, 1996.

Kalyvas, Stathis. "The Paradox of Terrorism in Civil War." *Journal of Ethics* 1, no. 1 (2004): 97–138.

Kalyvas, Stathis. "The Urban Bias in Research on Civil Wars." *Security Studies* 13, no. 3 (2004): 160–190.

Kalyvas, Stathis. *The Logic of Violence in Civil War.* Cambridge: Cambridge University Press, 2006.

Kalyvas, Stathis. "Ethnic Defection in Civil War." *Comparative Political Studies* 41, no. 8 (2008): 1043–1068.

Kamberović, Husnija. *Begovski zemljišni posjedi u Bosni i Hercegovini od 1878. do 1918. godine.* Zagreb: Hrvatski institut za povijest-Zagreb; Institut za istoriju-Sarajevo, 2003.

Katz, Jack. *Seductions of Crime: A Chilling Exploration of the Criminal Mind—from Juvenile Delinquency to Cold-blooded Murder.* New York: Basic Books, 1988.

Kaufmann, Chaim. "Possible and Impossible Solutions to Ethnic Civil Wars." *International Security* 20, no. 4 (1996): 136–175.

King, Charles. "Can There Be a Political Science of the Holocaust?" *Perspectives on Politics* 10, no. 2 (2012): 323–341.

King, Jeremy. *Budweisers into Czechs and Germans: A Local History of Bohemian Politics, 1848–1948*. Princeton, NJ: Princeton University Press, 2002.

Kisić Kolanović, Nada. *Muslimani i hrvatski nacionalizam, 1941.–1945*. Zagreb: Hrvatski institut za povijest; Školska knjiga, 2009.

Korb, Alexander. "Understanding Ustaša Violence." *Journal of Genocide Research* 12, nos. 1–2 (2010): 1–18.

Korb, Alexander. *Im Schatten des Weltkriegs. Massengewalt der Ustaša gegen Serben, Juden und Roma in Kroatien 1941–1945*. Hamburg: Hamburger Edition, 2013.

Kopstein, Jeffrey, and Jason Wittenberg. "Deadly Communities: Local Political Milieus and the Persecution of Jews in Occupied Poland." *Comparative Political Studies* 44, no. 3 (2011): 259–283.

Kotkin, Stephen. *Magnetic Mountain: Stalinism as a Civilization*. Berkeley: University of California Press, 1995.

Kreševljaković, Hamdija. *Kulen Vakuf*. Sarajevo: Islamska dionička štamparija, 1935.

Kreševljaković, Hamdija. *Kapetanije u Bosni i Hercegovini*. Sarajevo: Svjetlost, [1953] 1980.

Krizman, Bogdan. *Ante Pavelić i Ustaše*. Zagreb: Globus, 1978.

Krstić, Đorđo. *Agrarna politika u Bosni i Hercegovini*. Sarajevo: Štamparija "Bosanka pošta," 1938.

Kukuljević Sakcinski, Ivan. *Putovanje po Bosni*. Zagreb: Narodna tiskarnica dr. Ljudevit Gaja, 1858.

Kuper, Leo. *Genocide: Its Political Use in the Twentieth Century*. New Haven: Yale University Press, 1981.

Laitin, David. *Nations, States, and Violence*. Oxford: Oxford University Press, 2007.

Lefebvre, Georges. *The Great Fear of 1789: Rural Panic in Revolutionary France*. Translated by Joan White. New York: Pantheon Books, 1973.

Leites, Nathan, and Charles Wolf Jr. *Rebellion and Authority: An Analytic Essay on Insurgent Conflicts*. Chicago: Markham, 1970.

Lieberman, Benjamin. *Terrible Fate: Ethnic Cleansing in the Making of Modern Europe*. Chicago: Ivan R. Dee, 2006.

Lienhardt, Peter. "The Interpretation of Rumour." In *Studies in Social Anthropology: Essays in Memory of E.E. Evans-Pritchard by His Former Oxford Colleagues*, edited by J. H. M. Beattie and R.G. Lienhardt, 105–131. Oxford: Clarendon Press, 1975.

Longman, Timothy. *Christianity and Genocide in Rwanda*. Cambridge: Cambridge University Press, 2010.

Lohr, Eric. *Nationalizing the Russian Empire: The Campaign against Enemy Aliens during World War I*. Cambridge, MA: Harvard University Press, 2003.

London, Perry. "The Rescuers: Motivational Hypotheses about Christians Who Saved Jews From the Nazis." In *Altruism and Helping Behavior: Social Psychological Studies of Some Antecedents and Consequences*, edited by Jacqueline Macaulay and Leonard Berkowitz, 241–250. New York: Academic Press, 1970.

Lower, Wendy. "Pogroms, Mob Violence and Genocide in Western Ukraine, Summer 1941: Varied Histories, Explanations, and Comparisons." *Journal of Genocide Research* 13, no. 3 (2011): 217–246.

Lubkemann, Stephen C. *Culture in Chaos: An Anthropology of the Social Conditions in War*. Chicago: University of Chicago Press, 2008.

Luft, Aliza. "Toward a Dynamic Theory of Action at the Micro Level of Genocide: Killing, Desistance, and Saving in 1994 Rwanda." *Sociological Theory* 33, no. 2 (2015): 148–172.

Lukač, Dušan. *Ustanak u Bosanskoj Krajini.* Belgrade: Vojnoizdavački zavod, 1967.

Marijan, Davor. "Lipanjski ustanak u istočnoj Hercegovini 1941. godine." *Časopis za suvremenu povijest* 35, no. 2 (2003): 545–576.

Martin, Terry. *The Affirmative Action Empire: Nations and Nationalism in the Soviet Union, 1923–1939.* Ithaca, NY: Cornell University Press, 2001.

Maslak, Nijazija, et al. *Turističke informacije. Stari gradovi općine Bihać.* Bihać: Općina Bihać, 2008.

Mazower, Mark. *Hitler's Empire: How the Nazis Ruled Europe.* New York: Penguin Books, 2008.

Mazower, Mark. "Timothy Snyder's *Bloodlands.*" *Contemporary European History* 21, no. 2 (May 2012): 117–123.

McDoom, Omar Shahabudin. "Who Killed in Rwanda's Genocide? Micro-Space, Social Influence and Individual Participation in Intergroup Violence." *Journal of Peace Research* 50, no. 4 (2013): 453–467.

McDoom, Omar Shahabudin. "Antisocial Capital: A Profile of Rwandan Genocide Perpetrators' Social Networks." *Journal of Conflict Resolution* 58, no. 5 (2014): 866–894.

Midlarsky, Manus. *The Killing Trap: Genocide in the Twentieth Century.* Cambridge: Cambridge University Press, 2005.

Mikić, Đorđe. *Političke stranke i izbori u Bosanskoj Krajini, 1918–1941.* Banja Luka: Institut za istoriju, 1997.

Milgram, Stanley. *Obedience to Authority. An Experimental View.* New York: Harper-Perennial, [1974] 2009.

Naimark, Norman M. *Fires of Hatred: Ethnic Cleansing in Twentieth-Century Europe.* Cambridge, MA: Harvard University Press, 2001.

Nielsen, Christian. *Making Yugoslavs: Identity in King Aleksandar's Yugoslavia.* Toronto: University of Toronto Press, 2014.

Okamura, Jonathan Y. "Situational Ethnicity." *Ethnic and Racial Studies* 4, no. 4 (1981): 452–465.

Oliner, Samuel P., and Pearl M. Oliner. *The Altruistic Personality: Rescuers of Jews in Nazi-Europe.* New York: Free Press, 1988.

Orlovac, Anto. *Palme im rukama. Život i mučeništvo župnika Krešimir Barišić i uništenje župe Krnjeuša 1941. godine.* Banja Luka and Zagreb: Biskupski ordinarijat Banja Luka; Ekološki glasnik d.o.o., 2008.

Owens, Peter B., Yang Su, and David A. Snow. "Social Scientific Inquiry into Genocide and Mass Killing: From Unitary Outcome to Complex Processes." *Annual Review of Sociology* 39, no. 4 (2013): 4.1–4.16.

Patterson, Orlando. *Rituals of Blood: Consequences of Slavery in Two American Centuries.* New York: Basic Books, 1998.

Pavičić, Luka. *Kronika stradanja Hrvata južne Like.* Zagreb: D-GRAF, 1996.

Peterson, Roger D. *Understanding Ethnic Violence: Fear, Hatred, and Resentment in Twentieth Century Eastern Europe.* Cambridge: Cambridge University Press, 2002.

Politkovskaya, Anna. *A Small Corner of Hell: Dispatches from Chechnya.* Chicago: University of Chicago Press, 2003.

Popović, Vasilj. *Agrarno pitanje u Bosni i turski neredi za vreme reformnog režima Abdul-Medžida (1839–1861).* Belgrade: Srpska akademija nauka, 1949.

Portelli, Alessandro. "The Peculiarities of Oral History." *History Workshop* 12, no. 1 (1981): 96–107.

Posen, Barry. "The Security Dilemma and Ethnic Conflict." *Survival* 35, no. 1 (1993): 27–47.

Prunier, Gérard. *The Rwanda Crisis: A History of a Genocide.* London: Hurst & Company, [1995] 2010.

Prunier, Gérard. *Darfur: A 21st Century Genocide.* 3rd ed. Ithaca, N.Y.: Cornell University Press, 2008.

Prusin, Alexander V. *The Lands Between: Conflict in the East European Borderlands, 1870–1992.* Oxford: Oxford University Press, 2010.

Purivatra, Atif. "Političke partije prema agrarnoj reformi u Bosni i Hercegovini neposredno poslije 1918. godine." In *Nacionalni i politički razvitak Muslimana. Rasprave i članci,* edited by Atif Purivatra, 216–275. Sarajevo: Svjetlost, 1969.

Purivatra, Atif. *Jugoslavenska muslimanska organizacija u političkom životu Kraljevine Srba, Hrvata i Slovenaca.* Sarajevo: Bosanski kulturni centar, [1974] 1999.

Redlich, Shimon. *Together and Apart in Brzezany: Poles, Jews, and Ukrainians, 1919–1945.* Bloomington and Indianapolis: Indiana University Press, 2002.

Renwich Monroe, Kristen. *Ethics in an Age of Terrorism and Genocide: Identity and Moral Choice.* Princeton, NJ: Princeton University Press, 2011.

Robinson, Geoffrey. *The Dark Side of Paradise: Political Violence in Bali.* Ithaca, NY: Cornell University Press, 1995.

Ron, James. *Frontiers and Ghettos: State Violence in Serbia and Israel.* Berkeley: University of California Press, 2004.

Roy, Beth. *Some Trouble with Cows: Making Sense of Social Conflict.* New Delhi: Vistaar, 1994.

Rudé, George F. E. *The Crowd in the French Revolution.* Oxford: Oxford University Press, 1959.

Rudé, George F. E. *The Crowd in History: A Study of Popular Disturbances in France and England, 1730–1848.* New York: Wiley, 1964.

Sahlins, Marshall. "The Return of the Event, Again." In *Culture in Practice. Selected Essays,* edited by Marshall Sahlins, 293–352. New York: Zone Books, 2000.

Samardžija, Dušan D. *Bosanskodubičko područje u NOR-u i socijalističkoj revoluciji 1941–1945.* Bosanska Dubica: Društveno-političke organizacije i Skupština opštine Bosanska Dubica, 1984.

Sambanis, Nicholas, and Moses Shayo. "Social Identification and Ethnic Conflict." *American Political Science Review* 107, no. 2 (2013): 294–325.

Sarajlić, Abdulah, and Dragutin Strunjaš. "Prvi dani ustanka u Drvaru i okolini." *Godišnjak istorijskog društva Bosne i Hercegovine* II (1950): 5–18.

Sarić, Samija. "Prilog pregledu provođenja agrarne reforme u Bosni i Hercegovine 1918–1941. godine." *Glasnik arhiva i društva arhivskih radnika Bosne i Hercegovine* XVIII–XIX (1978–1979): 213–223.

Schama, Simon. *Citizens: A Chronicle of the French Revolution.* New York: Albert Knopf, 1989.

Schirmer, Jennifer. *The Guatemalan Military Project: A Violence Called Democracy.* Philadelphia: University of Pennsylvania Press, 1998.

Šehić, Nusret. *Četništvo u Bosni i Hercegovini, 1918–1941. Politička uloga i oblici djelatnosti četničkih udruženja.* Sarajevo: Akademija nauke i umjetnosti Bosne i Hercegovine, 1971.

Sémelin, Jacques. *Purify and Destroy: The Political Uses of Massacre and Genocide.* New York: Columbia University Press, 2007.

Sewell, William H., Jr. "Three Temporalities: Towards an Eventful Sociology." In *The Historic Turn in the Human Sciences*, edited by Terrence J. McDonald, 245–280. Ann Arbor: University of Michigan Press, 1996.

Škaljić, Abdulah. *Turcizmi u srpskohrvatskom jeziku.* Sarajevo: Svjetlost, 1966.

Skoko, Savo. *Pokolji hecegovačkih Srba '41.* Belgrade: Stručna knjiga, 1991.

Skoko, Savo, and Milan Grahovac. "Junski ustanak." In *Hercegovina u NOB, april 1941.–juni 1942, tom 2*, edited by Sveta Kovačević and Slavko Stijačić-Slavo, 409–439. Belgrade and Mostar: Vojnoidavački i novinski centar i Istorijski arhiv Hercegovina, 1986.

Smith, Sebastian. *Allah's Mountains: The Battle for Chechnya.* New York: I.B. Tauris, 2006.

Šljivo, Galib. *Omer-paša Latas u Bosni i Hercegovini, 1850–1852.* Sarajevo: Svjetlost, 1977.

Snyder, Timothy. "'To Resolve the Ukrainian Problem Once and for All': The Ethnic Cleansing of Ukrainians in Poland, 1943–1947." *Journal of Cold War Studies* 1, no. 2 (1999): 86–120.

Snyder, Timothy. "The Causes of Ukrainian-Polish Ethnic Cleansing, 1943." *Past and Present* 179, no. 1 (2003): 197–234.

Snyder, Timothy. "The Life and Death West Volhyinian Jewry, 1921–1945." In *The Shoah in Ukraine: History, Testimony, Memorialization*, edited by Ray Brandon and Wendy Lower, 77–113. Bloomington: Indiana University Press, 2008.

Snyder, Timothy. *Bloodlands: Europe between Hitler and Stalin.* New York: Basic Books, 2010.

Solonari, Vladimir. *Purifying the Nation: Population Exchange and Ethnic Cleansing in Nazi-Allied Romania.* Baltimore: Johns Hopkins University Press, 2010.

Spencer, Jonathan. "Popular Perceptions of the Violence: A Provincial View." In *Sri Lanka in Change and Crisis*, edited by James Manor, 187–195. London: Croom Helm, 1984.

Spencer, Jonathan. "Violence and Everyday Practice in Sri Lanka." *Modern Asian Studies* 24, no. 3 (July 1999): 603–623.

Stanisavljević, Đuro. "Pojava i razvitak četničkog pokreta u Hrvatskoj." *Istorija XX veka—Zbornik radova,* 5–140. Belgrade: Institut društvenih nauka, 1962.

Stanisavljević, Đuro. "Narodni heroj, Matić Ilije Stojan." In *Kotar Donji Lapac u Narodnooslobodilačkom ratu, 1941.–1945.*, edited by Gojko Vezmar and Đuro Zatezalo, 974–976. Karlovac: Historijski arhiv u Karlovcu, 1985.

Stojkov, Todor. "O takozvanom Ličkom ustanku 1932." *Časopis za suvremenu povijest* 2, no. 2 (1970): 167–180.

Stoll, David. *Between Two Armies in the Ixil Towns of Guatemala.* New York: Columbia University Press, 1993.

Stoll, David. *Rigoberta Menchú and the Story of All Poor Guatemalans.* Boulder, CO: Westview Press, 1999.

Straus, Scott. *The Order of Genocide: Race, Power, and War in Rwanda.* Ithaca, NY: Cornell University Press, 2006.

Straus, Scott. "Second-Generation Comparative Research on Genocide." *World Politics* 59, 3 (2007): 476–501.

Straus, Scott. "The Historiography of the Rwandan Genocide." In *The Historiography of Genocide*, edited by Dan Stone, 517–542. Basingstoke, England: Palgrave Macmillan, 2008.

Straus, Scott. "From 'Rescue' to Violence: Overcoming Local Opposition to Genocide in Rwanda." In *Resisting Genocide: The Multiple Forms of Rescue*, edited by Jacques Semelin, Claire Andrieu, and Sarah Gensburger, 331–343. Translated by Emma Bently and Cynthia Schoch. New York: Columbia University Press, 2011.

Straus, Scott. "'Destroy Them to Save Us': Theories of Genocide and the Logics of Political Violence." *Terrorism and Political Violence* 24, no. 4 (2012): 544–560.

Straus, Scott. "Retreating from the Brink: Theorizing Mass Violence and the Dynamics of Restraint." *Perspectives on Politics* 10, no. 2 (June 2012): 343–362.

Straus, Scott. *Making and Unmaking Nations: War, Leadership, and Genocide in Modern Africa.* Ithaca, NY: Cornell University Press, 2015.

Stuparić, Darko, ed. *Tko je tko u NDH. Hrvatska 1941.–1945.* Zagreb: Minerva, 1997.

Su, Yang. *Collective Killings in Rural China during the Cultural Revolution.* Cambridge: Cambridge University Press, 2011.

Suny, Ronald Grigor, and Terry Martin, eds. *A State of Nations: Empire and Nation-Making in the Age of Lenin and Stalin.* Oxford: Oxford University Press, 2001.

Tambiah, Stanley. *Levelling Crowds: Ethnonationalist Conflicts and Collective Violence in South Asia.* Berkeley: University of California Press, 1996.

Tec, Nechama. *When Light Pierced the Darkness: Christian Rescuers of Jews in Nazi-Occupied Poland.* Oxford: Oxford University Press, 1986.

Ther, Philipp, and Ana Siljak, eds. *Redrawing Nations: Ethnic Cleansing in East-Central Europe, 1944–1948.* Lanham, MD: Rowman & Littlefield, 2001.

Tishkov, Valery. "'Don't Kill Me, I'm a Kyrgyz!': An Anthropological Analysis of Violence in the Osh Ethnic Conflict." *Journal of Peace Research* 32, no. 2 (1995): 133–149.

Tomasevich, Jozo. *Peasants, Politics, and Economic Change in Yugoslavia.* Stanford: Stanford University Press, 1955.

Tomasevich, Jozo. *War and Revolution in Yugoslavia, 1941–1945: Occupation and Collaboration.* Stanford: Stanford University Press, 2001.

Truhelka, Ćiro. *Historička podloga agrarnog pitanja u Bosni.* Sarajevo: Zemaljska štamparija, 1915.

Tse-tung, Mao. *On Guerrilla Warfare.* Translated by Samuel B. Griffith. Mineola, NY: Dover, [1937] 2005.

Valentino, Benjamin. *Final Solutions: Mass Killing and Genocide in the Twentieth Century.* Ithaca, NY: Cornell University Press, 2004.

Valentino, Benjamin. "Why We Kill: The Political Science of Political Violence against Civilians." *Annual Review of Political Science* 17 (2014): 89–103.

Valentino, Benjamin, Paul Huth, and Dylan Balch-Lindsay. "Draining the Sea: Mass Killing and Guerrilla Warfare." *International Organization* 58, no. 2 (2004): 375–407.

Varshney, Ashutosh. *Ethnic Conflict and Civil Life. Hindus and Muslims in India.* New Haven: Yale University Press, 2002.

Verkaaik, Oskar. "Fun and Violence: Ethnocide and the Effervescence of Collective Aggression." *Social Anthropology* 11, no. 1 (2003): 3–22.

Vujačić, Veljko, and Victor Zaslavsky. "The Causes of Disintegration in the USSR and Yugoslavia." *Telos* 1991, no. 88 (1991): 120–140.

Vukmanović, Milan. *Ustaški zločini na području Bihaća u ljeto 1941. godine.* Banja Luka: Institut za istoriju u Banjaluci, 1987.

Wachtel, Andrew Baruch. *Making a Nation, Breaking a Nation: Literature and Cultural Politics in Yugoslavia.* Stanford: Stanford University Press, 1998.

Waller, James. *Becoming Evil: How Ordinary People Commit Genocide and Mass Killing.* New York: Oxford University Press, 2002.

Weinstein, Jeremy. *Inside Rebellion: The Politics of Insurgent Violence.* Cambridge: Cambridge University Press, 2007.

Weitz, Eric. *A Century of Genocide: Utopias of Race and Nation.* Princeton, NJ: Princeton University Press, 2003.

Wickman-Crowley, Timothy. "Terror and Guerrilla Warfare in Latin America, 1956–1970." *Comparative Studies in Society and History* 32, no. 2 (1990): 201–237.

Wimmer, Andreas. *Waves of War: Nationalism, State Formation, and Ethnic Exclusion in the Modern World.* Cambridge: Cambridge University Press, 2013.

Wolfgang, Marvin. *Patterns in Criminal Homicide.* Philadelphia: University of Pennsylvania, 1958.

Wood, Elisabeth Jean. "The Social Processes of Civil War: The Wartime Transformation of Social Networks." *Annual Review of Political Science* 11 (2008): 539–561.

Yeomans, Rory. *Visions of Annihilation: The Ustasha Regime and the Cultural Politics of Fascism, 1941–1945.* Pittsburgh: University of Pittsburgh Press, 2013.

Yosmaoğlou, İpek. *Blood Ties: Religion, Violence and the Politics of Nationhood in Ottoman Macedonia, 1878–1908.* Ithaca, NY: Cornell University Press, 2013.

Zahra, Tara. *Kidnapped Souls: National Indifference and the Battle for Children in the Bohemian Lands, 1900–1948.* Ithaca, NY: Cornell University Press, 2008.

Zahra, Tara. "Going West." *East European Politics and Societies* 25, no. 4 (2011): 785–791.

Żbikowski, Andrezj. "Local Anti-Jewish Pogroms in the Occupied Territories of Eastern Poland, June-July 1941." In *The Holocaust in the Soviet Union: Studies and Sources on the Destruction of Jews in the Nazi-Occupied Territories of the USSR, 1941–1945*, edited by Lucjan Dobroszycki and Jeffrey Gurock, 173–179. Armonk, NY: M.E. Sharpe, 1993.

Zimbardo, Philip. *The Lucifer Effect: Understanding How Good People Turn Evil.* New York: Random House, 2007.

INDEX

www.ingramcontent.com/pod-product-compliance
Lightning Source LLC
Chambersburg PA
CBHW020339100426
42812CB00029B/3190/J
* 9 7 8 1 5 0 1 7 0 4 9 2 5 *